Java Network Programming

Java Network Programming

SECOND EDITION

A complete guide to networking, streams, and distributed computing

MERLIN HUGHES

MICHAEL SHOFFNER

DEREK HAMNER

WITH A CHAPTER ON CORBA BY UMESH BELLUR
CONRAD HUGHES AND MARIA WINSLOW CONTRIBUTED MATERIAL TO THE FIRST EDITION

 **MANNING**

Greenwich
(74° w. long.)

For electronic browsing of this book, see http://www.manning.com

The publisher offers discounts on this book when ordered in quantity. For more information, please contact:

Special Sales Department
Manning Publications Co.
32 Lafayette Place
Greenwich, CT 06830

Fax: (203) 661-9018
email: orders@manning.com

Library of Congress Cataloging-in-Publication Data
Hughes, Merlin.
       Java network programming / Merlin Hughes . . . [et al.] — 2nd ed.
          p.   cm.
       Includes index.
       ISBN 1-884777-49-X
       1. Java (Computer program language) 2. Internet programming.
    I. Hughes, Merlin, 1972 –
    QA76.73.J38J377   1997
    005.2'762—dc21
                    CIP
97-17916

Manning Publications Co.   Copyeditor: Sherry Roberts
32 Lafayette Place   Typesetter: Tony Roberts
Greenwich, CT 06830   Cover designer: Leslie Haimes

Second printing, October 1999
Changes due to JAVA 2 v1.3 available at publisher's website: http://www.manning.com/Hughes

Printed in the United States of America
   2 3 4 5 6 7 8 9 10 – CR – 03 02 01 00 99

contents

contents in detail

Appendices

preface to the second edition

Well, here we are at edition two. Why did we do this again?

As before, our main reason for writing *Java Network Programming* is to provide you with useful techniques and code for networked applications development in Java.

With the recent updates to the Java platform, its capabilities for networking and distributed computing have expanded significantly. APIs now exist that offer new options for significant applications development.

The primary focus of this book is the fundamental networking technology provided by Java: streams and IP-based protocols such as TCP, UDP, and multicast. In this second edition we have added coverage of new API features relevant to these technologies, while, in addition, improving and extending the examples provided by the first edition to cover these changes and more.

In other areas, updates to the Java platform have introduced new networking capabilities such as RMI, CORBA, and servlets. To provide a good networking foundation in this book, we have added coverage of these important topics to the second edition. Of course, spatial limitations of the printed page limit the depth in which we can cover these specialized networking APIs. As a result we have attempted to introduce these topics sufficiently that you can make an informed choice about what technology to use, and should one catch your fancy, other dedicated books can serve you better than we could hope to.

Finally, with the Java 2 platform, a complete and far-reaching cryptography API has been added to Java's repertoire. Rather than attempting to shoehorn our cryptographic examples from the first edition into this new API, we have completely excised cryptography from this second edition, preferring to cover that in a separate book, *Applied Java Cryptography*, due out after the Java APIs stabilize.

In short, there was a lot of new stuff that needed coverage, some old stuff that needed revision, and then some other random things that happened to catch our attention. Plus, our publisher put a gun to our head so we didn't have any choice.

Enjoy!

preface to the first edition

We founded our company, Prominence Dot Com, with the commitment to provide clients with advanced Internet-based solutions for business needs. When we first set up shop, the hot new technology for the Internet was the World Wide Web. Applications-oriented Web sites became our first order of business.

We began evaluating Java for Web applications development during its alpha-2 phase, in the summer of 1995. At the time, CGI applications of various sorts represented the cutting edge of Web-based products. It was immediately apparent that Java presented unique and powerful features that enabled "real" distributed applications which could run over any TCP/IP network.

Of course, all of that is ancient history in Internet terms. Slightly more than a year later, Java is hotter than the coffee that inspired its name. In fact, at the time of this writing, the coffee market itself is in a bit of a lull, but Java's popularity continues to surge.

Java's appearance in the right place at the right time with the answers to hard problems is earning it a place in the toolkits of developers worldwide. From a developer's standpoint, Java's cross-platform, secure, object-oriented, and network-centric features make it useful. Its clean syntax makes it fun and relatively easy to use. Most importantly, its status as the only high-level cross-platform language with native Web browser support makes it a must for serious Web- and Internet-oriented development efforts—precisely the sort of efforts that require the use of the secure networking codebase and techniques developed in this book.

Java Network Programming arose out of a set of professional courseware that we developed in response to the widespread need for a comprehensive reference on advanced features of the Java language. This book, therefore, covers everything from the basics of Java networking to in-depth techniques for implementing high-level secure networked applications. It is simultaneously a complete tutorial on networking and cryptography, a Java networking API reference, and a collection of production codebase contained on a companion CD-ROM.

We sincerely hope and believe that the material in this book will be as useful to you as it has been to us. Please give *Java Network Programming* a good home and dogear it, so that it knows it is loved.

acknowledgments

Putting this book together brought us severe pain and torture. We would all be dead now were it not for the kind help of several people. Many thanks are owed to Marjan Bace, our publisher, and his cohorts, for their valuable advice along the way and their patience with missed deadlines, and to Len Dorfman for getting us started in the first place. Thanks to Kevin Jeffay for reviewing the appendix on networking, and to Grant Gainey and Dave Zimmerman for inspiring our original coverage of RMI. Much credit is also due Dinesh Manocha who demonstrated infinite patience during the writing of the first edition, and to Jeffay, Don Smith, Bert Dempsey, and Donal O'Mahony, who gave valued lectures on networking over the years.

We would all like to thank our friends and family for not abandoning us permanently even though we abandoned them temporarily, twice. Special thanks also to Dr. Dumas for much-needed sanity and reality checks.

Merlin would particularly like to thank Simon Rooney, David Graham and the TCD crowd for their support, and the folks at Baltimore Technologies for graciously accommodating his extended absences, and Michael wants to add special thanks to the old University of North Carolina Sunsite crew and the folks at UNC Geology for all of their help.

This second edition brought another round of pain and torture. But we're used to it now and we're hardened. In addition to all the folks from edition one, we'd like to thank Catherine O'Sullivan, Jill Greeson, Marq Singer, and Paul Jones for their much-needed patience and assistance, and Andy Wang, Roy Tal, Andrew Chen, Claude Duguay, Michael Andreano, Michael Brundage, Scott Zimmerman, and Victor A. Brennan for their greatly appreciated feedback.

Thanks are also due Tony and Sherry Roberts, Elizabeth Martin, Aaron and Heather Lyon, Margaret Marynowski, and Leslie Haimes for all actually implementing the book over the years, and to Kevin Hall for his guiding genius.

Without you all, it wouldn't have been possible.

Sa-lute!

guide to the reader

Intended audience

Java Network Programming offers something for every Java networker, from the beginner to the experienced developer. In addition to developing practical networking classes, advanced features such as custom streams and remote method invocation are covered in detail. For convenience, the library of code developed in the book is available online in a companion Web site, http://nitric.com/jnp/, where future updates also will be made available.

- *Beginners* can take advantage of the Preliminaries part of the book, which contains an overview of networking as well as highlights of the Java security model, exceptions, and multithreading. A comprehensive appendix also provides additional detailed background information on networking. Parts 2 and 3 of the book then provide complete introductions to the `java.io` and `java.net` packages, which are the fundamentals of network programming in Java and the foundation of the rest of the book.

- *Experienced Java programmers* will be able to jump right in at the point most appropriate for their needs. Programmers familiar with the original Java APIs can browse parts 2 and 3 for the new features introduced with the latest language updates, such as multicast and the character streams, accompanied by many significant examples. Then they can dive into parts 4 and 5, which cover message passing, RMI, CORBA, and servlets—among the most advanced topics covered by the book and some of the most powerful parts of networking with Java.

- *Experienced C and C++ programmers* will find that networking with Java is quite a bit cleaner and more rewarding than networking in C and C++. For example, Java's exception mechanism facilitates robust handling of common problems that occur during I/O and networking operations, and the threading facilities provide a way to easily implement powerful servers. Familiarity with Java is presumed; however, networking in Java should come naturally to C/C++ developers.

Changes to the second edition

This second edition presents many changes from the first edition of the book. These changes fall into three main categories: Additional coverage of new API features has been provided, all examples have been updated to reflect changes to the Java API, and the book has been expanded with more examples of varied networking applications.

Coverage of the language I/O facilities has been extended with full details of the character streams and enhanced coverage of the object streams. The networking part of the book now covers changes to the basic classes and provides extensive coverage of multicast facilities, in addition to new examples of complete networked applications including finger, nslookup, and a full-featured Web server. A new section now provides detailed coverage of RMI, CORBA and servlets, new capabilities provided with updates to the Java platform. Finally, the cryptography section has been excised, in favor of a dedicated book that can do better service to the new Java cryptographic APIs.

Networking with Java

The Java programming language is ideally suited to networked applications programming. The core API comes with a standard set of classes that provides uniform access to networking protocols across all of the platforms to which the Java Virtual Machine has been ported. The language abstracts away from issues such as hardware byte order so that programmers need not concern themselves with the traditional problems of cross-platform interoperability. Basic network access is provided through classes from the `java.net` package. These are complemented by classes from the `java.io` package that provide a uniform streams-based interface to communications channels. These classes can be extended to provide sophisticated high-level functionality to serve custom communications needs.

Both applications and embedded applets can benefit from the networked facilities provided by the language. Applets can communicate with central information storage to access a central information store and to provide true real-time collaboration between users distributed across the World Wide Web. Applications can also benefit in a number of ways above and beyond the usual advantages that Java enjoys over traditional programming languages. The secure and dynamically linked nature of Java permits development of servers which can be extended with new code at run time. Examples of this include a Web server that can dynamically and securely execute code supplied by a client, or a search engine that can accept searches in the form of "searchlet" code fragments.

Additional packages within the language API further abstract away from the underlying nuts and bolts of networking. These extensions include a remote method invocation API that provides transparent access to the methods of an object resident in a remote virtual machine. Parameters and results of remote method calls are implicitly transmitted over a network connection between the virtual machines. Another API and set of tools provides CORBA compatibility, providing universal access to CORBA objects. Additional packages provide a cryptographic framework, networked multimedia access and interfaces to telephony products, and a commerce framework. Further down the road, JavaSpace promises global tuple spaces for truly distributed applications.

Contents and layout

In this book, we cover the `java.io`, `java.net`, `java.rmi`, and `javax.servlet` packages extensively with examples covering all of the techniques that are necessary to develop networked applications in Java, including an introductory treatment of threads and exceptions, and details of some of the API support for CORBA. Aloing with API coverage, we document and discuss many practical examples of networked applications programming, including a high-level streams-based communications library. An overview of networking is provided for those readers less familiar with the topic.

The book is organized into six parts:

Part I provides preliminary information, including an introduction to networking, the Java security model, threads, and exceptions.

Part II covers the `java.io` package in detail, presenting API details, example code and extensions to the basic streams. It provides full details of all Java's major stream classes; the byte streams, character streams, and object streams.

Part III covers the `java.net` package, with extensive real-world examples including many TCP and UDP clients and servers, multicast examples, and complete coverage of the URL classes including example custom protocol handlers.

Part IV provides details of three specialized networking technologies supported by Java: remote method invocation (`java.rmi`), servlets (`javax.servlet`), and CORBA (`org.omg.CORBA`), with extensive examples along the way.

Part V discusses the development of a message-based networking library that can significantly ease the development of some networked applications, and serves as a foundation for many other potentially interesting streams-based networking libraries.

Part VI consists of appendices, including an in-depth overview of networking and some useful lists and tables.

The Java platform is undergoing constant revision. As bugs are fixed, APIs undergo cleanup and new features are added. A small marker has been added beside classes, interfaces, and methods that have been introduced by major *new* releases of the JDK and associated products. To be specific, details in this book are, to the best of the authors' abilities, correct as of the following release versions:

- JDK 1.2: Java 2 SDK, a.k.a. JDK 1.2

- JDK 1.1: JDK 1.1.7B

- JDK 1.0: JDK 1.0.2
- Java IDL: Java 2 SDK
- JSDK 2.1: JSDK 2.1 specification
- JSDK 2.0: JSDK 2.0
- JSDK 1.0: JSDK 1.0.1

Downloading the code

To save you the effort of typing in all the code from this book and the expense of purchasing an unnecessary CD-ROM, a companion Website at http://nitric.com/jnp/ provides all the source in various convenient downloadable formats.

The source code also can be downloaded from the publisher's Website, http://www.manning.com/Hughes2.

about the cover illustration

The cover illustration of this book is from the 1805 edition of Sylvain Maréchal's four-volume compendium of regional dress customs. This book was first published in Paris in 1788, one year before the French Revolution. Its title alone required no fewer than 30 words.

"Costumes Civils actuels de tous les peuples connus dessinés d'après nature gravés et coloriés, accompagnés d'une notice historique sur leurs coutumes, moeurs, religions, etc., etc., redigés par M. Sylvain Maréchal"

The four volumes include an annotation on the illustrations: "gravé à la manière noire par Mixelle d'après Desrais et colorié." Clearly, the engraver and illustrator deserved no more than to be listed by their last names—after all they were mere technicians. The workers who colored each illustration by hand remain nameless.

The remarkable diversity of this collection reminds us vividly of how distant and isolated the world's towns and regions were just 200 years ago. Dress codes have changed everywhere and the diversity by region, so rich at the time, has melted away. It is now hard to tell the inhabitant of one continent from another. Perhaps we have traded cultural divesrsity for a more varied personal life—certainly a more varied and interesting technology environment.

At a time when it is hard to tell one computer book from another, Manning celebrates the inventiveness and initiative of the computer business with book covers based on the rich diversity of regional life of two centuries ago, brought back to life by Maréchal's pictures. Just think, Maréchal's was a world so different from ours people would take the time to read a book title 30 words long.

PART I

Preliminaries

The Preliminaries part of this book provides the programmer with overviews of important concepts for Java networking and the Java security model. It also provides overviews of exceptions and multithreading, topics which are assumed during the rest of the book.

Chapter 1: Introduction to networking   This chapter presents the basics of networking with TCP/IP, including the concept of stacks and layers, IP, TCP, UDP, ports, sockets, and the TCP family of services.

Chapter 2: The Java security model   This chapter outlines browser restrictions on client resource access. The `SecurityManager` class places certain limitations on the operations that untrusted code may perform. An understanding of these limitations is useful if networked applications are to be embedded on the Web as applets. A brief discussion of considerations imposed by firewalls is also provided, along with an overview of Java's "sandbox" security model.

Chapter 3: Overview of exceptions   The Java exception handling model is introduced in this chapter, along with the relevant classes, how to make use of exceptions, how to define your own exceptions, and why.

Chapter 4: Overview of multithreading   The Java language natively supports multithreading, which can be important in writing powerful client and server applications. This chapter gives an overview of this capability, the relevant classes, and some of the issues that arise with multithreaded applications.

C H A P T E R   1

Introduction to networking

A network is simply a collection of interconnected information devices that speak the same data transmission protocol.

1.1 Stacks and layers

Networking involves moving data from one device on a network to other devices on the network. For devices to communicate, they must all speak the same data transmission language. Protocols provide that language.

When a given unit of data is being transferred across a network, an array of related networking protocols is involved in everything from pushing the relevant voltages (or pulses of light) over the physical links to delivering continuous data streams to applications that use the data. The relationship of these pro-

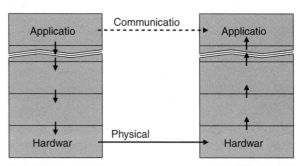

Figure 1.1   A network stack

tocols to one another is most naturally visualized as a *stack* or *layer* system, with the bottom layer being hardware and the top being the networked applications actually producing and consuming the data. The middle layers handle intermediate functions such as bridging different physical networks into larger networks. Each networking layer performs a discrete function and talks only to the layers immediately above and below it in the stack (figure 1.1).

The point of the stack abstraction is that each layer in the stack need handle only its specific function and may, in fact, be implemented by several different interchangeable protocols. For example, the standard Ethernet LAN (a datalink protocol with associated hardware) found in many office complexes may simultaneously carry IP, IPX (Novell), and AppleTalk, all of which are distinct network-layer protocols.

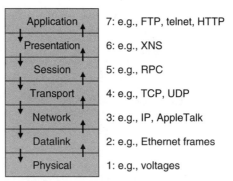

Figure 1.2   The OSI networking stack

1.1.1 OSI seven-layer model

The open systems interconnect (OSI) model is a seven-layer stack specified and implemented by the International Standards Organization. The actual OSI protocols never caught on in the United States, but the general model is a good one to use when designing network stacks. The OSI model is often used to illustrate principles of network layers (figure 1.2).

1.1.2 IP suite

Since the Internet and intranet are Internet Protocol (IP) networks, the IP suite is the stack of interest to the Internet/intranet applications programmer. The IP family of networking protocols subdivides networking functions into five conceptual layers instead of seven (figure 1.3).

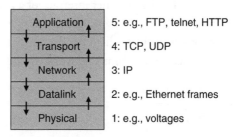

Figure 1.3   The IP networking stack

1.1.3 Encapsulation

Each layer talks only to the layers immediately below and above it in the stack. This arrangement is accomplished by means of encapsulation and decapsulation. *Encapsulation* is the process of embedding each layer's packets into the packets of the layer immediately below it (figure 1.4). *Decapsulation* is the reverse process—stripping lower level packets as the data moves up the receiving machine's protocol stack.

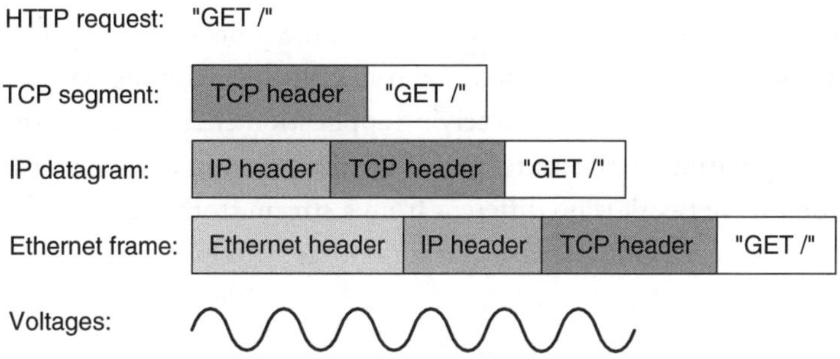

HTTP request: "GET /"

TCP segment: | TCP header | "GET /" |

IP datagram: | IP header | TCP header | "GET /" |

Ethernet frame: | Ethernet header | IP header | TCP header | "GET /" |

Voltages:

Figure 1.4   Encapsulation between protocol layers

1.1.4 In practice

The process works as follows: An application generates a stream of data. In the case of TCP/IP, this stream is handed to the transport layer, which encapsulates the data in TCP segments and performs other transport layer functions, such as error correction. TCP then passes the segments to the IP layer, which puts them into IP datagrams and performs other network layer functions, such as routing. The datagrams next go to the datalink layer, which in many cases is an Ethernet.

The Ethernet encapsulates the datagrams into frames, which it then prepares to put on the physical cable. The frames move onto the wire as a voltage, to be picked up by another Ethernet card or interface somewhere else on the physical network. If the original data stream is bound for a local machine, the Ethernet card of the local destination machine will pick up the frames directly from the wire. Otherwise they will be picked up by the Ethernet interface of a gateway of some sort, possibly an IP router. The IP router will then decapsulate the frames into IP packets, make routing decisions about them, re-encapsulate them for the correct outbound interface, and ship them off toward the destination machine's network (figure 1.5).

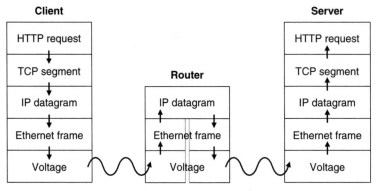

Figure 1.5   TCP/IP communication

When the remote host receives the frames addressed to it, the process of decapsulation begins. Each packet is stripped out of its containing packet as the incoming data are passed up the stack to the application layer. The receiving application ends up seeing the stream generated by the originating application. As far as the receiving application is concerned, the stream from the network is no different from a stream from the local file-system, keyboard, or other device, despite the fact that it may have originated thousands of miles away.

1.2 The Internet

An *internet* is a collection of more than one network with any-to-any connectivity based on a network (layer 3) protocol. The *Internet* is specifically the worldwide network of TCP/IP networks, which use IP addresses and protocols under the ultimate jurisdiction of the Internet Society (figure 1.6).

The networks that comprise the Internet are quite varied. They include everything from permanent enterprise-level corporate networks and university networks to SLIP/PPP accounts from Internet service providers (ISPs). All of these self-contained networks connect to larger regional providers via wide-area networking (WAN), which in turn connect at peering points to exchange Internet traffic. Most of the networks that

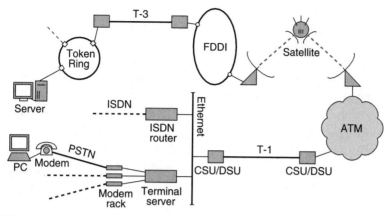

Figure 1.6 An internet

connect to the Internet are permanent local-area networks (LANs), but many are also transient dialup accounts, which originate from a pool of IP addresses provided by ISPs.

1.2.1 IP: the Internet protocol

TCP/IP is the most prevalent network protocol on the Internet. TCP/IP has as its foundation the IP. IP is a layer 3 (network) protocol for addressing hosts and routing data packets (datagrams) between them. IP overlays datalink layer networks of vastly different sorts to link machines on different types of physical networks as if they were on the same network. The current version of IP is formally known as IPv4.

1.2.2 IP addresses and networks

IP addresses take the form *x.x.x.x*, where each *x* is one byte, such as `152.2.254.81`. Every IP address falls into a *network*, which is a block of IP addresses grouped for administrative purposes.

Networks fall into different *classes*. The number of hosts in the network is determined by the class of which it is a member. There are five classes, and every network falls into only one of them, based on the first byte in its address.

- Class A: 1–126 (16M hosts each)
- Class B: 128–191 (65,536 hosts each)
- Class C: 192–223 (256 hosts each)
- Class D: 224–239 (multicast mode)
- Class E: 240–255 (reserved for future use)

The class scheme was designed to provide a range of network sizes so that organizations could match the network size to the actual number of hosts required. The class scheme subsequently had to be modified to avoid technical problems with routing table overload. These problems are discussed in appendix A, section A.4.7.

1.2.3 IP subnets

IP makes use of subnets, which are logical divisions of a network into smaller networks. Each subnet consists of a range of addresses from the original IP net. Subnets are necessary in order to configure an IP network that is made up of more than one broadcast-based network such as Ethernet. Each subnet contains its own broadcast address.

IP networks and subnets have a broadcast address. Packets to this address are picked up by every host on the network or subnet. A non-subnetted IP address uses a default broadcast address based on the class of the IP address. For example, the Class C address 198.86.40.81 has a default broadcast address of 198.86.40.255.

The netmask is a binary mask that covers the network number portion of the IP address. If the network is not subnetted, the netmask is the default netmask for whichever class of network contains the IP address. For example, a non-subnetted Class B address has a netmask of 255.255.0.0 and a non-subnetted Class C has the netmask

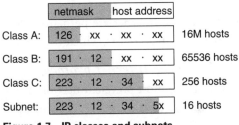

Figure 1.7 **IP classes and subnets**

255.255.255.0. For a subnetted address, the netmask will extend into some portion of the address beyond the default. The portion of the address that is not the network and subnet addresses is the host address (figure 1.7). All hosts that share a subnet are configured to have the same netmask and broadcast address.

1.2.4 ARP

The address resolution protocol (ARP) is used by IP to find the hardware address associated with a given IP address. When a host tries to send an IP packet, it first encapsulates the packet into the frames of the datalink layer protocol below it. It sends an ARP request, which is sent on the hardware broadcast address, to get the hardware address of the host in question. If the host is not on the local subnet, IP will use the broadcast to ask for the hardware address of the local IP gateway.

1.2.5 IP datagrams

An IP datagram consists of a header and a protocol data unit (PDU). The header contains information about fragmentation, length, time to live (TTL), and similar parameters. The PDU contains the data being encapsulated, which usually means a TCP segment or UDP packet.

IP uses Internet Control Message Protocol (ICMP) to correct routing problems on the fly. ICMP supports various messages for managing packet flow. The most important ICMP messages are:

- *Destination unreachable*   When a router destroys a packet because the destination is unreachable, it sends this message back to the originating host.

- *Redirect*   The redirect message is sent by a router to a host when it discovers that the host is using an inefficient route that is passing through it.

- *Echo*   An echo message asks the destination to respond with an echo reply message, which proves that the remote end is up and functioning. Programs like ping and traceroute use echo to debug network connectivity.

- *Source quench*   A source quench is sent to a packet source to get it to slow its transmission rate.

1.2.6 IP routing

Conceptually, IP networks are based on hosts and routers (figure 1.8). The hosts implement IP stacks and do transmission flow control, error-checking (if any), and other data processing. The routers concern themselves only with discovery of the optimal path through the network.

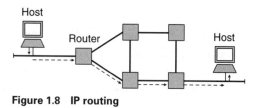

Figure 1.8   IP routing

The key to IP is its routing capability. An IP router has several network interfaces and examines each packet that appears on them. It then calculates a least-cost route to the destination, by means of its routing protocol, and forwards the packet down the appropriate interface toward the destination. A simple router does not need global knowledge of the network. It must simply know which of its local interfaces the packet should be forwarded to, based upon the destination address.

1.3   TCP: transmission control protocol

TCP is a connection-oriented transport protocol that sits on top of IP. TCP packets, called *segments*, are encapsulated into IP datagrams. TCP encoding and decoding occur at the hosts that form the endpoints of the communications channel. Along the way, the intermediate routers examine the IP packets only to make routing decisions.

TCP provides applications with data streams in which all transmitted data are guaranteed to appear at the destination host's applications layer in the order that they were transmitted. TCP is not isochronous, which means that it makes no guarantee about the exact arrival time or rate at which the segments will appear on the remote end, only that they will appear uncorrupted and in the correct order.

1.3.1 TCP's features

TCP provides a number of mechanisms to implement quality of service (QOS) over the connectionless, nonguaranteed IP layer:

- *Multiplexing (ports)*   A given host can support more than one TCP-based connection simultaneously because the TCP layer does multiplexing and demultiplexing based on port numbers (figure 1.9). Well-known services such as telnet, HTTP, and SMTP have port numbers assigned

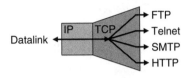

Figure 1.9   Multiplexing TCP virtual streams

by a central authority. Custom applications may make private use of other ports. Ports with numbers below 1024 are known as *privileged*, and are reserved for authorized services. Ports 255 and below should not be used by programmers, as they are typically allocated for system purposes.

- *Guaranteed, unique delivery*   A sequence number is assigned to each segment transmitted by the sending TCP. On the remote end, a checksum is performed; and if data are missing, the receiving end informs the sending end to retransmit. If the data are intact, the receiving end sends an acknowledgment, called an *ACK*. TCP automatically removes duplicate segments so that the receiving end sees each segment only once.

- *Streams*   TCP supports virtual streams across a network. Each TCP session is a connection between two machines and designated ports on those machines. TCP makes use of the network to present remote applications with a point-to-point connection that resembles a direct byte-oriented stream.

- *Slow start*   Congestion is the number one cause of packet loss in the Internet. This problem arises if packets are arriving at a router too quickly, and it must drop some to prevent buffer overflows. TCP uses a slow start algorithm that initially limits a new connection's bandwidth, so that it does not transmit excessive amounts of data if the network is congested. Slow start leads into TCP's flow control mechanism.

- *Flow control*   Flow control enables TCP to adjust the sender's send rate and, thereby, avoid buffer overflows on the receiving machine. TCP accomplishes this with a variable-length sending window, which both ends adjust based on data acknowledgment.

- *Full-duplex transmission*   TCP connections simultaneously transmit and receive, which saves the time required for a turnaround signal required by a half-duplex connection.

1.3.2 Ports and sockets

A socket represents a TCP connection between two applications across a TCP/IP network. It is specified by IP addresses and port numbers at both ends of the connection, although typically only the server's port number is encountered by the programmer. At the server, a process listens on a particular port. Every time a connection is made to the port, a TCP stream is created between the server and the client.

Sockets are the basis of most applications layer network communications. TCP is useful when net-

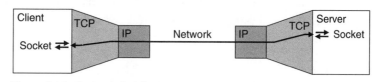

Figure 1.10   Ports and sockets

work overhead is not a significant problem and reliable data transfer is required (figure 1.10).

1.4 UDP: User Datagram Protocol

UDP is a connectionless transport layer protocol that sits on top of IP. Unlike TCP, UDP provides no state management and data integrity functions except for a checksum. It provides no congestion avoidance, and no packet delivery guarantees. If the receiving IP stack receives the packet and finds that the UDP datagram is corrupted, it simply throws it away.

1.4.1 UDP sockets

UDP provides sockets in much the same way that TCP does. A UDP socket is identified by the local IP address and the UDP port. Packets may be sent to anywhere or received from anywhere through a UDP socket.

1.4.2 Uses for UDP

UDP is appropriate when transport layer overhead must be minimized or

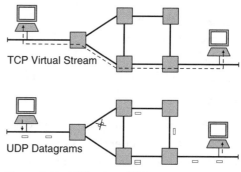

Figure 1.11   TCP versus UDP

data reliability is not crucial. This is the case when the application calls for small, independent packets. Examples of well-known services that use UDP are NFS, DNS, and SNMP. When using UDP, it is important to keep in mind that zero, one, or more than one copy of a datagram may get to the receiving end (figure 1.11).

UDP packet length is stored in 16 bits, so when using UDP it is important to limit data size. It is also particularly important to limit packet size to avoid fragmentation.

Fragmentation arises if a packet must be broken into several smaller packets for transmission purposes. This reduces the chances of data delivery because, if any of the fragments is lost, the entire packet will be discarded.

1.5 The IP family of services

The IP family of services is largely applications layer services that are usually found bundled into IP stacks or in system applications. The specific port numbers that the services use are specified and published by a central authority. All TCP/IP services are client/server in nature.

1.5.1 FTP

File transfer protocol is one of the original TCP/IP protocols. FTP is used for transferring documents and binary files. FTP works by allowing a user to log on and request documents for downloading or uploading. FTP uses TCP port 21 for initiating and controlling connections, and TCP port 20 for data transfer.

1.5.2 Telnet

Telnet is an application that allows users to log in to (telnet to) a machine and use the equivalent of a direct console or terminal. Telnet uses TCP port 23.

1.5.3 Gopher

Gopher is a precursor to HTTP that organizes and presents information in a text-based menu format. Gopher has been largely obviated by HTTP. Gopher uses TCP port 70.

1.5.4 Finger

The finger protocol is used to find out information about users on a particular host. It can also provide information about currently logged-in users. Finger uses TCP port 79. An example finger client is provided in chapter 5.

1.5.5 WAIS

Wide Area Information Server is a system of indexing and searching a filesystem. WAIS consists of two components: an indexer and a search engine. The indexer indexes information in a filesystem and creates a lookup table. The search engine accepts search strings from the user and queries the lookup table.

WAIS is becoming obsolete, replaced by more advanced systems that operate on similar principles over the Web.

1.5.6 NNTP

Network News Transport Protocol is used to transfer articles among servers (and NNTP-enabled clients) in the USENET Internet news system. NNTP uses a flooding protocol to make sure that a given article gets transferred to every server in the system. NNTP uses TCP port 119.

1.5.7 SMTP

Simple Mail Transfer Protocol is the protocol used to transfer email between mail transport agents (MTAs) over the Internet. Sendmail is the most widely used MTA. ESMTP is a new extended version of SMTP that supports additional commands for MTA communication. SMTP uses TCP port 25.

1.5.8 SNMP

Simple Network Management Protocol is used to remotely manage network devices. SNMP allows manipulation of a management information base (MIB) for a networked object. Network interface cards, Ethernet hubs, and routers are possible examples of SNMP-enabled network devices. SNMP uses UDP ports 161 and 162.

1.5.9 HTTP

Hypertext Transfer Protocol is the World Wide Web protocol. It uses TCP port 80. An example HTTP server is provided in chapter 17.

Standard HTTP is a stateless protocol. The client opens a connection to the server and makes a request. The server responds to the request by passing the requested information to the browser, and then closes the connection. HTTP documents consist of headers, which contain type and other information, and a data body. Normally, the browser masks the headers so that the user does not see them.

The Uniform Resource Locator URLs are used to point to resources of all types on the World Wide Web, including HTTP

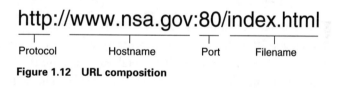

Figure 1.12   URL composition

documents. A URL is made up of a protocol part, a server designation, and a file (path) designation (figure 1.12).

Common Gateway Interface HTTP provides for server-side extensions that conform to the CGI standard. CGI programs typically reside in specified directories, usually called `cgi-bin`, on the server and are invoked by HTML browsers based on user action.

CGIs can be used in HTML documents as images, links, and as the action for forms. When the user activates the CGI, the browser opens a connection to the server and passes a set of information to it. The server then starts a copy of

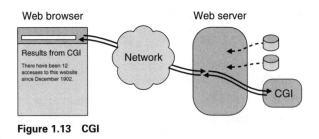

Figure 1.13   CGI

the CGI program and passes this information to it as environment variables and its standard input. Whatever the CGI writes to its standard output is sent back to the browser via the server (figure 1.13).

The browser can pass environment information to the server in three ways. The `get` method puts this information in an environment variable, usually called `QUERY_STRING`. The `post` method puts the information in the CGI's standard input. Information also may be encoded as the end part of the URL used to invoke the CGI; information appears in the `PATH_INFO` variable.

CGIs can indicate whether the server should process, or parse, the header information on the return trip or pass it through to the browser unparsed. In the default case, the server parses the data. To indicate to the server that it is not to parse the data, the CGI filename typically must begin with the string `nph-`, although this designation may differ depending on the server.

1.6 DNS

The Domain Naming System (DNS) is a distributed mapping system between host names and IP numbers. It allows hosts to have one or more names that resolve to a varying number of IP addresses. In general, each host on the Internet with a registered name has one name associated with its IP number. The entire host name, including the domain and subdomain component, is known as the host's fully qualified domain name (FQDN). Resolving the same FQDN to more than one IP address is known as round-robin DNS. Round-robin DNS is used to distribute load for one service, such as a Web host, across multiple machines.

DNS performs two functions. It provides lookup services, or name resolution, to hosts that are trying to find the IP number of a given host name. It also provides the database that defines these mappings. Both of these functions are provided by name servers, which are hosts that provide name resolution services.

DNS is implemented by a hierarchical system of name servers that resolve different components of the FQDN. The root level is maintained by InterNIC. InterNIC is responsible for assigning domain names in all root level domains, including .edu, .com,

.mil, .net, .org, and creating entries for each domain in the root name servers. These entries list the authoritative name servers for each domain (figure 1.14).

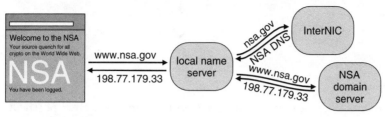

Figure 1.14   DNS in action

1.6.1 Authoritative and caching-only name servers

Authoritative name servers are specific machines on the Internet that provide listings for all of the machines and subdomains for a given organization's block of IP numbers. Authoritative name servers have entries that either give the host name-IP mappings directly or point to other name servers which give these mappings.

1.6.2 Host name lookup

Each host that needs to resolve host names is configured to use a DNS server to make name resolution queries. This server is provided by an ISP or the local network administration. When a new host name needs to be looked up, the host queries its name server. A special type of name server used only for lookups is known as a caching-only name server. Caching-only name servers diminish network traffic by performing a lookup only once and then retaining the results for a preset period, typically fourteen days.

1.6.3 Reverse lookups

Standard DNS is a one-way mapping from host name to IP number. Reverse mappings are sometimes useful, usually for verification purposes. Organizations may list their IP numbers and associated host name in a special domain, in-addr.arpa, to facilitate reverse lookups on their IP numbers.

1.7 Firewalls and proxy servers

For security reasons, many organizations choose to partition their internal networks from the Internet by means of firewalls (figure 1.15). Firewalls may be configured to restrict traffic in a variety of fashions; and, as a result, not all options will be open in certain situations. For example, a heavily firewalled site may permit traffic only to port 80

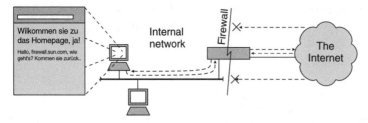

Figure 1.15 Firewalls

of the Web server, in which case a stand-alone server running on a dedicated port will not be accessible from a client running outside the firewall.

Firewalls come in two primary flavors: packet filters and application-layer gateways. Packet filtering happens at the IP layer, usually at routers with external interfaces. Packet filtering employs an access control list to allow or deny packet delivery to inside hosts based on the source and destination address in the packet. Attempts to reach hosts behind the firewall are blocked and sometimes logged.

Applications level gateways are also known as proxies. A proxy is a server that is interposed between an internal client and an outside service when the client attempts to make an outside connection. For example, an HTTP proxy server accepts connections from internal clients that are directed toward an outside host's port 80. It then makes the connection to the outside itself and relays the response to the client. This insulates the client and hides details about the internal network from the outside service. Proxies are typically able to do more logging and implement more sophisticated access control criteria than packet filters.

Proxies have the unfortunate effect of eliminating true streams between client and server. Since the HTTP proxy is in effect the server for the internal client, there is no way for the client and the actual remote server to communicate in any way except through the specific services the proxy supports. Supported service usually means only port 80 traffic. This effectively prevents many Web-based networked applications from operating through firewalls, except through HTTP requests.

1.8 Conclusion

TCP/IP networking fundamentals are the foundation of most Java networking, including the classes developed in this book. Java code based on these APIs and the core APIs may also utilize the TCP/IP family of applications layer services such as DNS, SMTP, and HTTP. Appendix A contains further information on these and other netowrking topics. Also see the books *Computer Networks* by Andrew S. Tannenbaum (Prentice Hall, 1996) and *Unix Network Programming: Network Apis: Sockets and Xti (Volume 1)* by W. Richard Stevens, (Prentice Hall, 1997).

C H A P T E R   2

The Java security model

A basic working knowledge of the Java security model is indispensable for any programmer who wishes to make use of Java for serious applications. Since Java is designed to be distributed and must, therefore, provide assurances of safety, Java implementations necessarily impose

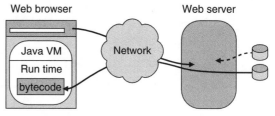

Figure 2.1   Java execution flow

restrictions on applet/application access to system resources such as networks and file systems (figure 2.1). This chapter provides an overview of the main points of the security model which affect the networked applications programmer.

Java provides two levels of security: low-level intrinsic security and resource-level security. Java's intrinsic security relates to the integrity of byte-codes that come across a network, and consists of a bytecode verifier and a `ClassLoader`. The verifier attempts to make sure that incoming byte-codes do not perform illegal type conversions, memory accesses, and other similar forbidden activities. The `ClassLoader` partitions the name spaces of classes loaded from across the network and prevents collisions and related name resolution problems. The `ClassLoader` also ensures that local classes are loaded first to prevent spoofing of system classes. On top of this, Java provides resource access restriction through a `SecurityManager` class (figure 2.2).

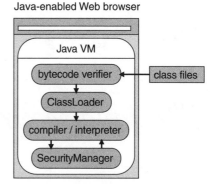

Figure 2.2   Java's security model

Java's intrinsic security measures are extremely important, but they are for the most part transparent to the programmer. Java's resource-level security restrictions are much more relevant because they directly affect the availability of higher-level system resources. Resource-level security is especially important for clients that are applets, because applets bear the brunt of security restrictions.

2.1   Untrusted and trusted code

Java's security model centers around the concept of trust. The security model defines a "sandbox," which is a limited set of resources considered safe for untrusted code. Properly authenticated, or "trusted," code may operate outside the sandbox and enjoy increased resource privileges.

At the time of writing, the majority of deployed Java-enabled browsers still only implement JDK 1.0.2, which treats all Java applets as untrusted and, therefore, restricts them all to the sandbox. The 1.1 API introduced mechanisms to create trusted applets; thus providing the potential for basic trusted applet support. However limitations of the 1.1 signing mechanism led to browser-specific signing technologies such as Netscape's capabilities API and Microsoft's Authenticode technology. Finally, JDK 1.2 introduced a powerful and general permissions API that could replace browser-specific techniques, however market penetration of this API is minimal. As a result, if you wish to deploy trusted applets then you must typically consult vendor-specific sites for details of their particular solutions.

2.2 SecurityManager and resources

Java's trust policy is implemented with the `SecurityManager` class, which determines the level of I/O access for run time objects. Since an applet in a Web page is instantiated and runs within the run time of the browser, the browser's built-in `SecurityManager` governs the applet's I/O capabilities (figure 2.3). The applet programmer cannot override the browser's `SecurityManager` to gain additional access to resources.

The `SecurityManager` imposes a variety of restrictions on resources, including file system access, access to native methods, thread modification, network resources, and access to system properties. Current browser `SecurityManager` classes allow untrusted applets no file system access, no ability to spawn processes on the client, and no native code execution.

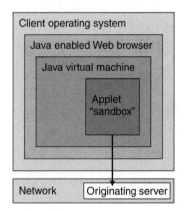

Figure 2.3 The Java sandbox model

2.2.1 System properties

Browsers provide read-only access to a limited set of system properties. These properties usually include those listed in table 2.1, among others, and are accessible through the `getProperty()` method of the `System` class. Web browsers usually provide a few properties in addition to these:

Table 2.1 Standard Java system properties

Property name	Property meaning
os.name	Operating system name
os.arch	Operating system architecture
file.separator	Local OS' file separator (e.g. "\" for Windows)

Table 2.1   Standard Java system properties

Property name	Property meaning
line.separator	Local OS' path separator (e.g. ";" for Windows
java.version	Java version
java.vendor	Java vendor's string
java.vendor.url	Java vendor's URL
java.class.version	Java class library version

2.2.2 Threads

Threads may not be modified by untrusted code that does not *own* them. This usually means that only the applet that created a thread may manipulate it; however, there are occasional implementation bugs that err on over-restrictiveness and others that err on laxity.

2.2.3 Network resources

Untrusted code is restricted from accessing network resources for security reasons: with unrestricted network access, an applet could leak information about a firewalled network, for example. The restrictions on network access are discussed more fully in section 2.3.

2.2.4 Process creation

For obvious security reasons untrusted code cannot start a process on the client machine. This means that an applet cannot execute a system command, even if the system command is relatively harmless.

2.2.5 File access

In general, untrusted code is not allowed access to any files on the local system. Some browsers are introducing special directories to which applets have limited access, but the details of such facilities vary among different environments.

2.2.6 Global API resources

Some classes in the Java API provide facilities for installing resources that affect the entire run time. These include the Socket class, which provides a SocketImplFactory for custom socket implementations, and the URL classes, which provide various global protocol and content handler frameworks. The SecurityManager governs access to these customization features, and prevents untrusted code from affecting the run time through these mechanisms.

2.3 Networked applets

Major browsers allow an untrusted applet to open sockets and URLs only to its source host. The applet source is the host that served the class files; this is usually the Webserver from which the original HTML page was served, unless the `codebase` parameter specifies an alternate host. Attempts to open sockets to any other host result in a `Security-Exception`.

In typical environments, the applet is served from the same host as the Web page that contains it. This means that for client/server Java applets, when the applet connects back to its server, its server must be running on the main Web server machine.

If your Web site is heavily loaded, you can reduce load on the primary machine by serving applets from, and running their servers on, a secondary machine running another Web server. To do this, you simply serve the main HTML document from the main Web server, but change the `codebase` in the `applet` tag so that the applet is loaded from the secondary server. In this case, the application's Java server will need to run on the secondary Web server along with the extra Web server, since that is the source of the applet (figure 2.4).

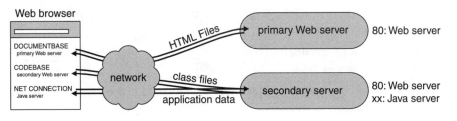

Figure 2.4   Load sharing with applets

Note that if you serve code from a secondary machine in this fashion, you will have to use the `getCodeBase()` call in your applets instead of `getDocumentBase()` in order to load images and audio files and do other types of networking. Otherwise you will get a `SecurityException` for trying to create a socket to the host that served the HTML instead of the host that served the applet.

2.3.1 URL protocols

Unfortunately, the access that applets have to different URL protocols is inconsistent from environment to environment. In general, if an applet is loaded from a `file` URL, then it has no network access. It can only access files relative to its `codebase`.

If an applet is loaded from an HTTP URL, then it has network access back to the host that served it and can use HTTP URLs to access other resources on that machine. It is not safe to assume that all environments will provide access to any other URL protocols, such as FTP or NTTP, even if some environments do presently offer these services.

Under most current browsers, if an applet is loaded from an HTTPS URL, that is, over an SSL-secured network connection then it can also use HTTPS to securely access documents from its originating server. Other browsers restrict applets to only using unsecured HTTP connections. Until a standard interface to such secure network connections is provided, it is not safe to rely on this feature for a browser-independent applet.

2.3.2 IP multicast

Java provides access to IP multicast in addition to traditional TCP and UDP unicast. Multicast allows applications within a multicast group to communicate between each other in a peer-to-peer fashion, providing that their network supports multicast. This eliminates the need for a traditional server. Instead, an application can transmit data once and it is automatically delivered to all other applications in the group.

For applets, security restrictions complicate matters. Some browsers do not support multicast at all; others support it in the following manner: An applet may create a multicast socket and join a multicast group, but it may only receive packets from the machine that served it. Packets received from other machines will simply be discarded. The applet may not transmit to the group at all; this would allow it to break the restriction that it can only communicate with the host that served it (figure 2.5).

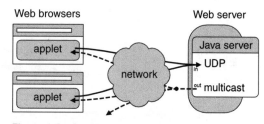

Figure 2.5   Applet access to IP multicast

To effectively transmit to a multicast group from an applet, the applet must unicast its data back to a central server (running beside the Web server, as usual) and then the central server can multicast the data to other multicast listeners in the group; see the multicast chapter for an example of this in action.

2.3.3 DNS

Applets are limited in the host name lookups that they can perform. DNS requests can theoretically be used as a *covert channel* that lets an applet leak information to a name server that is different from the host that served it. For this reason, an applet is permitted to perform name lookups only for the host that served it, as specified by its `codebase`. Attempts to look up other hosts will result in a `SecurityException`.

2.4 Firewalls

Firewalls effectively turn off all socket-based networking for Java applets, since the firewall usually blocks all unusual network traffic. HTTP proxy servers allow URL access, such as fetching images and the like, but other TCP/IP access is typically disallowed. The exceptions are if a hole is punched in the firewall on the port that the applet wants to use, or if a SOCKS system is in place.

2.4.1 HTTP proxy servers

A Web proxy allows HTTP from behind a firewall: all HTTP requests are directed from within the firewall to the proxy; the proxy then forwards these requests on to hosts out on the Internet. The Web proxy is usually specially secured against other outside access, and reveals nothing about the layout of the internal network (figure 2.6).

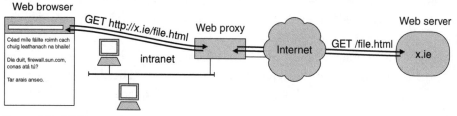

Figure 2.6   HTTP proxying

Web browsers inside a firewall must be configured to use the proxy instead of attempting a direct connection to requested URLs. URL proxying is enabled by default for applets running within such a browser. To take advantage of URL proxying from a Java application, simply set the system properties `http.proxyHost` and `http.proxy-Port` when the application is run:

```
java -Dhttp.proxyHost=proxy.myself.com -Dhttp.proxyPort=8080 MyApp
```

Any HTTP requests made by the URL classes will automatically be routed through the named Web proxy, except those made to hosts listed in the `http.nonProxyHosts` system property.

Alternatively, an application can set these properties manually through the `System.getProperties()` and `System.setProperties()` methods.

2.4.2 SOCKS

SOCKS is a middleware layer for TCP/IP that provides proxying for any TCP connection, not just HTTP. SOCKS traditionally has been used as a transport-layer *circuit-based firewall* to allow selected TCP/IP connections through firewalls. SOCKS clients route all TCP/IP traffic through SOCKS servers, which act as proxies to connect to the outside world (figure 2.7).

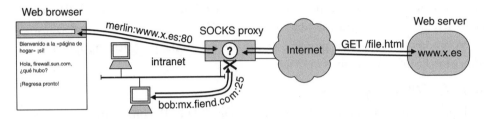

Figure 2.7 SOCKS proxying

Java provides automatic support for SOCKS socket connections with the system properties `socksProxyHost` and `socksProxyPort`. When `socksProxyHost` is set (a default port is used if none is specified), all socket connections are automatically routed through the specified SOCKS server. Currently, SOCKS proxying is only provided for TCP; in future, UDP may also be supported.

If an applet is running behind a SOCKS'ed firewall, from a browser that supports SOCKS, then any sockets that the applet creates will be automatically routed through the SOCKS server. The server will then permit or deny the connection according to its internal configuration.

An application can also make use of the SOCKS server by setting the system properties appropriately. The easiest way to achieve this is by specifying them when the application is run:

```
java -DsocksProxyHost=socks.me.com -DsocksProxyPort=1234 MyApp
```

For more details about SOCKS, see the SOCKS Web site at:
`http://www.socks.nec.com/notables/`

2.4.3 DNS behind firewalls

Many firewalls turn off DNS resolution entirely for nonlocal host names. If this is the case and a lookup is attempted, a `NoSuchHostException` will be thrown, which the `SecurityManager` will then rethrow as a `SecurityException`. If an applet needs to connect to its server from behind such firewalls, you must specify its `codebase` as an IP number so it does not need to do name lookup. Using a `codebase` of this form, however, may fail under some browsers that do not handle IP addresses correctly.

The reason that an applet can be loaded at all from within such a firewall is that the client machine does not need to perform name lookup to access HTTP documents. Instead, the request is passed verbatim to the Web proxy, which is allowed to perform name lookups.

2.5 The security API

Java provides a security API in various packages under the `java.security` hierarchy. The security API provides trust-management functionality such as signatures, message digests, and key management. A cryptographic extension is also available that provides encryption facilities but is restricted to U.S. distribution. Details of this API can be found online and in other books.

2.6 Conclusion

For stand-alone applications, resource usage is unrestricted, so few of the limitations that we have discussed apply except for the effects of firewalls. For applets, channels, and other embedded programs, resource restrictions are imposed by the respective environments' `SecurityManagers`. The exact scope of these restrictions is subject to change as new versions of browsers and other execution environments are released, although they are unlikely to change significantly from those that we have described.

As digital signatures and other authentication technologies become more widely supported, trusted applets which are subject to a different, relaxed set of restrictions will become available. Again, however, the exact restrictions will depend upon the user's choices and the environment's options.

Beyond applets and simple stand-alone applications, distributed systems such as RMI introduce new, different security implications involving the download of code from peer applications. We will discuss these issues further in the relevant chapters.

For further details, see *Securing Java* by Gary McGraw and Edward W. Felten (John Wiley & Sons, 1999) and the Web sites http://www.rstcorp.coom/javasecurity/ and http://nitric.com/jnp/codeSigning.html.

CHAPTER 3

An overview of exceptions

An *exception* is an occurrence, usually some form of error, that disrupts the normal execution flow of a Java program. When an exception occurs, the normal flow of program execution is stopped, and control is transferred to a block of code that has been designated to handle the exceptional condition. If no such code is specified, then the exception propagates up to stop the affected thread and display the exception.

Java's exception mechanism is a lot cleaner than having to check for a possible error value after every method call, such as is required in C. The Java compiler requires the programmer to catch all predictable exceptions; this is useful because it ensures that the programmer is aware of potential problems.

3.1 Exception catching

At the language level, all exceptions are themselves classes that subclass from the `java.lang.Throwable` class and are handled using the `try ... catch` mechanism. The `try` clause surrounds a block of code that may throw certain exceptions. The `catch` clause handles a particular class of exception that may be thrown by this block.

The process of handling different classes of exception obeys the Java inheritance chain (figure 3.1). A block of code that may throw an exception is surrounded with a `try` statement that has some associated `catch` clauses. Each `catch` clause indicates a particular class of exceptions to catch and has an associated handler. The `catch` clause will catch exceptions of the specified class, and any of its subclasses.

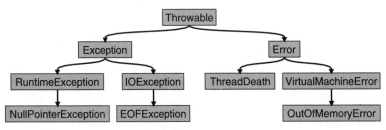

Figure 3.1   The exception inheritance chain

For example, catching exceptions of type `IOException` also catches any subclass of `IOException`, such as `EOFException`. This simplifies network programming because one does not have to name explicitly every possible exception that can occur. However, if a subclass must be dealt with in a different manner than the superclass, then either a `catch` clause for that class must be specified before the superclass `catch` clause, or the exception must be dealt with appropriately within the superclass' `catch` clause.

```
URL url;
try {
  url = new URL ("xyz");
  // ...
} catch (MalformedURLException ex) {
```

```
    // url is undefined.
} catch (IOException ex) {
    // any other IOExceptions
}
```

If an exception occurs as part of an assignment statement, then the assignment will not complete.

3.2 The major types of exceptions

In the Java environment, there are two major superclasses for exceptions, both of which themselves are subclasses of `Throwable`. The `RuntimeException` class also holds an important distinction worth noting.

3.2.1 Error

Exceptions that are a subclass of the class `Error` are serious errors in the Java run time system; and in a correct system, they should not occur. The major departure from this rule is the `ThreadDeath` exception that is used by the run time to stop a thread. `ThreadDeath` will be thrown when a thread's `stop()` method is called.

No normal code should attempt to catch a subclass of `Error`.

3.2.2 Exception

Exceptions that are a subclass of the `Exception` class are normal errors that can occur during program execution, corresponding to problems such as communications failures and so forth. Common subclasses of `Exception` include `IOException` and `InterruptedException`. These exceptions must be explicitly handled by user code. The Java compiler will complain if these exceptions are not either caught or explicitly passed on.

3.2.3 RuntimeException

`RuntimeException` is a subclass of the class `Exception` that encompasses all exceptions that can happen at run time but that cannot be predicted at compile time. This includes problems such as array bounds exceptions and null pointer exceptions. If one of these errors is encountered, then a `RuntimeException` will be thrown. It is not *necessary* to declare that a `RuntimeException` may be thrown or to provide a `try ... catch` clause; however, if you know that one may occur and wish to handle it, then the normal exception handling mechanisms can be used.

3.3 Generating exceptions

Exceptions may be generated in several ways:

3.3.1 Method calls

If a method or constructor is declared to throw an exception, then calling that method or constructor may result in an exception of the declared class or a subclass. By declaring that it throws particular exceptions, the method is permitted to throw those exceptions and does not have to catch them in the method body. It is a compile time error for a method body to throw an exception that is not declared in the throws clause, unless it is a subclass of RuntimeException.

```
int method () throws IOException ...
// ...
method (); // this call may throw an IOException
```

3.3.2 RuntimeException

A RuntimeException may occur even though the offending piece of code does not declare that it throws such an exception. Examples of RuntimeException include NullPointerException and ArrayIndexOutOfBoundsException. These exceptions can be thrown by a language statement or a method call. A RuntimeException is thrown by a method if the method executes a statement that throws the exception, and the method does not itself handle it.

```
int[] array;
// ...
int value = array[100]; // this can throw an ArrayIndexOutOfBoundsException
```

3.3.3 User-generated exceptions

Exceptions can be manually thrown with the throw statement. This statement takes a single argument that must be a subclass of Throwable. The programmer can either throw an existing subclass of Throwable or declare a new one.

```
throw new Exception ("Problem");
```

3.4 Handling exceptions

If a piece of code can generate an exception by any of the mechanisms above, then unless the exception is a RuntimeException, it must be either caught or passed on. If a RuntimeException is not caught, then it will be passed on by default.

3.4.1 Passing on exceptions

Passing on an exception refers to a method declaring that it can throw that class of exception (figure 3.2). The method body may then perform actions that can cause the

```
void method () throws IOException {
  // ...
  out.close ();_ _ _ IOException _ _ _
  // ...
}
```

Flow of Execution

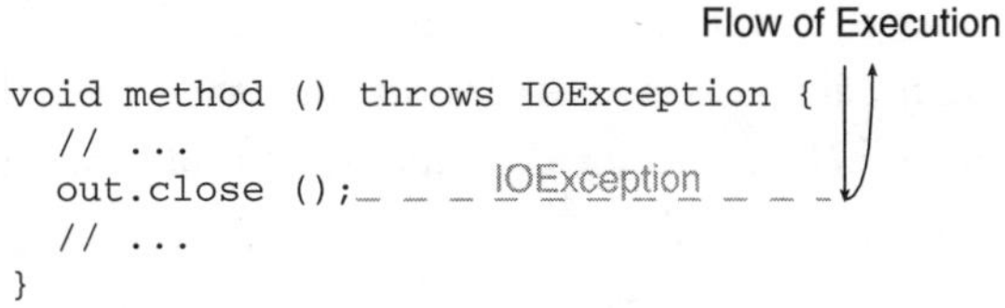

Figure 3.2 Passing on an exception

specified types of exception to be thrown. Should such an exception be thrown, then it will be passed on to the method's caller. Because the method has declared that it can throw a particular exception, the caller knows that it can occur, and must itself be able to catch the exception or pass it on. If an exception is not handled by any of the callers in the stack trace, then the current thread is stopped and the exception is printed to the terminal.

```
java.lang.NullPointerException
  at Consumer.extract(Consumer.java:47)
  at Consumer.run(Consumer.java:19) at
  java.lang.Thread.run(Thread.java)
```

3.4.2 Catching exceptions

Catching an exception refers to declaring that a block of code handles exceptions of a particular class. If an exception occurs, then execution transfers to the corresponding piece of handler code (figure 3.3).

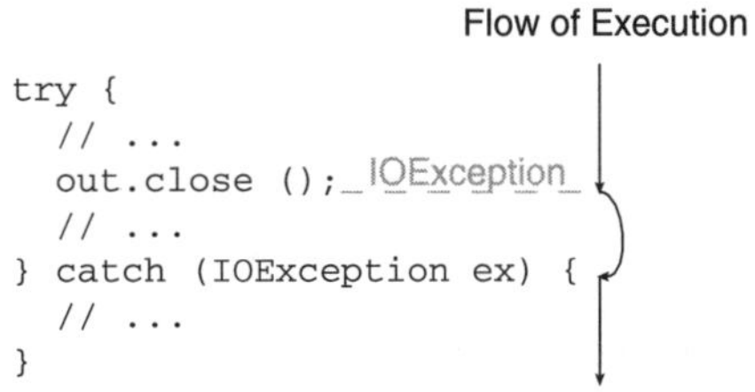

```
try {
  // block of code
} catch (ExceptionClass ex) {
  // handle exceptions of class ExceptionClass
} catch (OtherExceptionClass ex) {
  // handle exceptions of class OtherExceptionClass
}
```

Flow of Execution

```
try {
  // ...
  out.close ();_IOException_
  // ...
} catch (IOException ex) {
  // ...
}
```

Figure 3.3 Handling an exception

If the block of code here throws an exception that is of class `ExceptionClass` or any subclass, then execution will transfer to the first handler. Otherwise, if it throws an exception that is of class `OtherExceptionClass` or any subclass, execution will transfer to the second handler.

More details   In a block of code surrounded with a `try ... catch` statement, the `try` clause is the piece of code that is to be attempted. The `catch` clauses are the handlers for the various possible exceptions. There may be one or more `catch` clauses for a single `try` clause. If an exception of a caught type occurs, then the corresponding handler code is executed and the exception that was thrown is placed in the variable declared in the `catch` statement. Note that if exceptions of several types are to be caught, and one is a subclass of the other, then the `catch` clause for the subclass must appear before that for the superclass. Only the first handler that can handle the exception will be called.

```
try {
  // any code can throw a RuntimeException
} catch (NullPointerException ex) {
  // a NullPointerException occurred
  ex.printStackTrace (); // prints stack trace
} catch (RuntimeException ex) {
  // some other exception occurred
  System.err.println (ex); // prints ex.toString()
}
```

In this example, we want to distinguish between a `NullPointerException` and any other `RuntimeException`. If the `RuntimeException` clause came first, then it would always catch the `NullPointerException` and the other handler would never be executed.

3.4.3 The finally clause
A `finally` clause can be appended to a `try ... catch` statement as follows:

```
try {
  // ...
} catch (Exception ex) {
  // ...
} finally {
  // this clause is always executed
}
```

The `finally` clause is always executed after code leaves the `try` clause, regardless of the manner (figure 3.4). If the `try` clause completes naturally, then the `finally` clause is executed. If an exception occurs and is caught, then the `finally` clause is executed after the exception handler. If there is a `return` statement or other exit from the `try` clause, the `finally` clause will be executed before the exit occurs. Only if the JVM is forcibly aborted will the finally clause not be

```
                                      Flows of Execution
try {
  // ...
  out.close ();  IOException
  // ...
} catch (IOException ex) {
  // ...
} catch (Exception ex) {
  // ...
} finally {
  // ...
}
```

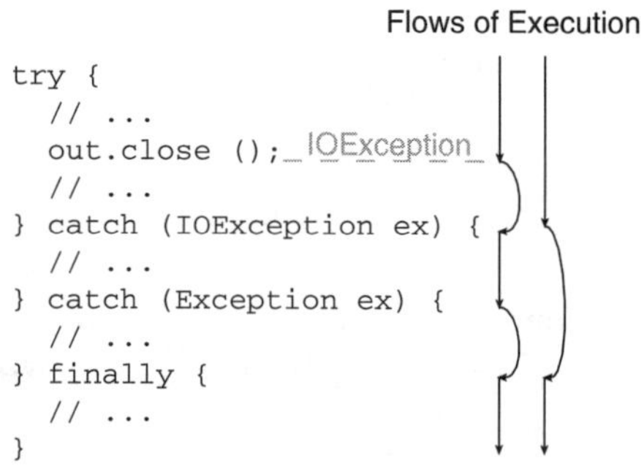

Figure 3.4   The finally clause

executed. The use of `finally` is, therefore, useful for performing cleanup after a particular piece of code, regardless of how the code exits.

3.5 Class Throwable

The `Throwable` class is the template for all exceptions, and most follow this model.

3.5.1 Constructors

`Throwable` has two constructors:

Throwable()　　This creates a `Throwable` object with no detail message. A detail message is a short description of the cause of the exception.

Throwable(String message)　　This creates a `Throwable` object with the specified detail message. A detail message is useful to help identify the cause when the exception stack trace is printed.

3.5.2 Useful methods

`Throwable` has several useful methods.

Throwable fillInStackTrace()　　This method inserts the current execution stack trace into the exception and returns the exception. The current stack trace is the list of method calls that has led up to the current point in execution; this is what is displayed when an exception is printed. Usually the exception constructor inserts the current stack trace, so when an exception is created, the list of method calls that led up to the exception being created will be automatically inserted. The `fillInStackTrace()` method can be used to alter an exception, so that it appears as if it originated at the rethrowing point, rather than at the original occurrence.

void printStrackTrace()　　This method prints the exception's stack trace, which displays the sequence of method calls that led to the exception being thrown. This method is useful for tracking down errors.

void printStrackTrace(PrintStream out)　　This version of `printStackTrace()` prints the exception's stack trace to the specified `PrintStream out`.

JDK 1.1　*void printStackTrace (PrintWriter writer)*　　This version of `print-StackTrace()` prints the exception's stack trace to the specified `Printwriter`, `writer`.

String getMessage()　　The `getMessage()` method returns the exception's detail message.

String getLocalizedMessage ()   The `getLocalizedMessage()` method returns a locale-specific version of the exception's detail message; the default implementation just returns `getMessage()`.

String toString()   The `toString()` method is overridden to include the exception class and the detail message.

3.6 User exceptions

Declaring your own exception is simply a case of declaring a class that subclasses the appropriate exception, and providing the appropriate constructors. You can then throw exceptions of the new class in the usual manner.

```
import java.io.IOException;

public class AuthException extends IOException {
   public AuthException () {
   }
   public AuthException (String detail) {
      super (detail);
   }
}
```

This code declares a new exception type that is a subclass of `IOException`. Networking code can throw exceptions of this type if an authentication error occurs. It is important to subclass an appropriate exception type; for most networking code, this will be `IOException` or a subclass. Many of the networking- and I/O-related methods are declared as throwing `IOExceptions`; we can safely throw this `AuthException` class from one of these methods, even though it did not exist when the original API classes were defined.

Because our new exception is a subclass of `IOException`, all existing code will be able to handle the new exceptions appropriately.

3.7 Wrapping up

Exceptions provide a clean error-handling mechanism for the language. Code can be written without explicit error checks, and the appropriate exception handling code will automatically be called if a problem arises.

We can define our own exceptions that will fit within the standard exception model, and we can use `finally` clauses to perform cleanup operations where necessary, regardless of how the corresponding block of code exits.

C H A P T E R   4

An overview of multithreading

Multithreading is an important aspect of network programming in Java. It lets us write efficient and robust servers that process separate client connections in separate threads. We can use this to insulate different client handlers from each other, and to insulate applications from communication failures. We make extensive use of threads for both clients and servers in this book, so an appropriate understanding of the wherewithals of thread usage is appropriate.

Traditionally, one considers only a single flow of execution through a program: execution begins at the start and flows along a single path until the program terminates (figure 4.1).

The concept of multithreading is that there can be multiple flows, or threads, of execution in the same program at the same time (figure 4.2). This is unlike multitasking, because the threads execute in the same data space; if a global variable is changed in one thread, all the other threads will observe the change.

On a multiprocessor machine, different threads may truly run concurrently on different processors. This provides an easy route to upgrading the processing power of a server, because even a single application will see the benefit.

Java supports threads natively at the language level. This makes programming with threads significantly easier than if a helper library must be used, as was traditionally the case.

The Java environment provides a `Thread` class for handling threads. There is a one-to-one correspondence between `Thread` objects and actual language threads. The language thread may be controlled by calling methods on its corresponding `Thread` object.

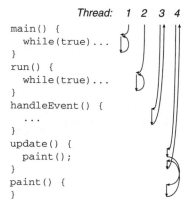

```
main() {
    execute();
}
execute() {
    logon();
    communicate();
    logoff();
}
logoff() {
}
communicate() {
}
logon() {
}
```

Figure 4.1 A single-threaded application

```
                    Thread:  1 2  3  4
main() {
    while(true)...
}
run() {
    while(true)...
}
handleEvent() {
    ...
}
update() {
    paint();
}
paint() {
}
```

Figure 4.2 A multithreaded application

4.1 Variable scope in threads

Variables, which are declared within the execution of a thread, are local to that thread. That is to say, modifications made to the local variables of one thread are not made to the local variables of another thread. *Local* in this context does not refer to instance variables, but to variables that are declared within a method; these are variables that are allocated memory in the thread's local stack.

`Static` class member variables will thus be common to all threads; other instance variables will be common to all threads accessing a particular instance of the class. All method parameters and local variables will be local to a single thread.

```
class Test {
   static int staticW;
   Vector instanceX;

   void aMethod (int paramY) {
      float localZ = staticW;
      instanceX.addElement (new Float (localZ));
   }
}
```

In this example, every thread that calls the `aMethod()` method will be allocated its own variables `paramY` and `localZ`. The `instanceX` instance variable will shared by all threads calling `aMethod()` on the same instance of the `Test` class, and the `staticW` will be shared among all threads in the run time.

Obviously, a locally declared reference variable may refer to a nonlocal object, in which case any changes to the object will be nonlocal in scope.

4.2 Synchronization

Threads introduce a need for synchronization. *Synchronization* is a mechanism to allow the relative execution of different threads to be controlled, to prevent certain undesirable paths of execution. Consider the following code:

```
int balance;

boolean withdraw (int amount) {
   if (balance - amount >= 0) {
      balance -= amount;
      return true;
   }
   return false;
}
```

Ordinarily, this code would be perfectly correct; the withdrawal is performed only if the new balance would be positive. Consider, however, two threads executing this method simultaneously. See figure 4.3 and figure 4.4.

Figure 4.3 Two threads execute a method at the same time

If thread 2 happens to interrupt thread 1 at a critical point, then the balance could become negative (table 4.1). To overcome this, we need synchronization.

Figure 4.4 Execution of a method rapidly switches between two threads

Table 4.1   Thread synchronization

Thread 1	Thread 2	balance
if (15 - 10 >= 0)		15
	if (15 - 10 >= 0)	15
balance -= 10		5
	balance -= 10	-5

A synchronized block is a region of code that can only be entered by a *single* thread at a time. In this thread example, two threads were executing in the withdraw() method at the same time. Note that we wish to restrict access to the balance variable of this object—not to the block of code itself.

In Java, the synchronized statement allows us to mark regions of code as being accessible to just a single thread at a time.

```
synchronized (anObject) {
   // critical statements
}
```

The Java run time will ensure that only one thread can execute the enclosed critical statements on anObject at a time.

4.2.1 Semaphores

Every class and object in Java has an associated semaphore. A semaphore is a special system object (not a Java object) that has two operations available on it: get and release. Only one thread can get a semaphore at a time; all other threads which attempt to get a semaphore that is already owned by another thread will be put to sleep. When the semaphore owner calls release, one of the waiting threads will succeed in its get request, and all the others will go back to sleep (figure 4.5). With this mechanism, access to facilities can be restricted to just a single thread at a time—that which owns the semaphore. The nature of semaphores is entirely hidden from the Java programmer with the synchronized abstraction.

Regions of code can be marked as being synchronized on a particular object or class. Before entering a synchronized block of code, a thread must obtain the semaphore

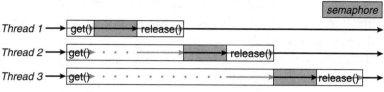

Figure 4.5   Using semaphores

on the specified object or class. If the semaphore is already taken, then the thread will block (go to sleep) until the semaphore is released.

In this manner, if a particular piece of code is a critical section for a certain object `object`, it can be placed within a `synchronized(object)` statement. In the previous example, the `withdraw()` method is a critical section for whichever instance of the object it is being called on.

Another use of the `synchronized` keyword is to declare that a method is synchronized. In this case, execution of that method must first obtain a semaphore on the object (or class, in the case of `static` methods). This is equivalent to surrounding the method body with a `synchronized(this)` statement.

4.2.2 Synchronizing

This code is a multithread-correct version of the previous example:

```
synchronized boolean withdraw (int amount) {
   if (balance - amount >= 0) {
     balance -= amount;
     return true;
   }
   return false;
}
```

Only one thread can execute this method on any particular object at any one time (figure 4.6). This has the same effect as the following:

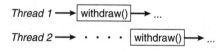

Figure 4.6   Only one thread can execute the method at one time

```
boolean withdraw (int amount) {
   synchronized (this) {
     if (balance - amount >= 0) {
       balance -= amount;
       return true;
     }
     return false;
   }
}
```

These examples state that the enclosed block of code cannot be executed until the semaphore of the corresponding object, this, has been obtained (this is a reference to the object on which the method was called).

If a thread already has the semaphore on a particular object and attempts to take that semaphore again, it automatically succeeds:

```
synchronized void a() {
    b(); // this method calls b while holding the current semaphore
}

// if called by a, the synchronized automatically succeeds
synchronized void b() {
}
```

If this were not the case, then method a() calling method b() would automatically block forever because the semaphore would be already taken.

It is frequently useful for an application that has multiple threads to be able to assign unique identifiers to each thread. The following code fragment allocates a unique identifier to every thread.

```
int id = 0;

public void run () {
    int myId;
    synchronized (this) {
        myId = id ++;
    }
}
```

By synchronizing around the assignment of the myId variable, we ensure that no other thread can interrupt the operation. Note, of course, that this is only of use if there are multiple threads in a single instance of an object. Extending this for all threads in an entire class, we need the following code:

```
static int classId = 0;

static synchronized int getId () {
    return classId ++;
}
```

By declaring that a static method is synchronized we require synchronization on the semaphore associated with the entire class, in order to execute. This permits only a single thread in the entire run time to execute the getId() method at any time. We can thus use the getId() method to allocate unique identifiers to any thread in the run time.

Declaring a synchronized static method in this manner is, in fact, exactly the same as synchronizing on the Class object of the class in question. The Java run time maintains a `Class` object corresponding to every class that has been loaded. Only one `Class` object exists per class per run time, so synchronizing on the `Class` object guarantees mutually exclusive access among all instances of a particular class. Thus, we can achieve the same effect with the following code:

```
int id;
synchronized (getClass ()) {
  id = classId ++;
}
```

This code fragment must be part of an instance method; the `getClass()` method returns a reference to the unique `Class` of the object on which it is called. In this case, it returns the `Class` object of the class containing this code.

4.2.3 Life without semaphores

Without semaphores or a similar atomic mechanism, there is no way to write multithread-correct code. It is impossible to manually recreate the function of a semaphore. In particular, remember that different threads may be running concurrently on different processors. (This task is still impossible in the presence of preemption, even if there is just one processor.)

4.2.4 Efficiency of synchronization

Synchronizing on an object is an expensive operation because it usually requires access to an atomic processor operation that may have to bypass the processor's cache. Synchronizing on an object for which you already hold the lock, on the other hand, is a significantly less costly operation. New versions of the JVM support fairly efficient synchronization; however, for the moment, if efficiency is a concern, then synchronization should be minimized. Of course, in many cases, synchronization is crucial; in such situations it should never be omitted. However, overuse of unnecessary synchronization can cause performance problems, can imped reusability, and can cause actual errors such as deadlock.

4.3 Class Thread

This class is the run time representation of a thread (figure 4.7). Given a `Thread` object, you can pause, resume, and stop the corresponding system thread. There are many constructors and methods, of which we will list only a few.

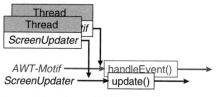

Figure 4.7 Class Thread

4.3.1 Constructors

These are the common constructors of `Thread`:

Thread(String name)   This creates a `Thread` having the name `name`. We can use thread names to identify the various threads of an application; this can make debugging easier because we can determine the purpose of the various threads that are active at any particular time.

Thread(Runnable target)   This creates a new `Thread` object; the corresponding thread will be asleep until the `start()` method is called. Calling the `start()` method on this new `Thread` object will result in the thread starting and calling the `run()` method of the `target` object.

Thread(ThreadGroup group, Runnable target)   This creates a new `Thread` object in the specified `ThreadGroup`, which will call the `run()` method of `target` when it is started. `ThreadGroups` allow us to group multiple threads and provide easy facilities to control the group of threads.

4.3.2 Static methods

There are several `static` methods that are useful for controlling the current thread (yourself) and finding out information about threads in the run time.

static int activeCount()   This returns the number of currently active threads.

static Thread currentThread()   This returns the `Thread` object corresponding to the currently executing thread (yourself).
```
Thread myself = Thread.currentThread ();
```

static void sleep(long millis) throws InterruptedException   This causes the current thread (yourself) to sleep for the specified number of milliseconds. Other threads will run during this time. If another thread has a reference to your `Thread` object and calls your `interrupt()` method, then you will be awakened with an `Interrupted-Exception`.

```
try {
  Thread.sleep (1000); // sleep for a second
} catch (InterruptedException ex) {
  System.out.println ("I was interrupted.");
}
```

static void yield()   This causes the current thread (yourself) to yield the processor to any other waiting threads. The language does not guarantee preemption, so you should call this method if you are performing long computations without any pauses.

```
for (int i = 0; i < 1000; ++ i) {
```

```
    // some large computation
    Thread.yield (); // permit other threads to run
}
```

static boolean interrupted()   This method returns whether the current thread (yourself) has been interrupted and then clears the interrupted flat. See the following discussion of `interrupt()`.

4.3.3 Instance methods

These instance methods control the thread represented by a `Thread` object.

void run()   This is the internal `Thread` method that is called when a thread is started. If you create a subclass of the `Thread` class, then this is the method that you should override and that will be executed by the language thread.

int getPriority()   This returns the thread's priority, a value between `Thread.MIN_PRIORITY` and `Thread.MAX_PRIORITY`.

void setPriority(int newPriority)   This sets the thread's priority. Higher priority threads will preempt lower priority threads when they become ready to run. Thread priorities can be any integer value between `Thread.MIN_PRIORITY` and `Thread.MAX_PRIORITY`, which are, respectively, 1 and 10.

```
Thread myself = Thread.currentThread();
myself.setPriority (Thread.MAX_PRIORITY); // raise my priority
```

A `ThreadGroup` can restrict the maximum priority of all of its member threads. As a result, this `setPriority()` method may not succeed.

void start()   This actually starts a thread. It is an error to call the `start()` method of a `Thread` that is currently alive. When you call this method, the corresponding language thread starts and enters the `run()` method. If the thread was created with a `Runnable` target, then this method will call the `run()` method of `target`.

```
Thread execution = new Thread (anObject);
// anObject must implement Runnable
execution.start ();
// a new thread starts and calls anObject.run()
```

void stop()   This stops a thread; it cannot subsequently be started again.

Warning: Use of this method is strongly discouraged. Because it can stop the target thread at any point in its execution, it is highly probable that it may leave critical data-structures in an inconsistent state. Instead, you should always use a flag or some similar mechanism to notify a thread that it should terminate itself. Use of a flag in conjunction with `interrupt()` to awaken a sleeping thread is a recommended alternative. See the following example of using `Runnable` for one possible implementation.

void suspend()   This suspends a thread; its execution is paused.
   Note: This method is no longer supported.

void resume()   This resumes a previously suspended thread.
   Note: This method is no longer supported.

void interrupt()   If the target thread is blocked in a method such as `sleep()` or `wait()` then this method will cause it to abort immediately with an `Interrupted-Exception`. If the thread is not in such a method but it subsequently enters one, then it will abort at that point. Many blocking I/O operations will also abort with an `InterruptedIOException` upon receipt of such an interrupt.
   The `interrupted()` method can be used by a thread to test for an outstanding interrupt; this is particularly useful as an alternative to `stop()`.

boolean isInterrupted()   This method returns whether the target thread has been interrupted and has not yet received an `InterruptedException`. Unlike the `interrupted()` method, this does not clear that condition if it is set.

void join() throws InterruptedException   The caller blocks until the thread upon whose method this was called has stopped. Thus, if you have created and started a `Thread` object and want to wait for the thread to finish executing, you call its `join()` method.

```
Thread execution = new Thread (anObject);
execution.start (); // start the thread
try {
  execution.join (); // wait for the thread to finish
} catch (InterruptedException ex) {
  // I was interrupted.
}
```

boolean isAlive()   This returns a value indicating whether the thread is currently alive; a thread is alive if it has been started and not yet stopped.

ThreadGroup getThreadGroup()   This method returns the thread's `ThreadGroup`.

4.3.4 SecurityException

The `SecurityManager` restricts the thread methods so that threads cannot take liberties with each other. This would be a problem if, for example, an applet were to stop all the threads of other applets running in the same browser. Calling any of the `Thread` class' methods may raise a `SecurityException` if the caller does not have permission to modify the target thread.

4.4 Interface Runnable

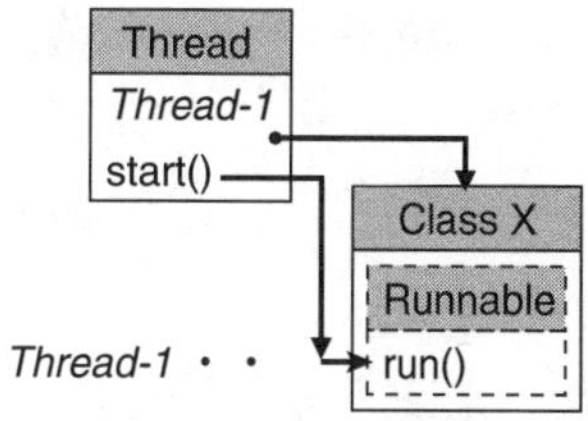

This interface is used to allow threads to easily be created in objects that do not extend the `Thread` class directly (figure 4.8). If a class implements this interface, then a new `Thread` can be created to automatically call a `Runnable` object's `run()` method.

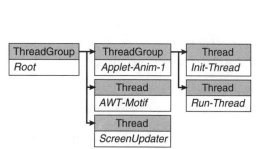

Figure 4.8   Interface Runnable

4.4.1 Methods

There is just one method defined:

void run()   The `Thread` class provides a constructor that takes a `Runnable` object as a parameter. When such a `Thread`'s `start()` method is called, a new thread will call this method. The thread stops automatically when this method completes.

4.5 Class ThreadGroup

The `ThreadGroup` class is used to group threads to ease the maintenance of multiple threads (figure 4.9). A limit can be placed on the maximum priority of any thread in a `ThreadGroup`. All the threads can be controlled with just a call to the `ThreadGroup`.

Figure 4.9   Class ThreadGroup

ThreadGroups can be used by Java-enabled browsers to keep different applets in separate execution spaces so that they can be more easily controlled.

4.5.1 Constructors

The are two constructors:

ThreadGroup(String name)   This creates a `ThreadGroup` with the specified name that is within the `ThreadGroup` of the currently executing thread (the caller).

ThreadGroup(ThreadGroup parent, String name)   This creates a `ThreadGroup` of the specified name that is within the specified `ThreadGroup`. You can have a hierarchy of `ThreadGroups` to ease thread management.

4.5.2 Methods

The methods of `ThreadGroup` can be used to control all of the threads in a `ThreadGroup` simultaneously.

int activeCount()   This returns the number of active threads within the group.

int enumerate(Thread[] list)   This fills in the array `list` with references to all active `Thread`s in the group, and returns the number inserted.

int activeGroupCount()   This returns the number of active `ThreadGroup`s within the group.

int enumerate(ThreadGroup[] list)   This fills in the array `list` with references to all active `ThreadGroup`s in this group, and returns the number inserted.

void setMaxPriority(int pri)   This sets the maximum priority that any `Thread` in the group can have.

```
ThreadGroup appletGroup = new ThreadGroup ("Applet Group");
appletGroup.setMaxPriority (Thread.MIN_PRIORITY);
```

int getMaxPriority()   This returns the current maximum `Thread` priority for the group.

void stop()   This stops all of the `Thread`s and groups within this group. Use of this method is strongly discouraged.

void suspend()   This suspends all of the `Thread`s and groups within the group. This method is no longer supported.

void resume()   This resumes all of the `Thread`s and groups within the group. This method is no longer supported.

void destroy()   This destroys a `ThreadGroup`. This method is not yet supported..

4.6 A Runnable example

One way to start a thread in an object is for the object to implement the `Runnable` interface. A `Thread` can be constructed with the object as an argument and then started. When the thread begins executing, it will call the target object's `run()` method. Many threads can be started in an object that implements `Runnable`, although we only use one in this example.

This is an example of using a thread in a `Runnable` application. We provide methods to start and stop the thread (figure 4.10).

```
public class ThreadDemo implements Runnable {
    // public synchronized void begin () ...
    // public synchronized void end () ...
    // public void run () ...
}
```

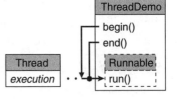

Figure 4.10   Class ThreadDemo

In this example, we implement the `Runnable` interface. This interface says that we must implement a `run()` method, which will be called when we start a thread in this object. The `begin()` method starts a new thread if there is none currently running, and the `end()` method stops it without using `stop()`.

```
protected Thread execution;

public synchronized void begin () {
   if (execution == null) {
      execution = new Thread (this);
      execution.setPriority (Thread.MIN_PRIORITY);
      execution.start ();
   }
}
```

This method is called to start executing a thread in this object. If this is the first call, we create a `Thread` object passing `this` as a parameter. This creates a thread which will call our `run()` method when it is started. We limit the thread's priority and then start it. We keep a reference to the new thread in the `execution` variable.

```
public synchronized void end () {
   if (execution != null) {
      execution.interrupt ();
      execution = null;
   }
}
```

This method is called to stop our thread. We first check to see if the thread is still running. If so, then we call its `interrupt()` method; this will wake it from any blocking operation with an `InterruptedException`. We then set the `execution` reference to `null` so we know that the thread has been stopped.

```
public void run () {
   try {
      Thread myself = Thread.currentThread ();
      while (execution == myself) {
         // body
      }
   } finally {
      synchronized (this) {
         execution = null;
      }
   }
}
```

The new thread calls this method. We perform our long-running task here; a server connection handler is a typical task. If this method completes for any reason—natural or exceptional—we set our thread reference to `null`. This will allow garbage collection to free any system resources held by the `Thread`. This is not always necessary, but it is an example of a possible implementation

Note that inside the main loop, we keep executing while the `execution` reference is still pointing to `myself` (a reference to the thread executing this code). You might wonder why we do this instead of simply testing for `null`. The problem is that testing for `null` may fail in the case where someone stops and then restarts this code in quick succession: When we go to test the `execution` variable, it may be pointing to the new thread and so would pass a test for non-`null`. This alternative is much more robust; it will only keep executing while this thread is still the active target of the class. An obvious alternative would be a call to `interrupted()`, however this is a bit more efficient.

Note also that inside the body of the loop if we call a method that may block and be woken with an `InterruptedException`, then the occurrence of such an exception is an indication that the thread should terminate itself as soon as possible.

4.7 A Thread subclass example

An alternative way to start a thread in an object is for the object to subclass `Thread` (figure 4.11). The `start()` method, when called on this object, will automatically create a thread that will enter through the `run()` method. Only one thread can be started in an object in this manner; there is a one-to-one mapping between `Thread` objects and language threads, so the `start()` method will affect only the one thread.

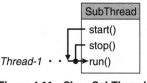

Figure 4.11   Class SubThread

```
public class SubThread extends Thread {
   public void run () {
      // ...
   }

   public static void main (String[] args) {
      SubThread subThread = new SubThread ();
      subThread.start ();
   }
}
```

In this example, we subclass `Thread` and override the `run()` method. When we create an instance of our `SubThread` class, a corresponding language thread is created. When we call the `start()` method on our `SubThread` object, the language thread starts and calls the `run()` method on our `SubThread` object.

4.8 Thread notification methods

The `Object` class defines some methods that are relevant to threads (figure 4.12). Because these methods are declared by the `Object` class, they are defined on every Java object. The methods permit efficient producer/consumer thread synchronization.

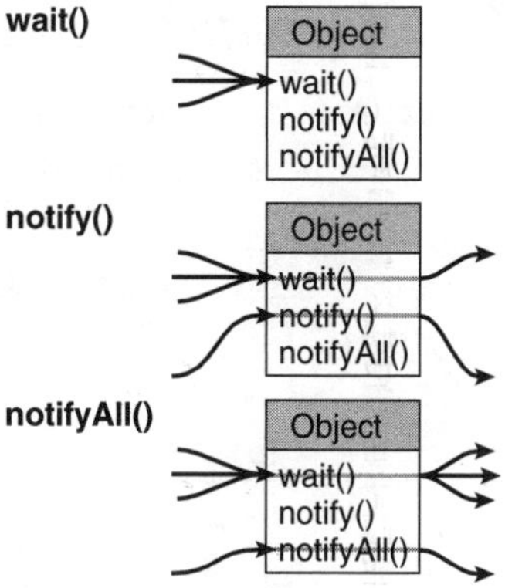

Figure 4.12   Thread notification methods

4.8.1 Methods

The following methods provide a mechanism for threads to await notification of an occurrence, and to notify other waiting threads of the occurrence.

void wait() throws InterruptedException   Any thread can call this method on any object. The thread will then block until another thread calls the `notify()` method of the same object.

For example, if a thread finds that a `Vector` has no elements, it can then call the `wait()` method to wait for another thread to insert an object. If another thread inserts an object into the `Vector`, then it can call the `Vector`'s `notify()` method to wake a sleeping thread.

void wait(long timeout) throws InterruptedException   This method waits for someone to call `notify()` on the object, or for the specified timeout to elapse. The granularity of the timeout is in milliseconds.

void wait(long timeout, int nanos) throws InterruptedException   This method waits for someone to call `notify()` on the object, or for the specified timeout to expire. This method allows the timeout to be specified in milliseconds plus nanoseconds.

void notify()   This method wakes one `Thread` that is waiting on the target object.

void notifyAll()   This method wakes all threads that are waiting on the target object; most will immediately go back to sleep, but one will succeed.

An important thing to note about the use of these methods is that a thread must be `synchronized` on the target object to call any of these methods. The `wait()` methods temporarily release the synchronization to let other threads access the target. After the `notify()` method has been called, and the caller of `notify()` releases the synchronization, the thread will regain synchronization on the object upon waking.

4.9 A producer-consumer example

This example demonstrates usage of the `wait()` and `notify()` methods to implement a simple producer/consumer (figure 4.13).

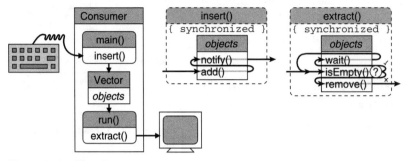

Figure 4.13   Class Consumer

```
import java.util.*;
import java.io.*;

public class Consumer extends Thread {
   protected Vector objects;

   // public Consumer () ...
   // public void run () ...
   // public void insert (Object object) ...
   // public static void main (String[] args)
   //     throws IOException, InterruptedException ...
}
```

This class represents a consumer. The class extends `Thread`; when the `start()` method is called, it proceeds to consume objects from the `objects` Vector. The `insert()` method allows producers to add objects to this Vector for consumption.

```
public Consumer () {
   objects = new Vector();
}
```

The constructor creates a `Vector`, which will hold the objects to be consumed.

```
public void run () {
   try {
      while (true) {
         Object object = extract ();
         System.out.println (object);
      }
   } catch (InterruptedException ignored) {
   }
}
```

```
// protected Object extract () throws InterruptedException ...
```

When the `start()` method is called on this consumer, a new thread enters the `run()` method. This thread repeatedly uses the `extract()` method to extract an object from `objects` and then prints this object.

```
protected Object extract () throws InterruptedException {
    synchronized (objects) {
        while (objects.isEmpty ()) {
            objects.wait ();
        }
        Object object = objects.firstElement ();
        objects.removeElementAt (0);
        return object;
    }
}
```

This method extracts an object from `objects`, using the `wait()` method to provide an efficient implementation. We synchronize on `objects`, and then sit in a loop that waits until the `Vector` is nonempty. Every time around the loop, we call the `wait()` method; this will sleep until another thread calls `notify()` on the object. If the `Vector` becomes nonempty, then we return the first element after removing it from the `Vector`.

Synchronizing on `objects` is necessary for two reasons. It allows us to call the `wait()` method; more importantly, it makes this code multithread-safe. To extract an object from the `Vector`, we must first call `firstElement()`, and then call `removeElementAt()`. If we were not synchronized on the `Vector`, then another thread could interrupt us between these two operations and remove the same object.

```
public void insert (Object object) {
    synchronized (objects) {
        objects.addElement (object);
        objects.notify ();
    }
}
```

This method adds an object to the `Vector` and then calls the `notify()` method. This will wake a thread that is waiting for the `Vector` to become nonempty. Note that we must be synchronized on the object to call its `notify()` method.

```
public static void main (String[] args)
    throws IOException, InterruptedException {
    Consumer consumer = new Consumer ();
    consumer.start ();
    BufferedReader keyboard = new BufferedReader (
        new FileReader (FileDescriptor.in));
    String line;
```

```
    while ((line = keyboard.readLine ()) != null) {
      consumer.insert (line);
      Thread.sleep (1000);
    }
  }
```

This method shows the `Consumer` class in action. We first create a consumer and start it; we then sit in a loop accepting input from the user. Every line that is entered is inserted into the consumer object. The `insert()` method will wake the consumer thread to consume the line and display it.

The `wait()` and `notify()` methods allow us to efficiently implement producer/consumer classes. We will, in fact, make use of a similar class in the applications part of this book.

4.10 Efficient multithreading

Unfortunately, the creation of Java threads can be a slow process, and some virtual machines suffer from thread-related memory leaks. For efficiency, it is thus sometimes worthwhile to reuse old `Threads` instead of always creating them, although advanced VMs already do this at the system level and so benefits will vary.

4.10.1 Class ReThread

This class is a simple thread-like class that maintains an internal list of Java `Threads`, adding to this list only when necessary and reusing old threads whenever possible (figure 4.14).

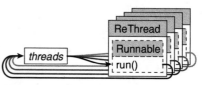

Figure 4.14 Reusing threads for efficiency

The interface provided by the class is similar to the `Thread` class when used with a `Runnable` target. Safeguards are built in to protect against erroneous access, such as repeated calls to `start()`.

```
import java.util.*;

public class ReThread implements Runnable {
  // public ReThread (Runnable target) ...
  // public synchronized void start () ...
  // public synchronized void interrupt () ...
  // public void run () ...
}
```

This class implements `Runnable`; language threads enter the `run()` method, which includes appropriate logic to allow them to be reused. A `Runnable` target must be specified in the constructor for this class; the `start()` method starts a new thread, or reuses an old thread, that enters the target's `run()` method. The `interrupt()` method can be used to interrupt this thread if it is still running. No `stop()` method is supported.

```java
protected Runnable target;

public ReThread (Runnable target) {
  this.target = target;
}
```

When this object is started, a thread will enter the `run()` method of the specified `Runnable target`.

```java
private static Vector threads = new Vector ();
private ReThread reThread;
private Thread thread;

private static int id = 0;
private static synchronized int getID () { return id ++; }

public synchronized void start () {
  if ((thread == null) && (reThread == null)) {
    synchronized (threads) {
      if (threads.isEmpty ()) {
        thread = new Thread (this, "ReThread-" + getID ());
        thread.start ();
      } else {
        reThread = (ReThread) threads.lastElement ();
        threads.setSize (threads.size () - 1);
        reThread.start0 (this);
      }
    }
  }
}

// protected synchronized void start0 (ReThread reThread) ...
```

The `start()` method causes a thread to enter the target's `run()` method. If either `thread` or `reThread` is non-null then the thread has already been started so we can ignore the request.

The `static Vector threads` maintain a list of dormant `ReThreads` that can be reused for future targets. If this is empty then we must create a `Thread`, `thread`, that enters this class' `run()` method and calls the target's `run()` method. We otherwise extract the last `ReThread` from the list and call its `start0()` method to service us.

```java
protected synchronized void start0 (ReThread reThread) {
  this.reThread = reThread;
  target = reThread.target;
  notify ();
}
```

This method will be called to awaken a dormant `ReThread`. We alter our target to that of the specified `ReThread` and then call `notify()` to awaken our sleeping language thread.

```
public synchronized void interrupt () {
  if ((target != null) && ((thread != null) ^ (reThread != null))) {
    if (thread != null) {
      thread.interrupt ();
    } else {
      reThread.interrupt0 (this);
    }
  }
}

// protected void interrupt0 (ReThread reThread) ...
```

The `interrupt()` method interrupts the thread represented by this `ReThread`. If the users's thread has finished or has not yet been started then we ignore the interrupt request. If we are using a language thread then we call its `interrupt()` method. Otherwise, we are reusing an existing `ReThread` so we call its `interrupt0()` method.

```
protected synchronized void interrupt0 (ReThread reThread) {
  if ((target != null) && (reThread == this.reThread)) {
    thread.interrupt ();
  }
}
```

This method is called to interrupt a `ReThread` that is being reused. We check to see that we are still servicing the caller; if not, we can ignore the request. We otherwise interrupt the language thread as expected.

```
public void run () {
  while (true) {
    try {
      target.run ();
    } catch (RuntimeException ex) {
      ex.printStackTrace ();
    }
    waitForTarget ();
  }
}

// protected synchronized void waitForTarget () ...
```

The `run()` method contains the logic for reusing threads. In an infinite loop, we call our target's `run()` method, catching and displaying any `RuntimeException` that may arise. After this we call `waitForTarget()`, which waits for a new target, and we then loop again to execute the new target.

```
protected synchronized void waitForTarget () {
  target = null;
  threads.addElement (this);
  while (target == null) {
    try {
      wait ();
    } catch (InterruptedException ignored) {
    }
  }
}
```

This method waits for a new target. We first reset our target to null; this will allow the garbage collector to work, if it needs to, and will stop any further attempts by the user to interrupt us. We then add ourselves to the list of dormant ReThreads in threads, and call wait() to sleep until we have a new target. When we are reused, the start0() method will assign a target and call notify() to wake us up.

All of these methods are synchronized; this is necessary to maintain coherence in such a moderately complex multithreaded system.

4.10.2 Putting it to use

This class can be used essentially anywhere that a normal thread would be used. Whenever one of the language threads completes—whether because it is stopped or because it completes its task—then it automatically requeues itself for reuse. For full function, we should also provide all of the standard setPriority() methods and such, however these would have a similar form to the interrupt() method. Another useful method would allow all queued threads to be disposed of when the framework is no longer needed. However, this is again omitted for clarity.

Users of this class should take care not to directly access the language threads that this creates; for example, by calling Thread.currentThread(). If the language threads are manipulated directly in such a manner then this framework can become inconsistent.

For clarity's sake, we only use this clase in one example: chapter 17, *Implementing a Web server*; in all other cases, we use plain language threads. For an actual production environment, use of this or a similar class is recommended.

4.11 Wrapping up

To make use of threads you must either implement the Runnable interface or extend the Thread class. Creating threads is fairly easy; however, managing synchronization issues can be more complex. Synchronization errors can be difficult to detect because they are not guaranteed to occur; they may occur only when some threads happen to be scheduled in a particular order. If you write a piece of code that is not multithread-correct, but does operate correctly under Java on one particular system, remember that multiprocessor machines are becoming widespread.

Efficiency is another important issue of multithreaded code. Minimizing the use of synchronization primitives, and reusing threads whenever possible, are both useful techniques for addressing this problem. Modern JVMs also incorporate some performance enhancements that can dramatically improve the performance of multithreaded code, so maintaining some familiarity with different JVMs and their relative strengths is worthwhile.

More details on threading can be found in *Concurrent Programming in Java* by Doug Lea (Addison-Wesley, 1998).

PART II

Streams

This part of the book introduces the classes and interfaces supplied in the `java.io` package. This package contains all the tools needed for communicating in a uniform manner within a virtual machine and among applications in different virtual machines.

Coverage of this package includes an exhaustive description of the available stream classes along with extensive examples of using and extending these classes. Streams are crucial in Java networking: they represent the programmer's connection to communications channels, providing access to I/O facilities such as pipes and memory channels as well as an extensible interface to networking facilities.

Chapter 5 An introduction to streams   A *stream* is a high-level abstraction representing a connection to a communications channel, which is any entity that may *receive* or *send* data. A network socket and a memory buffer could both be considered communications channels by this definition. Streams can either read from the channel or write to it, so they are divided into two classifications: input and output streams. In this chapter, we look at `InputStream` and `OutputStream` and their characteristics, and we put the abstract concepts into perspective with examples.

Chapter 6 File access through streams   File streams are available to use when it may be convenient to treat files as communications channels. Applications can then stream data to files in the same manner as they stream data to other channels. An overview of file-related classes is given in this chapter before moving on to the file streams, `FileInputStream` and `FileOutputStream`. We step through various examples, including how to create custom file streams.

Chapter 7 Extending streams with filters   Stream filters are wrappers (decorators) for the lower level streams that allow for a higher level of abstraction in communications. They connect to the simple streams and provide added function. In this chapter, we give an introduction to stream filters and their uses. The generic `FilterInputStream` and `FilterOutputStream` classes are introduced, a quick overview of the standard filters is given, and then we implement a few examples.

Chapter 8 Standard stream filters This chapter discusses the various stream filters provided with the API, including `DataInputStream` and `DataOutputStream`, `BufferedInputStream` and `BufferedOutputStream`, `SequenceInputStream`, and `PushbackInputStream`. These filters add additional function on top of the facilities provided by the various basic stream classes. An implementation of buffered streams is shown and described, as well as a custom stream that can seamlessly transmit data to several output streams simultaneously.

Chapter 9 Memory I/O streams The Java API provides two pairs of streams that use memory as a communications channel: `ByteArrayInputStream` and `ByteArrayOutputStream`, and `PipedInputStream` and `PipedOutputStream`. The byte array streams allow data to be streamed into and out of memory buffers; the piped streams allow data to be streamed between the threads of an application. This chapter begins with a description of these streams followed by examples, including an example of extending `ByteArrayOutputStream`.

Chapter 10 Character streams The character streams are a complementary set of stream classes to the byte-oriented streams that we have looked at thus far. They provide facilities for communicating character-based data within and among virtual machines. These streams inherit from `Reader` and `Writer`, and provide essentially the same facilities as the byte streams, but transport 16-bit characters instead of bytes. Automatic translation facilities are provided by the `InputStreamReader` and `OutputStreamWriter` classes to easily access alternative character encodings such as ASCII, ISO Latin 1, UTF-8, and so forth.

Chapter 11 Character stream filters This chapter introduces the character stream filters. They mirror most of the filters of the byte streams, but for character data. We look at the API for and examples of the various stream filters provided, including `BufferedReader` and `BufferedWriter`, `LineNumberReader`, `PrintWriter`, and `PushbackReader`, in addition to developing some custom character stream filters of our own.

Chapter 12 Memory-based character streams This chapter discusses the various character streams that transfer data into and out of memory buffers, including `CharArrayReader` and `CharArrayWriter`, `PipedReader` and `PipedWriter`, and various other derivatives. As with earlier chapters, we illustrate these classes with both API documentation and relevant examples.

Chapter 13 Object streams The object streams allows complete objects to be streamed across a communications channel, just as the data stream classes allow primitive values to be streamed. The `ObjectInputStream` and `ObjectOutputStream` classes are stream filters, derived from the data stream classes, that provide this object serialization facility. Persistence is a side-effect of object serialization, and can be used to maintain the state of objects while they are stored in an inactive state such as in a file. We demonstrate the use of these streams with examples, and discuss the issues that surround customizing and extending them.

CHAPTER 5

An introduction to streams

Streams are an extremely important part of network programming, and the Java API provides several stream classes with which to work. A *stream* is a high-level abstraction representing a connection to a communications channel, such as a TCP/IP network connection or a memory buffer. Streams can either read from a communications channel or write to it, so they are divided into two classifications: input and output.

In this chapter, we first discuss the characteristics of streams, then move on to the two generic stream classes: OutputStream and InputStream. These are the superclasses of all other streams. The methods of these classes are detailed, then demonstrated with examples. A brief discussion of the basic stream types supplied by the API concludes the chapter. We will look at all of these streams in detail in later chapters.

5.1 Overview

Streams are the underlying abstraction behind communications in Java. A stream represents an endpoint of a one-way communications channel, as shown in figure 5.1.

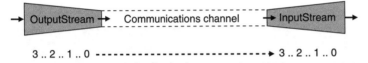

Figure 5.1   OutputStream and InputStream

The communications channel usually connects an output stream to a corresponding input stream. Everything that is written to the output stream can subsequently be read from the input stream. This connection can take the form of a link through a network, a memory buffer between threads, a file, or a terminal to the user. Streams provide a uniform data interface for applications, no matter what communications channel is actually used.

All of the I/O classes in Java are supplied by the package java.io.

5.1.1 FIFO

Streams are FIFO (first-in first-out). This means that the first thing that is written to an output stream will be the first thing that is read from the corresponding input stream. If a sequence of numbers is written to an output stream, then it will be read in the same order from the corresponding input stream.

5.1.2 Sequential access

Streams provide sequential access to the communications channel; you can write a sequence of bytes one after the other, or read a sequence of bytes in the order in which they were written. Most streams provide no random access; it is not possible to skip around and read or write bytes at just any position. Very little facility is provided for reading or writing data in anything other than a purely sequential manner: in order, one byte after another.

5.1.3 Read-only or write-only

The various stream classes provide either only reading functions or only writing functions. An output stream writes data into a communications channel; an input stream reads data out of a communications channel. There is no stream class that allows both reading and writing.

In cases where we wish to both write to and read from a single communications channel, we must use one stream to write (the output stream) and a different stream to read (the input stream). As we will see later when we look at networking applications, when you open a network connection, you obtain two streams—an input stream to read from the network and an output stream to write to the network.

5.1.4 Blocking

An important issue that arises with streams is *blocking*. If a thread tries to read from a user's keyboard, it cannot read any data until the user actually types something. While the thread is waiting for data to arrive (which, in this case, requires the user to type something in), it is blocking. Similarly, if a thread tries to write data to a disk, it may take a while for the data to actually be written; while the thread is waiting for the I/O operation to complete, it is blocking.

Blocking refers to a thread going to sleep because it attempts to read data and there is none available, or it attempts to write data and the operation does not happen immediately. The Java environment will let other threads run while one is blocking; the blocking thread will wake up only when data arrive or the I/O operation completes.

There is little facility for nonblocking I/O in Java. *Nonblocking I/O* refers to being able to read some data and return immediately if there is none available, or to write some data and to return immediately if there will be a delay. We will look at the existing nonblocking facilities when we start building network servers.

5.2 Character streams

In addition to these basic byte streams, there is a complementary set of character stream classes that derive from the superclasses `Reader` and `Writer`. Character streams are used to communicate 16-bit Unicode characters in the same way that conventional streams communicate byte-oriented data (figure 5.2). There is a complementary `Reader` or `Writer` class for almost every byte stream class that we will encounter, and in many situations, old text-oriented streams and methods of the byte streams have been deprecated in favor of the more efficient and generalized character streams.

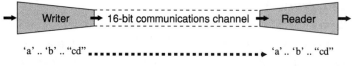

'a' .. 'b' .. "cd" ■■■■■■■■■■■■■■■■■■■■■■■■■■■■▶ 'a' .. 'b' .. "cd"

Figure 5.2 Reader and Writer

For all text-based communications, use of the character streams is recommended. General-purpose conversion classes are available that interface between byte streams and character streams. These can be used to interface to non-Unicode systems, such as native files and network streams. The generalized nature of these conversion classes allows text to be easily converted from Unicode to ASCII, ISO Latin 1, dingbats, or other appropriate byte encoding.

The character streams are covered in detail in chapters 10, 11, and 12. For the purposes of the following chapters, which provide examples that read text from the keyboard and write to the terminal, we will ignore issues of character conversion and consider input and output as consisting just of bytes.

5.3 Class OutputStream

The OutputStream class represents a gateway onto a communications channel: you can write data to an OutputStream, and it will travel down the attached communications channel.

5.3.1 Constructors

There are no usable constructors for the base class OutputStream. Simply creating an OutputStream by itself is meaningless; it must be connected to a communications channel. As such, OutputStreams can only be instantiated by creating a subclass such as a FileOutputStream to a file or a PipedOutputStream to a pipe, or any subclass which actually con-

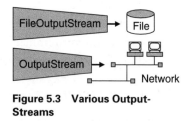

Figure 5.3 Various Output-Streams

nects to something. An OutputStream is like an entrance: you can't just create an entrance by itself; you must create an entrance to *something*, such as a cave or a room or a hallway. In the same way you must create an output stream to *something*, such as a file or network (figure 5.3).

Obviously, with Java's inheritance model, if you create a FileOutputStream, then you can subsequently pass it as just a generic OutputStream.

5.3.2 Methods

The `OutputStream` class provides the superclass for all concrete output stream implementations. As such, it declares the standard methods that you can expect of all output streams, whether to a file or to a network. In the same way that you can go through any entrance, whether it is to a cave or room, you can write bytes to any output stream, whether it is to a terminal or a memory buffer.

The `OutputStream` class provides a few simple methods for communication: you can write a byte or a sequence of bytes. It also provides control methods to flush or close the communications channel. Any of the methods may block the calling thread.

abstract void write(int b) throws IOException   This method accepts a single byte and writes it to the attached communications channel. The argument is of type `int` but only the bottom 8 bits are actually written.

This method is abstract because its implementation must be provided by a subclass that is attached to an actual communications channel such as a file.

void write(byte[] b, int off, int len) throws IOException

This method accepts an array of bytes b, an initial index `off`, and a number of bytes `len`, and writes `len` bytes from b starting from index `off` to the attached communications channel.

The default implementation of this method is to repeatedly call the single-byte `write()` method. Subclasses will usually override this with a more efficient implementation.

void write(byte[] b) throws IOException   This method accepts an array of bytes b and writes the entire array to the attached communications channel.

The default implementation of this method is to call the previous `write()` method on the entire array.

void flush() throws IOException   This method flushes any buffers that the `Output-Stream` may have. Sometimes, for reasons of efficiency, the data which are being sent to a communications channel are kept temporarily in memory buffers. This method forces any buffered data to actually be written.

This method only flushes buffers supplied by Java classes; it does not flush any underlying OS buffers. If necessary, OS buffers can sometimes be flushed through system-level access such as that provided by the `FileDescriptor` class.

void close() throws IOException   This method flushes and closes the underlying communications channel and then frees up any system resources which it is using. Any data that have been sent before this call is made will still be sent when the stream is flushed; this call may thus block until the data are written.

What actually happens when a stream is closed depends on the entity to which it is attached. If it is attached to a network connection, then the network connection is closed down; if it is attached to a memory buffer, then nothing happens.

5.3.3 IOException

Every `OutputStream` method can throw an exception of type `IOException`. The exact type of `IOException` thrown depends on the problem and the entity to which the stream is actually connected.

Even closing a stream can throw an exception: if a stream is buffered, then the data must be sent before the stream can be closed, and an error may occur at this point. For example, a file system may become full while there is still buffered data in memory. Closing a file stream requires that the data be actually written, and this may not be possible.

5.4 A simple OutputStream example

As noted, an `OutputStream` must always be attached to some underlying communications channel, whether it is a memory buffer or a network connection. The most easily accessible stream is `System.out`, which is connected to the system's standard output stream, as shown in figure 5.4.

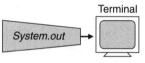

Figure 5.4   System.out

Every byte that is written to `System.out` is displayed on the user's terminal. For a stand-alone application, this will be the terminal where the application was run. For an applet, this will be the Java Console window or its equivalent.

The following piece of code prints out each of the command line parameters using a `println()` method that we will define next:

```
import java.io.*;

public class SimpleOut {
   public static void main (String[] args) throws IOException {
      for (int i = 0; i < args.length; ++ i) {
         println (args[i]);
      }
   }
   // public static void println (String msg) throws IOException ...
}
```

We declare that the `main()` method may throw exceptions of type `IOException`. We are not interested in actually handling exceptions that may be thrown by the `println()` method, and so we pass them on and let the main execution thread halt.

The comment describes the signature of the `println()` method; we will look at this method next.

```
public static void println (String msg) throws IOException {
   synchronized (System.out) {
      for (int i = 0; i < msg.length (); ++ i)
         System.out.write (msg.charAt (i) & 0xff);
      System.out.write ('\n'); // write one-byte LineFeed
   }
   System.out.flush ();
}
```

The `println()` method uses the `write()` methods of `System.out` to print out its argument.

All of the `write()` methods of class `OutputStream` are declared as throwing `IOException`, and so we must prepare for such exceptions. Since we are not interested in handling exceptions at this point, we simply pass them on by declaring that this method may throw any exceptions raised. In practice, `System.out` is unlikely to throw an exception. However, because the declaration of the `OutputStream` class states that exceptions may be thrown, we must be prepared for their occurrence.

We synchronize on `System.out` to ensure that no other threads can write to the terminal in the middle of this message and then print the `String`. We print the `String`, composed of 16-bit Unicode characters, by converting it into a series of bytes; the `Output-Stream` class can only transmit bytes. We loop through the message, extracting each character, masking it to a byte and writing it. Note that we simply discard the high bits of the character. We finally write out a newline character and flush the stream to ensure that any buffered data are displayed immediately.

Looping through each character is quite slow. The `String` class actually declares some `getBytes()` methods that efficiently convert the `String` into an array of bytes; the encoding used to convert characters to bytes can be specified as a parameter to the method call. With this approach, we can use the multibyte `write()` method of `Out-putStream` to efficiently write a `String`.

```
byte[] buffer = msg.getBytes ();
System.out.write (buffer);
```

This code fragment uses the `getBytes()` method to convert the `String` into an array of bytes, and then writes the array to `System.out`.

5.4.1 ASCII characters

In this example, we are writing to an ASCII device (the user's terminal) so we don't want to transmit full Unicode 16-bit characters. To convert Unicode to ASCII, we simply discard the high bits of each character. Unicode was designed as a superset of ASCII to help facilitate a transition away from that limited character set—the crude translation of just discarding the high bits will be correct for most common messages.

If, however, the message should include other Unicode characters, then this translation will garble the message. Therefore, to communicate with traditional ASCII programs and devices, we must restrict our messages to contain only ASCII characters. ASCII itself is a 7-bit character set; ISO Latin 1 is an extension of ASCII that adds an additional 128 international character above those of ASCII. A crude conversion from Unicode to ISO Latin 1 is to simply discard the top 8 bits of each character: Unicode characters 0–255 correspond exactly to those of ISO Latin 1; characters 0-127 correspond exactly to those of ASCII. The remaining Unicode characters are garbled by this conversion.

We can either perform this conversion explicitly, by looping and casting each character to a byte, or we can use the `getBytes()` method that mechanically performs this conversion for us. If we want to explicitly convert to ISO Latin 1, we can specify the encoding *latin1* in the call to `getBytes()`:

```
byte[] buffer = msg.getBytes ("latin1");
```

This effectively discards the high byte from each character and returns the result. In the earlier example, we did not specify a particular encoding with the call to `getBytes()`. In that case, the platform default encoding is used. Typically this will be ISO Latin 1; however, any appropriate encoding is possible. When writing to the console or a system-specific text file, it is appropriate to use the system default rather than assuming Latin 1.

For more details about character encodings and the different available conversions, see chapter 10. For the purposes of byte streams, however, this is the extent of knowledge that we will need.

5.4.2 Synchronization

Readers unfamiliar with the threading features and classes of Java should refer to chapter 4 for an overview of this topic.

The `println()` method synchronizes on `System.out`. While this is not important in this particular example, it might be useful in a more complex program. Synchronization ensures that no other thread may write to the terminal while this thread is writing the message and *newline* (figure 5.5).

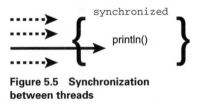

Figure 5.5 Synchronization between threads

`OutputStream` methods frequently block while writing, because communications channels are usually slow. Other threads can execute during this period, and so, it would be quite common for another thread to attempt to write to `System.out` in the middle of this thread's writing. Using synchronization prevents this problem.

Of course, synchronization helps only if other threads, which try to access `System.out`, are also synchronized on it. The various `print()` methods of class `PrintStream` are all synchronized so the user of these methods will be safe. Be aware, however, that the `write()` methods are not synchronized, and so, it is still possible to interrupt a message.

In this particular case, the problems of synchronization simply pose an aesthetic challenge. In a networked application, they pose real difficulties. It could be disastrous for two threads to simultaneously write messages to a single network connection without synchronization.

Figure 5.6 demonstrates how threads could interact badly. In this example, two threads are both printing *hello world!* to the same stream without synchronization. Because the message is written as a sequence of bytes, one thread may block at any point while its message is being written; during this time, the other thread may proceed to write its own message.

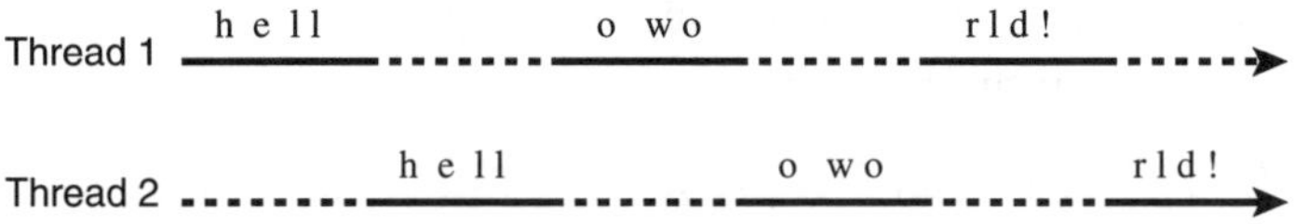

Thread 1   h e l l   o w o   r l d !

Thread 2   h e l l   o w o   r l d !

Figure 5.6 I/O without synchronization

5.5 *Class InputStream*

The `InputStream` class represents a gateway that lets us read data *out* of a communications channel. Data that have been written into a communications channel by an `OutputStream` can be read by a corresponding `InputStream`.

5.5.1 *Constructors*

The `InputStream` class is abstract, like the `OutputStream` class. A subclass must be constructed, such as a `FileInputStream`, that is actually attached to a communications channel. In the same way that the `OutputStream` is like an entrance, the `InputStream` class is like an exit. You cannot just create an exit, you must create an exit from *something* such as a room. By reading from a stream, you read data through the exit. In the case of an `InputStream`, you must create a concrete implementation such as a `FileInputStream` or a `PipedInputStream`. These streams let you read data from a file or a memory pipe (figure 5.7).

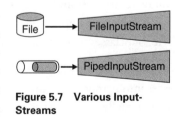

Figure 5.7 Various Input-Streams

5.5.2 Methods

The InputStream class is the superclass for all input streams. It declares those methods that will be supplied by all input streams, whether they read from files, network connections, or memory buffers.

The InputStream class provides methods for reading a byte or a sequence of bytes, as well as methods to determine the amount of data available for reading without blocking, to skip and reread data, and to close the communications channel.

Attempting to read from an InputStream that has no data ready will cause the caller to block until data become available. If the data have already arrived from the communications channel (for example, delivered by a network transport protocol), then they will be waiting in a memory buffer, and so, will be available immediately without the need to block.

abstract int read() throws IOException   This method reads and returns a single byte, blocking if none is available. The method returns -1 if the end of the file (EOF) is reached. EOF will be caused by reaching the end of a file, by reaching the end of a closed network connection, or by whatever is appropriate for the communications channel.

This method is abstract because its implementation must be provided by a subclass that is attached to an actual communications channel.

int read(byte[] b, int off, int len) throws IOException   This method attempts to read len bytes into array b, starting at index off. The array must already have been allocated. The method will block if no data are available, and will return the number of bytes successfully read or -1 if the end of the file is reached.

The method may not actually read len bytes for two possible reasons: if there are fewer bytes left in the stream before the end of the file, then only the remaining bytes will be read. Subsequent reads will return EOF. Alternatively, if some data are available to read immediately without blocking, but are fewer than the length of the subarray, then only those bytes will be read. More data may subsequently become available and will be returned from later reads.

The default implementation of this method is to repeatedly call read() for a single byte. Subclasses will usually override this with a more efficient implementation.

int read(byte[] b) throws IOException   This method attempts to read as many bytes into b as possible, up to the length of the array. The method returns the number of bytes actually read or -1 if the end of the file is reached. Again, fewer than b bytes may actually be read.

The default implementation of this method is to call the previous read() method for the entire array.

int available() throws IOException   This method returns the number of bytes that can be read from the stream without blocking. For example, an `InputStream` attached to a network connection will return the number of bytes that have actually been received down the network connection and are in memory but have not yet been read.

void close() throws IOException   This method closes the attached communication channel. Any data that have not yet been read will be discarded, and any system resources will be freed. In the case of an `InputStream` from a network connection, `close()` will close down the network connection.

long skip(long n) throws IOException   This method attempts to skip n bytes of input. This is useful if you know that you want to ignore a number of bytes, and is more efficient than just reading and ignoring them. It may not be possible for the method to actually skip as many bytes as were requested, so this method returns the number of bytes that were successfully skipped.

5.5.3 Mark and reset methods

The `mark()` and `reset()` methods allow a place in a stream to be marked, some data read, and then for the stream to be reset. Subsequent reads will reread data from the marked point onwards (figure 5.8).

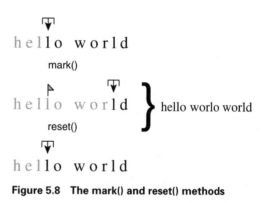

Figure 5.8   The mark() and reset() methods

This operation is frequently useful, particularly in a situation such as decoding an image of an unknown format. If an `InputStream` is attached to an image file, then it may be necessary to pass the stream to several image decoders to determine which one actually understands the format.

A GIF decoder must read 6 bytes before it can determine whether or not it can understand the file. If it is not a GIF file, it must return the bytes to the stream. The stream can then be passed to a JPEG decoder, which will read the first 11 bytes to determine whether it can understand the file, and so forth.

The GIF decoder should mark the beginning of the file before reading the header. If it cannot decode the file, then it can simply reset the stream so that the next decoder will start reading again from the beginning. Otherwise, there is no easy facility to return the 6 bytes to the stream; it would have to be closed and reopened for the next decoder.

As an example of this operation, consider an `InputStream` with 3 bytes, abc, available. If a program reads 1 byte, calls `mark()`, reads another byte, calls `reset()` and then reads 2 more bytes, it will have read abbc.

boolean markSupported()   None of the basic `InputStream` classes support `mark()` and `reset()`, but we will see later how to add mark/reset functions to any stream. The `markSupported()` method can be used to test whether a particular `InputStream` supports these methods.

void mark(int readlimit)   This instructs the stream to mark its current location. The parameter `readlimit` specifies the maximum number of bytes that may be unread before a subsequent call to `reset()`. If more than `readlimit` bytes are read, a call to reset may fail.

In the example given, a GIF decoder would specify 6 bytes, and a JPEG decoder would specify 11 bytes.

void reset() throws IOException   This instructs the stream to return to the previously marked location; subsequent reads will continue from the position in the stream where mark was last called. This may fail if more bytes have been read than were initially indicated.

5.5.4 IOException

All methods but `markSupported()` and `mark()` may throw an exception of type `IOException`. The nature of the `IOException` depends upon the problem and the underlying communications channel. Reaching the end of a file will not cause an `IOException` from a plain `InputStream`. Instead, the `read()` methods will return –1. Later we will see how some variants of `InputStream` may throw an `IOException` if a premature EOF occurs.

5.6 A simple InputStream example

This is a simple example that demonstrates reading from `System.in`. Terminal input to a Java application—keyboard input to a command-line application—is available through `System.in` (figure 5.9).

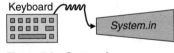

Figure 5.9   System.in

This stream is not frequently used by Java applications, but it is useful as an example `InputStream`.

The following piece of code reads bytes from `System.in` and writes them back to `System.out`:

```
import java.io.*;

public class SimpleIn {
    static public void main (String[] args) throws IOException {
        int charRead;
        while ((charRead = System.in.read ()) >= 0)
            System.out.write (charRead);
```

```
    }
}
```

We declare that the `main()` method may throw an `IOException`; this may occur from either the `read()` or `write()` call. We then sit in a loop, reading bytes from `System.in` and writing them out to `System.out`. The loop terminates when `read()` returns -1; this corresponds to the end of the file. This particular example is reading from the keyboard; EOF is signalled under UNIX when the user types CTRL+D, and under DOS when the user types CTRL+Z.

It is fairly inefficient to transfer individual bytes in this manner; it would be better to use a small buffer for reading and writing multiple bytes, as in the following piece of code:

```
byte[] buffer = new byte[8];
int numberRead;
while ((numberRead = System.in.read (buffer)) >= 0)
   System.out.write (buffer, 0, numberRead);
```

Here, we create a small buffer and read as many bytes as possible into it using the `read()` method. This call returns the number of bytes read or -1 at the end of the file. If some data have actually been read, we write out as many bytes as were read in and loop again.

Note that a newline is not printed after each buffer. The newlines that are printed are part of the input stream from the user, inserted whenever RETURN is typed, just like all other characters.

5.7 A Class Tee example

In this example, we implement a class that operates in a similar fashion to a plumbing tee joint. We will take input from one `InputStream` and allow it to be written out to multiple `OutputStreams`. This is not actually a stream. However later on we will develop a proper tee stream class.

We will define a class that reads data from an `InputStream` and stores it in an internal buffer. We will also provide a method that writes this buffer to an `OutputStream`. This method can be called repeatedly to write the buffer to multiple streams (figure 5.10):

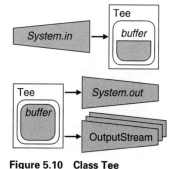

Figure 5.10   Class Tee

```
import java.io.*;
public class Tee {
   // public Tee (InputStream in, int initialCapacity) throws IOException ...
```

```
// public Tee (InputStream in) throws IOException ...
// public void writeTo (OutputStream out) throws IOException ...
}
```

The `Tee` class provides two constructors. Both require an `InputStream in` from which data will be read; the first also accepts an initial buffer size specification. The class provides one public method, `writeTo()`, that writes the buffered data to the specified `OutputStream out`:

```
protected byte[] buffer;
protected int bufferSize, bufferCapacity;

public Tee (InputStream in, int initialCapacity) throws IOException {
  bufferCapacity = initialCapacity;
  buffer = new byte[bufferCapacity];
  readFrom (in);
}

// protected void readFrom (InputStream in) throws IOException ...
```

To create a `Tee` object, you must supply an `InputStream` as a parameter to the constructor. It will read data from this stream until the end of the file, storing this data in the internal buffer.

We will store the data that we read in the `buffer` array. This array must be able to grow to accept as much data as is supplied, so we will also need to keep a record of the current size of the buffer, `bufferCapacity`, and the amount of data which we have read into it, `bufferSize`.

Because our buffer automatically grows, we can make the initial buffer as small or large as we like. Creating an initial buffer that is too small will be inefficient because we will need to increase the buffer size an unnecessary number of times. Creating one that is too large will simply waste memory. In this case, we let the user specify an initial size. We use the `readFrom()` method to actually fill the buffer from the supplied stream:

```
public Tee (InputStream in) throws IOException {
  this (in, in.available () + 1);
}
```

This constructor calls the previous constructor with a buffer size that is just larger than the number of bytes that are available for reading from `i`. If the value returned by `available()` happens to correspond to the entire amount of data that can be read, then we will not need to expand the buffer when reading:

```
public void readFrom (InputStream in) throws IOException {
  bufferSize = 0;
  int numberRead;
  while ((numberRead = in.read (buffer, bufferSize,
```

```
            bufferCapacity - bufferSize)) >= 0) {
        bufferSize += numberRead;

        if (bufferSize == bufferCapacity)
            increaseBufferSize ();
    }
}

// protected void increaseBufferSize () ...
```

The `readFrom()` method reads and buffers data from the specified `InputStream`, increasing the buffer size as necessary.

The `numberRead` variable corresponds to the number of bytes which we have actually read into the buffer; initially, we set this to zero. We then loop, reading from the `InputStream` into this buffer.

We use a multibyte `read()` method, specifying that it should read into our buffer, starting just beyond the data that we have already read. We attempt to read as many bytes as are left in the buffer; initially this will be the entire buffer size.

If the `read()` method returns -1, then we have reached EOF and can exit the loop. Otherwise, we add the number of bytes that we just read to the total number of bytes we have read altogether. If the buffer is then full, we must increase its size. So we call the `increaseBufferSize()` method:

```
protected void increaseBufferSize () {
    bufferCapacity *= 2;
    byte[] newBuffer = new byte[bufferCapacity];
    System.arraycopy (buffer, 0, newBuffer, 0, bufferSize);
    buffer = newBuffer;
}
```

This method allocates a new, larger buffer for incoming data. It is not possible to reallocate an existing buffer; so to increase the buffer size, we must first create a bigger buffer and then copy the contents of the old buffer into the new buffer.

To increase the buffer's size, we double it. By doubling its size, we allow the buffer to grow very rapidly. In only 20 calls to this method, we can grow a buffer from 1 byte up to 1 MB. We also make use of the `System.arraycopy()` method to efficiently copy the old buffer data to the new buffer. To start using the new buffer, we simply reassign our `buffer` reference. Garbage collection will take care of freeing memory allocated to the old buffer:

```
public void writeTo (OutputStream out) throws IOException {
    out.write (buffer, 0, bufferSize);
}
```

The last method in this class is the `writeTo()` method. This writes the current buffer contents to the specified `OutputStream`. We write all of the valid contents of `buffer`, that is, as many bytes as we have read.

5.8 Basic stream types

Streams can be connected to a variety of communications channels. Regardless of the underlying communications channel, the stream will provide the basic methods of `InputStream` or `OutputStream`. Depending upon what the stream is actually connected to, however, there may be some additional methods for manipulating the underlying channel.

Up to this point, we have referred to a *communications channel* as underlying streams. With some of the classes we shall look at, it may not be entirely obvious that there is a communications channel. We shall look at `ByteArrayOutputStream`, which just writes data into an array of bytes. This is a communications channel, because we can transport this array of bytes by any means we desire: IP datagram or carrier pigeon. Another thread somewhere else can then take this array of bytes and read out from it exactly what was written into it using a `ByteArrayInputStream`. So we have a communications channel, albeit an indirect one. A file is a similar indirect communications channel; you can read out of it what you formerly wrote into it.

In subsequent chapters, we will look at the various classes that provide streams access to different communications channels such as files, memory buffers, and network connections. The following is a quick listing of the main relevant classes (figure 5.11). You may notice that there is no stream specifically devoted to network connections. The actual stream classes corresponding to a network connection, `SocketInput-Stream` and `SocketOutput-Stream`, are not made public, and so we will see the streams only as a generic `Output-Stream` and `InputStream`.

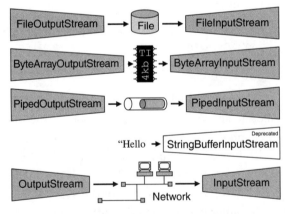

Figure 5.11 The different stream types

5.8.1 FileOutputStream and FileInputStream

These streams can be used to read and write files in a simple sequential manner. We will look at these classes in detail in the next chapter.

5.8.2 ByteArrayOutputStream and ByteArrayInputStream

These streams can be used to write data into an array of bytes and to read data out of an array of bytes. They are useful classes for producing complex streams, such as encrypted streams and message streams; we can write data into an array and manipulate it before transmission. They also provide an easy mechanism to temporarily buffer stream data.

5.8.3 PipedOutputStream and PipedInputStream

These streams can be used for streams-based communications between threads in a single application. They are usually created in pairs; everything that is written to the output stream of a pipe can subsequently be read on the corresponding input stream. This is useful for simple streams-based interthread communications.

5.8.4 StringBufferInputStream

This stream, now deprecated, provides a facility for reading bytes from a `StringBuffer` in a similar manner to the `ByteArrayInputStream` class. It has been replaced by the `StringReader` character stream class.

5.9 Wrapping up

This chapter has introduced the general concept of streams-based communications. Streams allow threads and applications to communicate over a variety of underlying communications channels in a uniform byte-I/O manner.

In the following chapters we will look at the various stream classes that are provided by the `java.io` package. These classes will provide us with a streams interface to files, networks, and other devices. We will also look at developing our own stream classes to provide us with function that is not provided by the supplied classes. Subsequently, we will look at the character streams that parallel the byte stream classes but provide facility for character-based I/O.

In later chapters, we will begin developing networked applications. Streams provide the basis for most networked interapplication communications, and we will see how to develop significant networking libraries using the streams interface. We will look at using custom streams to decode DNS responses as well as an entire custom message-streams framework.

C H A P T E R   6

File access through streams

`FileOutputStream` and `File-InputStream` (figure 6.1) are the two standard classes that supply byte-oriented streams access to

Figure 6.1 FileOutputStream and FileInputStream

files. This chapter is primarily concerned with a treatment of stream classes. Although files can also be accessed using the `RandomAccessFile` class, it is frequently useful to be able to access them through a streams interface: An application designed to read from a stream will accept input from the keyboard, a file, or a network connection without modification. The character-stream classes `FileReader` and `FileWriter` are also provided for streams-access to text files; these are discussed in detail in chapter 10.

Other file-related classes include `File` and `FileDescriptor`. We will begin this chapter with an overview of these classes as well as an introduction to `RandomAccess-File`. Because they are not strictly related to networking, we go no further than discussing their respective APIs; we provide a more thorough treatment of the file stream classes.

6.1 Class File

This class represents a system-independent file-name (figure 6.2). It provides various methods to determine information about the actual file of the specified name, as well as methods to modify the file's attributes. With this class, a programmer can query whether a file of a particular name exists, whether it is readable, and so on.

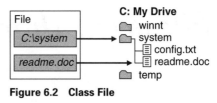

Figure 6.2 Class File

One possible use of the `File` class is to take a directory name and a filename and join them to obtain a complete path to the file. The directory separator is different in different operating systems. Therefore, it is not reasonable to simply append, for example, a / character to the pathname and then append the filename to this. As an example, the AWT `FileDialog` class returns a pathname and a filename; it is up to the programmer to join them, preferably using this class. The class can also, however, be used to rename files, to create directories, to get a listing of the files in a directory, and so forth.

6.1.1 Constructors

An instance of `File` can be created from an entire system-dependent pathname, from a pathname and a filename, or from an existing `File` object and a filename. In the latter case, the `File` object must be a directory. The new `File` object will then refer to a particular file in the directory.

File(String path)   This constructor creates a `File` object for the specified system-dependent pathname `path`. The file can subsequently be manipulated with the methods supplied by this class.

File(String path, String name)   This constructor creates a `File` object for the specified filename on the specified path `path`. Usually this involves concatenating the pathname and the filename, separated by the directory separator character.

File(File dir, String name)   This creates a `File` object for the specified filename in the specified directory `dir`.

6.1.2 Static variables

String separator   This variable contains the OS' file separator, which is the character sequence that separates the different directory names in a file path (/ under UNIX, \ under DOS). This is taken from the system property `file.separator`.

char separatorChar   This variable contains the first character of the file separator. Most file separators are a single character.

String pathSeparator   This variable contains the OS' path separator, which is the character sequence that separates different paths in a list of paths (: under UNIX, ; under DOS). This is the system property `path.separator`.

char pathSeparatorChar   This variable contains the first character of the path separator.

6.1.3 Methods

The `File` class provides various methods to test whether a file exists, whether it is a directory or a file, and so on. It also provides methods to create directories, and to remove and rename files. The `File` class is commonly used to provide a platform-independent naming mechanism, although it can also be used to provide these file management facilities.

Note that few of these methods throw `IOExceptions`. Instead, they usually return a flag indicating whether they were successful.

boolean exists()   This method returns `true` if the file or directory represented by this `File` exists.

boolean canRead()   This method returns `true` if the file or directory represented by this `File` exists and is readable.

boolean canWrite()   This method returns `true` if the file or directory represented by this `File` exists and is writable.

boolean isDirectory() This method returns `true` if this `File` corresponds to a directory.

boolean isFile() This method returns `true` if this `File` corresponds to a file.

JDK 1.1 *boolean isHidden()* This method returns `true` if this `File` corresponds to a hidden file or directory.

long lastModified() This method returns the time since the file or directory represented by this `File` was last modified, in milliseconds since the epoch (00:00:00 GMT, January 1, 1972), or 0 on error. See `java.util.Date`.

long length() This method returns the length of the file represented by this `File`.

String getName() This method returns the leaf name of this `File`; this is just the filename, without the preceding path.

String getParent() This method returns the parent directory of this `File`; this is the entire filename up to the leaf name.

JDK 1.2 *File getParentFile()* This method returns a `File` representing the parent directory of this `File`.

String getPath() This method returns the pathname of this `File`; that is, every element up to and including the leafname.

boolean isAbsolute() This method returns `true` if the pathname represented by this `File` is an absolute pathname.

String getAbsolutePath() This method returns the system-dependent absolute pathname of this `File`.

JDK 1.2 *File getAbsoluteFile()* This method returns a `File` representing the system-dependent absolute pathname of this `File`.

JDK 1.1 *String getCanonicalPath()* This method returns the canonical path of this `File`.

JDK 1.2 *File getCanonicalFile()* This method returns a `File` representing the canonical path of this `File`.

JDK 1.2 *URL toURL()* This method returns a `file:` URL corresponding to this `File`, with a trailing / if this represents a directory.

String[] list() This method returns an array of every filename in the directory represented by this `File`. No ordering of these filenames is guaranteed.

String[] list(FilenameFilter filter)   This method returns an array of every file matching the specified `FilenameFilter`, `filter` in the directory represented by this `File`. The `FilenameFilter` class provides a convenient way to select only those files in a directory with, for example, a particular suffix.

JDK 1.2 *File[] listFiles()*   This method returns an array of `Files` representing every file in the directory represented by this `File`.

JDK 1.2 *File[] listFiles(FilenameFilter filter)*   This method returns an array of `Files` representing every file matching the specified `FilenameFilter`, `filter` in the directory represented by this `File`.

JDK 1.2 *File[] listFiles(FileFilter filter)*   This method returns an array of `Files` representing every file matching the specified `FileFilter`, `filter` in the directory represented by this `File`.

JDK 1.2 *boolean createNewFile() throws IOException*   This method attempts to create an empty file corresponding to this `File`, succeeding if and only if no such file already exists. This methods returns `true` upon success or `false` if the corresponding file already exists. This operation is guaranteed to be *atomic* so you can use this for performing multiprocess-safe file locking.

boolean mkdir()   This method creates a directory corresponding to this `File`, returning `true` upon success.

boolean mkdirs()   This method creates a directory corresponding to this `File`, and as many parent directories as are necessary, returning `true` upon success.

boolean renameTo(File dest)   This method attempts to rename the file or directory represented by this `File` to the specified destination `dest`, returning `true` upon success.

boolean delete()   This method attempts to delete the file or directory represented by this `File`, returning `true` if successful.

JDK 1.2 *void deleteOnExit()*   This method schedules the file or directory represented by this `File` for deletion upon termination of the JVM. Use this to tidy up temporary files, and in particular atomic lock files. There is no way to abort a scheduled termination.

JDK 1.2 *boolean setReadOnly()*   This method sets the file or directory represented by this `File` to be read-only, returning `true` upon success.

JDK 1.2 *boolean setLastModified(long time)*   This method sets the last-modified attribute of the file or directory represented by this `File` to the specified value, time, in milliseconds since the epoch (00:00:00 GMT, January 1, 1972), returning `true` upon success.

6.1.4 Static methods

The following static methods are provided by the `File` class:

JDK 1.2 *File[] listRoots()* This method returns an array containing all the top-level directory names supported by the local machine. Under UNIX, for example, this will be just */*; under Windows, *A:*, *C:*, and so forth.

JDK 1.2 *File createTempFile(String prefix, String suffix, File directory) throws IOException* This method creates an empty file in the specified directory `Directory` and returns the corresponding `File`. The `prefix` parameter should be a `String`, at least three characters long, used to form the start of the temporary filename; `suffix` should be a `String` used to form the end of the temporary filename, or `null` for the default .tmp. Use of this method is typically accompanied by use of the `deleteOnExit()` method.

JDK 1.2 *File createTempFile(String prefix, String suffix) throws IOException* This method creates an empty file in the system temporary directory and returns the corresponding `File`. The system temporary directory is specified by the `System` property `java.io.tmpdir`. This is equivalent to calling the previous method with a `null` third parameter.

6.1.5 SecurityException

Access to files is restricted by the `SecurityManager`. Most of the methods listed above may fail with an exception of type `SecurityException` if the program is not permitted to perform the requested operation. Applications do not have a `SecurityManager`; so they can access files arbitrarily. Applets under most browsers currently may not open any file for reading or writing, or they may access only a certain restricted directory.

Note that a `SecurityException` may be thrown even though it is not listed in any `throws` clause. This is because it is a subclass of `RuntimeException`, which may be thrown at run time without being declared.

6.2 Class FileDescriptor

A `FileDescriptor` object is a handle to a low-level system file-descriptor. A file-descriptor represents an open file and includes information such as the current file position for reading and writing. This class is not commonly used.

6.2.1 Constructors

Java has no facilities for usefully creating `FileDescriptors` other than by the `RandomAccessFile`, `FileOutputStream`, and `FileInputStream` classes.

FileDescriptor()   This constructor creates an *uninitialized* `FileDescriptor` object. There is no public mechanism to initialize the `FileDescriptor` except through the related I/O classes, so this constructor is rarely of use.

6.2.2 Static variables

FileDescriptor in   This is a `FileDescriptor` for the standard input device (usually the keyboard). `System.in` is attached to this `FileDescriptor`.

FileDescriptor out   This is a `FileDescriptor` for the standard output device (usually the console). `System.out` is attached to this `FileDescriptor`.

FileDescriptor err   This is a `FileDescriptor` for the standard error device (usually the console). `System.err` is attached to this `FileDescriptor`. Error messages should be written to this device in preference to `out`.

6.2.3 Methods

boolean valid()   This method returns whether the `FileDescriptor` represents a valid, open system file descriptor.

(JDK 1.1) *void sync() throws SyncFailedException*   This method forces any operating system buffers for this `FileDescriptor` to be written to the underlying device or filesystem. Any attached Java buffers (such as from a `BufferedOutputStream`) should be flushed *before* this method is called.

6.2.4 **(JDK 1.1)** *SyncFailedException*

This exception is thrown if a call to `sync()` fails. This means that the operating system cannot guarantee that all buffers have been synchronized with the underlying medium.

6.3 Class RandomAccessFile

The `RandomAccessFile` class offers an easy way to handle files without using the streams interface of `FileOutputStream` and `File-InputStream` (figure 6.3). The advantage of using this class is that it provides both reading and writing methods and allows, as the name suggests, random access to the file. The file stream classes are limited by their streams nature to provide only sequential access, and either read-only access or write-only access through any single stream.

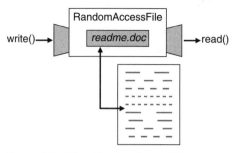

Figure 6.3   Class RandomAccessFile

6.3.1 Constructors

Random access files can be constructed from filenames or `File` objects. Whether access is read/write or read-only is specified in the constructor. Writing into an existing file overwrites the data at the current file-access position. It does not insert the data at the current position, and it does not truncate the file.

RandomAccessFile(String name, String mode) throws IOException   This constructor creates a `RandomAccessFile` with the specified system-dependent filename `name` and the specified mode `mode`. Mode `"r"` is for read-only, and mode `"rw"` is for reading and writing.

Remember that filenames are not portable across platforms. Under UNIX, a filename may have the form /etc/rc.d/rc.sysinit, while under DOS the filename may have the form C:\Windows\System.ini. Unless the user is supplying a filename, it is better to use the next constructor.

RandomAccessFile(File file, String mode) throws IOException   This constructor creates a `RandomAccessFile` from a specified `File` object `file` and mode `mode` (`"r"` or `"rw"`).

6.3.2 Methods

This class provides several methods that have similar signatures to those of `OutputStream` and `InputStream`. It provides facilities to read and write bytes, as well as many higher level functions, such as reading a line of ASCII text or reading an `int` value. These methods have the same signatures as the `DataOutputStream` and `DataInputStream` classes, which we shall look at in chapter 8. This class actually implements the `DataInput` and `DataOutput` interfaces that declare a standard set of these methods.

final FileDescriptor getFD() throws IOException   This method returns the system-level file-descriptor object that is being used by the `RandomAccessFile`.

int read() throws IOException   This method reads a byte of data. It returns the value -1 if the end of the file is reached.

int read(byte[] b, int offset, int len) throws IOException   This method reads a subarray as a sequence of bytes. It reads `len` bytes into array b, starting at index `offset`. The number of bytes successfully read is returned. As with the `InputStream` class, this method may not read the requested number of bytes.

int read(byte[] b) throws IOException   This method attempts to read a complete array of bytes using the previous `read()` method.

final void readFully(byte[] b, int off, int len) throws IOException   This method fully reads the specified subarray of b. If EOF is reached before enough bytes have been read, an exception of type `EOFException` is thrown.

final void readFully(byte[] b) throws IOException   This method fully reads the specified array b using the previous `readFully()` method.

int skipBytes(int n) throws IOException   This method skips the specified number of bytes n. It blocks until n bytes have been skipped, throwing an `EOFException` if EOF is detected prematurely. The returned value is meaningless because it is always n.

void write(int b) throws IOException   This method writes a byte of data. Although the parameter b is an `int`, only the low 8 bits are written.

void write(byte[] b, int off, int len) throws IOException   This method writes the specified subarray of `len` bytes from array b starting at index `off`.

void write(byte[] b) throws IOException   This method writes an array of bytes using the previous `write()` method.

long getFilePointer() throws IOException   This method returns the current location of the file pointer. This is the byte offset in the file at which the `RandomAccessFile` is currently reading or writing.

void seek(long pos) throws IOException   This method sets the file pointer to the specified absolute position.

long length() throws IOException   This method returns the length of the file.

void close() throws IOException   This method closes the file.

final boolean readBoolean() throws IOException   This method reads a `boolean` value, as written by the `writeBoolean()` method. All of these high-level methods throw an exception of type `EOFException` if a premature EOF is reached.

final byte readByte() throws IOException   This method reads a `byte` value. Unlike the `read()` method, this method throws an `EOFException` if the EOF is reached.

final short readShort() throws IOException   This method reads a `short` value, as written by the `writeShort()` method.

final int readInt() throws IOException   This method reads an `int` value. Note that this is read as 4 binary bytes; the value is not decoded from a text file.

final long readLong() throws IOException   This method reads a `long` value (8 bytes).

final int readUnsignedByte() throws IOException   This method reads an unsigned `byte` value; thus, the `byte` 255 will be treated as the `int` 255 and not −1.

final int readUnsignedShort() throws IOException   This method reads an unsigned `short` value, returning the corresponding `int`.

final float readFloat() throws IOException   This method reads a `float` value.

final double readDouble() throws IOException   This method reads a `double` value.

final char readChar() throws IOException   This method reads a 16-bit `char` value.

final String readUTF() throws IOException   This method reads a UTF formatted `String`. UTF format includes the `String` length and stores characters to full 16-bit precision, albeit in a special encoding. UTF format is briefly described with the `DataInputStream` and `DataOutputStream` classes, and documented more fully in appendix B.

final String readLine() throws IOException   This method reads a line of ASCII (ISO Latin 1) characters terminated by a newline or EOF. It only recognizes the newline character (`\n`) as the end of a line and does not return this character as part of the result. The method returns `null` at EOF.

final void writeBoolean(boolean b) throws IOException   This method writes a `boolean` value.

final void writeByte(int i) throws IOException   This method writes a single byte.

final void writeShort(int i) throws IOException   This method writes a 16-bit `short` as a sequence of 2 bytes, high byte first.

final void writeInt(int i) throws IOException   This method writes a 32-bit `int` as a sequence of 4 bytes, high byte first.

final void writeLong(long l) throws IOException   This method writes a 64-bit `long`.

final void writeFloat(float f) throws IOException   This method writes a 32-bit `float`.

final void writeDouble(double d) throws IOException   This method writes a 64-bit `double`.

final void writeChar(int c) throws IOException   This method writes a 16-bit `char` as a sequence of 2 bytes, high byte first.

final void writeChars(String s) throws IOException   This method writes a `String` as a sequence of 16-bit characters. Neither the string length nor a delimiting character is written.

final void writeUTF(String str) throws IOException   This method writes a `String` in UTF encoding.

final void writeBytes(String s) throws IOException   This method writes a `String` as a sequence of ASCII bytes. The top byte of every character in the `String` is ignored. This is effectively ISO Latin 1 encoding but without any checking for invalid characters.

6.3.3 IOException

All of the methods listed above may throw an `IOException` if there is a problem with the read or write. All of the higher level read methods (for integers, etc.) will throw an `EOFException` (a subclass of `IOException`) if the EOF is reached prematurely.

6.3.4 SecurityException

All file access is restricted by the current `SecurityManager`. Creating a `RandomAccessFile` may cause a `SecurityException` if the specified file access is prohibited.

6.4 Class FileOutputStream

The `FileOutputStream` class allows sequential data to be written to a file (figure 6.4). The usual constructors take a filename or `File` object and either create a corresponding new file, destroying any existing file having the same name, or append to an existing file.

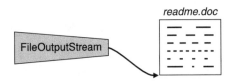

readme.doc

Figure 6.4 Class FileOutputStream

Note that if you open two appending file streams onto a single file, then each stream will overwrite data written by the other. They will not append to data written by the other. Use a single stream and synchronization if you wish to do this properly.

6.4.1 Constructors

Constructing a `FileOutputStream` will create the specified file and then provide the capability to write to it. The `close()` method should be called when writing to the file is finished. If this is not done, then the file and underlying `FileDescriptor` are automatically closed when the `FileOutputStream` is garbage collected.

FileOutputStream(String name) throws IOException   This constructor creates a file with the specified filename `name`, destroying any existing file having the same name. The `FileOutputStream` provides sequential write access to the new file.

FileOutputStream(File file) throws IOException   This constructor creates a file corresponding to the specified `File` object `file`, destroying any existing file having the same name. To use this constructor, a `File` object with the desired name must be created first, followed by the associated `FileOutputStream`.

FileOutputStream (String name, boolean append) throws IOException   This constructor creates a `FileOutputStream` for the specified file, `name`. The flag `append` specifies whether the stream should append to an existing file (`true`) or truncate it.

FileOutputStream(FileDescriptor fdObj)   This constructor allows a `FileOutputStream` to be constructed from the `FileDescriptor` of a file which is already open; for example, one which is open for random access. This constructor does not create the file; it takes an existing, open file and writes to it at the current read/write position.

This constructor will not throw an `IOException` because the `FileDescriptor` is assumed to be already attached to an open file.

6.4.2 Methods

The `FileOutputStream` class provides one method in addition to the usual methods of `OutputStream`.

FileDescriptor getFD() throws IOException   This method returns a `File-Descriptor` object for the file that is being written.

6.4.3 IOException

The methods and constructors described above may all throw exceptions of type `IOException` if an I/O error occurs. Possible causes include a filename being invalid, the file being locked, or the disk becoming full.

6.4.4 SecurityException

Creating a `FileOutputStream` may throw an exception of type `SecurityException` if the current `SecurityManager` does not permit file writing.

6.5 Class FileInputStream

The `FileInputStream` class allows one to read sequential data from a file (figure 6.5). The file must already exist. Creating a `FileInputStream` for a nonexistent file will throw an exception of type `IOException`.

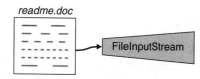

Figure 6.5   Class FileInputStream

6.5.1 Constructors

Constructing a `FileInputStream` opens a stream for reading from the specified file. The `close()` method should be called when reading from the file is complete. If this is not done, then the file and underlying `FileDescriptor` are automatically closed when the `FileInputStream` is garbage collected.

FileInputStream(String name) throws IOException   This constructor opens a file with the specified filename `name` for reading. The `FileInputStream` then provides sequential read access to this file. As before, be aware of the differences between filenames on different operating systems.

FileInputStream(File file) throws IOException   This constructor opens a file corresponding to the specified `File` object `file` for reading.

FileInputStream(FileDescriptor fdObj)   This constructor creates a `FileInput-Stream` attached to the existing `FileDescriptor fdObj`. The `FileDescriptor` must be a valid descriptor for a file that is open for reading.

6.5.2 Methods

The `FileInputStream` class provides one additional method to those of `InputStream`. The `markSupported()`, `mark()`, and `reset()` methods take their default implementations of unsupported.

FileDescriptor getFD() throws IOException This method returns a reference to the system-level `FileDescriptor` object to which the `FileInputStream` is attached. Creating a `FileInputStream` automatically creates such a `FileDescriptor` object.

6.5.3 IOException

Most of the methods and constructors described above may throw an exception of type `IOException`. The exact nature of the `IOException` depends upon the I/O error, but the most common cause is a file not existing. The `read()` methods do not throw an exception at EOF, but, as with `InputStream`, they return the value –1.

6.5.4 SecurityException

Creating a `FileInputStream` may throw an exception of type `SecurityException` if the operation is not permitted by the `SecurityManager`.

6.6 A simple file streams example

This example presents a trivial file copier (figure 6.6). It takes two filename parameters and copies the first file to the second.

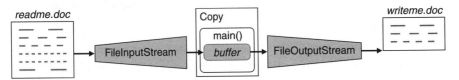

Figure 6.6   File copying

```
import java.io.*;

public class Copy {
   public static void main (String[] args) throws IOException {
      if (args.length != 2)
         throw (new IllegalArgumentException ("Syntax: Copy <src> <dst>"));
      FileInputStream in = new FileInputStream (args[0]);
      FileOutputStream out = new FileOutputStream (args[1]);

      byte[] buffer = new byte[16];
      int numberRead;
      while ((numberRead = in.read (buffer)) >= 0)
         out.write (buffer, 0, numberRead);

      out.close ();
      in.close ();
   }
}
```

All of the code resides in the `main()` method. We declare that this method may throw any exceptions that may occur from attempting to copy the file. We verify that the correct number of parameters has been supplied, and throw an explanatory exception if not.

We open a `FileInputStream` from the first parameter and a `FileOutputStream` to the second parameter. These provide the basic `InputStream` and `OutputStream` interfaces for accessing the files. We then copy the first file to the second file using a small intermediate buffer for efficiency. We have seen this type of loop in the previous chapter: we read as many bytes into the buffer as possible and then write them to the `OutputStream`.

When the `read()` method returns the value -1, we have reached the EOF so we exit the loop and close the two files.

6.7 Writing an overwriting FileOutputStream

We will now look at creating a custom `OutputStream`. This class is similar to a `File-OutputStream`, except that it will overwrite the contents of an existing file rather than either creating a file or appending to an existing file. The file will be created if it does not exist (figure 6.7).

```
import java.io.*;

public class SimpleOverwritingFileOutputStream extends OutputStream {
  // public SimpleOverwritingFileOutputStream (String filename)
      throws IOException ...
  // public void write (int datum) throws IOException ...
  // public void close () throws IOException ...
}
```

Our class extends `OutputStream` and provides the minimum number of methods necessary to actually implement an `OutputStream`.

```
  protected RandomAccessFile file;

  public SimpleOverwritingFileOutputStream (String filename)
    throws IOException {
    file = new RandomAccessFile (filename, "rw");
  }
```

We make use of the `RandomAccessFile` `file` to perform all I/O: the constructor creates this `RandomAccessFile` with the specified filename, `filename`. The `RandomAccessFile` class automatically creates the file if it does not exist, or else opens it for random access. After the file has been opened, it is automatically positioned at the beginning, so any written data will overwrite the original contents of the file.

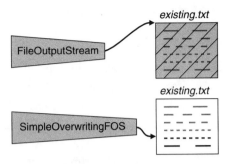

Figure 6.7   Class SimpleOverwriting-FileOutputStream

```
public void write (int datum) throws IOException {
   file.write (datum);
}
```

This method calls the `write()` method of the `RandomAccessFile`.

```
public void close () throws IOException {
   file.close ();
}
```

This method calls the `close()` method of the `RandomAccessFile`.

We could obviously implement the multibyte `write()` methods to call those of `RandomAccessFile`; however, for illustrative purposes, this is the minimum number of methods necessary to implement this class.

There are actually several alternative implementations for this class; we will now look at one of these.

6.7.1 An alternative overwriting FileOutputStream

One alternative implementation is to avail of the `FileOutputStream` constructor that attaches to an already open `FileDescriptor` object. We can open a file for random access using a `RandomAccessFile` and then create a `FileOutputStream` attached to the same underlying `FileDescriptor`.

```
import java.io.*;

public class OverwritingFileOutputStream extends FileOutputStream {
  // public OverwritingFileOutputStream (String filename)
       throws IOException ...
}
```

We extend `FileOutputStream` and provide just one constructor. Note that this implementation is simple because we inherit all of the methods of `FileOutputStream` that efficiently write to an internal `FileDescriptor`. It would obviously be prudent, in a final implementation, to also provide a constructor that accepts a `File` argument. However, for clarity we will omit this.

```
public OverwritingFileOutputStream (String filename) throws IOException {
   super (getFDOf (filename));
}

// protected static FileDescriptor getFDOf (String filename)
      throws IOException ...
```

In the constructor, we call the superclass constructor with a `FileDescriptor` argument. This `FileDescriptor` is returned by the method `getFDOf()` and corresponds to an open `FileDescriptor` positioned at the beginning of the specified file.

```
protected static FileDescriptor getFDOf (String filename)
    throws IOException {
  RandomAccessFile file = new RandomAccessFile (filename, "rw");
  return file.getFD ();
}
```

This `static` method creates a `RandomAccessFile` for the specified file, `fileName`, and returns its `FileDescriptor`. Creating a `RandomAccessFile` in this manner does not erase an existing file, so after the constructor call we will have a `FileOutputStream` attached to an existing file, but positioned at the beginning. The `RandomAccessFile` class does not automatically close when it is garbage collected, unlike `FileInputStream` and `FileOutputStream`, and so we can simply discard it.

We could replace this method with a superconstructor call of the form `super (new RandomAccessFile (fileName, "rw").getFD ())`. However, this extra method makes the code more legible.

6.8 Writing a seekable FileOutputStream

This example uses much the same technique as above to create what is essentially a random access `FileOutputStream`: it is a `FileOutputStream` with methods to read and modify the position at which the file is being written.

It is necessary to understand the `FileDescriptor` class to understand this class. Java creates a `FileDescriptor` object for every open file. This `FileDescriptor` includes information such as a reference to the actual file and a read/write position in the file. If a file is opened for reading twice, then each `FileInputStream` will have a different `FileDescriptor`. Reading from one will not affect the read position of the other. Alternatively, you can open a file once and create several file streams attached to the single `FileDescriptor`. Any operation that modifies the read/write position of this `File-Descriptor` will affect all of these streams.

In this case, we create a `RandomAccessFile` and a `FileOutputStream`, both of which are attached to the same `FileDescriptor`. We use the `FileOutputStream` for streams-based access to the file and the `RandomAccessFile` to provide random access.

```
import java.io.*;

public class SeekableFileOutputStream extends FileOutputStream {
  // public SeekableFileOutputStream (String filename) throws IOException ...
  // public SeekableFileOutputStream (File file) throws IOException ...
  // public void setPosition (long position) throws IOException ...
  // public long getPosition () throws IOException ...
  // public long getLength () throws IOException ...
}
```

This class is essentially the same as the `OverwritingFileOutputStream`, but with the addition of methods to read and modify the position at which the file is being written. We extend `FileOutputStream` and provide constructors that accept either a `File` or a `String` filename specification.

```
public SeekableFileOutputStream (String filename) throws IOException {
  this (new RandomAccessFile (filename, "rw"));
}

// protected SeekableFileOutputStream (RandomAccessFile file)
//     throws IOException ...
```

This constructor calls another constructor with a new `RandomAccessFile` attached to the specified file, `filename`.

```
public SeekableFileOutputStream (File file) throws IOException {
  this (file.getPath ());
}
```

This constructor calls the previous constructor with the specified `File` `file`'s path.

```
protected RandomAccessFile file;

protected SeekableFileOutputStream (RandomAccessFile file)
    throws IOException {
  super (file.getFD ());
  this.file = file;
}
```

This constructor accepts a `RandomAccessFile` as a parameter, calls the superclass constructor with its `FileDescriptor` and then leaves a reference to the `RandomAccessFile` in the variable `file`.

Unlike the previous example, we cannot use a `static` method because we must keep a reference to the `RandomAccessFile` in each instance of the `SeekableFileOutputStream`.

```
public void setPosition (long position) throws IOException {
  file.seek (position);
}
```

This method calls the `RandomAccessFile`'s `seek()` method to set the writing position to the specified location.

```
public long getPosition () throws IOException {
  return file.getFilePointer ();
}
```

This method returns the current writing position in the file. Because this stream and the `RandomAccessFile` share a common `FileDescriptor`, this value will be the same for both.

```
public long getLength () throws IOException {
  return file.length ();
}
```

This method returns the length of the file by calling the corresponding method of the `RandomAccessFile`.

This class can be used in any situation where random access is required at the same time as the streams interface. For example, random access could be combined with the use of the data streams, and so forth. Note that external buffering is incompatible with this class, unless the buffer is flushed every time the stream location is altered. Adding buffering to this class could, however, address this issue automatically.

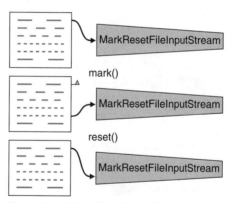

Figure 6.8 Class MarkResetFileInput-

A similar mechanism might be useful with an `InputStream` interface to provide random access for reading records from a flat database file. To achieve this, we can use exactly the same technique but subclass `FileInputStream` instead of `FileOutputStream`.

6.9 Building a mark/reset FileInputStream

In the previous chapter, we discussed the mark() and reset() methods of Input-Stream. The default FileInputStream does not provide these methods, even though they are provided by the underlying file system. In this example, we will create a FileInputStream that supports the mark() and reset() methods (figure 6.8).

```
import java.io.*;

public class MarkResetFileInputStream extends FileInputStream {
  // public MarkResetFileInputStream (String filename) throws IOException ...
  // public MarkResetFileInputStream (File file) throws IOException ...
  // public boolean markSupported () ...
  // public void mark (int readAheadLimit) ...
  // public void reset () throws IOException ...
}
```

This class has the same structure as the previous example, except that we extend FileInputStream and implement the markSupported(), mark(), and reset() methods. As before, we provide constructors that accept either a File or a String file specification.

```
public MarkResetFileInputStream (String filename) throws IOException {
  this (new RandomAccessFile (filename, "r"));
}

// protected MarkResetFileInputStream (RandomAccessFile file)
//     throws IOException ...
```

This constructor calls another constructor with a new RandomAccessFile attached to the specified file, fileName.

```
public MarkResetFileInputStream (File file) throws IOException {
  this (file.getPath ());
}
```

This constructor calls the previous constructor with the path of the specified File, file.

```
protected long markedPosition;
protected RandomAccessFile file;

protected MarkResetFileInputStream (RandomAccessFile file)
    throws IOException {
  super (file.getFD ());
  this.file = file;
  markedPosition = -1;
}
```

In this constructor, we accept a `RandomAccessFile` attached to the chosen file and then call the superclass constructor with the underlying `FileDescriptor` of this file. We keep a reference to the `RandomAccessFile` in `file`.

To perform `mark()` and `reset()`, we store the marked position in the `markedPosition` variable. We initially set the marked position to –1 to indicate that no position has been marked.

```
public boolean markSupported () {
   return true;
}
```

We override the default implementation of `markSupported()` to indicate that this class does indeed support the `mark()` and `reset()` operations.

```
public void mark (int readAheadLimit) {
   try {
      markedPosition = file.getFilePointer ();
   } catch (IOException ex) {
      markedPosition = -1;
   }
}
```

To mark a position in the file we must take note of the current reading position in the file. To do this, we can call the `getFilePointer()` method of the `RandomAccess-File`. Note that the `getFilePointer()` method may throw an `IOException`, but the signature for `mark()` specifies that it may not, so we must catch any potential exception and set the marked position to –1.

```
public void reset () throws IOException {
   if (markedPosition == -1)
      throw new IOException ("No mark set.");
   file.seek (markedPosition);
}
```

The `reset()` method first checks to see that a mark has been set. If none has, then we throw an explanatory `IOException`. Otherwise we use the `seek()` method of `RandomAccessFile` to reset the reading position of the underlying `FileDescriptor`. Both this `FileInputStream` and the `RandomAccessFile` are attached to the same `FileDescriptor`, so calling the `RandomAccessFile` `seek()` method will also reposition the reading position of the `FileInputStream`.

Using this stream, we can make use of the mark/reset `InputStream` methods to efficiently implement file format discriminators and other such classes. To implement this without using a `RandomAccessFile`, we would have to buffer the data as we read it and then reread from the buffer in case of a reset.

6.10 Wrapping up

In this chapter, we have looked at the file stream classes. More importantly, we have seen how we can extend these classes and provide additional function beyond what is provided by the basic API. The classes that we have developed are small because we can leverage off the existing code base. This ability is one of the tremendous advantages of object-oriented programming. In addition, we have provided all of these facilities on top of the uniform streams interface, so they are readily usable by any code that makes use of the stream classes.

The classes that we have implemented provide only additional functionality for file streams. They are not directly usable for byte array streams, networked streams, or indeed any other stream class. In the next chapters, we will look at stream filters that provide enhanced function on top of any underlying stream connection.

C H A P T E R   7

Extending streams with filters

Up to this point, we have looked only at simple streams that support writing bytes and byte arrays. Obviously, communication at such a level is more awkward than it need be. We have seen how to extend an existing stream and add function; however, this is limited because we can extend only a single stream, and so must implement the extension for all communication channels that we will use.

We would like to be able to develop streams that allow us to attach higher level functions to any type of stream in a generic manner. This chapter introduces the concept of a *stream filter*, a stream that provides additional function on top of an existing stream. We will be able to develop streams that allow us to communicate all of the primitive Java data types over any underlying stream connection, among other things.

7.1 *Providing higher level communications*

There are several obvious ways of providing higher level communications over a stream that can handle only bytes. Specifically, we can create a global utility class, subclass, or delegate. Said more explicitly, we can use general-purpose methods that convert data into bytes and transmit the bytes over a separate stream; alternatively, we can subclass a stream and provide these methods directly. The last and most general option is to make a stream filter that provides enhanced stream function on top of any other existing stream.

7.1.1 *General-purpose methods*

In this example, we implement a pair of general-purpose methods that write an integer as 4 bytes into an

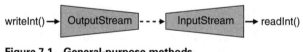

Figure 7.1 General-purpose methods

OutputStream and read an integer as 4 bytes from an InputStream (figure 7.1).

```
void writeInt (OutputStream out, int value) throws IOException {
   out.write (value >> 24);
   out.write (value >> 16);
   out.write (value >> 8);
   out.write (value);
}
```

This method writes the integer value to the OutputStream out as a series of 4 bytes, high byte first. Note that the write() method just writes the bottom 8 bits of the integer parameter.

The operator >> shifts the integer right by the specified number of bits, so the value value >> 24 is just the top byte of value (sign-extended).

```
int readInt (InputStream in) throws IOException {
   int v0, v1, v2, v3;
   if (((v3 = in.read ()) == -1) ||
```

```
      ((v2 = in.read ()) == -1) ||
      ((v1 = in.read ()) == -1) ||
      ((v0 = in.read ()) == -1))
    throw new IOException ("EOF while reading int");
  return (v3 << 24) | (v2 << 16) | (v1 << 8) | v0;
}
```

This method reads 4 bytes from the `InputStream in` and adds them together to produce the integer result. If we reach EOF before reading the entire integer, we throw an `IOException`. The operator << shifts the value left by the specified number of bits.

This manner of communication is quite adequate in a simple situation. Methods can be provided for communicating all of the default types. The problem with this approach is that every application that needs to communicate these types must agree on a format and provide the code in the form of these methods.

7.1.2 Enhanced streams

In the previous example, we read the integer from the stream, so it would be nice if the stream provided

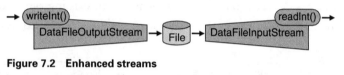

Figure 7.2   Enhanced streams

the method to read an integer directly; this is the nature of object-oriented programming. The following class extends the `FileOutputStream` class and provides a `writeInt()` method; we would obviously implement a corresponding `DataFileInputStream` that mimics the `readInt()` method (figure 7.2).

```
import java.io.*;

public class DataFileOutputStream extends FileOutputStream {
  // public DataFileOutputStream (String filename) throws IOException ...
  // public void writeInt (int value) throws IOException ...
}
```

This class extends `FileOutputStream` and adds a `writeInt()` method that writes an integer to the attached file as 4 bytes.

```
public DataFileOutputStream (String filename) throws IOException {
  super (filename);
}
```

In the constructor, we call the superclass constructor with the specified filename `filename`. For reasons of simplicity, we don't implement any of the other constructors.

```
public void writeInt (int value) throws IOException {
  write (value >> 24);
  write (value >> 16);
```

```
    write (value >> 8);
    write (value);
}
```

The `writeInt()` method writes the integer as 4 separate bytes, as before.

This approach is cleaner than the first approach; we can call the `writeInt()` method directly on the `OutputStream`. The drawback of this approach is that we must provide an implementation of `writeInt()` for every `OutputStream` available. We have demonstrated an implementation for a `FileOutputStream`; we also would have to provide an implementation for `PipedOutputStream` and so forth.

7.1.3 Stream filters

The preferred mechanism for adding higher level function to streams in Java is stream filters. A `FilterInputStream` is a stream that attaches to an existing `InputStream` and provides additional function on top of that which is already provided (figure 7.3). Similarly, a `FilterOutputStream` attaches to an existing `OutputStream` and enhances its function. In the rest of this chapter, we will look at some of the standard stream filters.

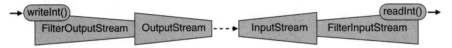

Figure 7.3   Stream filters

One important thing to note about stream filters is that they are subclasses of `OutputStream` and `InputStream`; they provide all of the normal methods of these superclasses. Usually the superclass methods will be passed on directly to the attached stream, so writing to a `FilterOutputStream` will write directly to the attached `OutputStream`. Because stream filters are themselves streams, we can attach several filters in series together and obtain their combined function.

7.2   Class FilterOutputStream

This class is a template for output stream filters. It does not provide any additional function other than the ability to attach to an existing `OutputStream` and to make use of its methods.

In fact, a plain `FilterOutputStream` is functionally indistinguishable from the `OutputStream` to which it is attached; all of the methods perform the relevant action on the attached stream. The `FilterOutputStream` can thus be passed as an `OutputStream` parameter with no visible difference. This class is used by subclasses which will add to the basic function provided here.

7.2.1 Constructors

FilterOutputStreams attach to existing OutputStreams, hence the single constructor:

protected FilterOutputStream(OutputStream out) This constructor creates a new FilterOutputStream attached to the OutputStream out. It is not possible to call this constructor directly; it may only be called by a subclass.

7.2.2 Methods

The default methods call the corresponding action on the attached stream.

void close() throws IOException This calls the corresponding method on the attached stream—closing a FilterStream closes the stream to which it is attached. It is thus not necessary to also close the attached stream.

void flush() throws IOException This calls the corresponding method on the attached stream.

void write(int b) throws IOException This calls the corresponding method on the attached stream.

void write(byte[] b) throws IOException This calls the following write() method with the entire byte array b:

void write(byte[] b, int off, int len) throws IOException This method writes the specified len-byte subarray of b, starting from offset off, as a series of single-byte writes to the attached stream. Subclasses should always override this with a more efficient implementation.

7.2.3 Variables

protected OutputStream out This is the attached OutputStream that was specified in the constructor. Subclasses can either access this stream directly through this variable or indirectly by calling methods of their FilterOutputStream superclass; the former is usually preferred.

7.3 Class FilterInputStream

This class is a template for input stream filters. It does not provide any function other than the ability to attach to an existing InputStream and to pass requests on to methods of this attached stream.

7.3.1 Constructors

FilterInputStreams attach to existing InputStreams, hence the single constructor:

protected FilterInputStream(InputStream in) This constructor creates a `Filter-InputStream` attached to the `InputStream` in. It is not possible to call this constructor directly; it may be called only by the constructor of a subclass.

7.3.2 Methods
The default methods call the corresponding action on the attached stream.

int available() throws IOException This returns the number of bytes available on the attached stream.

void close() throws IOException This closes the attached stream.

void mark(int readlimit) This calls the corresponding method on the attached stream.

boolean markSupported() This calls the corresponding method on the attached stream.

int read() throws IOException This calls the corresponding method on the attached stream.

int read(byte[] b) throws IOException This calls the following `read()` method with the entire byte array b:

int read(byte[] b, int off, int len) throws IOException This calls the corresponding method on the attached stream.

void reset() throws IOException This calls the corresponding method on the attached stream.

long skip(long n) throws IOException This calls the corresponding method on the attached stream.

7.3.3 Variables

protected InputStream in This is the attached `InputStream` that was specified in the constructor. Subclasses can either access this stream directly through this variable or indirectly by calling methods of their `FilterInputStream` superclass.

7.4 Standard stream filters

There are many possible uses for stream filters, and the Java environment comes with several such streams already defined. These are streams that can attach to any existing stream, including other stream filters, and provide additional function. We will cover these in detail in the following chapters, however, for reference, they include:

7.4.1 BufferedOutputStream and BufferedInputStream

These streams provide input and output buffering on top of an existing stream. Buffering is a useful function because it makes I/O more efficient (figure 7.4).

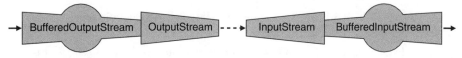

Figure 7.4   Buffered streams

Without buffering, every call to a stream will pass through to the local operating system, which can incur considerable overhead. By buffering the communications, the majority of reads and writes can occur directly to a memory buffer, and the operating system need be only occasionally called. Output buffers can be flushed using the `flush()` method; this writes any buffered data to the attached `OutputStream`. These streams will also flush automatically when necessary.

7.4.2 DataOutputStream and DataInputStream

These streams provide high-level communications capabilities on top of an existing stream, which can only read and write bytes. Methods are provided to communicate all of the primitive language types, such as `Strings` and floating point numbers (figure 7.5).

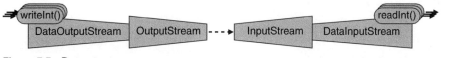

Figure 7.5   Data streams

7.4.3 PushbackInputStream

A pushback stream is an input stream that supports *unreading* of data: data can be pushed back into the input stream and will subsequently be available for

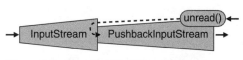

Figure 7.6   Class PushbackInputStream

rereading (figure 7.6). In an earlier chapter, we discussed using the `mark()` and `reset()` methods to permit, for example, a GIF decoder to read some of a file and then to restore the stream if it does not understand the image. We can achieve the same effect with a `PushbackInputStream` if a decoder needs only to read a small fixed amount of data to determine whether it can proceed. A single-byte pushback buffer is, in fact, a common requirement of a language scanner.

7.4.4 SequenceInputStream

This stream filter is interesting because it allows a series of Input-Streams to be sequenced one after another (figure 7.7). All of the data are read from the first stream until

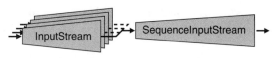

Figure 7.7   Class SequenceInputStream

the end of the file is reached, at which point reading switches to the next stream. End of file is signaled only when the end of the last InputStream is reached. Because this is a stream filter, it appears as just a single long InputStream, even though it reads sequentially from several underlying streams.

7.4.5 LineNumberInputStream

This stream, deprecated by the LineNumberReader class, provides rudimentary line numbering: it proceeds as a normal InputStream, but increments an internal

Figure 7.8   Class LineNumberInputStream

counter with every line that it reads (figure 7.8). The current line number can be queried using a special method; this permits an application to easily identify the line number of a text file which it is reading without having any additional code. The mark() and reset() methods are modified to restore the line number.

7.4.6 PrintStream

This class, deprecated by the PrintWriter class, provides the capability of ASCII textual data output. It provides methods for writing all of the standard data types to an Output-Stream, formatting the values as plain text.

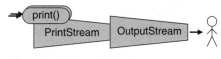

Figure 7.9   Class PrintStream

The System.out stream is, in fact, a PrintStream attached to the user's terminal; all data written to System.out using the print methods are thus formatted in ASCII for human use (figure 7.9).

7.5 Using stream filters

In this example, we will look at using a few stream filters together (figure 7.10). We will look at the various filters in detail in the next chapter. It should be noted that this example uses several deprecated features (features that have been replaced by other, better classes and methods). Their use, however, serves to make a more interesting example than would be otherwise possible using just byte streams. Notably, class LineNumberInputStream has been replaced by class LineNumberReader, and the readLine() method of class DataInputStream has been replaced by that of class BufferedReader.

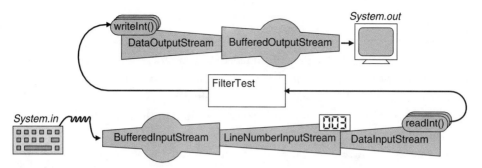

Figure 7.10   Using stream filters

In chapter 11, we will reimplement this example more properly using those replacements.

This example reads lines of input and writes them out again, in uppercase, preceded by the line number. What makes this unusual, other than using methods of `DataInput-Stream` and `DataOutputStream` to read and write ASCII lines, is that we buffer the input and the output. Buffering the input has little obvious effect; however, buffering the output has the effect of delaying the actual writing out of data until we flush the stream or until the buffer becomes full. Hence, we do not see our input written out again until either we have written a lot (512 bytes by default), or until we terminate the input using CTRL+D (UNIX) or CTRL+Z (DOS) and the output is flushed.

```java
import java.io.*;

public class FilterTest {
  public static void main (String[] args) {
    BufferedInputStream bufferedIn = new BufferedInputStream (System.in);
    BufferedOutputStream bufferedOut = new BufferedOutputStream (System.out);

    LineNumberInputStream lineNumberIn =
      new LineNumberInputStream (bufferedIn);

    DataInputStream dataIn = new DataInputStream (lineNumberIn);
    DataOutputStream dataOut = new DataOutputStream (bufferedOut);
    try {
      String line;
      while ((line = dataIn.readLine ()) != null) {
        String response = lineNumberIn.getLineNumber () + " : " +
        line.toUpperCase () + "\n";
        dataOut.writeBytes (response);
      }
      dataOut.flush ();
    } catch (IOException ex) {
      System.err.println (ex);
    }
  }
```

}

The first thing we do is create a `BufferedInputStream` `bufferedIn` and a `BufferedOutputStream` `bufferedOut` attached to the user's terminal. Everything that we read from or write to these streams ultimately comes from or goes to the user's terminal; however, memory buffers make the I/O more efficient. We attach a `LineNumber-InputStream` `lineNumberIn` to the input to keep a count of the current line number.

We subsequently create a `DataInputStream` `dataIn` and a `DataOutputStream` `dataOut` attached to these streams. Again, what we read and write goes through the buffered streams, which are attached to the user's terminal. These data streams provide us with a filter for higher level communications on top of the lower level streams, which can handle only bytes.

We subsequently read lines from the input, process them, and write them to the output. Notice here that we do this processing until the `readLine()` method returns `null`. Some methods of `DataInputStream` indicate to us that we have reached the end of the file by throwing an `EOFException`. The `readLine()` method simply returns `null`. Our loop is thus terminated when the user types CTRL+D (or CTRL+Z). We subsequently flush the output.

The use of a `DataOutputStream` is actually unnecessary here. We could have simply used the `println()` methods of `System.out`; however, this serves as an example of attaching multiple streams together.

This example is concerned with reading and writing text-based information, a task that is better served by the character streams. For comparison, we recreate this example in chapter 11 using the corresponding character-stream classes.

7.6 Building text stream filters

There are many uses for stream filters in networking, which we shall look at later. In this example, we will create a pair of stream filters that permit us to read and write data in textual format. We define a `TextOutputStream` and a `TextInputStream` that attach to an existing stream and provide methods to read and write strings and integers. The `TextOutputStream` is analogous to the predefined `PrintStream` class, which provides methods to write all of the standard data types in textual format. Streams such as these are useful for communicating with human beings, as well as with servers that communicate in plain text.

Text-based communications are now performed more properly with the character stream classes that support a wide variety of encoding options. It is still, however, a sufficiently common requirement to read and write raw textual data that the following examples are in fairly wide use.

7.6.1 Class TextOutputStream

This class is a `FilterOutputStream` that attaches to an existing stream and provides some capability for communicating in textual format over the stream. Because the normal `write()` methods are passed directly to the attached stream, these textual communication methods are provided in addition to the usual methods of `OutputStream`.

```
import java.io.*;

public class TextOutputStream extends FilterOutputStream {
   // public TextOutputStream (OutputStream out) ...
   // public void writeInt (int value) throws IOException ...
   // public void writeString (String string) throws IOException ...
}
```

This class extends `FilterOutputStream` and provides methods `writeInt()`, which writes an integer value in textual format, and `writeString()`, which writes a `String` in ISO Latin 1 encoding.

```
public TextOutputStream (OutputStream out) {
   super (out);
}
```

The constructor calls the superclass constructor, attaching to the specified `Output-Stream out`.

```
public void writeInt (int value) throws IOException {
   writeString (Integer.toString (value));
}
```

This method writes the integer `value` to the attached stream in textual format. We make use of the `toString()` method of class `Integer`, which converts an integer value into a `String`, and then use the `writeString()` method.

```
public void writeString (String string) throws IOException {
   write (string.getBytes ("latin1"));
}
```

This method writes the `String string` to the attached stream in ISO Latin 1 encoding. We perform the encoding conversion by using the `getBytes()` method of class `String` that converts a `String` into an array of bytes according to a specified encoding. In this case, we specify the encoding latin1, which is ISO Latin 1 or international ASCII. We then write this buffer to the attached `OutputStream` using the `write()` method. Note that when we call `write()` here, we are making use of the `write()` method that is inherited from the superclass `FilterOutputStream`. This inherited `write()` method simply calls the `write()` method of the attached stream.

7.6.2 Class TextInputStream

This stream is a `FilterInputStream` that attaches to an existing stream and provides rudimentary function for reading textual data from the stream. We provide a method `skipWhitespace()` that skips whitespace in the stream, a method `readInt()` that reads a textual integer from the stream, and a method `readWord()` that reads a word of text, where a word is considered to be any consecutive sequence of nonwhitespace characters.

```
import java.io.*;

public class TextInputStream extends FilterInputStream {
    // public TextInputStream (InputStream in) ...
    // public synchronized int read () throws IOException ...
    // public synchronized int read (byte[] data, int offset, int length)
    //      throws IOException ...
    // public synchronized long skip (long amount) throws IOException ...
    // public synchronized int available () throws IOException ...
    // public void skipWhitespace () throws IOException ...
    // public int readInt () throws IOException, NumberFormatException ...
    // public String readWord () throws IOException ...
}
```

This class extends `FilterInputStream` and adds methods to read textual data. To do this, we must provide a similar function to the `PushbackInputStream` class. For this reason, we provide new implementations of the `read()` methods that let us unread a single byte of data in addition to adding the `skipWhitespace()`, `readInt()`, and `readWord()` methods.

```
public TextInputStream (InputStream in) {
    super (in);
}
```

In the constructor we call the superclass constructor, attaching to the `InputStream` in.

```
protected int pushback = -2;

public synchronized int read () throws IOException {
    int datum = pushback;
    if (datum == -2)
        datum = super.read();
    else
        pushback = -2;
    return datum;
}
```

This `read()` method supports an unreading function that lets us insert a single byte back into the `InputStream`, so that a subsequent call to `read()` will reread this byte. The `pushback` variable holds this unread byte, or the value –2 if none has been unread. Our implementation of this method, therefore, checks to see whether a byte has been unread; if so, then we return this value and set `pushback` to –2. Otherwise, we read a byte from the attached stream.

The reason that we use the value –2 to indicate that no data have been unread, is that we wish to also support unreading of the EOF. The native `PushbackInputStream` does not support this because it assumes that only valid data will ever be unread.

This EOF pushback facility is important when reading from `System.in`, because when the user types CTRL+D (or CTRL+Z), EOF will be signaled only once. A subsequent call to `read()` will wait for another character to be entered on the keyboard. By unreading the EOF, we allow keyboard EOFs to be correctly processed by this stream.

```
public synchronized int read (byte[] data, int offset, int length)
    throws IOException {
  if (length <= 0)  {
    return 0;
  } else if (pushback == -2)  {
    return super.read (data, offset, length);
  } else if (pushback == -1)  {
    pushback = -2;
    return -1;
  } else {
    data[offset] = (byte) pushback;
    pushback = -2;
    return 1;
  }
}
```

This method implements the multibyte `read()` operation with unreading. We first check to see whether the read request was for zero bytes; if so, we return 0 (no bytes were read). Next, we check to see whether a byte has been unread; if not, then we return a multibyte read from the attached stream.

Otherwise, a byte has been unread. We check to see if this was the EOF; if so, then we reset `pushback` and return EOF. Otherwise we insert `pushback` into the array `data`, reset it, and return 1 (one byte was successfully read).

```
public synchronized long skip (long amount) throws IOException {
  if (amount <= 0) {
    return 0;
  } else if (pushback == -2) {
    return super.skip (amount);
  } else if (pushback == -1) {
    pushback = -2;
    return 0;
```

```
    } else {
      pushback = -2;
      return 1;
    }
  }
```

We override the `skip()` method to operate correctly with the pushback facility. If the request is to skip no data, then we ignore it. Otherwise, if there is no data in the pushback buffer, then we pass the call on to the superclass. We otherwise reset the pushback buffer, and return 0 if we were at EOF or 1 otherwise, to indicate that we have skipped the 1 byte from the pushback buffer.

```
public synchronized int available () throws IOException {
    return (pushback == -2) ? super.available () : (pushback >= 0) ? 1 : 0;
  }
```

We also provide a modified `available()` method that takes into account the single byte that may be in the pushback buffer.

```
protected synchronized void unread (int chr) throws IOException {
    if (pushback != -2)
      throw new IOException ("Pushback overflow");
    pushback = chr;
  }
```

This method unreads a single byte by placing it in the `pushback` variable. Note that you can only unread a single byte at a time.

```
public void skipWhitespace () throws IOException {
    int chr;
    do {
      chr = read ();
    } while ((chr != -1) && Character.isWhitespace ((char) chr));
    unread (chr);
  }
```

The `skipWhitespace()` method skips over any immediate whitespace in the stream. To skip whitespace, we use a loop that reads a character, tests to see whether it is the EOF or a whitespace character, and repeats the loop until a nonwhitespace character is encountered.

Once we encounter a nonwhitespace character, we discover our need for the unreading: this method is only supposed to skip whitespace, but we must loop until we actually read a nonwhitespace character. We must, therefore, undo the last read that we performed by calling our `unread()` method. Note that we will even push back the EOF.

When the user next calls `read()` after calling this method, it will, as expected, read the first nonwhitespace character in the stream.

```
public int readInt () throws IOException, NumberFormatException {
    StringBuffer result = new StringBuffer ();
    skipWhitespace ();
    int chr = read ();
    if ((chr == '-') || Character.isDigit ((char) chr)) {
        result.append ((char) chr);
        while (((chr = read ()) != -1) && Character.isDigit ((char) chr))
            result.append ((char) chr);
    }
    unread (chr);
    String value = result.toString ();
    if ((value.equals ("") || value.equals ("-")) && (chr == -1))
        throw new EOFException ("EOF reading int");
    return Integer.parseInt (value);
}
```

This method reads a textual integer from the attached stream. A textual integer is considered to be any consecutive sequence of digits on the attached stream, optionally preceded by a minus sign.

We first call the `skipWhitespace()` method to skip any immediate whitespace. We then read the first character of our number; this must either be a minus sign or a digit. If this is okay then we enter a loop that proceeds to read the remaining digits in our number until a terminating nondigit is read. Finally, we unread the last character that we read; this will either be the nondigit that terminated our loop or the character that failed our initial test.

If the number that we have read is empty or is just a minus sign, and we have reached the EOF, then we throw an `EOFException` that explains that the stream ended prematurely. Otherwise we attempt to parse the string using the `parseInt()` method of class `Integer` and return the result. If we failed to read a valid number then this will throw an appropriate `NumberFormatException`.

This `readInt()` method expects to encounter a nondigit character after the sequence of digits; however, the `writeInt()` method that we described earlier does not write any subsequent whitespace. It is up to the programmer to ensure that if two integers are to be written back-to-back, then a whitespace or other nondigit character separates them.

```
public String readWord () throws IOException {
    StringBuffer result = new StringBuffer ();
    skipWhitespace ();
    int chr;
    while (((chr = read ()) != -1) && !Character.isWhitespace ((char) chr))
        result.append ((char) chr);
```

```
    unread (chr);
    if (result.length () == 0)
       throw new EOFException ("EOF reading word");
    return result.toString ();
  }
```

This method reads a word of text from the attached stream. (Remember: A word is considered to be any contiguous sequence of nonwhitespace characters.) This method is similar to the readInt() method. We first skip any immediate whitespace characters using the skipWhitespace() method. We then read the characters of the word until we reach EOF or a whitespace character. As before, we must unread the last character that we read.

Finally, if we have reached the EOF without reading any characters, then we throw an explanatory EOFException. We otherwise return the String that we have just read.

These two streams, TextOutputStream and TextInputStream, provide us with basic functions to read and write textual values from or to any underlying streams-based communications channel. The TextInputStream is obviously extensible to allow us to read other plain text datatypes, and so can be useful for reading data from the user or from a text file. A generic method that could read a sequence of characters matching a specified search pattern would be an obvious aid to extending this class further.

7.6.3 Class StreamTokenizer

The StreamTokenizer class is a fairly involved class that provides the capability to parse an InputStream or a character stream as a sequence of language tokens (figure 7.11).

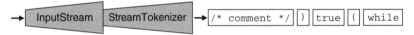

Figure 7.11   Class StreamTokenizer

The class is oriented around the Java language and is of most use to programmers who are interested in parsing Java source files. It does, however, provide facilities to parse numbers and other simple tokens that are of more general use. For this reason, it can be used as a replacement for the TextInputStream class. Use of this class typically takes the following form:

```
// StreamTokenizer tokenizer;
int token = tokenizer.nextToken ();
switch (token) {
  case StreamTokenizer.TT_EOF:
    // end of file
    break;
  case StreamTokenizer.TT_NUMBER:
    double theNumber = t.nval;
```

```
      break;
   case StreamTokenizer.TT_WORD:
      String theString = t.sval;
      break;
}
```

Calling `nextToken()` parses the next token from the stream and then returns its type. Its actual value can be determined as shown. Here, we switch among the various tokens: end of file, number, or word. Consult the API for full details.

7.7 *Wrapping up*

We have provided a broad introduction to stream filters in this chapter, and it should be obvious that they are powerful. We can essentially implement arbitrarily complex filters that extend the functions provided by existing stream filters and that work over any streams-based communications channel.

Considerable effort is expended in later chapters on developing powerful custom stream filters. Simply opening a communications channel between two remote applications is a trivial task. Where the complexity of networked applications arises is in the definition of application-level protocols that can operate in a robust fashion in the presence of problems such as concurrency issues and communications failures. We will see later that we can hide many of these protocol complexities behind a fairly clean and simple streams-based interface.

C H A P T E R   8

Supplied stream filters

We have already introduced the concept of stream filters and offered a terse overview of those provided by the language environment. In this chapter, we will take a detailed look at several of those streams, in addition to developing more of our own.

The important stream filters that we will examine are the data streams and the buffered streams. In addition, we will briefly look at the SequenceInputStream class prior to developing a similar output stream, and the PrintStream class.

8.1 Class DataOutputStream

This class provides function for high-level data communications by supplying methods to write all of the primitive language types over a byte-oriented OutputStream (figure 8.1). A corresponding DataInputStream can decode the written data at the remote end.

Figure 8.1   Class DataOutputStream

The methods here may be familiar because they are the same as those provided by RandomAccessFile. Both classes, in fact, implement a DataOutput interface that declares a standard set of methods for higher level data communications.

8.1.1 Network byte order

Values written by this class are written in *network byte order*, that is, high byte first. This is particularly important for interfacing with clients and servers that are not written in Java.

Network byte order is a widely recognized byte-ordering standard for network communications on the Internet. It specifies the order in which the constituent bytes of an int or short should be written when such a value is being sent across a network connection. Specifically, the high byte should be written first, and the low byte written last. In the writeInt() method from the previous chapter, we wrote the bytes in network byte order.

Applications written in C and C++ make use of the htons() and htonl() functions (host to network short, host to network long) to convert 16-bit and 32-bit values from the byte order of the machine architecture into that of the Internet. There are corresponding functions ntohs() and ntohl() for decoding data from the network. These functions are directly interoperable with the methods of DataOutputStream that write short and int values.

The issues of communicating text are usually solved by communicating in ASCII using the `writeBytes()` method of `DataOutputStream` or the appropriate methods of the character streams. The UTF format is also a public standard, so it is equally possible for non-Java applications to interpret Unicode strings, as written by the `writeUTF()` method.

8.1.2 Constructors

Like most stream filters, there is only one constructor:

DataOutputStream(OutputStream out)   This constructs a `DataOutputStream` attached to the specified `OutputStream out`. All data are broken down into bytes and transmitted over the attached stream.

8.1.3 Methods

These methods allow us to transmit high-level data across a communications channel; the various types are broken up into a sequence of bytes. There are several methods provided in addition to those that transmit the basic language types.

void writeBoolean(boolean v) throws IOException   This method writes a `boolean` value to the attached stream in a format that can be understood by a `DataInputStream`.

void writeByte(int v) throws IOException   This method writes a `byte` value to the attached stream.

void writeShort(int v) throws IOException   This method writes a `short` to the attached stream as 2 bytes, high byte first.

void writeInt(int v) throws IOException   This method writes an `int` to the attached stream as 4 bytes, high byte first.

void writeLong(long v) throws IOException   This method writes a `long` to the attached stream.

void writeFloat(float v) throws IOException   This method writes a `float` to the attached stream.

void writeDouble(double v) throws IOException   This method writes a `double` to the attached stream.

void writeChar(int v) throws IOException   This method writes a `char` to the attached stream as 2 bytes, high byte first.

void writeChars(String s) throws IOException   This method writes a `String` to the attached stream as a sequence of characters. Each character is written as a pair of bytes that can be read as a character by a `DataInputStream`. Neither the length of the `String` nor a terminator is written.

void writeUTF(String str) throws IOException   This method writes a `String` to the attached stream in modified Unicode UTF-8 format. This is the usual mechanism for communicating strings between Java applications. The UTF format specifies that the `String` be written in a special encoding such that each character is written as 1, 2, or 3 bytes. ASCII characters are written in just a single byte, whereas very rarely used characters are written as 3 bytes. The majority of text-based communications between applications are usually in ASCII, so this encoding is efficient for transmitting most common text.

The length of the encoded `String` is also written to the stream, so the encoded `String` can be automatically decoded by a `DataInputStream`. Note that the length of the UTF-encoded string is represented as 2 bytes, so it is only possible to write `String`s of up to 65,535 bytes in length. This is the length of the encoded `String`, so the original `String` can only have between 21,845 and 65,535 characters, depending on the particular characters involved. Details of the UTF encoding can be found in appendix B.

void writeBytes(String s) throws IOException   This method writes a `String` to the attached stream as a sequence of bytes. Only the low byte of each character in the `String` is written, so this is suitable for transmitting ASCII data to a device such as to a conventional terminal or a client written in the C programming language. The length of the `String` is not indicated; the programmer should usually terminate strings with a newline. When appropriate, character streams should be used in place of this method.

int size()   This method returns the number of bytes that have been written thus far to the attached stream.

8.1.4 Variables

protected int written   This is a count of the number of bytes written thus far by the `DataOutputStream`, as returned by `size()`.

8.1.5 IOException
All of the transmission methods make use of the `write()` methods of the attached stream and so can correspondingly throw exceptions of type `IOException`.

8.2 Class DataInputStream

This class provides methods to read all of the standard data types from a byte-oriented InputStream (figure 8.2).

Figure 8.2   Class DataInputStream

As with the DataOutputStream class, the methods that read short and int values are compatible with network byte order. They can read values that were written by a C program that uses the htons() and htonl() functions. ASCII text-based input should be performed using the new character streams (notably, the readLine() method from class BufferedReader).

These data stream classes are used by almost all networked applications; it is otherwise inconvenient to have to perform data communications at the byte level. Because this function is provided by stream filters, the basic OutputStream and InputStream classes can be simple; yet we can still achieve higher level function when desired.

8.2.1 Constructors

As with most stream filters, there is only one constructor:

DataInputStream(InputStream in)   This constructs a DataInputStream attached to the specified InputStream in. When a method is called to read a value, the individual bytes are read from in.

8.2.2 Methods

All of the methods to read data make use of the read() methods of the attached stream. Note that unlike the read() methods of InputStream, these higher level methods cannot simply return the value -1 to indicate that the end of the file has been reached. If, for example, we are reading an integer and the attached stream reaches EOF, then we cannot return the value -1 because that is a perfectly valid integer to read. Instead, these methods throw an EOFException to indicate that the EOF of the attached stream has been reached.

The simple read() methods to read bytes and arrays of bytes still return -1. It is vital that stream filters provide exactly the same function for these methods as an

InputStream; otherwise, we could not attach another stream filter to the data stream and get the desired result.

void readFully(byte[] b) throws IOException   This method fully reads an array of bytes. This is similar to the multibyte `read()` method, except that it blocks until all of the bytes have been read, and throws an `EOFException` if EOF is reached prematurely.

void readFully(byte[] b, int off, int len) throws IOException   This method fully reads a subarray of `len` bytes into array b at offset `off`. This is similar to the multibyte `read()` call, except that it blocks until all of the bytes have been read, and throws an `EOFException` if EOF is reached prematurely.

boolean readBoolean() throws IOException   This method reads a `boolean` value from the attached stream, as written by a `DataOutputStream`, throwing an `EOFExeption` on premature EOF.

byte readByte() throws IOException   This method reads a `byte` value from the attached stream, throwing an `EOFException` on premature EOF.

short readShort() throws IOException   This method reads a `short` value from the attached stream.

int readInt() throws IOException   This method reads an `int` value from the attached stream.

long readLong() throws IOException   This method reads a `long` value from the attached stream.

int readUnsignedByte() throws IOException   This method reads a `byte` value from the attached stream and treats it as an unsigned value, thus returning a positive `int`.

int readUnsignedShort() throws IOException   This method reads a `short` value from the attached stream and treats it as an unsigned value, thus returning a positive `int`.

float readFloat() throws IOException   This method reads a `float` value from the attached stream.

double readDouble() throws IOException   This method reads a `double` value from the attached stream.

char readChar() throws IOException   This method reads a `char` value from the attached stream.

String readUTF() throws IOException   This method reads a `String` in UTF encoding from the attached stream.

static String readUTF(DataInput in) throws IOException   This `static` method reads a `String` in UTF encoding from the specified `DataInput in`.

String readLine() throws IOException   This method, now deprecated, reads a `String` in ASCII. It reads a sequence of bytes until the EOF or end of line is reached and converts the result directly to a string. The character stream class `BufferedReader` now provides the preferred implementation of this method. This method is frequently used to read input from the keyboard or from another application written in C, which communicates using conventional ASCII data. This method returns `null` on EOF; it does not throw an `EOFException`.

8.2.3 IOException

All of the methods may throw an `IOException` if an error occurs in the underlying stream. The other exceptions thrown by this class (`EOFException` and `UTFDataFormat-Exception`) are subclasses of `IOException`, and so can be caught by a single catch clause.

8.2.4 EOFException

This is a subclass of `IOException` and indicates that the end of the file was reached while a method of `DataInputStream` was expecting more data. The most common cause of an `EOFException` is that a network connection has been closed.

8.2.5 UTFDataFormatException

This is a subclass of `IOException` and indicates that data were received by a `readUTF()` method that were not in UTF format. Typically this is a result of attempting to read a `String` when some other data have been written.

8.3 Class BufferedOutputStream

Buffering is used to make communications more efficient. This class buffers output until either `flush()` is called or the buffer becomes full. An output buffer is basically an area of memory in which data are stored between being written by an application and being written to the attached stream (figure 8.3). We buffer data because it is considerably more efficient to call an operating system `write()` function once using a 512-byte block than 512 times using 1-byte blocks. We can store data in a buffer until there are a reasonable number of them and then write them all at once to the operating system in a single operation.

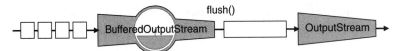

flush()

Figure 8.3 Class BufferedOutputStream

The DataOutputStream implementations of the high-level communications methods are much the same as methods we developed; they consist of a series of single-byte writes. Writing data using a DataOutputStream is thus a lot more efficient if it goes through a buffer, rather than directly to a communications channel.

Buffering is particularly important in a networked application. The network usually carries data in packets; each packet consists of a header (40 bytes in the case of TCP/IP) and the body data. If we attach a DataOutputStream directly to a network connection and then call writeInt(), it is highly probable that the first byte written will be sent in a packet of its own. This is inefficient because we are sending 41 bytes yet transporting only one useful byte. Efficiency may be even less if the packet travels over a datalink layer that has a minimum packet size. The minimum frame size over Ethernet is 64 bytes; higher values such as 576 are common for other media. Using a Buffered-OutputStream enables us to write a reasonable amount of data before calling flush() and to use the network more efficiently.

8.3.1 Constructors
There are two constructors for the BufferedOutputStream class; the stream can be created using either the default buffer size or a user-specified buffer size.

BufferedOutputStream(OutputStream out)   This creates a BufferedOutput-Stream attached to the specified OutputStream out with the default buffer size (which is usually 512 bytes). Data are written to the attached stream only when the Buffered-OutputStream is flushed or becomes full. When the buffer is flushed, its contents are written in a single call to the write() method of out.

BufferedOutputStream(OutputStream out, int size)   This creates a Buffered-OutputStream attached to the specified OutputStream out with the specified buffer size size.

8.3.2 Methods
The BufferedOutputStream class provides exactly those methods that are defined on an OutputStream and no more. The only difference is that the class performs internal buffering and implements the flush() method. It should be noted that the default

implementation of `close()` for all `FilterOutputStreams` is to first flush the stream, and then to close the buffer. This means that closing a buffered stream or a filter attached to a buffered stream will first flush any buffered data and then close the stream, so buffered data will not be lost.

8.3.3 Variables

protected byte[] buf   This variable is the array that stores buffered data to be written out.

protected int count   This variable indicates the number of valid bytes in `buf`, between zero and `buf.length`.

8.3.4 IOException

As with the `FilterOutputStream` class, many methods of `BufferedOutputStream` can throw exceptions of type `IOException`.

8.4 Class BufferedInputStream

This class adds buffering to an `InputStream` (figure 8.4). It may not be so obvious why this is useful, but it basically removes the need for every `read()` to call the operating system. When a `read()` method of this class is first called, the class attempts to read a full buffer from the attached stream. Subsequent `read()` calls just return bytes from this memory buffer, making the calls much more efficient. This `FilterInputStream` also implements the `mark()` and `reset()` methods; this permits us to add mark/reset functions to any `InputStream`.

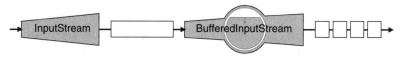

Figure 8.4   Class BufferedInputStream

8.4.1 Constructors

As with `BufferedOutputStream`, there are two constructors:

BufferedInputStream(InputStream in)   This creates a `BufferedInputStream` attached to the specified `InputStream` in, with the default buffer size. Subsequent `read()` calls to this class will buffer the data read from in and thus be more efficient.

BufferedInputStream(InputStream in, int size)   This creates a `BufferedInput-Stream` attached to the specified `InputStream` in, with a buffer of the specified size size.

8.4.2 Methods

This class provides all of the standard methods of InputStream, providing buffering on the read() methods and implementing the mark() and reset() methods.

8.4.3 Variables

protected byte[] buf This variable is the array that stores buffered data that have been read in from the attached stream.

protected int count This variable indicates the total number of valid bytes in buf, between zero and buf.length.

protected int pos This variable indicates the current reading offset in buf, between zero and count.

protected int markpos This variable indicates the last marked position in the stream, or -1 if no mark has been set.

protected int marklimit This variable indicates the maximum amount of data that can be read between a call to mark() and a successful call to reset().

8.4.4 IOException

As with the FilterInputStream class, many methods of BufferedInputStream can throw exceptions of type IOException.

8.5 Class PrintStream

We've looked at the most commonly used stream filters provided by the environment. Of the other filters, PrintStream is commonly used to print to the console through System.out; SequenceInputStream can be used to string together multiple streams; and PushbackInputStream provides a limited pushback buffer.

The PrintStream class, deprecated by the PrintWriter class, attaches to an existing stream and provides a series of print() and println() methods that write out all of the primitive language types in textual format (figure 8.5). The println() methods print a newline after every value, whereas the print() methods print the values with no newline.

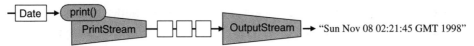

Figure 8.5   Class PrintStream

8.5.1 Constructors

By default, this stream flushes the attached stream whenever a newline is encountered, whether this is a result of `println()` or just a newline somewhere in a `String`. A second constructor is provided to override this behavior when it is inappropriate.

PrintStream(OutputStream out) This constructor creates a `PrintStream` attached to the specified `OutputStream`, `out`; the stream is flushed whenever a newline is encountered.

PrintStream(OutputStream out, boolean autoFlush) This constructor creates a `PrintStream` attached to the specified `OutputStream`, `out`; the flag `autoFlush` specifies whether the stream should flush automatically when a newline is encountered.

8.5.2 Methods

`PrintStream` has a few peculiarities. None of the methods will throw an `IOException`; this makes it considerably easier to write applications that print out information to the console because it is not necessary to handle exceptions whenever information is printed. Instead, a `checkError()` method is provided to query whether an exception has ever been encountered on the underlying stream. Exceptions can thus essentially be ignored.

void print(...) These methods print their parameter in textual format to the attached stream.

void println() This method prints the system-dependent line separator to the attached stream. This is the system property `line.separator`.

void println(...) These methods print their parameter in textual format to the attached stream, followed by the system-dependent line separator.

boolean checkError() This method returns whether an exception has ever been encountered on the attached stream.

JDK 1.1 *protected void setError()* This method sets a flag to indicate that an exception has been encountered on the attached stream.

8.5.3 In practice

Any of the system data types can be printed in textual format using the methods of `PrintStream`. No control is provided over the formatting of floating-point numbers; they are displayed to approximately their maximum precision.

```
// Object object ...
System.out.print ("The object is ");
System.out.print (object);
System.out.println ('.');
```

The `PrintStream` class provides `print()` and `println()` methods that take an `Object` parameter. With these methods, we can print any `Object` in textual format. These methods actually call the `toString()` method of the `Object` parameter and then print out this `String`.

The default `PrintStream` class is somewhat inefficient. If this is an issue, then an enhanced version of the `textOutputStream` that we developed in the previous chapter should probably be used.

8.6 Class SequenceInputStream

`SequenceInputStream` is a stream filter that allows us to sequence together several `InputStreams` to appear as a single long `Input-Stream` (figure 8.6). The observant

Figure 8.6   Class SequenceInputStream

reader will notice that it is not in fact a subclass of `FilterInputStream`. The default implementations of all the `FilterInputStream` methods are not particularly useful for this class, and so it is more appropriate to subclass `InputStream` and provide the implementations directly. The `FilterInputStream` class is simply a useful superclass to use if the implementation that it provides is appropriate for a particular filter. When `Filter-InputStream` is not a useful superclass, it is better to subclass `InputStream` directly.

8.6.1 Constructors
There are two constructors provided, one that attaches to just two streams and another that attaches to any number.

SequenceInputStream(InputStream s1, InputStream s2)   This constructor creates a `SequenceInputStream` that reads from `s1` until its EOF is reached, then closes it and switches to reading from `s2` until its EOF.

SequenceInputStream(Enumeration e)   This constructor creates a `SequenceInputStream` that reads in order from each stream in the `Enumeration e`.

8.6.2 Methods
`SequenceInputStream` provides all the usual methods of `InputStream`, reading in sequence from each of the attached streams. When the end of one attached stream is

reached, it is closed and then reading switches to the next. Closing a `SequenceInput-`
`Stream` closes all of the remaining attached streams.

8.6.3 IOException

As with most `InputStreams`, `SequenceInputStream` will pass on any exceptions that
are encountered while reading from the attached stream.

8.6.4 In practice

The following is a simple example using `SequenceInputStream`:

```
FileInputStream file1In = new FileInputStream ("file1.txt");
FileInputStream file2In = new FileInputStream ("file2.txt");
InputStream sequenceIn = new SequenceInputStream (file1In, file2In);
```

This example creates three streams. The first two are normal `FileInputStreams`
that read from files. The third is a `SequenceInputStream` constructed from the two file
streams.

Reading from the `InputStream sequenceIn` reads from `file1In` until the EOF is
reached and then reads from `file2In`, only reporting EOF when the end of this second
stream is reached. We can thus transparently read from the concatenation of several
`InputStreams`.

We could sequence together many streams by using `sequenceIn` as an input to yet
another `SequenceInputStream`. The following is another way of sequencing many
streams:

```
Vector vector = new Vector ();
vector.addElement (new FileInputStream ("file1.txt"));
vector.addElement (new FileInputStream ("file2.txt"));
vector.addElement (new FileInputStream ("file3.txt"));
InputStream sequenceIn = new SequenceInputStream (vector.elements ());
```

This uses an alternative constructor for `SequenceInputStream` that accepts an
`Enumeration` of `InputStreams` and sequences through all of the elements of this
`Enumeration`. `Enumeration` is an interface defined in the `java.util` package; the
`Vector` class provides a simple means by which to create an `Enumeration` of objects.

8.7 Class LineNumberInputStream

This class, deprecated by the `LineNumberReader` class, provides rudimentary facilities
to count the number of lines of text that have been read through an `InputStream`.

8.7.1 Constructors

Only one constructor is provided:

LineNumberInputStream(InputStream in)   This constructor creates a `LineNum-`
`berInputStream` that reads from the specified `InputStream`, `in`.

8.7.2 Methods

The `read()` and `skip()` methods are overridden to count every instance of newline,
carriage return, or carriage return/newline (`\n`, `\r`, `\r\n`) that is read through the
stream. The `mark()` and `reset()` methods are overridden to correctly save and restore
the line number. In addition, the following methods are added:

int getLineNumber()   This method allows the current line number to be read. The
line number is initially zero; after reading a single line of text, the value will be incremented to one, and so forth.

void setLineNumber(int lineNumber)   This method allows the line number to be
modified. Altering the line number only affects the stream's internal state variable; it
does not alter the stream's position.

8.7.3 IOException

As with any `InputStream`, reading from or manipulating a `LineNumberInputStream`
may result in an `IOException`.

8.8 Class PushbackInputStream

This `InputStream` provides the facility to *unread* data; any unread data are effectively
pushed back into the stream, to be read out again by subsequent calls to `read()`.

8.8.1 Constructors

There are two constructors for this class, allowing the size of the pushback buffer to be
optionally specified.

PushbackInputStream(InputStream in)   This constructor creates a `PushbackIn-`
`putStream` attached to the `InputStream` `in`, with the default pushback buffer size of
one: only a single byte may be stored in the pushback buffer.

(JDK 1.1) *PushbackInputStream(InputStream in, int size)*   This   constructor
creates a `PushBackInputStream` attached to the `InputStream` `in`, with the specified
pushback buffer size `size`.

8.8.2 Methods

The `unread()` methods that this class defines allow data to be inserted into an internal
pushback buffer. The `read()` and `skip()` methods are overridden to read any remaining data from this buffer before reading from the attached stream. Using this mecha-

nism, a class can read some data from an `InputStream`, determine whether it can proceed and, if not, return the data to the stream and allow other code to try. Note that the EOF cannot be pushed back; the `unread()` methods assume that only valid bytes will be supplied.

The `markSupported()` method is overridden to disable any mark/reset function supplied by the attached stream, as this is incompatible with the pushback operation.

void unread(int b) throws IOException   This method unreads the byte `b`; this byte is inserted into an internal pushback buffer, to be returned by subsequent calls to `read()`. If a call to `unread()` overflows the internal pushback buffer then an appropriate `IOException` is thrown. This would happen, for example, with a pushback buffer of size one if two calls were made to `unread()` without an intervening call to `read()`.

If a byte *x* is unread, followed by a byte *y*, then the next call to `read()` will return *y*, the next will return *x* and the next will return a byte of data from the attached stream.

JDK 1.1   *void unread(byte[] b, int off, int len) throws IOException*   This method unreads the subarray of length `len` from array `b`, starting at offset `off`. If a subarray containing the sequence *xyz* is unread, then subsequent calls to `read()` will return, as expected, *x*, *y*, then *z*.

JDK 1.1   *void unread(byte[] b) throws IOException*   This method unreads the entire array `b` by calling the previous `unread()` method.

8.8.3 Variables

JDK 1.1   *protected byte[] buf*   This is the internal buffer used to store pushback data. For efficiency, calls to `unread()` insert data into the array starting from the end.

JDK 1.1   *protected int pos*   This variable represents the current read index in the pushback buffer `buf`. If the buffer is empty (that is, no data has been pushed back), then `pos` holds the value `buf.length`. If the buffer is full, then `pos` is zero.

8.8.4 IOException

As with any `InputStream`, reading from or manipulating a `PushbackInputStream` may result in an `IOException`.

8.8.5 Using the PushbackInputStream

In this example, we pass a stream among various methods in order to determine which can process its contents:

```
import java.io.*;

public class PushbackProcessor {
  // public static InputStream process (InputStream in) throws IOException ...
}
```

This class provides one method, process(), that attempts to process an Input-Stream using internal processing methods (that do nothing in this example). This method returns null if the stream was processed, and otherwise returns an Input-Stream that should be used for subsequent processing of the initial stream (it will contain data which were unread).

```
public static InputStream process (InputStream in) throws IOException {
  PushbackInputStream pushbackIn = new PushbackInputStream (in, 2);
  if (processorA (pushbackIn)) {
    return null;
  } else if (processorXY (pushbackIn)) {
    return null;
  } else {
    return pushbackIn;
  }
}

// protected static boolean processorA (PushbackInputStream pushbackIn)
//     throws IOException ...
// protected static boolean processorXY (PushbackInputStream pushbackIn)
//     throws IOException ...
```

This method passes the InputStream in, with a 2-byte pushback buffer, to processorA(). If this method returns true, then the stream is processed and we are done; we otherwise pass the stream on to processorXY(). Any data read by processorA() will have been unread and so the stream will appear unaltered to this next function. Finally, if this cannot process the stream, then we return pushbackIn so that the caller can attempt to process the stream using additional code. Any data that were read will have been pushed back to the stream that is returned.

```
protected static boolean processorA (PushbackInputStream pushbackIn)
    throws IOException {
  int chr = pushbackIn.read ();
  if (chr == 'A') {
    // read from pushbackIn
    return true;
  } else {
    if (chr != -1)
      pushbackIn.unread (chr);
    return false;
  }
}
```

This method simply ascertains whether the stream starts with the byte *A*, and if so, processes the remaining data. We otherwise unread the single byte (if it was not the EOF) and return `false`.

```
protected static boolean processorXY (PushbackInputStream pushbackIn)
    throws IOException {
  byte[] buffer = new byte[2];
  int numberRead = pushbackIn.read (buffer);
  if ((numberRead == 1) && (pushbackIn.read (buffer, 1, 1) == 1))
    ++ numberRead;
  if ((numberRead == 2) && (buffer[0] == 'X') && (buffer[1] == 'Y')) {
    // read from pushbackIn
    return true;
  } else {
    if (numberRead > 0)
      pushbackIn.unread (buffer, 0, numberRead);
    return false;
  }
}
```

This method attempts to read 2 bytes into the array `buffer`. If the first call to `read()` returns just a single byte, then we try to read a second byte, updating number-Read accordingly. If 2 bytes were read and they constitute the header that we want, then we process the remaining data. We otherwise unread any data in the array and return `false`.

8.9 Writing a buffered input stream

In this example, we will look at implementing our own `BufferedInputStream`. We won't support `mark()` and `reset()`, as they add a fair amount of complexity to the code. This example should demonstrate the ease with which we can extend basic stream functions in a transparent manner.

The basic idea behind this implementation is simple: when we create the stream, we create a buffer to hold data. When a `read()` method is called, we check to see if our buffer currently contains any data. If the buffer is empty, we must refill it from the attached stream; otherwise we can efficiently return data straight from our buffer without making any operating system calls.

```
import java.io.*;
public class MyBufferedInputStream extends FilterInputStream {
  // public MyBufferedInputStream (InputStream in) ...
  // public MyBufferedInputStream (InputStream in, int bufferCapacity) ...
  // public synchronized int available () throws IOException ...
  // public synchronized int read () throws IOException ...
  // public synchronized int read (byte[] data, int offset, int length)
  //     throws IOException ...
  // public synchronized long skip (long amount) throws IOException ...
}
```

The class is a buffered `FilterInputStream`; we provide modified implementations of the `read()` methods, `available()` and `skip()`.

```
public MyBufferedInputStream (InputStream in) {
   this (in, 512);
}
```

This constructor calls the next constructor, with the default buffer size of 512 bytes.

```
protected byte[] buffer;
protected int bufferSize, bufferIndex, bufferCapacity;

public MyBufferedInputStream (InputStream in, int bufferCapacity) {
   super (in);
   this.bufferCapacity = bufferCapacity;
   buffer = new byte[bufferCapacity];
}
```

This constructor accepts an `InputStream` and a specified buffer size. It initially calls the superclass constructor with the attached stream, and then initializes the buffer.

Buffered data are stored in the byte array `buffer`; the length of this array is stored in `bufferCapacity`. The `bufferSize` variable indicates the quantity of valid data in the buffer; this is the amount of data that have been successfully read into the buffer, and may be less than `bufferCapacity`. The `bufferIndex` variable is the current read index in the buffer. The initial zero value of these variables indicates to the `read()` methods that the buffer must be filled immediately.

```
public synchronized int available () throws IOException {
   return (bufferSize < 0) ? 0 :
      (bufferIndex < bufferSize) ? bufferSize - bufferIndex : in.available ();
}
```

This method returns the number of bytes available to read without blocking. This is equal to the number of remaining bytes in our buffer or the number of bytes that can be read from the attached stream without blocking. The stream `in` is inherited from the `FilterInputStream` superclass, and corresponds to the attached stream.

```
public synchronized int read () throws IOException {
   if (bufferIndex >= bufferSize) {
      if (bufferSize < 0)
         return -1;
      fillBuffer ();
      if (bufferSize < 0)
         return -1;
   }
   return buffer[bufferIndex ++] & 0xff;
}
```

```
// protected void fillBuffer () throws IOException ...
```

This method reads a single byte. If the buffer is empty (the read index is beyond the valid data), we will need to call the `fillBuffer()` method, which will attempt to fill the buffer from the attached stream. If, however, before or after this, the buffer size is negative, then EOF has been reached and we return the value –1. Otherwise, we return a byte of buffered data at the current read index and then increment the index.

```
protected void fillBuffer () throws IOException {
    bufferIndex = 0;
    bufferSize = in.read (buffer, 0, bufferCapacity);
}
```

This is an internal method called by the `read()` methods when the internal buffer is empty and must be refilled. We first reset `bufferIndex` to zero and then set `bufferSize` to be the amount of data that we are able to read from the attached stream. If the end of the attached stream is reached, then our buffer size will be set to –1.

```
public synchronized int read (byte[] data, int offset, int length)
      throws IOException {
    int amount;
    if (length <= 0) {
      amouunt = 0;
    } else if (bufferIndex < bufferSize) {
      amount = Math.min (length, bufferSize - bufferIndex);
      System.arraycopy (buffer, bufferIndex, data, offset, amount);
      bufferIndex += amount;
    } else {
      if (bufferSize < 0)
        return -1;
      if (length < bufferCapacity) {
        fillBuffer ();
        amount = read (data, offset, length);
      } else {
        amount = in.read (data, offset, length);
        if (amount < 0)
          bufferSize = -1;
      }
    }
    return amount;
}
```

This method reads a subarray of bytes, ignoring attempts to read negative amounts. For maximum efficiency, our implementation is fairly complex.

The first case is when we have data in our internal buffer. We simply copy as many data as are requested and available from our internal buffer to the caller's buffer, updating `bufferIndex` as appropriate.

The second case is when there are no data in the internal buffer. If `bufferSize` is subzero then we have reached EOF so we return -1. Otherwise, if the caller is attempting to read fewer data than would fit in our internal buffer, then we first call `fillBuffer()` to fill up the buffer and then recursively call `read()` to read data out of this buffer; this will execute the first case.

The third and final case is when there are no data in the internal buffer and the caller wishes to read more data than we could fit in our internal buffer. For efficiency, we directly read from the attached stream into the caller's buffer, setting `bufferSize` to -1 if we reach EOF.

It is arguable whether we should go to this complexity to allow large reads to occur. If we did not take this effort, however, it would be inefficient to read a very large amount of data through this stream because it would be transferred in many small-buffer-sized amounts which would seem to contradict the purpose of this stream.

One final note. For maximum efficiency we would eliminate the recursion from this code, checking for EOF and directly copying from the internal buffer in case two. This, however, is left as an exercise for the reader.

```
public synchronized long skip (long amount) throws IOException {
  if ((amount <= 0) || (bufferSize < 0)) {
    return 0;
  } else if (bufferIndex < bufferSize) {
    int skip = (int) Math.min (amount, bufferSize - bufferIndex);
    bufferIndex += skip;
    return skip;
  } else {
    return in.skip (amount);
  }
}
```

This method attempts to skip over the specified number of bytes, `amount`. If this is less than zero or we have already reached the EOF, then we simply return. Otherwise, if our internal buffer is nonempty then we increment `bufferIndex` by the appropriate amount (which may be less than the caller requested); otherwise, we attempt to skip the data from the attached stream.

8.10 *Building a tee stream filter*

At the beginning of the discussion of streams, we developed a primitive tee joint for streams. It operated by buffering up data from an `InputStream`, and then subsequently writing this buffer to

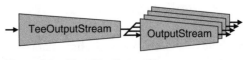

Figure 8.7   Class TeeOutputStream

several `OutputStreams`. In this example, we reimplement the tee joint as a stream filter (figure 8.7). We provide constructors to attach the tee stream to several `OutputStreams` (figure 8.7). We provide constructors to attach the tee stream to several `OutputStreams`. Everything that is written to the tee stream is written to all of the attached streams.

We will also make use of two helper exception classes, `MultiIOException` and `OutputStreamException`, that help with the potential problem of multiple exceptions occurring on multiple attached streams.

8.10.1 Class TeeOutputStream

To implement this stream, we keep a list of all of the `OutputStreams` to which we are attached and override the `write()` methods to write to each. We also override the other methods of `OutputStream` to call the appropriate method of all attached `Output-Streams`. In this manner, we can transparently take a single stream of data and redirect it to as many targets as we desire.

```
import java.io.*;
import java.util.*;

public class TeeOutputStream extends OutputStream {
   // public TeeOutputStream (OutputStream out0, OutputStream out1) ...
   // public TeeOutputStream (Enumeration outs) ...
   // public void flush () throws MultiIOException ...
   // public void close () throws MultiIOException ...
   // public void write (int datum) throws MultiIOException ...
   // public void write (byte[] data, int offset, int length)
        throws MultiIOException ...
}
```

Our class extends `OutputStream` instead of `FilterOutputStream` because none of the methods provided by `FilterOutputStream` is appropriate for this class. It is more appropriate in this case to subclass `OutputStream` directly. We provide implementations of all of the necessary methods of class `OutputStream`. Note that we don't provide an implementation of the full array `write()` method; we thus inherit the superclass implementation which just calls our subarray `write()` method.

```
protected Vector outVector;

public TeeOutputStream (OutputStream out0, OutputStream out1) {
   outVector = new Vector ();
   outVector.addElement (out0);
   outVector.addElement (out1);
}
```

This constructor allows us to attach the `TeeOutputStream` to two `OutputStreams`, `out0` and `out1`. We maintain a list of the target streams in the `Vector outVector`.

```
public TeeOutputStream (Enumeration outs) {
   outVector = new Vector ();
```

```
      while (outs.hasMoreElements ())
        outVector.addElement (outs.nextElement ());
  }
```

This constructor allows us to attach our `TeeOutputStream` to an arbitrary number of `OutputStreams` specified by the `Enumeration` outs. We create a `Vector` outVector as before, and transfer every element of the `Enumeration` into outVector. The caller can create an `Enumeration` of `OutputStreams` in many ways. One way to do this is to create a `Vector` of the `OutputStreams` and use its `elements()` method, much as we did in the `SequenceInputStream` example. We cannot repeatedly use the supplied `Enumeration` for the purposes of this class, because it is possible to iterate through the elements of an `Enumeration` only once. In this class, we must do it repeatedly, for every method call.

```
  public void flush () throws MultiIOException {
    MultiIOException problems =
      new MultiIOException ("Flush exceptions");
    for (int i = 0; i < outVector.size (); ++ i) {
      OutputStream out = (OutputStream) outVector.elementAt (i);
      try {
        out.flush ();
      } catch (IOException ex) {
        problems.addException (new OutputStreamException (out, ex));
      }
    }
    if (problems.hasMoreExceptions ())
      throw problems;
  }
```

When our `flush()` method is called, we wish to sequence through all of the attached `OutputStreams` and call the `flush()` method on each. This is complicated somewhat by the fact that any call to `flush()` may throw an `IOException`.

There are two ways we could handle this situation. One option would be to just call `flush()` and, if an `OutputStream` throws an exception, exit the loop and not flush the rest of the `OutputStreams`. Instead, however, we call `flush()` on each `OutputStream` and, if any throw an exception, we catch it, store it, and rethrow it only after we have flushed all of the `OutputStreams`. To achieve this, we store any exception that occurs in the `MultiIOException` problems, and after we have flushed all the streams, we rethrow this exception.

The `MultiIOException` class is a convenient container class that we develop next for holding multiple exceptions. The `OutputStreamException` class, in which we additionally wrap any exceptions, is another container; this time for an `IOException` and the `OutputStream` to which it occurred. If `IOExceptions` are encountered, then the caller will receive a `MultiIOException`, which it can query for all exceptions raised.

For each such exception, the caller will receive a OutputStreamException that contains both the IOException and the OutputStream to which it applies.

```
public void close () throws MultiIOException {
  MultiIOException problems =
    new MultiIOException ("Close exceptions");
  for (int i = 0; i < outVector.size (); ++ i) {
    OutputStream out = (OutputStream) outVector.elementAt (i);
    try {
      out.close ();
    } catch (IOException ex) {
      problems.addException (new OutputStreamException (out, ex));
    }
  }
  if (problems.hasMoreExceptions ())
    throw problems;
}
```

This method is similar to the flush() method; we sequence through all of the OutputStreams, calling their respective close() methods. If an exception occurs, we store it in a MultiIOException, which we rethrow after closing all the streams.

```
public void write (int datum) throws MultiIOException {
  MultiIOException problems =
    new MultiIOException ("Write exceptions");
  for (int i = 0; i < outVector.size (); ++ i) {
    OutputStream out = (OutputStream) outVector.elementAt (i);
    try {
      out.write (datum);
    } catch (IOException ex) {
      problems.addException (new OutputStreamException (out, ex));
    }
  }
  if (problems.hasMoreExceptions ())
    throw problems;
}
```

This method writes a single byte to each of the attached streams. This class thus presents all of the usual methods of OutputStream to the caller, but every byte that is written to this stream is transparently written to all of the attached streams. Again, we store and rethrow any exception that occurs, so if one OutputStream fails, then the data will still be sent to all the other attached streams.

```
public void write (byte[] data, int offset, int length)
    throws MultiIOException {
  MultiIOException problems =
    new MultiIOException("Write exceptions");
  for (int i = 0; i < outVector.size (); ++ i) {
    OutputStream out = (OutputStream) outVector.elementAt (i);
    try {
```

```
        out.write (data, offset, length);
      } catch (IOException ex) {
        problems.addException (new OutputStreamException (out, ex));
      }
    }
  }
  if (problems.hasMoreExceptions ())
    throw problems;
}
```

This method writes the specified subarray to all of the attached streams in much the same manner as the previous methods.

This stream allows us to direct a single stream of data to multiple recipients through a completely transparent streams interface. There are several potential uses, from a server communicating with multiple clients at once, through a client engaged in group collaboration.

8.10.2 Class MultiIOException

This `MultiIOException` class is simply a container for other `IOExceptions` (figure 8.8). The `TeeOutputStream` class stores any exceptions that occur during a method call in a `MultiIOEx-`

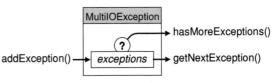

Figure 8.8   Class MultiIOException

ception and, if necessary, throws the `MultiIOException` at the end of the method call. The recipient of the `MultiIOException` can then extract the stored exceptions and handle each individually.

```
import java.io.*;
import java.util.*;

public class MultiIOException extends IOException {
  // public MultiIOException () ...
  // public MultiIOException (String detail) ...
  // public void addException (IOException ex) ...
  // public boolean hasMoreExceptions () ...
  // public synchronized IOException getNextException ()
      throws NoSuchElementException ...
  // public String toString () ...
}
```

This class is an `IOException` with the usual exception constructors, and the addition of various methods to add exceptions to the container and to extract exceptions from the container. The overridden `toString()` method returns the concatenation of all stored exceptions.

```
  public MultiIOException () {
```

```
}
```

This creates a `MultiIOException` with no detail message.

```
public MultiIOException (String detail) {
  super (detail);
}
```

This creates a `MultiIOException` with the specified detail message, `detail`.

```
protected Vector exceptions = new Vector ();

public void addException (IOException ex) {
  exceptions.addElement (ex);
}
```

This method adds the specified `IOException`, `ex`, to the `Vector` of exceptions, `exceptions`.

```
protected int index = 0;

public boolean hasMoreExceptions () {
  return index < exceptions.size ();
}
```

This method returns whether there are any further exceptions in the container. The variable `index` represent a read index into the `Vector` of exceptions.

```
public synchronized IOException getNextException ()
    throws NoSuchElementException {
  if (index >= exceptions.size ())
    throw new NoSuchElementException ("No more exceptions");
  return (IOException) exceptions.elementAt (index ++);
}
```

This method returns the next `IOException` from `exceptions`; if the read index is beyond the end of the `Vector` then we throw an appropriate `NoSuchElement-Exception`.

```
public String toString () {
  StringBuffer result = new StringBuffer (super.toString ());
  result.append (" {");
  for (int i = 0; i < exceptions.size (); ++ i) {
    if (i > 0)
      result.append (", ");
    result.append (exceptions.elementAt (i));
  }
  result.append ("}");
  return result.toString ();
}
```

This method returns a description that is the concatenation of the superclass description and all contained exceptions. We loop through all stored exceptions, accumulating the result in the `StringBuffer result`. Appending an `IOException` to `result` automatically results in a call to the appended exception's `toString()` method.

8.10.3 Class OutputStreamException

This is another container exception class, used to associate a stream with a particular exception (figure 8.9). Class `TeeOutput-Stream` uses this class to indicate to which `OutputStream` a particular exception has occurred; exceptions are wrapped in a `Output-`

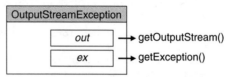

Figure 8.9   Class OutputStreamException

`putStreamException` before being stored in the `MultiIOException` container. Each `OutputStreamException` contains both an exception and the affected stream. The recipient of this exception can thus query the affected stream as well as the actual exception that occurred. An obvious extension to this class would be to additionally support `InputStream` exceptions; that would not be of particular use for this example, however.

```
import java.io.*;

public class OutputStreamException extends IOException {
  // public OutputStreamException (OutputStream out, IOException ex) ...
  // public OutputStreamException
  //     (String detail, OutputStream out, IOException ex) ...
  // public OutputStream getOutputStream () ...
  // public IOException getException () ...
  // public String toString () ...
}
```

The affected `OutputStream` as well as the contained exception are specified in the constructor, along with an optional detail message. The stream and exception can subsequently be queried through the `getOutputStream()` and `getException()` methods. Again, we provide an appropriate `toString()` method.

```
  protected OutputStream out;
  protected IOException ex;

  public OutputStreamException (OutputStream out, IOException ex) {
    this.out = out;
    this.ex = ex;
  }
```

This constructor accepts an affected `OutputStream`, out, and an affecting `IOException`, ex, and stores these in the instance variables out and ex.

CHAPTER 8   SUPPLIED STREAM FILTERS

```
   public OutputStreamException (String detail, OutputStream out, IOException
ex) {
   super (detail);
   this.out = out;
   this.ex = ex;
   }
```

This constructor accepts a detail message, detail; an affected OutputStream, out; and an affecting IOException, ex. We call the superclass constructor with the detail message and then store the stream and exception in our instance variables.

```
   public OutputStream getOutputStream () {
   return out;
   }
```

This method returns the affected OutputStream out.

```
   public IOException getException () {
   return ex;
   }
```

This method returns the IOException ex.

```
   public String toString () {
   return super.toString () + " [" + ex + "]";
   }
```

This method returns an appropriate description, which is the superclass description followed by that of the contained exception.

The combination of these two classes provides a convenient interface for the caller to appropriately handle a number of exceptions that may arise on a number of different streams as a result of just a single method call.

8.11 Wrapping up

The streams interface is a powerful mechanism for building a high-level communications library. The Java environment comes with a set of stream filters that adds the necessary fundamental features to communicate meaningful data over a communications channel. As we see, it is comparatively easy to enhance these with significant extensions that operate through the same streams interface and so can build on top of each other.

In the next chapter we will revisit the OutputStream and InputStream classes and look at two pairs of stream classes that provide new communications channels. The byte array stream classes allow us to read and write data into and out of memory buffers, and the piped stream classes allow us to communicate between different threads of an application using a memory pipe.

CHAPTER 9

Memory I/O streams

We have introduced the basic stream types and the concept of filter streams. In this chapter, we will look at two more types of basic streams: `ByteArrayInputStream` and `ByteArrayOutputStream`, and `PipedInputStream` and `PipedOutputStream`. The former pair permits communication into and out of a memory buffer; the latter pair permits streams-based communications between the threads of an application.

The byte array stream classes are useful because they provide a convenient mechanism to buffer data prior to manipulation by a class such as a block encryption function. The piped stream classes are less frequently used; however, they complete our coverage of Java's stream APIs.

9.1 Class ByteArrayOutputStream

This class is an `OutputStream` and, as such, provides the basic writing methods. This class is unusual in that it is not attached to any real underlying communications channel; all of the data written to a `ByteArray-`

Figure 9.1   Class ByteArrayOutputStream

`OutputStream` are written into an expanding memory buffer (figure 9.1). This buffer can then be extracted from the stream and used, for example, with a packet-based networking protocol.

We will make use of this class in later chapters to build UDP packets and to build a messaging library, so it is an important class to understand. In the first `Tee` class example that we developed, we copied data from an `InputStream` into an expanding buffer. This class uses much the same mechanism, but with an `OutputStream` interface to the buffer.

9.1.1 Constructors

There are two `ByteArrayOutputStream` constructors; an initial size for the buffer may be specified, or the default size may be used.

ByteArrayOutputStream()   This creates a `ByteArrayOutputStream` with the default initial buffer size (32). The buffer grows arbitrarily as it is filled, so the small initial size is of no matter, except where efficiency is important.

ByteArrayOutputStream(int size)   This creates a `ByteArrayOutputStream` with the specified initial buffer size `size`. If the buffer becomes full, then a new buffer of twice the capacity is allocated and the old buffer is copied into it. Unless message sizes are known in advance and efficiency is important, specifying an initial size is unnecessary.

9.1.2 Methods

As an `OutputStream`, this class supports all of the usual methods. In addition, the following methods also are provided to access the internal buffer:

void reset()   This method empties the internal buffer. The existing contents are abandoned, so subsequent writes will start anew.

int size()   This method returns the number of valid bytes in the internal buffer. This is equal to the number of bytes that have been written since the stream was created or last reset.

byte[] toByteArray()   This method returns an array of bytes, which is a copy of the valid data in the internal buffer. The internal buffer is not reset, so subsequent writes will continue to expand the buffer. The returned buffer is exactly as large as the quantity of valid data in the buffer.

String toString()   This method returns a `String` that is converted from the internal buffer according to the platform-default character encoding. The internal buffer is not reset.

JDK 1.1   *String toString(String enc)*   This method returns a `String` that is a copy of the internal buffer, converted from a byte array to a `String` according to the specified character encoding, `enc`. See chapter 10 for details of the different encodings available.

String toString(int hibyte)   This method, now deprecated, returns a `String` that is a copy of the internal buffer; each character of the `String` corresponds to a byte of the array with the top byte set to the specified value `hibyte`.

void writeTo(OutputStream out) throws IOException   This method writes the contents of the internal buffer to the specified `OutputStream out`. This is more efficient than calling the `toByteArray()` method and manually writing the returned copy to the `OutputStream`. The internal buffer is not reset.

9.1.3 Variables

protected byte[] buf   This array contains any buffered data. The array is automatically expanded as necessary to contain data that are written to this stream.

protected int count   This variable indicates the number of valid bytes in the buffer `buf`.

9.1.4 IOException

The `writeTo()` method may throw an `IOException` if an error occurs while writing to the specified `OutputStream`.

9.2 A simple ByteArrayOutputStream example

We will look at using these streams more usefully in our later dealings with networking. For the moment, we will look at a simple example, which writes data into a `ByteArray-OutputStream` and then extracts it again.

This example copies all user input into a `ByteArrayOutputStream`. At EOF, it writes the data back to the terminal and into every file specified on the command line. Before writing each file, it appends a message into the buffer (figure 9.2).

Figure 9.2   Using a ByteArrayOutputStream

```
import java.io.*;

public class ByteArrayOutputTest {
   static public void main (String[] args) throws IOException {
      ByteArrayOutputStream byteArrayOut = new ByteArrayOutputStream ();

      byte[] buffer = new byte[16];
      int numberRead;
      while ((numberRead = System.in.read (buffer)) > -1)
         byteArrayOut.write (buffer, 0, numberRead);

      System.out.println ("Read " + byteArrayOut.size () + " bytes.");
      System.out.write (byteArrayOut.toByteArray ());

      PrintStream printStream = new PrintStream (byteArrayOut);
      for (int i = 0; i < args.length; ++ i) {
         printStream.println ("Written to " + args[i] + ".");
         FileOutputStream fileOut = new FileOutputStream (args[i]);
         byteArrayOut.writeTo (fileOut);
         fileOut.close ();
      }
   }
}
```

We first create a `ByteArrayOutputStream` byteArrayOut into which we will write all of our data. We then create a small buffer and copy `System.in` into byteArrayOut through this buffer. At EOF, we print the size of `byteArrayOut` and dump its contents to the terminal.

Note that we use the `toByteArray()` method, which returns a copy of the buffer contents, and then use the multibyte `write()` method of `System.out` to write this to the terminal. We then create a `PrintStream` attached to `byteArrayOut` which we will use to append text to the buffer.

For every command-line parameter, we append a message to the `ByteArray-OutputStream` and dump its contents to a new `FileOutputStream`. This time around we use the `writeTo()` method; this is functionally identical to using the `toByte-Array()` method as before, but is more efficient. The only reason we use both alternatives is to demonstrate their application. Each file will thus contain the data typed in by the user and a list of all the files that the buffer has been written to thus far.

9.3 Class ByteArrayInputStream

This class is an `InputStream` that is constructed from an array of bytes. The `read()` methods read data from this array (figure 9.3).

Figure 9.3   Class ByteArrayInputStream

9.3.1 Constructors

There are two constructors:

ByteArrayInputStream(byte[] buf) This creates a `ByteArrayInputStream` from the entire specified array of bytes `buf`. Calls to `read()` will read sequentially from this buffer until the end of the buffer is reached.

ByteArrayInputStream(byte[] buf, int offset, int length) This creates a `Byte-ArrayInputStream` from the specified subarray of `buf` starting at `offset`, of length `length`. Calls to `read()` will read sequentially from this subarray until `length` bytes have been read, and then return EOF.

9.3.2 Methods

This class provides only those methods defined by the `InputStream` class. Calls to `read()` will read from the array of bytes specified in the constructor, and EOF is indicated when the end of the array or subarray is reached. `ByteArrayInputStream` supports the `mark()` and `reset()` methods. Note that if the `reset()` method is called without a prior call to `mark()`, then the stream will reset to the beginning of the array even if it was initially constructed from a non-zero-origin subarray.

We can make use of the `reset()` method in order to use a single `ByteArrayIn-putStream` to repeatedly read changing data from a single array.

9.3.3 Variables

protected byte[] buf   This array contains the data from which this stream reads. This is the array that was passed to the constructor; a copy is not made.

protected int pos   This variable indicates the current read index in the buffer.

protected int count   This variable indicates the amount of valid data in the buffer as a count from the beginning of the array.

protected int mark   This variable indicates the last marked index, initially zero.

9.4 A simple ByteArrayInputStream example

This example demonstrates the use of a `ByteArrayInputStream`; it echoes the user's input back to the terminal after the EOF is reached, preceding each line by its line number. Byte arrays are used intermediately (figure 9.4). Note that this example makes use of text-related classes and methods that have been deprecated by the character streams. Use of these facilities is convenient for explanatory purposes but should, in general, be avoided.

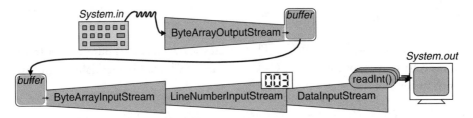

Figure 9.4   Using a ByteArrayInputStream

```
import java.io.*;

public class ByteArrayInputTest {
   static public void main (String[] args) throws IOException {
      ByteArrayOutputStream byteArrayOut = new ByteArrayOutputStream ();
      byte[] buffer = new byte[16];
      int numberRead;
      while ((numberRead = System.in.read (buffer)) > -1)
         byteArrayOut.write (buffer, 0, numberRead);

      ByteArrayInputStream byteArrayIn =
         new ByteArrayInputStream (byteArrayOut.toByteArray ());
      LineNumberInputStream lineNumberIn =
         new LineNumberInputStream (byteArrayIn);
      DataInputStream dataIn = new DataInputStream (lineNumberIn);
      String line;
      while ((line = dataIn.readLine ()) != null)
```

```
        System.out.println (lineNumberIn.getLineNumber () + " : " + line);
    }
}
```

We first copy the user's input into a `ByteArrayOutputStream` until EOF is reached, as in the previous example. We then create a `ByteArrayInputStream` byte-`ArrayIn` from the contents of the `ByteArrayOutputStream`. From this, we create a `LineNumberInputStream lineNumberIn` to count lines and a `DataInputStream` `dataIn` to read lines. We read one line at a time, and write out each line preceded by its line number.

In effect, a byte array is the communications channel connecting the user input to the code, which reads one line at a time. This is all streams-based, and so is functionally indistinguishable from just connecting the `LineNumberInputStream` to `System.in` initially, except that the response is written only after all input has been received.

This example really makes sense only if you consider that we could transmit the buffer over a packet-based network such as UDP, and still use the streams interface for communications.

9.5 Class PipedOutputStream

The `PipedOutputStream` and `PipedInputStream` classes provide a streams-based interthread communications mechanism. The idea is that we can create a connected pair of piped streams; a thread can read from one end of the pipe, and it will receive anything that is written into the other end by other threads (figure 9.5).

Piped streams are created in pairs; one end is created unconnected, and then the other is created and connected to the first. It is only necessary to attach one stream to the other, not both to each other. Usually, one thread will block reading from the `PipedInputStream` end of the pipe; other threads occasionally will write data into the pipe, thus waking the listening thread.

Figure 9.5   Class PipedOutputStream

9.5.1 Constructors
A `PipedOutputStream` can either be created and then manually connected to a `PipedInputStream`, or created and automatically connected to an existing `Piped-InputStream`.

PipedOutputStream()   This creates an unconnected `PipedOutputStream`. Writes will fail unless the stream is connected to a `PipedInputStream`.

PipedOutputStream(PipedInputStream snk) throws IOException   This creates
a `PipedOutputStream` and connects it to the specified `PipedInputStream` snk.

9.5.2 Methods

This class provides all of the standard methods of `OutputStream` and in addition, a
`connect()` method to attach to a `PipedInputStream`.

Writing to a `PipedOutputStream` throws an `IOException` with the message *Pipe
broken* if the thread that was reading from the attached `PipedInputStream` has terminated. This behavior is necessary because piped streams are implemented using a memory buffer. If this buffer becomes full, then a subsequent `write()` call will block until
some data are read from the buffer. If there is no thread reading from the buffer, then the
writer will block indefinitely.

void connect(PipedInputStream snk) throws IOException   This method attaches to the specified `PipedInputStream` snk. All data written to this stream will be
subsequently available for reading from snk.

9.5.3 InterruptedIOException

If a thread is blocked writing to a `PipedOutputStream` and is then interrupted by a call
to `interrupt()`, then the write operation will abort with an `InterruptedIOExcep-
tion`.

9.6 Class PipedInputStream

This is the corresponding read end for piped interthread communications (figure 9.6).

Figure 9.6   Class PipedInputStream

9.6.1 Constructors

A `PipedInputStream` can either be created and then connected to a `PipedOutput-
Stream`, or automatically connected to an existing `PipedOutputStream` upon creation.

PipedInputStream()   This creates an unconnected `PipedInputStream`.

PipedInputStream(PipedOutputStream src) throws IOException   This creates
a `PipedInputStream` and connects it to the specified `PipedOutputStream` src.

9.6.2 Methods

This class provides all of the standard methods of `InputStream` and also one to attach
to a `PipedOutputStream`.

Unlike a typical `InputStream`, reading from an empty `PipedInputStream` will
not always block. If the thread that was writing to the attached `PipedOutputStream`
has terminated, then if an attempt is made to read from the empty stream, an `IOExcep-`

tion with the message *Pipe broken* will be thrown. This behavior is necessary, because if there were no longer a thread writing to the stream, the reader would block indefinitely.

void connect(PipedOutputStream src) throws IOException
This method attaches to the specified PipedOutputStrean src. Subsequently all data written to src will be available for reading from this stream.

JDK 1.1 *protected void receive(int datum) throws IOException* This implementation-related method is called by the attachedPipedOutputStream to insert the specified byte datum into the internal buffer of this PipedInputStream, blocking if the buffer is full. This method is called for every byte written to the attached stream.

9.6.3 Variables

JDK 1.1 *protected static int PIPE_SIZE* This variable specifies the buffer size used by the piped streams.

JDK 1.1 *protected byte[] buffer* This array is a circular buffer that is used to store piped data while it is being written in and read out.

JDK 1.1 *protected int in* This variable is the write index at which data is written into buffer. This variable is set to –1 when the buffer is empty.

JDK 1.1 *protected int out* This variable is the read index from which data is read out of buffer.

9.6.4 InterruptedIOException

If a thread is blocked reading from a PipedInputStream and is then interrupted by a call to interrupt(), then the read operation will abort with an InterruptedIO-Exception.

9.7 A piped stream example

This example demonstrates piping data between two threads in an application (figure 9.7). The main thread reads from System.in and writes to a pipe; another thread reads from this pipe and writes to System.out in uppercase. Again, for didactic purposes, this example makes use of methods that are now deprecated: lines of text are more appropriately read using the character stream classes.

This begins to bring together several important concepts: a connected Piped-OutputStream and PipedInputStream pair are created; a thread is then created, reading lines from the read end of the pipe and writing them to the terminal in uppercase.

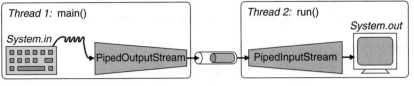

Figure 9.7 Using piped streams

The main thread sits in a loop reading user input and writing it to the write end of the pipe. We will use threads extensively in the networking sections.

```
import java.io.*;

public class PipeTest extends Thread {
   // public PipeTest (InputStream in) ...
   // public void run () ...
   // public static void main (String[] args)
      throws IOException, InterruptedException ...
}
```

The `PipeTest` class inherits from `Thread`; this is one of the simplest ways to use threads. To start a thread, all we need to do is to create an instance of the class and call the `start()` method. This creates a thread, which enters the `run()` method.

```
protected DataInputStream dataIn;

public PipeTest (InputStream in) {
   dataIn = new DataInputStream (in);
}
```

This is the constructor for our `PipeTest` class. The parameter `in` is the `Input-Stream` from which the thread will read. We create a `DataInputStream dataIn` attached to `in`.

```
public void run () {
   try {
      String line;
      while ((line = dataIn.readLine ()) != null)
         System.out.println (line.toUpperCase ());
      dataIn.close ();
   } catch (IOException ex) {
      ex.printStackTrace ();
   }
}
```

This method is called when the thread is started. The method reads lines from the piped input stream and writes them in uppercase to `System.out` until EOF is reached.

We surround the code with a `try ... catch` statement to catch any exception that should arise.

```
public static void main (String[] args)
    throws IOException, InterruptedException {
  PipedOutputStream pipedOut = new PipedOutputStream ();
  PipedInputStream pipedIn = new PipedInputStream (pipedOut);
  PipeTest pipeTest = new PipeTest (pipedIn);
  pipeTest.start ();

  byte[] buffer = new byte[16];
  int numberRead;

  while ((numberRead = System.in.read (buffer)) > -1) {
    pipedOut.write (buffer, 0, numberRead);
    Thread.sleep (1000);
  }
  pipedOut.close ();
}
```

This is the `main()` method of the class. We initially create a pair of connected piped streams and an instance of our `PipeTest` class that is attached to the read end of the pipe. We then sit in a loop, reading data from `System.in` and writing it to the pipe.

Something of note, although not particularly of interest, is that we sleep for a second after writing to the `PipedOutputStream`. The reason we do this is that under some operating systems, if one thread is blocking on reading from `System.in`, then another thread cannot write to `System.out`. By sleeping for a second, we give our other thread a chance to write to `System.out`. This particular behavior is unusual and not typical of streams; it is unique to `System.in` and `System.out`. If we were not writing to `System.out` or were not interested in seeing the response immediately, we could omit the `sleep()` call. The `sleep()` method can throw an `InterruptedException`; we ignore this and let the `main()` method throw the exception.

If the `main()` method were to exit and the other thread were to continue attempting to read from the `PipedInputStream`, then it would receive an `IOException` to indicate that the pipe was broken. Because we first close the pipe, the other thread should, however, exit naturally.

9.8 An autoresetting ByteArrayOutputStream

The `ByteArrayOutputStream` class does not automatically reset its internal buffer after it is extracted using the `toByteArray()` method. This is actually a common requirement; a lot of code ends up calling `reset()` immediately after every call to `toByteArray()`. This class is a simple variant of the `ByteArrayOutputStream` class that automatically resets the buffer after a call to `toByteArray()` or any of the other similar methods.

```
import java.io.*;

public class ResettingByteArrayOutputStream extends ByteArrayOutputStream {
    // public ResettingByteArrayOutputStream () ...
    // public ResettingByteArrayOutputStream (int initialCapacity) ...
    // public synchronized byte[] toByteArray () ...
    // public synchronized void writeTo (OutputStream out)
    //     throws IOException ...
}
```

This class extends `ByteArrayOutputStream` and overrides the default methods to call `reset()` automatically after calling the corresponding superclass method.

```
public ResettingByteArrayOutputStream () {
}
```

This constructor calls the default superclass constructor. A class does not inherit its parent's constructors, and so it is necessary to declare all the constructors that we wish to make available.

```
public ResettingByteArrayOutputStream (int initialCapacity) {
    super (initialCapacity);
}
```

This constructor calls the corresponding superclass constructor.

```
public synchronized byte[] toByteArray () {
    byte[] result = super.toByteArray ();
    reset ();
    return result;
}
```

We wish to automatically reset the stream after a call to this method. We first call the superclass `toByteArray()` method, keeping the result in a temporary variable. We reset the buffer using the `reset()` method, and then return the superclass result. The `toString()` methods call this method, and so we need not alter them.

```
public synchronized void writeTo (OutputStream out) throws IOException {
    super.writeTo (out);
    reset ();
}
```

This method calls the superclass `writeTo()` method and then resets the stream. If an exception occurs while writing to the `OutputStream`, then the stream is not reset. If we wished to reset the stream regardless of whether an exception was thrown, we could surround the superclass `writeTo()` call with a `try ... finally` clause that calls the `reset()` method regardless of whether the call exits naturally or because of an exception.

It is debatable whether a class that is as simple as this is actually useful; after all, is it such a burden to call `reset()` manually? If it turns out that a significant amount of code calls the `reset()` method manually, then it probably is worth using this class. However, in the situation of a small applet, or where efficiency is at a premium, it is probably more appropriate to use a normal `ByteArrayOutputStream` and manually call `reset()`.

9.9 Wrapping up

This chapter should have served to illustrate that streams-based communications need not be carried over a file or network connection, and that they can also be carried through memory buffers. Later chapters will make extensive use of buffers because they allow us to manipulate the data easily before and after transportation by a networking protocol.

Up to this point, we have dealt with just the basic byte-oriented streams, even though many of the examples were concerned with reading text from `System.in` and writing text to `System.out`. In the following chapters, we will look at the companion character stream classes that provide an efficient, generalized framework for character-oriented streams-based communications. We will subsequently examine the object streams, that allow entire `Objects` to be streamed, before going on to actually make use of these classes in the networking sections of the book.

C H A P T E R   1 0

Character streams

In this and the following two chapters, we will discuss the character streams, which are streams that parallel the byte streams, but are oriented around the transmission of character-based textual data.

10.1 Overview

With the basic byte-oriented streams, support for the communication of textual data was fairly limited. Other than some crude support from the data streams, all text communications were assumed to be in 8-bit ASCII (ISO Latin 1). This was clearly incommensurable with Java's cross-platform nature and the 16-bit Unicode character set supported by the language.

To address this deficiency, a parallel set of character-oriented stream classes was introduced that allows transport of true 16-bit Unicode character data (figure 10.1). These streams address not only the issue of character transport but also the issues of character-encoding conversion and efficiency.

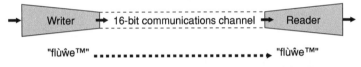

Figure 10.1 The character streams

The standard character streams mirror many of the byte-oriented stream classes, including filters, buffers, and file streams, all derived from the superclasses `Reader` and `Writer`. In addition, two bridge classes are defined, `OutputStreamWriter` and `InputStreamReader`, that bridge between byte streams and character streams. These two classes incorporate function to convert from characters to bytes and vice versa according to a specified encoding. This allows an ASCII data source to be easily converted to a Unicode character source, and similarly allows Unicode data to be easily written to a file according to the local character encoding, whether it be 8-bit dingbats, UTF-8, or 16-bit little-endian Unicode (figure 10.2).

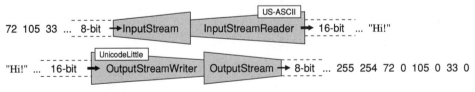

Figure 10.2 Encoding conversion

10.1.1 Correspondences

Table 10.1 lists the character streams that correspond to the various byte streams. There are no character stream equivalents for the byte streams that are concerned with actual binary data; similarly, the byte streams that were used to process text data have now been replaced by more appropriate character streams.

Table 10.1 Character- and byte-stream correspondences

byte streams	character streams
OutputStream	Writer
InputStream	Reader
FileOutputStream	FileWriter
FileInputStream	FileReader
ByteArrayOutputStream	CharArrayWriter
ByteArrayInputStream	CharArrayReader
—	StringWriter
StringBufferInputStream	StringReader
PipedOutputStream	PipedWriter
PipedInputStream	PipedReader
FilterOutputStream	FilterWriter
FilterInputStream	FilterReader
BufferedOutputStream	BufferedWriter
BufferedInputStream	BufferedReader
PushbackInputStream	PushbackReader
LineNumberInputStream	LineNumberReader
PrintStream	PrintWriter
DataOutputStream	—
DataInputStream	—
ObjectOutputStream	—
ObjectInputStream	—
SequenceInputStream	—
—	OutputStreamWriter
—	InputStreamReader

10.1.2 Deprecations

Table 10.2 lists the text-oriented methods and classes of the byte streams that have been deprecated by new features of the character stream classes. Note that for compatibility with common legacy systems, the `writeBytes()` method of class `DataOutputStream` remains.

Table 10.2   Deprecated classes and methods

deprecated class/method	replacement
LineNumberInputStream	LineNumberReader
PrintStream	PrintWriter
StringBufferInputStream	StringReader
DataInputStream.readLine()	BufferedReader.readLine()

10.2   Character encoding

When bridging between a character stream and a byte stream, it is necessary to specify the character encoding used by the byte stream; that is, what characters are represented by each byte or group of bytes (table 10.3). The name of the byte encoding is specified as a `String` that is passed to the constructor of the bridging `OutputStreamWriter` or `InputStreamReader`.

Table 10.3   Some example character encodings

encoding	char	bytes
US-ASCII	!	33
IBM-EBCDIC	!	90
ISO Latin	é	232
ISO Latin 2	č	232
UTF-8	é	195 168

Table 10.4 lists several of the supported encodings; appendix B lists more. The text-oriented methods of the byte streams are equivalent to latin1, which is also known as ISO Latin 1 or ISO 8859-1; this is an 8-bit encoding that matches exactly the first 256 characters of Unicode. Character-encoding names are, in general, case sensitive so you should use the encoding name exactly as it appears in these tables.

Table 10.4   Supported encodings

name	encoding
latin1	ISO 8859-1 (Europe, Latin America, Caribbean, Canada, Africa)
latin2	ISO 8859-2 (Eastern Europe)
latin3	ISO 8859-3 (SE Europe: Esperanto, Maltese, etc.)
latin4	ISO 8859-4 (Scandinavia)
cyrillic	ISO 8859-5 (Cyrillic)
arabic	ISO 8859-6 (Arabic)
greek	ISO 8859-7 (Greek)
hebrew	ISO 8859-8 (Hebrew)
latin5	ISO 8859-9 (ISO 8859-1 with Turkish)
ASCII	7-bit ASCII
Unicode	platform-default marked 16-bit Unicode
UnicodeBig	big-endian marked 16-bit Unicode
UnicodeBigUnmarked	big-endian unmarked 16-bit Unicode
UnicodeLittle	little-endian marked 16-bit Unicode
UnicodeLittleUnmarked	little-endian unmarked 16-bit Unicode
UTF8	Unicode transmission format

If latin1 encoding is used to bridge a character stream to a byte stream then characters 0–255 are transmitted unaltered as a single byte, and all other characters are replaced by the character ?. Similarly, if latin1 is used to bridge a byte stream to a character stream, then every byte that is read is converted directly into a Unicode character.

Alternatively, if UTF8 is used, then during writing, a character is converted into between one and three bytes and during reading, between one and three bytes are read and converted into a 16-bit Unicode character.

10.2.1 Default encoding

All character-byte conversion operations offer a default mode where no character encoding is specified. The actual encoding that is used is determined from the system property `file.encoding`; this is the encoding used to store files on the local platform. If that property is not set, a fallback of ISO Latin 1 is used. In Western locales, under most UNIX systems, the platform-default character encoding is ISO Latin 1 (latin1). Under Windows, as of the latest release of the JDK, it is Windows Latin 1 (Cp1252).

10.2.2 ASCII encoding

ASCII conversion is provided by the encoding named ASCII. Using this converter, the standard 7-bit U.S. ASCII character set maps exactly to Unicode characters 0–127. All other Unicode characters are mapped to ASCII character ? (code 63).

10.2.3 ISO encoding

There are ten supported ISO encodings, from ISO 8859-1 through ISO 8859-9 and ISO 8859-15. These are a standard set of international 8-bit character encodings; the characters from 0–127 are the usual U.S. ASCII characters and the remaining 128 are either control codes, accented characters, or other international characters.

10.2.4 Unicode encoding

There are several Unicode encodings that directly translate between 16-bit characters and two 8-bit bytes (table 10.5). Big- or little-endian conversion can be specified, along with optional *marking*. If the encoding Unicode is specified, then the platform-default endianness is used with marking.

Table 10.5   Unicode encodings

encoding	string	bytes
UnicodeBig	Hë!	254 255 0 72 0 235 0 33
UnicodeSmall	Hë!	255 254 72 0 235 0 33 0
UnicodeBigUnmarked	Hë!	0 72 0 235 0 33
UTF-8	Hë!	72 195 171 33

Marking means that a two-byte marker will be written initially, that specifies the endianness of encoding used. Marking is used by the encodings Unicode, UnicodeBig, and UnicodeLittle. To read from such a stream, you can simply use the encoding Unicode and the endianness of the stream can be determined automatically from the marker.

Alternatively, a stream can be written with the encoding UnicodeBigUnmarked or UnicodeLittleUnmarked and no marker will be written. It should then be read with the appropriate UnicodeBig or UnicodeLittle encoding because Unicode cannot automatically determine the encoding used.

The UTF8 encoding is identical to that used by `DataOutputStream` and `DataInputStream` except that the character zero is encoded as per the standard, with a single zero byte.

10.2.5 Network character sets

It is extremely important when using the character streams to communicate with network services, to verify that you are using a valid character encoding *and* valid line terminators. If you fail to verify this, then your application may appear to be correct—it will send valid data—but it will fail to communicate successfully with the remote service. More problematically, this problem may only manifest itself when communicating with certain implementations of a network service, or when certain data are transferred.

Gradually, with the introduction of MIME typing to Web and email data, character encodings are being explicitly specified along with data being transported. To communicate with any non-MIME-typed network service, however, you must verify that you are using the character encoding that is specified by the network protocol in use. For most services, the 8-bit character set ISO Latin 1 (latin1) is recognized as the standard, but you should always consult the appropriate documentation before assuming this. There are still a great number of legacy 7-bit protocols or services that will only accept U.S. ASCII (ASCII) data.

Use of the platform-default encoding (i.e., not explicitly specifying a character encoding) is incorrect because your application will behave differently on a UNIX machine than on a Windows machine, where ISO Latin 1 is not the default.

Similarly, use of the platform-default line terminator (i.e., use of any println() methods) is incorrect. Under UNIX, the line terminator is simply LF (ASCII character 10; Java character \n). Under Windows, the line terminator is CR-LF (ASCII characters 13 and 10; Java characters \r\n). Under MacOS, the line terminator is just CR (ASCII character 13; Java character \r). Always consult the appropriate protocol documentation to determine what line terminator is expected by the remote service that you will be communicating with, and always explicitly specify this terminator in calls to print(), and so forth.

10.3 [JDK 1.1] *Class Writer*

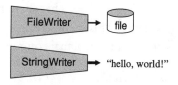

Figure 10.3 Some writers

Writer is the superclass of all character output streams. It provides similar methods to Output-Stream, but oriented around writing characters (figure 10.3).

10.3.1 Constructors

There are two constructors provided by this class. These constructors are protected. As with the byte-stream classes, you cannot create just a Writer; you must create some subclass.

protected Writer()   This constructor creates a Writer that uses itself as a lock object for synchronization purposes. This constructor is typically used by *sink* Writer classes, that is nonfilters, such as StringWriter or CharArrayWriter.

protected Writer(Object lock)   This constructor creates a Writer that uses the specified Object, lock, as a lock for synchronization purposes. FilterWriters usually pass their attached stream to this constructor for synchronization purposes. This synchronization mechanism is discussed in detail in the following discussion of the lock variable.

10.3.2 Methods

The Writer class provides methods to write characters either individually, from an array, or as part of a String, in addition to the flush() and close() methods.

Note that for efficiency, unlike OutputStream, the Writer class is oriented around writing arrays rather than individual characters. Thus, a subclass need only implement the character-subarray write() method, flush() and close(). Only where efficiency is at an absolute premium need the other write() methods be overridden.

void write(int c) throws IOException   This method writes the character c to the communications channel represented by this stream. The argument is of type int but only the bottom 16 bits are actually written. The default implementation of this method creates a single-character array and writes this with the character-subarray write() method.

void write(char cbuf[]) throws IOException   This method writes the entire array of characters cbuf to this stream. The default implementation of this method is to call the character-subarray write() method.

abstract void write(char cbuf[], int off, int len) throws IOException   This method writes len characters from array cbuf to the attached stream, starting from index off. This method is abstract because it must be implemented by a subclass that is attached to an actual communications channel, such as a file or another stream.

void write(String str) throws IOException   This method writes the specified String, str, to this stream. The default implementation of this method is to call the following substring write() method.

void write(String str, int off, int len) throws IOException   This method writes len characters of the String str to this stream, starting from offset off. The default implementation of this method extracts the substring into a character array and then calls the character-subarray write() method.

abstract void flush() throws IOException   This method flushes any buffers that the Writer may have; that is, it forces any buffered data to be written. This only flushes Java-specific buffers such as are provided by a buffered stream filter; it does not flush any OS buffers.

abstract void close() throws IOException   This method closes the attached communications channel. If a `Writer` implements internal buffering, it is appropriate for it to flush its buffers before closing.

10.3.3 Variables

protected Object lock   This variable should be used for synchronization by any `Writer` methods that require it. It is more efficient to use this common lock object than to declare synchronized methods.

The reasoning behind the use of this synchronization mechanism is that if a stream filter requires synchronization and it makes a call on an attached stream that also requires synchronization, then ordinarily the run time will obtain two semaphores: one on the stream filter and one on the attached stream. Using the new mechanism, both calls will synchronize on the same object so only one semaphore will be obtained. This efficiency obviously does not extend perfectly to a chain of several filters. However, long chains of character filters are fairly rare.

10.3.4 IOException

If a problem is encountered with the underlying communications channel, any of the methods of `Writer` may throw an exception of type `IOException` or a subclass.

10.4   JDK 1.1   Class Reader

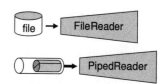

Figure 10.4   Some readers

`Reader` is the superclass of all character input streams. It provides similar methods to `InputStream`, but oriented around reading characters (figure 10.4).

10.4.1 Constructors

As with the `Writer` class, an optional lock object can be specified in the `Reader` constructor. This is used by subclasses for synchronization purposes.

protected Reader()   This creates a `Reader` that uses itself as a lock object. This is usually used by source character streams; that is, nonfilters such as `StringReader`.

protected Reader(Object lock)   This creates a `Reader` that uses the specified `Object`, `lock`, as a lock.

10.4.2 Methods

The `Reader` methods parallel those of the `InputStream` class, but the `available()` method has been replaced by a `ready()` method.

int read() throws IOException   This method reads a single character from the communications channel represented by this stream and returns this character, or –1 if the end of file is reached. This method will block if necessary until data are available. The default implementation of this method is to call the character-subarray `read()` method for a unit character-array.

int read(char cbuf[]) throws IOException   This method reads as many characters into the array `cbuf` as possible up to the size of the array, returning the number of characters read or –1 if the end of file is reached before any characters are read. This method will return immediately if some characters are available to read without blocking, and will otherwise block until some become available. The default implementation of this method is to call the character-subarray `read()` method for the whole array.

abstract int read(char cbuf[], int off, int len) throws IOException   This method reads as many characters as possible into the subarray of `cbuf` of length `len`, starting from index `off`, returning the number of characters read, or –1 if the end of file is reached before any characters are read.

This method will fail to read the requested number of characters if either the EOF is reached or some characters could be read without blocking, and attempting to read any more would block. If no characters can be read without blocking, the method will block until characters become available or the EOF is signaled.

This method is `abstract` because it must be implemented by a subclass that is attached to an actual communications channel.

long skip(long n) throws IOException   This method attempts to skip the specified number of characters, returning the number successfully skipped. If no characters can be immediately skipped, then the method will block; otherwise it will immediately skip as many as it can, up to the requested number. Upon reaching the EOF, this method returns 0. The default implementation simply reads and discards the specified number of characters.

boolean ready() throws IOException   This method returns whether the stream has data available to be read immediately without blocking. The character streams do not have an `InputStream`-style `available()` method that indicates the number of characters available to read because this is not possible in the presence of nonuniform byte-encodings such as UTF-8. If this method returns `true`, then characters can be read immediately without blocking. On the other hand, if this method returns `false`, then it does not necessarily mean that a call to `read()` will block. There are simply no guarantees being given either way.

abstract void close() throws IOException   This method closes the stream and releases any system resources that it holds. Subsequent calls to any of the other methods, including `read()`, will raise an `IOException`. Subsequent calls to `close()` will be ignored.

boolean markSupported()   This method returns whether the stream supports the mark/reset methods: not all streams support these methods.

void mark(int readAheadLimit) throws IOException   This method marks the current position in the stream. A subsequent call to `reset()` will rewind the stream to start reading again from this point, provided that no more than `readAheadLimit` characters were read before the call to `reset()`. Note that this method may throw an `IOException`, unlike that of `InputStream`.

void reset() throws IOException   This method rewinds the stream to start reading from the previously marked position. This method may fail if more than the specified number of characters were read since the call to `mark()`.

10.4.3 Variables

protected Object lock   This variable should be used for synchronization purposes by any `Reader` subclass.

10.4.4 IOException

An exception of type `IOException` or a subclass may be thrown by any of the methods of `Reader` but `markSupported()`. This usually indicates that some problem was encountered with the attached communications channel.

10.5 JDK 1.1 *Class OutputStreamWriter*

This class provides a character-oriented `Writer` bridge to a byte-oriented `Output-Stream` channel. Characters that are written to this `Writer` class are converted into bytes according to an encoding that is specified in the constructor and then written to the attached `OutputStream` (figure 10.5).

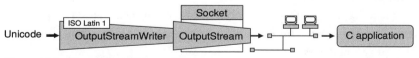

Figure 10.5   Class OutputStream Writer

This class provides internal buffering of the bytes that it writes to the attached stream. However, for efficiency, a `BufferedWriter` also should be attached in front of this to provide buffering prior to encoding conversion. This increases efficiency by reducing the number of calls to the character-to-byte converter.

10.5.1 Constructors

The encoding that is used by this class to convert characters into bytes is specified in the constructor, or else the platform default is used.

OutputStreamWriter(OutputStream out)   This constructor creates an `Output-StreamWriter` attached to the specified `OutputStream`, `out`, that uses the platform default encoding for converting characters into bytes before writing to the attached stream.

   This constructor should not in general be used for networked applications. While it is appropriate for writing to files or the console, it is inappropriate to assume that the local platform default is suitable for a network protocol.

OutputStreamWriter(OutputStream out, String enc) throws UnsupportedEncodingException   This constructor creates an `OutputStreamWriter`, attached to the `OutputStream out`, that uses the specified character encoding, `enc`, such as latin1, to convert characters into bytes for writing to the attached stream.

   This is the preferred constructor for use in networked applications. Text-based communications between Java applications should probably use either UTF8 or UnicodeBig. Text-based communications with conventional applications should probably use either latin1 (ISO Latin 1) or ASCII (7-bit US-ASCII). More encodings are listed in appendix B.

10.5.2 Methods

This class provides the usual `Writer` methods, as well as the following:

String getEncoding()   This method returns the name of the byte-encoding used to convert characters to bytes. This is the internal name of the encoding and may not be the name specified in the constructor: ISO_8859-1:1978, latin1, and ISO_8859-1 are but three aliases for the encoding that is internally called ISO8859_1.

10.5.3 UnsupportedEncodingException

If the requested encoding is not supported by the Java environment, an `UnsupportedEncodingException` is thrown. This is a subclass of `IOException`, so it will be caught by normal `IOException` handlers.

10.6 `JDK 1.1` *Class InputStreamReader*

This `Reader` represents a character-oriented bridge out of a byte-oriented `InputStream`. Bytes are read from the `Input-`

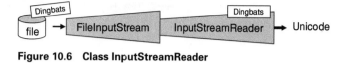

Figure 10.6   Class InputStreamReader

`Stream` and converted into characters according to the encoding specified in the constructor (figure 10.6).

This class provides internal buffering of the bytes that it reads from the attached stream. However, for efficiency, a `BufferedReader` also should be attached after this to provide buffering after encoding conversion. This increases efficiency by reducing the number of calls to the byte-to-character converter.

10.6.1 Constructors

The encoding that is used by this class to convert bytes into characters is specified in the constructor. Otherwise the platform default is used.

InputStreamReader(InputStream in)   This constructor creates an `InputStream-Reader`, attached to the `InputStream in`, which uses the platform-default encoding to convert from bytes to characters.

This constructor should not in general be used for networked applications. It should be restricted to reading from system-specific files or the console.

InputStreamReader(InputStream in, String enc) throws Unsupported-EncodingException   This constructor creates an `InputStreamReader`, attached to the `InputStream in`, which converts from bytes to characters according to the specified encoding, `enc`.

10.6.2 Methods

String getEncoding()   This method returns the name of the byte-encoding used by this stream to convert from bytes to characters. This is the internal name of the encoding and may not be the same name as that specified in the constructor.

10.6.3 UnsupportedEncodingException

If a requested encoding is not supported by the Java environment, an `UnsupportedEncodingException` will be thrown.

10.7 An encoding converter

This simple example demonstrates how the InputStreamReader and OutputStream-Writer classes can be used to convert a file using one character encoding to one using another (figure 10.7).

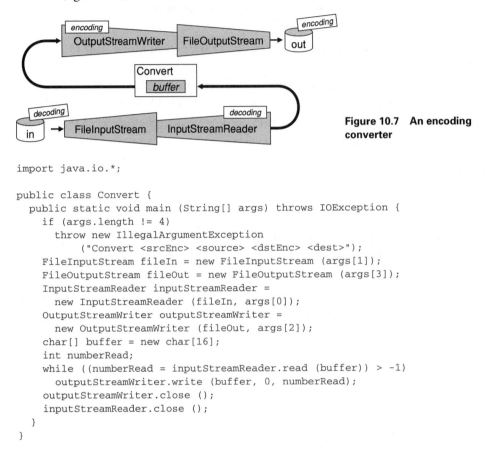

Figure 10.7 An encoding converter

```java
import java.io.*;

public class Convert {
  public static void main (String[] args) throws IOException {
    if (args.length != 4)
      throw new IllegalArgumentException
          ("Convert <srcEnc> <source> <dstEnc> <dest>");
    FileInputStream fileIn = new FileInputStream (args[1]);
    FileOutputStream fileOut = new FileOutputStream (args[3]);
    InputStreamReader inputStreamReader =
      new InputStreamReader (fileIn, args[0]);
    OutputStreamWriter outputStreamWriter =
      new OutputStreamWriter (fileOut, args[2]);
    char[] buffer = new char[16];
    int numberRead;
    while ((numberRead = inputStreamReader.read (buffer)) > -1)
      outputStreamWriter.write (buffer, 0, numberRead);
    outputStreamWriter.close ();
    inputStreamReader.close ();
  }
}
```

We first ensure that four arguments have been supplied to this program, throwing an explanatory exception if not. We then create a FileInputStream, fileIn, that reads from the chosen input file, and a FileOutputStream, fileOut, that writes to the chosen output file.

We then create an InputStreamReader, inputStreamReader, that reads from fileIn using the chosen input encoding, and an OutputStreamWriter, output-StreamWriter, that writes to fileOut using the chosen output encoding.

We use a simple copy loop that uses an array of characters to copy between the streams. We copy all data from inputStreamReader to outputStreamWriter and then close both streams.

The `InputStreamReader` performs automatic decoding from the byte-oriented input file to Unicode characters, and then the `OutputStreamWriter` performs automatic encoding from these characters to the byte-oriented output file.

Note that we perform no line-terminator modification; that is a higher-level issue than character encoding.

10.7.1 In practice

To use this example, we must have a source file and specify both an input encoding and an output encoding.

```
java Convert latin1 file.latin1 UnicodeBig file.unicode
```

This command will convert the file `file.latin1` from ISO Latin 1 to the Unicode file `file.unicode`. Examination of the output file will reveal that it consists of a 2-byte endian marker followed by two bytes for every character of the original file.

```
java Convert Unicode file.unicode ASCII file.ascii
```

This command will convert the file `file.unicode` from Unicode to the 7-bit US-ASCII file `file.ascii`. Because we used a marked Unicode encoding, the Unicode decoder can automatically determine the endianness used to encode the source file. If we encoded with UnicodeBigUnmarked, then we would have to decode with UnicodeBig.

10.8 ⬤JDK 1.1⬤ Class FileWriter

This `Writer` provides a character-streams interface to writing text files using the platform-default character encoding. Note that this is typically *not* 16-bit Unicode; more usually it is ISO Latin 1 or a similar 8-bit encoding (figure 10.8).

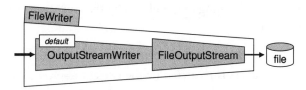

Figure 10.8   Class FileWriter

To manually specify the character encoding that is used to encode a file, simply use an `OutputStreamWriter` attached to a `FileOutputStream`, as in figure 10.8.

10.8.1 Constructors

Creating a `FileWriter` is exactly equivalent to creating an `OutputStreamWriter` using the platform-default character encoding, attached to a `FileOutputStream` constructed with the same parameters. This is how the class is implemented (it actually subclasses `OutputStreamWriter`).

FileWriter(String fileName) throws IOException   This creates a `FileWriter` that writes to the specified file, `fileName`, using the platform-default character encoding. Any existing file of that name will be first destroyed.

FileWriter(File file) throws IOException   This creates a `FileWriter` that writes to the specified file, `file`, using the platform-default character encoding. If the corresponding file already exists, it will be first destroyed.

FileWriter(String fileName, boolean append) throws IOException   This creates a `FileWriter` that writes to the specified file, `fileName`, using the platform-default character encoding. The flag `append` specifies whether data should be appended to an existing file or whether an existing file should be destroyed.

FileWriter(FileDescriptor fd)   This creates a `FileWriter` that writes to the specified `FileDescriptor`, `fd`. This must be a valid `FileDescriptor` that is already open for writing.

10.8.2 Methods

The `FileWriter` class provides all the usual methods of `Writer`. Writing characters to a `FileWriter` results in the characters being converted into bytes according to the platform-specific encoding and written to the attached file.

10.8.3 IOException

An `IOException` will be thrown by the methods of `FileWriter` if an error is encountered while writing to the file, or by the constructors if the chosen file cannot be created or written.

10.8.4 SecurityException

All file access is restricted by the current `SecurityManager`. Violation of access restrictions will result in a `SecurityException`.

10.9 JDK 1.1 Class FileReader

This `Reader` provides a character streams interface to reading text files using the platform-default character encoding. This allows you to read text files as streams of Unicode characters, without concern for the local character encoding (figure 10.9).

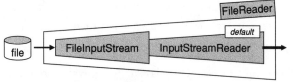

Figure 10.9   Class FileReader

To manually specify the character encoding that is used to decode a file, simply use an `InputStreamReader` attached to a `FileInputStream`, as in figure 10.9.

10.9.1 Constructors

Creating a `FileReader` is exactly equivalent to creating an `InputStreamReader` using the platform-default character encoding, attached to a `FileInputStream` constructed with the same parameter. This is how the class is implemented (it actually subclasses `InputStreamReader`).

FileReader(String fileName) throws FileNotFoundException This creates a `FileReader` that reads from the specified file, `fileName`, using the platform-default character encoding.

FileReader(File file) throws FileNotFoundException This creates a `FileReader` that reads from the specified file, `file`, using the platform-default character encoding.

FileReader(FileDescriptor fd) This creates a `FileReader` that reads from the specified `FileDecriptor`, `fd`. This must be a valid `FileDescriptor` that is already open for reading.

10.9.2 Methods

The `FileReader` class provides all the usual methods of `Reader`. Reading characters from a `FileReader` results in bytes being read from the attached file and converted into characters according to the platform-default encoding.

10.9.3 IOException

As usual, the methods of `FileReader` may all throw exceptions of type `IOException`. The constructors will throw a `FileNotFoundException` if the specified file does not exist or is not readable.

10.9.4 SecurityException

All file access is restricted by the current `SecurityManager`. Violation of access restrictions will result in a `SecurityException`.

10.10 Using the file streams

The following example demonstrates how the `FileReader` and `FileWriter` classes can be used to interface with the console. In earlier examples, when we used methods of `System.in` and `System.out`, we assumed that the console communicated using ISO Latin 1 (8-bit ASCII). Using the `FileReader` and `FileWriter` classes, on the other hand, assumes that it uses whatever is the default platform-specific file encoding.

This example simply echoes keyboard input back to the terminal in uppercase. Data are read and written a buffer at a time. Typically this will be equivalent to echoing every line typed (figure 10.10).

Figure 10.10   Class CharFiles

```
import java.io.*;

public class CharFiles {
  public static void main (String[] args) throws IOException {
    FileReader fileReader = new FileReader (FileDescriptor.in);
    FileWriter fileWriter = new FileWriter (FileDescriptor.out);
    char[] buffer = new char[256];
    int numberRead;
    while ((numberRead = fileReader.read (buffer)) > -1) {
      String upper = new String (buffer, 0, numberRead).toUpperCase ();
      fileWriter.write (upper);
      fileWriter.flush ();
    }
  }
}
```

Here, we attach the `FileReader fileReader` to `FileDescriptor.in`, which is the file descriptor from which keyboard input can be read (`System.in` is attached to this). We also attach the `FileWriter fileWriter` to `FileDescriptor.out`, which is the file descriptor to which console output should be written (`System.out` is attached to this).

We then loop, reading data into the character array `buffer`, converting this to the uppercase `String upper`, and then writing this to `out`. Note that we are not reading a line at a time; we are simply reading as much data as the `read()` method can obtain. Typically, when reading from the keyboard, this will be a line at a time. However this is unique to keyboard input. To properly read lines, see the `readLine()` method of class `BufferReader`. Note also that we are not inserting newlines; newlines in the output simply result from newlines in the input.

We flush after writing every buffer because the `FileWriter` class automatically obtains the output buffering that is provided by its `OutputStreamWriter` superclass.

10.11 Wrapping up

In this chapter we have presented the character streams needed to support character-oriented streams-based communications from Java. `Reader`, `Writer`, and their subclasses parallel closely the byte-oriented `InputStream` and `OutputStream` classes. Additionally, the `InputStreamReader` and `OutputStreamWriter` classes provide a bridge between character streams and byte streams.

It should not be misconstrued that character streams are always bridged to or from byte streams. In the following chapters we will look at the various character stream filters as well as piped and memory-based character streams that provide a true 16-bit end-to-end communications channel.

Many networked applications that involve text-based communications are only concerned with ASCII or ISO Latin 1 characters, which are easily accessed through the byte streams. However, it is still prudent in many cases to use the character streams for their better text support and increased efficiency, which comes from both their better synchronization support and their better use of internal arrays.

C H A P T E R   1 1

Character stream filters

The character stream classes provide the same filter mechanism as the byte stream filters for extending stream function. Character stream filters can be attached to existing character streams in order to extend and modify the basic stream operation.

The basic `FilterWriter` and `FilterReader` superclasses are extended to provide the same filters for the character streams as are provided for the byte streams, except where the filters are oriented specifically around binary data: `BufferedWriter` and `BufferedReader` provide buffering facilities, `LineNumberReader` provides line numbering, `PrintWriter` provides textual formatting of Java types, and `PushbackReader` provides an unreading facility.

11.1 JDK 1.1 Class FilterWriter

This is the superclass for all character stream filters. This stream attaches to another `Writer` and forwards all method calls to the attached stream. A stream filter implementation will usually extend this class and override its methods to implement the desired function (figure 11.1).

Figure 11.1   Class FilterWriter

11.1.1 Constructors

Only one constructor is provided:

protected FilterWriter(Writer out)   This creates a `FilterWriter` attached to the specified `Writer`, `out`. All method calls are forwarded to the attached stream; writing to this `Writer` thus writes to the attached stream. Note that this constructor is `protected`; it can only be called by a subclass. The attached stream, `out`, is used as the character-stream lock object.

11.1.2 Methods

This class overrides three of the `write()` methods of class `Writer` and forwards them to the attached stream. The other `write()` methods are inherited from the superclass and simply call these overridden methods. Thus, a subclass need only override the following three `write()` methods to change all writing operations:

void write(int c) throws IOException   This method calls the corresponding method on the attached stream.

void write(char[] cbuf, int off, int len) throws IOException   This method calls the corresponding method on the attached stream.

void write(String str, int off, int len) throws IOException   This method calls the corresponding method on the attached stream.

void flush() throws IOException   This method calls the corresponding method on the attached stream. A subclass should perform any necessary internal flushing and then flush the attached stream.

void close() throws IOException   This method calls the corresponding method on the attached stream. A subclass should first flush itself, if necessary, and then close the attached stream.

11.1.3 Variables

protected Writer out   This variable is the character stream to which this stream is attached. A direct subclass of `FilterWriter` should usually access this stream directly rather than make use of the methods of its superclass.

11.1.4 IOException

Any of the methods of class `FilterWriter` can, as expected, throw an exception of type `IOException`, whether from the attached stream or from the stream filter class itself.

11.2 JDK 1.1 *Class FilterReader*

This is the superclass for all `Reader` character stream filters. This stream attaches to another `Reader` and forwards all method calls to the attached stream. A stream filter implementation will usually extend this class and override its methods to perform the desired function (figure 11.2).

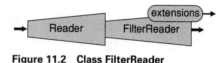

Figure 11.2   Class FilterReader

11.2.1 Constructors

One constructor is provided:

protected FilterReader(Reader in)   This creates a `FilterReader` attached to the specified `Reader`, `in`; all method calls are forwarded to the attached stream. Reading from this `FilterReader` thus reads from the attached stream. Note that this constructor is `protected`; it can only be called by a subclass. The attached stream, `in`, is used as the character stream lock object.

11.2.2 Methods

As with the `FilterWriter` class, not all of the `read()` methods have been overridden. Thus a subclass need override the following two `read()` methods to change all reading functions:

int read() throws IOException   This method calls the corresponding method on the attached stream.

int read(char[] cbuf, int off, int len) throws IOException   This method calls the corresponding method on the attached stream.

void close() throws IOException   This method calls the corresponding method on the attached stream.

long skip(long n) throws IOException   This method calls the corresponding method on the attached stream.

boolean ready() throws IOException   This method calls the corresponding method on the attached stream.

boolean markSupported()   This method calls the corresponding method on the attached stream.

void mark(int readAheadLimit) throws IOException   This method calls the corresponding method on the attached stream.

void reset() throws IOException   This method calls the corresponding method on the attached stream.

11.2.3 Variables

protected Reader in   This variable is the character stream to which this stream is attached. A subclass of `FilterReader` should usually access this stream directly rather than make use of its superclass' methods.

11.2.4 IOException

The methods of `FilterReader` all may throw exceptions of type `IOException` should such an exception arise while reading from the attached stream or because of an exception raised by the filter implementation.

11.3 `JDK 1.1` *Class BufferedWriter*

This `FilterWriter` provides write-buffering on the attached stream. All data written to this class are stored in an internal buffer until either the buffer becomes full, `flush()` is called, or `close()` is called, at which time the data are written to the attached stream in a single multicharacter `write()` call (figure 11.3).

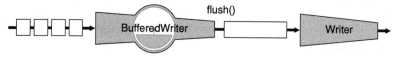

Figure 11.3   Class BufferedWriter

It is a good idea to use buffering with the `OutputStreamWriter` class (and, by consequence, with `FileWriter`). `OutputStreamWriter` provides output buffering, but not input buffering. Using a `BufferedWriter` in combination with an `OutputStream-Writer` can help minimize the overhead of the character-byte conversion. None of the memory-based streams need buffering except, perhaps, `PipedWriter`.

11.3.1 *Constructors*

There are two `BufferedWriter` constructors, one providing the option of specifying the buffer size:

BufferedWriter(Writer out)   This creates a `BufferedWriter` attached to the `Writer` out, with the default buffer size (8,192 characters).

BufferedWriter(Writer out, int sz)   This creates a `BufferedWriter` attached to the `Writer` out, with a buffer size of `sz` characters.

11.3.2 *Methods*

In addition to the usual methods of the `Writer` class, `BufferedWriter` provides a `new-Line()` method.

void newLine() throws IOException   This method writes the platform-local line separator to the attached stream; this is the system property `line.separator`, which is `\n` under UNIX and `\r\n` under MS-DOS/Windows.

11.3.3 *IOException*

As expected, any of the methods of `BufferedWriter` may throw an `IOException`.

11.4 ⬤JDK 1.1 *Class BufferedReader*

This class is a `FilterReader` that provides input buffering on the attached stream. Data are read in large chunks from the attached stream into an internal buffer and can then be efficiently read in smaller volumes from this buffer (figure 11.4).

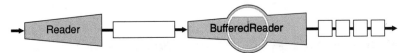

Figure 11.4   Class BufferedReader

It is a good idea to use buffering with the `InputStreamReader` class (and, by consequence, `FileReader`). Although `InputStreamReader` provides input buffering from the attached `InputStream`, attaching a `BufferedReader` to it can help minimize the cost of the subsequent byte-character conversion. The `LineNumberReader` class subclasses `BufferedReader` so it is not necessary to use buffering in combination with that class. None of the memory-based streams need buffering except, perhaps, `PipedReader`.

11.4.1 Constructors
Two constructors are exposed, one allowing the internal buffer size to be specified:

BufferedReader(Reader in)   This creates a `BufferedReader` that reads from the `Reader` in and uses an internal buffer of the default size (8,192 characters).

BufferedReader(Reader in, int sz)   This creates a `BufferedReader` that reads from the `Reader` in and uses an internal buffer size of `sz` characters.

11.4.2 Methods
`BufferedReader` provides the usual `Reader` methods and adds support for the `mark()` and `reset()` methods with a maximum read-ahead limit equal to the size of the internal buffer. In addition, this class provides the following method to read a line of text:

String readLine() throws IOException   This method reads and returns a single line of text, discarding the line terminator. This method copes with any standard line terminator: \n, \r or \r\n.

11.4.3 IOException
Any of the methods of `BufferedReader` may throw an exception of type `IOException`.

11.5 [JDK 1.1] *Class LineNumberReader*

This class is a `FilterReader` that adds rudimentary line-numbering facilities to the attached stream. As data are read through this stream, it maintains a count of the number of line terminators that it

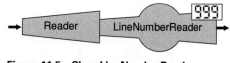

Figure 11.5   Class LineNumberReader

encounters. The internal line counter can be queried and modified as necessary. This class replaces the `LineNumberInputStream` class (figure 11.5).

Note that this is, in fact, a subclass of `BufferedReader`, so it automatically provides buffering for the attached stream.

11.5.1 *Constructors*

As a `BufferedReader`, this class exposes two constructors, one that allows the internal buffer size to be specified and one that uses the default.

LineNumberReader(Reader in)   This creates a `LineNumberReader` attached to the `Reader in`, with the default superclass buffer size.

LineNumberReader(Reader in, int sz)   This creates a `LineNumberReader` attached to the `Reader in`, with the specified buffer size of `sz` characters.

11.5.2 *Methods*

This class is a `BufferedReader` so it provides the usual `Reader` methods, as well as `BufferedReader`'s `readLine()` method. In addition, it provides the following line-number-related methods:

int getLineNumber()   This method returns the current line number. This is initially zero for a newly created stream, and is incremented by one for every line that is read. This means that after one call to `readLine()`, this method will return 1.

Note that this class monitors the `read()` method, so it will count lines whether they are read with `readLine()` or the usual `read()` methods.

void setLineNumber(int lineNumber)   This method sets the internal line number counter to the specified value, `lineNumber`.

11.6 *Using character stream filters*

This example mirrors the earlier example of using the byte-oriented stream filters. We connect a `FilterReader` to the console input stream and a `FilterWriter` to the console output stream. We then proceed to read lines of input and write them out in upper-case, preceded by the line number (figure 11.6).

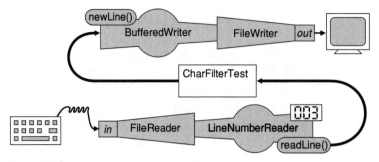

Figure 11.6 Using character stream filters

```
import java.io.*;

public class CharFilterTest {
  public static void main (String[] args) throws IOException {
    FileReader fileReader = new FileReader (FileDescriptor.in);
    FileWriter fileWriter = new FileWriter (FileDescriptor.out);
    LineNumberReader lineNumberReader = new LineNumberReader (fileReader);
    BufferedWriter bufferedWriter = new BufferedWriter (fileWriter, 256);
    String line;
    while ((line = lineNumberReader.readLine ()) != null) {
      String response = lineNumberReader.getLineNumber () + " : " +
        line.toUpperCase ();
      bufferedWriter.write (response);
      bufferedWriter.newLine ();
    }
    bufferedWriter.flush ();
  }
}
```

We attach the `FileReader fileReader` to the console input `FileDescriptor.in`, and the `FileWriter fileWriter` to the console output `FileDescriptor.out`. These streams automatically convert from and to the local character encoding. We then attach the `LineNumberReader lineNumberReader` to `fileReader` and the `BufferedWriter bufferedWriter` to `fileWriter`. As a `BufferedReader` subclass, `lineNumberReader` automatically provides buffering for the input stream.

We then proceed to read input, a line at a time, using `lineNumberReader`'s `readLine()` method. We convert each line to uppercase, prepend the line number and then write the line to `bufferedWriter` using the `write(String)` method. We follow each line with a newline using `bufferedWriter`'s `newLine()` method; this automatically writes the local newline character sequence. When `readLine()` returns `null`, then we have reached the EOF, so we can flush `bufferedWriter` and exit. This will occur in response to CTRL-D (UNIX) or CTRL-Z (DOS).

Note that, in practice, nothing will be displayed until the EOF is reached. After every 256 characters, `bufferedWriter` *will* write to `fileWriter`; however, the `FileWriter` class extends `OutputStreamWriter` which has a large output buffer. Thus, nothing will actually be written to the console until that buffer is flushed, which is after the user finishes the stream or types a lot of data (many kilobytes).

11.7 `JDK 1.1` *Class PrintWriter*

This `Writer` replaces the `PrintStream` class to provide methods for writing out data in textual format. It attaches to an existing stream and provides `print()` and `println()` methods that write out data in text format (figure 11.7). For convenience, all exceptions are suppressed; an internal flag is set if an exception arises while writing to the attached stream.

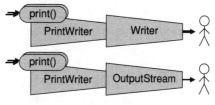

Figure 11.7   Class PrintWriter

Where more control is desired over the formatting of numbers and other data written by this class, the classes of the `java.text` package should be consulted.

11.7.1 *Constructors*

A `PrintWriter` can be connected to either a `Writer` or, for convenience, an `OutputStream`. Unlike the `PrintStream` class, this stream does not by default flush whenever a newline is written; an optional flag can, however, enable this feature. This only affects newlines written by the `println()` methods, and not those written through the `write()` methods.

PrintWriter(Writer out)   This creates a `PrintWriter` that writes to the specified `Writer`, `out`. Automatic flushing is disabled.

PrintWriter(Writer out, boolean autoFlush)   This creates a `PrintWriter` that writes to the specified `Writer`, `out`. If the flag `autoFlush` is `true`, then the `println()` methods automatically flush the attached stream after every line.

PrintWriter(OutputStream out)   This creates a `PrintWriter` that writes to the specified `OutputStream`, `out`, using the platform-default character encoding. This is equivalent to attaching a `PrintWriter` to a `BufferedWriter` to an `OutputStreamWriter` to `out`. Automatic flushing is disabled.

PrintWriter(OutputStream out, boolean autoFlush)   This creates a `PrintWriter` that writes to the specified `OutputStream`, `out`, using the platform-default character encoding, with optional automatic flushing.

11.7.2 Methods

This class provides various `print()` and `println()` methods to print text-formatted data to the attached stream. It also includes methods to set and query the current error status. Note that the `write()`, `flush()`, and `close()` methods are overridden to automatically suppress exceptions.

boolean checkError()   This method returns whether an error has ever been encountered while writing to the attached stream.

protected void setError()   This method can be called by a subclass to set the error flag.

void print(...)   These methods print their parameter to the attached stream, formatted as text. They make use of the `valueOf()` methods of class `String` to convert data types to text. Writing an `Object` is equivalent to calling its `toString()` method and writing that to the attached stream.

void println()   This method prints a newline to the attached stream; this value is taken from the system property `line.separator`. If autoflushing is enabled, the stream is subsequently flushed.

void println(...)   These methods print their parameters to the attached stream, formatted as text, followed by a newline. If autoflushing is enabled, the stream is subsequently flushed.

11.8   JDK 1.1 *Class PushbackReader*

This class provides a pushback buffer, in the same way as the `PushbackInput-Stream` class, that allows characters to be effectively *unread*. Such unread data are inserted into an internal buffer and returned from subsequent calls to `read()` (figure 11.8).

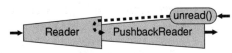

Figure 11.8   Class PushbackReader

This allows, for example, a language scanner to read from a stream until a certain character sequence is encountered and then to return those characters to the stream so that they will be reread by the next phase of scanning.

11.8.1 Constructors

The pushback buffer used by this class has a fixed size, thus limiting the amount of data that can be unread. If more data are unread than there is buffer capacity, an exception will be raised. The `PushbackReader` constructor allows the size of this buffer to be specified.

public PushbackReader(Reader in)   This creates a `PushbackReader` that reads from the specified `Reader`, in, and has a single-character pushback buffer. An exception will be raised if two or more characters are `unread()` in succession without an intervening `read()` call to empty the buffer.

public PushbackReader(Reader in, int size)   This creates a `PushbackReader` that reads from the specified `Reader`, in, and has a pushback buffer of the specified size, `size`. Up to `size` characters can be unread into the internal buffer.

11.8.2 Methods

The usual `Reader` methods are overridden to operate in conjunction with the unreading facility. This facility is incompatible with an underlying mark/reset facility, so `markSupported()` returns `false`. In addition, the following methods are provided:

void unread(int c) throws IOException   This method unreads the specified character, `c`: the character is inserted into the internal pushback buffer, to be returned by the next call to `read()`. If the pushback buffer overflows, an `IOException` will be thrown. The character `c` must be a valid Unicode character (i.e., not the EOF).

void unread(char[] cbuf, int off, int len) throws IOException   This   method unreads the `len`-character subarray of the character-array `cbuf`, starting from offset `off`. If you unread an array and then subsequently read it back in, whether a character at a time or as a whole array, then you will obtain the same array contents in the same order.

void unread(char[] cbuf) throws IOException   This method unreads the entire character array `cbuf` using the previous `unread()` method.

11.8.3 IOException

Reading from the attached stream may raise an `IOException`. In addition, unreading more data than can be stored in the internal buffer will result in an `IOException` (Pushback buffer overflow).

11.9 Building a textual data Reader

This example is similar to the `TextInputStream` that we developed in chapter 7, except that it reads from a character-oriented `Reader`

Figure 11.9   Class DataReader

and supports reading floating point numbers as well as decimal numbers (figure 11.9). The purpose of this is simply to demonstrate the construction of a FilterReader subclass, although the ability to read textual numeric data in this manner is fairly useful.

```
import java.io.*;

public class DataReader extends Reader {
  // public DataReader (Reader reader) ...
  // public int read () throws IOException ...
  // public int read (char[] data, int offset, int length)
       throws IOException ...
  // public long skip (long amount) throws IOException ...
  // public boolean ready () throws IOException ...
  // public void close () throws IOException ...
  // public String readWord () throws IOException ...
  // public long readLong () throws IOException, NumberFormatException ...
  // public double readDouble ()
       throws IOException, NumberFormatException ...
}
```

To implement the DataReader class, we extend the Reader class. Usually, when implementing a character stream filter, it is simply necessary to subclass FilterReader and add any additional methods desired. In this case, however, we need to modify the function of all the standard Reader methods, and so, none of the FilterReader methods are useful.

We must, therefore, override the standard Reader methods read(), skip(), ready(), and close() and modify their operation accordingly, in addition to defining the new readWord(), readLong(), and readDouble() methods. Note that this class is incompatible with the mark() and reset() methods; therefore we inherit the default markSupported() implementation that returns false.

```
  protected PushbackReader pushbackReader;
  public DataReader (Reader reader) {
    super (reader);
    pushbackReader = new PushbackReader (reader);
  }
```

This creates a DataReader that reads from the specified Reader, reader. We call the superconstructor, passing it reader as a lock. This is not a stream from which the Reader superclass will read; this is the lock object, which we will use for synchronization purposes.

We attach a PushbackReader to reader and keep a reference to this in the instance variable pushbackReader. We could attach the PushbackReader to a BufferedReader attached to reader; this would guarantee that we had efficient buffered input. Instead, however, we leave that task to the caller; the caller should be in a better position to decide whether buffering is necessary.

```
protected boolean eof = false;

public int read () throws IOException {
  synchronized (lock) {
    if (!eof)
      return pushbackReader.read ();
    else {
      eof = false;
      return -1;
    }
  }
}
```

This method reads a character from the attached stream and returns the result. To implement this stream, we require the facility to unread the EOF should it be encountered prematurely. The PushbackReader class only supports unreading of normal characters. So we must also keep a local variable eof that we set to true when the EOF is unread. In this read() method, we check to see if eof is true and, if so, we reset it and return –1.

Note that the synchronization object used by the character streams is the lock variable that is inherited from the Reader superclass. In our constructor, we passed the attached stream as a value for lock. The FilterReader class also uses the attached stream as a synchronization object and, therefore, so does the PushbackReader class. As a result, when we call read() on the PushbackReader, it will attempt to synchronize on lock, which we have already done.

It is much more efficient for a thread to synchronize on an object on which it is already synchronized than on an unlocked object. Therefore, this is more efficient than using synchronized methods, in which case this method would first obtain a lock on itself, and then the PushbackReader would obtain a separate lock on itself.

```
public int read (char[] data, int offset, int length) throws IOException {
  synchronized (lock) {
    if (!eof)
      return pushbackReader.read (data, offset, length);
    else {
      eof = false;
      return -1;
    }
  }
}
```

This method reads the specified subarray from the attached stream. If the EOF had been pushed back, we would reset eof and return –1.

```java
public long skip (long amount) throws IOException {
  synchronized (lock) {
    if (amount <= 0)
      return 0;
    else if (!eof)
      return pushbackReader.skip (amount);
    else {
      eof = false;
      return 0;
    }
  }
}
```

This method attempts to skip `amount` characters from the attached stream. If the EOF had been pushed back, we would reset `eof` and return `0`.

```java
public boolean ready () throws IOException {
  synchronized (lock) {
    return pushbackReader.ready ();
  }
}
```

This method returns `true` if there are characters available for immediate reading from the attached stream.

```java
public void close () throws IOException {
  synchronized (lock) {
    pushbackReader.close ();
    eof = false;
  }
}
```

This method closes the attached stream and resets `eof`. Subsequent calls to other methods will raise an `IOException` when they attempt to access `pushbackReader`.

```java
protected void unread (int chr) throws IOException {
  synchronized (lock) {
    if (eof)
      throw new IOException ("Pushback buffer overflow");
    if (chr == -1)
      eof = true;
    else
      pushbackReader.unread (chr);
  }
}
```

This method unreads the specified character `chr`. If the EOF has already been pushed back, then we throw an appropriate exception. Otherwise, we make use of our

PushbackReader's unread() method, unless the EOF is being pushed back in which case we set eof to true.

```
public String readWord () throws IOException {
  synchronized (lock) {
    readExp (WHITESPACE, ZERO_OR_MORE);
    String word = readExp (NON_WHITESPACE, ZERO_OR_MORE);
    if (word.equals ("") && eof)
      throw new EOFException ("EOF reading word");
    return word;
  }
}

// protected String readExp (int chars, int number) throws IOException ...
```

This method reads a word of text from the attached stream. We use a helper method readExp() that takes two parameters—a type of character and a volume—and attempts to read the requested volume of the requested type of character.

In this case, we first read as much whitespace as possible; this discards any immediate whitespace in the stream. We then read as much nonwhitespace as possible, stopping when whitespace is encountered. The result is the word that we will return. We first check to see whether we encountered a premature EOF in which case we throw an appropriate EOFException.

```
public long readLong () throws IOException, NumberFormatException {
  synchronized (lock) {
    readExp (WHITESPACE, ZERO_OR_MORE);
    String value = readExp ('-', ZERO_OR_ONE) +
      readExp (DIGITS, ZERO_OR_MORE);
    if ((value.equals ("") || value.equals ("-")) && eof)
      throw new EOFException ("EOF reading long");
    return Long.parseLong (value);
  }
}
```

This method reads a long value from the attached stream as a sequence of digits with an optional leading minus sign, and returns the result. We skip any immediate whitespace, and then use the readExp() method to read a sequence of digits. If we reach a premature EOF, we throw an EOFException. Otherwise we parse the digits using the Long class. This may throw a NumberFormatException if a valid number was not read.

Note that this method will not read numbers with a leading plus sign, octal numbers, hexadecimal numbers, or scientific notation. Adding support for these would be routine, if long-winded.

```
public double readDouble () throws IOException, NumberFormatException {
```

```
    synchronized (lock) {
      readExp (WHITESPACE, ZERO_OR_MORE);
      String value = readExp ('-', ZERO_OR_ONE) +
        readExp (DIGITS, ZERO_OR_MORE) + readExp ('.', ZERO_OR_ONE) +
        readExp (DIGITS, ZERO_OR_MORE);
      if (eof && (value.equals ("") || value.equals (".") ||
                  value.equals ("-") || value.equals ("-.")))
        throw new EOFException ("EOF reading double");
      return Double.valueOf (value).doubleValue ();
    }
  }
```

This method reads a `double` value from the attached stream as an optional minus sign, an optional sequence of digits, an optional period, and another optional sequence of digits. If we reach a premature EOF, we throw an `EOFException`. Otherwise we parse the value using the `Double` class. This may throw a `NumberFormatException` if a valid number was not read.

```
  protected String readExp (int type, int volume) throws IOException {
    synchronized (lock) {
      StringBuffer result = new StringBuffer ();
      boolean done = false;
      while (!done) {
        int chr = read ();
        if (isMatch (chr, type)) {
          result.append ((char) chr);
          done = (volume == ZERO_OR_ONE);
        } else {
          unread (chr);
          done = true;
        }
      }
      return result.toString ();
    }
  }

  // protected boolean isMatch (int chr, int type) ...
```

This method attempts to read the specified volume of the specified type of character type. The volume can be either `ZERO_OR_MORE` or `ZERO_OR_ONE`; the type can be either `WHITESPACE`, `NON_WHITESPACE`, `DIGITS`, or a normal Java character. We loop while the specified type of character is being read and we still need characters, appending the characters to the `StringBuffer result`. When a nonmatching character is encountered (this could be the EOF), we `unread()` the character and return the sequence of characters that were read. We make use of a method `isMatch()` to determine whether a character matches the desired type.

```
  protected static final int WHITESPACE = 0x10000,
    NON_WHITESPACE = 0x10001, DIGITS = 0x10002;
```

```
protected static final int ZERO_OR_MORE = 0,
  ZERO_OR_ONE = 1;

protected boolean isMatch (int chr, int type) {
  switch (type) {
    case WHITESPACE:
      return Character.isWhitespace ((char) chr);
    case NON_WHITESPACE:
      return !Character.isWhitespace ((char) chr);
    case DIGITS:
      return Character.isDigit ((char) chr);
    default:
      return (type == chr);
  }
}
```

This method returns whether the specified character chr matches the specified type type. We simply switch for the various wild card options, and default to an exact character match.

Using this class we can easily parse textual data files. We could add other methods in addition to readLong() and readDouble() in order to parse the other native data types, or else we can simply cast the result of those methods to the appropriate precision. Another facility that might be useful would be one to read data from a single line at a time. The following class implements such a facility; alternatively, investigate the StreamTokenizer class, which also can be configured to operate on a line-by-line basis.

11.10 LineAtATimeReader

This class is a FilterReader that attaches to another Reader and allows data to be read from the attached stream one line at a time. It

Figure 11.10   Class LineAtATimeReader

operates as a normal Reader, reading from the attached stream until an end-of-line sequence is encountered (\n, \r, \r\n) at which point the read() methods return EOF. The stream can then be instructed to skip to the next line at which point reading will resume as normal, until the next EOL is reached (figure 11.10).

```
import java.io.*;

public class LineAtATimeReader extends FilterReader {
  // public LineAtATimeReader (Reader reader) ...
  // public int read () throws IOException ...
  // public int read (char[] data, int offset, int length)
  //     throws IOException ...
  // public long skip (long amount) throws IOException ...
  // public void mark (int readAheadLimit) throws IOException ...
  // public void reset () throws IOException ...
```

```
    // public boolean nextLine () throws IOException ...
}
```

This class is a `FilterReader`, so we inherit the usual `Reader` methods that are forwarded to the attached stream. We override the necessary `read()` methods, `skip()`, `mark()`, and `reset()`, to operate in conjunction with the line-at-a-time reading methodology. In addition, we provide `nextLine()` that allows `read()` to start reading again from the next line.

```
public LineAtATimeReader (Reader reader) {
    super (reader);
}
```

In the constructor, we just call the superconstructor, attaching to the specified Reader, reader.

```
protected boolean eol, eof, skipLF;

public int read () throws IOException {
    synchronized (lock) {
        if (eol || eof)
            return -1;
        int chr = in.read ();
        if (skipLF && (chr == '\n'))
            chr = in.read ();
        skipLF = (chr == '\r');
        if ((chr == '\n') || (chr == '\r')) {
            eol = true;
            return -1;
        } else {
            eof = (chr == -1);
            return chr;
        }
    }
}
```

We override the `read()` method to support the line-at-a-time reading methodology. We maintain flags `eol`, `eof`, and `skipLF`, which indicate respectively that we have reached the end of a line, that we have reached the end of the attached stream, or that we should skip any immediate line feed character.

If we are at the end of the attached stream or the end of the current line, we return EOF (−1). Otherwise, we read a character from the attached stream. If it is a line feed character and `skipLF` is set, then we discard it and read another character; this allows us to cope with \r\n line terminators.

If we have just read an end-of-line character, we set `eol` to be `true` and return −1; any subsequent `read()` calls also will return EOF. Otherwise, we set `eof` if appropriate, and finally return the character that we just read, whether a normal character or the EOF.

```
public int read (char[] data, int offset, int length) throws IOException {
  if (length <= 0)
    return 0;
  int amount = 0;
  synchronized (lock) {
    int chr;
    while ((amount < length) && ((chr = read ()) != -1))
      data[offset + (amount ++)] = (char) chr;
  }
  return (amount > 0) ? amount : -1;
}
```

We override the character subarray `read()` method to read it as a sequence of single-character `read()` calls. This is inefficient and goes against the buffer-oriented nature of the character streams; however, it makes this example considerably simpler. We read as many characters as were requested, up to the end of line or end of file, and then return the number read, or -1 if the EOF or EOL was reached before any data.

```
public long skip (long amount) throws IOException {
  long skip = 0;
  synchronized (lock) {
    while ((skip < amount) && (read () != -1))
      ++ skip;
  }
  return skip;
}
```

We override the `skip()` method to make a sequence of single-character `read()` calls until the EOF is reached or enough characters have been skipped.

```
protected boolean oldEOF, oldEOL, oldSkipLF;

public void mark (int readAheadLimit) throws IOException {
  synchronized (lock) {
    in.mark (readAheadLimit);
    oldEOF = eof; oldEOL= eol; oldSkipLF = skipLF;
  }
}
```

This stream can support `mark()` and `reset()` if the attached stream does. We simply call the attached stream's `mark()` method and then store the old values of `eof`, `eol`, and `skipLF` in the variables `oldEOF`, `oldEOL`, and `oldSkipLF`. The inherited `markSupported()` method calls that of the attached stream.

```
public void reset () throws IOException {
  synchronized (lock) {
```

```
    in.reset ();
    eof = oldEOF; eol = oldEOL; skipLF = oldSkipLF;
  }
}
```

To reset this stream, we reset the attached stream and then restore the values of
eof, eol, and skipLF.

```
public boolean nextLine () throws IOException {
  synchronized (lock) {
    while (read () != -1);
    eol = false;
    return !eof;
  }
}
```

The nextLine() method skips to reading the next line of text. If we are not currently at the end of a line or the end of the attached stream, we repeatedly skip characters until we are. We then set eol to false so that read() can proceed with the next
line, and return true if we have not yet reached the end of the attached stream.

Note that if the last line in a text file ends with a newline sequence (as most do),
then this method will still return true after reading the last line because it will not be
aware that the end of file follows immediately. Subsequently calling read() will, of
course, return EOF. We could add a single-character look ahead to test for this case.
However, doing so would interfere with the operation of this stream when data is only
received one line at a time, such as from the keyboard.

11.10.1 In practice

Some FilterReaders, including the DataReader class, will not operate correctly when
reading from a stream such as this, that can return EOF and then later return more valid
data. In particular, in the case of the DataReader class, the DataReader will unread the
EOF that is returned from the end of a line. Even if nextLine() is called on this
stream, the attached DataReader will still return –1 from the next read() call. To use
these two streams together, it is necessary to have code of the following form:

```
// Reader reader;
LineAtATimeReader lineReader = new LineAtATimeReader (reader);
do {
  DataReader dataReader = new DataReader (lineReader);
  // read from dataReader
} while (lineReader.nextLine ());
```

This code attaches a LineAtATimeReader, lineReader, to the Reader reader
and then creates a DataReader for each iteration of the main loop. We stop looping
when the real EOF is reached, at which point nextLine() will return false. In the

next chapter, we will see an alternative way to implement this type of function using the `StringReader` class.

11.11 Wrapping up

The character streams support filters in much the same way the byte-oriented streams do. The primary difference between filters for the two types of stream are the new synchronization mechanism of the character streams and the fact that the character streams are oriented around reading data through arrays where the byte streams are implemented with more byte-by-byte operations.

In the next chapter, we will look at the memory-based character streams, including character pipes and various facilities to read from and write to character array-type data types. Those streams conclude our treatment of the character streams, from which point we will look at the object streams before proceeding with a detailed look at Java's networking facilities in part III.

C H A P T E R   1 2

Memory-based character streams

These character streams use memory as either the origin of the data that they produce or the destination of the data that they consume. Paralleling the byte-oriented streams, they provide piped communications facilities that allow for character streams-based communications among different threads within a virtual machine, as well as the facility to write characters into a String or array of characters, or to read characters out of a String or array of characters.

12.1 `JDK 1.1` *Class PipedWriter*

This class is a character-oriented piped stream. Piped streams allow for streams-based interthread communication within a virtual machine: one thread writes into a pipe and another thread reads from the pipe. Data emerge from the pipe in the same order that they were written in (figure 12.1).

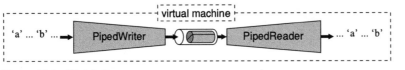

Figure 12.1   Piped streams

PipedWriter provides the write end of a piped stream. A PipedWriter must be connected to a PipedReader, and then any data written into the PipedWriter can be subsequently read from the PipedReader. These classes use a small 512-

Figure 12.2   Class PipedWriter

character internal buffer (they are actually implemented using the conventional byte-oriented piped streams); if this buffer becomes full, then writing into a PipedWriter will block the caller until some data are read from the pipe and space becomes available (figure 12.2).

12.1.1 Constructors

A PipedWriter can either be created unconnected and then connected to a PipedReader, or it can be created and automatically connected to an existing PipedReader. Only one thread should ever write to any particular PipedWriter; problems can arise if multiple threads use the same PipedReader, even if not concurrently.

It is only necessary to connect either a PipedWriter to a PipedReader, or a PipedReader to a PipedWriter. It is not necessary to connect each to the other.

PipedWriter()   This creates an unconnected PipedWriter. This can subsequently be connected to a PipedReader with the connect() method or the PipedReader constructor.

PipedWriter(PipedReader sink) throws IOException This method creates a `PipedWriter` and connects it to the specified `PipedReader`, `sink`.

12.1.2 Methods

The `PipedWriter` class provides the usual `Writer` methods in addition to the new `connect()` method. However, the `write()` methods are modified so that an attempt to write into a `PipedWriter` whose corresponding reading thread is no longer alive will result in an `IOException` (*Pipe broken*). This prevents a writer from potentially blocking forever if the internal buffer becomes full and there is no thread remaining to empty the buffer. The reading thread that is checked for liveness is the most recent thread to read from the attached `PipedReader`.

If a `PipedWriter` is closed, all data previously written will still be available to read from the attached `PipedReader`, after which the `PipedReader` will report EOF.

void connect(PipedReader sink) throws IOException This method connects this `PipedWriter` to the specified `PipedReader`, `sink`.

12.1.3 IOException

Connecting a `PipedWriter` to an already-connected `PipedReader` will result in an `IOException`, as will attempting to reconnect a connected `PipedWriter` or writing to a pipe whose reading thread is no longer alive.

12.1.4 InterruptedIOException

If a thread is blocked writing to a `PipedWriter` and is then interrupted by a call to `interrupt()`, then the write operation will abort with an `InterruptedIOException`.

12.2 [JDK 1.1] *Class PipedReader*

`PipedReader` provides the corresponding read end for character-oriented streams-based piped inter-thread communications. Any data written to the attached `PipedWriter` become available for reading from this stream. Attempting to read from an

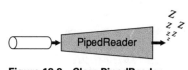

Figure 12.3   Class PipedReader

empty `PipedReader` will block the caller until data are written into the attached stream or it is closed (figure 12.3).

These piped streams can be used in exactly the same manner as the `PipedOutputStream` and `PipedInputStream` classes, except that they provide a true 16-bit character stream for interthread communications. Typically they are used in a producer/consumer scenario where the production and consumption of text data should not be tightly coupled. Production should be allowed to continue even if consumption is not as fast. Bear in mind that the small buffer limit will enforce lock-step execution after some time if consumption cannot keep up with production.

12.2.1 Constructors

As with the PipedWriter class, a PipedReader can either be created and then connected to a PipedWriter or created and automatically connected to an existing PipedWriter.

PipedReader()   This creates an unconnected PipedReader.

PipedReader(PipedWriter src) throws IOException   This creates a PipedReader and connects it to the specified PipedWriter, src.

12.2.2 Methods

The PipedReader class provides the usual Reader methods in addition to the new connect() method. The read() methods are modified so that an attempt to read from an empty, unclosed PipedReader whose corresponding writing thread is no longer alive will result in an IOException (*Pipe broken*). This prevents the reader from potentially blocking forever if there is no thread remaining to provide more data. The writing thread that is checked for liveness is the most recent thread to write to the attached PipedWriter.

void connect(PipedWriter src) throws IOException   This method connects this PipedReader to the specified PipedWriter, src. Any data written to src will subsequently become available to be read through this PipedReader.

12.2.3 IOException

Connecting to an already-connected PipedWriter, attempting to reconnect a connected PipedReader, or attempting to read from an open, empty pipe whose writing thread is no longer alive will raise an IOException.

12.2.4 InterruptedIOException

If a thread is blocked reading from a PipedReader and is then interrupted by a call to interrupt(), then the read operation will abort with an InterruptedIOException.

12.3 JDK 1.1 Class CharArrayWriter

This class provides a Writer interface to creating an array of characters: all data that are written to a CharArrayWriter are written into an expanding internal buffer, which can subsequently be

Figure 12.4   Class CharArrayWriter

extracted for processing. This is similar to the facility provided by the `ByteArrayOutputStream` class (figure 12.4).

12.3.1 Constructors

Although the internal character buffer used by a `CharArrayWriter` can expand as necessary to store any volume of data, it is more efficient if it is created initially with sufficient capacity to hold its final payload. Two constructors are therefore exposed: one uses a default small initial buffer size and the other allows the initial buffer size to be specified.

CharArrayWriter()   This creates a `CharArrayWriter` that has the default initial buffer size (32). Whenever the buffer becomes full, its capacity is doubled so it can grow rapidly to accommodate any amount of data.

CharArrayWriter(int initialSize)   This creates a `CharArrayWriter` that has the specified initial buffer size, `initialSize`. This buffer will be expanded as necessary if it is too small.

12.3.2 Methods

In addition to the usual methods of `Writer`, this class provides various means to manipulate the internal character array:

void reset()   This method resets the internal character buffer, discarding all data that have been written to the stream thus far. Subsequent data written to this stream will refill the buffer from the beginning.

int size()   This method returns the number of characters in the internal buffer, which is the amount of data that has been written to this stream since it was created or last reset.

char[] toCharArray()   This method extracts a copy of the contents of the internal character array. The result is an array exactly large enough to hold all the data that have been written to this stream since it was created or last reset. The internal buffer is not reset; so if more data are subsequently written to this stream, it will continue to expand.

String toString()   This method extracts a copy of the contents of the internal character array as a `String`. The internal buffer is not reset.

void writeTo(Writer out) throws IOException   This method writes the contents of the internal character array to the specified `Writer`, `out`. The internal buffer is not reset. This is more efficient than, but exactly equivalent to, extracting the character array and then writing it to out.

12.3.3 Variables

protected char buf[]   This variable is the internal buffer used to store data written to this stream.

protected int count   This variable indicates the amount of valid data stored in buf; This is the amount of data that have been written to this stream since it was created or last reset.

12.3.4 IOException

Although writing to a CharArrayWriter will not throw an IOException, writing the contents of its buffer to another stream may result in an IOException.

12.4 JDK 1.1 Class CharArrayReader

This class provides a complimentary reading facility, presenting a character-oriented streams interface for reading data from an array of characters. This is similar to the byte-oriented class Byte-ArrayInputStream (figure 12.5).

Figure 12.5   Class CharArrayReader

12.4.1 Constructors

A CharArrayReader can be constructed to read either from an entire character array or from a subarray thereof.

CharArrayReader(char buf[])   This creates a CharArrayReader that reads from the entire character array buf. Reading proceeds from the first element of the array through to the last, subsequently returning EOF.

CharArrayReader(char buf[], int offset, int length)   This creates a CharArrayReader that reads from the specified length-character subarray of buf, starting from index offset. Reading proceeds from the first element of this subarray through to the last, subsequently returning EOF.

12.4.2 Methods

The usual methods of class Reader are provided by this class, reading data from the array or subarray specified in the constructor. This class supports the mark() and reset() methods. Note that if reset() is called before mark() is ever called then the class resets to the very start of the array, regardless of whether the stream was initially constructed with a non-zero-offset subarray. The original absolute endpoint is, however, maintained.

This class reads from the same array that is passed in to the constructor; a copy is not made. Thus, the contents of the array may be externally modified and the stream reset to read the new data.

12.4.3 Variables

protected char buf[]   This is the character array passed in the constructor.

protected int pos   This is the current read index in `buf`.

protected int markedPos   This is the most recently marked position in `buf`, initially zero.

protected int count   This variable is the index one greater than the last valid character in `buf`. For a `CharArrayReader` constructed from an entire array, it is `buf.length`; for a `CharArrayReader` constructed from a subarray, it is `offset+length`. The `read()` methods read up to this index and then return EOF.

12.5 [JDK 1.1] *Class StringWriter*

This class provides a character-oriented stream interface for creating a `String` or `StringBuffer`. All data written to this stream are appended to an internal

'h' ... 'e' ... → StringWriter → "hello, world!"

Figure 12.6   Class StringWriter

`StringBuffer` and can be extracted as either a `String` or `StringBuffer`. This class is similar to, but more limited than, the `CharArrayWriter` class (figure 12.6).

12.5.1 Constructors

Two constructors are provided: One uses the default initial `StringBuffer` size; the other allows this initial size to be specified.

StringWriter()   This creates a `StringWriter` that uses the default initial `String-Buffer` size (16).

StringWriter(int initialSize)   This creates a `StringWriter` that uses the specified initial `StringBuffer` size, `initialSize`. Appropriately used, this constructor is more efficient than using the default size because fewer buffer increases may be necessary.

12.5.2 Methods

The contents of this `StringWriter` can be extracted as either a `String` or a `String-Buffer`.

String toString()   This method returns a `String` that is a copy of the contents of this `StringWriter`; that is, all data written to this stream thus far.

StringBuffer getBuffer()   This method returns the `StringBuffer` that is used internally to store data written to this stream. This `StringBuffer` can be subsequently manipulated as desired; calling `setLength(0)` on it is equivalent to the `CharArray-Writer reset()` method.

12.6   JDK 1.1 *Class StringReader*

This class provides a character-oriented streams-based interface to reading character data from a `String`. This is similar to, but more limited than, the `CharArrayReader` class (figure 12.7).

Figure 12.7   Class StringReader

12.6.1 Constructors

Only one constructor is provided:

StringReader(String s)   This creates a `StringReader` that reads from start to finish from the contents of `s`.

12.6.2 Methods

The usual methods of `Reader` are all supported, including `mark()` and `reset()`.

12.7 *Another line-at-a-time Reader*

The `LineReaderReader` class is similar to the `LineAtATimeReader` example of the previous chapter except that rather than inlining the line-at-a-time reading function with the standard `Reader` interface, we add a method `getLineReader()` that can be used to

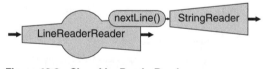

Figure 12.8   Class LineReaderReader

obtain a new, separate `Reader` for the next line of text (figure 12.8).

```
import java.io.*;

public class LineReaderReader extends BufferedReader {
  // public LineAtATimeReader (Reader reader) ...
  // public LineAtATimeReader (Reader reader, int bufferCapacity) ...
  // public Reader getLineReader () throws IOException ...
}
```

The `LineReaderReader` class extends `BufferedReader` because we wish to take advantage of both its efficient buffering facilities and its `readLine()` method. We inherit all of the usual `FilterReader`/`Reader` methods and the `readLine()` method.

```
public LineReaderReader (Reader reader) {
  super (reader);
}
```

This constructor calls the superconstructor to attach to the specified `Reader`, reader, and use the default buffer size.

```
public LineReaderReader (Reader reader, int bufferCapacity) {
  super (reader, bufferCapacity);
}
```

This constructor calls the superconstructor to attach to the specified `Reader`, reader, and use the specified buffer size, `bufferCapacity`.

```
public Reader getLineReader () throws IOException {
  String line = readLine ();
  if (line == null)
    return null;
  else
    return new StringReader (line);
}
```

This method returns a new `Reader` that reads data from only the next line of the attached character stream, or else returns `null` when the end of the attached stream is reached. We read a line of text using the inherited `readLine()` method, and then return a new `StringReader` that reads from this line of text.

12.7.1 In practice

To use this class, simply attach it to the desired character source and then repeatedly call the `getLineReader()` method, attaching any desired filters to the resulting stream.

```
// Reader reader;
LineReaderReader lineReaderReader = new LineReaderReader (reader);
Reader lineReader;
while ((lineReader = lineReaderReader.getLineReader ()) != null) {
  DataReader dataReader = new DataReader (lineReader);
  // read from dataReader
}
```

In this code fragment, we attach the `LineReaderReader` lineReaderReader to the `Reader` reader and then proceed to extract single-line `Reader`s using its `getLineReader()` method. We process each `Reader` as necessary and then repeat the loop until the EOF is reached.

12.8 Wrapping up

This concludes our treatment of the character streams, and of the simple streams in general. Streams form the underlying abstraction behind basic communications in Java—whether to a file, between threads, or through a network connection. The character streams provide a useful companion to the byte streams because they demonstrate a greater emphasis on efficiency and they allow for translation between the character encodings of different systems, as well as for easy raw character communications within a single application.

For many network applications, distributed object platforms, such as RMI and CORBA, remove the need for the programmer to develop at the level of streams and sockets. As these platforms become more popular, the need for developing at this low level may diminish; however it will never disappear. Efficient low-level network access will remain at the heart of many leading edge and legacy applications, for a long time to come.

In the next chapter we look at the object streams, `ObjectInputStream` and `ObjectOutputStream`, which provide the facility for writing arbitrary Java objects to a bytestream. These greatly simplify the storage of Java data structures because they obviate the need to break an object down into its component primitive data. This is automatically handled by the object stream classes.

CHAPTER 13

Object streams

In this chapter, we take a look at two stream classes that allow complete `Objects` to be written to a communications channel without much effort on the part of the programmer. These streams allow the programmer to send an `Object` to a stream as easily as an integer. This facility is extremely powerful. You are not restricted to just sending data types such as a `Color` or a `Vector`. You can, for example, transmit an entire applet, and it will be successfully recreated by the recipient.

When you transmit an object, the object streams take care to transmit every object to which the base object refers; the streams ensure that even complex object relationships are preserved. Special facilities are, however, available for restricting what data are included with an object during transmission and for performing postserialization cleanup if necessary, even including facilities for handling class version differences between sender and recpient.

13.1 Overview

An inherent characteristic of networked applications is the need to send data back and forth between two applications, possibly on remote machines. This is usually achieved in three stages, which we have already implemented in some form using the basic streams. These stages are, in sequence: packing up the data into a form that can be sent over some communications channel (marshaling), delivering the data, and unpacking the data into the original form at the other end (unmarshaling). See figure 13.1.

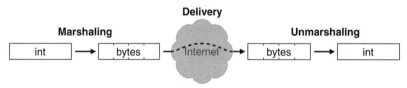

Figure 13.1 Data communications

13.1.1 Marshaling

Marshaling is the process of breaking data down into bytes so that they can be sent over a communications channel such as TCP. Using the normal streams, we transmitted an integer by breaking it down into 4 bytes and writing these to an `OutputStream`. Marshaling of the Java primitive types is handled for us by the `DataOutputStream` class, which does exactly this. If we want to send more complex data represented in whole objects, we have to break down the object manually into a form that can be reconstructed on the other end. If the object refers to other objects, this process can be very complex.

The object streams provide a streams-based interface to accomplish this at a high level, taking the complexity out of the hands of the programmer but allowing for all the flexibility of passing objects. *Object serialization* is the term used for marshaling actual objects so that they can be transmitted and later unmarshaled with all fields, even other reference types, intact.

13.1.2 Delivery

The delivery stage is the process of actually sending the data from source to destination. We have already encountered several streams-based transport mechanisms, including byte arrays, and pipes, and in future chapters we will see sreams-based network connections. The Java object streams provide object serialization facilities across the standard byte-oriented streams so we can access all of these existing transport mechanisms.

13.1.3 Unmarshaling

Unmarshaling refers to the unpacking of the data after they have been delivered. The serialization process reduces data into a stream of bytes, but it retains enough information to reconstruct the data correctly after delivery. With the object streams, deserialization is used to refer to unmarshaling.

13.1.4 Marshaling objects

Marshaling primitive types is fairly easy, but if there is a need to send reference types, it quickly becomes quite difficult. Objects typically have multiple fields, and may refer to many other objects. To faithfully reconstruct the object after delivery, all fields and outside references must be tracked and kept to ensure correct reconstruction.

The mechanism used by the object streams to preserve referential integrity is to maintain a history of transmitted objects, so that whenever an object reference is serialized, if it has already been serialized then a

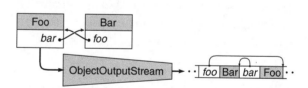

Figure 13.2   Serialization of inter-referential objects

back-reference is serialized instead of the raw object data. Note that the recipient receives a *copy* of the original object and every object to which it referred, even if it is within the same virtual machine as the origin. However, if one object is transmitted twice down the same stream, then the recipient will receive two references to just one copy (figure 13.2).

13.1.5 The object streams

The marshaling and unmarshaling processes in Java are achieved using the object streams, ObjectOutputStream and ObjectInputStream (figure 13.3). The delivery occurs when these streams are attached to an underlying communications channel, such as a file or a socket. Using these streams is actually quite easy, but a lot of behind-the-scenes work is being done to access internal class variables and preserve referential integrity.

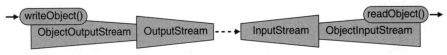

Figure 13.3   The object streams

13.2   JDK 1.1   *Class ObjectOutputStream*

The `ObjectOutputStream` class implements the `ObjectOutput` interface (an extension of `DataOutput`), and has all the methods defined there; in particular, the `write-Object()` method. As a `FilterOutputStream`, it attaches to an existing `Output-Stream` in the usual manner (figure 13.4).

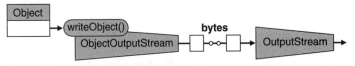

Figure 13.4   Class ObjectOutputStream

Both `ObjectOutputStream` and `ObjectInputStream` also implement the interface `ObjectStreamConstants`; this interface defines various constants that are of interest to people actually producing or analyzing a serialized byte stream. The only constants of relevance to this book relate to the stream protocol version, and are discussed with the `useProtocolVersion()` method.

13.2.1 Constructors

As a `FilterOutputStream`, the `ObjectOutputStream` class provides one standard public constructor:

ObjectOutputStream(OutputStream out) throws IOException   This creates an `ObjectOutputStream` attached to the `OutputStream out`. This constructor may throw an `IOException` because a header is immediately written to the attached stream. If the attached stream is buffered, then the caller may want to call `flush()` immediately so that the remote `ObjectInputStream` can read and verify the header without blocking until the stream is flushed later.

JDK 1.2   *protected ObjectOutputStream() throws IOException, SecurityException*   This method is used by subclasses that wish to entirely replace the default serialization protocol. This is not a topic that we will discuss.

13.2.2 Methods

When primitive types are being sent, the methods of `DataOutput` should be used. For example:

```
ObjectOutputStream objectOut = new ObjectOutputStream (out);
int answer = 42;
objectOut.writeInt (answer);
```

In this example, we send an integer using the `writeInt()` method, which `ObjectOutputStream` implements from the `DataOutput` interface.

In addition to the various methods of `DataOutput`, the `ObjectOutputStream` class provides several other methods that are related to the serialization process. The public methods provided are all described by the `ObjectOutput` interface which extends `DataOutput`, adding various object-related methods as well as all of the standard `OutputStream` methods.

void writeObject(Object o) throws IOException The `writeObject()` method is responsible for serializing objects and sending them to the stream. This method is used to send whole objects.

```
int[] array = new int[10];
objectOut.writeObject (array);
```

In this example, we send an array of integers using the `writeObject()` method. Objects of any type can be sent. Here is an example of sending a `Color`.

```
Color whiteish = new Color (240, 240, 240);
objectOut.writeObject (whiteish);
```

The `writeObject()` method can send *all* the fields of an `Object`, including `private` and `protected` fields that are not usually publicly accessible. Only fields marked `transient` or `static` will not be sent. Because of the security implications that this raises, a class must explicitly grant permission to be serialized by implementing either the `Serializable` interface or the `Externalizable` interface. Attempting to serialize an `Object` that does not implement one of these interfaces will result in a `NotSerializableException`.

void reset() throws IOException This method resets the `ObjectOutputStream` to a clean initial state, as if it had been just created.

Each `ObjectOutputStream` keeps track of every `Object` that it has ever sent. Thus, if the same `Object` is written to an `ObjectOutputStream` twice, then only a back-reference will be written the second time, even if the original `Object` has been modified. This is important because it means that if several inter-referential `Object`s are written over the course of several calls to writeObject(), then the recipient will still end up with the same reference structure as the sender.

After a call to reset(), all such information is discarded, so if an Object is sent again, then a new, fresh copy will be sent to the recipient. Care should be taken with the use of this method, especially when complex relations are transmitted.

void defaultWriteObject() throws IOException   This method writes the calling Object (i.e., the Object that called this method) to the ObjectOutputStream. This is only used by a custom writeObject() implementation. (This is discussed more in section section 13.8.3 on page 229.)

protected void writeStreamHeader() throws IOException   When an ObjectOutputStream is first created, this method is called to transmit a header to the attached stream (including an identifier and version number, for future compatibility). An ObjectOutputStream subclass can override the writeStreamHeader() to append or prepend its own additional header information, if it so desires.

protected Object replaceObject(Object obj) throws IOException   This method is used by ObjectOutputStream subclasses to replace certain Objects with others before transmission. This is useful, for example, when you wish to serialize a final class that does not implement Serializable. Instead, you replace it with another Object that is suitable for transmission, and upon receipt convert this back to the original. This reconversion is handled by the resolveObject() method of class ObjectInputStream. Every Object that is written to an ObjectOutputStream will be passed to this method. To leave it unchanged, simply return obj; otherwise return a serializable replacement. (This is discussed more in section 13.9.2 on page 236.)

Under JDK 1.2, the writeReplace() method provides an alternative, more general mechanism for objects to explicitly designate their own replacement before serialization.

protected boolean enableReplaceObject(boolean enable) throws SecurityException   Because the replaceObject() method introduces certain security issues, it is not initially enabled. To enable object replacement, it is necessary to first call this enableReplaceObject() method; it will either enable or disable Object replacement, according to the enable parameter. Under JDK 1.1, if there is *any* SecurityManager installed then this method will raise a SecurityException. Under JDK 1.2, if the caller does not have the SerializablePermission enableSubstitution then a SecurityException will be raised.

protected void annotateClass(Class cl) throws IOException   This   method   is used by ObjectOutputStream subclasses to write additional information when the class cl is being transmitted. This will occur the first time that an object of this class is transmitted through the stream. The object streams usually only specify the class name and version information; a subclass could add, for example, the location of the class' byte-codes, should the recipient not have them available locally.

protected void drain() throws IOException   This method writes out any internally buffered data that the `ObjectOutputStream` may have, without actually flushing the attached stream.

JDK 1.2   *protected void writeObjectOverride(Object object) throws IOException*   This method should be implemented by subclasses that are completely replacing the default serialization protocol, to serialize the specified `Object`, object.

JDK 1.2   *void useProtocolVersion(int version) throws IOException*   JDK 1.2 introduced some changes to the object serialization protocol that are incompatible with earlier versions of the JDK. This method allows you to specify the protocol version that this stream will write; the default is the new version, `ObjectStream-Constants.PROTOCOL_VERSION_2`, which is only compatible with JDK 1.1.7+ and JDK 1.2+. To retain compatibility with earlier versions of the JDK, specify `Object-StreamConstants.PROTOCOL_VERSION_1`.

JDK 1.2   *ObjectOutputStream.PutField putFields() throws IOException*   This method returns an object that can be used for explicitly defining the fields of your object that will be serialized to an object stream. Initialize this datastructure and then call `writeFields()` to actually transmit the fields.

JDK 1.2   *void writeFields() throws IOException*   This method provides a compatible alternative to calling `defaultWriteObject()` to write your fields to an object stream. Whereas that method reads the fields directly from the caller, this allows the caller to provide an `ObjectOutputStream.PutField` datastructure in which the fields are explicitly specified. Calling this method inappropriately will raise a `NotActive-Exception`.

13.2.3   **JDK 1.2**   *ObjectOutputStream.PutField*
This inner class is a datastructure that represents the fields of an object to be serialized out to a byte-stream. The use of this class is unnecessary for most typical applications.

13.2.4 *IOException*
Certain objects may refuse to be serialized, for security reasons, and will throw a `NotSe-rializableException` if such an attempt is made. In particular, when you serialize an object, any `private` fields will be exposed. This presents a security risk, because these

fields can be extracted from the transmission byte stream. For this reason, Java requires that all serializable classes explicitly declare permission. The default operation will be to refuse to serialize an object unless it declares permission.

The mechanism for declaring permission to be serialized is to implement either the `Serializable` or `Externalizable` interface, and to implement any required support methods. This process is discussed in detail in section 13.8 on page 227. Most of the core API classes that you would expect support serialization by implementing the `Serializable` interface, including `String`, `Rectangle`, and the `Components`, but not classes such as `InputStream` or `Socket`.

There are many other `IOExceptions` that can be thrown by the `writeObject()` method; these are outlined in section 13.4 on page 224. If an exception occurs during a call to `writeObject()`, then special data are serialized so that the recipient will receive a `WriteAbortedException` when it tries to read the object.

13.3 ⬤JDK 1.1⬤ *Class ObjectInputStream*

The `ObjectInputStream` class implements the `ObjectInput` interface (an extension of `DataInput`), and thus has all the methods defined there; in particular, `readObject()`. As a `FilterInputStream`, the constructor attaches to an existing `InputStream`, from which all data will be read. Primitive types are read in the normal way, but there are new methods for dealing with reference types. See figure 13.5.

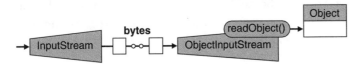

Figure 13.5   Class ObjectInputStream

13.3.1 *Constructors*

As a `FilterInputStream`, the `ObjectInputStream` class provides one standard public constructor:

ObjectInputStream(InputStream in) throws IOException   This   creates   an `ObjectInputStream` attached to the `InputStream` in. This constructor may throw an `IOException` because a header is immediately read from the attached stream to ensure compatibility with the remote `ObjectOutputStream`.

⬤JDK 1.2⬤   *protected ObjectInputStream() throws IOException, SecurityException* *tion*   This method is used by subclasses that wish to replace the entire default serialization protocol. This is not a topic that we will discuss.

13.3.2 Methods

When primitive types are being read, the methods of `DataInput` should be used. For example:

```
ObjectInputStream in = new ObjectInputStream (socket.getInputStream ());
int value;
value = in.readInt ();
```

This simply reads 4 bytes and reconstructs an integer.

In addition to the methods of `DataInput`, the `ObjectInputStream` provides various methods related to the deserialization process. These include methods to resolve unknown class files. The public methods provided are all described by the `ObjectInput` interface which extends `DataInput`, adding various object-related methods as well as all of the standard `InputStream` methods.

Object readObject() throws IOException, ClassNotFoundException   The `readObject()` method is responsible for deserializing objects from a communications stream.

```
Color color;
color = (Color) objectIn.readObject ();
```

This example reads a `Color` object. The `readObject()` method returns an `Object` that we must cast to the appropriate type.

Note that transmitting a `Class` object with the object streams does not transmit the bytecodes of the actual class. Instead, only the class name and its signature will be transmitted. Upon receipt, the `ObjectInputStream` class will attempt to load the named class from the local class path.

`ObjectInputStream` provides protection against erroneously attempting to read raw binary data from a stream with the normal `read()` methods when a serialized `Object` is the next item, or attempting to read a serialized `Object` when the next item is raw binary data. Attempting to read normal data when the next item in a stream is an `Object` will return an EOF. Attempting to read an `Object` when the next item in a stream is normal data will result in an `OptionalDataException`.

void defaultReadObject() throws IOException, ClassNotFoundException
This method reads the fields of the calling `Object` (i.e., the `Object` that called this method) from the `ObjectInputStream`. This is only used by a custom `readObject()` implementation. Calling this method inappropriately will raise a `NotActive-Exception`. This is discussed in detail in section 13.8.3 on page 229.

protected void readStreamHeader() throws IOException When an `Object-InputStream` is first created, this method is called to read a header from the attached stream. An `ObjectInputStream` subclass can override the `readStreamHeader()` to read any additional header information that a corresponding `ObjectOutputStream` writes. A `StreamCorruptedException` should be thrown if the header data are not valid.

protected Object resolveObject(Object obj) throws IOException This method is used by `ObjectInputStream` subclasses to replace certain `Objects` with others after reception. This is usually used in association with the `replaceObject()` method of a remote `ObjectOutputStream` to allow transmission of objects that are usually not serializable. This method must always return an `Object` that is compatible with the original class; that is, an instance of the original class or a subclass. For example, a `FileInputStream` object could be replaced for transmission by a `SerializedFileInputStream` object that includes just the associated filename. Upon reception, the `resolveObject()` method can replace this by a new `FileInputStream`. This is discussed in detail in section 13.9.5 on page 239.

Under JDK 1.2, the `readResolve()` method provides an alternative, more general mechanism for objects to explicitly designate their own replacement before serialization.

protected boolean enableResolveObject(boolean enable) throws SecurityException Because the object replacement mechanism introduces certain security issues related to access of private data, it is not initially enabled. To enable `Object` resolution by an `ObjectInputStream`, it is necessary to first call this `enableReplaceObject()` method; it will either enable or disable `Object` replacement, according to the `enable` parameter. Under JDK 1.1, if there is *any* `SecurityManager` installed this method will raise a `SecurityException`. Under JDK 1.2, if the caller does not have the `SerializablePermission enableSubstitution` then a `SecurityException` will be raised.

protected Class resolveClass(ObjectStreamClass v) throws IOException, ClassNotFoundException This method is used by `ObjectInputStream` subclasses to read additional information written by the `annotateClass()` method of the remote `ObjectOutputStream`, and from this to resolve the corresponding `Class` object. For example, an `ObjectOutputStream` could transmit the actual bytecodes of a class (or its location) and an `ObjectInputStream` could then use these to create the class if it is not already available locally.

void registerValidation(ObjectInputValidation validator, int priority) throws NotActiveException, InvalidObjectException   A class that provides a custom `readObject()` implementation can call this method from within that method to install a postreading validator. The `validateObject()` method of this validator will be called just before the *original* call to `readObject()` returns. This allows postprocessing to be performed after an entire `Object` structure has been deserialized, but before it is returned to the caller.

Registration of a validator is only possible from a custom `readObject()` implementation and will only remain in effect for the execution of the main `readObject()` call. If multiple validators are registered during the deserialization of a single `Object`, then the validators will be called in order of their registered priority level, `priority` (highest priority first).

JDK 1.2   *protected Object readObjectOverride() throws IOException*   This method should be implemented by subclasses that are completely replacing the default serialization protocol, to deserialize and return the next object in the stream.

JDK 1.2   *ObjectInputStream.GetField readFields() throws IOException, ClassNotFoundException*   This method provides a compatible alternative to calling `defaultReadObject()` to read in your serialized fields from a stream. Whereas that method reads the fields directly into the caller, this returns an `ObjectInput-Stream.GetField` datastructure that allows the fields to be explicitly examined. Calling this method inappropriately will raise a `NotActiveException`.

13.3.3   **JDK 1.2**   *ObjectInputStream.GetField*
This inner class is a datastructure that represents the fields of an object, as read out of a serialized byte-stream. The use of this class is unnecessary for most typical applications.

13.3.4 *IOException*
As expected the methods of `ObjectInputStream` may throw various `IOExceptions` if there is a problem with the deserialization process or with reading from the stream.

13.3.5 *ClassNotFoundException*
A `ClassNotFoundException` will be thrown if the class of a received object cannot be located by the receiving virtual machine. The object streams do not transmit the bytecodes for classes that are not known to the recipient; the classes of all received objects must be either available on the local file system, or made available by some other mechanism; in particular, the `annotateClass()` and `resolveClass()` methods.

13.4 ⬤JDK 1.1 *Object stream exceptions*

The object streams may throw a variety of exceptions, whether IOExceptions resulting from access to the underlying stream, or ObjectStreamExceptions (a subclass of IOException) relating to the serialization process. The various ObjectStreamExceptions are:

InvalidClassException   This exception indicates that a local class cannot be used to deserialize an object from a stream, even though the serialized object goes by the same name as the local class. This may arise from a variety of problems, usually a versioning issue or simply a naming conflict between the sender and receiver.

NotSerializableException   This exception may be thrown either during reading or writing, and indicates that the Object being read or written (or one of its fields) does not support serialization.

StreamCorruptedException   This exception indicates that the stream does not contain valid object stream data, or that the stream header information is incorrect.

NotActiveException   This exception is thrown if one of the custom object stream serialization methods is accessed from anywhere other than a custom serialization implementation.

InvalidObjectException   This exception is thrown if an object failed its postread validation test.

OptionalDataException   This exception is thrown if an attempt is made to read an object from a stream that contains primitive data. The exception contains a field, length, that indicates the number of remaining bytes of primitive data and a field eof that indicates if there is no remaining primitive data.

WriteAbortedException   This exception is thrown when attempting to read an object which failed to be written because an exception occurred during the writing process. The exception contains a field detail that is the actual exception that the writer received.

13.5 ⬤JDK 1.1 *Interface Serializable*

The Serializable interface is a marker interface that is used by classes to indicate that they may be serialized by the default serialization mechanism. The interface defines no methods or data; it is simply a flag that lets the object streams know that serializing instances of the class will not reveal sensitive information or open up potential security holes.

If a subclass of a nonserializable class wishes to implement the `Serializable` interface, the immediate superclass *must* provide a constructor that takes no arguments. It is the responsibility of the subclass to serialize any of the superclass' data using the following customization methods:

13.5.1 Customization methods

Classes that wish to provide custom serialization in addition to the default mechanism can provide either of both of the following methods:

private void writeObject(ObjectOutputStream out) throws IOException
This method will be called when an instance of this class is being serialized to the `ObjectOutputStream out`. It should call the `defaultWriteObject()` method of `out` before writing any of its own custom data using the standard `ObjectOutputStream` methods, even if it has no data that will be serialized by the default mechanism. This will ensure compatibility with future versions of the class that wish to take advantage of the default serialization option. For full details see section 13.9 on page 235.

private void readObject(ObjectInputStream in) throws IOException, ClassNotFoundException   This method will be called when an instance of this class is being deserialized from the `ObjectInputStream in`. It should call the `defaultReadObject()` method of `in` before reading any of its own custom data and performing any subsequent initialization of `transient` fields. For full details see section 13.9 on page 235.

13.5.2 Self-replacement & resolution methods

These methods can be provided by serializable objects that wish to delegate their serialized form to another class. This is useful because it separates serialization details from a class' actual implementation, which can be important when the serialization details become fairly involved because of versioning issues.

JDK 1.2   *private Object writeReplace() throws ObjectStreamException*
This method should return a replacement of this object for serialization purposes. When a class that implements this method is written to an `ObjectOutputStream`, this method will be called and the returned object will instead be serialized. Of course, the returned object itself must be serializable. Typically, it will also implement the following `readResolve()` method so that it can be translated back to the original type upon deserialization. For full details see section 13.9.6 on page 241.

JDK 1.2   *private Object readResolve() throws ObjectStreamException*   This method should return a replacement of this object for deserialization purposes. When a class that implements this method is read from an `ObjectInputStream`, this method will be called and the resulting object will instead be returned. This will typically be an instance of a class that originally provided a `writeReplace()` method. For full details see section 13.9.6 on page 241.

13.6 `JDK 1.1` *Interface Externalizable*

This interface should be implemented by classes that wish to provide entirely manual serialization facilities. The object streams will only write the name of the class to the stream; all other data must be communicated through this interface. Classes that use this mechanism gain none of the versioning facilities provided by the default serialization mechanism.

Note that an `Externalizable` object must provide a no-arg constructor by which an instance will be created, prior to deserialization from the stream.

13.6.1 Methods

This interface declares two methods for serialization:

void writeExternal(ObjectOutput out) throws IOException　This method will be called when an instance of this class is being serialized. It can write all of its data to the `ObjectOutput out`, using the various methods that declares.

void readExternal(ObjectInput in) throws IOException　This method will be called when an instance of this class is being deserialized. It can read all of its data from the `ObjectInput in`, using the various methods that declares. An instance will be created using the class' no-arg constructor, after which this method will be called.

13.6.2 Self-replacement & resolution methods

The JDK 1.2 self-replacement and resolution methods can also be used with the `Externalizable` serialization mechanism. An `Externalizable` class that wishes to support self-replacement or self-resolution can implement either or both of `writeReplace()` and `readResolve()`, and upon serialization or deserialization the appropriate method will be called automatically.

13.7 `JDK 1.1` *Interface ObjectInputValidation*

This interface must be implemented by classes that perform postprocessing after a call to `readObject()` has completed. Validators can be registered by a received `Object`'s `readObject()` method through `ObjectInputStream`'s `registerValidation()` method.

13.7.1 Methods

Only one method is declared by this interface:

void validateObject() throws InvalidObjectException This method will be called after a complete `Object` structure has been deserialized. If the object fails its self-validation, it should throw an `InvalidObjectException`.

13.8 Creating a serializable class

We will now look at how a serializable class can be implemented. Implementing a serializable class raises security considerations because a serialized object exposes its internal state to being read and manipulated. If this is inappropriate, then a class should not be serializable. Versioning considerations are also raised because a serialized object may later be read back into an environment with an older or newer version of the actual class files. Versioning issues are discussed in brief detail in section 13.10 on page 241.

When you implement a serializable class, you must decide what part of your class' state will be serialized. By default, all non-`static` and non-`transient` data will be serialized. This means that if you don't want certain variables to be serialized, then you should declare them as being `transient`. If you choose to do this, however, you must employ the `readObject()` and `writeObject()` methods to ensure that the `transient` field is correctly initialized upon deserialization; otherwise, it will wind up with its default value (`null` or `0`) and your class may fail to function correctly.

JDK 1.2 also introduced an alternative mechanism for declaring which fields should be serialized. If a class declares a static array of `ObjectStreamFields` named `serialPersistentFields`, then only the fields specified in this array will be serialized. This mechanism is only typically of use for applications that have special serialization needs, and so we will not discuss it further in this book.

Ignoring this aspect of serialization, there are essentially four different ways to create a serializable class.

13.8.1 Subclassing a serializable class

If you subclass a class that is already serializable then, by transitivity, your subclass will automatically be serializable (figure 13.6).

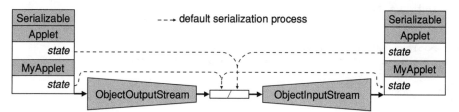

Figure 13.6   Subclassing a serializable class

```
import java.awt.*;
import java.applet.*;
```

```
public class MyApplet extends Applet {
  private Label label;

  public void init () {
    label = new Label (getParameter ("label"));
  }
}
```

The `MyApplet` class subclasses `Applet`, which ultimately extends from the serializable class `Component`. As a result, our new `MyApplet` class is automatically serializable. The object streams transparently take care of transmitting all of our applet's state, including any superclass data as well as any new data such as the `Label label`.

13.8.2 Implementing the Serializable interface

By implementing the `Serializable` marker interface, a new class can take advantage of the transparent serialization features of the object streams (figure 13.7):

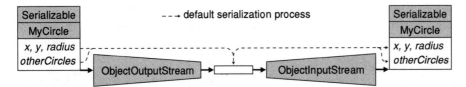

Figure 13.7   Implementing the Serializable interface

```
import java.io.*;
import java.util.*;

public class MyCircle implements Serializable {
  protected double x, y, radius;
  private Vector otherCircles = new Vector ();

  public MyCircle (double x, double y, double radius) {
    this.x = x;
    this.y = y;
    this.radius = radius;
  }

  public boolean isWithin (double x, double y) {
    return (this.x - x) * (this.x - x) + (this.y - y) * (this.y - y) <=
        radius * radius;
  }
}
```

The `Serializable` interface declares no methods; it is simply a marker to the object streams that they may extract the internal state of this class and transport it through a communications channel. Although the variables x, y, radius, and other-Circles are not normally publicly accessible, they *are* accessible to the object streams.

The Vector class is serializable so our Vector and all of its elements will be transmitted successfully, as long as all of its elements are themselves serializable. In this case, the Vector would hold other MyCircle objects; the entire structure of MyCircles and their otherCircles inter-references will be correctly reconstructed for the recipient.

13.8.3 *Using the custom serialization methods*

There are many cases where it is useful to customize the serialization process somewhat. In particular, this is useful when a class includes data that are either not serializable, that are unique to a virtual machine and should not be transmitted to another, or of which transmission is simply unnecessary.

To provide custom serialization of this form, a class must implement Serializable and provide special writeObject() and readObject() methods. Note that these methods may be declared to throw any type of exception. However, the programmer *must* ensure that they only throw those exceptions declared by the corresponding writeObject() and readObject() methods of the object streams: readObject() may only throw IOException, ClassNotFoundException or a subclass, and writeObject() may only throw IOException or a subclass.

```
import java.io.*;
import java.net.*;

public class MoreCircle extends MyCircle {
  private transient double radiusSquared;
  private transient int id;
  private transient Socket socket;

  private static int globalId;
  private synchronized static int getId () { return globalId ++; }

  public MoreCircle (double x, double y, double radius) throws IOException {
    super (x, y, radius);
    radiusSquared = radius * radius;
    id = getId ();
    String host = System.getProperty ("circle.server.host");
    int port = Integer.parseInt (System.getProperty ("circle.server.port"));
    socket = new Socket (host, port);
  }

  public boolean isWithin (double x, double y) {
    return (this.x - x) * (this.x - x) + (this.y - y) * (this.y - y) <=
        radiusSquared;
  }

  // private void writeObject (ObjectOutputStream objectOut)
      throws IOException ...
```

```
// private void readObject (ObjectInputStream objectIn)
    throws IOException, ClassNotFoundException ...
}
```

In this somewhat arbitrary `MoreCircle` class, we add some `transient` and `static` data to the `MyCircle` class (figure 13.8).

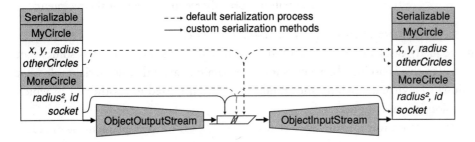

Figure 13.8   Custom serialization methods

Remember, the object streams do not transmit `transient` data, data that by nature are unique to a virtual machine. We must provide custom `writeObject()` and `readObject()` methods to send and restore `transient` data appropriately.

Neither do the object streams transmit `static` data such as `globalID`. Static data is global to a virtual machine and so it makes no sense to transmit it with a single instance of a class. Instead, when the receiving machine initially loads the appropriate class file, its `static` data will be initialized as normal.

In this class, we add a variable `radiusSquared`; this is equal to `radius*radius` and makes the `isWithin()` calculation more efficient. It is unnecessary to transmit this with each object because it is trivial to reconstruct it at the receiving end. We therefore mark it as `transient`.

We also add a VM-unique identifier, `id`: each instance of `MoreCircle` within a virtual machine will have a unique value for `id`. It makes no sense to transmit this because we cannot guarantee that the receiving VM will not have already used up the identifier. There is no need for identifiers to match across VMs, just to be unique within a VM, so we again mark this `transient` and therefore noncommunicable.

We finally add a `Socket`, `socket`. We are not particularly concerned with the semantics of the `Socket` class, except that it is not serializable so we must mark it as `transient` and add special code to allow serialization.

```
private void writeObject (ObjectOutputStream objectOut) throws IOException {
  objectOut.defaultWriteObject ();
  objectOut.writeObject (socket.getInetAddress ());
  objectOut.writeInt (socket.getPort ());
}
```

The writeObject() method will be called when this object is being serialized. Note that this is just a magic method with a specific signature, it is not part of the Serializable interface.

We first call out's defaultWriteObject() method. The semantics of this call are somewhat unusual: it serializes *this* Object to the ObjectOutputStream out using the default serialization mechanism; that is, all nontransient and non-static data will be serialized. For our custom serialization, we then simply transmit socket's address and port using the usual methods of ObjectOutputStream. We don't need to transmit any of the other transient data.

Note that calling defaultWriteObject() in this particular case will not actually transmit any data since this class declares no new serializable fields. However, it allows us to add default-serializable fields to future versions of this class and remain compatible.

```
private void readObject (ObjectInputStream objectIn)
    throws IOException, ClassNotFoundException {
  objectIn.defaultReadObject ();
  radiusSquared = radius * radius;
  id = getId ();
  InetAddress address = (InetAddress) objectIn.readObject ();
  int port = objectIn.readInt ();
  socket = new Socket (address, port);
}
```

The readObject() method will be called to deserialize this object. Again, this is a magic method with a specific signature, it is not part of the Serializable interface.

We first call objectIn's defaultReadObject() method to deserialize *this* Object from the ObjectInputStream objectIn, using the default deserialization mechanism. We then fill in all of our transient data: we recompute radiusSquared from the value of radius that was initialized by the normal serialization of the superclass. We assign a new id, unique to *this* virtual machine, and finally connect the Socket socket to the host and port that were transmitted by the remote writeObject() method.

If we required post-reading validation after the complete object had been deserialized, for example to verify integrity, then we would register a validator from this method by calling the objectIn.registerValidation() method.

13.8.4 Implementing the Externalizable interface

The Externalizable interface is an alternative mechanism for a class to provide serializability without taking advantage of the usual serialization mechanisms. When an Externalizable Object is written to a stream, a header is written consisting of essentially just the class' name, and then the class is entirely responsible for its own serialization and deserialization (figure 13.9).

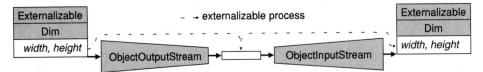

Figure 13.9   Implementing the Externalizable interface

```
import java.io.*;

public class Dim implements Externalizable {
  private int width, height;

  public void writeExternal (ObjectOutput objectOut) throws IOException {
    objectOut.writeInt (width);
    objectOut.writeInt (height);
  }

  public void readExternal (ObjectInput objectIn) throws IOException {
    width = objectIn.readInt ();
    height = objectIn.readInt ();
  }
}
```

The `Dim` class implements `Externalizable` and provides manual methods for serialization and deserialization. In this case, we write the class' data as a series of integers. To deserialize a `Dim`, we read back the fields in the same format as they were written. As an `Externalizable` object, we must provide a public no-arg constructor by which we will initially be created. The object streams do not call any superclass `Externalizable` methods; instead, we must explicitly call the superclass methods if we subclass an `Externalizable` object.

Note that this implementation provides no versioning facilities; so if a new version of the `Dim` class uses a different format for its fields, it will not be compatible with instances that were serialized before the change. Versioning is an important feature that is provided by the normal serialization process and discussed more in section 13.10 on page 241.

13.8.5 Inheritance and custom serialization

The custom writeObject() and readObject() methods are private and, therefore, not inherited. If you extend a class that provides custom serialization and add new custom serialization methods to the

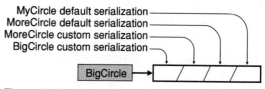

Figure 13.10 **Inheritance and custom serialization**

subclass, then the object streams will automatically call, in sequence, all of the custom methods from the topmost Serializable class down to the bottommost. It is not necessary to call the defaultWriteObject() or defaultReadObject() methods to get this behavior; those methods are only concerned with serializing the data for the exact class that calls them (figure 13.10).

```java
import java.io.*;

public class BigCircle extends MoreCircle {
  public BigCircle (double x, double y, double radius) throws IOException {
    super (x, y, radius);
  }

  private void writeObject (ObjectOutputStream objectOut) throws IOException {
    // custom writing
  }

  private void readObject (ObjectInputStream objectIn) throws IOException {
    // custom reading
  }
}
```

This class extends MoreCircle and so is also Serializable. We provide custom serialization methods for this subclass; however, we don't call the default serialization methods. We may, for example, have only provided some additional transient data and so there is no data to be transmitted by the usual mechanism. The problem with this is that if a future version of this class adds some serializable fields, then we cannot take advantage of the default serialization process and remain compatible with this version. Instead, we would have to manually serialize those fields with these methods.

If we serialize an instance of BigCircle, some header information will be written to the OutputStream and the MyCircle data will be written using the default serialization mechanism. Then, MoreCircle's writeObject() method will be called; this calls the defaultWriteObject() method to serialize its non-transient, non-static data, and then adds any additional data that it wants. BigCircle's writeObject() method will then be called; this will write its own custom data. A subclass of a serializable object can thus refuse to be serialized by throwing a `NotSerializableException` from a custom `writeObject()` method.

Upon deserialization, first the `MyCircle` data will be read in. Then, `MoreCircle`'s `readObject()` method will be called; this calls `defaultReadObject()` to read the usual data and then reads its own data. Finally, `BigCircle`'s `readObject()` method will be called to read its own data.

13.8.6 *Object self-replacement and resolution*

Sometimes it is useful for a serializable class to make use of a helper class to actually handle details of the serialization process. This can help maintain the distinction between implementation issues of the main class and incidental issues such as serialization. The `writeReplace()` and `readResolve()` methods provide a convenient mechanism for achieving this distinction. A skeletal example of the use of these methods follows:

```
import java.io.*;

public class Foo implements Serializable {
  // main class body
  private Object writeReplace () throws ObjectStreamException {
    return new FooHolder (this);
  }
}
```

Here we have the skeleton of a class `Foo` that is `Serializable`. Instead of containing all serialization-related code in this class, however, we implement a `writeReplace()` method and use a helper class `FooHolder` to handle serialization. Note that this method is not declared by the `Serializable` interface; it is simply a method with a particular signature. If an instance of `Foo` is written to an `ObjectOutputStream`, then its `writeReplace()` method will automatically be called and the object that this returns will instead be serialized. In this case, an instance of `FooHolder` will be serialized and so will be responsible for the serialization process.

```
class FooHolder implements Serializable {
  FooHolder (Foo foo) {
    // extract state from foo
  }
  // handle serialization and deserialization issues
  private Object readResolve () throws ObjectStreamException {
    Foo foo = /* create a new Foo */;
    return foo;
  }
}
```

Here we have the skeleton of a `Serializable` class `FooHolder` that is responsible for the serialization and deserialization of instances of the `Foo` class. This class implements `readResolve()` because upon deserialization we want instances of this class to be resolved back into instances of `Foo`. The constructor is responsible for extracting a copy of the state of `foo`; it should extract sufficient state that it can recreate a copy of the original object upon deserialization. Additionally, we must implement other serialization methods such as `writeObject()` and `readObject()`. Finally, when an instance of `FooHolder` is fully deserialized, its `readResolve()` method will automatically be called; this method must return an instance of the original class `Foo`.

As this brief example should have shown, using the `writeReplace()` and `readResolve()` methods we can effectively delegate all responsibility for handling serialization issues to a helper class. This mechanism helps maintain a clean division between the actual implementation of our main class and subordinate issues such as serialization.

Other uses do, of course, exist for these methods, beyond delegating to helper classes for serialization. One particular use is an object that wishes to perform some tidying up before serialization; it can simply return a tidied-up instance of itself from a `writeReplace()` method and, if necessary, an untidied instance from `readResolve()`.

13.9 Subclassing the object streams

In some cases, it is necessary to subclass the object streams, usually to provide transmission facilities for classes that are not serializable and cannot be easily replaced by serializable alternatives.

In the following example, we provide subclassed object streams that allow the `DatagramPacket` class to be transmitted, even though it does not implement `Serializable` and is `final` so cannot be subclassed to add serializability. We also modify the serialization of the `File` class, so that serialized `File` objects are altered to include the absolute path of their referenced file instead of just its relative path. For example, the `File` readme.txt created by an application that is executing in the directory /home/merlin is serialized as /home/merlin/readme.txt.

13.9.1 Interface MyOSConstants

To enforce version compatibility between different object streams executing on different virtual machines, we will include headers that identify the streams and specify their version number. If there is a header mismatch between connected object streams, communications will not be possible.

```
interface MyOSConstants {
  final short myOSMagick = (short) 0x1359;
  final short myOSVersion = (short) 0x0010;
```

}

We use the interface `MyOSConstants` to declare these constants; this is a convenient way for constants to be shared among different classes. In this case, we declare the value `myOSMagick` (chosen arbitrarily), which uniquely identifies this type of stream, and `myOSVersion`, which identifies the version of the class. If we were to later modify these streams, we would increment `myOSVersion` and leave `myOSMagick` unchanged.

13.9.2 Class MyObjectOutputStream

This class subclasses `ObjectOutputStream` and modifies its behavior to allow serialization of `DatagramPackets`, and to modify the transmission of `Files` (figure 13.11).

Figure 13.11   Class MyObjectOutputStream

```
import java.io.*;
import java.net.*;

public class MyObjectOutputStream extends ObjectOutputStream
        implements MyOSConstants {
  // public MyObjectOutputStream (OutputStream out) throws IOException ...
  // protected void writeStreamHeader () throws IOException ...
  // protected Object replaceObject (Object object) throws IOException ...
}
```

We extend `ObjectOutputStream` and implement the `MyOSConstants` interface; this gives us convenient access to the constants that it declares. We provide the usual constructor and implementations of the `writeStreamHeader()` and `replace-Object()` methods that implement our desired behavior.

```
  public MyObjectOutputStream (OutputStream out) throws IOException {
    super (out);
    enableReplaceObject (true);
  }
```

In the constructor, we call the superconstructor, attaching to the specified `Output-Stream`, out, and then call `enableReplaceObject()` to enable our modified `repla-ceObject()` method. The `enableReplaceObject()` method ensures that there is no `SecurityManager` present or, under JDK 1.2, that the caller has the `Serializable-Permission enableSubstitution`. If this class is used by an applet without permission, then a `SecurityException` will be thrown.

If we were modifying `ObjectOutputStream` but not using the `replaceObject()` method, we would not need to make this call and this class could be used by an applet or other untrusted application.

```
protected void writeStreamHeader () throws IOException {
  super.writeStreamHeader ();
  writeShort (myOSMagick);
  writeShort (myOSVersion);
}
```

Our modified `writeStreamHeader()` method writes the superclass header followed by our own stream's magic number, myOSMagick, and version number, myOSVersion.

```
protected Object replaceObject (Object object) throws IOException {
  if (object.getClass () == DatagramPacket.class)
    return new MyDatagramPacket ((DatagramPacket) object);
  else if (object.getClass ().getName ().equals ("java.io.File"))
    return new MyFile ((File) object);
  else
    return object;
}
```

The `replaceObject()` method is responsible for substituting `Objects` before serialization. In this case, we replace any instances of `DatagramPacket` with our own `MyDatagramPacket` class, and any instances of `File` with our own `MyFile` class. We otherwise return the original `Object`, object. Any object that we return must be serializable, either through the `Externalizable` interface or the `Serializable` interface. If this is not the case, the usual `NotSerializableException` will be thrown later in the serialization process.

Note that we do not use the `instanceof` operator in this method; it is not sufficient that the serialized object be a `File` or a subclass, or a `DatagramPacket` or a subclass (ignoring its finality). Instead, we will only replace instances of the exact original class. We do not know what extra data may be included by a subclass of these classes, so an attempt to transport them based only on their superclass information would almost certainly fail. We can verify this exact equivalence using either of the above two methods.

13.9.3 Class MyDatagramPacket

This class provides a serializable container for instances of the `DatagramPacket` class. The `readObject()` method of class `MyObjectInputStream` reads instances of this class and converts them back into `DatagramPackets` for the recipient (figure 13.12).

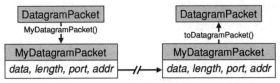

Figure 13.12   Class MyDatagramPacket

```java
import java.io.*;
import java.net.*;

public class MyDatagramPacket implements Serializable {
  private byte[] data;
  private int length, port;
  private InetAddress address;

  MyDatagramPacket (DatagramPacket packet) {
    data = packet.getData ();
    length = packet.getLength ();
    address = packet.getAddress ();
    port = packet.getPort ();
  }

  DatagramPacket toDatagramPacket () {
    return new DatagramPacket (data, length, address, port);
  }
}
```

MyDatagramPacket is a simple container class that stores the entire contents of the specified `DatagramPacket`, `packet`, and implements `Serializable` to avail of the default serialization mechanism. We are not particularly interested in the meaning of these fields, just that they are all themselves serializable. An extractor method `toDatagramPacket()` is provided that returns a new `DatagramPacket` constructed from these contents.

13.9.4 Class MyFile

This class is a subclass of `File` that inherits its serializability and assumes the absolute path of the `File` that is passed to its constructor (figure 13.13).

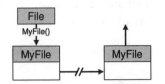

Figure 13.13   Class MyFile

```java
import java.io.*;

public class MyFile extends File {
  private String originalPath;

  MyFile (File file) {
```

```
    super (file.getAbsolutePath ());
    originalPath = file.getPath ();
  }

  public String getOriginalPath () {
    return originalPath;
  }
}
```

MyFile simply calls the superconstructor with the absolute path of the File that it is passed. For convenience, we also keep a copy of the original path in the variable originalPath, accessible through the getOriginalPath() accessor.

The File class is itself serializable so we automatically inherit serializability. Note that the superclass automatically takes care of translating path separators from machine to machine. It transmits the path separator character along with the actual path, so the receiving machine can translate automatically. The originalPath variable will not receive this treatment because it is stored as a plain String. This is, however, not of particular importance because this class is only really useful for transport among virtual machines running on the same physical host or on homogenous machines with a shared file system. Given the expository nature of this example, such considerations are not really of concern.

13.9.5 Class MyObjectInputStream

The MyObjectInputStream class is a complementary ObjectInputStream to the MyObjectOutputStream class that performs the necessary input-processing on its serialized objects (figure 13.14).

Figure 13.14 Class MyObjectInputStream

```
import java.io.*;
import java.net.*;

public class MyObjectInputStream extends ObjectInputStream
        implements MyOSConstants {
  // public MyObjectInputStream (InputStream in) throws IOException ...
  // protected void readStreamHeader () throws IOException ...
  // protected Object resolveObject (Object object) throws IOException ...
}
```

We extend ObjectInputStream and implement MyOSConstants to gain easy access to the constants that it declares. We provide the usual constructor, and appropriately modified readStreamHeader() and resolveObject() methods.

```
public MyObjectInputStream (InputStream in) throws IOException {
  super (in);
  enableResolveObject (true);
}
```

In the constructor, we call the superconstructor, attaching to the specified Input-Stream, in. To take advantage of the object resolution facilities provided by the resolveObject() method, we must call enableResolveObject(). This verifies that the stream is used by a trusted application; that is, that there is no SecurityManager.

It is not always necessary for an ObjectInputStream to use the resolveObject() method, even if the corresponding ObjectOutputStream is using replaceObject(), so it is possible for applets and other untrusted applications to modify ObjectInput-Stream and not suffer this security restriction.

```
protected void readStreamHeader () throws IOException {
  super.readStreamHeader ();
  if (readShort () != myOSMagick)
    throw new StreamCorruptedException
      ("Incompatible myOSMagick number");
  if (readShort () > myOSVersion)
    throw new StreamCorruptedException
      ("Incompatible myOSVersion number");
}
```

In the readStreamHeader() method, we call the superclass readStream-Header() method and then verify that our own header is correct. If the magic numbers do not match, then we are probably not hearing from a MyObjectOutputStream. If the version number is more recent than ours, we are speaking to an incompatible MyObjectOutputStream. We presume compatibility with earlier versions of these streams.

```
protected Object resolveObject (Object object) throws IOException {
  if (object instanceof MyDatagramPacket)
    return ((MyDatagramPacket) object).toDatagramPacket ();
  else
    return object;
}
```

In the resolveObject() method, we replace instances of MyDatagramPacket with genuine DatagramPacket instances, constructed from the contents of our serializable container class. We simply return any other objects, unmodified. If a remote application transmits a DatagramPacket, it will thus be converted into a MyDatagram-Packet, transported, and then converted back into a DatagramPacket.

Note that we don't resolve the MyFile class which is a subclass of File and so can be transparently used in place of a File by the recipient. The recipient should remain unaware that it is using a doppelgänger. In some cases, of course, this is not true; for example, if the recipient uses one of the equality tests that we use. Use of a nonidentical replacement should thus only be exercised in limited circumstances over which you have complete control.

13.9.6 Class MyAltDatagramPacket

Under JDK 1.2, the `readResolve()` interface would actually allow us to eliminate `MyObjectInputStream` entirely. We would obviously have to remove the version header from `MyObjectOutputStream`. Beyond that, however, `MyDatagramPacket` (and optionally `MyFile`) could implement `readResolve()` and automatically resolve themselves correctly to their original form without the help of `MyObjectInputStream`. The same is not true of `writeReplace()`, however; that method can only be used with classes over which you have control, so it could not take the place of `MyObjectOutputStream`.

The resulting `MyAltDatagramPacket` class, a replacement for `MyDatagramPacket`, would have the following form:

```
import java.io.*;
import java.net.*;

public class MyAltDatagramPacket extends MyDatagramPacket {

  MyAltDatagramPacket (DatagramPacket packet) {
    super (packet);
}

  private Object readResolve () {
    return toDatagramPacket ();
  }
}
```

By implementing `readResolve()`, our `MyAltDatagramPacket` class will automatically be resolved back into a `DatagramPacket` upon deserialization.

13.10 Class versioning

An important feature of the object streams is their support for class versioning. This allows an object to be serialized from one version of a class and then successfully deserialized into another, whether more or less recent. This allows for compatibility between different virtual machines with different versions of an application. It also allows an application to be dynamically upgraded while retaining access to previously serialized data.

13.10.1 Unique class identifiers

All versioned classes except an original version (i.e., all but the first version of a class) must contain a special identifier in a `static` variable `serialVersionUID`. This is a unique identifier computed from the original class' name, interfaces, methods, and fields. This variable is unique to a particular class, regardless of its version. All versions of a particular class will have the same UID; however, *no other* class will have this UID. The JDK comes with a special utility `serialver` that computes this value:

```
serialver MyClass
MyClass: static final long serialVersionUID = -2467320932749741192L;
```

The utility accepts a class name as a command-line parameter and prints out the value of the class' unique identifier. This UID is used to identify when different object streams are using different classes with the same name. If the signatures of the two classes (their methods and fields) differ in any way then the two classes will have different UIDs.

So, *before* you modify a class, you must run `serialver` to compute its UID. Then, add the class variable `serialVersionUID` to the class before proceeding with your modifications. All future versions of the class will retain this value.

```
public class MyClass { // version 1
  ...
}
```

The first version of `MyClass` does not have a `serialVersionUID` variable. Before we modify it, we compute this value and then proceed with the modifications:

```
public class MyClass { // version 2+
  static final long serialVersionUID = -2467320932749741192L;
  ...
}
```

When an `ObjectOutputStream` serializes a `Class` object (i.e., the first time that it serializes an instance of the class), it will send the class name and this value, if present. When an `ObjectInputStream` reads the class information, it will load the named class from its local class path and then verify that the `serialVersionUID` of the loaded class matches the value in the stream, throwing an `InvalidClassException` if not. If a class does not contain a `serialVersionUID` variable, the object streams compute a value in exactly the same way as the `serialver` command.

In practice, the suggested way of computing the UID is clumsy: it requires that you remember to compute the UID *before* making any changes to a class. An alternative and equally valid way of versioning is to simply compute a random UID for every class that you create, and to use this UID from the *very first* version of each class. There is no practical difference between these two methods, if you have a good random number generator. The `serialver` command is really just trying to generate a good random number. The `java.security.SecureRandom` class is a good alternative.

13.10.2 *Maintaining class compatibility*

Serialization of objects using the default mechanism maintains compatibility between different versions of a class by storing all data symbolically, so the value of field x is stored along with the name *x*. Upon deserializing this field, it can be correctly inserted into the new empty object by locating the field x and inserting the deserialized value therein. If a field is deserialized and the local version of the class does not contain that field, it will be ignored. If the local version of a class contains a field that is not present in the stream, then it is assigned its default value.

The programmer must obey certain basic guidelines to ensure that new versions of a class support compatibility using the default versioning mechanism. Other than basic issues such as maintaining the same class semantics, these are not changing the serialization mechanism of the class (`Serializable` or `Externalizable`), not changing the variables of a class in an incompatible manner (deleting a variable, changing the type of a variable), and not significantly altering the class hierarchy.

It is, of course, sometimes useful to perform some manual migration between versions of a class. In this case, simply add an instance variable to the class that stores the current class version. When an object is deserialized, you can query its version and perform appropriate migration:

```
import java.io.*;

public class MigrationExample implements Serializable {
    static final long serialVersionUID = 1234081623487162347L;
    private static final short classVersion = 2;
    // increment this version number as the class changes
    private short instanceVersion = classVersion;

    private void readObject (ObjectInputStream objectIn)
        throws IOException, ClassNotFoundException {
      objectIn.defaultReadObject (); // restores instanceVersion
      switch (instanceVersion) {
        case 0:
          // perform migration from version 0
          break;
        case 1:
          // perform migration from version 1
          break;
      }
      instanceVersion = classVersion;
    }
}
```

Here, we simply store the class version in the variable `classVersion`, which is mirrored in the instance variable `instanceVersion`. When an instance of this class is serialized, the `instanceVersion` variable will be automatically stored. When it is deserialized, we can query the version and perform appropriate migration. After migration, the object will effectively have the new version so we must update `instanceVersion` appropriately; this allows the deserialized object to be correctly reserialized at a later stage.

Classes that use the `Externalizable` interface or custom serialization must use their own mechanism for maintaining version compatibility of the data that they write.

13.11 Wrapping up

The object streams are important because they allow serialization of standard objects without significant effort on the part of the programmer, and they support controlled evolution of classes. Instead of manually breaking up objects into their component fields, the programmer can instead automatically serialize entire complex objects. The fact that you can serialize a complete applet and recreate it in a remote machine has remarkable implications. In addition, because the object stream classes leverage off the standard streams interface, the technology can be applied to a wide variety of applications.

Object persistence is a side effect of object serialization, and proves to be useful and convenient for a whole range of applications, particularly storing objects in object databases.

In chapter 23, we will discuss remote method invocation. This uses the object streams to allow method calls between virtual machines. Method parameters and results are transparently communicated over object streams between the VMs, so networked applications can be developed using a simple, convenient method-call interface.

13.12 Conclusion

This concludes our treatment of the `java.io` package and the byte streams, character-streams and object streams that it provides. These form the basis of the networked communications mechanisms that we will deal with in this book—notably, streams, sockets and RMI.

Although the basic streams provide many useful facilities, a significant part of our later development will involve extending the stream classes to provide additional function, including simple streams-based interfaces to Internet protocols and a streams-based message-passing framework.

Some other streams that we have not discussed thus far include a package of streams, `java.util.zip`, that supports compression and decompression in a variety of formats, including *zip* and *gzip*. These streams can be useful for networked applications because they can help reduce the bandwidth required by an application. However we will not discuss them here further.

Part III

Networking

This part of the book is a comprehensive description of the classes of the `java.net` package, with extensive API details and accompanying examples. Together, the `java.io` and `java.net` packages contain all the tools needed for building complex networked applications.

We look at both client-side and server-side networking using TCP/IP, UDP/IP, and multicast. Among the many examples included are a complete Web server; finger, nslookup, and ping clients; and various chat systems using TCP, UDP, and multicast. Along the way we also touch on a treatment of the URL classes, including a basic implementation of HTTP and how to extend this framework to support additional protocols such as finger.

Chapter 14 Client-side networking   This chapter begins the discussion of networking with TCP/IP in Java. IP is the low-level network protocol that makes up the transport layer of the Internet. TCP is an Internet protocol, running on top of IP, that establishes a virtual connection over an IP-based network. The `InetAddress` class represents a unique address on the network; every device on the Internet has at least one IP address. Once a client has obtained a remote machine's IP address, a socket is used to establish a connection to that machine. The `Socket` class represents a TCP connection to a particular IP address. This chapter introduces these classes, with examples, and discusses various aspects of developing TCP clients in Java.

Chapter 15 Some example clients   This chapter puts the concepts developed in the previous chapter into practice, by implementing some TCP/IP clients that communicate using real-world Internet protocols. We develop a client that uses the finger protocol to determine information about users connected to a remote (usually UNIX) machine. We also develop a comprehensive suite of classes that implement the DNS protocol, allowing us to write a Java nslookup program that performs DNS resolution. This framework lets us look up information about domain names and host names, such as their IP addresses, authoritative name servers, and mail exchangers.

Chapter 16 Server-side networking   The `ServerSocket` class is used to implement servers; its purposes is to receive TCP/IP connections from remote clients. This class is described, along with a simple echo server that demonstrates the principles involved in developing servers. Issues that make server-side programming more complex than client-side programming are discussed. This chapter also gives examples of a nonblocking server and a more sophisticated server that makes use of the multithreading features of Java to cleanly handle multiple simultaneous connections.

Chapter 17 Building a Web server   This chapter applies the treatment of server-side TCP/IP networking to the development of a full-featured Web server that supports HTTP/1.0, CGI/1.0, and an internal Java server extension mechanism. This brings together issues of multithreading, security, and real applications development, involving multiple classes, custom streams, dynamic extensibility, and the execution of native applications.

Chapter 18 Client/server Internet applications   In this chapter, we implement two real-world client/server Internet applications. We start out by building a simple chat client and a multithreaded broadcast server. This is the first example of a full client/server system that uses entirely our own protocols for communication. The multithreading model of the server is useful for many similar servers, and the system can easily be modified for deployment on the Web. We then provide a TCP/IP implementation of a distributed list datastructure; this is a `Vector`-like datastructure that is distributed across a network, allowing multiple clients to concurrently read from and write to the list. This provides an interesting abstraction away from raw networking because the list appears to a client as a simple local datastructure, while behind the scenes it is transparently distributed among potentially many users.

Chapter 19 The URL classes   The URL-related classes provide a framework for accessing networked and local data through a common URL interface. The `URL` class represents the location of an object, usually on the World Wide Web, and provides methods to allow the object to be easily accessed and downloaded in a useful local form. Several classes and interfaces form a framework that allows additional protocols and content types to be easily integrated. The API of these classes is discussed, and then examples are given of implementing the HTTP and finger protocols, and automatically processing plain text documents.

Chapter 20 Datagram networking   Datagram networking uses the UDP protocol in place of TCP. UDP is a packet-based protocol that provides no guarantees of data delivery or correct ordering of data. Because of this, it does not have the overhead of TCP, so it can be used when network latency is a serious concern but the guarantees of correct and complete delivery that TCP provides are not required. This chapter gives an overview of `DatagramSocket` and `DatagramPacket`, the classes relevant to UDP, along with various examples. A discussion of when to use UDP rather than TCP concludes the chapter.

Chapter 21 Some datagram applications   This chapter applies the issues of datagram networking into the development of a few real-world UDP clients and servers. We extend the DNS system developed in chapter 15 to transmit queries as UDP datagrams: DNS data can be transported over either TCP or UDP. We also look at a simple ping client that evaluates whether remote hosts are reachable and computes the average latency of communicating with them. Finally, we look at a server that implements the Internet daytime protocol, a simple protocol that allows remote hosts to query the local time at a server.

Chapter 22 Multicast networking   Multicast is an important protocol that is becoming increasingly widespread on the Internet. It provides support for efficient communications among multiple hosts. Using multicast, a single packet can be placed onto a network and automatically transported to multiple interested recipients, replicating only as necessary. Along with a description of the `MulticastSocket` class that provides Java support for multicast, this chapter provides two examples of multicast-based chat systems. One uses a pure peer-to-peer model; the other uses a relay server in the manner mandated by the Java security model for untrusted applets. We also discuss broadcast and the various security and implementation concerns of using multicast.

C H A P T E R   1 4

Client-side networking

Networking in Java is accomplished with the streams-related classes that we have already covered, and classes from the package `java.net` which provide access to IP addresses, TCP, UDP, and various URL-related mechanisms.

In this chapter, we will begin to look at the client side of networking with TCP. TCP provides a virtual-stream connection across a network that supports IP. This virtual stream provides streams-based facility to transport data from either end of the connection to the other.

IP addresses, which are used to address the target of TCP connections, are provided by the `InetAddress` class. TCP connections are created using the `Socket` class. Once a connection has been created, we can obtain streams to and from the remote application, and then communicate through the streams interface. We can use filter streams to add higher-level functions to this byte-oriented communications channel.

14.1 Class InetAddress

An IP address is the address of a computer on the Internet; it is currently a 4-byte value. Data can be sent onto a network, addressed to a specific IP address, and will be delivered to the target machine.

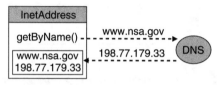

Figure 14.1   Class InetAddress

The `InetAddress` class provides abstracted access to IP addresses (figure 14.1). The advantage of using this class to represent an IP address over, for example, a 32-bit `int`, is that applications will be transparently portable to IPv6, which will provide 128-bit addresses.

14.1.1 Constructors

There are no constructors for this class. Instances must instead be created by using the `static` methods `getByName()`, `getLocalHost()`, and `getAllByName()`.

14.1.2 Static methods

The following `static` methods are provided to create `InetAddress` objects:

InetAddress getLocalHost() throws UnknownHostException   This method returns an `InetAddress` object corresponding to the local machine. In some cases, such as from behind a firewall, this may simply be the loopback address `127.0.0.1`.

InetAddress getByName(String host) throws UnknownHostException   This method returns an `InetAddress` object for the specified host, `host`. The host can be specified either by name (`proxy0.att.com`) or by IP address (`127.0.0.1`). There is no other client-side mechanism to construct an `InetAddress` for a remote host.

InetAddress[] getAllByName(String host) throws UnknownHostException
This method returns an array of `InetAddress` objects corresponding to every known IP address for the specified host, `host`. Typically, high-traffic Web sites will register several IP addresses for a single host name to distribute the load across several machines.

14.1.3 Instance methods

The following methods are provided to get information from an `InetAddress`:

byte[] getAddress()   This method returns an array of bytes corresponding to the IP address represented by this `InetAddress`. The array is in network byte order, that is, high byte first. Currently, under IPv4 this array will only be 4 bytes long. Future versions of IP will support longer addresses.

String getHostName()   This method returns the name of the host represented by this `InetAddress`. If the host name is not already known, an attempt is made to look it up using DNS, based upon the IP address. If this lookup fails, the numeric IP address is returned in `String` form.

For reasons of security, name lookups may be denied if an application is running behind a firewall.

(JDK 1.1)   *String getHostAddress()*   This method returns the IP address of the host represented by this `InetAddress` as a `String` such as `127.0.0.1`.

(JDK 1.1)   *boolean isMulticastAddress()*   This method returns whether the `Inet-Address` represents a multicast (class D) IP address; that is, whether the first byte of the address lies between 224 and 239 (inclusive).

14.1.4 UnknownHostException

This exception is a subclass of `IOException` and indicates that the named host could not be successfully identified.

14.1.5 SecurityException

A `SecurityException` may be thrown if the `SecurityManager` does not permit a specific operation. An untrusted applet may only construct an `InetAddress` for the hostname of the Web server from which it originated (its codebase).

14.2 An InetAddress example

This example introduces the basics of creating and using `InetAddress` objects. It first prints out the local machine's address and then sits in a loop accepting host names and looking them up. The loop terminates on EOF.

```java
import java.net.*;
import java.io.*;

public class InetExample {
  // public static void main (String[] args) ...
}
```

This example is just a demonstration of the application of `InetAddress` objects. The `main()` method makes use of a few `static` methods to print out `InetAddress` objects.

```java
public static void main (String[] args) {
  printLocalAddress ();

  Reader kbd = new FileReader (FileDescriptor.in);
  BufferedReader bufferedKbd = new BufferedReader (kbd);
  try {
    String name;
    do {
      System.out.print ("Enter a hostname or IP address: ");
      System.out.flush ();
      name = bufferedKbd.readLine ();
      if (name != null)
        printRemoteAddress (name);
    } while (name != null);
    System.out.println ("exit");
  } catch (IOException ex) {
    System.out.println ("Input error:");
    ex.printStackTrace ();
  }
}

// static void printLocalAddress () ...
// static void printRemoteAddress (String name) ...
```

The `main()` method first calls the `printLocalAddress()` method to print out the local machine name and address. It then sits in a loop that reads host names from the keyboard and uses the `printRemoteAddress()` method to print `InetAddress` information about every host name that is entered. We flush `System.out` because we use the `print()` method, which does not automatically flush output.

If an exception occurs while we are reading from the keyboard, then we display the exception and exit; otherwise, we execute until EOF is reached.

```java
static void printLocalAddress () {
  try {
    InetAddress myself = InetAddress.getLocalHost ();
    System.out.println ("My name : " + myself.getHostName ());
    System.out.println ("My IP : " + myself.getHostAddress ());
    System.out.println ("My class : " + ipClass (myself.getAddress ()));
  } catch (UnknownHostException ex) {
```

```
        System.out.println ("Failed to find myself:");
        ex.printStackTrace ();
    }
}

// static char ipClass (byte[] ip) ...
```

This method uses the `getLocalHost()` method of `InetAddress` to get the IP address of the local machine. We print out the name of the local machine using the `getHostName()` method, its address using the `getHostAddress()` method, and its network class using the `getAddress()` and `ipClass()` methods.

```
static char ipClass (byte[] ip) {
    int highByte = 0xff & ip[0];
    return (highByte < 128) ? 'A' : (highByte < 192) ? 'B' :
      (highByte < 224) ? 'C' : (highByte < 240) ? 'D' : 'E';
}
```

This method takes the first byte from an IP address and returns the corresponding IP address class. We must first mask the value with `0xff` to turn it into an unsigned integer; otherwise, bytes with the high bit set (non-class A) would be considered negative. We then return the corresponding address class: `'A'` for addresses up to 127 through `'E'` for addresses 240 and above.

```
static void printRemoteAddress (String name) {
    try {
        System.out.println ("Looking up " + name + "...");
        InetAddress machine = InetAddress.getByName (name);
        System.out.println ("Host name : " + machine.getHostName ());
        System.out.println ("Host IP : " + machine.getHostAddress ());
        System.out.println ("Host class : " +
                            ipClass (machine.getAddress ()));
    } catch (UnknownHostException ex) {
        System.out.println ("Failed to lookup " + name);
    }
}
```

This method takes a host name `name` and uses the `getHostName()`, `getHostAddress()`, and `getAddress()` methods of the returned `InetAddress` object to display its name, IP number, and address class. If the name that the user entered was a numeric IP address, we will find the corresponding host name only if it is registered for reverse DNS lookup. If the name that the user entered was a host name, we will now know one of its IP addresses.

14.3 Class Socket

A `Socket` is the Java representation of a TCP network connection (figure 14.2). Using this class, a client can establish a streams-based communications channel with a remote host.

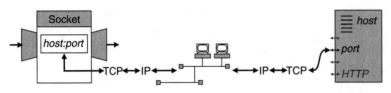

Figure 14.2 Class Socket

To communicate with a remote host using TCP/IP, the client must first create a `Socket` to the remote host. This automatically establishes a TCP connection, throwing an exception if it fails. In addition to specifying a host name, it is necessary to specify a port; this is an integer between 1 and 65,535. Effectively, there are 65,535 different addresses on every host. To connect to a host, you must specify the address on the host that you wish to connect to. There must be a server actively listening on the specified port, or the connection attempt will fail.

We have omitted some deprecated constructors and implementation-related methods from the following description.

14.3.1 Constructors

Creating a `Socket` automatically connects to the specified host and port. There must be a server listening on the host port; otherwise, an exception of type `IOException` will be thrown (*Connection refused*). Other possible errors result from network failures and unknown host names.

JDK 1.1 *protected Socket()*   This constructor creates an unconnected `Socket` object. This `Socket` can be subsequently attached to an incoming connection by a `ServerSocket`. Note that this constructor can only be called by a subclass as part of a custom socket framework.

JDK 1.1 *protected Socket(SocketImpl impl)*   This constructor is only of use for providing a custom socket implementation.

Socket(String host, int port) throws IOException   This creates a `Socket` and connects to the specified port `port` of the specified host `host`. The host is specified by name or by textual IP address; the port must be in the range 1–65,535.

Socket(InetAddress address, int port) throws IOException   This creates a `Socket` and connects to the specified port `port` of the specified host `address`. The port must be in the range 1–65,535.

JDK 1.1   *Socket(String host, int port, InetAddress localAddr, int localPort) throws IOException*   This creates a `Socket`, binds it to the local address `localAddr` and port `localPort`, and connects to the remote host `host` on port `port`. If `local-Addr` is `null`, the default local address is used. If `localPort` is `0`, a random unused local port is used.

Every TCP connection in fact consists of the local and remote IP address, and a local and remote port number. When a `Socket` is created and connected to a remote host, it is usually assigned a random unused local port number.

This constructor allows the local IP address and port to be specified. Specifying the local port number can sometimes be useful for connecting to servers that require a connection from a particular port or where it is required by a firewall. Specifying the local address is similarly useful: it can only be used by a multihomed machine (a machine with multiple network interfaces), and it allows the outgoing interface to be specified. For access control purposes, it makes the connection appear to come from the specified IP address. For network purposes, packets will be sent through the corresponding interface. This can be useful if different interfaces are connected to different networks because it allows the best interface to be chosen manually.

JDK 1.1   *Socket(InetAddress address, int port, InetAddress localAddr, int localPort) throws IOException*   This creates a `Socket`, binds it to the local address `localAddr` and port `localPort`, and connects to the remote host `address` on port `port`. If `localAddr` is `null`, the default local address is used. If `localPort` is `0`, a random unused local port is used.

14.3.2 Methods

The methods of class `Socket` permit identification of the remote host, and the local and remote port numbers, as well as extraction of streams for the purposes of bidirectional communication.

To perform communications across a TCP connection, you must first create a `Socket`, and then use the `getInputStream()` and `getOutputStream()` methods to obtain streams with which to communicate with the remote server. Thus, the client and server will each have both an `InputStream` and an `OutputStream` for the purposes of communication.

InputStream getInputStream() throws IOException   This method returns an `InputStream` that permits streams-based communications across the TCP connection. All data written by the server at the far end of the connection may be read from this `InputStream`.

This method returns a stream of type `InputStream`. In the current implementation, it in fact returns a private `SocketInputStream` class that is a subclass of `FileInputStream`, attached to a system-level socket filedescriptor.

Ultimately, data written to a `Socket` are segmented into packets for communication across IP. For all intents and purposes, however, the connection provides a continuous stream of data. For reasons of efficiency, `Socket` streams should be buffered.

OutputStream getOutputStream() throws IOException   This method returns an `OutputStream` that permits streams-based communications across the TCP connection. All data written to this stream may be read by the server at the far end of the connection. For reasons of efficiency, this `OutputStream` should be buffered; otherwise, the first byte of a message frequently will be sent in an independent packet, wasting bandwidth.

```
// OutputStream out;
void writeInt (int x) throws IOException {
   out.write (x >> 24);
   out.write (x >> 16);
   out.write (x >> 8);
   out.write (x);
}
```

This method is typical of many of the methods of `DataOutputStream` and demonstrates the reason why `Socket` streams should be buffered. If the TCP connection is idle and then this method is called, it is highly probable that the first `write()` call will result in a packet with just a single byte being sent. The subsequent three bytes will then be sent in a later packet. By buffering the stream, we can ensure that small packets like this are not inadvertently sent.

void close() throws IOException   This method closes the `Socket`, releasing any network and system resources being used. Any data sent before this call will be successfully delivered to the remote end unless there is a network failure.

Note that if the `Socket`'s `OutputStream` has been buffered with a `BufferedOutputStream`, the `BufferedOutputStream` should be closed in preference to the `Socket`. Otherwise any data remaining in the buffer will be lost. Closing either the `Socket`'s `InputStream` or `OutputStream` will close down the network connection, so it is only necessary to close `Socket`, its `InputStream` or its `OutputStream`. No facility is provided for performing a partial socket shutdown.

InetAddress getInetAddress()   This method returns the IP address of the remote host.

int getPort()   This method returns the port number of the remote host to which the `Socket` is connected.

`JDK 1.1` *InetAddress getLocalAddress()*   This method returns the local address to which this `Socket` is bound; that is, the local IP interface through which packets are sent.

int getLocalPort()   This method returns the local port number to which this `Socket` is bound. This value is assigned randomly if no port is specified in the constructor.

`JDK 1.1` *void setSoTimeout(int timeout) throws SocketException*   This method sets a time-out, in milliseconds, after which a blocking read operation on this `Socket` will automatically abort. A value of zero disables the time-out, so operations will block indefinitely. This method is useful if you wish to only wait a certain length of time for a client to respond with some data. If a `read()` call times out, then an `Interrupt-edIOException` will be thrown.

`JDK 1.1` *int getSoTimeout() throws SocketException*   This method returns the current socket time-out value. A value of `0` indicates that there is no time-out; that is, any socket operations will block indefinitely (the default).

`JDK 1.1` *void setTcpNoDelay(boolean on) throws SocketExceptiont*   This method can be used to disable the use of Nagle's algorithm over a socket connection. Nagle's algorithm is used to make TCP more efficient by delaying the writing of small amounts of data until either enough data has been buffered that a large packet can be sent or there is no unacknowledged data en route to the server.

Nagle's algorithm makes normal unbuffered communications much more efficient in terms of network usage, but it can introduce an unacceptable delay for certain specialized applications. In such a case, calling this method with a parameter of `true` will disable the algorithm.

`JDK 1.1` *boolean getTcpNoDelay() throws SocketException*   This method returns whether Nagle's algorithm is currently disabled. It defaults to `false`; that is, Nagle's algorithm is enabled by default.

JDK 1.1 *void setSoLinger(boolean on, int val) throws SocketException*   This method allows a client to set a maximum linger time-out on a TCP socket. TCP guarantees to successfully deliver all data transmitted to a socket. This means that when a socket is closed, the network connection is not immediately terminated; it will remain open while all unsent data are delivered and acknowledged. Setting a linger value means that the operating system will only wait the specified time after closing a socket before closing down the network connection. If data have not been successfully transmitted by this time, the network connection is aborted.

When a socket connection is closed naturally, there is usually a four-minute period during which an identical connection cannot be recreated (from the same client port to the same server port; this is only of significance if the client port is specified in the constructor). This normal delay is required to protect against *wandering duplicate* packets on the network: these are packets which were delayed en route to the destination and then retransmitted by the source. Setting a linger time-out will override this default operation. If an old connection is aborted, and a new identical connection is established before the delayed packet times out, the delayed packet could arrive successfully and be inserted into the conversation. Because of this potential problem, it is generally best to avoid use of linger time-outs.

JDK 1.1 *int getSoLinger() throws SocketException*   This method returns the current linger setting, or -1 if the option is disabled.

JDK 1.2 *void setSendBufferSize(int size) throws SocketException*   This method requests that the operating system set this socket's send buffer size (SO_SNDBUF) to the specified value, `size`. Increasing the buffer size can increase performance for sending large volumes of data. The operating system may ignore the value that you request.

JDK 1.2 *int getSendBufferSize() throws SocketException.* This method returns this socket's current send buffer size.

JDK 1.2 *void setReceiveBufferSize(int size) throws SocketException*   This method requests that the operating system set this socket's receive buffer size (SO_RCVBUF) to the specified value, `size`. Increasing the buffer size can increase performance for receiving large volumes of data; decreasing it can reduce backlogged data. The operating may ignore the value that you request.

JDK 1.2 *int getReceiveBufferSize() throws SocketException*   This method returns this socket's current receive buffer size.

static void setSocketImplFactory(SocketImplFactory factory) throws IOException This `static` method can be used to install a custom socket implementation for the entire JVM. This method can only be called once, and is vetted by the `Security-Manager`.

14.3.3 IOException

Many of the methods and constructors of the `Socket` class may throw `IOException` if an error is encountered.

14.3.4 SocketException

This `IOException` is a superclass for some common socket exceptions that allows for more fine-grained handling of networking exceptions. Subclasses are:

JDK 1.1 *BindException* This `SocketException` indicates that the requested local port or address could not be bound. Typically, this occurs when the requested local port is already in use or is a system port, or when the specified local address is not a valid local network interface.

JDK 1.1 *ConnectException* This `SocketException` indicates that the connection attempt was refused because there was no server listening on the specified port of the remote machine.

JDK 1.1 *NoRouteToHostException* This `SocketException` indicates that the remote host could not be reached, typically because of a network problem or a firewall.

14.3.5 SecurityException

The `SecurityManager` restricts the creation of `Sockets`. Untrusted applets, for example, may not open `Sockets` to anywhere other than the host from which they were served. Another significant restriction is that an applet behind a firewall may not be permitted to perform a DNS lookup, so it may be necessary to use a numeric IP address to target the connection instead of a host name.

14.3.6 Socket implementation

The `Socket` class is actually an intermediary between networked applications and a `SocketImpl` class that provides the implementation of network connection setup and control. In some situations, it is useful to be able to provide a custom implementation; this allows, for example, the `Socket` class to automatically connect through a local proprietary firewall proxy or to transparently perform data encryption. Any class that uses the `Socket` class will then automatically use this new implementation and take advantage of the facilities that it provides.

The steps involved in installing a custom socket implementation are as follows:

- Create a subclass of `SocketImpl` that implements the necessary connection setup and control methods.

- Create a `SocketImplFactory` that returns instances of this new `SocketImpl` class.

- Register this `SocketImplFactory` with the `Socket` class through its `setSocketImplFactory()` method.

- Provide, if necessary, a corresponding implementation at the server.

The registered factory is used for *all* future sockets created in the JVM. For this reason, access to this feature is controlled by the `SecurityManager`; a `SecurityException` will be thrown if an untrusted class attempts to install a socket factory.

Creating an actual socket implementation requires either the use of native methods in order to access the OS' networking facilities, or else the insertion of a class within the `java.net` package to extend the default package-local `PlainSocketImpl` class. The latter is not recommended, but examining the `PlainSocketImpl` source can be of use during an implementation using native methods.

We will not discuss this aspect of network programming further; a more common and practical alternative since JDK 1.1 is to simply subclass the existing socket classes.

14.3.7 SOCKS proxying

Java `Socket`s support the SOCKS v4 TCP proxy mechanism in most environments. If the system property `socksProxyHost` is set, the `Socket` class automatically makes a connection to the specified SOCKS proxy on port 1080 (or the value of the system property `socksProxyPort` if that is different) and transmits a SOCKS connection request using the username from the system property `user.name`.

The SOCKS proxy checks the origin host and port, the username, and the destination host and port against its internal access list and determines whether to set up a proxy connection. The `Socket` class throws an appropriate exception if the connection is refused. Note that SOCKS may make use of the `identd` protocol to verify the indicated username.

Through a SOCKS firewall, an organization can provide fine-grained control over Internet access from within the firewall, choosing who can connect to what, from where, and can log all such activity. The advantage of this type of proxy over a Web proxy is that it can proxy *all* TCP data, not just HTTP.

14.4 Getting Web pages with a socket

In this example, we will look at using a `Socket` to download pages from the Web. The program sits in a loop waiting for the user to type in URLs; for each URL entered, it creates a `GrabPage` object. This object

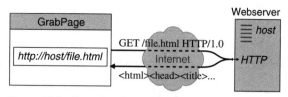

Figure 14.3   Downloading a Web page

attempts to connect to the Web server and download the specified page. If successful, it displays the page contents to the screen (figure 14.3).

We can achieve this same result automatically using just the URL class; however, it is instructive to perform the process manually to see what is involved in the World Wide Web protocols.

```
import java.net.*;
import java.io.*;

public class GrabPage {
   // public GrabPage (String textURL) throws IOException ...
   // public void grab () throws IOException ...
   // public static void main (String[] args) throws IOException ...
}
```

This class downloads and displays the Web page specified in its constructor. In the constructor, we parse the specified URL. When the `grab()` method is called, we connect to the server, issue an HTTP request, and display the response.

The `main()` method demonstrates the application of this class by requesting URLs from the user and displaying the corresponding Web pages.

```
public GrabPage (String textURL) throws IOException {
   dissect (textURL);
}

// protected void dissect (String textURL) throws MalformedURLException ...
```

The constructor simply calls on the `dissect()` method to dissect the specified URL into its component parts.

```
protected String host, file;
protected int port;

protected void dissect (String textURL) throws MalformedURLException {
   URL url = new URL (textURL);
   host = url.getHost ();
   port = url.getPort ();
```

```
      if (port == -1)
        port = 80;
      file = url.getFile ();
  }
```

The URL class is provided for processing and downloading documents; typically from the Web, but other protocols can also be supported. In this method, we use the URL class to dissect what the user types in. If the user types in the URL *http:// www.att.com:8080/index.html*, we dissect it into the hostname host (*www.att.com*), the port port (8080), and the file file (*/index.html*). If the port number is omitted from the URL, then –1 is returned, so we need to use the default, which for HTTP is 80.

```
public void grab () throws IOException {
  connect ();
  try {
    fetch ();
  } finally {
    disconnect ();
  }
}

// protected void connect () throws IOException ...
// protected void fetch () throws IOException ...
// protected void disconnect () throws IOException ...
```

This method fetches and displays the page specified in the constructor. We first connect to the Web server using the connect() method. Next, we call fetch() to actually download this page. Finally, we disconnect with the disconnect() method.

The fetch() method will throw an IOException if an error occurs. To prevent resource leakage, we should still close the connection to the server, regardless of whether we finish successfully or with an exception. To ensure that the connection is always closed, we surround the fetch() call with a try ... finally clause which calls the disconnect() method no matter how the body completes.

```
protected Writer writer;
protected BufferedReader reader;

protected void connect () throws IOException {
  Socket socket = new Socket (host, port);

  OutputStream out = socket.getOutputStream ();
  writer = new OutputStreamWriter (out, "latin1");

  InputStream in = socket.getInputStream ();
  Reader reader = new InputStreamReader (in, "latin1");
  this.reader = new BufferedReader (reader);
}
```

This method connects us to the server. We open a `Socket` to the host and port determined by the `dissect()` method. If this succeeds (no exception is thrown), we create the `Writer writer` and `BufferedReader reader`, which allow us to communicate with the remote HTTP server. We use the character encoding latin1 to translate between the byte-oriented network connection and Unicode `Strings`. We don't buffer the output stream because `OutputStreamWriter` provides sufficient buffering.

```
protected void fetch () throws IOException {
  writer.write ("GET " + file + " HTTP/1.0\r\n\n");
  writer.flush ();

  PrintWriter console = new PrintWriter (System.out);
  String input;
  while ((input = reader.readLine ()) != null)
    console.println (input);
  console.flush ();
}
```

This method sends an HTTP 1.0 request to the remote server and displays the server's response. A typical request has the form:

```
GET /index.html HTTP/1.0
```

This tells the remote server that we want to get the file /index.html and that this is an HTTP version 1.0 request. By specifying HTTP/1.0, we tell the server that we may send some qualifying headers with this request and that we want it to send back extra HTTP 1.0 headers in response.

Note that we must follow the request with two newline characters. HTTP 1.0 requests are terminated by a blank line. We could optionally follow the request by various headers that specify the types of file that we can understand before we send the terminating blank line. We must also flush `writer` because the `OutputStreamWriter` class provides buffering; our request would otherwise just sit in the buffer. See appendix B for more details of HTTP requests, and the example Web server in chapter 17.

After sending the request, we display the server's response. We use the `readLine()` method of class `BufferedReader`; this reads a line of text, stripping off any carriage-return/newline characters. We print each line to the console through a `PrintWriter` attached to `System.out`; this automatically converts to the local console's character encoding and uses the platform-default line terminator.

The response from an HTTP version 1.0-compliant server will consist of some headers, a blank line, and the contents of the file that we requested—or an appropriate error response. An old HTTP version 0.9 response consists of just the requested file.

```
protected void disconnect () throws IOException {
```

```
    reader.close ();
  }
```

This method closes down the network connection by closing `reader`, which in turn closes the attached socket stream, which closes the socket connection. We pass on any exceptions that may occur.

```java
public static void main (String[] args) throws IOException {
  Reader kbd = new FileReader (FileDescriptor.in);
  BufferedReader bufferedKbd = new BufferedReader (kbd);
  while (true) {
    String textURL;
    System.out.print ("Enter a URL: ");
    System.out.flush ();
    if ((textURL = bufferedKbd.readLine ()) == null)
      break;

    try {
      GrabPage grabPage = new GrabPage (textURL);
      grabPage.grab ();
    } catch (IOException ex) {
      ex.printStackTrace ();
      continue;
    }

    System.out.println ("- OK -");
  }
  System.out.println ("exit");
}
```

In the `main()` method, we sit in a loop prompting the user to type in a URL. We create and run a new `GrabPage` object for each such URL; this attempts to display the specified page. On EOF, we exit the loop using the `break` statement.

We surround our use of `GrabPage` with a `try ... catch` statement to catch any exceptions that should occur. If an exception occurs, we print it and restart the loop using the `continue` statement. If the `grab()` method succeeds, we have successfully displayed a page and so we display the message - *OK* -.

We declare that the `main()` method can throw `IOException` because the read-Line() call that reads from the keyboard declares that it may throw such an exception, and we wish to exit if this occurs.

Note that the code is a lot cleaner, because instead of handling exceptions at every possible occurrence, we pass them up and handle them at the highest level, which in this case is the `main()` method.

14.5 Building a PostOutputStream class

In this example, we will develop an `OutputStream` class that performs an HTTP post operation.

To perform a post, you must open a connection to the Web server as before, and send the following header in ASCII:

```
POST filename HTTP/1.0
Content-type: type
Content-length: length
```

You must fill in the filename, content type, and content length yourself. The content type specifies the format of the following data; we use the MIME type *application/x-www-form-urlencoded*. The content length specifies the length of the remaining data. Following this header you must transmit the body of the request; as before, it must be separated from the header by a blank line.

The body for this content-type (the content type that is submitted by standard HTML forms) has the following form (spacing is just for legibility):

```
key1 = value1 & key2 = value2 ...
```

You must fill in the keys and values for all of the variables that you want to send. The key and value text must be encoded in a special URL-encoding; this involves replacing any non-ASCII characters and certain ASCII characters with an escape sequence that consists of a percent character followed by the two-byte hexadecimal encoding of the character.

14.5.1 Class PostOutputStream

This is an `Output-Stream` class that performs an HTTP post operation. It buffers up all of the data that are written to it, and when the `post()` method is

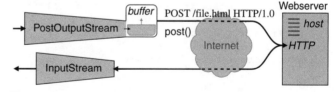

Figure 14.4 Performing an HTTP post operation

called, it connects to the specified URL and posts the data, returning an `InputStream` from which the server response can be read (figure 14.4).

As with the previous example, we can perform the same process using just the URL class; however, it is useful to understand how to do this manually. We will look at actually using the URL classes in a later chapter.

In addition to `post()` and the usual methods of `OutputStream`, this class provides a `writeString()` method that writes a `String` in ASCII; a `writeTag()` method that writes a variable-value pair in URL-encoding; and a `writeTags()` method that writes a `Hashtable` of variable-value pairs in URL-encoding.

```java
import java.io.*;
import java.net.*;
import java.util.*;

public class PostOutputStream extends FilterOutputStream {
  // public PostOutputStream (URL url) ...
  // public PostOutputStream (URL url, String contentType) ...
  // public void writeString (String string) throws IOException ...
  // public void writeTag (String attr, String value) throws IOException ...
  // public void writeTags (Hashtable tags) throws IOException ...
  // public InputStream post () throws IOException ...
}
```

This class extends `FilterOutputStream`. We will use the `FilterOutputStream` methods to buffer up data in a `ByteArrayOutputStream` prior to posting.

```java
public PostOutputStream (URL url) {
   this (url, "application/x-www-form-urlencoded");
}
```

This constructor takes a single parameter `url`, which specifies the URL that will be the target of the post request, and uses the default content-type for form-encoded data.

```java
protected ByteArrayOutputStream byteArrayOut;
protected URL url;
protected String contentType;

public PostOutputStream (URL url, String contentType) {
   super (new ByteArrayOutputStream ());
   byteArrayOut = (ByteArrayOutputStream) out;
   this.url = url;
   this.contentType = contentType;
}
```

This constructor accepts both a target URL `url` and a content encoding `content-Type`. It passes a new `ByteArrayOutputStreem` to the superclass constructor. We make a local reference to this in `byteArrayOut` for convenience; the `out` variable that we use corresponds to the attached stream (what we supplied to the superclass constructor) and is inherited from the superclass. All data that are written to this `PostOutputStream` will be written to `byteArrayOut` and buffered up pending the actual post request.

```java
public void writeString (String string) throws IOException {
   write (string.getBytes ("latin1"));
```

```
    }
```

This method writes a `String` in ASCII by using the `getBytes()` method of class `String`, specifying the character encoding latin1.

```
public void writeTag (String attr, String value) throws IOException {
   if (byteArrayOut.size () > 0)
     write ('&');
   writeString (encode (attr));
   write ('=');
   writeString (encode (value));
}

// protected String encode (String string) ...
```

This method writes a variable-value pair in URL-encoding. We first check whether the `ByteArrayOutputStream` is empty; if not, we assume that this is not the first variable-value pair and so we write an ampersand separator. We then URL-encode the variable name `attr` and write this out, followed by the equals separator, and the URL-encoded value `value`.

```
protected String encode (String string) {
   StringBuffer encoded = new StringBuffer ();
   for (int i = 0; i < string.length (); ++ i)
     encoded.append (encode ((char) (string.charAt (i) & 0xff)));
   return encoded.toString ();
}

// protected String encode (char chr) ...
```

This method URL-encodes the specified `String string`. We create a `String-Buffer encoded` in which to accumulate the result. We then loop through every character of `string`, appending the encoded character to `encoded`. We mask every character by 255 because the character encoding method only works for 8-bit values. This method is equivalent to the `static encode()` method of class `URLEncoder`.

```
protected String encode (char chr) {
   if (chr < 16) {
     return "%0" + Integer.toString (chr, 16);
   } else if ((chr < 32) || (chr > 127) || (" +&=%/~".indexOf (chr) >= 0)) {
     return "%" + Integer.toString (chr, 16);
   } else {
     return String.valueOf (chr);
   }
}
```

This method URL-encodes a single character `chr`. We return the escaped version of `chr` if it is nonprintable (less than 32 or greater than 127) or one of space, plus, ampersand, equals, percent, slash, or tilde. Otherwise, we just return the character unmodified.

The escaped version of a character consists of a percent sign followed by the two-digit hexadecimal encoding of the character; plus becomes %2B, and so on. We special-case those characters that encode in a single hexadecimal digit (those less than 16) to insert a leading 0.

```
public void writeTags (Hashtable tags) throws IOException {
   Enumeration attrs = tags.keys ();
   while (attrs.hasMoreElements ()) {
      String attr = (String) attrs.nextElement ();
      writeTag (attr, (String) tags.get (attr));
   }
}
```

This method writes an entire `Hashtable` of attribute-value pairs. Every key in the `Hashtable` must be a `String` that maps to another `String`. We loop through every key, extracting the key and its corresponding value. We then use the `writeTag()` method to write out this variable-value pair.

```
public InputStream post () throws IOException {
   int port = url.getPort ();
   if (port == -1)
     port = 80;
   Socket socket = new Socket (url.getHost (), port);
   try {
     OutputStream out = socket.getOutputStream ();
     Writer writer = new OutputStreamWriter (out, "latin1");
     writer.write ("POST " + url.getFile () + " HTTP/1.0\r\n");
     if (contentType != null)
       writer.write ("Content-type: " + contentType + "\r\n");
     writer.write ("Content-length: " + byteArrayOut.size () + "\r\n\n");
     writer.flush ();
     byteArrayOut.writeTo (out);
     byteArrayOut.reset ();
     return socket.getInputStream ();
   } catch (IOException ex) {
     try {
       socket.close ();
     } catch (IOException ignored) {
     }
     throw ex;
   }
}
```

This method performs the CGI post operation and returns an `InputStream` from which to read the server response. We first open a `Socket` connection to the server, extracting the host name and port using the `getHost()` and `getPort()` methods of URL.

We then transmit a post header as described at the start of this section; as always, we must flush `writer`'s internal buffers before data will be transmitted. The post target comes from the URL's `getFile()` method. The content type is as specified in the constructor, or unspecified if `null` was passed. And the content length can be determined from the amount of data present in `byteArrayOut`.

After sending this header and a blank line, we transmit the contents of `byteArrayOut` using its `writeTo()` method. Finally, we return an `InputStream` from which to read a response. The caller should close the `InputStream` when finished.

We surround the entire post operation with a `try ... catch` expression to catch any `IOException` that is encountered. If an `IOException` is encountered, we can close the `Socket` connection before rethrowing the exception.

We could have extended the `ByteArrayOutputStream` class directly and added our new methods to this. We would then be able to buffer the data ourselves and use our own `writeTo()` method to send the request. The problem with doing this is that we would then have to make the standard `ByteArrayOutputStream` methods public, which, while not particularly problematic, does not provide the cleanest public interface that extending `FilterOutputStream` does.

14.6 Wrapping up

Client-side networking with TCP is fairly easy: once you have established a connection to a server, it is simply a case of communicating using the standard streams interface with which we have been working. Interfacing with most existing programs requires us to engage in ASCII communications, which we can transparently achieve using the character streams and selecting ISO Latin 1 or whatever is the appropriate character encoding. Interfacing with other existing applications may require transmitting data in network byte order; this is provided by the data streams: `DataInputStream` and `DataOutputStream`.

An easy way to experiment with client-side networking is to write programs that interface with existing applications, of which HTTP is just one example. Most UNIX workstations support a number of standard TCP services. For example, if you open a TCP connection to port 79 of a public UNIX host and transmit a username, it will respond with finger information about that user. If you open one to port 7, it will echo everything that you send; port 13 responds to every connection with the current time. The beauty of networking is that you don't need to own a UNIX workstation to communicate with one.

In the next chapter, we will look at developing some simple TCP clients that connect with existing Internet services, such as the finger service (port 79) and the domain naming system (port 53). These examples should demonstrate the application of streams and sockets for communicating with conventional servers. Later in the book, we will look at client/server systems built entirely from Java, and how these let us take full advantage of Java's I/O facilities.

C H A P T E R   1 5

Some example TCP/IP clients

In this chapter, we examine the implementation of some simple TCP clients that interact with existing Internet protocols. Specifically, we will look at a finger client (RFC 1288) and a DNS client (RFC 1035), the equivalent of the nslookup command. These clients can serve as the basis for implementations of other Internet protocols that possess similar structures.

15.1 Internet protocols

An important prerequisite for the implementation of an Internet protocol is a correct and current specification. In the case of the protocols that we shall look at, the specifications exist in the form of Internet requests for comments (RFCs) and standards (STDs): public documents that describe information of relevance to the Internet community. Although in many cases there are sample client implementations available, it is important to use the actual specification as a basis for an implementation. The Internet RFCs and Standards are available for public download from the location ftp://ds.internic.net/. The specification documents for various common Internet protocols are listed in table 15.1.

Table 15.1   Internet protocol specification documents (from STD 1)

Protocol	Name	RFC	STD
—	Internet Official Protocol Standards	1920	1
—	Assigned Numbers	1700	2
—	Host Requirements - Communications	1122	3
—	Host Requirements - Applications	1123	3
IP	Internet Protocol	791	5
—	IP Subnet Extension	950	5
—	IP Broadcast Datagrams	919	5
—	IP Broadcast Datagrams with Subnets	922	5
ICMP	Internet Control Message Protocol	792	5
IGMP	Internet Group Multicast Protocol	1112	5
UDP	User Datagram Protocol	768	6
TCP	Transmission Control Protocol	793	7
TELNET	Telnet Protocol	854, 855	8
FTP	File Transfer Protocol	959	9
SMTP	Simple Mail Transfer Protocol	821	10
SMTP-SIZE	SMTP Service Ext for Message Size	1870	10
SMTP-EXT	SMTP Service Extensions	1869	10
MAIL	Format of Electronic Mail Messages	822	11
CONTENT	Content Type Header Field	1049	11
NTPV2	Network Time Protocol (Version 2)	1119	12

Table 15.1   Internet protocol specification documents (from STD 1)

Protocol	Name	RFC	STD
DOMAIN	Domain Name System	1034, 1035	13
DNS-MX	Mail Routing and the Domain System	974	14
SNMP	Simple Network Management Protocol	1157	15
SMI	Structure of Management Information	1155	16
Concise-MIB	Concise MIB Definitions	1212	16
MIB-II	Management Information Base-II	1213	17
NETBIOS	NetBIOS Service Protocols	1001, 1002	19
ECHO	Echo Protocol	862	20
DISCARD	Discard Protocol	863	21
CHARGEN	Character Generator Protocol	864	22
QUOTE	Quote of the Day Protocol	865	23
USERS	Active Users Protocol	866	24
DAYTIME	Daytime Protocol	867	25
TIME	Time Server Protocol	868	26
TFTP	Trivial File Transfer Protocol	1350	33
TP-TCP	ISO Transport Service on top of the TCP	1006	35
ETHER-MIB	Ethernet MIB	1643	50
PPP	Point-to-Point Protocol (PPP)	1661	51
PPP-HDLC	PPP in HDLC Framing	1662	51
IP-SMDS	IP Datagrams over the SMDS Service	1209	52
FINGER	Finger User Information Protocol	1288	–

15.2 A finger client

A finger client is a comparatively simple tool that lists the users logged into a remote machine and displays detailed information about a specific user on the machine (figure 15.1).

To use the client, you specify a host to which to connect and an optional username. The typical syntax is finger @host to list the users on the machine host, or finger username@host to find out information about the specified user, username.

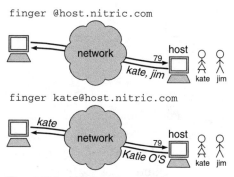

Figure 15.1   The finger protocol

There are two further details relevant to the protocol: Finger supports an optional verbose flag (`-l` in this implementation), which can be used to obtain more detailed information. It also supports a finger forwarding service whereby a finger request can be forwarded from one machine to another. The command `finger username@hostA@hostB` connects to the machine `hostB` which in turn forwards the finger request to machine `hostA` (figure 15.2).

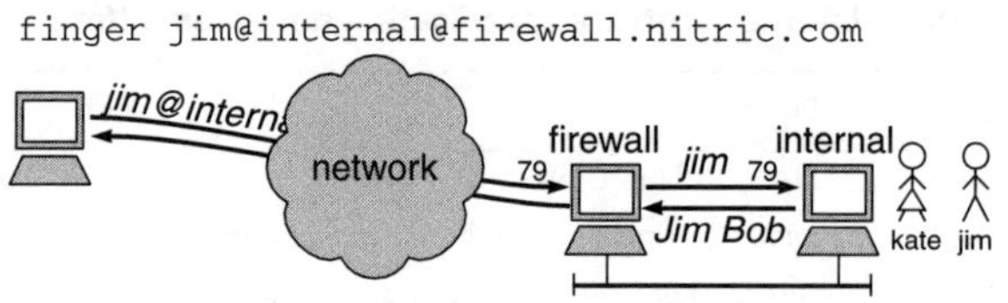
finger jim@internal@firewall.nitric.com
jim@intern
network
firewall
79
jim
79
internal
Jim Bob
kate
jim
Figure 15.2 Finger forwarding

15.2.1 Protocol specification

The finger protocol is specified in RFC 1288. The specification states that the client machine should make a TCP connection to port 79 of the remote machine and transmit a finger query in 8-bit ASCII; the host will respond with an ASCII result. For this purpose, we'll use the ISO Latin 1 character set.

The client's query (table 15.2) is basically taken from RFC 1288.

Table 15.2 Client's query

{Q1}	::=[{U} | {W} | {W}{S}{U}] {C}
{Q2}	::=[{W}{S}] [{U}] {H}{C}
{U}	::=username
{H}	::=@*hostname* | @*hostname* {H}
{W}	::=/W
{S}	::=<SP> | <SP> {S}
{C}	::=<CRLF>

This type of specification is typical of the RFCs and should be interpreted as follows: {Q1} is the symbol Q1, technically called a nonterminal: every nonterminal is assigned a definition that states what values it can hold. In the case of the finger protocol, there are two types of queries: Q1 and Q2. The format of a Q1 query is defined in the first line; the format of a Q2 query is defined in the second line.

Each definition has the form {LHS} ::= RHS, which states that nonterminal on the left hand side can hold the value indicated on the right hand side.

The right hand side of a definition consists of a sequence of nonterminals and terminals that define the values that the left-hand-side symbol may hold. A *terminal* is a final value, such as a username, that will appear in an actual instance of the symbol.

A vertical bar (|) represents OR, meaning that a symbol can hold either the value on the left side of the bar or the right side. Square brackets ([]) enclose optional parts of a symbol's definition. Angle brackets (<>) enclose terminal values such as space or carriage return.

In the finger specification above, the symbols *U*, *W*, and *C* represent exactly the value on the right side of their definitions. The symbol *S* can represent either a space or a space followed by another symbol *S*. This other *S* can represent again, by definition, either a space or a space followed by another symbol *S*. In other words, the symbol *S* represents a sequence of one or more spaces. Similarly, the symbol *H* represents a sequence of one or more @*hostname* values, such as @hostA@hostB.

Symbol Q1 represents all or part of a /W header followed by whitespace, a username, and a newline sequence. Symbol Q2 represents all or part of a /W header followed by whitespace, a username, a sequence of @*hostname* values, and a newline sequence. Expanding the various possibilities, table 15.3 lists the possible rewritings of Q1 and Q2, or the valid types of query that a finger client may make.

Table 15.3

Definition	Symbols	Value	e.g.
Q1	{C}	<CRLF>	\r\n
Q1	{U}{C}	*username* <CRLF>	merlin\r\n
Q1	{W}{C}	/W <CRLF>	/W\r\n
Q1	{W}{S}{U}{C}	/W <SP>+ *username* <CRLF>	/W jim\r\n
Q2	{H}{C}	@*hostname*+ <CRLF>	@x.com@y.com@z.com\r\n
Q2	{U}{H}{C}	*username* @*hostname*+ <CRLF>	ego@nitric.com\r\n
Q2	{W}{H}{C}	/W <SP>+ @*hostname*+ <CRLF>	/W @int@gw.x.com\r\n
Q2	{W}{S}{U}{H}{C}	/W <SP>+ *username* @*host*+ <CRLF>	/W ego@nitric.com\r\n

Spacing here is just for legibility; the <SP> terminal represents actual space characters. A plus sign (+) indicates that the adjacent value may occur one or more times.

Note that these queries are not what the user types on the command line. They are the queries that the finger client sends to the remote machine. Queries of type Q1 are used to obtain information about users on the target machine; Q2 queries are forwarded from the target machine to another machine. Finger forwarding can be used to pass finger requests through a firewall gateway; however, it is usually considered a security risk and so disabled. Multiple levels of forwarding are permitted.

15.2.2 Command syntax

The syntax for the finger client that we develop is fairly simple:

```
java Finger [-l] [<username>][@[<hostname>{@<hostname>}][:<port>]]
```

The -l flag indicates that a verbose query should be made; the body of the finger request follows, consisting of an optional username, a sequence of host name specifications, and an optional port number. If no host is specified, the local host is queried. If more than one host name is specified, a forwarded finger query is sent to the last listed host. If no port is specified, the default port 79 is used.

```
java Finger -l
```

This produces a verbose listing of all users on the local machine.

```
java Finger merlin@sadhbh.nitric.com:8079
```

This requests information about user merlin on host sadhbh.nitric.com, using the nonstandard port number 8079.

```
java Finger -l merlin@sadhbh.nitric.com@fw.nitric.com
```

This requests verbose information about user merlin on host sadhbh.nitric.com; this request is sent to host fw.nitric.com, which forwards the query to host sadhbh. If sadhbh is an internal machine and fw is a firewall that supports finger forwarding, this allows external users to obtain potentially sensitive information about internal users, which is why it is usually disabled.

15.2.3 Class Finger

The finger client is implemented by a single class, Finger. The class is instantiated with two parameters: the actual finger request and a verbosity flag. Methods are provided to execute the finger request and to display the resulting information.

```
import java.io.*;
import java.net.*;
import java.util.*;

public class Finger {
  public static final int DEFAULT_PORT = 79;

  // public Finger (String request, boolean verbose) throws IOException ...
  // public Finger (String query, String host, int port, boolean verbose)
  //     throws IOException ...
  // public Reader finger () throws IOException ...
  // public static void display (Reader reader, Writer writer)
  //     throws IOException ...
```

```
// public static void main (String[] args) throws IOException ...
}
```

The `Finger` class is designed to be both a reusable class and a standalone applica-tion. The first constructor accepts a `String` request, `request`, and verbosity flag, `verbose`. The request should have the form [*<username>*][@[*<hostname>*]{@*<host-name>*}[:*<port>*]]; this is automatically parsed into its component parts. An alternative constructor allows the parts to be specified separately. The `finger()` method connects to the remote host, sends the query, then returns a `Reader` from which the result can be read. A helper method, `display()`, displays the result of a finger query to a specified `Writer`. The `main()` method allows the `Finger` class to be run as a standalone applica-tion.

```
protected boolean verbose;
protected int port;
protected String host, query;

public Finger (String request, boolean verbose) throws IOException {
  this.verbose = verbose;
  int at = request.lastIndexOf ('@');
  if (at == -1) {
    query = request;
    host = InetAddress.getLocalHost ().getHostName ();
    port = DEFAULT_PORT;
  } else {
    query = request.substring (0, at);
    int colon = request.indexOf (':', at + 1);
    if (colon == -1) {
      host = request.substring (at + 1);
      port = DEFAULT_PORT;
    } else {
      host = request.substring (at + 1, colon);
      port = Integer.parseInt (request.substring (colon + 1));
    }
    if (host.equals (""))
      host = InetAddress.getLocalHost ().getHostName ();
  }
}
```

In this constructor, we keep a copy of the flag `verbose` and parse the request `String` into the `port`, `host`, and `query` variables. If no host was specified, `localhost` is used. If no port was specified, the default is used.

To parse the request, we separate the actual user and forwarding information from the host specification (which follows the last occurence of @). We then separate the host specification into a host name and port number. If no port was specified, we use the default; otherwise, we parse the specified value. If no host was specified, we obtain the local host name from class `InetAddress`.

```
public Finger (String query, String host, int port, boolean verbose)
    throws IOException {
  this.query = query;
  this.host = host.equals ("") ?
    InetAddress.getLocalHost ().getHostName () : host;
  this.port = (port == -1) ? DEFAULT_PORT : port;
  this.verbose = verbose;
}
```

This constructor simply allows the various parts of the request to be specified separately. We use the same defaults as before if a host or port are omitted.

```
public Reader finger () throws IOException {
  Socket socket = new Socket (host, port);
  OutputStream out = socket.getOutputStream ();
  OutputStreamWriter writer = new OutputStreamWriter (out, "latin1");
  if (verbose)
    writer.write ("/W");
  if (verbose && (query.length () > 0))
    writer.write (" ");
  writer.write (query);
  writer.write ("\r\n");
  writer.flush ();
  return new InputStreamReader (socket.getInputStream (), "latin1");
}
```

This method connects to the remote host and writes the finger request, returning a `Reader` from which the result can be read. We first create an `OutputStreamWriter` using ISO Latin 1 character encoding. If the verbose flag was specified, then we write out /W, and optionally a space. We then write the request and line terminator, and flush the output stream. We don't need to add a `BufferedWriter` because `OutputStreamWriter` provides sufficient internal buffering.

We actually specify a character encoding here rather than using the default because the default may not be appropriate for the protocol. RFC 1288 specifies an international ASCII character set, of which ISO Latin 1 is the most prevalent.

```
public static void display (Reader reader, Writer writer)
    throws IOException {
  PrintWriter printWriter = new PrintWriter (writer);
  BufferedReader bufferedReader = new BufferedReader (reader);
  String line;
  while ((line = bufferedReader.readLine ()) != null)
    printWriter.println (line);
  reader.close ();
}
```

This method reads a finger response from the `Reader reader` and prints it to the `Writer writer`. We create a `BufferedReader` using ISO Latin 1 character encoding and then proceed to read and print lines of text.

```
public static void main (String[] args) throws IOException {
    if (((args.length == 2) && !args[0].equals ("-l")) || (args.length > 2))
        throw new IllegalArgumentException
            ("Syntax: Finger [-l] [<username>][{@<hostname>}[:<port>]]");

    boolean verbose = (args.length > 0) && args[0].equals ("-l");
    String query = (args.length > (verbose ? 1 : 0)) ?
        args[args.length - 1] : "";

    Finger finger = new Finger (query, verbose);
    Reader result = finger.finger ();
    Writer console = new FileWriter (FileDescriptor.out);
    display (result, console);
    console.flush ();
}
```

This method allows the `Finger` class to be executed as a standalone application. We verify that the parameters are valid, throwing an explanatory exception if not. We set the flag `verbose` if `-l` is specified, and we set `query` to be any remaining argument or an empty `String` if no further arguments are supplied. We then create a `Finger` object with these values and call its `finger()` method; if an exception occurs here, we simply pass it on. Otherwise, we create a new `Writer`, `console`, and print and flush the finger information to it.

15.2.4 Using it

The `Finger` class can either be used as part of a separate program or executed as a standalone application. Examples of standalone use follow:

```
java Finger
Login       Name                TTY  Idle   When       Bldg.     Phone
merlin      Merlin Hughes       *s0  159d   Sun 22:53
id          Rev. Blue           s6   4:13   Mon 09:00
```

This just fingers the users connected to the local machine.

```
java Finger -l
Login name: merlin          (messages off)  In real life: Merlin Hughes
Directory: /org/merlin/home/merlin      Shell: /bin/rc
On since Oct 30 22:53:17 on pty/ttys0 from alpha0
159 days Idle Time
Plan:
9 from outer space
"The good Christian should beware of mathematicians and all those
who make empty prophecies.    The danger already exists that the
```

```
mathematicians have made a covenant with the devil to darken   the
spirit and to confine man in the bonds of hell."    - St Augustine

Login name: id                         In real life: Rev. Blue
Directory: /com/disinfo/home/id        Shell: /bin/sh
On since Apr  7 09:00:45 on pty/ttys6 from ultra1
4 hours 14 minutes Idle Time
No Plan.
```

Here, we request verbose information about these users.

```
java Finger merlin@sadhbh.nitric.com@fw.nitric.com
Remote finger not allowed: merlin@sadhbh.nitric.com
```

We finally try finger forwarding: our request is refused. For further details, chapter 19 provides an example of using this class in a different manner by integrating it with the URL framework.

15.3 A DNS client

The DNS is a globally distributed database, specified in RFC 1035, that maintains the mapping from Internet host names to IP addresses, in addition to various other data including the reverse mapping. Some details of the DNS system can be found in the networking introduction. However, for the purposes of this example it is sufficient to know that a client can request the IP address of a given host name from a machine called a name server, and it will return the requested information. Behind the scenes, the name server may require contact with various other machines; however, this process is mostly transparent to the client.

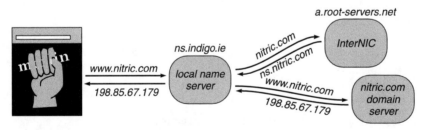

Figure 15.3   The domain name system

Most organizations and all ISPs have at least one name server to serve their connected machines. To determine a local name server that you can use with this example, either examine your own machine's DNS configuration or try similar names for your own domain or ISP as `ns.inch.com` or `ns1.aol.com`, or whatever is appropriate. A common convention is that the name server is the first machine on a subnet (e.g., host 198.85.67.193 on subnet 198.85.67.192).

The client that we develop here allows you to query a name server for information about a given host name or domain name. This can be used to determine a machine's IP address, to determine the mail exchanger for a domain, and so forth. The client framework is fairly generic and extensible and is intended to demonstrate the implementation of a more complex protocol than the finger client. We use a custom stream class as well as various other helper classes in the implementation.

To use the client, you must specify a name server to query and a host name that you wish to look up. The client connects to the name server, requests information about the name, and prints the result. There are many DNS options that are supported by the framework but, for brevity, not accessible through the simple command-line interface.

15.3.1 Protocol specification

The protocol specification for DNS is fairly complex so we shall only provide a brief and incomplete overview. For full details, consult RFC 1035.

Essentially, a client constructs a query and sends it to a name server over either TCP or UDP. The query includes some flags and a host name or domain name in which the client is interested.

The server will then respond with a series of resource records (RRs) which are basically answers to the particular question, along with additional related information. Each resource record includes one piece of information, such as the IP address of a particular host or the name of an authoritative name server for the host.

The query that is sent from a client to a name server and the response that is returned from the name server have the same form (figure 15.4).

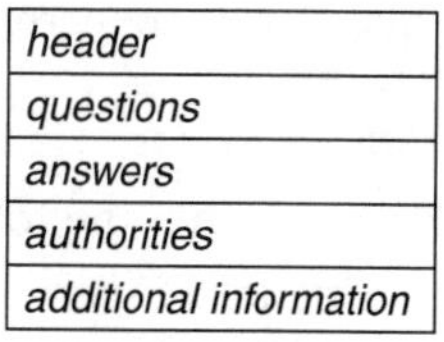

The header specifies some flags and information about the request or response. The questions block includes one or more questions. The answers block includes zero or more answers to those questions. The authorities block includes zero or more authoritative name servers for the requested name, and the additional information block includes zero or more additional pieces of information.

| header |
| questions |
| answers |
| authorities |
| additional information |

Figure 15.4 DNS queries and responses

Header The same header is used for queries and responses, and has the following format (figure 15.5):

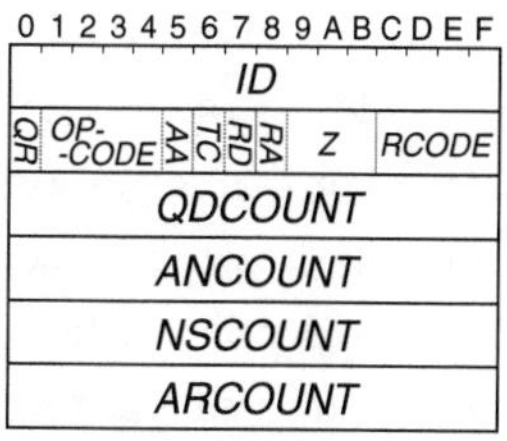

ID is a 16-bit identifier that the client assigns to the request; the server will include this in its response. All data is written in network byte order (high-byte first).

The next 16 bits are the query/response flags: *QR* should be 0 for a query and 1 for a response; *OPCODE* indicates the type of query, usually 0. *AA* is set in a response if it

```
0 1 2 3 4 5 6 7 8 9 A B C D E F
```

| ID |
| QR | OP-CODE | AA | TC | RD | RA | Z | RCODE |
| QDCOUNT |
| ANCOUNT |
| NSCOUNT |
| ARCOUNT |

Figure 15.5 DNS headers

is an authoritative answer; *TC* means that the response is truncated; *RD* is set in a query if recursion is desired (the nameserver should forward the query to other nameservers); *RA* is set in a response if recursion is available from the server. The *Z* bits are reserved, and *RCODE* is a response code: An *RCODE* of zero means there was no error; otherwise, some error was encountered.

The next four fields indicate the number of questions, answers, authoritative answers, and additional resource records following the header. Each is an unsigned 16-bit value. For a query, there will usually be one question and no other resource records. For a response, the question will be returned, followed by various resource records that answer the question and provide extra information.

Questions Each question has the following format (figure 15.6):

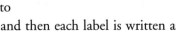

Figure 15.6 DNS questions

QNAME is the domain name or host name with which the question is concerned. The name is split into its component labels (such as *www*, *nitric*, and *com*) and then each label is written as a single-byte length followed by the label's characters. The maximum label length is 63 bytes; a complete host or domain name is terminated by a zero byte. *QTYPE* is an unsigned 16-bit value that indicates the type of resource record desired; usually 255, meaning that all information is desired, or 1, meaning that an IP address for the name is desired. *QCLASS* is an unsigned 16-bit value that indicates the network class with which this question is concerned; usually 1, the Internet.

Resource records Each resource record has the following format (figure 15.7):

NAME	TYPE	CLASS	TTL	RDLEN	DATA
n	2	2	2	2	n

Figure 15.7 DNS resource records

NAME is the domain name or host name to which the resource record applies. *TYPE* is an unsigned `short` indicating the type of the resource record; *CLASS* is an unsigned `short` indicating the class of the resource record; *TTL* is an unsigned `int` indicating the number of seconds for which the resource record is valid. These fields are followed by *RDLEN*, an unsigned `short` indicating the length of the following data and *DATA*, which are data specific to the particular type of resource record.

Address records (A, type 1) contain a 4-byte data part, which consists of just the IP address of the corresponding host. Mail exchanger records (MX, type 15) contain a variable-length data part consisting of a 16-bit preference value followed by a domain name.

For details of the format of the remaining resource records, consult the RFCs. For more details of the format and meaning of the various fields that we have mentioned, look at the following implementation. We include rudimentary comments about the various values that some of the fields can hold.

15.3.2 Implementation

The implementation that we provide uses a number of classes, including:

DNS   This class contains various constants that are used by the DNS-related classes, including the default DNS port number and the values of the various DNS request and response codes.

DNSQuery   This class represents a DNS query. It includes details of the host name being queried and the type of query, and provides methods to allow this query to be transmitted and a response to be received.

DNSRR   This class represents a DNS resource record, which is the encapsulation of a piece of DNS information. The response to a DNS query consists of a series of resource records; each RR has a type and some accompanying information. After a DNSQuery has been transmitted and a response received, the returned information can be extracted from the DNSQuery as a sequence of DNSRRs.

DNSRR is actually an abstract superclass for the different types of possible resource records; we will document some of these, but for brevity's sake, the remainder will only be available on the book's accompanying Web site.

record.Address   This class in the record package represents an address record, which is a DNS response that gives the IP address of a particular host name.

record.MailExchanger   This class represents a mail exchanger record, which is a DNS response that gives the name and priority of the machine to which mail for a particular domain should go.

DNSInputStream   This class is an InputStream that provides helper methods to decode the typical data that are returned in a DNS response.

NSLookup   This is a command-line nslookup client that uses these DNS classes to perform DNS resolution.

In essence, the NSLookup command constructs a DNSQuery for the host name and information in which it is interested. It then transmits this query to a name server and receives a response. The DNSQuery class then uses a DNSInputStream to decode this response into a series of DNSRR records. The NSLookup class can then extract and process these responses using the general DNSRR methods and the resource-record-specific DNSRR subclass methods.

15.3.3 Command syntax

The syntax for the nslookup client that we develop is as follows:

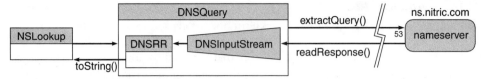

Figure 15.8 The DNS framework

```
java NSLookup <hostname>[@<nameserver>]
```

Host name is the name of a host or domain name about which we wish to find information. This must be a fully qualified domain name such as www.att.com or crypto.org; a partial name such as www is not valid. The name server is the optional name of a name server to query; if none is specified, a default name ns is used. Usually you must use the name of your local name server here, or if you wish to query another name server, then supply its name or address.

15.3.4 Class DNS
This class contains various DNS-related constants and some helper methods.

```
public final class DNS {
}
```

This class simply provides constants so we don't need to subclass anything.

```
public static final int
   DEFAULT_PORT = 53;
```

The default TCP and UDP port for DNS requests is number 53.

```
public static final int
   TYPE_A      = 1,    // address
   TYPE_NS     = 2,    // nameserver
   TYPE_MD     = 3,    // mail domain
   TYPE_MF     = 4,    // mail forwarder
   TYPE_CNAME  = 5,    // canonical name
   TYPE_SOA    = 6,    // start of authority
   TYPE_MB     = 7,    // mail box
   TYPE_MG     = 8,    // mail group
   TYPE_MR     = 9,    // mail rename
   TYPE_NULL   = 10,   // null
   TYPE_WKS    = 11,   // well-known services
   TYPE_PTR    = 12,   // pointer
   TYPE_HINFO  = 13,   // host info
   TYPE_MINFO  = 14,   // mail info
   TYPE_MX     = 15,   // mail exchanger
   TYPE_TXT    = 16,   // text
   TYPE_AXFR   = 252,  // zone transfer request
   TYPE_MAILB  = 253,  // mailbox request
```

```
    TYPE_MAILA = 254, // mail agent request
    TYPE_ANY   = 255; // request any
```

Every DNS request includes a value that indicates the *type* of record desired; it can be any one of these values, including TYPE_ANY which indicates that all relevant resource records are wanted. Each resource record in the response includes a value that indicates its type; it is common to receive additional types of record than those requested. The last four types are for requests only; a response will only be of type TYPE_A through TYPE_TXT.

```
public static final int
    CLASS_IN = 1,     // internet
    CLASS_CS = 2,     // csnet
    CLASS_CH = 3,     // chaos
    CLASS_HS = 4,     // hesiod
    CLASS_ANY = 255;  // request any
```

The domain naming system was designed to cater to different types of networks other than just the Internet. Therefore, requests and responses must also state the *class* in which they are interested or to which they correspond. CLASS_IN is most common, although CLASS_ANY may be used for a request.

```
public static final int
    SHIFT_QUERY = 15,
    SHIFT_OPCODE = 11,
    SHIFT_AUTHORITATIVE = 10,
    SHIFT_TRUNCATED = 9,
    SHIFT_RECURSE_PLEASE = 8,
    SHIFT_RECURSE_AVAILABLE = 7,
    SHIFT_RESERVED = 4,
    SHIFT_RESPONSE_CODE = 0;
```

These values indicate the bit locations of pieces of information in the *flag* field of a DNS header.

```
public static final int
    OPCODE_QUERY = 0,
    OPCODE_IQUERY = 1,
    OPCODE_STATUS = 2;
```

These are the various values that the opcode part of the header flags may take.

```
private static final String[] typeNames = {
    "Address", "NameServer", "MailDomain", "MailForwarder",
    "CanonicalName", "StartOfAuthority", "MailBox", "MailGroup",
    "MailRename", "Null", "WellKnownServices", "Pointer",
    "HostInfo", "MailInfo", "MailExchanger", "Text"
};
```

```
public static String typeName (int type) {
   return ((type >= 1) && (type <= 16)) ? typeNames[type - 1] : "Unknown";
}
```

This method returns a textual representation of the specified resource record type, type, or Unknown if it is not a valid type.

```
private static final String[] codeNames = {
  "Format error", "Server failure", "Name not known",
  "Not implemented", "Refused"
};

public static String codeName (int code) {
  return ((code >= 1) && (code <= 5)) ?
    codeNames[code - 1] : "Unknown error";
}
```

This method returns a textual representation of the specified error code, code, or Unknown error if it is not a known error code.

15.3.5 Class DNSQuery

This class represents a DNS query. It is constructed with a host name about which information is desired, a query type, and a query class. It then provides support for transmission to a remote host and decoding the response.

```
import java.io.*;
import java.util.*;

public class DNSQuery {
  // public DNSQuery (String host, int type, int clas) ...
  // public String getQueryHost () ...
  // public int getQueryType () ...
  // public int getQueryClass () ...
  // public int getQueryID () ...
  // public byte[] extractQuery () ...
  // public void receiveResponse (byte[] data, int length)
  //     throws IOException ...
  // public boolean isAuthoritative () ...
  // public boolean isTruncated () ...
  // public boolean isRecursive () ...
  // public Enumeration getAnswers () ...
  // public Enumeration getAuthorities () ...
  // public Enumeration getAdditional () ...
}
```

The DNS query information is specified in the constructor. The query can be converted into a byte-array for transmission to a name server with the extractQuery() method, and then the response can be decoded with the receiveResponse() method.

After a response has been decoded, it can be queried through the remaining methods of this class.

```
private String queryHost;
private int queryType, queryClass, queryID;
private static int globalID;

public DNSQuery (String host, int type, int clas) {
  StringTokenizer labels = new StringTokenizer (host, ".");
  while (labels.hasMoreTokens ())
    if (labels.nextToken ().length () > 63)
      throw new IllegalArgumentException ("Invalid hostname: " + host);
  queryHost = host;
  queryType = type;
  queryClass = clas;
  synchronized (getClass ()) {
    queryID = (++ globalID) % 65536;
  }
}
```

In the constructor, we verify that the host name is valid (each element must be shorter than 64 characters) and then store the supplied query information in the variables queryHost, queryType, and queryClass. We also allocate a VM-unique identifier, queryID, that is used to identify the DNS query.

```
public String getQueryHost () {
  return queryHost;
}
```

This method returns the host about which this DNSQuery is seeking information.

```
public int getQueryType () {
  return queryType;
}
```

This method returns the resource record type in which this DNSQuery is interested.

```
public int getQueryClass () {
  return queryClass;
}
```

This method returns the resource class in which this DNSQuery is interested.

```
public int getQueryID () {
  return queryID;
}
```

This method returns the identifier that was allocated to this DNSQuery.

```
public byte[] extractQuery () {
```

```
  ByteArrayOutputStream byteArrayOut = new ByteArrayOutputStream ();
  DataOutputStream dataOut = new DataOutputStream (byteArrayOut);
  try {
    dataOut.writeShort (queryID);
    dataOut.writeShort ((0 << DNS.SHIFT_QUERY) |
      (DNS.OPCODE_QUERY << DNS.SHIFT_OPCODE) |
      (1 << DNS.SHIFT_RECURSE_PLEASE));
    dataOut.writeShort (1); // # queries
    dataOut.writeShort (0); // # answers
    dataOut.writeShort (0); // # authorities
    dataOut.writeShort (0); // # additional
    StringTokenizer labels = new StringTokenizer (queryHost, ".");
    while (labels.hasMoreTokens ()) {
      String label = labels.nextToken ();
      dataOut.writeByte (label.length ());
      dataOut.writeBytes (label);
    }
    dataOut.writeByte (0);
    dataOut.writeShort (queryType);
    dataOut.writeShort (queryClass);
  } catch (IOException ignored) {
  }
  return byteArrayOut.toByteArray ();
}
```

This method returns this DNS query encoded as a byte array in the correct format
for transmission to a name erver. We create the query array by attaching a DataOutput-
Stream, dataOut, to a ByteArrayOutputStream, byteArrayOut, and writing the
query using the standard DataOutputStream methods.

We first write the query identifier, followed by the flags and the number of queries,
answers, authorities, and additional resource records in this query. We next write the
query, which consists of the host name, the query type, and the query class. We encode
the host name by breaking it into its component parts (such as www, nitric, com) and
then writing each part preceded by a byte that indicates the length of the part. We terminate the host name with a zero byte.

For this purpose, we could have created a DNSOutputStream that subclasses Byte-
ArrayOutputStream and adds these data-writing methods. However, we would only
use the stream once so the additional class would not serve much purpose.

Writing to a ByteArrayOutputStream will not throw an IOException, so we add
a dummy exception handler and simply return the contents of byteArrayOut.

```
private Vector answers = new Vector ();
private Vector authorities = new Vector ();
private Vector additional = new Vector ();

public void receiveResponse (byte[] data, int length) throws IOException {
  DNSInputStream dnsIn = new DNSInputStream (data, 0, length);
```

```
    int id = dnsIn.readShort ();
    if (id != queryID)
      throw new IOException ("ID does not match request");
    int flags = dnsIn.readShort ();
    decodeFlags (flags);
    int numQueries = dnsIn.readShort ();
    int numAnswers = dnsIn.readShort ();
    int numAuthorities = dnsIn.readShort ();
    int numAdditional = dnsIn.readShort ();

    while (numQueries -- > 0) { // discard questions
      String queryName = dnsIn.readDomainName ();
      int queryType = dnsIn.readShort ();
      int queryClass = dnsIn.readShort ();
    }
    try {
      while (numAnswers -- > 0)
        answers.addElement (dnsIn.readRR ());
      while (numAuthorities -- > 0)
        authorities.addElement (dnsIn.readRR ());
      while (numAdditional -- > 0)
        additional.addElement (dnsIn.readRR ());
  }   catch (EOFException ex) {
      if (!truncated)
        throw ex;
    }
  }

// protected void decodeFlags (int flags) throws IOException ...
```

This method decodes a DNS response, which must be in the form of a byte array. We use byte arrays rather than streams because DNS requests can be transported over either UDP or TCP; abstracting to byte arrays allows us to use either transport mechanism.

We create a DNSInputStream from the response array and read data from this stream. The header of the response has the same format as the request: We read the response ID and verify that it matches our own, throwing an appropriate IOException if not. We then read the response flags and the number of queries, answers, authorities, and additional resource records that will follow.

We loop through, reading and discarding the query data; this is exactly what we send out in the initial query. We could verify that this matches the query that we sent out, but that is probably unnecessary.

We finally read the resource records that were returned in response to our request. We use the readRR() method to decode these from the stream, inserting them into the appropriate Vector: answers, authorities, or additional. If the response was truncated and an EOFException occurs, then we simply ignore it and return with as much data as we have managed to decode.

```
private boolean authoritative, truncated, recursive;

protected void decodeFlags (int flags) throws IOException {
  boolean isResponse = ((flags >> DNS.SHIFT_QUERY) & 1) != 0;
  if (!isResponse)
    throw new IOException ("Response flag not set");
  int opcode = (flags >> DNS.SHIFT_OPCODE) & 15;
  // could check opcode
  authoritative = ((flags >> DNS.SHIFT_AUTHORITATIVE) & 1) != 0;
  truncated = ((flags >> DNS.SHIFT_TRUNCATED) & 1) != 0;
  boolean recurseRequest = ((flags >> DNS.SHIFT_RECURSE_PLEASE) & 1) != 0;
  // could check recurse request
  recursive = ((flags >> DNS.SHIFT_RECURSE_AVAILABLE) & 1) != 0;
  int code = (flags >> DNS.SHIFT_RESPONSE_CODE) & 15;
  if (code != 0)
    throw new IOException (DNS.codeName (code) + " (" + code + ")");
}
```

This method decodes the specified flags, `flags`. We verify that the response flag is set. We could check other fields such as opcode and recurse request, but this is probably unnecessary. We extract whether this is an authoritative response, whether it is truncated, and whether recursion was available. We also check the response code; if this is non-zero, an error was encountered so we throw an appropriate exception.

```
public boolean isAuthoritative () {
  return authoritative;
}
```

This method queries whether the response is authoritative, which means that it came from a name server that holds authoritative data for the requested domain.

```
public boolean isTruncated () {
  return truncated;
}
```

This method queries whether the response was truncated; this will happen if there was too much data in the response to fit into the transport limit. UDP responses are limited to just 512 bytes; any more data will simply be discarded.

```
public boolean isRecursive () {
  return recursive;
}
```

This method returns whether the response was the result of a recursive query; this means that the name server had to forward the query to another name server in order to determine the information.

```
public Enumeration getAnswers () {
```

```
        return answers.elements ();
    }
```

This method returns an `Enumeration` of the resource records from the answers section of the DNS response. These are the direct answers to the specified request.

```
    public Enumeration getAuthorities () {
        return authorities.elements ();
    }
```

This method returns an `Enumeration` of the resource records from the authorities section of the DNS response. This is a list of the authoritative name servers for the specified request. If the original question was not answered, one of these should be asked instead.

```
    public Enumeration getAdditional () {
        return additional.elements ();
    }
```

This method returns an `Enumeration` of the resource records from the additional information section of the DNS response. This is a list of additional information, such as the addresses of the listed authoritative name servers.

15.3.6 Class DNSInputStream

This class is a `ByteArrayInputStream` that provides special methods related to reading data from a DNS response. We directly subclass `ByteArrayInputStream` and add these methods rather than implementing a stream filter because some features of the DNS format require essentially random access to data that have previously been read.

```
import java.io.*;
import java.util.*;

public class DNSInputStream extends ByteArrayInputStream {
    // public DNSInputStream (byte[] data, int off, int len) ...
    // public int readByte () throws IOException ...
    // public int readShort () throws IOException ...
    // public long readInt () throws IOException ...
    // public String readString () throws IOException ...
    // public String readDomainName () throws IOException ...
    // public DNSRR readRR () throws IOException ...
}
```

We extend `ByteArrayInputStream` and add methods that allow us to read the various DNS datatypes including unsigned `bytes`, `shorts`, `ints`, `Strings`, domain names, and resource records.

```
    protected DataInputStream dataIn;
```

```
public DNSInputStream (byte[] data, int off, int len) {
  super (data, off, len);
  dataIn = new DataInputStream (this);
}
```

Our constructor calls the superconstructor to read from the specified `len`-byte sub-array of `data`, starting from offset `off`. We also attach a `DataInputStream`, `dataIn`, to `this`, to provide easy read access through the basic methods that provides.

```
public int readByte () throws IOException {
  return dataIn.readUnsignedByte ();
}
```

This method reads an unsigned `byte` from this stream.

```
public int readShort () throws IOException {
  return dataIn.readUnsignedShort ();
}
```

This method reads an unsigned `short` from this stream.

```
public long readInt () throws IOException {
  return dataIn.readInt () & 0xffffffffL;
}
```

This method reads an unsigned `int` from this stream, returning the resulting `long`.

```
public String readString () throws IOException {
  int len = readByte ();
  if (len == 0) {
    return "";
  } else {
    byte[] buffer = new byte[len];
    dataIn.readFully (buffer);
    return new String (buffer, "latin1");
  }
}
```

This method reads a `String`, encoded as we wrote the parts of a domain name in the DNSQuery class: we read a byte, `len`, which is the length of the `String`, and then read the indicated number of bytes, returning the result as a `String`.

```
public String readDomainName () throws IOException {
  if (pos >= count)
    throw new EOFException ("EOF reading domain name");
  if ((buf[pos] & 0xc0) == 0) {
    String label = readString ();
    if (label.length () > 0) {
      String tail = readDomainName ();
```

```
        if (tail.length () > 0)
          label = label + '.' + tail;
      }
      return label;
    } else {
      if ((buf[pos] & 0xc0) != 0xc0)
        throw new IOException ("Invalid domain name compression offset");
      int offset = readShort () & 0x3fff;
      DNSInputStream dnsIn =
        new DNSInputStream (buf, offset, buf.length - offset);
      return dnsIn.readDomainName ();
    }
  }
}
```

This method reads a domain name. As we saw, when writing a domain name in the
DNSQuery class, the name is simply split into its component parts and then each is written, preceded by its length, followed ultimately by a zero-byte.

For the purposes of
space efficiency in the
response, however, a special
compression option is supported: if any length-byte

Figure 15.9   DNS name compression

has either of its top 2 bits set, then it and the next byte form a pointer to part of a
domain name somewhere else in the response. This way, for example, www.nitric.com
and ns.nitric.com can be encoded in a single response as www, nitric, and com, and ns
followed by a pointer to the earlier occurrence of nitric.com.

In the readDomainName() method, we examine the next length byte: if both the
top bits are clear, it is a normally encoded string; otherwise it is a back reference pointer.
If it is a normal string, we can use readString() to read it, followed by readDomain-
Name() for the rest of the name.

Otherwise, we read the encoded pointer by reading a short and discarding the top
2 bits. We can then construct a temporary new DNSInputStream that reads from the
specified offset, and call readDomainName() on this new stream to decode the rest of
the domain name stored there. This decompression process may be recursive if the
remainder of the domain name itself contains a pointer reference.

```
public DNSRR readRR () throws IOException {
  String rrName = readDomainName ();
  int rrType = readShort ();
  int rrClass = readShort ();
  long rrTTL = readInt ();
  int rrDataLen = readShort ();
  DNSInputStream rrDNSIn = new DNSInputStream (buf, pos, rrDataLen);
  pos += rrDataLen;
  try {
```

```
        String myName = getClass ().getName ();
        int periodIndex = myName.lastIndexOf ('.');
        String myPackage = myName.substring (0, 1 + periodIndex);
        Class theClass = Class.forName
            (myPackage + "record." + DNS.typeName (rrType));
        DNSRR rr = (DNSRR) theClass.newInstance ();
         rr.init (rrName, rrType, rrClass, rrTTL, rrDNSIn);
         return rr;
      } catch (ClassNotFoundException ex) {
        throw new IOException ("Unknown DNSRR (type " +
          DNS.typeName (rrType) + " (" + rrType + "))");
      } catch (IllegalAccessException ex) {
        throw new IOException ("Access error creating DNSRR (type " +
          DNS.typeName (rrType) + ')');
      } catch (InstantiationException ex) {
        throw new IOException ("Instantiation error creating DNSRR " +
          "(type " + DNS.typeName (rrType) + ')');
      }
    }
  }
```

This method reads a resource record. The resource record consists of a domain name, a resource record type and class, a time to live, and a length followed by the resource record-specific data. We read the initial data and then extract a substream for the resource record data. This substream reads from just the resource record data part of this stream.

We finally construct a DNSRR and initialize it with the data that we have read. Rather than combining all resource records into a single DNSRR class, we use a generic DNSRR superclass and then provide a subclass for each type of resource record. The name of the subclass is constructed by joining "record." and the name of the resource record type. We use Class.forName().newInstance() to create an instance of this subclass, using the type name returned by the typeName() method of class DNS. We then initialize this resource record with the data that we read and the substream that we created. We rethrow any exceptions that arise during this process, or else return the resulting DNSRR instance.

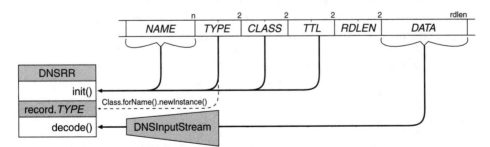

Figure 15.10 Reading a resource record

15.3.7 Class DNSRR

This is the generic superclass for all resource record classes. This superclass provides the methods that are supported by all resource records, including methods to query the standard resource record data. Subclasses may add whatever extra methods are appropriate for the data that they represent.

```java
import java.io.*;

public abstract class DNSRR {
    // public String getRRName () ...
    // public int getRRType () ...
    // public int getRRClass () ...
    // public long getRRTTL () ...
    // public boolean isValid () ...
}
```

The DNSRR superclass provides methods to query the basic resource record data that are found at the start of every resource record. We declare this class abstract because it must be extended by a subclass that is appropriate for a particular resource record type.

```java
    private String rrName;
    private int rrType, rrClass;
    private long rrTTL, rrCreated;

    void init (String name, int type, int clas, long ttl, DNSInputStream dnsIn)
        throws IOException {
        rrName = name;
        rrType = type;
        rrClass = clas;
        rrTTL = ttl;
        rrCreated = System.currentTimeMillis ();
        decode (dnsIn);
    }

    // protected abstract void decode (DNSInputStream dnsIn)
        throws IOException ...
```

This method is called by a DNSInputStream to initialize the DNSRR with the basic resource record data. We keep local copies of this information and the current time, and then call the decode() method to decode the supplied stream, which is a DNSInputStream attached to just the data that is specific to this resource record.

```java
    protected abstract void decode (DNSInputStream dnsIn) throws IOException;
```

A subclass must implement this method to decode the specified DNSInputStream, dnsIn, and extract any resource record-specific data.

```java
    public String getRRName () {
```

```
    return rrName;
  }
```

This method returns the name of the host or domain to which this resource record applies.

```
public int getRRType () {
  return rrType;
}
```

This method returns the type of this resource record; this will be one of the types defined in the DNS class.

```
public int getRRClass () {
  return rrClass;
}
```

This method returns the class of this resource record; this will be one of the classes defined in the DNS class.

```
public long getRRTTL () {
  return rrTTL;
}
```

This method returns the time to live (TTL) of this resource record, which is the number of seconds for which it is valid. After this time has expired, another query should be made to determine accurate and fresh information. A TTL of zero means that this resource record is only valid for the current transaction.

```
public boolean isValid () {
  return rrTTL * 1000 > System.currentTimeMillis () - rrCreated;
}
```

This method returns whether this resource record is still valid; that is to say, whether its time to live has not yet expired. This does not cater to a TTL of zero; the caller must be prepared to handle that case manually.

15.3.8 Class record.Address

This class represents a DNS address record, which is a resource record that specifies the IP address of a particular host.

```
package record;
import java.io.*;
import java.net.*;

public class Address extends DNSRR {
  // public byte[] getAddress () ...
  // public InetAddress getInetAddress () ...
```

```
// public String toString () ...
}
```

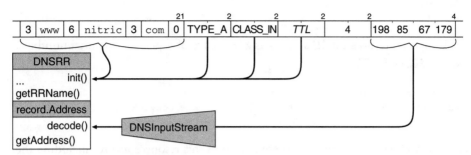

Figure 15.11   Class record.Address

We extend the DNSRR class and add a method getAddress() that returns the 4-byte IP address represented by this resource record. We also add a getInetAddress() method that returns this value as an InetAddress object and a toString() method that returns a useful String representation of this class.

```
private int[] ipAddress = new int[4];

protected void decode (DNSInputStream dnsIn) throws IOException {
  for (int i = 0; i < 4; ++ i)
    ipAddress[i] = dnsIn.readByte ();
}
```

The decode() method reads 4 bytes from the DNSInputStream dnsIn and stores these in the array ipAddress.

```
public byte[] getAddress () {
  byte[] ip = new byte[4];
  for (int j = 0; j < 4; ++ j)
    ip[j] = (byte) ipAddress[j];
  return ip;
}
```

This method creates and returns a new 4-entry byte array containing the IP address from ipAddress.

```
public InetAddress getInetAddress () throws UnknownHostException {
  return InetAddress.getByName (toByteString ());
}

// private String toByteString () ...
```

This method returns a new InetAddress, created from the result of the toByteString() method.

```
private String toByteString () {
  return ipAddress[0] + "." + ipAddress[1] + "." +
    ipAddress[2] + "." + ipAddress[3];
}
```

This method returns the IP address as a sequence of 4 period-separated numbers, for example, *12.34.56.78.*

```
public String toString () {
  return getRRName () + "\tinternet address = " + toByteString ();
}
```

This method returns a `String` representation of this resource record, including the target host, as returned by `getRRName()` and its IP address, as returned by `toByteString()`.

15.3.9 Class record.MailExchanger

This class represents a DNS mail exchanger record. These records indicate the host that should receive mail for a particular domain. Each record includes a host name that should receive mail and a preference that indicates in what order the mail exchangers should be tried. Domains typically have several mail exchangers that are tried in sequence; should one go down then another can receive mail until the primary exchanger is reanimated.

```
package record;
import java.io.*;

public class MailExchanger extends DNSRR {
  // public String getMX () ...
  // public int getPreference () ...
  // public String toString () ...
}
```

We extend DNSRR and add `getMX()`, `getPreference()`, and `toString()` methods that return the mail exchanger and its preference, and a useful `String` representation of this resource record.

```
private int preference;
private String mx;

protected void decode (DNSInputStream dnsIn) throws IOException {
  preference = dnsIn.readShort ();
  mx = dnsIn.readDomainName ();
}
```

In the `decode()` method, we read the preference as an unsigned `short` and the mail exchanger's domain name, which is encoded in the usual domain name encoding.

```
public String getMX () {
  return mx;
}
```

This method returns the mail exchanger's host name.

```
public int getPreference () {
  return preference;
}
```

This method returns the mail exchanger's preference.

```
public String toString () {
  return getRRName () + "\tpreference = " + preference +
    ", mail exchanger = "+ mx;
}
```

This method returns a `String` representation of this resource record.

This is the last resource record implementation that we will look at here; all others follow essentially the same pattern, reading data with the methods of DNSInputStream and then supplying methods to query this information. Implementations of the other fourteen types are available from the accompanying online site.

15.3.10 Class NSLookup

This class implements a simple DNS resolver client, similar in nature to the `nslookup` command. To run this example, specify a host name and optional name server. It will construct a DNSQuery, send it to the name server, receive a response, and print the resulting information.

This client uses TCP/IP and automatically requests all Internet-class resource records for the specified host name or domain name.

```
import java.io.*;
import java.net.*;
import java.util.*;

public class NSLookup {
  // public static void main (String args[]) ...
  // public static void sendQuery (DNSQuery query, Socket socket)
      throws IOException ...
  // public static void getResponse (DNSQuery query, Socket socket)
      throws IOException ...
  // public static void printRRs (DNSQuery query) ...
}
```

We provide a main() method that decodes the arguments; constructs a DNSQuery; opens a Socket to the name server; and then uses the sendQuery(), getResponse(), and `printResult()` methods to transmit the query, receive the response, and print the resulting resource records.

```
public static void main (String[] args) {
   if (args.length != 1)
     throw new IllegalArgumentException
        ("Syntax: NSLookup <hostname>[@<nameserver>]");

   int atIdx = args[0].indexOf ("@");
   String nameServer = (atIdx > -1) ? args[0].substring (atIdx + 1) : "ns";
   String hostName = (atIdx > -1) ? args[0].substring (0, atIdx) : args[0];

   System.out.println ("Nameserver: " + nameServer);
   System.out.println ("Request: " + hostName);

   DNSQuery query = new DNSQuery (hostName, DNS.TYPE_ANY, DNS.CLASS_IN);

   try {
     Socket socket = new Socket (nameServer, DNS.DEFAULT_PORT);
     socket.setSoTimeout (10000);
     sendQuery (query, socket);
     getResponse (query, socket);
     socket.close ();

     printRRs (query);
   } catch (IOException ex) {
     System.out.println (ex);
   }
}
```

In the `main()` method, we first verify that an argument has been supplied, throwing an appropriate exception if not. We then decode the argument into its component parts: If just a host name was specified, we assume a default name server called *ns*. Otherwise, we split the argument into a host name, `hostName`, and name server, `nameServer`.

We construct a `DNSQuery`, `query`, for the specified host name, requesting *any* resource records in the `Internet` class. We open a `Socket` to the name server on the default DNS port, transmit the query and then await a response. If the name server does not exist or is not operational, an exception will be thrown. Sometimes a name server will simply not respond at all, so we set a 20-second receive timeout. Note that the connection attempt, when we create the `Socket`, may in some cases take a long time to fail if there is a network problem.

We finally call upon the `printRRs()` method to display the returned resource records.

```
public static void sendQuery (DNSQuery query, Socket socket)
   throws IOException {
```

```
    BufferedOutputStream bufferedOut =
      new BufferedOutputStream (socket.getOutputStream ());
    DataOutputStream dataOut = new DataOutputStream (bufferedOut);
    byte[] data = query.extractQuery ();
    dataOut.writeShort (data.length);
    dataOut.write (data);
    dataOut.flush ();
  }
```

This method sends the specified DNSQuery, query, out the specified Socket, socket. We create a buffered DataOutputStream, dataOut, attached to the Socket's output stream. We extract the query into a byte array using its extractQuery() method; we write its length to the output stream using the writeShort() method and then write the entire query before flushing the output stream. When sending a DNS query over TCP, it is necessary to precede the query by its length; this is not necessary over UDP because UDP packets automatically contain the payload length.

```
  public static void getResponse (DNSQuery query, Socket socket)
      throws IOException {
    InputStream bufferedIn =
      new BufferedInputStream (socket.getInputStream ());
    DataInputStream dataIn = new DataInputStream (bufferedIn);
    int responseLength = dataIn.readUnsignedShort ();
    byte[] data = new byte[responseLength];
    dataIn.readFully (data);
    query.receiveResponse (data, responseLength);
  }
```

This method reads a response from the specified Socket, socket, into the specified DNSQuery, query. We create a buffered DataInputStream, dataIn, attached to the Socket's input stream. We read an unsigned short, which indicates the length of the following response, and then read the entire response using the readFully() method. We then call query's receiveResponse() method to decode the received data.

```
  public static void printRRs (DNSQuery query) {
    Enumeration answers = query.getAnswers ();
    if (answers.hasMoreElements ())
      System.out.println (query.isAuthoritative () ?
        "\nAuthoritative answer:\n" :
        "\nNon-authoritative answer:\n");
    while (answers.hasMoreElements ())
      System.out.println (answers.nextElement ());

    Enumeration authorities = query.getAuthorities ();
    if (authorities.hasMoreElements ())
      System.out.println ("\nAuthoritative answers can be found from:\n");
    while (authorities.hasMoreElements ())
      System.out.println (authorities.nextElement ());
```

```
    Enumeration additional = query.getAdditional ();
    if (additional.hasMoreElements ())
      System.out.println ("\nAdditional information:\n");
    while (additional.hasMoreElements ())
      System.out.println (additional.nextElement ());
  }
```

This method prints out the responses received for our query. We extract all the direct answers into the Enumeration answers; we print whether the result is authoritative or not, and then print each answer. We then print out all the authorities returned with this request, followed by any additional resource records that were returned.

This example is, perforce, simple. A more complex implementation would automatically use some of the resource record-specific methods of the returned data in order to provide increased function. For example, if no answers were returned to a request except for a list of authoritative name servers, we could automatically query those listed name servers. Similarly, we could automatically obtain additional information about returned canonical name records and so forth.

15.3.11 Using it

The NSLookup class is most easily demonstrated when used as a stand-alone application.

```
java NSLookup nitric.com
Nameserver: ns
Request: nitric.com

Authoritative answer:

prominence.com  start of authority
        origin = ns.nitric.com
        mail address = hostmaster.nitric.com
        serial = 1062
        refresh = 14400
        retry = 3600
        expire = 604800
        minimum TTL = 86400
nitric.com  nameserver = ns.nitric.com
nitric.com  internet address = 198.85.67.179
nitric.com  preference = 1000, mail exchanger = mail2.catalogue.com
nitric.com  preference = 10, mail exchanger = mailman.nitric.com
nitric.com  preference = 100, mail exchanger = mail.catalogue.com

Authoritative answers can be found from:

nitric.com  nameserver = ns.nitric.com

Additional information:

mailman.nitric.com      internet address = 198.85.67.179
mail.catalogue.com      internet address = 198.85.68.40
```

This looks up information about the domain nitric.com using our local name server, ns.

```
java nslookup.NSLookup internic.net@ns.isi.edu
Nameserver: ns.isi.edu
Request: internic.net

Authoritative answer:

internic.net    start of authority
        origin = ops.internic.net
        mail address = markk.internic.net
        serial = 970506000
        refresh = 3600
        retry = 3600
        expire = 432000
        minimum TTL = 86400
internic.net    nameserver = rs0.internic.net
internic.net    nameserver = ds0.internic.net
internic.net    nameserver = noc.cerf.net
internic.net    nameserver = ns.isi.edu
internic.net    text = WP-DAP://c=US@o=NSFNET@ou=InterNIC
internic.net    text = WP-SMTP-EXPN-Finger://internic.net
internic.net    preference = 100, mail exchanger = rs.internic.net
internic.net    internet address = 198.41.0.8
internic.net    internet address = 198.41.0.9
internic.net    internet address = 198.41.0.6
internic.net    internet address = 198.41.0.5

Authoritative answers can be found from:

internic.net    nameserver = rs0.internic.net
internic.net    nameserver = ds0.internic.net
internic.net    nameserver = noc.cerf.net
internic.net    nameserver = ns.isi.edu

Additional information:

rs0.internic.net       internet address = 198.41.0.5
ds0.internic.net       internet address = 198.49.45.10
noc.cerf.net    internet address = 192.153.156.22
ns.isi.edu      internet address = 128.9.128.127
rs.internic.net internet address = 198.41.0.8
rs.internic.net internet address = 198.41.0.9
rs.internic.net internet address = 198.41.0.12
rs.internic.net internet address = 198.41.0.5
rs.internic.net internet address = 198.41.0.6
rs.internic.net internet address = 198.41.0.7
```

This looks up information about the domain internic.net, querying the specified name server ns.isi.edu.

For a further example of the usage of these classes, chapter 21 demonstrates a UDP version of this command.

15.4 Wrapping up

In this chapter, we have looked at the implementations of two TCP clients. The first, finger, we implemented with a single class that performed all necessary function for the protocol. For the sake of reusability, we did not inline all code as `static` methods called by `main()` but instead provided a `Finger` object that could be constructed with desired parameters and then printed to any desired `Writer`. Because we provide this reusable interface, we will be able to use this class again in our discussion of the URL classes.

The DNS client, on the other hand, was implemented with many supporting classes. We could have implemented it in a single monolithic class, but the implementation that we chose has the advantage that it can be used by many different pieces of code. We demonstrated transport of DNS requests over TCP. In a later chapter, we will reuse these classes to provide DNS transport over UDP. Similarly, it is possible to make use of the DNS classes in a SMTP (mail) client. We can make a DNS request to determine the mail exchanger for a particular domain and can then connect appropriately. When mail is sent to the user x@nitric.com, a DNS request is made to determine the mail exchanger for the domain nitric.com; a TCP connection is then made to the SMTP port of the indicated machine. Because we have a generic reusable framework in place, we can simply use the classes of this example to query records of type `DNSRR_MX` and determine the domain information that we require (figure 15.12).

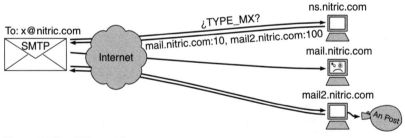

Figure 15.12   MX records

The trade-off between a simple but nonflexible approach (one class with `static` methods) and a generalized but slightly more voluminous approach is fairly common. The appropriate use of the powerful language mechanisms to provide a generalized solution is a better choice in almost all cases. Our use of a `DNSInputStream` class is much more elegant than explicitly dissecting an array of bytes in the main class, although the latter approach requires less initial design.

Following this introduction to TCP network clients we will now look at some servers. The next chapters cover the server API with some fairly simple examples, followed by an implementation of a real-world protocol: HTTP.

CHAPTER 16

Server-side networking

We have just seen some examples of network client programming. To build a client, we open a connection to a server and communicate over streams, using the server's application-layer protocol. The HTTP protocol is a fairly simple, text-based application-layer protocol, although we admittedly looked at only a small part of it. There are many other protocols in use, such as FTP and IRC, and we can develop similar clients for these.

In this chapter, we introduce the server side of networking with TCP. At first glance, it is even simpler than client-side programming. A server picks a port number and listens for connections; whenever a client connects, the server receives a `Socket` through which to communicate with the client.

The complexities of developing servers arise with multithreading issues and the definition of an application-layer protocol that governs how clients will communicate with the server. This is complicated further if we want clients to be able to communicate with each other through the server. In part V of this book, we will develop stream classes that provide a higher level transport layer that runs on top of TCP and provides many of these functions.

16.1 Class ServerSocket

The `ServerSocket` class is the mechanism by which a server can accept connections from clients across a network. The basic procedure for implementing a server is to open a `ServerSocket` on a particular local port number, and then to wait for connections. Clients will connect to this port, and a connection will be established.

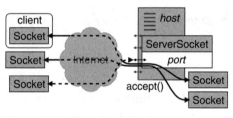

Figure 16.1 Class ServerSocket

The `ServerSocket` class creates a `Socket` for each client connection (figure 16.1); the server then can handle these connections in the usual manner, typically by extracting an `InputStream` and an `OutputStream` and communicating with the client through the streams interface.

16.1.1 Constructors

`ServerSockets` are constructed by choosing a port on the local machine. This port number must be in the range 1–65,535; however, ports 1–1,023 are reserved for system services and so can usually be used only by the machine administrator.

There is no easily accessible mechanism in the Internet for allocating port numbers to user applications; if you are serious, you must write to the Internet Assigned Numbers Authority (IANA). Usually, an application just selects a port and sticks to it; ideally this port number will be user-configurable. Alternatively, if a port number of 0 is specified, the operating system will select an arbitrary valid and free port every time that the application is run. The chosen port number can then be communicated to prospective clients by some other mechanism.

A server must explicitly accept a connection from a `ServerSocket` to obtain a `Socket` connection to a client. However, the operating system will actually start accepting connections from clients as soon as the `ServerSocket` is created. These connections will be placed in a queue and removed one-by-one as the server calls the `accept()` method. The `ServerSocket` constructor allows a server to specify how many connections it wishes the operating system to queue; the operating system will refuse any further connection requests that occur if the queue is full.

ServerSocket(int port) throws IOException   This constructs a `ServerSocket` that listens on the specified port `port` of the local machine; the default limit on outstanding connection requests (50) will be used. This means that the operating system should accept at most fifty clients in its queue of pending clients. Any additional connection attempts above this limit will be refused.

This is not a limit on the number of connections that the server can handle at once. It is a limit on the number that will be queued if the server is being slow about accepting new connections.

ServerSocket(int port, int backlog) throws IOException   This constructs a `ServerSocket` that listens on the specified port `port` of the local machine. The `backlog` parameter specifies the number of outstanding connection requests that should be queued by the operating system.

JDK 1.1 *ServerSocket(int port, int backlog, InetAddress bindAddr) throws IOException*   This creates a `ServerSocket` that listens on the specified port `port` of the local machine, with a limit of `backlog` outstanding connections. This `ServerSocket` will only accept connections to the local address `bindAddr`; this is useful on a multihomed machine to prevent connections to other local addresses from being accepted. A bind address of `null` accepts connections to any local address.

16.1.2 Methods

These methods permit connections to be accepted and information about the `ServerSocket` to be queried.

Socket accept() throws IOException   This method blocks (waits) until a client makes a connection to the port on which this `ServerSocket` is listening. A `Socket` is returned, corresponding to a TCP connection to the client. This `Socket` can be handled in the usual manner; frequently, it is passed off to a separate handler and the main server loop returns to waiting in an `accept()` call.

void close() throws IOException   This method closes the `ServerSocket`. It does *not* close any of the connections which have been accepted and not yet closed, so a server may close its `ServerSocket` and maintain connections to its existing clients. Instead, this call instructs the operating system to stop accepting new client connections.

InetAddress getInetAddress()   This method returns the local address to which this `ServerSocket` is bound. If no local address was specified in the constructor, this will return an `InetAddress` corresponding to any local address—typically `0.0.0.0`.

int getLocalPort()   This method returns the port on which this `ServerSocket` is listening. This is useful if you have specified a port number of 0 and so been assigned an available, unused port.

(JDK 1.1) *void setSoTimeout(int timeout) throws SocketException*   This method sets a time-out value, in milliseconds, after which an unanswered call to accept() will abort with an `InterruptedIOException`. A value of zero, the default, inhibits the timeout so that accept() will block forever.

(JDK 1.1) *int getSoTimeout() throws IOException*   This   method   returns   the current time-out value, or zero if none is set.

(JDK 1.1) *protected void implAccept(Socket s) throws IOException*   This method should be called by a `ServerSocket` subclass to initialize an empty `Socket` with a newly accepted connection.

static void setSocketFactory(SocketImplFactory factory) throws IOException
This static method can be used to install a custom server socket implementation for the entire JVM. This method can only be called once, and is vetted by the `SecurityManager`.

16.1.3 IOException
Creating a server socket can fail for various reasons, such as the requested port being a system port or if another application is already running on it. Other methods may also throw exceptions of this type.

16.1.4 SecurityException
Untrusted applets may not act as servers, so the `SecurityManager` will throw a `SecurityException` if an applet attempts to create a `ServerSocket`.

16.1.5 Socket implementation
This class also supports a `static setSocketFactory()` method that allows a custom factory to be installed for the `ServerSocket` class. This allows a subclass of `Socket` to

be returned by the `accept()` method, for use usually with an accompanying client-side `Socket` implementation. This mechanism is less commonly used than simply subclassing the `ServerSocket` class directly and returning a custom `Socket` implementation from the `accept()` method.

16.2 Building an echo server

This simple server accepts one connection and then echoes everything received on that connection back to the sender.

The server takes a single command-line parameter which is the port that it will listen on. It then waits for a connection, and subsequently echoes everything on that connection back to the sender (figure 16.2).

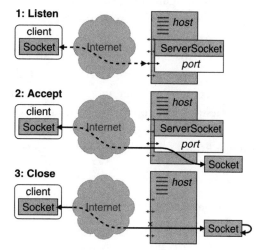

Figure 16.2   A single-threaded echo server

```
import java.net.*;
import java.io.*;

public class STServer {
  // public static void main (String[] args) throws IOException ...
}
```

The echo server is a simple single-threaded application that executes in the `main()` method.

```
public static void main (String[] args) throws IOException {
    if (args.length != 1)
        throw new IllegalArgumentException ("Syntax: STServer <port>");

    Socket client = accept (Integer.parseInt (args[0]));

    try {
        InputStream in = client.getInputStream ();
        OutputStream out = client.getOutputStream ();
        out.write ("You are now connected to the Echo Server.\r\n"
                   .getBytes ("latin1"));

        int x;
        while ((x = in.read ()) > -1)
            out.write (x);
    } finally {
        System.out.println ("Closing");
        client.close ();
    }
```

```
    }

    // static Socket accept (int port) throws IOException ...
```

When this application is run, the `main()` method is called. We first ensure that a port number argument has been provided and then call our own `accept()` method to accept a client connection on the specified port. Parsing the port number will throw a `NumberFormatException` if the number cannot be parsed. This is a `Runtime-Exception` that will abort the application; it is assumed that any code can throw a `RuntimeException` so we don't need to declare it.

We extract the input and output streams from the resulting `Socket`, print a welcome message, and commence echoing back to the client everything that is received. We use a `finally` clause to close the `Socket` regardless of whether we terminate gracefully from an EOF, or due to an `IOException` from some problem.

```
static Socket accept (int port) throws IOException {
    System.out.println ("Starting on port " + port);
    ServerSocket server = new ServerSocket (port);

    System.out.println ("Waiting");
    Socket client = server.accept ();
    System.out.println ("Accepted from " + client.getInetAddress ());

    server.close ();
    return client;
}
```

This method accepts a single connection from a client on the specified port `port`. We first create a `ServerSocket` listening on the specified port, `port`; opening this may throw an `IOException` which we pass on. We then accept a single connection from a single client; we immediately close the server socket so that no more connection attempts can be made.

16.2.1 Testing the server

This server can be tested by using a telnet application to connect to the server. You can specify the host address `127.0.0.1` if you are connecting from the same machine that is running the server, and you must specify the port number that you have chosen.

The IP address `127.0.0.1` is a special address called the *loopback address* that directs IP packets back to the sending machine. Usually, you can also refer to this with the name *localhost*. You can easily test client/server applications on a single machine that is not connected to the Internet by running the server and then connecting to the loopback IP address.

16.3 Building a nonblocking server

A simple server, as described, is adequate for handling one connection at a time. However, it is unsuited to handling multiple connections. The `read()` method blocks if there are no data, and so if the server attempts to read from a client that has not transmitted any data, then the server will block.

There are two ways to get around this problem. One solution is to write a nonblocking server; the other is to write a multithreaded server. The multithreaded alternative is almost always considered a better solution.

This example demonstrates the operation of a nonblocking server. Earlier in the book, we said that there is no real capability for nonblocking I/O in Java. The `available()` method does, however, provide us with a crude workaround. The amount of nonblocking I/O that we can achieve is the ability to call a `read()` method that returns immediately if there are no data. We can simulate this by preceding every call to `read()` with a call to `available()` to ensure that there are data available.

The following server accepts two client connections and loops, echoing data between the clients. It uses the `available()` methods to simulate nonblocking I/O (figure 16.3). This is effectively a simple two-person chat server.

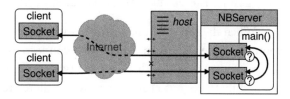

Figure 16.3   A nonblocking server

```
import java.net.*;
import java.io.*;

public class NBServer {
  // public static void main (String[] args) throws IOException ...
}
```

The server is a single thread that executes in the `main()` method.

```
static InputStream in0, in1;
static OutputStream out0, out1;

public static void main (String[] args) throws IOException {
  if (args.length != 1)
    throw new IllegalArgumentException ("Syntax: NBServer <port>");

  try {
    accept (Integer.parseInt (args[0]));
    int x0, x1;
    while (((x0 = readNB (in0)) != -1) &&
           ((x1 = readNB (in1)) != -1)) {
      if (x0 >= 0)
```

```
            out1.write (x0);
          if (x1 >= 0)
            out0.write (x1);
        }
      } finally {
      System.out.println ("Closing");
      close (out0);
      close (out1);
    }
  }

  static void close (OutputStream out) {
    if (out != null) {
      try {
        out.close ();
      } catch (IOException ignored) {
      }
    }
  }

  // static void accept (int port) throws IOException ...
  // static int readNB (InputStream in) ...
```

When the server is run, we first ensure that a port number has been specified on the command line. We then accept two connections using the `accept()` method, and commence echoing data between the two connections. We make use of the `readNB()` method that uses `available()` to test if there are any data to be read. If there are no data to be read, it returns the value -2; otherwise, it returns a byte of data.

Communication with the clients occurs through the streams `in0` and `out0` for the first client, and `in1` and `out1` for the second client; these are initialized by the `accept()` method.

We surround the entire body of this method with a `try ... finally` clause that serves to close both client connections when we exit. Note that even the `close()` call may throw an exception, so we must catch any exceptions that may occur, and thus ensure that both `Socket`s are closed.

Going to such lengths to close `Socket`s is not important for this particular server; when it exits, all `Socket`s will be closed anyway. It is usually, however, important that we clean up correctly when a client exits. Most servers will stay operational for a long time, possibly tying up system resources if sockets are not correctly closed.

```
  static void accept (int port) throws IOException {
    System.out.println ("Starting on port " + port);
    ServerSocket server = new ServerSocket (port);
    try {
      System.out.println ("Waiting..");
      Socket client0 = server.accept ();
      System.out.println ("Accepted from " + client0.getInetAddress ());
```

```
    in0 = client0.getInputStream ();
    out0 = client0.getOutputStream ();
    out0.write ("Welcome. Please wait.\r\n".getBytes ("latin1"));
    System.out.println ("Waiting..");
    Socket client1 = server.accept ();
    System.out.println ("Accepted from " + client1.getInetAddress ());
    in1 = client1.getInputStream ();
    out1 = client1.getOutputStream ();
    out1.write ("Welcome.\r\n".getBytes ("latin1"));
    out0.write ("Proceed.\r\n".getBytes ("latin1"));
  } finally {
    server.close ();
  }
}
```

This method accepts two client connections. We open a `ServerSocket server` on the specified port `port`, and then accept two connections, attaching the streams `in0`, `out0`, `in1`, and `out1` to the two `Socket`s.

Again, we surround the body of this method with a `try ... finally` clause that ensures to close `server`, regardless of how the method exits. If an exception is thrown when accepting the second connection, then the first connection will be closed by the `finally` clause of the `main()` method.

```
static int readNB (InputStream in) throws IOException {
  if (in.available () > 0)
    return in.read ();
  else
    return -2;
}
```

This method performs a nonblocking read from the specified `InputStream`, `in`, by first querying the `available()` method, and returning the value `-2` if there are no data available to be read.

Note that this method may not become aware when the client attached to `in` exits; the `available()` method will still return `0`, even if the network connection has terminated. This is a major problem with nonblocking servers of this form: The only way to determine that a client has quit is to periodically write data to the client. If they are no longer listening, an `IOException` will be thrown eventually.

16.3.1 Using a socket time-out value

An alternative approach to this server is to use a socket time-out value to abort a `read()` call after a short time-out. This still requires us to constantly poll the two

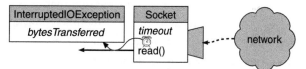

Figure 16.4 Using a socket time-out value

connections for data but has the advantage that it will notice when a socket connection is closed (figure 16.4).

For this approach we must set a time-out value on the two accepted connections and then alter the `readNB()` method:

```
client0.setSoTimeout (10);
client1.setSoTimeout (10);
```

Inside the `accept()` method we give each client a 10 millisecond time-out. Note that calling `setSoTimeout()` on the `ServerSocket` only affects calls to `accept()`; it does not set a time-out on the received connections. We must, therefore, set one for each connection as it arrives.

```
static int readNB (InputStream in) throws IOException {
  try {
    return in.read ();
  } catch (InterruptedIOException ex) {
    return -2;
  }
}
```

Here we simply read a byte of data from the `InputStream in`. If this call takes more than 10 milliseconds, an `InterruptedIOException` will be thrown and we can return -2, indicating that there are no data available to be read. If the connection is closed, the `read()` call should correctly return -1 indicating EOF.

Note that in neither of these examples do we attempt to address the problem of a call to `write()` blocking, although this may happen if OS write-buffers fill up and the write call must block until space becomes available. Other than the use of multiple threads, there is no means to address this problem in Java.

16.3.2 Simulating nonblocking with threads

Another alternative nonblocking mechanism is to use a special `InputStream` that uses an active thread to read from the attached stream into an internal pipe. This thread usually will sit in a blocking wait, reading data from the attached stream and inserting this data into the pipe (figure 16.5).

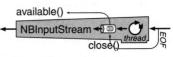

Figure 16.5 Simulating nonblocking with threads

Such a class can be used in the same manner as the nonblocking server example; that is, by querying its `available()` method before attempting to read data. The difference with the former example is that this active alternative will successfully identify when the attached stream is closed because the reading thread will receive an EOF and can then close the pipe.

Ultimately, however, such a class serves little purpose when compared with a full-blown multithreaded server because the latter is more flexible, powerful, and efficient.

16.3.3 A select() method

The Berkeley sockets' `select()` function allows a caller to supply a list of file descriptors, such as a list of `Socket`s and `ServerSocket`s, and to determine which of those are ready for reading or writing. This allows a single-threaded server to poll a list of `Socket`s and determine which have new data available for reading and which are ready to accept data to be written. It can also poll a `ServerSocket` to see if incoming connections are waiting. Using this mechanism, a server need never block on an I/O operation because it will only perform the operation when it knows that it will not block. Unfortunately, there is currently no Java interface to this useful facility although proposals apparently exist for its introduction.

Using native methods, it is possible to provide an equivalent call, but the solution is complex: native methods can access nonpublic fields of the various Java library classes. To *select* on a `Socket` or `ServerSocket`, it is necessary to violate Java's access security and extract the package-private `SocketImpl` field `impl`. The underlying file descriptor of this `SocketImpl` can then be accessed by extracting its `FileDescriptor` field `fd`. This `FileDescriptor` object has a private `int` field `fd` that can be extracted, and that corresponds to the underlying OS file descriptor of the `Socket` or `ServerSocket`, which can then be passed on to the usual C `select()` function. It should also be noted that some JVMs use a value one higher than the underlying OS file descriptor, so an implementation may have to take this into account.

It is beyond the scope of this book to provide details of a full native-method implementation of this call; however, the following C fragment demonstrates the native implementation of a method that prints out the underlying file descriptor of a `Socket` or `ServerSocket`. The extension to use an array of parameters and actually call `select()` should be routine, if arduous, for an experienced native-methods programmer.

```
JNIEXPORT jint JNICALL Java_Selector_getFD
(JNIEnv *env, jclass myclass, jobject socket) {
  /* extract the field: java.net.SocketImpl impl */
  jclass socketClass = (*env)->GetObjectClass (env, socket);
  jfieldID implId = (*env)->GetFieldID
    (env, socketClass, "impl", "Ljava/net/SocketImpl;");
  jobject impl = (*env)->GetObjectField (env, socket, implId);
  /* extract the field: java.io.FileDescriptor fd */
  jclass implClass = (*env)->GetObjectClass (env, impl);
  jfieldID fdId = (*env)->GetFieldID
    (env, implClass, "fd", "Ljava/io/FileDescriptor;");
  jobject fd = (*env)->GetObjectField (env, impl, fdId);
  /* extract the field: int fd */
```

```
  jclass fdClass = (*env)->GetObjectClass (env, fd);
  jfieldID osFdId = (*env)->GetFieldID (env, fdClass, "fd", "I");
  jint osFd = (*env)->GetIntField (env, fd, osFdId);
  /* return the result */
  return osFd;
}
```

The `jobject socket` is the parameter (a `Socket` or `ServerSocket`) that we wish to dissect. We determine `socketClass`, its class, and `implId`, the field identifier of its `SocketImpl` field `impl`. We then extract this field into the `jobject impl`. Again, we determine the class of this object, `implClass`, and the field identifier `fdId` of its `FileDescriptor` field `fd`. We extract this field into the `jobject fd` and determine `fdClass`, its class, `osFdId`, the field identifier of its `int` field `fd`. We then extract this into the `jint` variable `osFd`. We finally return this value which is the file descriptor that we would pass to `select()` in a full implementation.

This solution is complex and obviously only readily applicable to a server situation where a shared library or DLL can be deployed to provide the native `select()` function. The solution is, however, a useful alternative to multithreading. Note that implementation of this is somewhat dependent upon the JVM and the native threads being used. The *green threads* package that is used by most JavaSoft JVMs does not appear to currently support (at the time of writing) `select()`. Instead, you must use a JVM that uses native OS threads, such as the Solaris native-thread JVM.

16.4 Building a multithreaded echo server

Multithreaded servers overcome the blocking I/O problems by launching one or more threads per client connection. The main server thread will concern itself with accepting client connections, while the handler threads will serve existing connections. A handler thread can block on reading data from a client while all other threads keep processing.

This type of server has many advantages over the nonblocking alternative. Exceptions and other problems with a single connection are localized to the thread that is processing the connection; this generally leads to a more robust server. Under normal loads, all of the threads will spend most of their time blocking on I/O, unlike the nonblocking server, which must constantly monitor all client connections. The handler class also leads to a clean server implementation; all the code dedicated to accepting connections can be

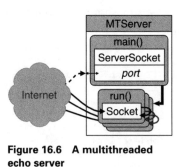

Figure 16.6   A multithreaded echo server

located in one class, and all of the code dedicated to handling a connection will be located in another.

This server is a multithreaded version of the first echo server that we looked at. The main thread accepts connections, launching a new handler for each one. Each handler echoes all received data back to the sender (figure 16.6).

```java
import java.net.*;
import java.io.*;

public class MTEchoServer extends Thread {
  // MTEchoServer (Socket socket) ...
  // public void run () ...
  // public static void main (String[] args) throws IOException ...
}
```

The MTEchoServer class extends Thread; we use the same class for both the mainline and the handlers. The main thread runs in the main() method, accepting new connections and creating MTEchoServer threads to process these connections. When we start a client's handler thread, the run() method takes care of echoing data back to the client.

```java
protected Socket socket;

MTEchoServer (Socket socket) {
  this.socket = socket;
}
```

In the constructor, we accept a reference to the Socket that this handler will process. The caller must manually call our start() method to start a thread processing this connection.

```java
public void run () {
  try {
    InputStream in = socket.getInputStream ();
    OutputStream out = socket.getOutputStream ();
    out.write ("Welcome to the multithreaded echo server.\r\n"
               .getBytes ("latin1"));
    byte[] buffer = new byte[1024];
    int read;
    while ((read = in.read (buffer)) >= 0)
      out.write (buffer, 0, read);
  } catch (IOException ex) {
    ex.printStackTrace ();
  } finally {
    try {
      socket.close ();
    } catch (IOException ignored) {
    }
  }
}
```

The thread that will process this connection enters the run() method. We open streams to and from the client, and send an introductory message. We then loop, echoing any received data back to the client; we use a small buffer buffer to make this transfer more efficient. The copy loop reads data into this buffer; the read variable indicates how many data were just read. If this is a positive amount, then we echo the data back to the client; otherwise, EOF has been reached and we exit the loop.

As usual, when dealing with I/O, we must deal with exceptions. If an exception occurs in the body of the run() method, we print the exception and close down; the thread will halt when we leave the run() method. We use a finally clause to ensure that we close the Socket, regardless of whether we exit because of an exception or naturally from an EOF.

```
public static void main (String[] args) throws IOException {
   if (args.length != 1)
      throw new IllegalArgumentException ("Syntax: MTEchoServer <port>");
   System.out.println ("Starting on port " + args[0]);
   ServerSocket server = new ServerSocket (Integer.parseInt (args[0]));
   while (true) {
      Socket client = server.accept ();
      MTEchoServer echo = new MTEchoServer (client);
      echo.start ();
   }
}
```

The main() method is responsible for accepting new connections. We ensure that a port number has been specified on the command line, and then open a new ServerSocket that listens on this port. We can then have a simple main loop that just accepts new Sockets and starts a new handler thread for each such connection. These handler threads will process the connections independently from this mainline.

Building a multithreaded server allows us to separate accepting connections from actually processing these connections. This leads to a cleaner implementation and also protects the server from problems with individual connections. An example of this type of problem is the write() method blocking. TCP guarantees that any data that are successfully written to a Socket *will* be delivered to the client (or an error will be raised). In the case of client or network problems, this may mean that a write() method will take time to complete. If we only have a single thread handling multiple clients, this blocking will delay all other clients. With multiple threads, such problems are isolated to just the offending connection.

16.5 *Wrapping up*

This chapter introduced the ServerSocket API, using comparatively simple examples. There has been no application-level protocol to deal with; we have just echoed data back to the clients. In the following chapters, we will look at developing servers that have actual application-level protocols with which we must interface.

In the next chapter we develop a fairly complex Web server application that follows similar lines to the last multithreaded server example: a main loop accepts client connections, which are processed by separate handler threads. In the following chapter, we develop a multithreaded client/server Internet chat system that introduces communication among the handler threads: when data is received from any client, it is rebroadcast to all connected clients. This introduces problems, because a single thread must write to many clients and so must deal with the associated potential communication errors. Later in the book, in the message streams section, we will revisit multithreaded servers and look at solutions to some of these problems.

CHAPTER 17

Building a Web server

The World Wide Web is a distributed client/server system for publishing and delivering content over the Internet using HTTP. Resources on the Web are located on Web servers, which are made available and maintained by anyone who wants to publish content.

In this chapter, we develop a multithreaded Web server that is HTTP 1.0 and CGI 1.0 compliant. The server also provides a special interface to support Java server extensions that produce dynamic content. This is similar to, albeit much simpler than, the Java servlet API which we will discuss in chapters 26 and 27.

In this chapter, we will start with an overview of the relevant standards to our server; notably, HTTP and the CGI standard. Then we will discuss the architecture of the server that we will implement, and finally, we will take a look at the actual implementation.

17.1 Resources on the Web

Resources on the Web are identified with URL syntax (protocol://host/resource) with http as the protocol portion of the URL. Standard Web servers operate on TCP port 80, but Web servers can be run on other ports as well. In this case, a URL trying to access their resources will also include the relevant port number (http://host:port/resource). URLs are also referred to as URIs, or Uniform Resource Identifiers. URIs encompass many different ways of identifying resources, including URLs, which specify the location of a resource, and Uniform Resource Names (URNs), which simply specify the location-independent name of a resource. For details, see RFCs 1630, 1738, 2141, and 2396.

The Web is request-driven. A Web client, such as Netscape Navigator, asks for a content resource from a Web server. The server responds by either delivering

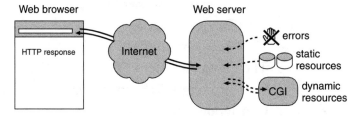

Figure 17.1 Resources on the Web

the requested resource to the client or returning a message indicating why the resource cannot be delivered (figure 17.1).

17.1.1 Static resources

Web servers provide two types of resources to clients: *static* and *dynamic*. Static resources are files such as HTML documents, text documents, images, and audio clips. When a static resource is requested, the server loads it from the file system and sends it to the client, encapsulated in an HTTP response. Static information can usually be cached for efficiency because it will not often change.

17.1.2 Dynamic resources

Dynamic resources are generated as the result of a request to a URL that represents a program or database access instead of a static file. In the case of a program, the server launches the requested program, routes client information to it, and passes the program's output back to the client as the response to the request. For database access, the client's request is translated into a database query and the result is formatted and returned to the client.

17.2 The HyperText Transfer Protocol

HTTP is a simple application-layer protocol that enables message passing between Web clients and Web servers, including intermediate proxy layers.

An HTTP *conversation* between client and server consists of a client request and a server response over a single TCP connection. The client initiates the conversation with an HTTP request to the server. The server then fulfills the request, for example by returning an HTML document or sending an error message as the response, and then closes the connection. More recent versions of HTTP support multiple transactions across a single connection (keepalive); however, we will not address that issue here.

The HTTP protocol is fundamentally a stateless protocol. This means that each client request is serviced by the server independently of any other requests, and no information about a client is maintained at the server after a connection has closed. A number of extensions to HTTP have been implemented to circumvent some of the problems arising from statelessness, including hidden fields in HTML forms and cookies. These extensions are useful but are not mandatory for a fully functional basic server such as the one in this chapter.

17.2.1 HTTP versions

Web servers and Web clients communicate and transfer data using HTTP. The latest version of HTTP is 1.1, which is detailed in RFC 2068. HTTP version 1.0, which is implemented by the server in this chapter, is documented in RFC 1945. An HTTP 1.0 compliant server also must support HTTP version 0.9, or *simple* HTTP.

HTTP 1.1 has in fact progressed somewhat since RFC 2068. At the time of writing, revision 5 to that document has been proposed as an Internet standard. Details of the progress of HTTP, including discussion of HTTP-NG, can be found on the World Wide Web Consortium's site at http://www.w3.org/Protocols/.

17.3 HTTP requests

An HTTP *request* contains information about a resource on the server and the action the client wishes the server to perform on the resource. The request line is the first line of a request:

```
GET /document.html HTTP/1.0
```

The first element of the request line is called the *method*; it specifies what action the server is to perform on the resource. The second element is the *request URI*, which denotes the resource in question. A third element, which is present in HTTP 1.0 and 1.1 requests, indicates the *version* of HTTP understood by the client.

HTTP requests come in two forms: simple and full. Simple (HTTP 0.9) requests consist of only one of two methods (*get* or *post*) and a request URI. Full requests can employ an additional method, called *head*. Full requests always include the client HTTP version as a third element of the request line. Full requests may also follow the request with various headers, which give more information about the request and the client.

17.3.1 Simple get request

A simple get request follows the old HTTP 0.9 specification which, while still in use, is essentially obsolete.

```
GET /document.html[CRLF]
```

17.3.2 Full get request

A full get request follows the HTTP 1.0 (or later) specification. It includes the HTTP version number in the request. The request must be followed by a blank line.

```
GET /document.html HTTP/1.0[CRLF]
[LF]
```

17.3.3 Full get request with headers

HTTP/1.0 supports optional headers in a request. The following request tells the server the type of browser being used and requests that the document only be returned if it has been modified more recently than the specified date. This particular header allows the browser to use a cached version of the document if the original has not changed. The request must be followed by a blank line.

```
GET /document.html HTTP/1.0[CRLF]
User-Agent: Surfer/1.01 libhttp/0.1[CRLF]
If-Modified-Since: Sun, 20 Oct 1996 04:07:51 GMT[CRLF]
[LF]
```

17.3.4 Post request

A post request allows the client to include a significant body of data in a request. Post is used, for example, to submit a large body of information to a CGI script or to upload a file to a Web server, to be processed by a target script. The content-length header is mandatory with a post request; the request headers must be followed by a blank line.

```
POST /cgi-bin/code.cgi HTTP/1.0[CRLF]
Content-type: application/octet-stream[CRLF]
Content-length: 2048[CRLF]
[LF]
body
```

Some Web servers and Web proxies also require that the post body be followed by a CRLF sequence; this should not be counted in the content-length header.

17.3.5 Head request

Head requests return only the headers of the resource, or the headers of an error message if an error occurs. This is useful to find out information about a document without the expense of transmitting the actual document. This method is illegal in a simple request since HTTP 0.9 does not support head requests.

```
HEAD /index.html HTTP/1.0[CRLF]
[LF]
```

17.3.6 Request URIs and virtual paths

The main function of the request URI portion of the request line (the second token) is to specify a virtual path to the resource that the client is requesting.

A URI consists of both a virtual path and an optional query string, separated by a query character (?):

```
/cgi-bin/code.cgi?query-string
```

The virtual path is a pathlike string that identifies a document or service being requested; the query string is some optional additional information that will be supplied to a dynamic resource. The virtual path is *virtual* because it always uses a / path-element separator, independent of the client or server operating system. Although it looks like a path, it will not be an absolute path on the Web server; it may refer to CGI script or other dynamic resources, and will almost certainly be translated according to aliasing rules to prevent external users from accessing arbitrary documents on the host machine (figure 17.2).

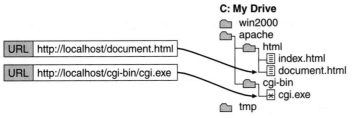

Figure 17.2   Request URIs and virtual paths

17.3.7 URI encoding

The request URI portion of the request line may be sent from the client in an encoded form; this allows arbitrary textual characters to be transmitted in unambiguous ASCII format. Therefore, before the server can process it, the request URI must be decoded to change + characters to space characters. Also, certain characters are encoded to a hexadecimal value, denoted by a preceding %.

Because of the fact that the raw request URI from the client may contain '..' and '.' path elements, it must finally be canonicalized to

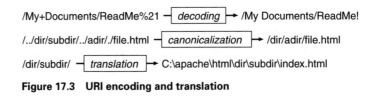

Figure 17.3   URI encoding and translation

remove these before translation to the physical file system location (figure 17.3). Failure to do so allows a client to access data outside of the server's document root, which is a serious security threat; for example, a client could request /../../etc/passwd which would refer to a document outside of the Web server's HTML directory.

17.4 HTTP responses

The Web server's response varies with the type of request and whether or not the request could be serviced.

17.4.1 Simple response

A simple response is only returned in response to an HTTP 0.9 request. It consists of the body of the requested resource with no headers.

body

CHAPTER 17   BUILDING A WEB SERVER

17.4.2 Full response

A full response includes a status line followed by the body of the document. The status line consists of the HTTP version of the response and a status code, which indicates how successfully the request was serviced.

```
HTTP/1.0 200 OK[CRLF]
[LF]
body
```

17.4.3 Full response with headers

A full response also may include some headers that include additional information about the server and requested document, such as its content type, whether it is compressed, and when it was last modified.

```
HTTP/1.0 200 OK[CRLF]
Server: Apache/1.2b11[CRLF]
Content-type: text/html[CRLF]
Content-encoding: x-gzip[CRLF]
[LF]
body
```

17.4.4 HTTP response codes

Table 17.1 lists the status codes that are included with HTTP 1.0 responses. The most common status code is 200, which means that the request was serviced successfully; 301 means that the document has moved (the response headers will include the new location); 404 means that the document was not found.

Table 17.1   HTTP response codes

Code	Meaning
200	OK
201	Created
202	Accepted
204	No Content
301	Moved Permanently
302	Moved Temporarily
304	Not Modified
400	Bad Request
401	Unauthorized
403	Forbidden
404	Not Found
500	Internal Server Error
501	Not Implemented

Table 17.1   HTTP response codes

502	Bad Gateway
503	Service Unavailable

17.4.5 MIME types

Multipurpose Internet Mail Extensions (MIME) is a mechanism, originally designed for email, to associate a type with a message so that the message receiver will understand how to decode/view it. MIME is defined in RFC 1521. The seven top-level MIME types defined in RFC 1521 are *text, image, audio, video, multipart, application,* and *message*. The most common subtypes associated with HTTP include *text/html, text/plain, image/gif, image/jpeg,* and *application/octet-stream*. More are listed in appendix B.

HTTP 1.0 and 1.1 support MIME typing as the means for servers to indicate the type of information contained in a response. To do this, the server sends a content-type header with the MIME type and subtype of the data being returned.

17.5 The Common Gateway Interface

CGI programs are the most widespread type of software for generating dynamic Web content. CGI enables developers to write custom request-handling software that automatically interfaces with any CGI-compliant Web server. A CGI or CGI script is a piece of software, usually written in Perl, C/C++, or a shell scripting language, that conforms to the CGI standard. For security reasons, CGIs are usually restricted to a central server directory, historically called *cgi-bin*.

When the server receives a request for a URI that refers to a CGI, it creates a process to execute the CGI, providing the CGI with certain information about the request. The server then forwards the CGI's output back to the client as the HTTP response. The server finally closes down the client connection when the CGI finishes executing (figure 17.4.

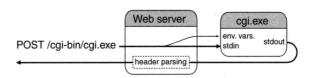

Figure 17.4   CGI processes

This section provides some details on CGI; for more information, consult the CGI spec, located at http://www.w3.org/CGI/ and http://hoohoo.ncsa.uiuc.edu/cgi/.

17.5.1 Environment variables

When the server launches a CGI process, it provides it with data required by the CGI specification. The majority of this information is contained in environment variables, the most interesting of which are:

QUERY_STRING   This variable contains the portion of the client's request following the *?* symbol; it is not decoded by the server. The query string is usually used by a client using the get request method in order to pass information to the CGI. For example, in the following request:

```
GET /cgi-bin/process.cgi?name=jim&address=pine+haus
```

The `QUERY_STRING` variable will contain `name=jim&address=pine+haus`.

PATH_INFO   This variable contains the portion of the request beyond the path to the CGI. This information is decoded by the server and may be canonicalized as well. For example, in the following request:

```
GET /cgi-bin/colorchange.cgi/blue/red
```

The `PATH_INFO` variable will contain `/blue/red`. Note the leading /.

REQUEST_METHOD   This variable contains the method used in the request; that is, GET, POST, or HEAD.

CONTENT_TYPE   This variable may contain the content type of the information being passed to the server in a post request. Data encoded from an HTML form has content type application/x-www-form-urlencoded.

CONTENT_LENGTH   This variable will contain the value of the `Content-Length` request header. This header is mandatory for a post request; it indicates the volume of data included in the client's request. The CGI will be able to read this volume of data (in bytes) from its input stream.

Request headers   All request headers from the client are translated into environment variables by changing instances of the - character into _ and prepending HTTP_ to each variable name. For example, `Content-Length` is also supplied to a CGI script as the variable `HTTP_CONTENT_LENGTH`.

17.5.2 CGI input

A script executed with the post method has the opportunity to access `QUERY_STRING` and `PATH_INFO` variables, just like a script executed using get. In addition, it receives the body of the client's post request as its standard input, and may read CONTENT_LENGTH bytes from this source.

17.5.3 CGI output

The CGI writes its output to the server on its standard output. The server then directs this output back to the client after header processing, if any.

17.5.4 CGI header parsing

In an HTTP 1.0 response, the client expects a standard header preceding any response from the server. The server can handle the issue of headers for the CGI's response in one of two ways. The default behavior is to parse any headers that the CGI sends, insert a status line and any other headers the server wants, and send the whole resulting header to the client followed by the remaining body of the CGI's response.

The other option is for the server to simply send the content produced by the CGI directly to the client without parsing its headers at all. This is called no parse headers (NPH). NPH CGIs are responsible for explicitly sending the appropriate status line and headers to the client themselves. The server treats any CGI that begins with a special filename designation (typically nph-) as an NPH program.

17.6 Implementing a Web server

The Web server that we will implement provides the following facilities:

HTTP 1.0 compliance   To provide HTTP support, we implement facilities for parsing HTTP 0.9 and HTTP 1.0 requests and producing HTTP 0.9 and HTTP 1.0 responses.

CGI 1.0 compliance   For CGI compliance, we use the Runtime.exec() method to execute native programs; we provide the CGI 1.0-defined environment variables and use multiple threads to copy data between the client and CGI program. We support get and post to native nonheader-parsed CGI programs.

Dynamic Java extension facility   The Java extension facility allows clients to access Java extension classes that implement a special support interface; these extension classes can provide similar functions to traditional CGI programs but without the overhead of executing native programs. This facility uses Java's Class.forName().newInstance() dynamic instantiation capability.

Efficient thread reuse   Finally, we use the ReThread class that we developed in chapter 4 to allow efficient thread reuse.

17.6.1 Architecture

The architecture of our Web server is depicted in figure 17.5.

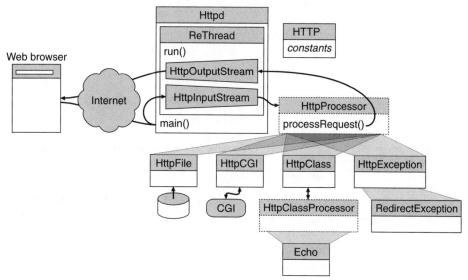

Figure 17.5 Web server architecture

Httpd   The mainline of our Webserver is provided by the Httpd class. This provides both a main() method that opens a ServerSocket and accepts client connections, and support for processing individual client connections in separate threads.

HttpProcessor   The actual processing of client requests is deferred to classes that implement the HttpProcessor interface. This interface simply describes how the Httpd class can call on the processor to respond to a client request.

HttpInputStream   This InputStream provides specialized support for reading HTTP requests, including parsing the request line and reading any request headers.

HttpOutputStream   This OutputStream provides specialized support for writing HTTP responses, including constructing the response line and setting response headers.

HttpFile   This implementation of the HttpProcessor interface provides support for serving static files from the local file system. This is used for the majority of Web server requests.

HttpCGI   This implementation of the HttpProcessor interface provides support for executing CGI programs in response to client requests. This supports both get and post requests.

HttpClass   This implementation of the `HttpProcessor` interface provides support for Java server-extension classes that provide similar pure-Java facilities to those provided by CGI. It allows the Web server to be dynamically extended with added capabilities.

HttpClassProcessor   This interface must be implemented by server-extension classes accessed through the `HttpClass` interface.

HttpException   This `IOException` subclass is used to return HTTP errors to the client. It implements the `HttpProcessor` interface so when raised in response to a client request, it can send an appropriate HTTP error message to the client.

RedirectException   This `HttpException` subclass provides special support for returning HTTP redirect messages to the client.

HTTP   This support class provides predefined constants and utility methods for use by other classes of this Web server.

Echo   This is a simple implementation of the `HttpClassProcessor` interface that demonstrates a server extension that echoes back the client's query string.

17.6.2 Class Httpd

The `Httpd` class is the main server class. It consists of both a mainline that opens a `ServerSocket` and accepts incoming connections, and support for actually processing these connections. With each connection accepted by the mainline, a new `Httpd` is created that will handle the client's request and a new thread is launched to execute this handler.

For efficiency, we use the `ReThread` class for threading purposes. This class maintains a pool of threads that have finished with previous clients and that are automatically awakened and reused for new tasks. A complete discussion of thread usage and efficiency is included at the end of this chapter.

```
import java.io.*;
import java.net.*;
import java.util.*;

public class Httpd implements Runnable {
  // public static void main (String[] args) throws IOException ...
  // protected Httpd (Socket client) ...
  // public void run () ...
}
```

Our `Httpd` class provides a `main()` method that performs the mainline of the Web-server (accepting incoming client connections) and implements `Runnable`, providing a run() method in order to actually handle client Socket connections in separate threads.

```
public static void main (String[] args) throws IOException {
  ServerSocket server = new ServerSocket (HTTP.PORT);
  while (true) {
    Socket client = server.accept ();
    Httpd httpd = new Httpd (client);
    ReThread reThread = new ReThread (httpd);
    reThread.start ();
  }
}
```

The main() method opens a new ServerSocket on the default port defined in the HTTP class and then loops, accepting incoming connections and passing each such connection off to a new Httpd for processing. We use the ReThread class for threading purposes instead of the normal Thread class. This makes our server more efficient because old threads are reused instead of the server having to constantly create threads and dispose of old ones.

```
protected Socket client;

public Httpd (Socket client) {
  this.client = client;
}
```

Our constructor takes a copy of the client Socket, for processing by a separate thread in the run() method.

```
public void run () {
  try {
    InputStream in = client.getInputStream ();
    HttpInputStream httpIn = new HttpInputStream (in);
    HttpProcessor processor = getProcessor (httpIn);
    OutputStream out = client.getOutputStream ();
    HttpOutputStream httpOut = new HttpOutputStream (out, httpIn);
    processor.processRequest (httpOut);
    httpOut.flush ();
  } catch (IOException ex) {
    ex.printStackTrace ();
  } finally {
    try {
      client.close ();
    } catch (IOException ignored) {
    }
  }
}

// protected HttpProcessor getProcessor (HttpInputStream httpIn) ...
```

Our run() method performs the high-level stages of processing a client requests. We first construct an HttpInputStream on the client's input stream; this class provides facilities to read in and parse HTTP requests. Then we call on the getProcessor() method to obtain a processor for the client's request; remember, our architecture defers the processing of requests to HttpProcessor classes that implement different services such as serving files, CGI scripts, or server support classes.

Next we construct an HttpOutputStream on the client's output stream; this class provides facilities to format and write out HTTP responses. We then call our processor's processRequest() method to process the request; then we flush the output stream and finally close the client socket. We provide minimal, appropriate, and necessary exception handling.

When the processor thread exits this method, it will return to the ReThread thread pool for future reuse. Note the simplicity of our architecture; the mainline of processing a request follows a few major steps that we abstract out into separate support classes, resulting in a simple, understandable, and extensible implementation.

```
protected HttpProcessor getProcessor (HttpInputStream httpIn) {
  try {
    httpIn.readRequest ();
    if (httpIn.getPath ().startsWith (HTTP.CGI_BIN))
      return new HttpCGI (httpIn, client.getInetAddress ());
    else if (httpIn.getPath ().startsWith (HTTP.CLASS_BIN))
      return new HttpClass (httpIn);
    else
      return new HttpFile (httpIn);
  } catch (HttpException ex) {
    return ex;
  } catch (Exception ex) {
    StringWriter trace = new StringWriter ();
    ex.printStackTrace (new PrintWriter (trace, true));
    return new HttpException (HTTP.STATUS_INTERNAL_ERROR,
                   "<PRE>" + trace + "</PRE>");
  }
}
```

This method obtains an appropriate HttpProcessor for the client's request. We call on the input stream to parse the client's request, and then determine whether the requested URI starts with /cgi-bin/ or /class-bin/, returning an HttpCGI or HttpClass processor if so. Otherwise, the request is for a plain file, and so, we return a HttpFile processor.

Note in our exception handling that the HttpException class itself implements HttpProcessor, constructing an appropriate HTTP error response in its process-Request() method, so if any of the earlier methods raise a HttpException, we can simply return that as an appropriate processor. If any other exception arises, we return a new internal-error `HttpException` containing the original exception's stack trace. This stack trace will then be displayed in the client's browser.

17.6.3 Interface HttpProcessor

This interface describes a class that will produce an HTTP response in response to a client's HTTP request. The mechanism for initializing the processor with the request information is entirely dependent upon the particular processor; what this interface describes is simply how the class will produce a response.

```
import java.io.*;

public interface HttpProcessor {
  public void processRequest (HttpOutputStream out) throws IOException;
}
```

We declare a single method, `processRequest()`, that accepts an `HttpOutputStream` into which the processor's response should be written.

It is important that a processor throw any `HttpException` resulting from the client's request during its initialization stages, and not from the `processRequest()` method. By the time `processRequest()` is called, it is assumed that the request is valid and so an `HttpException` will simply be ignored.

17.6.4 Class HttpInputStream

The `HttpInputStream` class is a specialized `InputStream` that provides support for reading HTTP requests. For efficiency, we subclass `BufferedInputStream`, adding HTTP-related methods to the buffering that class provides.

We primarily add two HTTP-related facilities: the first is a general-purpose `readLine()` method that reads a line of text; the second is the facility to parse an HTTP request, including separating the components of the request line into the method, request path, query string, and protocol version; and reading any subsequent request headers. It is not possible to determine the path info of the request in a fully general way at this level, and so we defer that to the caller.

```
import java.io.*;
import java.net.*;
import java.util.*;

public class HttpInputStream extends BufferedInputStream {
  // public HttpInputStream (InputStream in) ...
  // public void readRequest () throws IOException ...
  // public String readLine () throws IOException ...
  // public String getMethod () ...
  // public String getPath () ...
  // public String getQueryString () ...
  // public float getVersion () ...
```

```
  // public String getHeader (String name) ...
  // public Enumeration getHeaderNames () ...
}
```

Our `HttpInputStream` class extends `BufferedInputStream`, adding a read-
Request() method that reads in and parses an HTTP request, a `readLine()` method
that reads a single line of text, and various accessor methods that allow the caller to
extract the different components of the preparsed HTTP request.

```
public HttpInputStream (InputStream in) {
  super (in);
}
```

The constructor simply passes the attached stream on to the superconstructor.

```
protected String method, path, queryString;
protected float version;
protected Hashtable headers = new Hashtable ();

public void readRequest () throws IOException {
  String request = readLine ();
  if (request == null)
    throw new HttpException (HTTP.STATUS_BAD_REQUEST, "Null query");
  StringTokenizer parts = new StringTokenizer (request);
  try {
    parseMethod (parts.nextToken ());
    parseRequest (parts.nextToken ());
  } catch (NoSuchElementException ex) {
    throw new HttpException (HTTP.STATUS_BAD_REQUEST, request);
  }
  if (parts.hasMoreTokens ())
    parseVersion (parts.nextToken ());
  else
    version = 0.9f;
  if ((version < 1.0f) && (method == HTTP.METHOD_HEAD))
    throw new HttpException (HTTP.STATUS_NOT_ALLOWED, method);
  if (version >= 1.0f)
    readHeaders ();
}

// protected void parseMethod (String method) throws HttpException ...
// protected void parseRequest (String request) throws HttpException ...
// protected void parseVersion (String verStr) throws HttpException ...
// protected void readHeaders () throws IOException ...
```

The `readRequest()` method reads in and parses an HTTP request. We read the
first line, which consists of a request method, URI, and optional version number, calling
on the `parseMethod()`, `parseRequest()`, and `parseVersion()` methods to parse
each component of the request line. If this is an HTTP version 1.0 or greater request, we
finally call on the `readHeaders()` method to read the subsequent request headers.

Note that at any point, if we encounter an incongruity with the request, we simply throw an appropriate HttpException. The caller—Httpd, in this case—will automatically take care of transforming this exception into an error response being returned to the client.

```
protected void parseMethod (String method) throws HttpException {
  if (method.equals (HTTP.METHOD_GET))
    this.method = HTTP.METHOD_GET;
  else if (method.equals (HTTP.METHOD_POST))
    this.method = HTTP.METHOD_POST;
  else if (method.equals (HTTP.METHOD_HEAD))
    this.method = HTTP.METHOD_HEAD;
  else
    throw new HttpException (HTTP.STATUS_NOT_IMPLEMENTED, method);
}
```

This method parses the request method. If it is not one supported by this server, we throw a notimplemented HttpException. Otherwise, we assign the method instance variable to refer to HTTP.METHOD_GET, HTTP.METHOD_POST, or HTTP.METHOD_HEAD, allowing the efficient == referential-equality operator to be used.

```
protected void parseRequest (String request) throws HttpException {
  if (!request.startsWith ("/"))
    throw new HttpException (HTTP.STATUS_BAD_REQUEST, request);
  int queryIdx = request.indexOf ('?');
  if (queryIdx == -1) {
    path = HTTP.canonicalizePath (request);
    queryString = "";
  } else {
    path = HTTP.canonicalizePath (request.substring (0, queryIdx));
    queryString = request.substring (queryIdx + 1);
  }
}
```

This method parses the request URI. We simply separate it into the virtual path and query string and then canonicalize the path, removing any //, /./, and /../ elements.

```
protected void parseVersion (String verStr) throws HttpException {
  if (!verStr.startsWith ("HTTP/"))
    throw new HttpException (HTTP.STATUS_BAD_REQUEST, verStr);
  try {
    version = Float.valueOf (verStr.substring (5)).floatValue ();
  } catch (NumberFormatException ex) {
    throw new HttpException (HTTP.STATUS_BAD_REQUEST, verStr);
  }
}
```

This method parses the request version, if present. The version number must have the form *HTTP/x.y.*

```
protected void readHeaders () throws IOException {
  String header;
  while (((header = readLine ()) != null) && !header.equals ("")) {
    int colonIdx = header.indexOf (':');
    if (colonIdx != -1) {
      String name = header.substring (0, colonIdx);
      String value = header.substring (colonIdx + 1);
      headers.put (name.toLowerCase (), value.trim ());
    }
  }
}
```

This method reads any request headers that follow the request line. We read lines until we encounter a blank line, separating each line into the header name and value and inserting these into headers.

```
public String readLine () throws IOException {
  StringBuffer line = new StringBuffer ();
  int c;
  while (((c = read ()) != -1) && (c != '\n') && (c != '\r'))
    line.append ((char) c);
  if ((c == '\r') && ((c = read ()) != '\n') && (c != -1))
    -- pos;
  return ((c == -1) && (line.length () == 0)) ? null : line.toString ();
}
```

This method reads a line of text. We read until we encounter the end of the attached stream, a \n or a \r. If we encounter a \r, we read one more character to see if this line ends with \r\n. If so, we discard the second character; otherwise we unread it by stepping back the superclass read index. We finally return the line we have just read, or null if we've reached the EOF.

```
public String getMethod () {
  return method;
}
```

This method returns the preparsed request method, one of get, post, or head. For efficiency, we actually ensure that this will be referentially equal to HTTP.METHOD_GET, HTTP.METHOD_POST, or HTTP.METHOD_HEAD, meaning that a simple == can be used for comparison purposes.

```
public String getPath () {
  return path;
}
```

This method returns the canonicalized request path.

```
public String getQueryString () {
  return queryString;
```

```
  }
```

This method returns the query string, if any, or else an empty string.

```
public float getVersion () {
  return version;
}
```

This method returns the request protocol version.

```
public String getHeader (String name) {
  return (String) headers.get (name.toLowerCase ());
}
```

This method returns the value of the specified request header or else `null`. The case of the header name is ignored.

```
public Enumeration getHeaderNames () {
  return headers.keys ();
}
```

This method returns an `Enumeration` of all the request header names.

17.6.5 Class HttpOutputStream

The `HttpOutputStream` class is a specialized `OutputStream` that provides support for writing HTTP responses. For efficiency, we subclass `BufferedOutputStream`, adding HTTP-related methods to the buffering that class provides.

We add support for forming and sending the header of the HTTP response, including the initial status line and any subsequent headers. We also add support for sending `Strings`. This class provides internal support for automatically suppressing the headers of HTTP 0.9 responses and suppressing the body of HTTP 1.0 head-request responses.

```
import java.io.*;
import java.net.*;
import java.util.*;

public class HttpOutputStream extends BufferedOutputStream {
  // public HttpOutputStream (OutputStream out, HttpInputStream in) ...
  // public void setCode (int code) ...
  // public void setHeader (String attr, String value) ...
  // public boolean sendHeaders () throws IOException ...
  // public void write (String msg) throws IOException ...
  // public void write (InputStream stream) throws IOException ...
}
```

Our `HttpOutputStream` class extends `BufferedOutputStream`, adding set-Code(), setHeader(), and sendHeaders() methods for forming and transmitting the response header, as well as two new `write()` methods—one that writes a string of text and another that writes out the contents of an `InputStream`.

```
protected int code;
protected boolean sendHeaders, sendBody;
protected Hashtable headers = new Hashtable ();

public HttpOutputStream (OutputStream out, HttpInputStream in) {
  super (out);
  code = HTTP.STATUS_OKAY;
  setHeader ("Server", HTTP.SERVER_INFO);
  setHeader ("Date", new Date ().toString ());
  sendHeaders = (in.getVersion () >= 1.0);
  sendBody = !HTTP.METHOD_HEAD.equals (in.getMethod ());
}
```

Our constructor passes the attached stream on to the superconstructor and then performs some basic setup. We set a default response code, assign some default headers, and then set the `sendHeaders` and `sendBody` flags, based on the client's request, that indicate whether headers should be transmitted (HTTP 1.0 requests) and whether a body should be transmitted (for all but head requests).

```
public void setCode (int code) {
  this.code = code;
}
```

This method sets the response code that will be sent in the status line of this HTTP response.

```
public void setHeader (String attr, String value) {
  headers.put (attr, value);
}
```

This method adds a header that will be returned at the start of this HTTP response.

```
public boolean sendHeaders () throws IOException {
  if (sendHeaders) {
    write ("HTTP/1.0 " + code + " " + HTTP.getCodeMessage (code) + "\r\n");
    Enumeration attrs = headers.keys ();
    while (attrs.hasMoreElements ()) {
      String attr = (String) attrs.nextElement ();
      write (attr + ": " + headers.get (attr) + "\r\n");
    }
    write ('\n');
  }
  return sendBody;
}
```

This method actually sends the HTTP headers that have been initialized with the `setCode()` and `setHeader()` methods and then returns whether the caller should send a subsequent body. If not, it will be because this is a head request and no body is required.

```
public void write (String msg) throws IOException {
   write (msg.getBytes ("latin1"));
}
```

This method writes a line of text; we convert the `String` into an array of bytes in ISO Latin 1 encoding and then write these raw bytes to the attached stream. It is up to the caller to add any end-of-line characters, if desired.

```
public void write (InputStream in) throws IOException {
   int n, length = buf.length;
   while ((n = in.read (buf, count, length - count)) >= 0)
      if ((count += n) >= length)
         out.write (buf, count = 0, length);
}
```

This method writes out the content of the specified `InputStream in`. We read the contents of the `InputStream` directly into the superclass output buffer, flushing this buffer whenever it becomes full. To do this we access the superclass variables `buf` and `count`.

17.6.6 Class HttpFile

The `HttpFile` class is an `HttpProcessor` that handles get and head requests for static file resources. This processor returns a response containing the contents of the file as well as any necessary headers.

```
import java.io.*;

public class HttpFile implements HttpProcessor {
   // public HttpFile (HttpInputStream in) throws IOException ...
   // public void processRequest (HttpOutputStream out) throws IOException ...
}
```

Our `HttpFile` class implements `HttpProcessor` and the `processRequest()` method. The client's request for a file is passed into the constructor which throws any exceptions that result from the client's request; for example, if the file does not exist, is not readable, and so forth.

```
protected File file;

public HttpFile (HttpInputStream in) throws IOException {
   if (in.getMethod () == HTTP.METHOD_POST)
```

```
      throw new HttpException (HTTP.STATUS_NOT_ALLOWED,
        "<TT>" + in.getMethod () + " " + in.getPath () + "</TT>");
    file = new File (HTTP.HTML_ROOT, HTTP.translateFilename (in.getPath ()));
    if (in.getPath ().endsWith ("/"))
      file = new File (file, HTTP.DEFAULT_INDEX);
    if (!file.exists ())
      throw new HttpException (HTTP.STATUS_NOT_FOUND,
        "File <TT>" + in.getPath () + "</TT> not found.");
    if (file.isDirectory ())
      throw new RedirectException (HTTP.STATUS_MOVED_PERMANENTLY,
          in.getPath () + "/");
    if (!file.isFile () || !file.canRead ())
      throw new HttpException (HTTP.STATUS_FORBIDDEN, in.getPath ());
  }
```

In the constructor, we fully parse the client's request. If the client attempts to post to a file, we throw an appropriate HttpException; remember, this will be translated into an appropriate HTTP response. We otherwise translate the request into a file within the local HTML document directory, appending index.html if the request ends in /.

Finally, we can verify the document requested by the client. If the document does not exist, we throw a not-found exception. If the document is a directory, we throw a RedirectException (a subclass of HttpException that sends special redirect headers), appending a / to the original request path. Otherwise, if the document is not a file or is not readable, we throw a forbidden exception.

```
  public void processRequest (HttpOutputStream out) throws IOException {
    out.setHeader ("Content-type", HTTP.guessMimeType (file.getName ()));
    out.setHeader ("Content-length", String.valueOf (file.length ()));
    if (out.sendHeaders ()) {
      FileInputStream in = new FileInputStream (file);
      out.write (in);
      in.close ();
    }
  }
```

This method will be called when it is time to send a response. We set the Content-type and Content-length headers; then call sendHeaders() to send the headers; and, finally, transmit the body of the file if necessary. Remember, the sendHeaders() method only sends the response headers if this is an HTTP 1.0 conversation, and it returns a flag indicating whether we should transmit a response body. We use the write(InputStream) method of class HttpOutputStream to transmit the contents of the requested file and then close the file.

An additional facility that is important to add for static documents, but that we will not add here, is a Last-modified header that indicates to the client when a file was last modified and adds support for the If-modified-since request header. This allows clients and proxies to efficiently cache documents that have not changed. Unfortunately, up until JDK 1.2, the `lastModified()` method of the `File` class returned a system-dependent value that could not be universally transformed into a standard date format, and so could not be used to implement this facility.

17.6.7 Class HttpCGI

The `HttpCGI` class implements the necessary function to handle get, post, and head requests for CGI resources.

The implementation is a bit more involved than that of `HttpFile` because the execution of native programs involves a moderate degree of complexity. First, it is neces-

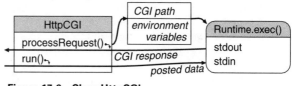

Figure 17.6   Class HttpCGI

sary to set up an environment variable array for the CGI. Then a new process must be forked to execute the script. Next, for post requests it is necessary start a new thread to copy the request data to the CGI. Finally, the output of the CGI script must be copied back to the client (figure 17.6).

Note that we do not support parse-header CGIs; a CGI is responsible for forming the entire HTTP response, including headers. To add header parsing, we would have to parse the start of the CGI's response, form and transmit our own headers, and then copy the body of the CGI response to the client.

```
import java.io.*;
import java.net.*;
import java.util.*;

public class HttpCGI implements HttpProcessor, Runnable {
  // public HttpCGI (HttpInputStream in, InetAddress ip)
       throws IOException ...
  // public void processRequest (HttpOutputStream out) throws IOException ...
  // public void run () ...
}
```

The `HttpCGI` class implements `HttpProcessor` and `processRequest()` as an implementation of an HTTP processor for CGI scripts, and `Runnable` and `run()` in order to support a separate thread for copying posted client data.

```
    protected HttpInputStream in;
    protected String scriptName, pathInfo;
    protected File cgiScript;
    protected int contentLength;

    public HttpCGI (HttpInputStream in, InetAddress ip) throws IOException {
```

```
      this.in = in;
      extractScriptName ();
      if (!cgiScript.exists ())
        throw new HttpException (HTTP.STATUS_NOT_FOUND,
          "CGI <TT>" + scriptName + "</TT> not found.");
      if (!cgiScript.isFile ())
        throw new HttpException (HTTP.STATUS_FORBIDDEN, scriptName);
      if (!cgiScript.getName ().startsWith ("nph-"))
        throw new HttpException (HTTP.STATUS_NOT_IMPLEMENTED,
                                 "Parse-header CGI unimplemented");
      if (in.getMethod () == HTTP.METHOD_POST) {
        try {
          contentLength = Integer.parseInt (in.getHeader ("Content-length"));
        } catch (NumberFormatException ex) {
          throw new HttpException (HTTP.STATUS_BAD_REQUEST,
                                   "Invalid content-length");
        }
      }
      initEnv (ip);
    }

    // protected void extractScriptName () ...
    // protected void initEnv (InetAddress ip) ...
```

The constructor accepts the client's request as an `HttpInputStream` and the IP address of the remote client. We determine the CGI script being executed by the client and verify that it exists and is a file, and that the actual script name starts with nph-. This is a simple way to verify that the client does not attempt to access a nonsupported parse-header CGI script. In addition, if the client is making a post request, we ensure that a valid Content-length header has been included. We finally initialize the CGI environment variables by calling `initEnv()`.

```
  protected void extractScriptName () {
    String path = in.getPath ();
    int pathIdx = path.indexOf ('/', 1);
    if ((pathIdx >= 0) && ((pathIdx = path.indexOf ('/', 1 + pathIdx)) >= 0)) {
      scriptName = path.substring (0, pathIdx);
      pathInfo = path.substring (pathIdx);
    } else {
      scriptName = path;
    }
    cgiScript = new File (HTTP.SERVER_LOCATION,
                          HTTP.translateFilename (scriptName.substring (1)));
  }
```

The method converts the path requested by the client into the script to be executed and the subsequent path info, if any. We assume that the script will be in the top level of the cgi-bin directory so that the path info will start at the third /. For example, the request /cgi-bin/script/index.html gets converted into the script /cgi-bin/script and path info /index.html. Supporting more flexibility would require us to compare the request against the local file system, which is more effort than this example warrants. Altogether, we construct the variables `scriptName` (the name of the script being executed), `pathInfo` (any path information following the script name) and `cgiScript` (the location of the CGI on the local file system).

```
protected String[] env;

protected void initEnv (InetAddress ip) {
  Vector environment = (Vector) HTTP.environment.clone ();
  environment.addElement ("SERVER_PROTOCOL=" + "HTTP/" +
    in.getVersion ());
  environment.addElement ("REQUEST_METHOD=" + in.getMethod ());
  if (pathInfo != null) {
    environment.addElement ("PATH_INFO=" + pathInfo);
    environment.addElement ("PATH_TRANSLATED=" + new File (
      HTTP.HTML_ROOT, HTTP.translateFilename (pathInfo)));
  }
  environment.addElement ("SCRIPT_NAME=" + scriptName);
  environment.addElement ("QUERY_STRING=" + in.getQueryString ());
  environment.addElement ("REMOTE_ADDR=" + ip.getHostAddress ());
  environment.addElement ("REMOTE_HOST=" + ip.getHostName ());
  if (in.getMethod () == HTTP.METHOD_POST) {
    environment.addElement ("CONTENT_LENGTH=" + contentLength);
    String type = in.getHeader ("Content-type");
    if (type != null)
      environment.addElement ("CONTENT_TYPE=" + type);
  }
  Enumeration headerNames = in.getHeaderNames ();
  while (headerNames.hasMoreElements ()) {
    String name = (String) headerNames.nextElement ();
    environment.addElement ("HTTP_" + name.toUpperCase ()
      .replace ('-', '_') + "=" + in.getHeader (name));
  }
  env = new String [environment.size ()];
  environment.copyInto (env);
}
```

This method sets up the environment for the CGI, using static data from the HTTP class and dynamic data from the current request. We fill in a `Vector` with the environment variables, including all of the client's request headers translated as per the CGI specification, and then copy this into the `env` environment array.

```
protected static Runtime jvm = Runtime.getRuntime ();
protected Process cgi;

public void processRequest (HttpOutputStream out) throws IOException {
  ReThread drain = null;
  try {
    if (in.getMethod () != HTTP.METHOD_POST) {
```

```
      cgi = jvm.exec (cgiScript.getPath (), env);
      cgi.getOutputStream ().close ();
      out.write (cgi.getInputStream ());
    } else {
      cgi = jvm.exec (cgiScript.getPath (), env);
      drain = new ReThread (this);
      drain.start ();
      out.write (cgi.getInputStream ());
    }
  } catch (IOException ex) {
    StringWriter trace = new StringWriter ();
    ex.printStackTrace (new PrintWriter (trace, true));
    HttpException httpEx = new HttpException
      (HTTP.STATUS_INTERNAL_ERROR, "<PRE>" + trace + "</PRE>");
    httpEx.processRequest (out);
  } finally {
    if (drain != null)
      drain.interrupt ();
    if (cgi != null)
      cgi.destroy ();
  }
}
```

As is to be expected, the processRequest() method does the main request processing work for HttpCGI. Since a CGI needs to run in its own process, we must obtain a new subprocess from the Java run time. We call Runtime.exec() to create the CGI process, passing in the name of the CGI script and the predefined environment array.

If the request method on the CGI is get or head, then we simply launch the CGI, close its input stream, and pipe its output back to the client using HttpOutputStream's write(InputStream) method. If, however, the method is post, we have to launch a separate thread that copies the client's post body into the CGI and then we can copy the CGI's output back to the client here, as usual. If we were to parse the CGI's headers, we would do it in this method, before writing data out to the client. At the very end, we use a finally clause to ensure that we clean up any resources that we have allocated when this method exits.

```
public void run () {
  OutputStream out = cgi.getOutputStream ();
  try {
    byte [] buffer = new byte [256];
    int len;
    while (!Thread.interrupted () && (contentLength > 0) &&
          ((len = in.read (buffer)) != -1)) {
      out.write (buffer, 0, len);
      contentLength -= len;
    }
    out.flush ();
  } catch (IOException ex) {
    ex.printStackTrace ();
```

```
    } finally {
      try {
        out.close ();
      } catch (IOException ignored) {
      }
    }
  }
```

This method copies the client's post body into the CGI's standard input. The purpose of using a separate thread for this is to prevent a possible deadlock, which might arise if we did this copying in the processRequest() method before reading the CGI output: It is possible that the CGI script would first produce a large amount of output before reading its input. As we are not reading its output, it will simply be buffered by the OS; similarly, it will not be reading its input so this too will be buffered. If the OS buffers become full, it is possible that both our thread and the CGI could block and become deadlocked.

17.6.8 Class HttpClass

HttpClass is an HttpProcessor that allows Java class files that implement the Http-ClassProcessor interface to process HTTP requests. HttpClassProcessor implementations have similar capabilities to CGIs, but without the cost of forking a new subprocess for each request.

```
import java.io.*;

public class HttpClass implements HttpProcessor {
  // public HttpClass (HttpInputStream in)
       throws IOException, IllegalAccessException, InstantiationException ...
  // public void processRequest (HttpOutputStream out) throws IOException ...
}
```

This class implements HttpProcessor, accepting the client's request in the constructor and producing a result with the processRequest() method.

```
  protected HttpClassProcessor processor;

  public HttpClass (HttpInputStream in) throws IOException,
      IllegalAccessException, InstantiationException {
    String classPath = in.getPath ().substring (HTTP.CLASS_BIN.length ());
    int idx = classPath.indexOf ('/');
    String className = (idx  < 0) ? classPath : classPath.substring (0, idx);
    try {
      Class theClass = Class.forName (className);
      processor = (HttpClassProcessor) theClass.newInstance ();
    } catch (ClassNotFoundException ex) {
      throw new HttpException (HTTP.STATUS_NOT_FOUND,
        "Class <TT>" + className + "</TT> not found.");
    }
```

```
      processor.initRequest (in);
  }
```

The `HttpClass` constructor takes the client's request path and converts it into a server-extension class name. We take the class name as the second element of the path; that is, the second element of /class-bin/package.ClassName/pathInfo. We then use `Class.forName().newInstance()` to create an instance of this class. If this fails with a `ClassNotFoundException`, we throw a not-found `HttpException`; otherwise, we pass on any exceptions to be rethrown as internal errors. Otherwise, we initialize the `Http-ClassProcessor`, with the client's request; this too can throw an `HttpException` if there is a problem with the request.

```
  public void processRequest (HttpOutputStream out) throws IOException {
      processor.processRequest (out);
  }
```

The `processRequest()` method simply delegates the HTTP request processing to the processor class.

17.6.9 Interface HttpClassProcessor

Interface `HttpClassProcessor` is the interface to be implemented by any class that wishes to be executed with our Java-based server-extension facility.

```
import java.io.*;

public interface HttpClassProcessor extends HttpProcessor {
  public void initRequest (HttpInputStream in) throws IOException;
}
```

Our interface extends the `HttpProcessor` interface. The new `initRequest()` method allows the processor to be initialized with the client's request. The inherited `processRequest()` method produces a response.

17.6.10 Class HttpException

The `HttpException` class is an `IOException` that itself implements `HttpProcessor`. If an HTTP-related problem occurs during the handling of a request, an appropriate instance of `HttpException` will be created and thrown. The `Httpd` class will then transfer processing of the client's request to this `HttpException`, which will return the correct HTTP error message to the client.

```
import java.io.*;

public class HttpException extends IOException implements HttpProcessor {
  // public HttpException (int code, String detail) ...
  // public void processRequest (HttpOutputStream out) throws IOException ...
}
```

Every `HttpException` is constructed with the appropiate HTTP error code and a detail message that will become the body of the HTTP response. We implement `Http-Processor` and provide a `processRequest()` method that will return an appropriate HTTP response when one of these exceptions is raised.

```
protected int code;

public HttpException (int code, String detail) {
  super (detail);
  this.code = code;
}
```

The constructor accepts the HTTP error code `code` and detail message `detail`; the detail message is passed on to the superconstructor.

```
public void processRequest (HttpOutputStream out) throws IOException {
  out.setCode (code);
  out.setHeader ("Content-Type", "text/html");
  if (out.sendHeaders ()) {
    String msg = HTTP.getCodeMessage (code);
    out.write ("<HTML><HEAD><TITLE>" + code + " " +
      msg + "</TITLE></HEAD>\n" + "<BODY><H1>" + msg + "</H1>\n" +
      getMessage () + "<P>\n</BODY></HTML>\n");
  }
}
```

The `processMethod()` method sends the HTTP error message represented by this exception to the client, encapsulated in HTML. We first set the `HttpOutputStream` error code, then set a Content-type header, and finally send an HTML body.

17.6.11 Class RedirectException

The `RedirectException` class is a subclass of `HttpException` that is specialized for sending redirect messages to the client.

```
import java.io.*;

public class RedirectException extends HttpException {
  // public RedirectException (int code, String location) ...
  // public void processRequest (HttpOutputStream out) throws IOException ...
}
```

The constructor for this class accepts the error code (one of the standard redirect codes) and the location to which the client should be redirected. We simply override the `processRequest()` method to set the appropriate redirect headers.

```
protected String location;

public RedirectException (int code, String location) {
```

```
  super (code, "The document has moved <A HREF=\"" +
    location + "\">here</A>.");
  this.location = location;
}
```

The constructor passes the error code and an appropriate response body to the superconstructor. It keeps a copy of the redirect location in the `location` variable.

```
public void processRequest (HttpOutputStream out) throws IOException {
  out.setHeader ("Location", location);
  super.processRequest (out);
}
```

The `processRequest()` method sets the Location redirect header and then calls the superclass `processRequest()` method.

17.6.12 Class HTTP

This final class related to the actual Web server implementation provides a set of related constants and utility methods.

```
import java.io.*;
import java.net.*;
import java.util.*;

public class HTTP {
  // public static String getCodeMessage (int code) ...
  // public static String canonicalizePath (String path) ...
  // public static String translateFilename (String filename) ...
  // public static String decodeString (String str) ...
  // public static String guessMimeType (String fileName) ...
}
```

In addition to many constants, we provide the method `getCodeMessage()` that returns a textual description of an HTTP error code, `canonicalizePath()` that strips relative elements from a path, `translateFilename()` that translates an HTTP filename to a local path, `decodeString()` that decodes a URL-encoded string, and `guessMimeType()` that guesses the MIME type of a filename.

```
public static final String SERVER_INFO = "JNP-HTTPD/1.0";
public static final String CGI_BIN = "/cgi-bin/";
public static final String CLASS_BIN = "/class-bin/";
public static final File SERVER_LOCATION =
  new File (System.getProperty ("user.dir"));
public static final File HTML_ROOT =
  new File (SERVER_LOCATION, "html");
public static final int PORT = 8888;
public static final String DEFAULT_INDEX = "index.html";
```

These constants provide configuration information for the Web server, including the location of HTML documents and so forth.

```
public static final String METHOD_GET = "GET";
public static final String METHOD_POST = "POST";
public static final String METHOD_HEAD = "HEAD";
```

These constants define the HTTP methods understood by this Web server.

```
public static final int STATUS_OKAY = 200;
public static final int STATUS_NO_CONTENT = 204;
public static final int STATUS_MOVED_PERMANENTLY = 301;
public static final int STATUS_MOVED_TEMPORARILY = 302;
public static final int STATUS_BAD_REQUEST = 400;
public static final int STATUS_FORBIDDEN = 403;
public static final int STATUS_NOT_FOUND = 404;
public static final int STATUS_NOT_ALLOWED = 405;
public static final int STATUS_INTERNAL_ERROR = 500;
public static final int STATUS_NOT_IMPLEMENTED = 501;
```

These constants are some standard HTTP error codes.

```
public static String getCodeMessage (int code) {
  switch (code) {
    case STATUS_OKAY:                return "OK";
    case STATUS_NO_CONTENT:          return "No Content";
    case STATUS_MOVED_PERMANENTLY:   return "Moved Permanently";
    case STATUS_MOVED_TEMPORARILY:   return "Moved Temporarily";
    case STATUS_BAD_REQUEST:         return "Bad Request";
    case STATUS_FORBIDDEN:           return "Forbidden";
    case STATUS_NOT_FOUND:           return "Not Found";
    case STATUS_NOT_ALLOWED:         return "Method Not Allowed";
    case STATUS_INTERNAL_ERROR:      return "Internal Server Error";
    case STATUS_NOT_IMPLEMENTED:     return "Not Implemented";
    default:                         return "Unknown Code (" + code + ")";
  }
}
```

This method converts an HTTP error code into an error description.

```
protected static final Vector environment = new Vector ();
static {
  environment.addElement ("SERVER_SOFTWARE=" + SERVER_INFO);
  environment.addElement ("GATEWAY_INTERFACE=" + "CGI/1.0");
  environment.addElement ("SERVER_PORT=" + PORT);
  environment.addElement ("DOCUMENT_ROOT=" + HTML_ROOT.getPath ());
  try {
    environment.addElement
      ("SERVER_NAME=" + InetAddress.getLocalHost ().getHostName ());
  } catch (UnknownHostException ex) {
    environment.addElement ("SERVER_NAME=localhost");
  }
```

```
          }
```

The Vector environment lists some static environment variables to be passed into CGI programs.

```
public static String canonicalizePath (String path) {
  char[] chars = path.toCharArray ();
  int length = chars.length;
  int idx, odx = 0;
  while ((idx = indexOf (chars, length, '/', odx)) < length - 1) {
     int ndx = indexOf (chars, length, '/', idx + 1), kill = -1;
    if (ndx == idx + 1) {
      kill = 1;
    } else if ((ndx >= idx + 2) && (chars[idx + 1] == '.')) {
      if (ndx == idx + 2) {
        kill = 2;
      } else if ((ndx == idx + 3) && (chars[idx + 2] == '.')) {
        kill = 3;
        while ((idx > 0) && (chars[-- idx] != '/'))
           ++ kill;
      }
    }
    if (kill == -1) {
      odx = ndx;
    } else if (idx + kill >= length) {
      length = odx = idx + 1;
    } else {
      length -= kill;
      System.arraycopy (chars, idx + 1 + kill,
                        chars, idx + 1, length - idx - 1);
      odx = idx;
    }
  }
  return new String (chars, 0, length);
}
// protected static int indexOf
    (char[] chars, int length, char chr, int from) ...
```

This method strips all relative components from a path, including //, /./, and /../, returning the resulting properly canonicalized path. For example, the path /../a/ /b/./c/../d/ becomes /a/b/d/. This method is somewhat convoluted because for efficiency we perform this process in-place; we essentially iterate through the path elements, removing // and /./, and removing /../ along with the preceding path element. We assume that the path begins with a /; this is required by the HTTP specification.

```
protected static int indexOf
    (char[] chars, int length, char chr, int from) {
  while ((from < length) && (chars[from] != chr))
    ++ from;
```

```
    return from;
  }
```

This helper method returns the index of the character `chr` in the `length`-character array `chars`, starting from index `from`.

```
public static String translateFilename (String filename) {
  StringBuffer result = new StringBuffer ();
  int idx, odx = 0;
  while ((idx = filename.indexOf ('/', odx)) != -1) {
    result.append (filename.substring (odx, idx)).append (File.separator);
    odx = idx + 1;
  }
  result.append (filename.substring (odx));
  return result.toString ();
}
```

This method translates an HTTP filename (e.g., /dir/file.html) into a local path-name (e.g., \dir\file.html).

```
public static String decodeString (String str) {
  String replaced = str.replace ('+', ' ');
  StringBuffer result = new StringBuffer ();
  int idx, odx = 0;
  while ((idx = str.indexOf ('%', odx)) != -1) {
    result.append (replaced.substring (odx, idx));
    try {
      result.append ((char) Integer.parseInt
        (str.substring (idx + 1, idx + 3), 16));
    } catch (NumberFormatException ex) {
    }
    odx = idx + 3;
  }
  result.append (replaced.substring (odx));
  return result.toString ();
}
```

This method decodes a URL-encoded string, converting all + characters to spaces and all $\%xy$ hex-encodings to their decoded values. This method duplicates the function of the JDK 1.2 class `URLDecoder` that provides a `decode()` method to do just this.

```
protected static final Hashtable mimeTypes = new Hashtable ();
static {
  mimeTypes.put ("gif", "image/gif");
  mimeTypes.put ("jpeg", "image/jpeg");
  mimeTypes.put ("jpg", "image/jpeg");
  mimeTypes.put ("html", "text/html");
  mimeTypes.put ("htm", "text/html");
}

public static String guessMimeType (String fileName) {
```

```
    int i = fileName.lastIndexOf (".");
    String type = (String) mimeTypes.get (
      fileName.substring (i + 1).toLowerCase ());
    return (type != null) ? type : "text/plain";
  }
```

This method guesses the MIME type of a file based on its filename. This is more comprehensively implemented by the static `URLConnection` method `guessContent-TypeFromName()`.

17.6.13 Class Echo

This class is an example implementation of the `HttpClassProcessor` interface. It accepts HTTP get requests and responds with the client's plain text query string.

```
import java.io.*;

public class Echo implements HttpClassProcessor {
  // public void initRequest (HttpInputStream in)
  //     throws IOException ...
  // public void processRequest (HttpOutputStream out)
  //     throws IOException ...
}
```

Our class implements the `HttpClassProcessor` interface and provides both methods it defines.

```
  protected String message;

  public void initRequest (HttpInputStream in) throws IOException {
    if (in.getMethod () != HTTP.METHOD_GET)
      throw new HttpException (HTTP.STATUS_NOT_ALLOWED,
        "Request method <TT>" + in.getMethod () + "</TT> not allowed.");
    message = HTTP.decodeString (in.getQueryString ());
  }
```

Our `initRequest()` method verifies that the client is accessing this resource with a get request, throwing a not-allowed `HttpException` if not. We then decode the query string and store this in the `message` variable.

```
  public void processRequest (HttpOutputStream out) throws IOException {
    out.setHeader ("Content-type", "text/plain");
    if (out.sendHeaders ())
      out.write (message + "\r\n");
  }
```

The `processRequest()` method sets a Content-type header and writes out the client's query string. A more useful `HttpClassProcessor` could perform any number of complex tasks, such as database queries.

17.6.14 In practice

To execute this Web server, set up an html directory with an index.html file (and others) and a cgi-bin directory with any CGI scripts. Install any Java extensions in your Java class path. Configure the Web server by editing and recompiling the HTTP class, and then run the Web server as follows:

```
java Httpd
```

Access the local Web server by pointing a browser at http://localhost:8888/ or http://localhost:8888/class-bin/Echo?hello+world.

17.6.15 Discussion

We have shown a simple but full-featured, extensible Web server that demonstrates several aspects of server-side Java programming including object-oriented design, custom streams, dynamic extensibility, and even integration with non-Java programs. A primary concern of server-side Java is efficiency, and so we will now discuss some related details.

By using the ReThread class, we are saved the expense of constantly creating and disposing of threads. Instead, old threads are reused for new connections in a completely transparent manner. This saves us from both the speed impact of thread creation and the memory leaks that are associated with some Java virtual machines. There are, however, several mechanisms by which we could improve on our current implementation.

For one, we have placed no limit on the number of threads that can be created. It probably would be prudent to add a limit such that the ReThread constructor will block, when a certain limit is reached, until an old thread becomes available for reuse. This is particularly important on some JVMs that experience significant slowdowns when a large number of threads are created. To protect against runaway support classes, we also could implement a time-out that forcibly terminates threads that have not completed within a certain amount of time.

Another thread-related improvement is to add prespawning of support threads. In the current implementation, if there are no threads available for reuse, the caller must wait while a new thread is created. We can eliminate this delay by adding a support thread that manually spawns new idle threads whenever the idle queue falls below a certain threshold.

Further efficiency improvements can be implemented by minimizing the number of objects that we create and reusing old objects whenever possible—in particular, by not creating a new Httpd for each client, not creating new HTTP streams for each client, and so forth. Such changes usually impact the clarity of the server, and so, are left as afterthoughts to be added if absolutely necessary.

17.7 Conclusion

This chapter has illustrated how to put together a reasonably complex server-side application that takes advantage of Java's networking and threading features. In addition, the Web server is relatively full-featured and can be easily tweaked to provide additional services and to test out new ideas. It demonstrates that Java is a viable and elegant language for implementing server-side systems, which the later chapters on servlets will reinforce.

It should be noted that it *is* possible to write a Web server in one class; it is even possible to write a Web server on a single line in a single method. What we are interested in here is not a toy example of simply implementing a server but how to implement clear, maintainable, and extensible applications. By delegating HTTP parsing to separate streams and delegating request processing to different support classes, we can produce a solution that is not only efficient, but is also robust and easy to maintain and extend.

For those interested in a more complete pure-Java Webserver, a free Java Webserver called Jigsaw is maintained and available, with source, from the W3 consortium at http://www.w3.org/Jigsaw/.

C H A P T E R   1 8

Client/server Internet applications

In this chapter, we develop and discuss two multithreaded client/server systems. The first, a simple example of a client/server chat system, is intended to demonstrate how to build TCP/IP applications using the streams available in the standard API. In later chapters, we will develop a set of classes that provide higher level facilities for building clients and servers with more complex application protocols.

The second example uses the object streams to implement a distributed list datastructure. This example is intended to demonstrate both how to use the object streams for networking and how to implement a generic subsystem that can abstract out the networking implementation of an application. On the accompanying Web site, http://nitric.com/jnp/, we show a few examples of using this datastructure to develop networked applications that completely separate their network implementation (this datastructure) from their application implementation (a whiteboard, for example).

18.1 Building a chat client

We will start with a simple graphical chat client. It takes two command-line parameters—the server name and the port number to connect to. It makes a socket connection and then opens a window with a large output region and a small input region (figure 18.1).

After the user types text into the input region and hits Return, the text is transmitted to the server. The server echoes back everything that is

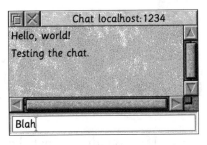

Figure 18.1 The ChatClient interface

sent by the client. The client displays everything received from the server in the output region. When multiple clients connect to one server, we have a simple chat system.

In this example, we will use the `readUTF()` and `writeUTF()` methods of the data streams to transmit text, instead of using the character streams. The character streams provide a continuous character-oriented data stream; the `readUTF()` and `writeUTF()` methods, on the other hand, provide encapsulated `String` transmission: whenever a `String` is written, it is preceded by its length. In this way we can easily identify each separate message, which makes processing the communications simpler.

18.1.1 Class ChatClient

This class implements the chat client, as described. This involves setting up a basic user interface, handling user interaction, and receiving messages from the server.

```
import java.net.*;
import java.io.*;
import java.awt.*;
import java.awt.event.*;
```

```
public class ChatClient implements Runnable, WindowListener, ActionListener {
  // public ChatClient (String host, int port) ...
  // public synchronized void start () throws IOException ...
  // public synchronized void stop () throws IOException ...
  // public void run () ...
  // public void windowOpened (WindowEvent event) ...
  // public void windowClosing (WindowEvent event) ...
  // public void actionPerformed (ActionEvent event) ...
  // public static void main (String[] args) throws IOException ...
}
```

The `ChatClient` class implements the `Runnable` interface so that we can start a thread that receives from the server, and the `WindowListener` and `ActionListener` interfaces so that we can handle events from the user interface. The constructor performs the basic setup of the GUI. The `start()` method connects to the server, displays the chat `Frame`, and starts a thread that enters the `run()` method to receive messages from the server. The `stop()` method can be used to close the `Frame` and the network connection. The `windowOpened()`, `windowClosing()`, and `actionPerformed()` methods handle user interface events, and the `main()` method executes this chat client as a stand-alone application.

```
protected String host;
protected int port;
protected Frame frame;
protected TextArea output;
protected TextField input;

public ChatClient (String host, int port) {
  this.host = host;
  this.port = port;
  frame = new Frame ("ChatClient [" + host + ':' + port + "]");
  frame.addWindowListener (this);
  output = new TextArea ();
  output.setEditable (false);
  input = new TextField ();
  input.addActionListener (this);
  frame.add ("Center", output);
  frame.add ("South", input);
  frame.pack ();
}
```

The constructor takes two parameters: the host and port to connect to, `host` and `port`. We keep a copy of these two parameters and construct the user interface, consisting of the `TextArea` output, the `TextField` input, and the `Frame` frame. We register this `ChatClient` as a listener for the useful user-interface events of these components, and pack the `Frame`.

```
protected DataInputStream dataIn;
protected DataOutputStream dataOut;
protected Thread listener;

public synchronized void start () throws IOException {
  if (listener == null) {
    Socket socket = new Socket (host, port);
    try {
      dataIn = new DataInputStream
        (new BufferedInputStream (socket.getInputStream ()));
      dataOut = new DataOutputStream
        (new BufferedOutputStream (socket.getOutputStream ()));
    } catch (IOException ex) {
      socket.close ();
      throw ex;
    }
    listener = new Thread (this);
    listener.start ();
    frame.setVisible (true);
  }
}
```

The start() method makes a Socket connection to the chat server; extracts the buffered communication streams dataIn and dataOut; starts a Thread, listener, which accepts messages from the server; and finally opens the chat Frame. We simply pass on any exceptions that occur.

```
public synchronized void stop () throws IOException {
  frame.setVisible (false);
  if (listener != null) {
    listener.interrupt ();
    listener = null;
    dataOut.close ();
  }
}
```

The stop() method interrupts the listener thread, hides the chat Frame, and closes the network connection. Because of the way the JVM is implemented, simply stopping or interrupting the listener thread may not abort a blocked call to read(). Instead we must actually close the network connection (or one of its streams) in order to cause read() to exit.

```
public void run () {
  try {
    while (!Thread.interrupted ()) {
      String line = dataIn.readUTF ();
      output.append (line + "\n");
    }
  } catch (IOException ex) {
    handleIOException (ex);
```

```
      }
    }

    // protected synchronized void handleIOException (IOException ex) ...
```

When the listener thread enters the run() method, we sit in a loop reading Strings from the input stream. We use the readUTF() method to read a String in the format that is written by the server. When a String arrives, we append it to the output region and repeat the loop. Our loop will terminate when the thread is interrupted or an IOException occurs; in that event, we call handleIOException() to properly handle the problem.

```
protected synchronized void handleIOException (IOException ex) {
    if (listener != null) {
        output.append (ex + "\n");
        input.setVisible (false);
        frame.validate ();
        if (listener != Thread.currentThread ())
            listener.interrupt ();
        listener = null;
        try {
            dataOut.close ();
        } catch (IOException ignored) {
        }
    }
}
```

This method is called to handle IOExceptions. If listener is null then this chat has been stopped. The exception is probably a result of the socket being closed so we ignore it. Otherwise, we display the exception in the output region, hide the input region, interrupt the listening thread (if necessary) and close the network connection.

```
public void windowOpened (WindowEvent event) {
    input.requestFocus ();
}
```

When the Frame becomes visible, we automatically set the input focus to the input region.

```
public void windowClosing (WindowEvent event) {
    try {
        stop ();
    } catch (IOException ex) {
        ex.printStackTrace ();
    }
}
```

When the user attempts to close the window, we call the `stop()` method to gracefully shut down the client. We must catch the `IOException` that may result from closing the network connection.

```
public void windowClosed (WindowEvent event) {}
public void windowIconified (WindowEvent event) {}
public void windowDeiconified (WindowEvent event) {}
public void windowActivated (WindowEvent event) {}
public void windowDeactivated (WindowEvent event) {}
```

These methods handle other events that may be generated by the `Frame`, in which we have no interest.

```
public void actionPerformed (ActionEvent event) {
  try {
    input.selectAll ();
    dataOut.writeUTF (event.getActionCommand ());
    dataOut.flush ();
  } catch (IOException ex) {
    handleIOException (ex);
  }
}
```

When the user hits Return in the input region, an event is passed to this method. We write the user's message to the output stream and call `flush()` to ensure that it is sent immediately. The output stream is a `DataOutputStream` so we can use `writeUTF()` to easily transmit a Unicode `String`. If an `IOException` occurs, we call `handleIOException()` to take appropriate action. Ideally, we would actually perform this I/O in a separate thread, so as not to stall the GUI event thread; however, that is more effort than this example warrants.

```
public static void main (String[] args) throws IOException {
  if ((args.length != 1) || (args[0].indexOf (":") < 0))
    throw new IllegalArgumentException ("Syntax: ChatClient <host>:<port>");

  int idx = args[0].indexOf (":");
  String host = args[0].substring (0, idx);
  int port = Integer.parseInt (args[0].substring (idx + 1));

  ChatClient client = new ChatClient (host, port);
  client.start ();
}
```

The `main()` method starts the client. We ensure that the correct argument has been supplied, and then we create and start a `ChatClient` that connects to the specified chat server. Starting the `ChatClient` may throw an exception, which will exit this method and be displayed.

18.2 Building a multithreaded server

We will now develop a chat server that can accept multiple connections and that will broadcast everything it reads from any client. It is hardwired to read and write `String`s in UTF format.

There are two classes in this program. The main class, `ChatServer`, is a server that accepts connections from clients and assigns them to new connection handler objects. The `ChatHandler` class actually does the

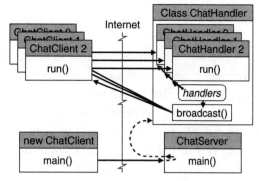

Figure 18.2   The chat system framework

work of listening for messages and broadcasting them to all connected clients. One thread (the main thread) handles new connections; there is a separate thread for each client.

Every new `ChatClient` will connect to the `ChatServer`. This `ChatServer` will hand the connection to a new instance of the `ChatHandler` class, which will receive messages from the new client (figure 18.2). A list of the current handlers is maintained within the `ChatHandler` class. The `broadcast()` method uses this list to transmit a message to all connected `ChatClients`.

18.2.1 Class ChatServer

This class is concerned with accepting connections from clients and launching handler threads to process them.

```
import java.io.*;
import java.net.*;
import java.util.*;

public class ChatServer {
  // public static void main (String[] args) throws IOException ...
}
```

This class is a simple stand-alone application. We supply a `main()` method that performs all the work.

```
public static void main (String args[]) throws IOException {
    if (args.length != 1)
      throw new IllegalArgumentException ("Syntax: ChatServer <port>");
    int port = Integer.parseInt (args[0]);
    ServerSocket server = new ServerSocket (port);
    while (true) {
      Socket client = server.accept ();
```

```
        System.out.println ("Accepted from " + client.getInetAddress ());
        ChatHandler handler = new ChatHandler (client);
        handler.start ();
    }
}
```

This method, which performs all of the work of the server, is fairly simple. We first verify and parse the port to run on, `port`. We then create a `ServerSocket` and enter a loop, accepting clients with the `accept()` method of `ServerSocket`. For each connection, we create a new instance of the `ChatHandler` class, passing the new `Socket` as a parameter. After we have created this handler, we start it with its `start()` method. This starts a new thread to handle the connection, and so, our main server loop can continue to wait on new connections.

Simply passing on exceptions, as we do, may not be the best choice for a production server. It is possible that the `accept()` call may fail for a single connection but that the `ServerSocket` will remain functioning. Ideally, we would actually catch and process exceptions within this loop, providing some protection against the `ServerSocket` truly failing.

18.2.2 Class ChatHandler

This class is concerned with handling individual connections. We must receive messages from the client and resend them to all other connections. We maintain a list of the connections in a `static Vector`. An alternative implementation would be to create the handlers `Vector` in the `ChatServer` class, and to pass this into the `ChatHandler` constructor. Minimizing the use of `static` data is often a preferable choice. This is, in fact, the approach that we will take in the distributed list server later in this chapter.

```
import java.io.*;
import java.net.*;
import java.util.*;

public class ChatHandler implements Runnable {
    // public ChatHandler (Socket socket) ...
    // public synchronized void start () ...
    // public synchronized void stop () ...
    // public void run () ...
}
```

We implement `Runnable` to allow a separate thread to process the associated client. The constructor accepts a `Socket` to which we attach; the `start()` method starts a new thread to run this handler; the `run()` method, called by this new thread, performs the actual client processing; the `stop()` method stops this handler.

```
    protected Socket socket;

    public ChatHandler (Socket socket) {
```

```
    this.socket = socket;
}
```

The constructor simply keeps a reference to the client's socket, `socket`.

```
protected DataInputStream dataIn;
protected DataOutputStream dataOut;
protected Thread listener;

public synchronized void start () {
  if (listener == null) {
    try {
      dataIn = new DataInputStream
        (new BufferedInputStream (socket.getInputStream ()));
      dataOut = new DataOutputStream
        (new BufferedOutputStream (socket.getOutputStream ()));
      listener = new Thread (this);
      listener.start ();
    } catch (IOException ignored) {
    }
  }
}
```

The `start()` method opens an input and an output stream; we use buffered data streams to provide us with efficient I/O, and methods to communicate high-level datatypes—in this case, `Strings`. We then start a new `Thread`, `listener`, to process this client. If an `IOException` occurs while opening the streams, then we silently fail.

```
public synchronized void stop () {
  if (listener != null) {
    try {
      if (listener != Thread.currentThread ())
        listener.interrupt ();
      listener = null;
      dataOut.close ();
    } catch (IOException ignored) {
    }
  }
}
```

The `stop()` method interrupts the listener thread and then closes `dataOut`. This will cause the listener thread to abort with an `IOException` if it is blocked reading from the socket.

```
protected static Vector handlers = new Vector ();

public void run () {
  try {
    handlers.addElement (this);
    while (!Thread.interrupted ()) {
      String message = dataIn.readUTF ();
```

```
          broadcast (message);
      }
    } catch (EOFException ignored) {
    } catch (IOException ex) {
      if (listener == Thread.currentThread ())
        ex.printStackTrace ();
    } finally {
      handlers.removeElement (this);
    }
    stop ();
  }

  // protected void broadcast (String message) ...
```

The run() method is where our thread enters. First we add our thread to the Vector of ChatHandlers, handlers. This Vector keeps a list of all of the current handlers. It is a static variable, and so, there is one instance of the Vector for the whole ChatHandler class and all of its instances. Thus, all ChatHandlers can access the list of current connections.

Note that it is important for us to remove ourselves from this list afterwards if our connection fails; otherwise, all other handlers will try to write to us when they broadcast information. This type of situation, where it is imperative that an action be done upon completion of a section of code, is a prime use of the try ... finally construct.

The body of this method receives messages from a client and rebroadcasts them to all other clients using the broadcast() method. When the loop exits, whether because of an exception reading from the client or because this thread is stopped, the finally clause is guaranteed to be executed. In this clause, we remove our thread from the list of handlers and then finally call stop().

```
protected void broadcast (String message) {
  synchronized (handlers) {
    Enumeration enum = handlers.elements ();
    while (enum.hasMoreElements ()) {
      ChatHandler handler = (ChatHandler) enum.nextElement ();
      try {
        handler.dataOut.writeUTF (message);
        handler.dataOut.flush ();
      } catch (IOException ex) {
        handler.stop ();
      }
    }
  }
}
```

This method broadcasts a message to all clients. We first synchronize on the list of handlers. We don't want people joining or leaving while we are looping, in case we try to broadcast to someone who no longer exists. This forces them to wait until we are finished.

Within this `synchronized` block we get an `Enumeration` of the current handlers. The `Enumeration` class provides a convenient way to evaluate every element of a `Vector`. Our loop writes the message to every element of the `Enumeration`. If an exception occurs while writing to a `ChatClient`, we call the client's `stop()` method. This stops the client's thread and, therefore, performs the appropriate cleanup, including removing the client from `handlers`.

Note that the `writeUTF()` method is not `synchronized`; however, we can guarantee that only one thread will be writing to any stream at a time because of the synchronization on the global `handlers` object. We could implement more fine-grained synchronization if this proves to be a performance bottleneck. However, the overhead of extra synchronization might counteract any potential benefit. Also, the manner in which we directly access the internal variables of each handler and how we handle exceptions clearly violates propriety to some degree. In the next distributed list example, we demonstrate a cleaner way to implement this type of server.

18.3 Networking with the object streams

In the last example, we took the comparatively simple approach of encapsulating each message of a chat system within a UTF-formatted text string. Frequently, such a simple approach is insufficient: We wish to include more data than just some text. However, we wish to retain the idea of sequential independent messages in a stream (figure 18.3).

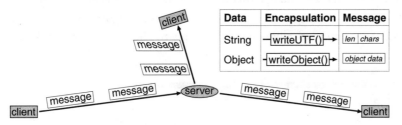

Figure 18.3 Message encapsulation

In part V, we will develop a stream-based framework that provides extended message-based communication facilities with the ability to route arbitrary data among selected clients in a generic and extensible manner. In this example, we leverage the flexibility of the object streams, `ObjectOutputStream` and `ObjectInputStream`, to provide similar function, encapsulating arbitrary data inside objects that are relayed through a central server.

The application that we will consider is a whiteboard (figure 18.4). The graphical part of this application is more extensive than we can hope to cover in the space available here, so instead we will make that code available in the accompanying Web site (http://nitric.com/jnp/) and focus here on the networking aspects of the application. A brief discussion of the graphical side of the whiteboard is available in the JavaWorld article "Drawing the world: Web-based whiteboards," available at http://www.javaworld.com/javaworld/jw-11-1997/jw-11-step.html.

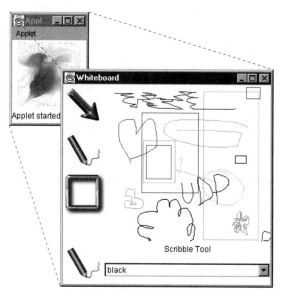

Figure 18.4 A simple whiteboard

The structure of the whiteboard is fairly unusual. Each whiteboard client knows nothing of the networking aspects of the framework; instead, the clients are based around a distributed list datastructure. This is a `Vector`-like datastructure that can be manipulated through a standard API. The whiteboard clients use this list as if it were a typical datastructure. However, any change that a client makes is transparently communicated to all other clients through a centralized data server (figure 18.5). In this manner, our application is automatically networked simply by the fact that our underlying datastructure is networked.

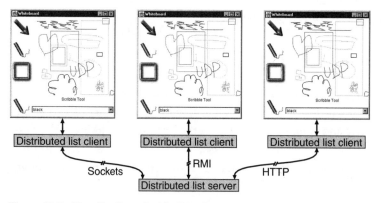

Figure 18.5 The distributed whiteboard structure

The advantage of this approach (where the client is not strongly coupled with details of the networking implementation) is that we can easily change the underlying networking implementation without having to make many changes to the client implementation. We will demonstrate the flexibility of this approach by showing various implementations of the distributed list. Here, we will use Sockets and the object streams; in chapter 24, we will demonstrate an implementation using RMI, and in chapter 27 we will show an implementation using servlets and the Java servlet API.

Note that this development approach (and this distributed list implementation) are applicable to many tasks other than just whiteboards. Many networked applications can be written in this manner, allowing for both code reuse and network independence. As you will see, we can easily provide the same datastructure API on top of many different networking facilities.

18.4 A distributed list datastructure

Our whiteboard framework is built around a distributed list datastructure. This is a list of elements (much like a Vector); however, we do not expose element indexes. Instead, elements can only be accessed by Enumeration or by value (figure 18.6). No facility is provided for accessing the *n*th element of the list, as this is incompatible with transparent distribution. Internally, list implementations usually associate identifiers with their contents instead of using indices. These identifiers are stored coherently among all clients of a central server, so if any client wishes to change an element of the list, it can refer to the element by its identifier, and all other clients will know which element is being addressed.

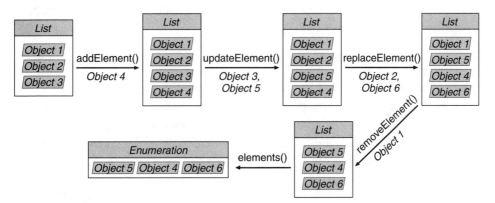

Figure 18.6 The list datastructure

In a nondistributed environment we would simply address elements by their index, much like the elements of an array. Extending this to a distributed environment is not so easy because multiple clients may attempt simultaneous updates to the same element. Without unique identifiers, we cannot easily resolve the conflicts that may arise in such a situation.

18.4.1 Interface DistributedList

This interface describes the basic interface to the list datastructure. We will provide various distributed implementations of this interface for different network protocols.

In addition to the expected datastructure accessor methods, we provide a callback mechanism that informs interested parties whenever the datastructure is changed. In this manner, the whiteboard will be able to refresh itself whenever changes are made to the datastructure by remote clients.

```
import java.util.*;

public interface DistributedList {
    // public abstract void addElement (Object element) ...
    // public abstract void updateElement
        (Object oldElement, Object newElement) ...
    // public abstract void replaceElement
        (Object oldElement, Object newElement) ...
    // public abstract void removeElement (Object element) ...
    // public abstract Enumeration getElements () ...
    // public abstract void addChangeListener (ChangeListener listener) ...
    // public abstract void removeChangeListener (ChangeListener listener) ...
}
```

The `DistributedList` interface declares various methods to access elements of the datastructure. It is important that all elements that are added to an `DistributedList` be `Serializable`; this allows us to use the object streams and, later, RMI to transport the elements of the datastructure.

```
public abstract void addElement (Object element);
```

This method adds the element `element` to the end of this datastructure. Note that because of the distributed nature of potential implementations, the caller should not assume that the element will be added immediately; the process may have to be relayed over a slow network. Instead, the `ChangeListener` callback mechanism will notify the caller when changes actually occur.

```
public abstract void updateElement (Object oldElement, Object newElement);
```

This method updates an element in the datastructure by in-place replacing the element `oldElement`, if it is still present, with the element `newElement`. No change is made to the datastructure if `oldElement` is not present.

```
public abstract void replaceElement (Object oldElement, Object newElement);
```

This method replaces an element in the datastructure by removing the element `oldElement`, if it is still present, and adding the element `newElement` to the end of the list. No change is made to the datastructure if `oldElement` is not present.

```
public abstract void removeElement (Object element);
```

This method removes the element `element` from the datastructure, if it is still present.

```
public abstract Enumeration getElements ();
```

This method returns an `Enumeration` of the elements of the datastructure.

```
public abstract void addChangeListener (ChangeListener listener);
```

This method adds the `ChangeListener` `listener` to be notified when this datastructure is modified.

```
public abstract void removeChangeListener (ChangeListener listener);
```

This method removes the `ChangeListener` `listener` from being notified when this datastructure changes.

18.4.2 Interface ChangeListener

This interface describes an object that should be notified of changes to an `DistributedList`:

```
import java.util.*;

public interface ChangeListener extends EventListener {
  public abstract void changeOccurred (ChangeEvent changeEvent);
}
```

The `changeOccurred()` method will be called on all listeners of an `DistributedList` whenever a change is made to the datastructure. The actual change is communicated as an object of type `ChangeEvent`.

18.4.3 Class ChangeEvent

This event describes a change to an `DistributedList`. The current implementation contains no special payload. A more complex implementation might indicate the type of change that occurred; whether an element was added or removed or, if a replacement occurred—what was replaced by what.

```
import java.util.*;
```

```
public class ChangeEvent extends EventObject {
  public ChangeEvent (Object source) {
    super (source);
  }
}
```

The `DistributedList` that was the source of the change event is specified in the constructor for this class. We pass this to the superconstructor where it is stored internally. This origin can be later queried through the inherited `getSource()` method.

18.4.4 Class ID

This class is a simple representation of an object identifier. The identifier is contained as an `int`. We will use this in the following `IDList` class.

```
import java.io.*;

public class ID implements Serializable {
  protected int id;

  public ID (int id) {
    this.id = id;
  }

  public boolean equals (Object other) {
    return (other != null) && (other instanceof ID) && (((ID) other).id == id);
  }

  public int hashCode () {
    return id;
  }
}
```

Our class is a simple `Serializable` object. An integer identifier is specified in the constructor and stored in the `id` variable.

We provide appropriate implementations of the `equals()` and `hashCode()` methods in order that our class can be used with the `Vector` and `Hashtable` classes.

18.4.5 Class IDList

This class is a simple nondistributed datastructure that provides a similar API to `DistributedList`, but that exposes the underlying identifiers assigned to its elements. We will use this class as the basis for various distributed list implementations (figure 18.7).

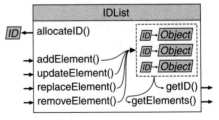

Figure 18.7   Class IDList

Internally, the storage of elements and identifiers is achieved with the standard `Vector` class.

```java
import java.io.*;
import java.util.*;

public class IDList implements Serializable {
  // public IDList () ...
  // public synchronized ID allocateID () ...
  // public synchronized boolean addElement (ID id, Object element) ...
  // public synchronized boolean updateElement
  //     (ID oldID, ID id, Object element) ...
  // public synchronized boolean replaceElement
  //     (ID oldID, ID id, Object element) ...
  // public synchronized boolean removeElement (ID id) ...
  // public synchronized ID getID (Object element) ...
  // public Enumeration getElements () ...
  // public synchronized Object clone () ...
}
```

The `IDList` class implements `Serializable` so we can easily transport it, and provides various methods similar to those of the `DistributedList` interface but that all accept preassigned object identifiers. We also provide an `allocateID()` method that generates a new identifier, suitable for use with these methods.

```java
protected Vector ids, elements;

public IDList () {
  ids = new Vector ();
  elements = new Vector ();
}
```

In the constructor, we allocate the `ids` and `elements` `Vectors` that will be used to store the elements and identifiers of this list.

```java
protected int id;

public synchronized ID allocateID () {
  return new ID (id ++);
}
```

This method returns a new identifier that is an `ID` object containing the value of the postincremented counter `id`.

```java
public synchronized boolean addElement (ID id, Object element) {
  if (ids.contains (id))
    return false;
  ids.addElement (id);
  elements.addElement (element);
  return true;
```

```
    }
```

The `addElement()` method adds a specified element to this list. If the specified identifier `id` is already present, we do nothing and return `false`; otherwise, we add the identifier `id` and element `element`, and return `true`.

```
public synchronized boolean updateElement
    (ID oldID, ID id, Object element) {
    int index = ids.indexOf (oldID);
    if (index < 0)
      return false;
    ids.setElementAt (id, index);
    elements.setElementAt (element, index);
    return true;
}
```

The `updateElement()` method updates a specified element in-place in this list. If the specified identifier `oldID` is not present, we do nothing and return `false`; otherwise, we replace the old identifier with the value `id`, replace the associated element with `element`, and return `true`.

```
public synchronized boolean replaceElement
    (ID oldID, ID id, Object element) {
    int index = ids.indexOf (oldID);
    if (index < 0)
      return false;
    ids.removeElementAt (index);
    elements.removeElementAt (index);
    ids.addElement (id);
    elements.addElement (element);
    return true;
}
```

The `replaceElement()` method replaces a specified element in this list. If the specified identifier `oldID` is not present, we do nothing and return `false`; otherwise, we remove the old identifier and its associated element, add the new identifier `id` and element `element` to the end of our list, and return `true`.

```
public synchronized boolean removeElement (ID id) {
    int index = ids.indexOf (id);
    if (index < 0)
      return false;
    ids.removeElementAt (index);
    elements.removeElementAt (index);
    return true;
}
```

The removeElement() method removes a specified element from this list. If the specified identifier id is not present, we return false; otherwise, we remove the identifier and its associated element and return true.

```
public synchronized ID getID (Object element) {
  int index = elements.indexOf (element);
  if (index < 0)
    return null;
  else
    return (ID) ids.elementAt (index);
}
```

The getID() method returns the identifier associated with the specified element, element, or null if the element is not present.

```
public Enumeration getElements () {
  return ((Vector) elements.clone ()).elements ();
}
```

The getElements() method returns an Enumeration of the elements of this list in a thread-safe manner by cloning the elements array and then returning an Enumeration of this clone.

```
public synchronized Object clone () {
  try {
    IDList idList = (IDList) super.clone ();
    idList.ids = (Vector) ids.clone ();
    idList.elements = (Vector) elements.clone ();
    return idList;
  } catch (CloneNotSupportedException ignored) {
    return null;
  }
}
```

The clone() method returns a clone of this list. We first call the superclass clone() method; this returns a shallow copy of this object. We then replace the clone's ids and elements arrays with clones; this provides sufficient depth of cloning for our purposes.

18.5 A Socket-based distributed list

Our Socket-based distributed implementation of the DistributedList interface follows the client-server model of the chat system that we have just looked at, except that it uses the object streams for encapsulating messages. The client side of the framework is the SocketListClient class that implements the DistributedList interface but routes all accesses through a central server, SocketListServer (figure 18.8). Both client and server implementations use the IDList class internally.

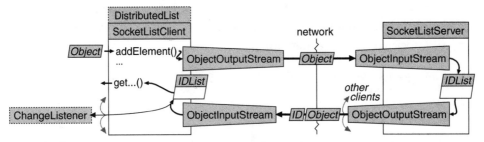

Figure 18.8   The Socket-based distributed list framework

Messages from the `SocketListClient` class are encapsulated in `IDListMsg` objects that are transmitted to the server. The server deserializes these objects, processes the contained information, and responds with messages that are again encapsulated in `IDListMsg` objects.

18.5.1 The distributed list protocol

The distributed list protocol is comparatively simple; however, it is also extremely powerful. We will consider five types of client messages and five types of server messages. There are obviously more that we might consider should we wish to provide an extended API. However, this is sufficient for our present needs (figure 18.9).

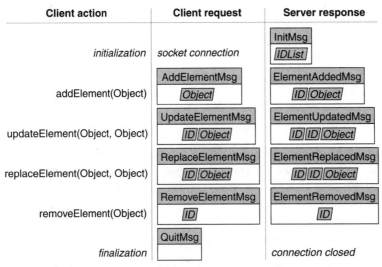

Figure 18.9   The socket-based distributed list protocol

```
import java.io.*;
public class IDListMsg implements Serializable {
}
```

The `IDListMsg` class provides typesafe encapsulation of all messages between the client and server; it implements `Serializable`, indicating that all messages can be safely transported by the object streams.

```
public class InitMsg extends IDListMsg {
  protected IDList idList;

  public InitMsg (IDList idList) {
    this.idList = idList;
  }

  public IDList getIDList () {
    return idList;
  }
}
```

When a client first connects to the server, it will receive a message of type `InitMsg` that contains the initial contents of the central `IDList`. This can be extracted with the `getIDList()` method.

```
public class AddElementMsg extends IDListMsg {
  protected Object element;

  public AddElementMsg (Object element) {
    this.element = element;
  }

  public Object getElement () {
    return element;
  }
}
```

If a client wishes to add an element to the distributed list, an `AddElementMsg` will be sent to the server containing the element to be added.

```
public class ElementAddedMsg extends AddElementMsg {
  protected ID id;

  public ElementAddedMsg (ID id, Object element) {
    super (element);
    this.id = id;
  }

  public ID getID () {
    return id;
  }
}
```

If a client addition is approved, the server will distribute an `ElementAddedMsg` to all clients, consisting of the new element and its allocated identifier. We simply extend `AddElementMsg`, adding an identifier field `id`.

```java
public class UpdateElementMsg extends IDListMsg {
  protected ID oldID;
  protected Object element;

  public UpdateElementMsg (ID oldID, Object element) {
    this.oldID = oldID;
    this.element = element;
  }

  public ID getOldID () {
    return oldID;
  }

  public Object getElement () {
    return element;
  }
}
```

If a client wishes to update an element in the list—for example, to change its color—then it will send an `UpdateElementMsg` containing the identifier of the element to be updated and the element with which to replace it.

```java
public class ElementUpdatedMsg extends UpdateElementMsg {
  protected ID id;

  public ElementUpdatedMsg (ID oldID, ID id, Object element) {
    super (oldID, element);
    this.id = id;
  }

  public ID getID () {
    return id;
  }
}
```

If a client update is approved (i.e., if the element is still in the server's copy of the list and the client has sufficient privilege), the server will respond to all clients with an `ElementUpdatedMsg` containing the old element identifier along with the replacement element and its identifier.

```java
public class ReplaceElementMsg extends IDListMsg {
  protected ID oldID;
  protected Object element;

  public ReplaceElementMsg (ID oldID, Object element) {
    this.oldID = oldID;
```

```
      this.element = element;
    }

  public ID getOldID () {
    return oldID;
    }

  public Object getElement () {
    return element;
    }
}
```

If the client wishes to replace an element in the list, it will send a `ReplaceEle-`
`mentMsg` containing the old identifier and the new element.

```
public class ElementReplacedMsg extends ReplaceElementMsg {
  protected ID id;

  public ElementReplacedMsg (ID oldID, ID id, Object element) {
    super (oldID, element);
    this.id = id;
    }

  public ID getID () {
    return id;
    }
}
```

The server will respond with an `ElementReplacedMsg` containing the old identifier, the new identifier, and the new element.

```
public class RemoveElementMsg extends IDListMsg {
  protected ID id;

  public RemoveElementMsg (ID id) {
    this.id = id;
    }

  public ID getID () {
    return id;
    }
}
```

If a client wishes to remove an element from the list, a `RemoveElementMsg` will be
sent to the server containing the identifier to be removed.

```
public class ElementRemovedMsg extends RemoveElementMsg {
  public ElementRemovedMsg (ID id) {
    super (id);
    }
}
```

The server will respond with an `ElementRemovedMsg` containing the identifier that is to be removed.

```
public class QuitMsg extends IDListMsg {
  public QuitMsg () {
  }
}
```

Finally, when the client wishes to notify the server that it is disconnecting, it sends an empty `QuitMsg` to the server.

18.5.2 Class SocketListServer

The `SocketListServer` class implements the server side of the `Socket`-based distributed list framework. A master copy of the list state is stored on this server in an `IDList`.

The server follows the basic form of the previous chat server: A main thread opens a `ServerSocket` and then awaits client connections. When a client connects, a new handler is spawned that processes all requests from the client. This handler initially sends a complete copy of the master list and then enters a loop, reading and processing client requests (figure 18.10).

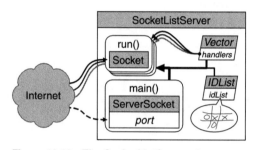

Figure 18.10   The SocketListServer class

When a client requests a change, the handler attempts to make the change to the central `IDList`. If this succeeds, the change is broadcast to all connected clients, including the client that actually made the request. In this manner, when a client actually requests a change, it does not immediately alter its local `IDList`; it must instead wait until the server actually broadcasts back the change (figure 18.11).

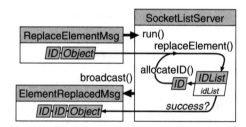

Figure 18.11   The SocketListServer lifecycle

In this implementation, the server allocates identifiers for all objects that are added by clients; in this way we can coherently maintain globally unique identifiers for every element of the list.

We have to pay special attention to synchronization issues in this system; otherwise, it would be possible for clients to fall out of step, and the global coherence of the distributed list could be lost.

```
import java.io.*;
import java.net.*;
import java.util.*;

public class SocketListServer implements Runnable {
  // public SocketListServer
      (Socket socket, Vector handlers, IDList idList) ...
  // public synchronized void start () ...
  // public synchronized void stop () ...
  // public void run () ...
  // public static void main (String[] args) throws IOException ...
}
```

The SocketListServer class serves as both the master server that accepts new client connections and the connection handler that processes each client connection. The main() method opens a ServerSocket, creates the master IDList, and then accepts client connections. For each such connection, it creates a new SocketListServer to handle the connection and calls start() to start that handler. We implement Runnable so that the start() method can create a new Thread that enters the run() method and processes the client network connection. The stop() method closes down the operation of a handler.

```
  protected Vector handlers;
  protected IDList idList;
  protected Socket socket;

  public SocketListServer (Socket socket, Vector handlers, IDList idList) {
    this.socket = socket;
    this.handlers = handlers;
    this.idList = idList;
  }
```

In the constructor for this class, we specify the client Socket, socket; the Vector of SocketListServer handlers, handlers; and the master IDList, idList. We simply store these in instance variables.

```
  protected Thread listener;

  public synchronized void start () {
    if (listener == null) {
      listener = new Thread (this);
      listener.start ();
    }
  }
```

The start() method starts a thread to process the client connection. We create a Thread, listener, that enters the run() method and processes the connection. We use appropriate synchronization to ensure that the handler can only be started once.

```
public synchronized void stop () {
  if (listener != null) {
    if (listener != Thread.currentThread ())
      listener.interrupt ();
    listener = null;
    try {
      socket.close ();
    } catch (IOException ignored) {
    }
  }
}
```

The stop() method shuts this handler down; we interrupt the listener thread and then close the network connection. Closing the socket will result in a blocked read() call throwing an IOException, which we can handle normally in the listener thread.

```
public void run () {
  try {
    init ();
    try {
      execute ();
    } finally {
      handlers.removeElement (this);
    }
  } catch (IOException ex) {
    if (listener == Thread.currentThread ())
      ex.printStackTrace ();
  } catch (ClassNotFoundException ex) {
    ex.printStackTrace ();
  }
  stop ();
}

// protected void init () throws IOException ...
// protected void execute () throws IOException, ClassNotFoundException ...
```

The run() method is executed by a separate thread to process data from the client. We first call init() to set up the network streams, register ourself in the list of handlers, and send our initial state to the client. We then call execute() to process the client connection. We use a try ... finally clause to automatically deregister ourself from handlers when we finish this block of code. If an exception occurs then we catch and display it. If, however, an IOException occurs as a result of the socket being closed, we can safely ignore the exception. Finally, we call stop() to close down.

```
protected ObjectInputStream objectIn;
```

```
    protected ObjectOutputStream objectOut;

    protected void init () throws IOException {
      objectOut = new ObjectOutputStream (
        new BufferedOutputStream (socket.getOutputStream (), 2048));
      objectOut.flush ();
      objectIn = new ObjectInputStream (
        new BufferedInputStream (socket.getInputStream ()));
      synchronized (handlers) {
        handlers.addElement (this);
        transmit (new InitMsg (idList));
      }
      flush ();
    }

    // protected void transmit (IDListMsg msg) ...
    // protected void flush () ...
```

The init() method performs our basic setup. We first create the object streams objectOut and objectIn, connected to the client. Remember that creating an ObjectOutputStream sends some header information and creating an ObjectInput-Stream reads some header information, so we must create and flush objectOut before we create objectIn. This guarantees that we will not encounter a deadlock situation exchanging object stream headers with the client.

We then synchronize on handlers (this is the object that we use for global thread safety), register ourself in this Vector, transmit a new InitMsg containing the initial IDList data, and flush our outward stream. We must use synchronization here to ensure that another client does not transmit a message to this new client before we send it the initial IDList contents. We defer the flush() call to outside our synchronized block to avoid holding the lock excessively. Because our ObjectOutputStream is attached to a BufferedOutputStream, the InitMsg (provided that it is small enough) will initially be written to a memory buffer so the delay of actually transmitting the data will not occur until outside of the synchronized block.

```
    protected void transmit (IDListMsg msg) {
      if (listener != null) {
        try {
          synchronized (objectOut) {
            objectOut.writeObject (msg);
          }
        } catch (IOException ex) {
          stop ();
          ex.printStackTrace ();
        }
      }
    }
```

The `transmit()` method transmits the `IDListMsg msg` to the attached client. If this handler has been stopped, we do nothing; otherwise we transmit `msg` using `objectOut`'s `writeObject()` method. We must synchronize on `objectOut` because `ObjectOutputStream`'s methods are not thread-safe; errors will occur if two calls are made to the stream simultaneously. In this case, `flush()` might be called during our call to `writeObject()`, which would cause problems. If an `IOException` occurs then we simply call `stop()` to close down this handler gracefully.

```
protected void flush () {
  if (listener != null) {
    try {
      synchronized (objectOut) {
        objectOut.flush ();
      }
    } catch (IOException ex) {
      stop ();
      ex.printStackTrace ();
    }
  }
}
```

The `flush()` method flushes `objectOut`. We must perform exactly the same checks as with the `transmit()` method, using synchronization to ensure thread safety and a `try ... catch` clause to catch exceptions appropriately.

```
protected void execute () throws IOException, ClassNotFoundException {
  while (listener != null) {
    IDListMsg msg = (IDListMsg) objectIn.readObject ();
    synchronized (handlers) {
      if (msg instanceof AddElementMsg) {
        ID id = idList.allocateID ();
        Object element = ((AddElementMsg) msg).getElement ();
        if (idList.addElement (id, element))
          broadcast (new ElementAddedMsg (id, element));
      } else if (msg instanceof UpdateElementMsg) {
        ID oldID = ((UpdateElementMsg) msg).getOldID ();
        ID id = idList.allocateID ();
        Object element = ((UpdateElementMsg) msg).getElement ();
        if (idList.updateElement (oldID, id, element))
          broadcast (new ElementUpdatedMsg (oldID, id, element));
      } else if (msg instanceof ReplaceElementMsg) {
        ID oldID = ((ReplaceElementMsg) msg).getOldID ();
        ID id = idList.allocateID ();
        Object element = ((ReplaceElementMsg) msg).getElement ();
        if (idList.replaceElement (oldID, id, element))
          broadcast (new ElementReplacedMsg (oldID, id, element));
      } else if (msg instanceof RemoveElementMsg) {
        ID id = ((RemoveElementMsg) msg).getID ();
        if (idList.removeElement (id))
          broadcast (new ElementRemovedMsg (id));
```

```
        } else if (msg instanceof QuitMsg) {
          break;
        } else {
          throw new IOException ("Unknown message: " + msg);
        }
      }
    }
    flushAll ();
  }
}
// protected void broadcast (IDListMsg msg) ...
// protected void flushAll () ...
```

The execute() method processes messages from the client. We repeat, while the
listener Thread is not null, reading a message (encapsulated as an IDListMsg
object) from objectIn and taking the appropriate action.

We use a sequence of instanceof comparisons to identify the message type; if the
client is adding an element (AddElementMsg), we allocate an identifier, attempt to add
the element to idList, and broadcast the change if this succeeds. Similarly, if the client
is updating an element (UpdateElementMsg), replacing an element (ReplaceElement-
Msg), or removing an element (RemoveElementMsg), we attempt to perform the
requested action on idList and broadcast the change if successful. If we receive a Quit-
Msg from the client, we simply exit this loop; this will result in the surrounding finally
clause calling stop(). The message is otherwise of an unknown type, so we throw an
appropriate IOException and abort. At the end of processing each normal message, we
call flushAll() to flush all outbound streams.

You will note that we again synchronize on handlers to ensure global thread safety,
and that we defer flushing the streams until outside of this synchronization to ensure
that we hold handler's lock for the least time possible.

```
protected void broadcast (IDListMsg msg) {
  synchronized (handlers) {
    for (int i = 0; i < handlers.size (); ++ i) {
      SocketListServer handler = (SocketListServer) handlers.elementAt (i);
      handler.transmit (msg);
    }
  }
}
```

The broadcast() method loops through all the elements of handlers, transmitting the specified IDListMsg msg to each handler. If any of the transmit() methods
encounters an IOException, it will take care of shutting down its own handler. This is a
cleaner implementation than the broadcast method of the previous chat server.

The broadcast() method is only ever called from within the synchronized block
of execute(), so we don't actually need to explicitly synchronize on handlers.

However, doing so ensures that, if at a later point we need to use this method from somewhere else, we won't run into unexpected problems.

```
protected void flushAll () {
  Vector handlers = (Vector) this.handlers.clone ();
  for (int i = 0; i < handlers.size (); ++ i) {
    SocketListServer handler = (SocketListServer) handlers.elementAt (i);
    handler.flush ();
  }
}
```

The `flushAll()` method loops through all the elements of `handlers`, flushing each `ObjectOutputStream`. For thread safety here, we clone `handlers` before looping through it; we don't want to hold the synchronization lock on the global `Vector` while we are performing the slow `flush()` operation.

```
public static void main (String[] args) throws IOException {
  if (args.length != 1)
    throw new IllegalArgumentException ("Syntax: SocketListServer <port>");
  int port = Integer.parseInt (args[0]);
  Vector handlers = new Vector ();
  IDList idList = new IDList ();
  ServerSocket serverSocket = new ServerSocket (port);
  while (true) {
    Socket client = serverSocket.accept ();
    SocketListServer handler =
      new SocketListServer (client, handlers, idList);
    handler.start ();
  }
}
```

The `main()` method performs the expected main server operation: We parse the command-line parameters to determine the port on which to execute, create the global `Vector handlers` and `IDList idList`, and then create a `ServerSocket serverSocket` that listens on the chosen port.

We then sit in a loop, accepting client connections, creating `SocketListServer` handlers, and starting threads that process the clients. It is important that we do not perform the object streams setup in the constructor as you might expect us to; if we did this, then the main server thread would have to wait while the object streams exchanged headers and would have to handle the exceptions that might result. Instead, we have deferred that operation to be performed by each client's own handler thread.

18.5.3 Class SocketListClient

The `SocketListClient` class implements the `DistributedList` interface and communicates with a `SocketListServer` to provide the distributed list datastructure.

An application, such as the whiteboard, will use this `SocketListClient` class just as it would a normal nondistributed implementation of the `DistributedList` interface. Transparently, and unbeknown to the application, the datastructure will be networked, and so we can easily implement a collaborative distributed application.

The `SocketList-Client` is implemented with an internal `IDList` object that reflects the state of the central `SocketList-Server`'s `IDList`. Whenever a client makes a change to a `SocketListClient`, the change is transmit-

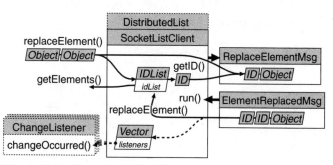

Figure 18.12   Class SocketListClient

ted as a request to the central server. If the server approves the change, it broadcasts a change message to all connected clients. When a `SocketListClient` receives such a change message, it alters its internal `IDList` accordingly, and then notifies any registered listeners of the change. Listeners can then query the `SocketListClient` through the standard `DistributedList` interface and they will receive details of the new state from the local `IDList` copy (figure 18.12).

```
import java.io.*;
import java.net.*;
import java.util.*;

public class SocketListClient implements DistributedList, Runnable {
    // public SocketListClient (String host, int port) ...
    // public synchronized void start () throws IOException ...
    // public synchronized void stop () throws IOException ...
    // public void run () ...
    // public synchronized void addElement (Object element) ...
    // public synchronized void updateElement
    //     (Object oldElement, Object newElement) ...
    // public synchronized void replaceElement
    //     (Object oldElement, Object newElement) ...
    // public synchronized void removeElement (Object element) ...
    // public Enumeration getElements () ...
    // public void addChangeListener (ChangeListener listener) ...
    // public void removeChangeListener (ChangeListener listener) ...
}
```

The `SocketListClient` class implements the `DistributedList` interface and all methods thereof, and the `Runnable` interface; we need an active thread that listens for messages from the central server. We also provide `start()` and `stop()` methods to control the threading and networking.

When `start()` is called, a `Socket` is created to the central server and a listener thread is created that enters the `run()` method to listen for messages from the server. Calling `stop()` closes the `Socket` and stops the listener thread. The update methods will only affect this list while it is running.

```
protected String host;
protected int port;
protected IDList idList;

public SocketListClient (String host, int port) {
  this.host = host;
  this.port = port;
  idList = new IDList ();
}
```

In the constructor, we create a local `IDList` and keep a note of the server address. Actually creating a `Socket` is deferred to the `start()` method.

```
protected Thread listener;
protected ObjectInputStream objectIn;
protected ObjectOutputStream objectOut;

public synchronized void start () throws IOException {
  if (listener == null) {
    Socket socket = new Socket (host, port);
    try {
      objectOut = new ObjectOutputStream
        (new BufferedOutputStream (socket.getOutputStream ()));
      objectOut.flush ();
      objectIn = new ObjectInputStream (
        new BufferedInputStream (socket.getInputStream ()));
    } catch (IOException ex) {
      socket.close ();
      throw ex;
    }
    listener = new Thread (this);
    listener.start ();
  }
}
```

In the `start()` method, we create a `Socket` to the central `SocketListServer`. If this connection attempt fails, we pass on the resulting `IOException`. We otherwise create the object streams `objectOut` and `objectIn`. As before, we create and flush `objectOut` before creating `objectIn`. If an exception occurs here, we close the socket and then rethrow the exception. We finally create a `Thread listener` that enters the `run()` method and processes messages from the server.

```
public synchronized void stop () throws IOException {
  if (listener != null) {
    if (listener != Thread.currentThread ())
      listener.interrupt ();
    listener = null;
    try {
      objectOut.writeObject (new QuitMsg ());
      objectOut.flush ();
    } finally {
      objectOut.close ();
    }
  }
}
```

In the `stop()` method, we ensure that we are still running. We then interrupt our thread and set the `listener` reference to `null`, transmit a `QuitMsg` that indicates to the server that we are about to exit, and close our `Socket`. If the listener thread is blocked on receiving a message from the server, it will wake up with an `IOException` at this point.

Technically, we don't actually need to interrupt the thread here. The use of `interrupt()` is only necessary if the listener thread might block in a Java API call such as `sleep()` or `wait()`, which will abort upon interruption. Our use of `interrupt()` is mainly a safeguard against our potentially changing the code in future to use such an API call.

```
public void run () {
  try {
    execute ();
  } catch (IOException ex) {
    if (listener == Thread.currentThread ())
      ex.printStackTrace ();
  } catch (ClassNotFoundException ex) {
    ex.printStackTrace ();
  } finally {
    try {
      stop ();
    } catch (IOException ignored) {
    }
  }
}
// protected void execute () throws IOException, ClassNotFoundException ...
```

In the `run()` method, we call `execute()` to receive messages from the server. We use a `try ... catch ... finally` sequence to catch and print out any exceptions that may occur, and to finally call `stop()` to close down the network connection. Remember, `stop()` will be called whether we exit as a result of an exception or due to natural causes.

One special case to note is that, if an IOException occurs and the listener reference is no longer to this thread, then it is most likely that the IOException occurred in response to a call to stop(), so we don't display the exception.

```
protected void execute () throws IOException, ClassNotFoundException {
  Thread myself = Thread.currentThread ();
  while (listener == myself) {
    IDListMsg msg = (IDListMsg) objectIn.readObject ();
    if (msg instanceof InitMsg) {
      InitMsg initMsg = (InitMsg) msg;
      idList = initMsg.getIDList ();
      fireChangeEvent (new ChangeEvent (this));
    } else if (msg instanceof ElementAddedMsg) {
      ElementAddedMsg addedMsg = (ElementAddedMsg) msg;
      idList.addElement (addedMsg.getID (), addedMsg.getElement ());
      fireChangeEvent (new ChangeEvent (this));
    } else if (msg instanceof ElementUpdatedMsg) {
      ElementUpdatedMsg updatedMsg = (ElementUpdatedMsg) msg;
      idList.replaceElement (updatedMsg.getOldID (), updatedMsg.getID (),
                             updatedMsg.getElement ());
      fireChangeEvent (new ChangeEvent (this));
    } else if (msg instanceof ElementReplacedMsg) {
      ElementReplacedMsg replacedMsg = (ElementReplacedMsg) msg;
      idList.replaceElement (replacedMsg.getOldID (), replacedMsg.getID (),
                             replacedMsg.getElement ());
      fireChangeEvent (new ChangeEvent (this));
    } else if (msg instanceof ElementRemovedMsg) {
      ElementRemovedMsg removedMsg = (ElementRemovedMsg) msg;
      idList.removeElement (removedMsg.getID ());
      fireChangeEvent (new ChangeEvent (this));
    } else {
      throw new IOException ("Unknown message " + msg);
    }
  }
}

// protected void fireChangeEvent (ChangeEvent changeEvent) ...
```

The execute() method loops while we are not stopped, receiving messages from the server and processing them accordingly. We use the instanceof operator to determine the message type and apply the change to idList. Because we have an exact local copy of the server's IDList, we can guarantee that every change that we receive will be valid.

After making any change, we call fireChangeEvent() with a new ChangeEvent that will indicate to all registered listeners the change that has occurred. In this case, we don't distinguish between the different types of change. In a more full-featured implementation, we would distinguish among the changes with the ChangeEvent that we fire.

```
  public synchronized void addElement (Object element) {
    if (listener != null) {
      try {
        objectOut.writeObject (new AddElementMsg (element));
        objectOut.flush ();
      } catch (IOException ignored) {
        try {
          stop ();
        } catch (IOException ignored2) {
        }
      }
    }
  }
```

The `addElement()` method, defined by the `DistributedList` interface, adds the specified element `element` to this list. If we are still executing, then we send a new `AddElementMsg` to the server containing the element to be added. If this addition is approved, the server will respond with an `ElementAddedMsg` containing this element and its allocated identifier, which will be processed by the `execute()` method.

Note that calling `addElement()` will *not* add the element immediately; the addition will occur at some point after the initial method call, and notification of the change will be provided asynchronously through the `ChangeListener` callback mechanism. If an exception occurs sending our message, we call `stop()` to close down cleanly. In some situations, it might be useful to switch to a nonnetworked mode of operation if this occurs; such a choice depends on the application being used.

```
  public synchronized void updateElement
      (Object oldElement, Object newElement) {
    if (listener != null) {
      ID id = idList.getID (oldElement);
      if (id != null) {
        try {
          objectOut.writeObject (new UpdateElementMsg (id, newElement));
          objectOut.flush ();
        } catch (IOException ignored) {
          try {
            stop ();
          } catch (IOException ignored2) {
          }
        }
      }
    }
  }
```

The `updateElement()` method, defined by the `DistributedList` interface, updates an element in this list. We call `getID()` to determine the identifier of the element to be replaced; if this returns `null`, the element is no longer present so we do nothing. Otherwise, we send an `UpdateElementMsg` to the server containing the identifier of the element to be updated and the element with which to update it. We can't send an index to the server because the server may already have removed the element in response to another client's request. Instead, sending the identifier allows us to uniquely identify the element that we want updated. We process exceptions as before.

```
public synchronized void replaceElement
    (Object oldElement, Object newElement) {
  if (listener != null) {
    ID id = idList.getID (oldElement);
    if (id != null) {
      try {
        objectOut.writeObject (new ReplaceElementMsg (id, newElement));
        objectOut.flush ();
      } catch (IOException ignored) {
        try {
          stop ();
        } catch (IOException ignored2) {
        }
      }
    }
  }
}
```

The replaceElement() method, defined by the DistributedList interface, replaces an element in this list. If appropriate, we send a ReplaceElementMsg to the server containing the identifier of the element to be replaced and the element with which to replace it.

```
public synchronized void removeElement (Object element) {
  if (listener != null) {
    ID id = idList.getID (element);
    if (id != null) {
      try {
        objectOut.writeObject (new RemoveElementMsg (id));
        objectOut.flush ();
      } catch (IOException ignored) {
        try {
          stop ();
        } catch (IOException ignored2) {
        }
      }
    }
  }
}
```

The removeElement() method, defined by the DistributedList interface, removes an element from this list. If appropriate, we send a RemoveElementMsg to the server containing the identifier of the element to be removed.

```
public Enumeration getElements () {
  return idList.getElements ();
}
```

The getElements() method, defined by the DistributedList interface, returns an Enumeration of the elements of this list. This is a snapshot of the state at the time of the call to getElements(). The Enumeration will not be updated with any new elements that may be added to the list after this call returns.

```
protected Vector listeners = new Vector ();

public void addChangeListener (ChangeListener listener) {
  listeners.addElement (listener);
}
```

The addChangeListener() method, defined by the DistributedList interface, adds the ChangeListener listener to be notified of any changes to this list. We store our list of ChangeListeners in the listeners Vector.

```
public void removeChangeListener (ChangeListener listener) {
  listeners.removeElement (listener);
}
```

The removeChangeListener() method, defined by the DistributedList interface, removes the ChangeListener listener from being notified of any changes to this list.

```
protected void fireChangeEvent (ChangeEvent changeEvent) {
  Vector listeners = (Vector) this.listeners.clone ();
  for (int i = 0; i < listeners.size (); ++ i)
    ((ChangeListener) listeners.elementAt (i)).changeOccurred (changeEvent);
}
```

The fireChangeEvent() method notifies all registered ChangeListeners of a change to this list. We clone the listeners Vector for thread safety, and then loop through all the elements thereof, calling each element's changeOccurred() method. As a result of our list implementation we can guarantee that the changeOccurred() method will be sequentially called once in response to every change to this list. In an extremely high-throughput system, we might amortize multiple changes into a single call to changeOccurred().

18.5.4 Extending the framework

There are several extensions that we could make to this framework. As we discussed before, we could include an indication of the change in the ChangeEvent that we fire; we would include the type of change and the actual elements that were affected. An extended `ChangeListener` interface (with methods such as `elementAdded()` and `elementUpdated()`) would simplify the delivery of these events.

An obvious speed improvement that we could make would be to replace our use of `instanceof` (a fairly slow operation) with an integer message-type variable included in each message. When we received a message, we then would `switch` on the message type (add a `getMessageType()` method to the `IDListMsg` class) instead of using the large `if ... then ... else` sequence.

Finally (at least for the purpose of this discussion), we could add some methods to the `DistributedList` interface. An obvious omission of the current implementation is a `removeAllElements()` method. The implementation of such a method would follow the structure of all the methods that we have looked at thus far.

18.5.5 Discussion

When using the distributed list classes for a simple whiteboard, we store all the elements of the whiteboard in a distributed list, adding and replacing elements thereof just as if the list were not distributed. Because the list is transparently distributed, if we connect multiple whiteboards to the same server, we have achieved collaboration with almost no application-level effort. Implementing a text-based chat system would be just as simple. Instead of transmitting and receiving `Strings` through a central server, we would store the whole conversation in a distributed list. To send a message, simply add the `String` to your list; this change will then be broadcast to all clients. Furthermore, if a client joins late, then they will automatically receive a copy of the entire discussion to date.

Other opportunities for using the distributed list as a basis for networked applications abound. Furthermore, we can easily implement other distributed datastructures based upon this paradigm. A distributed `Hashtable` can be crudely implemented as just a distributed list of key-value pairings. Greater efficiency requires a lower-level implementation, but can build from the techniques that we have just looked at.

18.6 Wrapping up

Multithreading is essential for servers with any sophistication. In this chapter, we developed a multithreaded broadcast chat server that used data streams to read and write messages in UTF format. Although this certainly makes more sense than breaking everything down into bytes, there is one drawback to this implementation: We can communicate only single `String` messages between clients. If we wish to communicate different information, then we must change both the client *and* the server. This can be a serious limitation when we want the server to perform a more generalized purpose, or when we want to extend the system to handle more than just text. One solution is to use the object streams, as we do with our list server; this allows us to encapsulate arbitrary data inside actual objects. We will also look at another solution to this problem in the later chapters on developing a message-streams library.

Our distributed list datastructure is intended to show an alternative—and often more effective—paradigm of network programming. In this paradigm we hide all aspects of networking—or, at least, as many as we can—from the application. This lets the application programmer concentrate on the important aspects of application programming and leave the networking to separate support classes—in this case, a distributed list datastructure. In later chapters, we will see how the RMI and CORBA distributed computing technologies allow us to achieve a similar dislocation of application programming from network implementation.

CHAPTER 19

The URL classes

In this chapter, we look at the URL classes from the networking API. The purpose of these classes is to provide an extensible framework, which, once in place, provides the programmer with a simple interface for retrieving objects from the network. URL objects are automatically downloaded and converted from their native formats to one that is usable from Java, so images can be automatically converted to `Image` objects that can be drawn to the screen, and so forth.

At the time of this writing, the standard Java environment provides facilities for automatically collecting and processing HTTP and file URLs, and for processing some multimedia datatypes. Capability also exists, although is not part of the public API, for retrieving FTP data, and so forth.

The `java.net` package provides this framework through several interfaces and abstract classes. By subclassing and implementing the classes and interfaces of this framework, it is possible to define custom

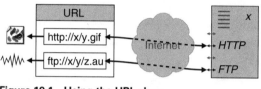

Figure 19.1   Using the URL class

ways of handling different types of data that are accessible through the URL addressing mechanism (figure 19.1). Later in this chapter, we will develop some examples that collect and handle URLs of MIME type text/plain, retrieving data from the Web and with the finger protocol. This could easily be extended to handle more unusual content types and protocols.

19.1 Overview

We will encounter six different classes and interfaces related to the URL classes, all of which are involved in downloading URL-addressable content. We will begin with a brief overview of these classes.

The ultimate goal of these classes is to enable an application to create a URL object using the standard URL addressing scheme, such as http://x.y.z/images/logo.gif or ftp:// sunsite.unc.edu/pub/sound/screams.au, and then simply call the `getContent()` method to download and decode the addressed object. For the first example, the URL classes must connect to the Web server, issue a request, parse the HTTP response headers, and decode the GIF image data, resulting in an `Image` object. For the second example, they must connect to the specified FTP site, log in, change directories, and download and decode the sound file, resulting in an appropriate `AudioClip` object.

To achieve this result, there are two chains of control. The first chain is based on the protocol (http or ftp) and allows us to obtain an `InputStream` from any URL-addressable object, based on the URL's protocol and address. The framework is extensible, so we can add new protocols such as nntp, and address objects across many different information systems.

The second chain of control is based on the type of the object, whether it is an image, formatted text, a soundclip, and so forth. The protocol chain identifies the type of the object and chooses an appropriate decoder. The decoder is responsible for reading from the protocol `InputStream` and constructing a useful Java representation of the object.

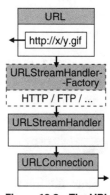

The first chain is achieved with the URL, URLStreamHandlerFactory, URLStreamHandler, URLConnection chain of classes (figure 19.2). The URL object addresses the object; its `getContent()` method calls on a URLStreamHandlerFactory to return a URLStreamHandler appropriate for the URL's protocol. This URLStreamHandler is responsible for creating a URLConnection object that can open an `InputStream` for reading from the addressed object.

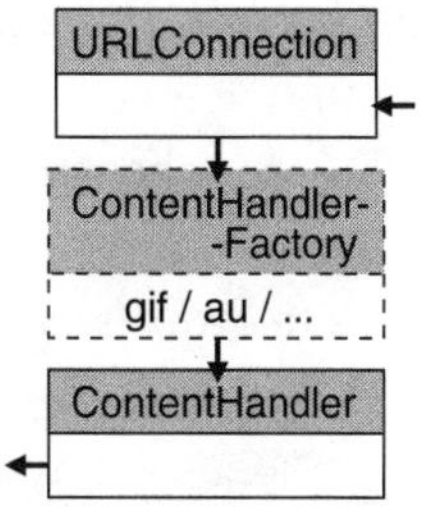

Figure 19.2 The URL protocol chain

The second chain of control, URLConnection, ContentHandlerFactory, ContentHandler, is then called upon to decode the object (figure 19.3). The URLConnection class must be able to identify the content type of the addressed object; it then calls on a ContentHandlerFactory to return a ContentHandler appropriate for the content type. This ContentHandler must be able to decode a useful Java representation of the object.

Figure 19.3 The URL content-type chain

What follows is a description of the API of these classes, followed by an actual implementation of a simple HTTP protocol chain, a text/plain content chain and finally a finger protocol chain.

19.2 Class URL

The URL class represents a URL, as used on the World Wide Web. A URL consists of four fields: the protocol, host name, port number, and filename.

19.2.1 Constructors
There are several constructors for the URL class:

URL(String url) throws MalformedURLException   This constructor creates a URL from a complete textual specification, typically of the form http://www.nsa.gov/index.html.

URL(String protocol, String host, String file) throws MalformedURL-Exception   This constructor assumes a default port number for the URL. The actual port used depends on the protocol and must be handled by a protocol handler. Internally, the port is set to –1.

URL(String protocol, String host, int port, String file) throws Malformed-URLException   This constructor creates an absolute URL from scratch. The protocol is the first field of the URL, typically http or ftp. The host and port specify the server where the URL object resides, and `file` specifies the object filename on the server.

JDK 1.2   *URL(String protocol, String host, int port, String file, URLStream-Handler handler) throws MalformedURLException*   This constructor creates an absolute URL from scratch, with a custom `URLStreamHandler`, `handler`. This is the recommended mechanism for JDK 1.2 applets to make use of custom protocol handlers. For security reasons, use of this constructor requires the `NetPermission` `specifyStreamHandler` (this is part of the JDK 1.2 permissions API).

URL(URL context, String relative)   This constructor creates a URL from an existing URL, `context`, and a relative textual URL, `relative`. If `relative` is an absolute URL, then the result is just a URL corresponding to `relative`; otherwise, the result is a URL that consists of `relative`, relative to the context `context`. For example, if `context` refers to http://server/ and `relative` is document.html, then the result will be a URL for http://server/document.html. Applets will often use this constructor, using the result of `getCodeBase()` as a context.

URL(URL context, String relative, URLStreamHandler handler)   This constructor creates a URL from an existing URL, `context`, and a relative textual URL, `relative`, with a custom `URLStreamHandler`, `handler`. By default, the new URL would inherit a `URLStreamHandler` from `context`. This is the recommended mechanism for JDK 1.2 applets to make use of custom protocol handlers. For security reasons, use of this constructor requires the `NetPermission` `specifyStreamHandler`.

19.2.2 Methods
The following methods allow a URL to be dissected and the data to which it refers to be obtained:

String getProtocol()   This method returns the protocol part of the URL. This will be *http*, *ftp*, *mailto*, and so forth.

String getHost()   This method returns the host name part of the URL.

int getPort()   This method returns the port number part of the URL. If none was specified, then -1 is returned and the protocol default should be used.

String getFile()   This method returns the file part of the URL.

String getRef()   This method returns the reference part of the URL. This is the part of the URL following the # symbol, if present.

boolean sameFile(URL other)   This method returns whether this URL is equal to other, ignoring the reference part, if present. This means that the protocol, host, port, and file parts must all match.

String toExternalForm()   This method returns a String representation of this URL, e.g. http://x.y.z:80/file.html#ref. This method also is used by the toString() method.

URLConnection openConnection() throws IOException   This method returns a URLConnection object, which represents a protocol connection to the URL object. We can then use this class to access the contents of the URL. This class is described in detail later in this chapter.

   Note that a URL can be used to create multiple URLConnection objects; this is useful if you will be repeatedly accessing the same service on a Web server. Each URLConnection can, however, only be used once.

InputStream openStream() throws IOException   This method opens a connection to the URL and returns an input stream for reading its contents.

   In the case of the HTTP protocol, calling openStream() automatically sends an HTTP request and parses the resulting headers, so the stream returned will just read from the contents of the object.

   This call is equivalent to first calling the openConnection() method, and then calling the getInputStream() method of the resulting URLConnection object.

Object getContent() throws IOException   The getContent() method collects the contents of the URL and returns it as an Object type. The actual type returned depends on the contents of the URL. If the URL refers to an image and an appropriate handler is installed, an object of type Image should be returned. Similarly, if we have installed an appropriate handler for text files, a text object should be returned as a String, and so forth.

   This method performs a series of operations to get the result: a connection must be made to a server, a request must be made, and the response must be processed. The response may indicate that the object actually resides elsewhere, in which case an appropriate protocol handler will automatically connect to the new address without any intervention from the user.

In practice, this method uses the `openConnection()` method to call on the protocol chain to make a connection, and then passes the result to the content chain for automatic parsing.

protected void set(String protocol, String host, int port, String file, String ref) This protected method allows a URL subclass to change the values of the various URL fields: `protocol`, `host`, `port`, `file`, and `ref`.

static void setURLStreamHandlerFactory(URLStreamHandlerFactory factory)
This method sets the global `URLStreamHandlerFactory` for the current application. We will use this method when we look at developing a custom protocol handler. The `URLStreamHandlerFactory factory` must be able to return an appropriate handler for the supported URL protocol types. This method can be called only once; however, the Java environment comes with default protocol handlers that can support at least HTTP, and usually others.

Access to this method is restricted by the current `SecurityManager`. Untrusted applets are not permitted to set the global `URLStreamHandlerFactory`. For this reason, statically extending the URL hierarchy is really useful only for applications; applets must instead make do with the protocols that are supported by the browser run time or, under JDK 1.2, they must manually specify an alternative `URLStreamHandler` for each URL that they construct.

19.2.3 IOException
Many of the methods of this class may throw `IOExceptions` if an I/O problem arises.

19.2.4 MalformedURLException
A `MalformedURLException` can be thrown by any of the URL constructors. It indicates an attempt to create a URL object from incorrectly formed fields. This is a subclass of `IOException`.

19.3 Using the URL class

The default JDK comes with a protocol handler for HTTP, so we can use the URL class to easily access content on the Web without having to manually install a suite of protocol and content handlers.

The following code fragment downloads a configuration file using the URL class.

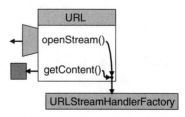

Figure 19.4 Class URL

```
URL url = new URL
  ("http://java.sun.com/index.html");
InputStream in = url.openStream ();
Reader reader = new InputStreamReader (in, "latin1");
BufferedReader bufferedReader = new BufferedReader (reader);
PrintWriter console = new PrintWriter (System.out);
String line;
while ((line = bufferedReader.readLine ()) != null)
  console.println (line);
console.flush ();
bufferedReader.close ();
```

In this example we create a URL for JavaSoft's homepage. We then call its open-Stream() method to get the InputStream in to read from this file, and attach the Reader reader (using ISO Latin 1 character translation) and BufferedReader buff-eredReader that let us read text, a line at a time.

We then create the PrintWriter console that lets us print to the console using the local character encoding. We read lines of text from bufferedReader and print these directly to the console. When we are done, we flush console and close buffere-dReader which closes the URL network connection.

Obviously, if an error is encountered (such as the server being down), then an IOException will be thrown by this piece of code.

Behind the scenes, when we call openStream(), the default HTTP protocol handler sends an HTTP get request to the Web server that the URL references, parses the resulting headers, and returns an InputStream that lets us read from the contents of the referenced file.

Using the URL class in this manner is the preferred method for an applet to read files from its server; usually with URLs created relative to the applet's codebase. The default HTTP handling is particularly useful because a proxy server is automatically used if the client is so configured.

19.4 Class URLConnection

The URLConnection class represents a protocol-specific connection to a URL object. This class is abstract; the protocol chain is responsible for providing suitable protocol-specific implementations.

JDK 1.1 introduced a subclass of this, HttpURLConnection, that provides additional HTTP-specific methods that are commonly used, and are implemented by the default HTTP protocol handler. Subsequently, JDK 1.2 introduced an additional subclass, JarURLConnection, that provides jar-specific methods that are commonly of use for accessing jar-encapsulated data.

19.4.1 Constructors

The one constructor provided by this class is `protected`; it should be called by a subclass that provides a protocol implementation.

protected URLConnection(URL url)   This constructor creates a `URLConnection` for the `URL url`. This constructor can only be called by a subclass that provides an implementation of the various `URLConnection` methods for a particular protocol.

19.4.2 Methods

This class represents a protocol-specific connection to a remote object. After a `URLConnection` is created, it should be initialized by calling the various methods that control how it will operate. It can then be connected to the remote server and the results of the connection can be queried.

It is the responsibility of a `URLConnection` subclass (i.e., an actual implementation of a protocol) to implement all the methods mentioned below that explicitly require implementation, and to take into account all the user options that it should support. For example, all of the configuration methods described below simply set internal variables; it is up to an implementation to actually make use of these variables during execution of its protocol.

URL getURL()   This method returns the `URL` to which this `URLConnection` is attached.

void setDoInput(boolean doInput)   This method sets whether or not this `URLConnection` will be used for input. Call this before connecting, if you will not be reading from this connection.

boolean getDoInput()   This method returns whether or not this `URLConnection` will be used for input; the default is `true`.

void setDoOutput(boolean doOutput)   This method sets whether or not this `URLConnection` will be used for output. Call this before connecting, if you will be writing to this connection.

boolean getDoOutput()   This method returns whether or not this `URLConnection` will be used for output; the default is `false`.

void setAllowUserInteraction(boolean allow)   This method sets whether or not this `URLConnection` should allow user interaction. A common example is access to a password-protected Web page; the `URLConnection` must ask the user for a username and password with which to access the page. If this is supported, an implementation of

URLConnection must itself provide additional functions for configuring how this user interaction will take place.

boolean getAllowUserInteraction()   This method returns whether or not this URL-Connection allows user interaction. The default is `false`.

void setUseCaches(boolean use)   This method sets whether or not this URLConnection should use existing cached data, if available, for the object that it references.

boolean getUseCaches()   This method returns whether or not this URLConnection will use cached data. The default is `true`.

void setRequestProperty(String key, String value)   This method sets the specified request property, `key`, to the specified value, `value`. This information will be included in the headers that are sent with the protocol request; for example, a header of the form key: value will be included with an HTTP request. A subclass of URLConnection should implement this method if it supports request properties.

String getRequestProperty(String key)   This method returns the value associated with the specified request property, `key`, or `null` if no value has been set. A subclass of URLConnection should implement this method if it supports request properties.

void setIfModifiedSince(long ifModified)   This method configures this URLConnection to only download the target object if it has been modified more recently than specified value, `ifModified` (milliseconds since January 1, 1970, GMT).

long getIfModifiedSince()   This method returns the `if-modified-since` value of this URLConnection, or `0` if none has been set.

abstract void connect() throws IOException   This method should connect to the server that was specified in the constructor. A subclass of URLConnection will provide an implementation of this method appropriate for a particular protocol. Typically it is not necessary for the user to explicitly call this method; it will be called automatically when the content of this URLConnection is accessed.

OutputStream getOutputStream() throws IOException   This method returns an `OutputStream` that allows an application to write to this URLConnection. This should be used, for example, to perform an HTTP post operation. This method must be implemented by a URLConnection subclass if it supports output; the default implementation throws an `UnknownServiceException` with the message protocol doesn't support output.

InputStream getInputStream() throws IOException   This method returns an `InputStream` that can be used to read from the `URL` object. If we have a `URLConnection` object, we can call this method to obtain a raw stream to read from the target. This bypasses the content-handler chain used by the `getContent()` method. This method must be implemented by a `URLConnection` subclass if it supports input; the default implementation throws an `UnknownServiceException` with the message protocol doesn't support input.

Object getContent() throws IOException   This method retrieves the contents of the URL. Since the contents could be anything, the return value has type `Object`. The actual class returned will depend on the content type, as processed by the content handler chain.

String getHeaderField(String name)   This method returns the value associated with the specified response header, `name`, or `null` if the header was not returned. This method should only be called after this connection has been opened. A subclass of `URL-Connection` should implement this method if it supports response headers.

String getHeaderFieldKey(int n)   This method returns the key of the n'th response header, counting from zero, or `null` if the key does not exist. A subclass of `URLConnection` should implement this method if it supports response headers.

String getHeaderField(int n)   This method returns the value of the n'th response header, counting from zero, or `null` if the value does not exist. A subclass of `URLConnection` should implement this method if it supports response headers.

int getHeaderFieldInt(String name, int alt)   This method returns the value associated with the specified response header, `name`, parsed as an integer, or else `alt` if the header was not returned.

long getHeaderFieldDate(String name, long alt)   This method returns the value associated with the specified response header, `name`, parsed as a `Date` by the `java.util.Date` class, or else `alt` if the header was not returned. Values are in milliseconds since January 1, 1970, GMT.

int getContentLength()   This method returns the value of the content-length response header, or `-1` if the header was not returned.

String getContentType()   This method returns the value of the content-type response header, or `null` if the header was not returned.

String getContentEncoding()   This method returns the value of the content-encoding response header, or `null` if the header was not returned.

long getExpiration()   This method returns the value of the expires response header, or `0` if the header was not returned. This is in the usual URL date encoding.

long getDate()   This method returns the value of the date response header, or `0` if the header was not returned. This is in the usual URL date encoding.

long getLastModified()   This method returns the value of the last-modified response header, or `0` if the header was not returned. This is in the usual URL date encoding.

(JDK 1.2) *Permission getPermission()*   This method returns the JDK 1.2 `Permission` object that the caller must possess in order to be able to access the document identified by this `URLConnection`. For example, if this corresponds to a file URL then permission to read from the file system is required; if it is an http URL then permission to communicate the remote server is required.

void setDefaultUseCaches(boolean defaultUse)   This method returns the default use of cached data for `URLConnections`. This is initially `true`. This method should be `static` but isn't.

boolean getDefaultUseCaches()   This method sets the default use of cached data for all future `URLConnections`. This method should be `static` but isn't.

19.4.3 Static methods
The following static methods are supported by this class:

void setDefaultAllowUserInteraction(boolean defaultAllow)   This method sets the default permissibility of user interaction for all future `URLConnections`.

boolean getDefaultAllowUserInteraction()   This method returns the default permissibility of user interaction for `URLConnections`. This is initially `false`.

void setDefaultRequestProperty(String key, String value)   This method should set the specified request property for all future `URLConnections`. At the time of writing, the JDK does not support this method.

String getDefaultRequestProperty(String key)   This method should return the specified default request property. However, it is currently unimplemented.

protected String guessContentTypeFromName(String fname)   This method can be used to try to determine a content type based on just the URL filename. We use this method in a later example to guess the content type of a URL before we have opened a connection. The method operates by looking up the filename extension in an internal table and is provided as an aid to the programmer.

String guessContentTypeFromStream(InputStream is) throws IOException This method attempts to determine the contents of a URL by reading a few bytes from the `InputStream is`. It uses the `mark()` and `reset()` methods so that some data can be read and subsequently unread. This method is provided as an aid to the programmer.

JDK 1.1 *FileNameMap getFileNameMap()*   This method returns the global `FileNameMap` used by the `guessContentTypeFromName()` method. This method was introduced with JDK 1.1.6; previously, a `public static` variable named `fileNameMap` was used.

JDK 1.1 *void setFileNameMap(FileNameMap map)*   This method sets the global `FileNameMap` used by the `guessContentTypeFromName()` method. This method was introduced with JDK 1.1.6; previously, a `public static` variable named `fileNameMap` was used. Access to this method is vetted by the current `Security-Manager`.

void setContentHandlerFactory(ContentHandlerFactory factory)   This method sets the `static ContentHandlerFactory` for the `URLConnection` class. This `ContentHandlerFactory factory` will be called upon to determine an appropriate content handler based on the content type of a URL. This method can be called only once.

As with the URL class' `setURLStreamHandlerFactory()` method, access to this method is restricted by the current `SecurityManager`. Applets are not permitted to change the global `ContentHandlerFactory`. Instead, they must make do with the content handlers supplied by the run time, or else they can call `getInputStream()` and parse the data directly.

19.4.4 Variables

All of the following variables except `connected` will be initialized before the `URLConnection` is connected to its target. An implementation of the `connect()` method should use the values of these variables to determine how to proceed and should then set the `connected` variable to `true`. Note that these variables ignore any global defaults that may have been set; the appropriate way to use these values is thus to query the variable value, and if this is unset, then to use the global default.

protected URL url   This variable represents the URL to which this URLConnection is attached.

protected boolean doInput   This variable indicates whether this URLConnection should support input.

protected boolean doOutput   This variable indicates whether this URLConnection should support output.

protected boolean allowUserInteraction   This variable indicates whether this URL-Connection should allow user interaction.

protected boolean useCaches   This variable indicates whether this URLConnection should use cached data.

protected long ifModifiedSince   The contents of this URLConnection should only be fetched if they have been modified more recently than this date.

protected boolean connected   This variable should be set to true when the URL-Connection is connected.

19.4.5 IOException

As usual, problems with accessing a URL through a URLConnection are signaled by IOExceptions.

19.5 Using the URLConnection class

The URLConnection class gives us more control over a connection than just using a URL object. Most implementations of the JDK provide HTTP support for both get and post requests. In the following code fragment, we use methods of URLConnection to perform a HTTP post operation. This can be used, for example, to submit information from an applet to a CGI program residing on a Web server.

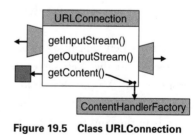

Figure 19.5   Class URLConnection

```
// String user, password;
URL url = new URL (getCodeBase (), "/cgi-bin/update.cgi");
URLConnection connection = url.openConnection ();
connection.setDoOutput (true);
OutputStream out = connection.getOutputStream ();
Writer writer = new OutputStreamWriter (out, "latin1");
writer.write ("user=" + URLEncoder.encode (user));
```

```
writer.write ("&password=" + URLEncoder.encode (password));
writer.close ();
InputStream in = connection.getInputStream ();
Reader reader = new InputStreamReader (in, "latin1");
BufferedReader bufferedReader = new BufferedReader (reader);
PrintWriter console = new PrintWriter (System.out);
String line;
while ((line = bufferedReader.readLine ()) != null)
  console.println (line);
console.flush ();
bufferedReader.close ();
```

We first create a URL url that points to the CGI program /cgi-bin/update.cgi on the Web server that served this applet. Provided by the Applet class, getCode-Base() returns the URL from which an applet's class files were served, and thus the only server than an untrusted applet may connect to.

Then we call openConnection() to create the URLConnection connection that corresponds to a protocol-specific connection to this URL object. The URLConnection is not initially connected. We call the setDoOutput() method to indicate that we wish to send data through this connection. For HTTP, this corresponds to using a post operation as opposed to the usual read-only get operation. We then call getOutputStream() to get the OutputStream out to which we can send our data. Some protocols do not support sending and will throw an appropriate IOException at this point.

We send our data to this stream using the character streams interface; we attach an OutputStreamWriter using ISO Latin 1 encoding and then send some data. In this case, we send two URL-encoded attribute/value pairs—a user and password. We use the URLEncoder class to encode the values. We finally close this OutputStream and call getInputStream() to get the InputStream in that lets us read a response from the server.

Only when we call getInputStream() will the protocol handler actually make a connection to the Web server, send a post command, and transmit the data that we wrote to out. We can then read the server's response from the returned stream. In this case, we read the response as a sequence of ISO Latin 1 lines of text, printing them directly to the console as with the previous example.

19.6 `JDK 1.1` *Class HttpURLConnection*

This class is an abstract subclass of URLConnection that provides specialized support for the HTTP protocol. When you open a URLConnection to a *http* URL then you can invoke methods defined here for additional protocol-specific control.

19.6.1 *Constructors*
The following constructors are provided:

protected HttpURLConnection(URL url)   A subclass will call this constructor with the URL object to which to connect.

19.6.2 Methods
The following methods are provided:

void setRequestMethod(String method) throws ProtocolException   This method sets the HTTP request method to be used by this URLConnection. This can only be called before connecting to the remote server, and the value is restricted to the values *GET, POST, HEAD, OPTIONS, PUT, DELETE* or *TRACE*.

String getRequestMethod()   This method returns the HTTP request method that will be used by this URLConnection. The default value, if none other is specified, is *GET* for read-only connections and *POST* for read-write.

int getResponseCode() throws IOException   This method returns the HTTP response code that was returned by the Web server in response to this request, or −1 if no response code was returned. For example, 404 is returned for the status line *HTTP/1.1 404 Not Found*. If the server has not yet been contacted then this method will contact it in order to retrieve the status line.

String getResponseMessage() throws IOException   This method returns the HTTP response message that was returned by the Web server in response to this request, or null if no response code was returned. For example, *Method Not Allowed* is returned for the status line *HTTP/1.1 405 Method Not Allowed*.

abstract void disconnect()   A subclass will implement this method to disconnect from the server.

boolean abstract usingProxy()   A subclass will implement this method to return whether a Web proxy was used to make this HTTP connection.

19.6.3 Static methods
The following static methods are provided:

void setFollowRedirects(boolean set)   This method allows the URL framework to be configured to automatically follow HTTP redirects (response codes in the 300 range with a *Location* header) or not. The default value is true; that is, follow redirects. The standard SecurityManager prevents untrusted code from calling this method.

boolean getFollowRedirects()   This method returns whether redirects are automatically followed or not.

19.6.4 Variables

The following instance variables are defined; values for these variables are assigned by the methods described above.

protected String method   This is the request method being used; by default, *GET.*

protected int responseCode   This is the HTTP response code that was returned (e.g., 200), or −1 if none could be determined.

protected String responseMessage   This is the HTTP response message that was returned (e.g., *Not found*), or `null` if none could be determined.

19.6.5 Static variables

The following static variables are provided, describing the various standard HTTP response codes:

Table 19.1   Success codes

Variable	Value
HTTP_OK	200
HTTP_CREATED	201
HTTP_ACCEPTED	202
HTTP_NOT_AUTHORITATIVE	203
HTTP_NO_CONTENT	204
HTTP_RESET	205
HTTP_PARTIAL	206

Table 19.2   Redirect codes

Variable	Value
HTTP_MULT_CHOICE	300
HTTP_MOVED_PERM	301
HTTP_MOVED_TEMP	302
HTTP_SEE_OTHER	303
HTTP_NOT_MODIFIED	304
HTTP_USE_PROXY	305

Table 19.3   Client error codes

Variable	Value
HTTP_BAD_REQUEST	400

Table 19.3   Client error codes

Variable	Value
HTTP_UNAUTHORIZED	401
HTTP_PAYMENT_REQUIRED	402
HTTP_FORBIDDEN	403
HTTP_NOT_FOUND	404
HTTP_BAD_METHOD	405
HTTP_NOT_ACCEPTABLE	406
HTTP_PROXY_AUTH	407
HTTP_CLIENT_TIMEOUT	408
HTTP_CONFLICT	409
HTTP_GONE	410
HTTP_LENGTH_REQUIRED	411
HTTP_PRECON_FAILED	412
HTTP_ENTITY_TOO_LARGE	413
HTTP_REQ_TOO_LONG	414
HTTP_UNSUPPORTED_TYPE	415

Table 19.4   Server error codes

Variable	Value
HTTP_SERVER_ERROR	500
HTTP_INTERNAL_ERROR	501
HTTP_BAD_GATEWAY	502
HTTP_UNAVAILABLE	503
HTTP_GATEWAY_TIMEOUT	504
HTTP_VERSION	505

19.6.6 For example

This example demonstrates the basic use of this class:

```
URL url = new URL ("http://nitric.com/jnp/index.html");
URLConnection conn = url.openConnection ();
HttpURLConnection httpConn = (HttpURLConnection) conn;
int responseCode = httpConn.getResponseCode ();
if (responseCode == HttpURLConnection.HTTP_OK) {
  InputStream in = httpConn.getInputStream ();
  ...
}
```

Here, we create a URL object using the HTTP protocol. We then open a HttpURL-Connection and call getResponseCode() to connect to the server and determine whether the connection was successful. If it was, then we call `getInputStream()` to read the successful response.

19.7 Interface URLStreamHandlerFactory

The `URLStreamHandlerFactory` interface represents the first part of a custom protocol-handler chain. A class that implements this interface is responsible for creating `URL-StreamHandler` instances that support different URL protocols (figure 19.6).

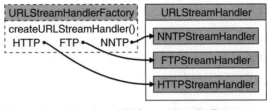

Figure 19.6   Interface URLStreamHandlerFactory

19.7.1 Methods

The `URLStreamHandlerFactory` interface declares one method:

URLStreamHandler create URLStreamHandler(String protocol)   This method should create a new `URLStreamHandler` that can handle the specified protocol `protocol`.

When the `URL` class attempts to open a connection to a `URL` object, it calls upon its `URLStreamHandlerFactory` to return an appropriate `URLStreamHandler` object for the protocol in question. For example, if the protocol type is ftp, an FTP stream handler would be created.

To implement the protocol chain, a class must implement this interface, and then actually be installed using the `setURLStreamHandlerFactory()` method of class `URL`.

Note that under JDK 1.2, this interface may be bypassed entirely because a per-URL `URLStreamHandler` may be specified, permitting a more fine-grained approach to protocol handling.

19.7.2 Default protocol handlers

If a custom `URLStreamHandlerFactory` returns `null`, the `URL` class continues on to search a default set of packages for a `URLStreamHandler` that supports the desired protocol: It tries to locate a class called `Handler` in the package prefix.protocol, where prefix is one of a set of default package names and protocol is the URL's protocol. The packages names that it searches are any listed in the `System` property java.protocol.handler.pkgs, followed finally by a default sun.net.www.protocol.

For example, if the `System` property java.protocol.handler.pkgs contains the value nitric.url.protocols|personal.protocols and a URL with the protocol *xyz* is created, then first the installed `URLStreamHandlerFactory`, if any, will be queried for a `URLStream-`

Handler that supports *xyz*. If that returns null, the URL class will attempt to locate a class nitric.url.protocols.xyz.Handler. If that does not exist, it will search for personal.protocols.xyz.Handler, then sun.net.www.protocol.xyz.Handler.

At the time of writing, JDK 1.1 is shipped with handlers within the sun.net.www.protocol packages for the following protocols: appletresource, doc, file, ftp, gopher, http, mailto, netdoc, systemresource, verbatim; JDK 1.2 adds support also for the protocol: jar.

The permanent presence of these protocols should not be relied upon, particularly from within a browser, as JavaSoft provides no guarantee that classes within the sun package hierarchy will remain available. However, their immediate presence can be useful for certain applications based on known versions of the JDK.

19.8 Class URLStreamHandler

The final class involved in the protocol chain is the abstract class URLStreamHandler. This class is responsible for actually creating instances of the

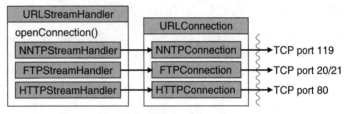

Figure 19.7   Class URLStreamHandler

URLConnection class that are capable of serving a particular protocol, such as HTTP (figure 19.7).

To implement a complete protocol chain, it is thus necessary to implement URLStreamHandlerFactory, URLStreamHandler, and also to provide URLConnection implementations for the various protocols that are to be supported. Usually, a single URLStreamHandler class will be provided for supporting multiple protocols.

19.8.1 Methods

Class URLStreamHandler defines one public method, to create a URLConnection, and various helper methods for URLStreamHandler implementations.

protected abstract URLConnection openConnection(URL url) throws IOException   This method should create an appropriate URLConnection object for the specified URL, url.

protected void parseURL(URL url, String spec, int start, int limit)   This method parses the host/port/file substring of the textual URL, spec, from start up to limit, into the target URL, url. The start index should be the first character after the :

following the protocol specification, if any. The limit index should be the end of the string, or the # reference delimiter. This method is not commonly used except internally by the URL class. The default implementation handles HTTP-style URL syntax; it should be overridden by URLStreamHandlers that support non-HTTP-style URLs.

protected String toExternalForm(URL url)   This method converts the URL url into a textual form. The default implementation handles HTTP-style URL syntax; it should be overridden by URLStreamHandlers that support non-HTTP-style URLs.

protected void setURL(URL url, String protocol, String host, int port, String file, String ref)   This method is provided for URLStreamHandler subclasses that need to modify the fields of a URL. This is usually only required by the parseURL() method if that is being overridden.

19.9 Interface ContentHandlerFactory

The ContentHandlerFactory interface represents the first part of the content handler chain. A class that implements this interface will be responsible for returning instances of the Content-Handler class appropriate for different

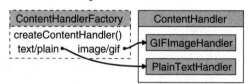

Figure 19.8   Interface ContentHandlerFactory

MIME types (figure 19.8). Typical MIME types include text/plain, image/jpeg, and so forth.

19.9.1 Methods
This interface defines just one method:

ContentHandler createContentHandler(String mimetype)   This method should create a ContentHandler that can read an object of the specified content type mimetype.

The URLConnection class provides methods that can determine the content type of a particular URL. It uses the object name, as well as the first few bytes of the object itself, to determine this information. It then calls on its ContentHandlerFactory to return an appropriate handler for the object type that it has identified. For example, if the type of an object is text/html, an HTML content handler should be returned.

To implement a content-handler chain, a class must implement this interface and then be registered with the URLConnection class through its setContentHandler-Factory() method.

19.9.2 Default content handlers

If a custom `ContentHandlerFactory` returns `null`, the `URLConnection` class continues on to search a default location for a `ContentHandler` that supports the desired protocol: It tries to locate an appropriate class under the package `sun.net.www.content`. The exact classname that it looks for is based on the MIME type: the slash character is replaced by period and all nonalphanumerics are replaced by an underscore. As a result, each major MIME type falls into a separate package, and each subtype will be a separate class within that package.

For example, if an object of MIME type image/x-xpixmap is being accessed, then first the installed `ContentHandlerFactory`, if any, will be queried for a `ContentHandler` for this type. If that returns `null`, the `URLConnection` class will attempt to locate a class `sun.net.www.content.image.x_xpixmap` (note the hyphen is replaced by an underscore). At the time of writing, JDK 1.1 is shipped with handlers within the `sun.net.www.content` packages for the following content types: text/plain, image/gif, image/jpeg, image/x-xbitmap, image/x-xpixmap.

As before, the permanent presence of these handlers should not be relied upon.

19.10 Class ContentHandler

This class is responsible for actually decoding the contents of a `URL` and producing a result that is usable by the Java run time (figure 19.9). When the `getContent()` method of class `URL` is called, the protocol chain will make a connection to the object, and the content chain will call upon an instance of this class to actually decode the object.

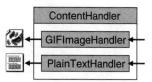

Figure 19.9   Class ContentHandler

19.10.1 Methods

An implementation of `ContentHandler` must provide just one method:

abstract Object getContent(URLConnection connection) throws IOException
This method should use the methods of the supplied `URLConnection`, `connection` to read the contents of the target object and to parse them as appropriate for the content type.

The actual type of the returned object will depend upon the application in question; however, for some types, the result should be obvious. If this `ContentHandler` parses image files of some unusual format, it should return an `Image` object. Similarly, if it parses HTML files, it should return an appropriate HTML object.

Only one `ContentHandler` will be created by the `ContentHandlerFactory` for a given MIME type; this `ContentHandler` will then be responsible for decoding all subsequent URLs of this type. For these reasons, content handlers should be threadsafe and capable of processing multiple objects.

19.11 An HTTP protocol handler

As we have seen, Web browsers send requests of the form GET /document HTTP/1.0 to download documents from a Web server over HTTP 1.0. The Web server responds with a series of headers, followed by the file. These headers can be examined to determine the type of the file, and the appropriate handler can then be invoked to deal with it.

In the following classes, we will implement the URL framework necessary to retrieve data using the HTTP protocol, and in the next section to automatically convert plain text data (figure 19.10). Later in this chapter we will look at supporting the finger protocol through this URL framework.

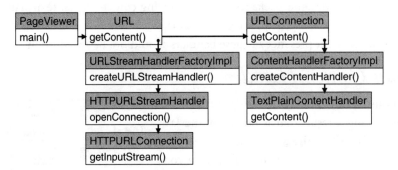

Figure 19.10   A URL-based plain-text HTTP framework

Support for the HTTP protocol requires us to provide an implementation of the URLStreamHandlerFactory interface that returns an appropriate URLStreamHandler for HTTP URLs. This in turn must return an implementation of URLConnection that actually implements HTTP. All of this, as we will see, is fairly simple given our knowledge of TCP/IP:

19.11.1 Class URLStreamHandlerFactoryImpl

This class must return a URLStreamHandler appropriate for the protocol, in this case, HTTP.

```
import java.io.*;
import java.net.*;

public class URLStreamHandlerFactoryImpl implements URLStreamHandlerFactory {
   public URLStreamHandler createURLStreamHandler (String protocol) {
      if (protocol.equalsIgnoreCase ("http"))
         return new HTTPURLStreamHandler ();
```

```
        else
          return null;
      }
}
```

This implementation of `URLStreamHandlerFactory` is simple; it checks for a protocol type of http and returns an `HTTPURLStreamHandler`.

More complex implementations would check for several protocols and return the stream handler for the appropriate protocol. If we wished to also implement the FTP protocol, we could return an `FTPURLStreamHandler` for the protocol ftp. Thus we can easily extend the URL framework to handle new protocols.

19.11.2 Class HTTPURLStreamHandler

This class must return a `URLConnection` appropriate to the protocols that it supports.

```
import java.io.*;
import java.net.*;

public class HTTPURLStreamHandler extends URLStreamHandler {
   protected URLConnection openConnection (URL url) throws IOException {
     return new HTTPURLConnection (url);
   }
}
```

This example can handle only the HTTP protocol, and so returns a new `HTTPURL-Connection` (not to be confused with the JDK 1.1 API class `HttpURLConnection`) from its `openConnection()` method. Were we to support multiple protocols, we could call `getProtocol()` to determine `url`'s protocol and then return an appropriate result based on this.

19.11.3 Class HTTPURLConnection

This is the class that does most of the work of retrieving a URL. It must open a connection to the server, send appropriate requests, and determine the content type of the resulting information.

Note that a production implementation of a `URLConnection` class for HTTP must perform much more processing than we do here. An HTTP response includes a status field that indicates the success of the request. Among the various responses possible is a response that indicates that the client should try retrieving an alternative URL. A more complete `URLConnection` would parse these headers and automatically perform this redirection if necessary. Additionally, we should also support the extra methods provided by the JDK 1.1 API class `HttpURLConnection`.

```
import java.net.*;
import java.io.*;
import java.util.*;
```

```
import java.text.*;

public class HTTPURLConnection extends URLConnection {
   // public HTTPURLConnection (URL url) ...
   // public void setRequestProperty (String name, String value) ...
   // public String getRequestProperty (String name) ...
   // public void connect () throws IOException ...
   // public InputStream getInputStream() throws IOException ...
   // public String getHeaderFieldKey (int index) ...
   // public String getHeaderField (int index) ...
   // public String getHeaderField (String key) ...
}
```

Our HTTPURLConnection extends the URLConnection class and implements some of the methods that are provided by the URLConnection class. These include setting request properties, the connect() method to connect to the server, getInputStream() to read the server's response, and various methods to read the headers that were returned by the server.

```
protected Hashtable requestProperties;
protected Vector keys;
protected Hashtable headers;

public HTTPURLConnection (URL url) {
   super (url);
   requestProperties = new Hashtable ();
   keys = new Vector ();
   headers = new Hashtable ();
}
```

In our constructor, we call the superclass constructor with the specified URL url. We initialize the Hashtable requestProperties, the Vector keys and the Hashtable headers; these are used to hold the request properties that are transmitted to, and the headers that are returned by the server.

```
public void setRequestProperty (String name, String value) {
   if (connected)
      throw new IllegalStateException ("Already connected.");
   requestProperties.put (name, value);
}
```

This method sets the specified request property, name, to the value, value, throwing an IllegalStateException if we're already connected.

```
public String getRequestProperty (String name) {
   return (String) requestProperties.get (name);
}
```

This method returns the request property of the specified name, name, or else null.

```
protected InputStream in;

public synchronized void connect () throws IOException {
  if (!connected) {
    String host = url.getHost ();
    int port = (url.getPort () == -1) ? 80 : url.getPort ();
    Socket socket = new Socket (host, port);
    sendRequest (socket.getOutputStream ());
    in = new BufferedInputStream (socket.getInputStream ());
    readHeaders ();
    connected = true;
  }
}

// protected void sendRequest (OutputStream out) throws IOException ...
// protected void readHeaders () throws IOException ...
```

The connect() method is responsible for connecting to the Web server, issuing our request and parsing the server's response. We use the sendRequest() method to send our request, the readHeaders() method to read the headers of the server's response and then set the connected variable to indicate that we are now connected.

```
protected void sendRequest (OutputStream out) throws IOException {
  setRequestProperty ("User-Agent", "JNP-HTTP/2e");
  if (ifModifiedSince != 0) {
    Date since = new Date (ifModifiedSince);
    SimpleDateFormat formatter =
      new SimpleDateFormat ("EEE, d MMM yyyy hh:mm:ss z");
    formatter.setTimeZone (TimeZone.getTimeZone ("GMT"));
    setRequestProperty ("If-Modified-Since", formatter.format (since));
  }
  StringBuffer request = new StringBuffer ("GET ");
  request.append (URLEncoder.encode (url.getFile ()));
  request.append (" HTTP/1.0\r\n");
  Enumeration keys = requestProperties.keys ();
  while (keys.hasMoreElements ()) {
    String key = (String) keys.nextElement ();
    request.append (key);
    request.append (": ");
    request.append (requestProperties.get (key));
    request.append ("\r\n");
  }
  request.append ('\n');
  out.write (request.toString ().getBytes ("latin1"));
}
```

The sendRequest() method creates a standard HTTP get request in the String-Buffer request and writes this as a byte array to the OutputStream out after ISO Latin 1 conversion.

We include all the user-specified request properties as standard HTTP headers in this request, including two of our own: User-Agent identifies the client application making the request (this URL framework) and If-Modified-Since specifies that the client doesn't want documents that remain unchanged since a specified date (formatted in the IETF standard manner; e.g., Tue, 10 Nov 1998 18:50:23 GMT).

```
protected void readHeaders () throws IOException {
  String status = readLine ();
  String header;
  while (((header = readLine ()) != null) &&
         (!header.trim ().equals ("")))) {
    int colon = header.indexOf (":");
    if (colon >= 0) {
      String key = header.substring (0, colon).trim ();
      String value = header.substring (colon + 1).trim ();
      keys.addElement (key);
      headers.put (key.toLowerCase (), value);
    }
  }
}

// protected String readLine () throws IOException ...
```

The readHeaders() method is called to read the HTTP headers from the server's response. These headers consist of a status line followed by a series of headers of the form key: value, followed by a blank line. For the purposes of this example, we are completely ignoring the server's status line. Ideally we would make the status available to the caller. Furthermore, we ought to check that a status is indeed returned; otherwise, if we connected to a legacy HTTP/0.9 server which returns no header information, then we will obliterate the start of its response.

Ignoring these issues, we simply read a line at a time, placing each header key into the Vector keys and each key-value pair into the Hashtable headers. The various methods that query the headers will read from these two data structures.

We keep reading lines until we encounter the end of the stream or a blank line. The data that follow these headers are the body of the URL object; we leave this data untouched, to be processed by a content handler.

```
protected String readLine () throws IOException {
  StringBuffer result = new StringBuffer ();
  int chr;
  while (((chr = in.read ()) != -1) && (chr != 10) && (chr != 13))
    result.append ((char) chr);
  if ((chr == -1) && (result.length () == 0))
    return null;
  if (chr == 13) {
    in.mark (1);
    if (in.read () != 10)
```

```
      in.reset ();
    }
  return result.toString ();
}
```

This method reads a single line of text from the `URLConnection`'s `InputStream`, `in`, where a line can be terminated by either LF, CR, or CRLF. We enter a loop, reading characters from `in`, and appending these to the `StringBuffer result` until we reach the EOF, a new line, or carriage return. If we reached the EOF without encountering any data, we return `null`. Otherwise, we test for CRLF; if we encountered a CR, we mark `in`'s current read position, read another character, and if that was not an LF character, we return it. In this manner, we can cater for any of the valid line terminators.

Note that we can't attach a `BufferedReader` to an `InputStreamReader` to in, and read a line from this. We want to be able to switch back to reading binary data after reading this text. The `InputStreamReader` class uses internal buffering, and so, will read more data from the attached stream than just the text that we read through it.

```
public InputStream getInputStream () throws IOException {
  if (!doInput)
    throw new IllegalStateException ("Input disabled.");
  connect ();
  return in;
}
```

This method calls the `connect()` method and returns the `InputStream` that is connected to the server. The contents of the URL can subsequently be read from this stream; the headers will already have been stripped by the `connect()` method.

```
public String getHeaderFieldKey (int index) {
  if (!connected)
    throw new IllegalStateException ("Not connected.");
  if (index < keys.size ())
    return (String) keys.elementAt (index);
  else
    return null;
}
```

This method allows for lookup of header keys (not values) by index, starting from zero.

```
public String getHeaderField (int index) {
  if (!connected)
    throw new IllegalStateException ("Not connected.");
  if (index < keys.size ())
    return getHeaderField ((String) keys.elementAt (index));
  else
    return null;
```

```
    }
```

This method allows for lookup of header values by index; again, indexing starts from zero.

```
public String getHeaderField (String key) {
   if (!connected)
      throw new IllegalStateException ("Not connected.");
   return (String) headers.get (key.toLowerCase ());
}
```

This method allows for lookup of header values by key. Using this we can, for example, look up the value corresponding to the key content-type. If the server provided a header Content-type: text/html, we would return text/html.

19.12 A plain text content handler

We will now look at implementing support for automatically downloading and decoding documents of type text/plain. This lets an application simply call the getContent() method of a text URL and receive an appropriate String in return. Given appropriate knowledge, we could easily extend this framework to support different content types.

To implement this framework, we must simply provide an implementation of the ContentHandlerFactory interface that returns an implementation of ContentHandler that can decode plain text. To demonstrates our HTTP protocol chain and plain text content chain in action, we conclude this section with a simple class that downloads and displays documents using the URL class.

19.12.1 Class ContentHandlerFactoryImpl

This class is responsible for returning the appropriate content handler for any MIME content types that we will support.

```
import java.io.*;
import java.net.*;

public class ContentHandlerFactoryImpl implements ContentHandlerFactory {
   public ContentHandler createContentHandler (String mimeType) {
      if (mimeType.equalsIgnoreCase ("text/plain"))
         return new TextPlainContentHandler ();
      else
         return null;
   }
}
```

The createContentHandler() method is the only method of the ContentHandlerFactory interface. In this case, we are only supporting simple text, so we return a `TextPlainContextHandler` for the MIME type text/plain and `null` for any other content types.

As with the `URLStreamHandlerFactory` implementation, we can easily add facilities to support new MIME types by simply returning an appropriate content handler for different content types. For testing purposes, a good idea might be to return the `Text-PlainContentHandler` for all MIME types beginning with text/.

19.12.2 Class TextPlainContentHandler

This class collects the contents of a plain text URL. We return a `String` object consisting of the URL contents surrounded by descriptive comments.

```
import java.net.*;
import java.io.*;

public class TextPlainContentHandler extends ContentHandler {
  public Object getContent (URLConnection connection) throws IOException {
    InputStream in = connection.getInputStream ();
    Reader reader = new InputStreamReader (in, "latin1");
    BufferedReader bufferedReader = new BufferedReader (reader);
    StringBuffer content = new StringBuffer ();
    String line;
    while ((line = bufferedReader.readLine ()) != null)
      content.append (line).append ('\n');
    bufferedReader.close ();
    return content.toString ();
  }
}
```

The only method we need to implement is `getContent()`. This method takes a `URLConnection` object as a parameter and should return an appropriate content object. We attach a `BufferedReader` to the `URLConnection`'s `InputStream`, read the contents of the stream into a `StringBuffer` and then return this result. In this example, we always decode the server's response using ISO Latin 1 encoding. It would ultimately be more appropriate to examine `connection`'s response headers, if any, and to choose a character encoding based on the information provided there. Doing so, however, is more than we wish to support at this point.

If we were handling a more complex content type, we probably obviously need to do more processing here. An image/gif content-handler would have to decode the URL contents and create an `Image` based on the image data. However, with just this simple implementation, we now have an entire framework together for downloading and automatically decoding text documents from the Web, as we will now demonstrate:

19.12.3 Class PageViewer

The `PageViewer` class is a simple application that takes a URL as a command-line argument, and downloads and displays the page. If the content of the page is not plain text (HTML files are not considered to be plain text), then this example will not print out a useful content object.

```
import java.io.*;
import java.net.*;

public class PageViewer {
   public static void main (String args[]) throws IOException {
      if (args.length != 1)
         throw new IllegalArgumentException ("Usage: PageViewer <url>");
      URL.setURLStreamHandlerFactory
         (new URLStreamHandlerFactoryImpl ());
      URLConnection.setContentHandlerFactory
         (new ContentHandlerFactoryImpl ());
      URL url = new URL (args[0]);
      System.out.println (url.getContent ());
   }
}
```

This class sets two custom factories to put the URL framework in place. For the URL class, we install our `URLStreamHandlerFactoryImpl` class. For the `URLConnection` class, we install our `ContentHandlerFactoryImpl` class. We now have our protocol and content handlers in place.

We can then simply create a URL corresponding to the requested document, call its `getContent()` method to retrieve the contents, and then print this to `System.out`. Contrast this with the efforts we went to in earlier chapters, parsing the URL, sending requests, and receiving responses. Of course, we still have to implement all of the networking, but this is hidden from the application within the URL framework.

To use this framework, simply try it out as follows:

```
java PageViewer http://nitric.com/jnp/file.txt
hello, world!
```

19.13 A finger protocol handler

Knowing the basics of the URL framework, it is fairly easy to add support for new protocols and content types. In this example, we add support for the finger protocol; we provide two `URLStreamHandlers` to support URLs of the following forms:

```
finger://nitric.com/merlin
finger://firewall.nitric.com/internal/#verbose
rawfinger:merlin@nitric.com
rawfinger:@internal@firewall.nitric.com#verbose
```

URLs with the finger or rawfinger protocol return the plain-text result of the finger request. This is largely based around the finger client that we developed in chapter 5; familiarity with that example is presumed.

We add three classes: FingerURLStreamHandler, RawFingerURLStreamHandler, and FingerURLConnection. We presume that our URLStreamHandlerFactoryImpl has been appropriately modified to return instances of our FingerURLStreamHandler for the finger protocol and instances of our RawFingerURLStreamHandler for the rawfinger protocol (figure 19.11).

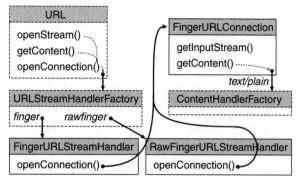

Figure 19.11   The finger URL framework

19.13.1 Class FingerURLStreamHandler

This class is a URLStreamHandler that will be returned by the URLStreamHandlerFactory in response to the finger protocol. This handler supports URLs of the form:

```
finger://nitric.com/merlin
finger://firewall.nitric.com/internal.nitric.com/#verbose
```

The first request is asking for information about user merlin on host nitric.com. The second request is asking host firewall.nitric.com to forward a query for verbose information about all users onto host internal.nitric.com. This class is comparatively simple because the actual conversion from this URL format into a finger request is performed by the FingerURLConnection class.

```
import java.io.*;
import java.net.*;

public class FingerURLStreamHandler extends URLStreamHandler {
  protected URLConnection openConnection (URL url) throws IOException {
    return new FingerURLConnection (url);
  }
}
```

We simply provide an openConnection() method that returns a new FingerURLConnection connected to the specified URL, url.

19.13.2 Class FingerURLConnection

The `FingerURLConnection` class extends `URLConnection`, providing support for the finger protocol using the `Finger` class that we developed earlier.

```
import java.io.*;
import java.net.*;
import java.util.*;

public class FingerURLConnection extends URLConnection {
  // public FingerURLConnection (URL url) ...
  // public void connect () throws IOException ...
  // public InputStream getInputStream () throws IOException ...
  // public String getContentType () ...
}
```

Our `FingerURLConnection` class provides the usual constructor, a `connect()` method, a `getInputStream()` method, and a `getContentType()` method. We inherit the default implementation of all other methods. This means that calling `getOutputStream()` will raise an exception and trying to read any headers will return `null`.

```
public FingerURLConnection (URL url) {
  super (url);
}
```

Our constructor calls the superconstructor, attaching to the URL `url`.

```
protected InputStream in;

public synchronized void connect () throws IOException {
  if (!connected) {
    StringBuffer query = new StringBuffer ();
    String file = url.getFile ().substring (1);
    StringTokenizer files = new StringTokenizer (file, "/", true);
    while (files.hasMoreTokens ())
      query.insert (0, files.nextToken ().replace ('/', '@'));
    Finger finger = new Finger (query.toString (), url.getHost (),
      url.getPort (), "verbose".equalsIgnoreCase (url.getRef ()));
    Reader reader = finger.finger ();
    in = new ReaderInputStream (reader, "latin1");
    connected = true;
  }
}
```

In the `connect()` method, we must translate the file part of our URL into a format suitable for a finger request. This involves removing the leading /, reversing the file components and replacing all instances of / with @. We achieve this with a `StringBuffer` and a `StringTokenizer`. Then we can create an instance of our `Finger` class using the hostname and port specified in our URL, and execute the finger request by calling finger(). We convert the resulting `Reader` into an `InputStream` using a `ReaderInput-Stream` (described next) and store this in the variable `in`, finally setting the superclass variable `connected` to `true`.

We could, of course, do away with the `ReaderInputStream` class by exposing an alternative `Finger` method that returns an `InputStream`, or by reading the entire contents of `reader` into a buffer and returning the contents of this as a `ByteArrayInput-Stream`; however, this alternative implementation is a little bit more interesting.

```
public InputStream getInputStream () throws IOException {
  connect ();
  return in;
}
```

The `getInputStream()` method calls `connect()` and returns our `InputStream`. The finger response can be read from this as plain text.

```
public String getContentType () {
  return "text/plain";
}
```

The `getContentType()` method returns text/plain; the response to any finger request is always plain text. As a result, the URL framework that we have developed will use our `TextPlainContentHandler` to parse the result of any finger request.

19.13.3 Class ReaderInputStream

This class transforms a `Reader` into an `InputStream` according to a specified encoding; essentially the opposite task of an `InputStreamReader`. This class is necessitated by the fact that our `Finger` class uses character streams, while the URL classes only use byte streams. The implementation of this class follows similar lines to our implementation of a buffered `InputStream` in chapter 8.

```
import java.io.*;

public class ReaderInputStream extends InputStream {
  // public ReaderInputStream (Reader reader) ...
  // public ReaderInputStream (Reader reader, String encoding)
  //     throws UnsupportedEncodingException ...
  // public int read () throws IOException ...
  // public int read (byte[] data, int off, int len) throws IOException ...
  // public int available () throws IOException ...
  // public void close () throws IOException ...
}
```

This class extends `InputStream`, providing constructors that accept a `Reader` from which to read and, optionally, an encoding with which to byte-encode the character data, along with the standard methods `read()`, `available()`, and `close()`. We don't support `mark()` or `reset()`.

```
protected Reader reader;
protected ByteArrayOutputStream byteArrayOut;
protected Writer writer;
protected char[] chars;
protected byte[] buffer;
protected int index, length;

public ReaderInputStream (Reader reader) {
  this.reader = reader;
  byteArrayOut = new ByteArrayOutputStream ();
  writer = new OutputStreamWriter (byteArrayOut);
  chars = new char[1024];
}
```

This constructor initializes the stream for character-to-byte conversion according to the platform-default character encoding. We store a reference to the `Reader` from which to read in `reader`, set up the `OutputStreamWriter` `writer` connected to the `ByteArrayOutputStream` `byteArrayOut` using the platform-default encoding, and then allocate the character buffer `chars`.

```
public ReaderInputStream (Reader reader, String encoding)
    throws UnsupportedEncodingException {
  this.reader = reader;
  byteArrayOut = new ByteArrayOutputStream ();
  writer = new OutputStreamWriter (byteArrayOut, encoding);
  chars = new char[1024];
}
```

This constructor initializes the stream for character-to-byte conversion according to the specified character encoding, `encoding`. We perform the same setup as before, but with a specified character encoding.

```
public int read () throws IOException {
  if (index >= length)
    fillBuffer ();
  if (index >= length)
    return -1;
  return 0xff & buffer[index ++];
}

// protected void fillBuffer () throws IOException ...
```

This method reads a single byte of data. If our internal buffer is empty, we call `fillBuffer()` to fill it up. If, after this, the buffer is still empty then we have reached the EOF and we return -1. Otherwise we return a byte from the buffer.

```
protected void fillBuffer () throws IOException {
  if (length < 0)
    return;
  int numChars = reader.read (chars);
  if (numChars < 0) {
    length = -1;
  } else {
    byteArrayOut.reset ();
    writer.write (chars, 0, numChars);
    writer.flush ();
    buffer = byteArrayOut.toByteArray ();
    length = buffer.length;
    index = 0;
  }
}
```

This method fills up our internal buffer with data from `reader`. If `length` is sub-zero then we have reached the EOF and so return immediately. Otherwise we read characters into our internal buffer, write these into `writer`, extract the resulting bytes from `byteArrayOut` and then reassign our internal state to read from this new buffer (figure 19.12).

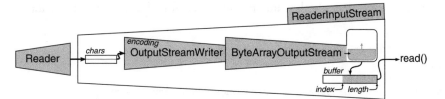

Figure 19.12   Class ReaderInputStream

```
public int read (byte[] data, int off, int len) throws IOException {
  if (index >= length)
    fillBuffer ();
  if (index >= length)
    return -1;
  int amount = Math.min (len, length - index);
  System.arraycopy (buffer, index, data, off, amount);
  index += amount;
  return amount;
}
```

This method reads a subarray of bytes. We refill our internal buffer, if necessary, and then copy as many bytes as we can from this buffer to the destination array.

```
public int available () throws IOException {
  return (index < length) ? length - index :
    ((length >= 0) && reader.ready ()) ? 1 : 0;
}
```

This method returns the number of bytes available to read from this stream: If our buffer is nonempty, then we return the number of bytes therein; otherwise, if we have not yet reached the EOF and `reader` has available data, then we return 1 (our best guess); otherwise, 0.

```
public void close () throws IOException {
  reader.close ();
}
```

This method closes this stream by closing `reader`.

19.13.4 Class RawFingerURLStreamHandler

This class is a `URLStreamHandler` that will be returned by the `URLStreamHandler-Factory` in response to the rawfinger protocol. This class is more complex than the earlier `FingerURLStreamHandler` because we support nonstandard URLs with the conventional finger syntax:

```
rawfinger:merlin@nitric.com
rawfinger:@internal.nitric.com@firewall.nitric.com#verbose
```

These two URLs have exactly the same meaning as before, but use the new syntax.

```
import java.io.*;
import java.net.*;
import java.util.*;

public class RawFingerURLStreamHandler extends URLStreamHandler {
  // protected void parseURL (URL url, String spec, int start, int limit) ...
  // protected String toExternalForm (URL url) ...
  // protected URLConnection openConnection (URL url) throws IOException ...
}
```

We implement the `parseURL()` method to parse a URL from finger-style textual form into the URL `url`, and the `toExternalForm()` method that performs the reverse process. We also provide an `openConnection()` method that creates an appropriate `URLConnection`.

```
protected void parseURL (URL url, String spec, int start, int limit) {
  String query = spec.substring (start, limit);
  int at = query.lastIndexOf ("@");
  String user = (at > -1) ? query.substring (0, at) : query;
  StringBuffer revUser = new StringBuffer ();
  StringTokenizer t = new StringTokenizer (user, "@", true);
  while (t.hasMoreTokens ())
    revUser.insert (0, t.nextToken ().replace ('@', '/'));
  revUser.insert (0, '/');
  String location = (at > -1) ? query.substring (at + 1) : "";
  int colon = location.indexOf (":");
```

```
      int port = ((colon > -1) && (colon < location.length () - 1)) ?
        Integer.parseInt (location.substring (colon + 1)) : -1;
      String host = (colon > -1) ? location.substring (0, colon) : location;
      setURL (url, url.getProtocol (), host, port,
            revUser.toString (), url.getRef ());
  }
```

In the parseURL() method, we must dissect the textual URL, spec, into the URL url. We extract the relevant substring into the variable query and dissect this in the same manner as with the original finger client. We convert the conventional finger-style syntax into the new URL style and call the setURL() method to insert the dissected parts into url.

For example, if the user enters a URL of the form rawfinger:merlin@internal@fire-wall.nitric.com:79#verbose, this method will be called with the substring merlin@inter-nal@firewall.nitric.com:79. We extract the host, firewall.nitric.com; the port, 79; and the file, merlin@internal, which we reverse to be internal/merlin. The resulting URL is internally represented as rawfinger://firewall.nitric.com:79/internal/merlin, compatible with the FingerURLConnection class.

```
  protected String toExternalForm (URL url) {
     StringBuffer result = new StringBuffer ();
     String file = url.getFile ().substring (1);
     StringTokenizer files = new StringTokenizer (file, "/", true);
     while (files.hasMoreTokens ())
        result.insert (0, files.nextToken ().replace ('/', '@'));
     result.insert (0, ':').insert (0, url.getProtocol ());
     if ((url.getHost ().length () > 0) || (url.getPort () != -1))
        result.append ('@');
     result.append (url.getHost ());
     if (url.getPort () != -1)
        result.append (':').append (url.getPort ());
     if (url.getRef () != null)
        result.append ('#').append (url.getRef ());
     return result.toString ();
  }
```

The toExternalForm() performs the reverse process, converting the URL url from its internal format into the standard finger textual form using the StringBuffer result to accumulate its result.

```
  protected URLConnection openConnection (URL url) throws IOException {
     return new FingerURLConnection (url);
  }
```

The openConnection() method returns a new FingerURLConnection connected to the specified URL, url. The internal fields of the URL are set up by the parseURL() method to be suitable for processing by this class.

To see these example in action, we can simply test finger and rawfinger URLs using the PageViewer class with which we tested our plain-text HTTP framework. We'll now take a brief look at the remaining URL-related API classes before moving on.

19.14 Class URLEncoder

The URLEncoder class is a utility class for encoding data in x-www-form-urlencoded format; this is the format that Web servers expect form data to be encoded, and thus a conversion that is often needed for accessing resources on the Web.

19.14.1 Static methods

This class provides all its function through a single static method:

String encode(String decoded)   This method returns the specified String, decoded, encoded as per the standard as follows:

Alphanumeric characters (*A–Z, a–z, 0–9*), minus, underscore, period and asterisk are left unchanged; spaces are replaced with plus symbols (+); all other characters are replaced by the three-character encoding *%xy* where *xy* is the two-digit upper-case hexadecimal encoding of the character's ASCII code. For example, the *!* character (ASCII character 33) is encoded as *%21*.

It should be noted that the Unicode characters of the String are converted into bytes, prior to hex encoding, with the aid of character streams using the platform-default character-byte encoding. For most environments this means Latin 1 encoding; standard characters will be encoded correctly and nonrepresentable characters will be encoded as a question mark.

19.15 〔JDK 1.2〕 Class URLDecoder

The URLDecoder class is a utility class for decoding data from x-www-form-urlencoded format; this is the format that Web servers expect form data to be encoded, and thus a conversion that is often needed for implementing Web server facilities.

19.15.1 Static methods

This class provides all its function through a single static method:

String decode(String encoded)   This method returns the specified String, encoded, decoded as per the standard as follows:

Plus symbols are replaced by spaces; all *%xy* sequences are replaced by the character resulting from hex-decoding *xy*, and all other characters are left unchanged. For example, hello%2c+world%21 is decoded to *hello, world!*

It should be noted that the decoded byte-stream is converted into a `String` using the platform-default byte-character encoding. For most environments this means Latin 1 encoding; care should be taken where this is not true.

19.16 Wrapping up

The URL-related classes provide a framework for easily accessing and decoding data from information systems such as the Web or a file system. Use of these classes is comparatively easy, and extending them to support new protocols and types is fully supported, making them an extremely powerful capability of Java.

The advantage of going to the effort of adding protocols and types to this framework is that an application can then use a simple and standard interface to access any addressable object. The `getContent()` method performs all of the protocol- and content-specific actions necessary to download and decode the referenced object; alternatively, `getInputStream()` can be used to bypass the content decoding. The JDK even provides support for most standard protocols, so most common data access needs are available immediately without any implementation being required.

The protocol handler that we provided for HTTP is obviously lacking in many respects. Anyone who is seriously considering implementing a protocol handler should first obtain complete documentation for the desired protocol. However, our examples should hopefully have shown where to begin.

C H A P T E R   2 0

Datagram networking

UDP is a *connectionless* transport layer protocol that operates on top of IP. It is packet-based and revolves around constructing packets of information and dispatching them into the network for delivery if possible. Delivery is not guaranteed, but assurance as to the basic integrity of packets that are delivered is provided by a 16-bit CRC.

The difference between TCP and UDP connections is best described with the following analogy. TCP is like a phone call: the number is dialed once, a connection is established, and the connection is available to both parties until someone closes the connection (hangs up the phone). UDP, on the other hand, is equivalent to having that same phone conversation through bionic couriers. Each message would be sent as a distinct package, and would arrive separately, requiring addressing each time. UDP packets can be lost and can overtake each other; they can even be duplicated. If a packet arrives, however, you can be sure that it is intact. Both TCP and UDP operate over IP, and so both ultimately result in individual IP packets; UDP, however, brings the programmer much closer to the raw IP layer.

20.1 Class DatagramPacket

Sending a UDP packet involves creating a `DatagramPacket` object that consists of the message body and the target address (figure 20.1); this `DatagramPacket` can then be placed into the network for delivery.

**Figure 20.1
Class Datagram-
Packet**

Receiving a UDP packet involves creating a `DatagramPacket` object and then accepting a UDP packet into it from the network. Upn receipt, the source address and contents can be extracted from the `DatagramPacket`.

20.1.1 Constructors

There are two constructors for UDP datagrams. One is used for sending packets and requires the address to be specified; the other is used for receiving packets and requires only that a memory buffer be provided.

DatagramPacket(byte buffer[], int length)   This constructor is used for receiving datagrams. The `buffer` parameter is the byte array that will hold the packet contents when it arrives; you must provide a preallocated array to hold the packet. The `length` parameter is the maximum number of bytes that should be read into this buffer. Any extra data that are received in a UDP packet will be discarded.

DatagramPacket(byte buffer[], int length, InetAddress address, int port)   This constructor is used to create a datagram packet for transmission. The packet body consists of the first `length` bytes of array `buffer`. The packet will be delivered to the specified port `port` on the specified host `address`; there must be a UDP server listening on the target port to receive the packet. Note that UDP and TCP port numbers are completely independent, so you can have both a UDP server and a TCP server listening on the same port number.

20.1.2 Methods

The contents and address of the `DatagramPacket` can be queried and modified with the following methods. If the packet was received, then the addresses correspond to the source host; if the packet was created for transmission, then the addresses correspond to the destination host.

InetAddress getAddress()   This method returns the IP address of the packet source (or destination).

int getPort()   This method returns the port number of the packet source (or destination). This information allows you to respond to a UDP packet easily, because you can determine the source server's port number directly.

byte[] getData()   The `getData()` method is used to extract the packet data into a byte array. This will be the same buffer that was specified in the constructor; it will, therefore, have the initial buffer size, and not the exact packet size.

int getLength()   This method is used to find the length of the actual UDP packet; which can be less than the actual buffer size.

(JDK 1.1) *void setAddress(InetAddress address)*   This method changes the address of this `DatagramPacket` to the specified address, `address`.

(JDK 1.1) *void setPort(int port)*   This method changes the port of this `Datagram-Packet` to the specified value, `port`.

(JDK 1.1) *void setData(byte[] buffer)*   This method changes the data payload of this `DatagramPacket` to the specified byte array, `buffer`.

(JDK 1.1) *void setLength(int length)*   This method changes the payload length of this `DatagramPacket` to the specified value, `length`.

20.2 Class DatagramSocket

This class is used to both send and receive `DatagramPackets`. After creating a `DatagramSocket`, you can send and receive packets (figure 20.2). As with TCP, a

`DatagramSocket` must listen on a particular port number between 1 and 65,535; ports 1–1,023 are reserved for system applications.

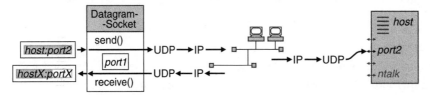

Figure 20.2 Class DatagramSocket

Remember that UDP is connectionless, so you use a single `DatagramSocket` to send packets to different destinations and receive packets from different sources. There is no way to control which hosts you will receive packets from; you will simply receive all those addressed to your port.

20.2.1 Constructors

A `DatagramSocket` will listen on a particular UDP port of the local machine for incoming packets. You can either specify a port for the `DatagramSocket` or let the operating system assign one to you. Usually a server will pick a particular port on which to operate, and clients will allow a random port to be assigned. The client's port number will be automatically inserted into every packet that it sends. Facility is also provided to bind a `DatagramSocket` to a particular local address on a multihomed machine.

DatagramSocket() throws SocketException   This constructor creates a `DatagramSocket` with a randomly chosen port number.

DatagramSocket(int port) throws SocketException   This constructor creates a `DatagramSocket` that listens on the specified port `port`. To bind to a random free port, as with the previous constructor, simply specify a port number of zero.

⬤ JDK 1.1   *DatagramSocket(int port, InetAddress local) throws Socket-Exception*   This constructor creates a `DatagramSocket` that listens on the specified port, `port`, and is bound to the specified local address, `local`. For multihomed machines, packets are sent through the corresponding network interface and, therefore, appear to come from the specified IP address. Incoming packets will only be received on this address. Specify port O to be assigned a random, unused port.

20.2.2 Methods

The `DatagramSocket` class provides methods to send and receive `DatagramPacket`s as well as methods to close the socket, to determine the local address information, and to set a receive timeout.

void send(DatagramPacket packet) throws IOException   This method sends the packet `packet` into the network. If you persist in sending packets to an unreachable or nonlistening destination, you may eventually receive an `IOException` although this is not guaranteed.

void receive(DatagramPacket packet) throws IOException   This method receives a single UDP packet into the specified `DatagramPacket`, `packet`. The packet can then be inspected to determine its source IP address and port, its contents, and the length of the data. This method blocks until it has successfully received a packet or a timeout occurs.

JDK 1.1   *InetAddress getLocalAddress()*   This method returns the local address to which this `DatagramSocket` is bound.

int getLocalPort()   This method returns the port number on which the `Datagram-Socket` is listening.

void close()   This method closes the `DatagramSocket`.

JDK 1.1   *void setSoTimeout(int timeout) throws SocketException*   This method sets a socket time-out of the specified value, `timeout`. The `receive()` method will only block for the specified number of milliseconds to receive a UDP packet, after which it will abort with an `InterruptedIOException`. A time-out of 0 disables this feature; socket operations will block forever.

JDK 1.1   *int getSoTimeout() throws SocketException*   This method returns the current socket time-out, or `0` if none is set (the default).

JDK 1.2   *void setSendBufferSize(int size) throws SocketException*   This method requests that the operating system set this socket's send buffer size (`SO_SNDBUF`) to the specified value, `size`. UDP packets larger than the send buffer size cannot be transmitted. The operating system may ignore the value that you request.

JDK 1.2   *int getSendBufferSize() throws SocketException*   This method returns this socket's current send buffer size.

JDK 1.2   *void setReceiveBufferSize(int size) throws SocketException*   This method requests that the operating system set this socket's receive buffer size (`SO_RCVBUF`) to the specified value, `size`. UDP packets larger than the receive buffer size cannot be received. The operating system may ignore the value that you request.

JDK 1.2 *int getReceiveBufferSize(int size) throws SocketException* This method returns this socket's current receive buffer size.

JDK 1.2 *void connect(InetAddress address, int port) throws SocketExcept ion* This method *connects* this socket to the specified remote address and port. Use this method only for performance reasons; it is not required for normal UDP operation.

This method checks with the current `SecurityManager` whether communication with the specified remote address and port is permitted, throwing a `SecurityException` if not. If this method succeeds, then all packets transmitted to and received from this socket will be verified against the chosen address and port without a security check: If a packet is sent to a different address then an `IllegalArgumentException` will be thrown; if a packet is received from a different address then it will be discarded. Without the use of this method, the `SecurityManager` is invoked for *every* packet that is sent to or received from a `DatagramSocket`. This can cause performance problems for applets.

JDK 1.2 *void disconnect()* This method disconnects this socket, if connected.

JDK 1.2 *InetAddress getInetAddress()* This method returns the `InetAddress` to which this socket is connected, or else `null` if it is not connected.

JDK 1.2 *int getPort()* This method returns the port to which this socket is connected, or else `-1` if it is not connected.

20.2.3 IOException
Creating a `DatagramSocket`, and sending and receiving packets may all throw `IOExceptions` if a problem arises. The `SocketException` class is also a subclass of `IOException` that conveys more specific problem detail.

20.2.4 SecurityException
The `SecurityManager` restricts access to UDP transmission and reception. Untrusted applets may neither send packets to nor receive packets from a server other than the one that originally served them. The receipt restrictions are performed by verifying the source address of every packet that is received; if the packet comes from an invalid source, it is silently dropped and the `receive()` method continues to wait for a valid packet (with the corresponding incorrect time-out semantics).

20.3 Receiving UDP packets

In this example, we step through the process of receiving a UDP packet (figure 20.3).

Figure 20.3   Receiving a UDP packet

```
DatagramSocket socket = new DatagramSocket (port);
```

We first create a `DatagramSocket` on a specified port. Specifying the port is optional; however, we want to pick our own port when we are planning on receiving unsolicited packets so that we can give other applications an address to which to send their packets.

```
byte buffer[] = new byte[65508];
DatagramPacket packet = new DatagramPacket (buffer, buffer.length);
```

We next construct a reception packet. Remember that there are two constructors for the `DatagramPacket` class—one for transmission and one for reception; when receiving, we don't specify a destination address. The byte array, `buffer`, is the buffer into which we will receive the packet.

Note that the byte array is declared with a length of 65,508 bytes. This is the maximum size of any UDP packet; the UDP packet size is specified in just two bytes of the UDP header and there is some protocol overhead. If we know that we will receive packets of a particular size, we can choose a more appropriate value. If, however, we provide a buffer that is too small, part of the received packet will be discarded.

```
socket.receive (packet);
```

The `receive()` method is called to wait for a packet to arrive. It takes a `DatagramPacket` as its parameter, and copies the received UDP packet into it.

```
InetAddress fromAddress = packet.getAddress ();
int fromPort = packet.getPort ();
int length = packet.getLength ();
byte[] data = packet.getData ();
// ...
```

Here we use methods of the `DatagramPacket` to determine its source address, port number, and data length. We then call `getData()` to get the packet contents; note that this is, in fact, the same buffer that we initially provided.

We can now dissect the data, and if necessary, respond to the application that originated the packet.

```
socket.close ();
```

When finished, we close the socket. This stops further reception and buffering of UDP packets.

20.4 Transmitting UDP packets

In this example, we step through the process of sending a UDP packet (figure 20.4).

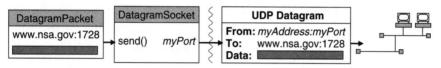

Figure 20.4   Transmitting a UDP packet

```
DatagramSocket socket = new DatagramSocket ();
```

We first construct a `DatagramSocket` for UDP transmission. UDP transfer is connectionless, but we still use a socket for transmission. In this case, we don't care about our local port number, so we accept a random one chosen by the operating system.

```
DatagramPacket packet = new DatagramPacket
   (data, data.length, InetAddress.getByName ("www.nsa.gov"), 1728);
```

We next create a `DatagramPacket` for transmission. We assume in this example that the `data` variable is an array of bytes. We construct a new `DatagramPacket` with this byte array, the length of the array, an `InetAddress` destination, and a port. These specify the destination to which the packet will be delivered; in this case, we are delivering to a server on port 1728 of the host www.nsa.gov. Remember that each packet must have its own addressing information, so we must use the constructor intended for transmission for each packet.

```
socket.send (packet);
```

Calling the `send()` method places the packet into the network for delivery to the target. On its way, it may be delivered out of order with earlier or later packets, it may be duplicated, or it may be lost. The local address and port number are automatically transmitted as part of the UDP header.

```
socket.close ();
```

We close the `DatagramSocket` when we are done.

20.5 A UDP example

It is often desirable to use UDP when latency is an issue; the overhead is considerably less than when TCP is used. Packet loss is, however, an obvious concern. This example uses an alarm to trigger a resend if no response is received to a transmission. We assume that the packet has been lost if we don't receive a prompt reply.

The server is a simple echo server; however, we have added code to simulate packet loss so that the behavior is easier to observe. UDP packets usually will be lost only if a network is congested. Across the Internet this may be quite common, but within a small LAN it is rare.

It is not advisable to use a much more complex mechanism than this to ensure reliable delivery with UDP. The more function you add, the closer you get to reimplementing TCP. TCP, however, has many special mechanisms that prevent network congestion and other problems. It is unlikely that a simple implementation of reliable delivery on top of UDP will address these issues successfully. If your data must get through intact, then use TCP, unless you are in a multiclient situation where reliable multicast is a consideration (see chapter 22).

20.5.1 Class Alarm

We will use this class in our UDP client to provide an alarm call mechanism (figure 20.5). This allows us to schedule a callback to occur after a specified delay. In this example, we will send a packet and then wait for a response from the server; we schedule an alarm call to resend the request if we get no response within a reasonable time.

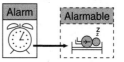

Figure 20.5 Class Alarm

This class implements the alarm mechanism using `Runnable`. When the thread is started, it sleeps for a while and then issues an alarm call on its target object. An `Alarm` can be started by calling `start()` and stopped by calling `stop()`.

```
public class Alarm implements Runnable {
   // public Alarm (int time, Alarmable target) ...
   // public Alarm (int time, Alarmable target, Object arg) ...
   // public synchronized void start () ...
   // public synchronized void stop () ...
   // public void run() ...
}
```

This class uses a `Thread` that calls the `alarmCall()` method of the target object after a specified time out. There are two constructors for the class: the time out and target for the alarm call must be specified. An additional parameter can optionally be specified to help identify the cause of an alarm callback.

```
public Alarm (int time, Alarmable target) {
    this (time, target, null);
}
```

This constructor calls the following constructor with a `null` arg value.

```
protected Alarmable target;
protected Object arg;
protected int time;

public Alarm (int time, Alarmable target, Object arg) {
    this.time = time;
    this.target = target;
    this.arg = arg;
}
```

This constructor takes three parameters: `time` is the number of milliseconds to sleep before issuing an alarm call; `target` is the object whose `alarmCall()` method should be called; and `arg` is an arbitrary value that can be used to indicate the cause of the alarm call. One possible use of `arg` is as a `String` description of the cause for alarm.

```
protected Thread alarm;

public synchronized void start () {
    if (alarm == null) {
        alarm = new Thread (this);
        alarm.start ();
    }
}
```

This method starts the alarm, if it has not already been started.

```
public synchronized void stop () {
    if (alarm != null) {
        alarm.interrupt ();
        alarm = null;
    }
}
```

This method stops the alarm, if it is still running, by calling its `interrupt()` method.

```
public void run () {
    try {
        Thread.sleep (time);
        synchronized (this) {
            if (Thread.interrupted ())
                return;
            alarm = null;
        }
        target.alarmCall (arg);
```

```
    } catch (InterruptedException ignored) {
    }
  }
```

This method is called when the `Alarm` is started; we sleep for the specified time, then call the `alarmCall()` method of the target object. If we are stopped while sleeping, an `InterruptedException` will be raised and we can exit gracefully. Otherwise we assign the `alarm` reference to `null` to indicate that we cannot be stopped. Out of paranoia, however, we first check to make sure that we were not stopped between waking and entering this `synchronized` block. If so, then we just return immediately.

20.5.2 *Interface Alarmable*

This is the interface that must be implemented by any object that wishes to receive alarm calls. An `Alarmable` object is thus any object that might receive an alarm call to signal an event. In this example, we will use this mechanism to resend lost packets.

```
public interface Alarmable {
  public void alarmCall (Object arg);
}
```

The `alarmCall()` method is called when an `Alarm` reaches its time-out; the `arg` value is that which was passed to the `Alarm` object when the callback was initiated. This can be used to help determine the cause of the alarm call.

20.5.3 *Class UDPEchoServer*

This class implements a UDP echo server. It creates a UDP socket, then waits for packets, echoing back what it receives (figure 20.6).

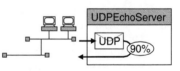

Figure 20.6   Class UDPEchoServer

```
import java.net.*;
import java.io.*;

public class UDPEchoServer {
  // public UDPEchoServer (int port) ...
  // public void execute () throws IOException ...
  // static public void main (String[] args) throws IOException ...
}
```

This is a simple class that listens on a specified UDP port and echoes back every packet that it receives to the sender.

```
  protected int port;

  public UDPEchoServer (int port) {
    this.port = port;
  }
```

The constructor stores the specified port number, `port`.

```
public void execute () throws IOException {
  DatagramSocket socket = new DatagramSocket (port);
  while (true) {
    DatagramPacket packet = receive (socket);
    if (Math.random () < .9) {
      sendEcho (socket, packet);
    } else {
      System.out.println ("Dropped!");
    }
  }
}

// protected DatagramPacket receive (DatagramSocket socket)
//     throws IOException ...
// protected void sendEcho (DatagramSocket socket, DatagramPacket packet)
//     throws IOException ...
```

The `execute()` method opens a `DatagramSocket socket` that listens on the chosen port for incoming UDP packets, and then loops, receiving UDP packets and echoing them back to the sender. We can easily return a packet to its sender because the source address and port are automatically provided by the networking protocol.

We simulate 10 percent packet loss to more clearly demonstrate the function of the subsequent client. Although UDP may drop packets naturally due to network congestion, this is not commonly observable on a small LAN.

```
protected DatagramPacket receive (DatagramSocket socket)
    throws IOException {
  byte buffer[] = new byte[65508];
  DatagramPacket packet = new DatagramPacket (buffer, buffer.length);
  socket.receive (packet);
  return packet;
}
```

This method is essentially the same as the UDP reception code fragment shown earlier in the chapter. We create a new `DatagramPacket`, and a buffer into which to read the packet. We then receive a packet into the buffer using the `receive()` method of `socket`. Note that this server would be more efficient if we reused the same packet for every packet that we receive.

```
protected void sendEcho (DatagramSocket socket, DatagramPacket packet)
    throws IOException {
  DatagramPacket response =
    new DatagramPacket (packet.getData (), packet.getLength (),
                        packet.getAddress (), packet.getPort ());
  socket.send (response);
}
```

This method creates a `DatagramPacket` from the specified packet's contents and transmits it to the packet's origin. Note again that this could be much more efficient: The fields of `packet` are already set up to form a reply so we could simply send `packet` to `socket` and the echo would be complete.

```
public static void main (String[] args) throws IOException {
    if (args.length != 1)
        throw new IllegalArgumentException ("Syntax: UDPEchoServer <port>");
    UDPEchoServer server = new UDPEchoServer (Integer.parseInt (args[0]));
    server.execute ();
}
```

This method creates a `UDPEchoServer` and calls the `execute()` method, which listens on the port specified as a command-line parameter and echoes back every packet that is received.

20.5.4 Class SureDelivery

The `SureDelivery` class is a client to demonstrate the `UDPEchoServer`. This class attempts to protect against packet loss by resending a request if no response is received within a certain time-out. We use the `Alarm` class to perform this callback (figure 20.7).

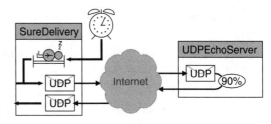

Figure 20.7   Class SureDelivery

```
import java.net.*;
import java.io.*;

public class SureDelivery implements Alarmable {
    // public SureDelivery (String message, String host, int port) ...
    // public void alarmCall (Object arg) ...
    // public static void main (String[] args)
    //     throws InterruptedException, IOException ...
}
```

The `SureDelivery` class sends a message specified in the constructor to the specified UDP server and awaits a response. An `Alarm` is used to resend the message if no response is received within a ten-second time-out. For brevity, all the processing is performed in the constructor.

```
protected DatagramSocket socket;
protected DatagramPacket packet;
protected Alarm alarm;

public SureDelivery (String message, String host, int port)
    throws IOException {
```

```
    socket = new DatagramSocket ();
    buildPacket (message, host, port);
    try {
      sendPacket ();
      receivePacket ();
    } finally {
      alarm.stop ();
      socket.close ();
    }
  }

// protected void buildPacket
//     (String message, String host, int port) throws IOException ...
// protected void sendPacket () throws IOException ...
// protected void receivePacket () throws IOException ...
```

In the constructor, we create a `DatagramSocket socket` to be used for sending and receiving packets. We call the `buildPacket()` method to create a `Datagram-Packet packet`, which consists of the specified message and is addressed to the specified server.

We next send the packet and wait to receive a response. The `sendPacket()` method automatically starts an `Alarm alarm` that will alert us if no response is received within ten seconds. When a response is received, we stop the alarm and terminate. Note the use of `finally` here—we wish to stop the alarm and close the socket, regardless of how we exit the constructor.

```
protected void buildPacket
    (String message, String host, int port) throws IOException {
  ByteArrayOutputStream byteArrayOut = new ByteArrayOutputStream ();
  DataOutputStream dataOut = new DataOutputStream (byteArrayOut);
  dataOut.writeUTF (message);
  byte[] data = byteArrayOut.toByteArray ();
  packet = new DatagramPacket (data, data.length,
    InetAddress.getByName (host), port);
}
```

The `buildPacket()` method takes a `String message` as a parameter, and a target host `host` and port `port`. We use a `ByteArrayOutputStream byteArrayOut` to create a byte array `data` that contains the specified message. We then construct a `Datagram-Packet` with `data` as the contents, addressed to the specified host and port. We use the `getByName()` method of class `InetAddress` to obtain the IP address of the host.

Note that we are using the `ByteArrayOutputStream` class to create a UDP packet; we can thus use the streams interface to communicate over UDP. We attach a stream filter `dataOut` to `byteArrayOut` and then write high-level data into this buffer. The `toByteArray()` method of `byteArrayOut` lets us subsequently extract the data as an array of bytes. Although in this case, the same effect could be achieved with a call to `getBytes()` with the encoding UTF8, this is an example of how higher-level data can easily be transmitted over UDP.

```
protected void sendPacket () throws IOException {
  socket.send (packet);
  System.out.println ("Sent packet.");
  alarm = new Alarm (10000, this);
  alarm.start ();
}
```

This method sends the previously constructed packet `packet` over the `Datagram-Socket socket`, and starts a new `Alarm alarm` to warn us if no response is received within ten seconds. Note that we don't need to explicitly provide an address or port for the server to respond to; this is taken care of by the UDP protocol.

```
protected boolean received;

protected void receivePacket () throws IOException {
  byte buffer[] = new byte[65508];
  DatagramPacket packet = new DatagramPacket (buffer, buffer.length);
  socket.receive (packet);
  received = true;
  ByteArrayInputStream byteArrayIn =
    new ByteArrayInputStream (packet.getData (), 0, packet.getLength ());
  DataInputStream dataIn = new DataInputStream (byteArrayIn);
  String result = dataIn.readUTF ();
  System.out.println ("Received " + result + ".");
}
```

The `receivePacket()` method creates a buffer `buffer` and a new `Datagram-Packet packet`, then awaits a UDP response from the server. When we receive a response, we create a `ByteArrayInputStream byteArrayIn` that reads from the contents of the packet. We attach a `DataInputStream dataIn` to this and display the contents of the packet.

Note that the `ByteArrayInputStream` class lets us use the familiar streams interface to read the contents of a UDP packet, even though the UDP communications channel is itself not streams-based.

```
public synchronized void alarmCall (Object object) {
  try {
    System.out.println ("Alarm!");
    if (!received)
      sendPacket ();
  } catch (IOException ex) {
    ex.printStackTrace ();
  }
}
```

This method is specified by the `Alarmable` interface and will be called by `alarm` after a certain period of time if we don't first stop it.

We use this method to resend the request if an echo response is not received within a certain timeout. We presume that this means that a packet must have been lost—either our request or the response—and so we must resend our request.

In this method, we resend the original packet using the `sendPacket()` method, displaying any exception that should occur. The `sendPacket()` method automatically schedules another alarm call should this request also be lost. We can thus simply return after calling `sendPacket()`.

There is a small race condition between receiving a response and stopping the alarm call, and the alarm call going off and triggering another send. We crudely circumvent this by checking the `received` boolean before triggering a resend. It is possible that an extra request may be sent before the alarm is shut down, but this is not a particular concern for this application.

```
public static void main (String[] args)
    throws InterruptedException, IOException {
  if (args.length != 3)
    throw new IllegalArgumentException
      ("Syntax: SureDelivery <host> <port> <message>");
  while (true) {
    new SureDelivery (args[2], args[0], Integer.parseInt (args[1]));
    System.out.println ("Pause...");
    Thread.sleep (2000);
  }
}
```

The `main()` method tests the classes we have discussed in these examples by repeatedly creating instances of the `SureDelivery` class that ping the server and await a response, resending requests if no response is received.

To run the example, first start the `UDPEchoServer`, then start the `SureDelivery` to ping the server machine. The output clearly shows what happens when a packet is dropped and the alarm call issues a resend.

20.6 Wrapping up

It is important to understand what UDP is useful for before planning applications based on it. Because UDP is a connectionless protocol, the overhead is quite a bit lower than TCP, which must perform connection setup and ensure reliable delivery with automatic retransmission and flow control. TCP uses a transmission window to make this process more efficient; however, UDP is still a more efficient protocol, with lower overhead.

On the other hand, UDP does not guarantee delivery. It does not guarantee that the order of reception is the same as the order of transmission, and it does not guarantee that packets will not be duplicated. If you send a packet once, it may be received several times. UDP also has a limited packet size, and no network congestion control; if a large UDP packet is sent, it is likely to be broken into smaller IP packets which significantly increases the likelihood that a complete packet will be lost.

An example of when *not* to use UDP is in long data communications. If packets are reordered or lost, then the information becomes unusable. TCP is best in this case, when data requires correct and complete delivery. For data that does not have this requirement, UDP may be a good choice. Video and audio communications are good examples, since a few lost or reordered packets will not be very noticeable, and the lower overhead makes a real difference in delivery feasibility. Pinging a time server is another appropriate use of UDP; a server can listen for incoming UDP packets and respond to each one with the current time, incurring minimal network overhead.

C H A P T E R   2 1

Some datagram applications

In this chapter, we examine the development of simple UDP applications, both client and server. Our purpose is to investigate the implementation of real-world protocols. However this is complicated somewhat by UDP's limited applicability: it is extremely useful for broadcast and multicast applications, which we shall look at in the next chapter. Outside of these domains, however, it is only commonly used for simple query operations (such as domain-name lookups or timeserver queries), for network analysis (determining if a host is alive), or for real-time applications (such as streamed media), which are hard to demonstrate in a simple example (figure 21.1).

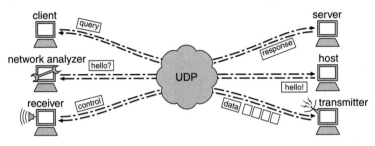

Figure 21.1 UDP applications

In an effort to examine some of these common domains, we will look at implementing a ping client that operates like the `ping` command, allowing the user to determine whether a host is alive and also to determine the round-trip time of packets sent to the host. We also look at a variant of the earlier TCP/IP `nslookup` command, but this time we use UDP as a transport layer. The last example is a simple server that mimics the UDP daytime protocol, responding to every UDP packet with a response that gives the current time at the server.

We will not look at an example of UDP streaming; however, the typical configuration for such a system, whether unicast, multicast, or broadcast, is for the client(s) and server to agree on a transmission rate and then for the server simply to transmit data at the chosen rate. The client receives and processes packets as they arive, typically discarding duplicate packets or packets that arrive out of order. The content must be able to handle data loss (audio and video are a typical example). Resending lost data is sometimes useful, providing that enough data are buffered that the resend can arrive in time. However downgrading the transmission rate in response to high data loss is usually also required in such a case.

21.1 A ping client

This class implements a ping client that operates in the same manner as the `ping` command, allowing the user to determine whether a remote host is alive, and also to determine the round-trip time of packets sent to the host. This can be useful to help determine network connectivity. Ping can be used to investigate progressively more remote hosts and, thereby, to determine where network delays or outages are occurring.

For the purposes of this client, we use the UDP *echo* service that many hosts support. This service simply echoes back any packets that are received on port 7 (RFC 862, STD 20) (figure 21.2). We can thus send

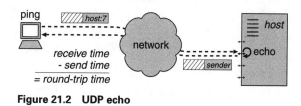

Figure 21.2   UDP echo

packets to port 7 of the machine in question. If it responds, then it is alive, and we can perform calculations on the round-trip response time. Not all machines support this service, so sometimes `ping` will receive no response although a remote host is up. Similarly, a firewall may block these UDP echo packets before they can reach their target.

ICMP, another IP protocol (like TCP and UDP), would actually be more appropriate than UDP for this purpose because it supports a lower-level ping protocol (ICMP 8/0: echo request and ICMP 0/0: echo reply) that does not rely on an application-level echo service. However, ICMP is not accessible from Java. Using ICMP, it also would be possible to do more extensive network investigation than just ping, such as the `traceroute` command, which enumerates all routers through which packets travel enroute to a remote host.

21.1.1 Command syntax
The `ping` command supports a fairly comprehensive set of options:

```
Ping [-c <count>] [-i <wait>] [-s <packetsize>] [-f] <hostname>[:<port>]
```

The basic operation of this command is to select a target host and optional port, and then to transmit a number of packets to the remote echo service. Round-trip time statistics are collected as responses are received.

The `-c` option specifies how many packets to send. The default is `32`; a value of `0` indicates to keep on sending until the command is aborted.

The `-i` option specifies the delay, in milliseconds, to wait between sending packets. The default is `1` second; the minimum is `10` milliseconds.

The `-s` option specifies the packet size to use. This is the size of IP packet to send across the network. The default is `64` bytes; the minimum is `40`.

The `-f` option indicates to operate in flood mode: in this mode, packets are sent out very rapidly (as soon as the response to an earlier packet is received or every 10 milliseconds, whichever is sooner). This option should be used with care, because it can result in significant network traffic.

21.1.2 Class Ping

This class implements the `ping` command. It is not likely that this code would be reusable for other purposes so we simply implement it as a singlethreaded application (figure 21.3).

We send packets to the remote machine and await responses. In flood mode, we print a period for every

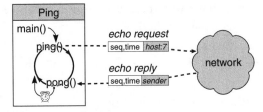

Figure 21.3   Class Ping

packet sent and a backspace for every packet received. Otherwise we print statistics with every response received.

```
import java.io.*;
import java.net.*;

public class Ping {
  // public static void main (String[] args) throws IOException ...
}
```

The entire operation of this class is accessed through the `main()` method. We parse the arguments, initialize the program, and proceed to ping the requested machine. When finished, we digest the timing information and report our results. We pass on any exceptions that may arise.

```
static final int DEFAULT_PORT = 7;
static final int UDP_HEADER = 20 + 8;
static final int BACKSPACE = 8;

public static void main (String[] args) throws IOException {
  parseArgs (args);
  init ();
  for (int i = 0; (i < count) || (count == 0); ++ i) {
    long past = System.currentTimeMillis ();
    ping (i, past);
    try {
      pong (i, past);
    } catch (InterruptedIOException ignored) {
    }
  }
  socket.close ();
  printStats ();
}

// static void parseArgs (String args[]) ...
// static void init () throws IOException ...
// static void ping (int seq, long past) throws IOException ...
// static void pong (int seq, long past) throws IOException ...
// static void printStats () ...
```

The `main()` method calls upon the `parseArgs()` method to parse any arguments and the `init()` method to initialize the program. We then loop for `count` iterations, or forever if that is `0`. We determine the current time, `past`, transmit a packet with the `ping()` method, and then wait to receive a response with the `pong()` method. The `pong()` method may abort early with an `InterruptedIOException`, if no response is received; we simply catch and ignore this exception. Finally, when done, we close `socket` and print out any statistics that we have obtained with the `printStats()` method. For simplicity, instead of using one thread to transmit and another to receive, we interleave transmission and reception in just one thread.

This class uses the constants `DEFAULT_PORT`, which is the default UDP echo port: `UDP_HEADER`, which is the header size of a UDP packet (20 bytes of IP header and 8 bytes of UDP header); and `BACKSPACE`, which is the ASCII code for backspace.

```
static String host = null;
static int port, count = 32, delay = 1000, size = 64;
static boolean flood = false;

static void parseArgs (String args[]) {
  for (int i = 0; i < args.length; ++ i) {
    if (args[i].startsWith ("-")) {
      if (args[i].equals ("-c") && (i < args.length - 1))
        count = Integer.parseInt (args[++ i]);
      else if (args[i].equals ("-i") && (i < args.length - 1))
        delay = Math.max (10, Integer.parseInt (args[++ i]));
      else if (args[i].equals ("-s") && (i < args.length - 1))
        size = Integer.parseInt (args[++ i]);
      else if (args[i].equals ("-f"))
        flood = true;
      else
        syntaxError ();
    } else {
      if (host != null)
        syntaxError ();
      int colon = args[i].indexOf (":");
      host = (colon > -1) ? args[i].substring (0, colon) : args[i];
      port = ((colon > -1) && (colon < args[i].length () - 1)) ?
        Integer.parseInt (args[i].substring (colon + 1)) : DEFAULT_PORT;
    }
  }
  if (host == null)
    syntaxError ();
}

// static void syntaxError () ...
```

In the `parseArgs()` method, we step through the command-line arguments. If an argument begins with –, it is an option. If we encounter -c, we parse a new value for the number of iterations `count`. If we encounter -i, we parse a new value for the inter-ping delay `delay` (minimum 10). If we encounter -s, we parse a new value for the packet size `size`. If we encounter -f, we set the flood flag `flood`. Otherwise, if an unknown switch is encountered or if one of the previous options was not followed by a value, we call the `syntaxError()` method to throw an appropriate exception.

The argument is otherwise a host specification, which we dissect into the host `host` and optional port `port`, using the default port if none is specified. After parsing all arguments, we display an error if no host was specified.

```
static void syntaxError () {
  throw new IllegalArgumentException
    ("Ping [-c count] [-i wait] [-s packetsize] [-f] <hostname>[:<port>]");
}
```

This method throws an explanatory exception if incorrect arguments are passed to the program.

```
static DatagramSocket socket;
static byte[] outBuffer, inBuffer;
static DatagramPacket outPacket, inPacket;

static void init () throws IOException {
  socket = new DatagramSocket ();

  outBuffer = new byte[Math.max (12, size - UDP_HEADER)];
  outPacket = new DatagramPacket (outBuffer, outBuffer.length,
    InetAddress.getByName (host), port);

  inBuffer = new byte[outBuffer.length];
  inPacket = new DatagramPacket (inBuffer, inBuffer.length);
}
```

The `init()` method performs network setup. We create a `DatagramSocket`, `socket`. We then create an outbound `DatagramPacket`, `outPacket`, and an inbound `DatagramPacket`, `inPacket`. The respective buffers, `outBuffer` and `inBuffer`, hold the requested amount of data or a minimum of 12 bytes.

```
static int sent = 0;

static void ping (int seq, long past) throws IOException {
  writeInt (seq, outBuffer, 0);
  writeLong (past, outBuffer, 4);

  socket.send (outPacket);
  ++ sent;
  if (flood) {
    System.out.write ('.');
    System.out.flush ();
  }
}
```

```
// static final void writeInt (int datum, byte[] dst, int offset) ...
// static final void writeLong (long datum, byte[] dst, int offset) ...
```

The `ping()` method accepts two parameters: a sequence number, `seq`, and a time, `past`. We write these values into the outbound buffer `outBuffer` and then transmit the enclosing `DatagramPacket outPacket`. We increment `sent`, a count of the number of packets transmitted. If we are in flood mode, we write a period.

```
static final void writeInt (int datum, byte[] dst, int offset) {
  dst[offset] = (byte) (datum >> 24);
  dst[offset + 1] = (byte) (datum >> 16);
  dst[offset + 2] = (byte) (datum >> 8);
  dst[offset + 3] = (byte) datum;
}
```

This method writes the `int datum` as 4 bytes into the byte array `dst` at offset `offset`. For efficiency, we don't use a `DataOutputStream`.

```
static final void writeLong (long datum, byte[] dst, int offset) {
  writeInt ((int) (datum >> 32), dst, offset);
  writeInt ((int) datum, dst, offset + 4);
}
```

This method writes the `long datum` as 8 bytes into the byte array `dst` at offset `offset`.

```
static int received = 0;

static void pong (int seq, long past) throws IOException {
  long present = System.currentTimeMillis ();
  int tmpRTT = (maxRTT == 0) ? 500 : (int) maxRTT * 2;
  int wait = Math.max (delay, (seq == count - 1) ? tmpRTT : 0);
  do {
    socket.setSoTimeout (Math.max (1, wait - (int) (present - past)));
    socket.receive (inPacket);
    ++ received;
    present = System.currentTimeMillis ();
    processPong (present);
  } while ((present - past < wait) && !flood);
}

// static void processPong (long present) ...
```

The `pong()` method accepts two parameters: a sequence number, `seq`, and a start time, `past`. We simply wait for replies from the remote host, updating our statistics accordingly. The UDP echo service responds to the same host and port that sent the request, so we must listen on the same socket through which the initial packet was sent.

We wait for the inter-ping delay `wait`, accepting any packets that may arrive within this time period. Each time around, we set a socket time-out that is the remaining time between the present time, `present`, and `wait` milliseconds beyond when this method started. We then wait for an incoming packet, increment `received`, the number of packets received, and update our statistics with the `processPong()` method. We repeat this process while there remains time before the next packet should be sent.

There are a few special cases here: If a time-out occurs and no packet is received within our calculated delay, an `InterruptedIOException` will be thrown, which will exit this method for another packet to be sent. If we are in flood mode, we only wait for one packet to be received and then exit immediately. Finally, if this is the last packet to be received, we increase our waiting period to be twice the maximum round-trip time so far experienced, `maxRTT`. This means that if packets are taking a long time to return, we will probably not miss the last responses. We special-case the situation where a few packets are sent quickly and we reach this end point before any response can be received to compute `maxRTT`, using a default of 500 milliseconds in this case.

We go to this complication because we may send several packets before any responses are received, and we could equally receive several responses within the space of a single inter-ping delay. We must process all responses promptly in order to obtain meaningful timing statistics.

```
static long minRTT = 100000, maxRTT = 0, totRTT = 0;

static void processPong (long present) {
  int seq = readInt (inBuffer, 0);
  long when = readLong (inBuffer, 4);
  long rtt = present - when;

  if (!flood) {
    System.out.println ((inPacket.getLength () + UDP_HEADER) +
      " bytes from " + inPacket.getAddress ().getHostName () +
      ": seq no " + seq + " time=" + rtt + " ms");
  } else {
    System.out.write (BACKSPACE);
    System.out.flush ();
  }

  if (rtt < minRTT) minRTT = rtt;
  if (rtt > maxRTT) maxRTT = rtt;
  totRTT += rtt;
}

// static final int readInt (byte[] src, int offset) ...
// static final long readLong (byte[] src, int offset) ...
```

This method processes the current response: we read from the incoming packet the original sequence number, seq, and transmission time, when; we can compute from this the round-trip time, rtt. We print out statistics for the current packet and then update the minimum round-trip time minRTT, the maximum round-trip time maxRTT, and the total round-trip time of all received packets totRTT.

```
static final int readInt (byte[] src, int offset) {
  return (src[offset] << 24) | ((src[offset + 1] & 0xff) << 16) |
    ((src[offset + 2] & 0xff) << 8) | (src[offset + 3] & 0xff);
}
```

This method reads an int as 4 bytes from array src at offset offset.

```
static final long readLong (byte[] src, int offset) {
  return ((long) readInt (src, offset) << 32) |
    ((long) readInt (src, offset + 4) & 0xffffffffL);
}
```

This method reads a long as 8 bytes from array src at offset offset.

```
static void printStats () {
  System.out.println (sent + " packets transmitted, " +
                      received + " packets received, " +
                      (100 * (sent - received) / sent) + "% packet loss");
  if (received > 0)
    System.out.println ("round-trip min/avg/max = " + minRTT + '/' +
                        ((float) totRTT / received) + '/' + maxRTT + " ms");
}
```

This method prints statistics about all packets transmitted: the number of packets sent and received, the number lost, and statistics about the round-trip times.

21.1.3 Using it

The Ping class can only be used as a stand-alone application:

```
java Ping -c 4 nitric.com
64 bytes from nitric.com: seq no 0 time=9 ms
64 bytes from nitric.com: seq no 1 time=1 ms
64 bytes from nitric.com: seq no 2 time=2 ms
64 bytes from nitric.com: seq no 3 time=1 ms
4 packets transmitted, 4 packets received, 0% packet loss
round-trip min/avg/max = 1/3.25/9 ms
```

This is a fairly mundane execution sequence. Note that there is usually some additional overhead on the first packet; this may be a result of many factors, mostly local setup time but with some additional overhead at routers along the path. For more accurate statistics, timing from this first packet should be ignored.

```
java Ping -c 8 -s 40 -i 100 flashgordon.maths.tcd.ie
40 bytes from flashgordon.maths.tcd.ie: seq no 0 time=491 ms
40 bytes from flashgordon.maths.tcd.ie: seq no 2 time=552 ms
40 bytes from flashgordon.maths.tcd.ie: seq no 1 time=908 ms
40 bytes from flashgordon.maths.tcd.ie: seq no 4 time=537 ms
40 bytes from flashgordon.maths.tcd.ie: seq no 5 time=511 ms
40 bytes from flashgordon.maths.tcd.ie: seq no 6 time=601 ms
8 packets transmitted, 6 packets received, 25% packet loss
round-trip min/avg/max = 491/600/908 ms
```

Note here that packets may be lost and occasionally reordered. They also may be duplicated. However, that is a rare occurrence.

```
java Ping -c 1024 -f -i 10 firewall
....1024 packets transmitted, 1020 packets received, 0% packet loss
round-trip min/avg/max = 4/9.163726/63 ms
```

Here, we execute in flood mode: four packets were not acknowledged before we terminated.

21.2 DNS over UDP

In this example, we look at transporting DNS requests over UDP. This uses the same DNS request framework that we developed in chapter

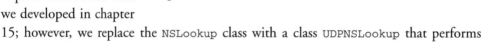

Figure 21.4   DNS over UDP

15; however, we replace the NSLookup class with a class UDPNSLookup that performs UDP transport (figure 21.4).

The basic protocol is the same as we looked at earlier: we construct a DNSQuery for the host in question, extract this into a byte array, and transmit it to a selected name server. We then await a response, decode this with the DNSQuery, and print out the resulting information.

Note that to transport DNS requests over TCP we preceded every transmission with 2 bytes that indicated the length of the subsequent data. This is not necessary for UDP because the payload length is automatically encoded in each UDP packet. Note also that all DNS transmissions over UDP are restricted to 512 bytes, so it is more probable that truncation will occur in a UDP DNS response.

21.2.1 Class UDPNSLookup

The UDPNSLookup class is similar to the NSLookup class that we developed earlier. The main() method performs the name lookup, constructing a query and communicating with the name server using helper methods. The significant change is that, to cope with

UDP's unreliability, we resend our query after a short time if no response is forth-coming.

```
import java.io.*;
import java.net.*;
import java.util.*;

public class UDPNSLookup {
  // public static void main (String[] args) ...
  // public static void sendQuery (DNSQuery query, DatagramSocket socket,
  //     InetAddress nameServer) throws IOException ...
  // public static void getResponse (DNSQuery query, DatagramSocket socket)
  //     throws IOException ...
}
```

The main() method parses any arguments supplied, constructs a DNSQuery for the requested host name, transmits this to the name server using the sendQuery() method, receives a response with the getResponse() method, and prints out any resulting information.

```
public static void main (String[] args) {
  if (args.length != 1)
    throw new IllegalArgumentException
      ("Syntax: UDPNSLookup <hostname>[@<nameserver>]");

  int atIdx = args[0].indexOf ("@");
  String nameServer = (atIdx > -1) ? args[0].substring (atIdx + 1) : "ns";
  String hostName = (atIdx > -1) ? args[0].substring (0, atIdx) : args[0];

  System.out.println ("Nameserver: " + nameServer);
  System.out.println ("Request: " + hostName);

  DNSQuery query = new DNSQuery (hostName, DNS.TYPE_ANY, DNS.CLASS_IN);

  try {
    boolean received = false;
    int count = 0;

    DatagramSocket socket = new DatagramSocket ();
    socket.setSoTimeout (5000);
    try {
      while (!received) {
        try {
          sendQuery (query, socket, InetAddress.getByName (nameServer));
          getResponse (query, socket);
          received = true;
        } catch (InterruptedIOException ex) {
          if (count ++ < 3) {
            System.out.println ("resend..");
          } else {
            throw new IOException ("No response received from nameserver");
```

```
          }
        }
      }
    } finally {
      socket.close ();
    }
    NSLookup.printRRs (query);
  } catch (IOException ex) {
    System.out.println (ex);
  }
}
```

In the `main()` method, we first parse the arguments into a host name, `hostName` and name server, `nameServer`; the syntax is the same as the `NSLookup` command. We then create a `DNSQuery`, `query`, that requests any Internet-class resource records for the specified host name.

We open a `DatagramSocket` `socket` with a 5-second timeout. We then loop, transmitting the query to the name server with the `sendQuery()` method and awaiting a response with the `getResponse()` method. If a timeout occurs and an `Interrupte-dIOException` is thrown, we repeat the loop up to 3 times; otherwise, we abort. We finally close the `DatagramSocket` and, if we successfully received a response, then we print out any received resource records using the `printRRs()` method of class `NSLookup`.

We could use a separate thread to perform the automatic resends; for example, using the `Alarm` class of the previous chapter. Using a single thread and socket timeouts, however, is more straightforward for an application of this simplicity.

```
public static void sendQuery (DNSQuery query, DatagramSocket socket,
    InetAddress nameServer) throws IOException {
  byte[] data = query.extractQuery ();
  DatagramPacket packet = new DatagramPacket
    (data, data.length, nameServer, DNS.DEFAULT_PORT);
  socket.send (packet);
}
```

This method transmits the `DNSQuery` `query` to the specified host, `nameServer`, through the `DatagramSocket` `socket`. We extract the query into a byte array, `data`; create a `DatagramPacket`, `packet`, that encloses this, addressed to the default DNS port of the specified name server. We then transmit this `DatagramPacket` and return, passing on any exceptions that may occur.

```
public static void getResponse (DNSQuery query, DatagramSocket socket)
    throws IOException {
  byte[] buffer = new byte[512];
  DatagramPacket packet = new DatagramPacket (buffer, buffer.length);
  socket.receive (packet);
```

```
    query.receiveResponse (packet.getData (), packet.getLength ());
  }
```

This method awaits a response for the DNSQuery query on the DatagramSocket socket. We create a buffer that is large enough to hold the DNS response; all UDP DNS transmissions are restricted to 512 bytes. We enclose this in the DatagramPacket packet, and then await a UDP packet from the network. If receive() returns successfully, then we decode the response with the receiveResponse() method of query. Otherwise, we pass on the exception, whether it is a genuine error or a time-out. Note that if a response is truncated (the response cannot fit into 512 bytes) then an IOException will be raised, even though some of the data could be usefully parsed.

21.2.2 Using it
This class can be used in exactly the same manner as the earlier NSLookup class; refer to section 15.3 for details.

21.3 A daytime server

In this example, we implement a simple UDP server that supplies the Internet *daytime* service (RFC 867, STD 25). This service simply replies

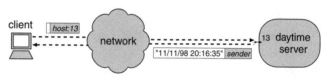

Figure 21.5   The daytime service

to every incoming packet with a packet that contains the current date and time in ASCII text format. There is no mandated format for the response so we can use any format that we desire (figure 21.5).

For testing purposes, we also supply a simple client that tests this service.

21.3.1 Class DaytimeServer
The daytime server listens on a command line-specified port and responds to every received packet with a packet the contains the current time. The entire code resides in the main() method. We use a single thread to receive packets and respond to them.

```
import java.io.*;
import java.net.*;

public class DaytimeServer {
  public static final int DEFAULT_PORT = 13;
  public static void main (String[] args) throws IOException {
    if (args.length > 1)
      throw new IllegalArgumentException ("Syntax: DaytimeServer [<port>]");
    DatagramSocket socket = new DatagramSocket (args.length == 0 ?
      DEFAULT_PORT : Integer.parseInt (args[0]));
```

```
      DatagramPacket packet = new DatagramPacket (new byte[1], 1);
      while (true) {
        socket.receive (packet);
        System.out.println
          ("Received from: " + packet.getAddress () + ":" + packet.getPort ());
        byte[] outBuffer = new java.util.Date ().toString ()
          .getBytes ("latin1");
        packet.setData (outBuffer);
        packet.setLength (outBuffer.length);
        socket.send (packet);
      }
    }
  }
}
```

In the `main()` method, we first verify that a port number has been specified as an argument, using the default port of 13 otherwise. We create a `DatagramSocket`, `socket`, that listens on this port and a `DatagramPacket`, `packet`, that we will use to receive incoming UDP packets. On most multiuser systems, user applications may not access system port numbers, so you should usually choose your own to test this application.

In our main loop we call `receive()` and wait for a packet to arrive. When a packet arrives, we print out information about its origin and then create a new byte array, `outBuffer`, that consists of the current time and date. We use the `java.util.Date` class for this. We use `packet`'s `setData()` and `setLength()` methods to alter its contents to be the new data and then send the packet back to its originator.

Note that the `DatagramPacket` already contains the port and address of the incoming packet's origin so we can simply reuse this information. Another implementation would be to just create a `DatagramPacket` to send back. However, the two approaches are essentially identical.

21.3.2 Class DaytimeClient

This class can be used to test the `Daytime` server. It sends a packet to the specified port of the specified machine, awaits a response, and then prints out the contents of the response.

```
import java.io.*;
import java.net.*;

public class DaytimeClient {
  public static void main (String[] args) throws IOException {
    if ((args.length != 1))
      throw new IllegalArgumentException
        ("Syntax: DaytimeClient <host>[:<port>]");

    int idx = args[0].indexOf (":");
    int port = (idx > -1) ? Integer.parseInt (args[0].substring (idx + 1)) :
```

```
        DaytimeServer.DEFAULT_PORT;
     String hostName = (idx > -1) ? args[0].substring (0, idx) : args[0];
     InetAddress host = InetAddress.getByName (hostName);

     DatagramSocket socket = new DatagramSocket ();
     socket.setSoTimeout (5000);
     DatagramPacket packet = new DatagramPacket (new byte[256], 1, host, port);
     socket.send (packet);
     packet.setLength (packet.getData ().length);
     socket.receive (packet);
     socket.close ();

     byte[] data = packet.getData ();
     int length = packet.getLength ();
     System.out.println (new String (data, 0, length, "latin1"));
  }
}
```

In the `main()` method, we verify that a host, `host`, and optionally port, `port`, have been specified, using the default port if none is specified. We create a `DatagramSocket`, `socket`, with a 5-second receive time-out, and a `DatagramPacket`, `packet`, with a 256-byte buffer but only a data length of 1, addressed to the remote server.

When we transmit this packet, we transmit a UDP packet with just a single-byte payload; this is sufficient to get a response. We then reassign `packet`'s payload length to 256 and await a response; we can thus accept a response up to 256 bytes long. When we receive a response, we close the `DatagramSocket` and print out the contents of the received packet. If no response was received within 5 seconds, we will abort with an `InterruptedIOException`.

21.4 Wrapping up

This concludes our treatment of unicast datagram networking. UDP applications are generally complicated by the fact that enough state must be maintained to handle lost and misordered data. However, this is countered by the fact that, in many cases, UDP applications can simply ignore this problem because the data being transported are essentially immune to this.

When used for a simple query-response protocol, the client can resend its request. When used for streamed data, lost and misordered data can either be ignored or buffered and a resend facility can be used. When an application begins to acquire significant complexity in an effort to handle the unreliability of datagram networking, it is probably appropriate to consider using TCP instead as a reliable transport layer.

In the next chapter, we examine multicast and broadcast networking. These extend the idea of one-to-one networking to the idea of one-to-many networking: a single packet can be transmitted and it will reach many listeners. In some ways, this changes the paradigm of networking, because instead of working in a client/server architecture, we can move to a peer-to-peer model. With the current organization of the Internet, however, a client/server architecture may still make sense for many multicast applications. We discuss many of these issues in the accompanying examples.

CHAPTER 22

Multicast networking

Multicast and broadcast are datagram network protocols that allow an application to place a single packet on a network and have that packet transported to multiple recipients. On a simple network such as a single Ethernet wire, this is comparatively simple provided that all machines on the wire know to listen for packets sent to a particular address. Then a packet need only be placed on the wire once, and all interested parties can pick up that data. Across an internet, or network of networks, this process is more complex because routers must know to pick up these multicast packets and deliver them to other attached networks.

The difference between multicast and broadcast is that a broadcast packet can be picked up only by interested machines on a single network (such as a single Ethernet) and will not, in general, be transported by a router, while a multicast packet can be transported by routers across multiple networks to a widespread set of interested recipients (figure 22.1). Broadcast only requires that the underlying network supports broadcast, whereas multicast requires that hosts and routers alike be multicast aware: hosts and routers must support IGMP and know to pick up and process packets sent to multicast addresses.

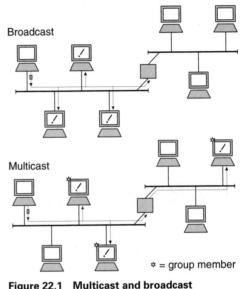

Figure 22.1   Multicast and broadcast

22.1 *Multicast*

Multicast is much like UDP, except that instead of sending a packet to a single destination, you send a packet to a *multicast group*. The underlying network protocols attempt to transport the packet to all interested recipients; the sender does not even need to know who the recipients are. As with UDP, multicast is packet-based and does not guarantee reliability. Packets may be lost, duplicated, and/or reordered; furthermore, successful delivery may obviously be different for different recipients.

22.1.1 *Multicast groups*

A multicast group is simply an IP address that falls into IP class D (224.0.0.0–239.255.255.255). Recipients express an interest in receiving packets addressed to a particular multicast group, and the underlying network protocols take care of announcing this interest to relevant routers on the network. To send a packet to a multicast group, a client simply inserts a packet into the network with the appropriate target address. A sender need not be a member of the group and does not know who will receive the packet.

The packet will be picked up by any machines on the immediate network that are interested in that group. In addition, it will be picked up by routers that will forward it as appropriate to adjacent networks that are interested. The significant complexity of multicast is how routers will know what adjacent networks are interested in the data; a packet may require forwarding among many routers in order to be delivered to all interested recipients (figure 22.2).

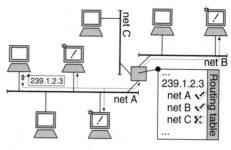

Figure 22.2   Multicast routing

The choice of which multicast group to use is currently somewhat arbitrary. Some multicast addresses are officially assigned to particular applications, and there are proposals for the dynamic assignment of multicast addresses, but within an organization it is usually possible to use internally assigned addresses. All multicast addresses beginning with 239 are reserved for such internal assignment, so it is safe to use any address in this range on your own network.

22.1.2 The MBone

Multicast is currently not widely deployed on the Internet so it is not possible to have a multicast conversation with just anyone on the Internet. The largest deployment of multicast on the Internet is the MBone, which is an experimental multicast framework that transports multicast packets through TCP/IP *tunnels* between multicast-enabled *islands* (figure 22.3). These tunnels overcome the problem of conventional routers knowing how to route multicast packets: an island is a network or group of adjacent networks that support multicast. A multicast packet is transported

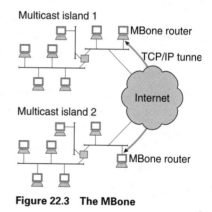

Figure 22.3   The MBone

as usual within an island, but is also picked up by router hosts that transmit the data through TCP tunnels to other router hosts on other islands. These other hosts can then multicast the data within their islands as normal. These router hosts use a routing protocol to determine which islands should receive data, communicating among each other using conventional unicast protocols.

Because of its popularity, the MBone is now widely deployed, at least in academia. So it is possible to use multicast fairly widely among participating systems. It is usually also possible to enable multicast within a LAN, or to use multicast between machines on a multicast-enabled network such as an Ethernet. It is expected that multicast will be widely deployed on the Internet in the future; for the moment, however, consult your local network administrator to determine how well multicast is supported within your environment.

22.1.3 TTL

Multicast packets include a TTL field that limits how far a packet will be propagated across an internet. In essence, every time a packet is relayed by a router or through a tunnel, the TTL is decremented. If it reaches zero, the packet is discarded and not relayed any further. A small TTL thus restricts a packet to be communicated only among "close" networks (figure 22.4).

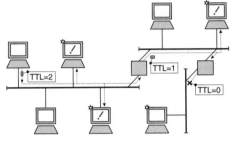

Figure 22.4   TTL

The exact meaning of the field depends on the routing protocol in use and how the multicast routers have been configured. With DVMRP, the routing protocol of the MBone, a packet sent with a TTL of 64 or less will, by default, not be forwarded through any IP tunnels. This allows an organization to easily have a multicast conversation that will not be broadcast to the Internet at large (figure 22.5). With appropriate adminis-

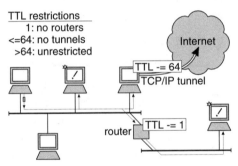

Figure 22.5   TTL in the MBone

tration, an internal network can be further partitioned. It is important to use the TTL field appropriately to prevent unnecessary Internet traffic.

22.1.4 Reliability

Neither multicast nor broadcast supports reliable data transfer (figure 22.6). To achieve reliability, you require potentially as much state as individual TCP connections among all participants (i.e., every participant requires transport state for every other participant), so it's not a good idea.

One option, if reliability is desired, is to use TCP through a central server for communications that require reliability and multicast for noncritical data. If you try adding reliability to a UDP-based protocol, you end up reimplementing TCP, but without the experience of TCP's original (and subsequent) designers.

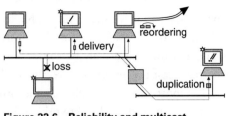

Figure 22.6   Reliability and multicast

Should it be necessary, there are reliable multicast protocols such as MTP, RAMP, RMP, RMTP, RTP, TMTP, or XTP. A Web search on this topic provides a wealth of information. Other options include multipoint transport layers such as T.120, which provides a peer-to-peer communications substrate that supports reliable group conversations. This is internally implemented as a TCP/IP tree structure that is overlaid on the participants. In general, however, use of these protocols may involve using native code to access an existing library, or else a fairly significant development effort to implement the protocol.

22.2 Broadcast

Broadcast is similar at a local level to multicast: every broadcast-based network (such as an Ethernet) has a broadcast address. This is an IP address that is received by all hosts on the network. A UDP packet can be transmitted to this address, and it will be picked up by every host on the network (figure 22.7). Thus, clients

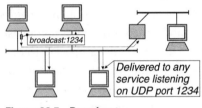

Figure 22.7   Broadcast

must choose a UDP port number on which to operate; packets that are transmitted to this port number on the local broadcast address will be picked up by all hosts that are listening on that port. Other than the special address, broadcast is otherwise essentially normal UDP.

The local broadcast address is usually the last address on the local subnet; for example, the broadcast address for the class C network 192.1.2.0 is 192.1.2.255. The broadcast address for the 16-host subnet 197.84.66.192 is 197.84.66.207. Your network administrator should be able to help you determine your broadcast address. Some hosts are configured to disallow broadcast transmissions from nonprivileged users; a broadcast attempt will usually raise a permission-error IOException. Enabling broadcast may require setting a socket option (SO_BROADCAST), that is not possible from Java without using native methods.

22.2.1 Multicast or broadcast

Given a choice, it is usually preferable to use multicast instead of broadcast. The only real reason that broadcast should be used is if some involved hosts are not multicast aware, and this can usually be solved with an OS upgrade. More often than not, however, multicast is supported correctly, but broadcast results in a permission error.

On most networks, multicast and broadcast result in exactly the same traffic: a single packet is placed on the network, and it is picked up by all interested hosts. Multicast, however, gives the choice of multiple multicast groups, whereas any given network only has a single broadcast address. Broadcast packets will be picked up by every host on a network, while multicast packets will only be processed by interested hosts. Additionally, from Java, only a single client can listen to broadcasts to a particular port on a single machine, while many clients can engage in the same multicast conversation from a single machine.

As a replacement for broadcast, multicast should be used with a TTL of 1, which means that data will not be related by any routers or through any tunnels.

22.3 JDK 1.1 *Class MulticastSocket*

The `MulticastSocket` class extends the `DatagramSocket` class and adds support for IP multicast. As a result, it provides all the methods of `DatagramSocket` as well as methods to control group membership plus an additional `send()` method that allows the TTL of a multicast packet to be specified.

It should be noted that multicast, broadcast, and unicast all share the same set of UDP ports. If a packet is received by a machine on a particular UDP port, it will be delivered to whatever applications are listening on that port, regardless of whether they are expecting a unicast packet, a broadcast packet, or a multicast packet—and regardless of whether the packet was broadcast, multicast, or unicast. Java does not support querying the destination address of a received packet, so it is up to every application to manually determine whether or not any received packet is actually addressed to itself. Because TCP/IP is a reliable stream between two endpoints, it does not suffer from this problem.

22.3.1 Constructors

`MulticastSocket` does not provide all the constructors of the `DatagramSocket` class. The facility to bind to a specific local address is instead provided with the `setInterface()` method.

MulticastSocket()   This creates a `MulticastSocket` that listens and transmits on an arbitrary free UDP port.

MulticastSocket(int port)   This creates a `MulticastSocket` that listens and transmits on the specified UDP port, `port`.

Note that multiple `MulticastSockets` can listen to the same port on the same machine (this is not true of `DatagramSockets`). However, a `MulticastSocket` cannot listen to a port on which a `DatagramSocket` is already listening. Incoming packets are distributed to all clients listening on the port; this allows multiple clients on the same machine to join in a multicast conversation. To achieve this, the `MulticastSocket` class internally sets the `SO_REUSEADDR` socket option.

22.3.2 Methods

This class provides all the usual `DatagramSocket` methods as well as specialized methods to control multicast group membership, transmission time-to-live values, and the local network interface to use.

The `send()` methods automatically verify that they are used to transmit multicast packets, falling back to normal UDP operation when packets are sent to a nonmulticast address. This means that the TTL value is ignored when this class is used to send unicast datagrams. If the sender is a member of the destination multicast group of any packet that it transmits, it also will receive a copy of its own transmission.

void joinGroup(InetAddress group) throws IOException   This method announces interest in the specified multicast group, `group`. Network protocols (IGMP in particular) will propagate this interest to the relevant routers, so that packets sent to the multicast group `group` will become available to read through this socket. Remember that you do not need to be a member of a group to send packets to it; you only need to join the group if you wish to receive such packets.

One `MulticastSocket` can be used to listen to multiple multicast groups. However, there is usually an OS-specific limit to how many groups a single socket can join. For safety's sake, it is usually a better idea to use separate sockets for separate groups.

void leaveGroup(InetAddress group) throws IOException   This method is used to leave the specified multicast group, `group`.

JDK 1.2   *void setTimeToLive(int ttl) throws IOException*   This method sets the default time-to-live value for all multicasts packets transmistted through this socket to the specified value, between 1 and 255.

Every time a packet is transported by a router or through a tunnel its TTL is decremented by a network-specific amount; when this reaches zero, the packet is no longer forwarded. A TTL of 1 restricts a packet to just the attached network; it is not forwarded by any routers. Under the MBone, a TTL of 64 or less restricts a packet to just the local multicast island.

void setTTL(byte ttl) throws IOException   This method sets the time-to-live value for this socket to the specified unsigned 8-bit value `ttl`. This method has been deprecated by JDK 1.2.

JDK 1.2   *int getTimeToLive() throws IOException*   This method returns the current time-to-live value for this socket as an integer between 1 and 255.

byte getTTL() throws IOException   This method returns the current time-to-live value for this socket. This value is an unsigned byte from 1 through 255; it should, therefore, be cast to a signed integer by masking with the value 255 (`getTTL() & 255`). This method has been deprecated by JDK 1.2.

void send(DatagramPacket packet, byte ttl) throws IOException   This method sends the `DatagramPacket`, `packet`, to its destination address and provides an option to specify the TTL for the packet, `ttl`. This value temporarily overrides any value set with the `setTTL()` method. The normal `send()` method should be used if the current setting is correct.

Note that this `send()` method is synchronized; the default `send()` method is not. This means that you cannot use this `send()` method on a `MulticastSocket` that is blocking in `receive()` because `receive()` is also synchronized. You can, however, call `setTTL()` and the default `send()` method on a blocking `MulticastSocket` because those methods are not synchronized.

void setInterface(InetAddress address) throws SocketException   This   method sets the network interface to be used for multicast packets sent through this socket; this is useful for multihomed hosts. This is equivalent to the alternative constructor provided by the `DatagramSocket` class. Most operating systems actually allow the network interface to be set on a per-group basis. However, Java does not yet support this, making separate sockets a necessity in some cases.

InetAddress getInterface() throws SocketException   This method returns the current network interface used for multicast packets by this socket.

22.3.3 IOException
As expected, the methods of `MulticastSocket` may all throw exceptions of type `IOException` or a subclass (including `SocketException`) if there is some network or protocol problem. An additional `IOException` to expect, however, is an exception with the message *Protocol not available* which indicates that the host or VM does not support multicast.

22.3.4 SecurityException

Access to multicast is restricted by the current `SecurityManager`. Most browsers do not allow untrusted applet access to multicast. However, there is a particular subset of multicast that may be permitted by some browsers: the subset where the applet never transmits a multicast packet and only receives multicast packets from a single host (that which served it). (See figure 22.8). Use of the inherited JDK 1.2 `connect()` method enforces this communication restriction for multicast data.

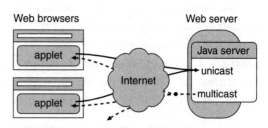

Figure 22.8 Untrusted use of multicast

Although this configuration may seem limited, it can still be useful, in particular, when a central server streams data to many clients simultaneously over multicast. This saves tremendously on bandwidth; however, it requires multicast, which is not widespread, to be deployed between the server and the clients. This may also introduce security implications from the use of IGMP that remain to be investigated.

22.4 Using multicast

Using multicast is similar to using UDP; the following two code fragments demonstrate the primary differences.

22.4.1 Sending a multicast packet

Sending a packet to a multicast group follows exactly the same model as sending a normal datagram packet, except that a TTL can be specified when a packet is sent through a `MulticastSocket`. The following code fragment demonstrates the process of sending a multicast packet (figure 22.9):

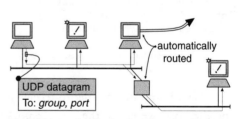

Figure 22.9   Sending a multicast packet

```
// byte[] data
// InetAddress multicastGroup
// int multicastPort

MulticastSocket socket = new MulticastSocket ();
DatagramPacket packet =
  new DatagramPacket (data, data.length, multicastGroup, multicastPort);
socket.send (packet, (byte) 64);
socket.close ();
```

We first create a `MulticastSocket`, `socket`; we will not be receiving packets, so we don't specify a port number. We next create a `DatagramPacket`, `packet`, addressed to the specified multicast group, `multicastGroup`, and port, `multicastPort` (e.g. group 239.1.2.3, port 5000). We finally send the packet into the network with the specified time-to-live; in this case, we choose 64, which will restrict the packet to just our own multicast island if we are using the MBone.

22.4.2 Receiving a multicast packet

Receiving a multicast packet involves one more step than receiving a normal datagram packet. We must explicitly announce interest in a multicast group before waiting for packets to arrive. The following code fragment demonstrates receiving a multicast packet (figure 22.10):

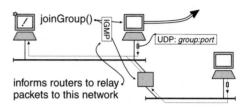

Figure 22.10   Receiving a multicast packet

```
// InetAddress multicastGroup
// int multicastPort

MulticastSocket socket = new MulticastSocket (multicastPort);
socket.joinGroup (multicastGroup);
byte[] buffer = new byte[65508];
DatagramPacket packet = new DatagramPacket ();
socket.receive (packet);
InetAddress fromAddr = packet.getAddress ();
int fromPort = packet.getPort ();
int length = packet.getLength ();
byte[] data = packet.getData ();
// ...
socket.leaveGroup (multicastGroup);
socket.close ();
```

As with unicast, in order to receive packets we must create a socket that listens to a specific port; we create the `MulticastSocket socket` listening on the port `multicastPort`. We next announce interest in a particular multicast group; in this case, group `multicastGroup`. We create a `DatagramPacket`, `packet`, into which we will receive a packet from the network. We then call `receive()`, which blocks until a datagram packet arrives. We can then use the usual methods of the `DatagramPacket` class to extract information about the sender and the contents of the datagram. We finally leave the multicast group and close the socket when we are done.

22.5 A peer-to-peer multicast chat system

Multicast and broadcast allow the development of true peer-to-peer applications. In such a configuration, there is no central server; instead, all clients communicate among each other as equals. This is different from the examples that we have examined thus far because there is no central application that can maintain coherence of the group's state. Instead, it is up to clients to perform all such administration.

In this example, we develop a multicast-based chat system. Clients in the chat system join a multicast group and communicate among each other using datagram packets that contain text messages (figure 22.11).

Note that since this is based on multicast, which is a UDP-based protocol, delivery of messages is not guaranteed. For the purposes of a chat system, this does not matter. No catastrophe other than mild con-

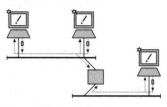

Figure 22.11 Peer-to-peer multicast

fusion will occur if some clients do not receive a message, if they receive a message in duplicate, or different clients receive messages in different orders. By including a sequence number in each message we could, however, identify losses, correct misorderings and ignore duplicates if we so desired.

22.5.1 Class MulticastChat

This chat system consists of just a single class. There is no server involved; instead, all clients communicate as peers. The `MulticastChat` class opens a simple chat `Frame` with the usual output and input regions and starts a thread that listens for incoming packets.

```java
import java.io.*;
import java.net.*;
import java.awt.*;
import java.awt.event.*;

public class MulticastChat implements Runnable, WindowListener,
        ActionListener {
  // public MulticastChat (InetAddress group, int port) ...
  // public synchronized void start () throws IOException ...
  // public synchronized void stop () throws IOException ...
  // public void windowOpened (WindowEvent event) ...
  // public void windowClosing (WindowEvent event) ...
  // public void actionPerformed (ActionEvent event) ...
  // public void run () ...
  // public static void main (String[] args) throws IOException ...
}
```

The `MulticastChat` class implements `Runnable`, `WindowListener`, and `Action-Listener` so we can handle GUI events and use a thread to listen for incoming messages. The constructor accepts a multicast group to join and a port number on which to communicate. The `start()` method shows the chat `Frame` and opens communications with the group; the `stop()` method closes the `Frame` and disconnects.

We implement `windowOpened()`, `windowClosed()`, and `actionPerformed()` to handle GUI events, and `run()` for the listener thread. The `main()` method opens a `MulticastChat` that communicates with the group specified in the command-line arguments.

```
protected InetAddress group;
protected int port;

public MulticastChat (InetAddress group, int port) {
  this.group = group;
  this.port = port;
  initAWT ();
}

// protected void initAWT () ...
```

In the constructor, we simply keep copies of the multicast group `group` and port `port`, and call `initAWT()` to initialize the chat `Frame`.

```
protected Frame frame;
protected TextArea output;
protected TextField input;

protected void initAWT () {
  frame = new Frame
    ("MulticastChat [" + group.getHostAddress () + ":" + port + "]");
  frame.addWindowListener (this);
  output = new TextArea ();
  output.setEditable (false);
  input = new TextField ();
  input.addActionListener (this);
  frame.setLayout (new BorderLayout ());
  frame.add (output, "Center");
  frame.add (input, "South");
  frame.pack ();
}
```

The `initAWT()` method creates and lays out the chat. We create the `Frame frame` and register as a listener for its events. We then create the output `TextArea`, `output`, and the input `TextField`, `input`, and register to receive events from the `TextField`. We finally lay out the components and pack the frame.

```
protected Thread listener;
```

```
public synchronized void start () throws IOException {
  if (listener == null) {
    initNet ();
    listener = new Thread (this);
    listener.start ();
    frame.setVisible (true);
  }
}

// protected void initNet () throws IOException ...
```

The `start()` method starts the chat system. We first call `initNet()` which initializes the network connection. We then show the chat `Frame` and start a new `Thread`, `listener`, that receives incoming packets.

```
protected MulticastSocket socket;
protected DatagramPacket outgoing, incoming;

protected void initNet () throws IOException {
  socket = new MulticastSocket (port);
  socket.setTimeToLive (1);
  socket.joinGroup (group);
  outgoing = new DatagramPacket (new byte[1], 1, group, port);
  incoming = new DatagramPacket (new byte[65508], 65508);
}
```

The `initNet()` method initializes the network connection. We create a `MulticastSocket`, `socket`, that listens and transmits on the port `port`. We set its TTL to 1; this means that packets will only be received by hosts directly attached to the local network. We create an outbound `DatagramPacket`, `outgoing`, that sends to the chosen multicast group, `group`, and an inbound `DatagramPacket`, `incoming`, that will be used to receive data.

```
public synchronized void stop () throws IOException {
  frame.setVisible (false);
  if (listener != null) {
    listener.interrupt ();
    listener = null;
    try {
      socket.leaveGroup (group);
    } finally {
      socket.close ();
    }
  }
}
```

The `stop()` method stops the chat system. We hide the chat `Frame`, interrupt the listener thread, and close the `DatagramSocket`. Closing the `MulticastSocket` will cause the blocking listener thread to abort.

```
public void windowOpened (WindowEvent event) {
  input.requestFocus ();
}
```

When the `Frame` is displayed, we send the input focus to the input `TextField`.

```
public void windowClosing (WindowEvent event) {
  try {
    stop ();
  } catch (IOException ex) {
    ex.printStackTrace ();
  }
}
```

When the user tries to close the frame, we call `stop()` to shut down.

```
public void windowClosed (WindowEvent event) {}
public void windowIconified (WindowEvent event) {}
public void windowDeiconified (WindowEvent event) {}
public void windowActivated (WindowEvent event) {}
public void windowDeactivated (WindowEvent event) {}
```

These methods are required by the `WindowListener` interface, but unused in this example.

```
public void actionPerformed (ActionEvent event) {
  try {
    byte[] utf = event.getActionCommand ().getBytes ("UTF8");
    outgoing.setData (utf);
    outgoing.setLength (utf.length);
    socket.send (outgoing);
    input.setText ("");
  } catch (IOException ex) {
    handleIOException (ex);
  }
}

// protected synchronized void handleIOException (IOException ex) ...
```

The `actionPerformed()` method is called when the user hits return in the Text-Field. We alter the payload of the `DatagramPacket` `outgoing` to be the user's message and transmit this through `socket`. Finally, we clear the `TextField`. Note that we also will receive a copy of this multicast message, so we don't need to add it to the output region at this point.

```
protected synchronized void handleIOException (IOException ex) {
  if (listener != null) {
    output.append (ex + "\n");
    input.setVisible (false);
    frame.validate ();
    if (listener != Thread.currentThread ())
      listener.interrupt ();
    listener = null;
    try {
      socket.leaveGroup (group);
    } catch (IOException ignored) {
    }
    socket.close ();
  }
}
```

This method is called to handle `IOExceptions`. If `listener` is `null` then this chat has been stopped. The exception is probably a result of the socket being closed so we ignore it. Otherwise, we display the exception in the output region, hide the input region, stop the listening thread and leave the multicast group.

```
public void run () {
  try {
    while (!Thread.interrupted ()) {
      incoming.setLength (incoming.getData ().length);
      socket.receive (incoming);
      String message = new String
        (incoming.getData (), 0, incoming.getLength (), "UTF8");
      output.append (message + "\n");
    }
  } catch (IOException ex) {
    handleIOException (ex);
  }
}
```

This method loops forever, receiving messages and displaying them in the output region. We first reset the buffer length of the inbound `DatagramPacket`, `incoming`; this will have been modified by any previously received packet. We then call `receive()` to receive a `DatagramPacket`, and then extract the message from this packet. We finally append this message to the output region and loop again to receive the next message.

This loop will be terminated as a result of either an `IOException` or the thread being interrupted. The exceptional case includes the case of our receiving a misformatted message and the `String` conversion throwing an exception. We could add a special `try ... catch` statement to ignore format errors of this kind if we wished. In the case of an exception, we simply call `handleIOException()` to tidy up, as before.

```
public static void main (String[] args) throws IOException {
  if ((args.length != 1) || (args[0].indexOf (":") < 0))
```

```
        throw new IllegalArgumentException
            ("Syntax: MulticastChat <group>:<port>");

    int idx = args[0].indexOf (":");
    InetAddress group = InetAddress.getByName (args[0].substring (0, idx));
    int port = Integer.parseInt (args[0].substring (idx + 1));

    MulticastChat chat = new MulticastChat (group, port);
    chat.start ();
}
```

The main() method allows this chat system to be run as a stand-alone application. We verify that a valid argument has been supplied: a multicast group (usually as a dot-format IP address) and a port on which to communicate. We create a MulticastChat, chat, and then start it; it opens a chat Frame and starts to listen for incoming messages.

22.5.2 Using it

When you run this chat system, you can essentially just choose any internal multicast group, such as 239.1.2.3 and then start several clients. Because we set a low TTL, messages will not stray far, even if your network is multicast aware. If your host is not multicast capable, you usually will encounter an exception; sometimes only when execution reaches the setTTL() method.

This particular system cannot be run as an untrusted applet; the SecurityManager will raise an exception when you attempt to transmit to the group because it is not the same address from which the applet was served. Additionally, any incoming packets that do not come from the Web server will be discarded. In the next example, we look at overcoming this by communicating through a central server that can reside on the same machine as the Web server.

22.6 A client/server multicast chat system

In this variant of the multicast chat system, we combine unicast and multicast to produce a multicast-based chat system that is compatible with Java's standard applet security model.

Instead of each client multicasting its message to the others, each client unicasts its message to a central server, which then multicasts it back to all clients. As a result, clients will only be transmitting to a single machine and receiving from a single machine. So if the server is correctly installed at the Web server's location, this system will be usable as an applet (figure 22.12).

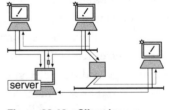

Figure 22.12   Client/server multicast

This system consists of two classes. Mixed-castChat is an extension of the MulticastChat class that unicasts messages back to a central server. `MixedcastServer` is a server that relays incoming messages back out to a multicast group on which the `MixedcastChat` clients are listening.

22.6.1 Class MixedcastChat

For the sake of simplicity, we extend the `MulticastChat` class and modify its operation appropriately. In a production environment, it would be more efficient to create a completely independent class.

```
import java.io.*;
import java.net.*;
import java.awt.*;
public class MixedcastChat extends MulticastChat {
  // public MixedcastChat (InetAddress group, int port,
       InetAddress server, int serverPort) ...
  // public static void main (String[] args) throws IOException ...
}
```

The constructor for this class accepts the multicast group and port, as well as a server address with which to communicate. The constructor only sets up the user interface; it is still necessary to call `start()` to start this system. We override the `initNet()` method to modify the outbound network connection so that it just unicasts back to a central server. As always, we provide a `main()` method that starts the chat client.

```
  protected InetAddress server;
  protected int serverPort;

  public MixedcastChat (InetAddress group, int port, InetAddress server,
      int serverPort) {
    super (group, port);
    this.server = server;
    this.serverPort = serverPort;
    frame.setTitle ("MixedcastChat [" + group.getHostAddress () + ":" + port +
      "/" + server.getHostName () + ":" + serverPort + "]");
  }
```

In the constructor, we call the superconstructor with the multicast group `group`, and port `port`. We also keep a copy of the central server's address, `server`.

```
  protected void initNet () throws IOException {
    super.initNet ();
    outgoing.setAddress (server);
    outgoing.setPort (serverPort);
  }
```

We override the `initNet()` method to call the superclass `initNet()` method and then modify the outbound `DatagramPacket`, `outgoing`, to be a unicast packet whose destination is the central server. Note that we will still transmit through a `Multicast-`

Socket; however, because this is a unicast address, the packet is transmitted as a conventional datagram.

```
public static void main (String[] args) throws IOException {
  if ((args.length != 2) || (args[0].indexOf (":") < 0) ||
      (args[1].indexOf (":") < 0))
    throw new IllegalArgumentException
      ("Syntax: MixedcastChat <group>:<port> <server>:<port>");

  int idx = args[0].indexOf (":");
  InetAddress group = InetAddress.getByName (args[0].substring (0, idx));
  int port = Integer.parseInt (args[0].substring (idx + 1));
  idx = args[1].indexOf (":");
  InetAddress server = InetAddress.getByName (args[1].substring (0, idx));
  int serverPort = Integer.parseInt (args[1].substring (idx + 1));

  MixedcastChat chat = new MixedcastChat (group, port, server, serverPort);
  chat.start ();
}
```

The `main()` method verifies the command-line arguments and then starts the client with the specified multicast group, port, and central server address.

22.6.2 Class MixedcastServer

This class is a simple single-threaded datagram relay: it retransmits all incoming unicast packets to an outgoing multicast group.

This class is intended for use with the `MixedcastChat` client. In the context of a Web-based chat system, it must be running on the same machine as the Web server that serves the client applet.

```
import java.io.*;
import java.net.*;

public class MixedcastServer {
  // public static void main (String[] args) throws IOException ...
}
```

We provide a `main()` method that executes the relay as a stand-alone application.

```
public static void main (String[] args) throws IOException {
  if ((args.length != 2) || (args[1].indexOf (":") < 0))
    throw new IllegalArgumentException
      ("Syntax: MixedcastServer <server port> <group>:<port>");

  int serverPort = Integer.parseInt (args[0]);
  int idx = args[1].indexOf (":");
  InetAddress group = InetAddress.getByName (args[1].substring (0, idx));
  int port = Integer.parseInt (args[1].substring (idx + 1));

  init (serverPort, group, port);
```

```
      while (true) {
        relay ();
      }
    }

    // protected static void init (int serverPort, InetAddress group, int port)
    //     throws IOException ...
    // protected static void relay () throws IOException ...
```

In the `main()` method, we first verify that a server port and multicast group and port have been specified as command-line arguments. We then initialize networking with the `init()` method and proceed to loop, calling the `relay()` method to relay incoming unicast packets to the outgoing multicast group.

```
    protected static DatagramSocket inSocket;
    protected static MulticastSocket outSocket;
    protected static DatagramPacket incoming, outgoing;

    protected static void init (int serverPort, InetAddress group, int port)
        throws IOException {
      inSocket = new DatagramSocket (serverPort);
      outSocket = new MulticastSocket ();
      outSocket.setTimeToLive (1);
      byte[] buffer = new byte[65508];
      incoming = new DatagramPacket (buffer, buffer.length);
      outgoing = new DatagramPacket (buffer, buffer.length, group, port);
    }
```

In the `init()` method, we create a `DatagramSocket`, `inSocket`, that we use to receive incoming unicast data from clients. We then create a `MulticastSocket`, `outSocket`, that we use to transmit outgoing multicast datagrams. We set the TTL on this socket to 1; this limits transmissions to just the attached network.

We then create a buffer, `buffer`, that is large enough to hold the biggest datagram that we could receive; we attach two `DatagramPackets`, `incoming` and `outgoing`, to this buffer. We will receive datagrams into `incoming` and then resend them with `outgoing`. These two `DatagramPackets` share the same buffer so we won't need to do any data copying. The outbound destination is simply the multicast group on which the clients are listening.

```
    protected static void relay () throws IOException {
      incoming.setLength (incoming.getData ().length);
      inSocket.receive (incoming);
      outgoing.setLength (incoming.getLength ());
      outSocket.send (outgoing);
    }
```

In the `relay()` method, we reset `incoming`'s packet size to be the full size of its buffer; this prevents new packets from being truncated to the size of the previously received packet. We receive an incoming packet, modify `outgoing`'s packet size accordingly, and retransmit the data to the multicast group.

22.6.3 Using it

To use this chat system, it is necessary to first start the server and then to start the clients. This chat can be installed as an applet providing that the client browsers support JDK 1.1 and multicast. Possibly the best choice is the applet viewer or HotJava. Some browsers may never permit multicast access from a Java applet, even when, as with this example, it does not violate the traditional communication restrictions.

To properly deploy the server, change the TTL to whatever is needed by your network. If you are running across a single broadcast-based network such as an Ethernet wire, a TTL of 1 is adequate. Otherwise, you will need to increase it as needed to cross the routers between your Web server and chat clients; the routers will also need to be configured to support IGMP and multicast. You can then start the server at a central location and connect clients into the system (figure 22.13).

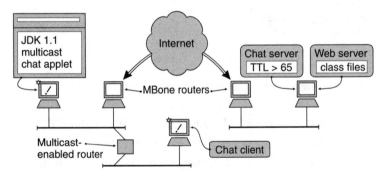

Figure 22.13   Deploying the chat system

Deployed as a Web-based chat system, the server must run on the same machine as the Web server. Clients can only connect if they are multicast-connected to the server; this can either be over the MBone, over a single broadcast-based network, or within a multicast-enabled network local to the server.

22.7 Wrapping up

Multicast has the tremendous advantage over unicast that it saves greatly on network bandwidth: a single packet is placed in the network, and it is only replicated as necessary to reach all interested clients. Using unicast, a server must maintain a list of all current clients and sequentially send a copy of the data to every one. The disadvantage of multicast is that its deployment across the Internet is still in its infancy. Using the MBone, it is possible to hook into an ever-growing multicast-enabled network. However, penetration of the MBone at large is still too small to be viable for some applications.

Looking beyond this limitation, however, multicast is interesting because it supports large-scale multiuser applications that are impractical with unicast protocols. In this chapter, we have looked at both a peer-to-peer multicast chat system and a client/server multicast chat system. As multicast becomes more widely deployed, it will see increased usage on the Internet and intranet for important broadcast and collaborative applications.

22.8 Conclusion

This concludes our treatment of the basic networking support in Java. We started by discussing TCP/IP, which provides a virtual stream across IP-based networks. Using this protocol, we have implemented clients that use standard Internet protocols, and we have discussed how to implement efficient multithreaded servers that can support multiple concurrent clients. Built on top of this protocol, the URL framework provides a convenient high-level mechanism for accessing MIME objects across network protocols such as HTTP and FTP, and we have seen how to extend this to support user protocols.

In addition, we have discussed UDP/IP and multicast, which provide efficient—albeit unreliable—packet-based data transfer. These protocols are particularly useful for specialized applications, such as multiuser collaboration, that either require extremely low network overhead, or require efficient multiclient communication.

We will now shift our focus to higher-level networking protocols; and, in particular, RMI, CORBA, and servlets. RMI and CORBA provide a high-level distributed-object interface to networking. This eliminates the need to directly establish network connections yourself; instead, an underlying networking infrastructure performs all the networking for you. Servlets, on the other hand, are a high-level mechanism for implementing network extensions; in particular, for Web servers. In essence, servlets do for servers what the URL classes do for clients.

All of these alternative technologies allow you to develop network applications at a much higher level than before. In some cases, use of these technologies can provide a significant development cost saving, and can present opportunities for developing significantly complex network applications with great ease.

Part IV

Alternative technologies

Up to this point we have looked at various applications that explicitly access the network, either through TCP, UDP, or multicast. These applications have been characterized by the explicit establishment of network connections, transmission of data, and handling of exceptions. In this part of the book we examine some networking technologies that abstract away from this low-level of networking, providing a higher-level API to gaining access to the network. Specifically, we will look at the RMI and CORBA distributed-object technologies which allow objects to communicate across the network through high-level method calls instead of low-level data transfer. After this, we look at servlets, a new Java technology for extending network servers. Servlets allow existing servers to be easily extended with custom capabilities.

Chapter 23 Remote method invocation   The remote method invocation API provides a framework for creating network-accessible distributed objects. Distributed objects are a high-level alternative to communicating with streams and sockets. Using this new API, it is possible to invoke methods on objects in remote virtual machines just as if they were normal local objects. Details of the transmission of method parameters, results and exceptions are handled in a completely transparent manner. In this chapter we introduce this technology and provide details of the Java RMI API.

Chapter 24 RMI in practice   In this chapter we develop several practical applications that demonstrate the use of RMI. We start out with two alternative implementations of a text-based chat system, one using polling and the other using server callback. We then provide an RMI implementation of the distributed list datastructure introduced earlier in chapter 18; this provides a transparent collaboration substrate for arbitrary network applications. Finally we provide a simple example of a peering server for establishing peer-to-peer network interconnects.

Chapter 25 CORBA   CORBA is an alternative technology for developing network-accessible distributed objects. It is a comprehensive industry standard for distributed objects that is supported by multiple languages and that is in use by many existing network systems. In this chapter we provide an overview of the CORBA architecture and development process, and provide a simple example of implementing a CORBA system using JDK 1.2.

Chapter 26 Servlets   Servlets are a comparatively new Java technology that allow network servers to be dynamically extended with Java services. Servlets can be used to extend any type of server; however, they are currently of most common use for extending Web servers. In this chapter we introduce the Java servlet framework, API and development process, including basic examples of the various mechanisms by which servlets can be invoked.

Chapter 27 Servlets in practice   In this chapter we put the servlet API into practice, including examples of adding persistence to servlets, a basic servlet access counter, and a full-fledged implementation of a distributed list datastructure. This datastructure has already been implemented with sockets and RMI; with this example, we provide a full suite of different implementations that serve to compare the different available networking technologies.

C H A P T E R   2 3

Remote method invocation

499

The Java remote method invocation (RMI) framework provides in intermediate network layer that allows Java objects residing in different virtual machines to communicate

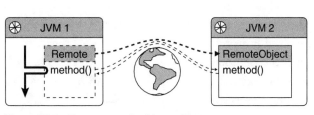

Figure 23.1   Remote method invocation

using normal method calls. As long as the hosts can communicate via TCP/IP (for example, computers connected to the Internet), networked applications can be developed without streams and sockets (figure 23.1).

This allows the programmer to avoid complex communication protocols between applications, and instead adopt a higher level method-based design.

23.1 Introduction

The whole purpose of the Java remote method invocation implementation is to provide a framework for Java objects to communicate via their methods, regardless of their location. This means that a client should be able to access a server on the local machine or on the network as if they were executing in the same run-time system. From the programmer's point of view, the networking detail necessary for distributed applications disappears. All network communications are performed transparently, under the guise of standard method calls.

To create a class that will be remotely accessible, we first define an interface which declares those methods that we wish to make public. Parameters and return values may be of any type; data transfer is handled by object streams

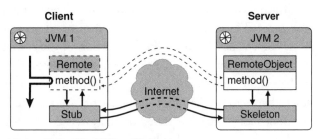

Figure 23.2   The RMI architecture

automatically. The class must implement this interface, plus any other interfaces and methods it needs for its own local use. A *stub* and *skeleton* must then be generated using rmic, a tool available in the JDK. The stub is a class that automatically translates remote method calls into network communication setup and parameter passing. The skeleton is a corresponding class that resides on the remote virtual machine, and which accepts these network connections and translates them into actual method calls on the actual object (figure 23.2).

The final setup involved in using RMI is that the remote object must be registered with a naming service that allows clients to locate where it is running. The

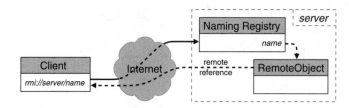

Figure 23.3   The naming registry

client connects to a naming registry and asks for a reference to a service registered under a given name (such as Chat Server). The naming registry then returns a remote reference to the object listed under that name (figure 23.3).

Under the current RMI architecture, this reference includes the host where the remote object is running, the port on which it is listening, and the object's internal RMI identifier. All of these details are, however, hidden from the programmer. The programmer simply receives a stub that implements the required interfaces and automatically translates method calls on these into remote method calls on the real object.

After the client has obtained a remote reference, it can proceed to invoke methods on the remote object. The RMI framework takes care of all low-level communications; the client is able to make method calls on the remote object just as if it were making calls on the object locally. The RMI framework even includes support for remote exceptions to be returned and for distributed garbage collection, so that remote objects will not be garbage-collected while remote references to them remain.

Tracing the method call in figure 23.2, the client appears to invoke the method on the remote object directly, as shown by the dotted lines. The call is actually being passed to the stub, which handles all of the details of the communication setup and transmits the call and parameters to the skeleton. The skeleton then makes the actual method call on the remote object. The return value is finally sent back from the skeleton to the stub, which then returns the result to the client as if the method call had been made locally. Exceptions, of course, are passed back, as well as correct results.

If the remote object has been set up correctly, then all of this work is transparent to both the remote object and the client. This does not mean that objects may be turned into remote objects without prior knowledge and intent; specific interfaces must be implemented and specific class files must be generated. It also does not mean that any method of the remote object may be invoked; only those methods declared in the remote interface are accessible to clients. However, bearing these differences in mind, the RMI framework is an extremely powerful mechanism because it allows networked applications to be developed as if everything is just a method call away.

23.1.1 The remote object

A remote object is any object that has been set up to accept method calls from another object running in a remote Java virtual machine. This is achieved with two parts: an interface describing the methods of the object and an implementation of this interface.

Defining the remote interface An interface must be written for the remote object defining all methods that should be public. This interface must extend `java.rmi.Remote`, a marker that simply identifies remotely accessible interfaces (figure 23.4).

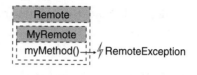

Figure 23.4   The remote interface

For example, to write a remote object with one method, the interface might look like this:

```
import java.rmi.Remote;
import java.rmi.RemoteException;

public interface MyRemote extends Remote {
   public int remoteHash (String s) throws RemoteException;
}
```

Here, we declare an interface, which can be implemented by any remote object and which declares a single remotely accessible method, `remoteHash()`, that takes a `String` parameter and returns an `int`. Note that all methods declared in a remote interface must declare that they can throw exceptions of type `java.rmi.RemoteException`. A method may, of course, declare that it can throw other exceptions of its own choosing.

The remote object implementation must extend `java.rmi.server.RemoteObject` or a subclass, and must implement each of the remote interfaces that it wishes to support. In practice, `java.rmi.server.Unicast RemoteObject` is most likely to be

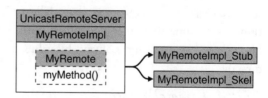

Figure 23.5   The remote object implementation

used as a superclass; this class provides an implementation of all the behavior of a typical remote object (figure 23.5).

An implementation of the interface shown above should look something like this:

```
import java.rmi.*;
import java.rmi.server.*;

public class MyRemoteImpl extends UnicastRemoteObject implements MyRemote {
   public MyRemoteImpl () throws RemoteException {
   }
```

```
  public int remoteHash (String string) {
    return string.hashCode ();
  }
}
```

We extend `UnicastRemoteObject` and implement the remote interface that we just declared. Note that the constructor for the superclass `UnicastRemoteObject` may throw exceptions of type `RemoteException`, so we must also declare a constructor that passes on exceptions of this type.

23.1.2 The stub and skeleton
Stub and skeleton objects must next be generated with the `rmic` tool. This tool takes the name of the implementation class as a parameter, and generates two class files: one for the stub and one for the skeleton.

```
rmic -d . MyRemoteImpl
```

This command produces the files `MyRemoteImpl_Stub.class` and `MyRemote-Impl_Skel.class`. Both of these classes are required to execute the remote object implementation (the server). A client of the remote object, however, only needs access to the stub class file.

23.1.3 Marshaling, delivery, and unmarshaling
The autogenerated client stub and remote object skeleton contain all the code involved in serializing details of a remote method call, dynamically invoking the remote method and serializing the results back to the caller. To perform data marshaling, they use a customized `ObjectOutputStream` class; delivery is performed over TCP/IP socket connections, and unmarshaling is performed with a customized `ObjectInputStream` class. Note that object passing is always by value, as it was when we used the object streams directly.

23.1.4 RemoteException
`RemoteException` is the superclass of all exceptions that can occur in the RMI run time. This exception is thrown whenever a remote method invocation fails. All methods in a remote interface must declare that they can throw this type of exception.

23.1.5 The naming registry

Clients can invoke methods on remote objects only if they have a remote reference to the object. A simple naming registry is provided in the RMI framework for obtaining such references (figure 23.6). A naming registry can either be manually started with the `rmiregistry` command or programmatically with methods of the `LocateRegistry` class, discussed later.

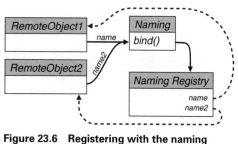

Figure 23.6   Registering with the naming service

Remote objects can register themselves using the `java.rmi.Naming` class using a URL-like naming scheme. Note that the naming registry is itself a simple RMI client, so it must have access to the stub files for all classes that will be registered therein; that is, it must be run with the location of the stub files in its `CLASSPATH`, or else it must be able to use RMI's automatic class file distribution mechanism.

When an object registers itself with the naming registry, it specifies a name under which it should be listed. Clients can then use the `java.rmi.Naming` class to obtain a remote reference to the object from the registry. The object is simply identified with a URL containing the host name on which the naming registry is running and the name under which the object is listed (figure 23.7).

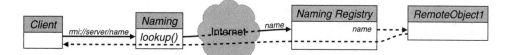

Figure 23.7   Locating a remote object with the naming service

23.2 An RMI date server

This example demonstrates remote method invocation with a simple date server that allows clients to determine the date and time at the server using remote method calls.

To create the date server application, we need to execute a number of steps. This is a general task list that can be used when implementing any application that uses RMI.

- Define the remote interface. This is the interface through which remote clients will access your server.

- Implement the remote interface. Remote method calls from the client will ultimately be made upon this implementation. This should register itself in a naming registry so that it can be remotely located.

- Generate the stub and skeleton classes using the `rmic` command.
- Write a client that locates your server in the naming registry and then calls remote methods.
- Start the naming registry using `rmiregistry`. Alternatively, your server can start a registry itself.
- Start the server.
- Run the client.

23.2.1 Interface DateServer

The first step is to write an interface that describes all the methods we want the client to be able to invoke. In this case, we have only one method to make public, and it will return a `Date` object.

```
import java.rmi.Remote;
import java.rmi.RemoteException;
import java.util.Date;

public interface DateServer extends Remote {
   public Date getDate () throws RemoteException;
}
```

We extend the `Remote` interface because we are implementing a remote interface. The `getDate()` method must be declared to throw `RemoteException`, which can occur during any problem with the remote method invocation.

23.2.2 Class DateServerImpl

The second step is to write an implementation of the remote object interface. We extend `UnicastRemoteObject` and implement `DateServer`.

All remote object implementations must extend `RemoteObject` or one of its subclasses. `UnicastRemoteObject` is provided with the JDK and is a useful implementation for use in TCP-networked client/server settings. This class automatically prepares to accept RMI connections for remote method calls when its constructor is called.

```
import java.rmi.*;
import java.rmi.server.*;
import java.util.Date;

public class DateServerImpl
    extends UnicastRemoteObject implements DateServer {
  // public DateServerImpl () throws RemoteException ...
  // public Date getDate () ...
  // public static void main (String[] args) ...
}
```

We extend `UnicastRemoteObject` and implement the remote interface that we have defined. We must provide a constructor that passes on any `RemoteException` that may be thrown by the superconstructor, and implement the methods of our remote interface.

For this example, we also declare a `main()` method that creates an instance of this class and registers it with the RMI naming registry.

```
public DateServerImpl () throws RemoteException {
}
```

For this class, we simply pass on the `RemoteExceptions` that can occur in the superclass constructor; for example, if the networking cannot be set up to receive remote method calls. If our object needs any other initialization, that too can be performed here.

```
public Date getDate () {
  return new Date ();
}
```

Our implementation of `getDate()` simply creates and returns a `Date` object. Note that in this case, our implementation doesn't throw any exceptions. We would only need to declare a `RemoteException` here if we made remote method calls from within this code. As it is, the only `RemoteExceptions` that can occur will arise within the RMI code involved in invoking this method; not actually from within this method.

```
public static void main (String[] args) throws Exception {
  DateServerImpl dateServer = new DateServerImpl ();
  Naming.bind ("Date Server", dateServer);
}
```

The `main()` method creates a new `DateServerImpl dateServer`, and registers this object with the naming service under the name Date Server. We declare that this method may throw exceptions of type `Exception`, as a simple catch-all for the various exceptions that can be thrown by the remote object and naming registry.

The `dateServer` object is registered with the naming registry using the `bind()` method of the `Naming` class. If an object is already bound with the name Date Server, an `AlreadyBoundException` will be thrown. We could alternatively use the `rebind()` method, described later, to overcome this.

After we have registered this object, remote clients can get a reference to it by making a connection to the registry running on this machine and requesting a reference to the object listed under the name Date Server.

23.2.3 Generating the stub and skeleton

To generate the stub and skeleton, we compile the `DateServerImpl` class and then use `rmic` with the Date Server implementation class name as the parameter:

```
rmic DateServerImpl
```

Two class files will be generated: one for the stub (`DateServerImpl_Stub`) and one for the skeleton (`DateServerImpl_Skel`).

23.2.4 Class DateClient

This client looks up the Date Server in the naming registry, collects a reference to it, makes a call to its `getDate()` method and then prints the result.

```java
import java.rmi.Naming;
import java.util.Date;

public class DateClient {
  public static void main (String[] args) throws Exception {
    if (args.length != 1)
      throw new IllegalArgumentException ("Syntax: DateClient <hostname>");
    DateServer dateServer = (DateServer) Naming.lookup
      ("rmi://" + args[0] + "/Date Server");
    Date when = dateServer.getDate ();
    System.out.println (when);
  }
}
```

The client has only a `main()` method. We verify the arguments, locate the remote server, and determine its date.

The `lookup()` method of `Naming` is used to collect a reference to the remote `Date-Server` implementation. A URL with the protocol field rmi is used to name this object; the rmi part may be optionally omitted, so we could just use the URL //server/object.

The URL specifies two things: the machine on which the naming registry is running, and the name with which the object has been registered there. In this case, the host is specified on the command line (localhost is useful for testing), and the name of the object is Date Server.

23.2.5 Running the application

To run the example, start the registry on the server machine:

```
rmiregistry
```

This registry is then accessible to remote clients on a standard (well-known) port. You must usually start this from a directory containing the stub classes for objects that will be registered. Next, start the server on the same machine:

```
java DateServerImpl
```

When we run this class, an instance of the `DateServerImpl` class is created and registered with the local registry. Note that the registry must be executing on the server machine before this registration can occur. Finally, run the client on any machine:

```
java DateClient localhost
```

When we run the client, we must specify the name of the host that is running the naming registry. The client connects to the naming registry, obtains a reference to the remote object, and calls its `getDate()` method; this returns the current date on the server machine. This is useful if your watch is slow.

Behind the scenes, the `Naming` class connects to the registry that is running on the specified host and then queries it for the object matching the specified name.

The object returned by this call is a remote reference (actually an instance of the stub) that implements whatever remote interfaces have been implemented by the remote server. Therefore, we must cast the result to the expected remote interface, and *not* the remote implementation class name: Only the methods declared in remote interfaces are accessible over RMI.

When a remote reference to the object has been obtained, we can invoke methods declared in its remote interfaces. In this case, we make a call to the `getDate()` method and print the response. When we make this method call, the local stub connects to the remote skeleton, which calls the remote object method, obtains a result, and streams this back down to the stub which returns it to our client for display.

23.3 RMI class file locations

When you build an RMI-based application, you end up with five primary sets of classes: the client implementation classes, the server implementation classes, the remote interfaces, the stub classes, and the skeleton classes.

To simply distribute an RMI client, for example, by placing it on a Web server for access by a Web browser, you must include the client implementation classes (these are what will be run by the client), the remote interface classes (these are how the client will access the server), and the stub classes (these are the classes that convert client remote-method calls into network connections).

To simply distribute an RMI server, for example, by installing it on a Web server, you must include the server implementation classes, the remote interfaces, the stub classes, and the skeleton classes. All of these classes are required during the execution of the server. Although the stub classes are only executed by the client, they are also required by the server when it is exporting itself for remote access.

Some RMI applications will, of course, not separate the client and server as cleanly as this. One of the great strengths of RMI is that the server can make remote method calls on the client, just as the client can make remote method calls on the server. Indeed, pure peer-to-peer applications that have no distinction between end points are possible with RMI. In these cases, you should distribute class files just as described above, but apply the heuristics on a per-remote-object basis instead of completely distinguishing the client and server applications. So, include all class files where the remote object will actually reside, and include just the interface and stub class files where it will be remotely accessed.

The RMI framework also includes the capability for automatic distribution of implementation-related class files such as the stub files. Using this mechanism, an RMI application needs access only to its own specific class files and any remote interfaces that it uses. Any other class files that it encounters as part of a remote method call will be automatically downloaded. When the application obtains a reference to a remote object, it will automatically download the object's stub files from an appropriate location. This capability is discussed in detail in the remainder of this section.

The primary advantage of this facility is that a client does not need to know what class is actually implementing a remote interface; all it needs to know is that the remote interface is implemented by the remote object. The appropriate stub for the remote object will be automatically and transparently downloaded, along with any other classes that are involved in the object implementation but of no direct concern to the client.

23.3.1 Automatic class file distribution

One of the limitations of RMI, as we have looked at it thus far, is that the client and naming registry must have access to the stub file for the remote service being accessed and that the server needs access to the stub and skeleton files, even though user code never directly accesses these classes. Similarly, both client and server must have access to the class files of all classes that they will exchange as parameters and return values of remote method calls. For example, if a client is expecting a remote method to return an object of type DBEntry and the server actually returns a subclass MyDBEntry, then the client must also have access to the MyDBEntry class file.

This is an unnecessary limitation, because in many cases the client and server will access the problematic classes only through a standard interface (such as the remote interface implemented by the server, or in the last example, through the API of DBEntry) and will never need direct access to the underlying classes.

For this reason, RMI comes with a facility for automatically distributing class files. Using this mechanism, when an unknown class name is encountered, the RMI framework will automatically download the corresponding class file from a standard location.

Under JDK 1.2, this mechanism is exposed through the `MarshalledObject` class, should it be of use in other situations.

23.3.2 Class file loading

When the RMI framework (either a client or server) encounters a class name that it does not recognize, it attempts to load the class from the following locations (figure 23.8):

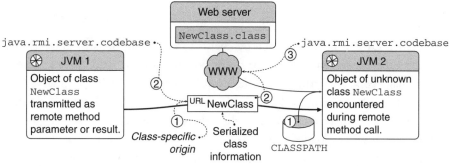

Figure 23.8 RMI class file loading

1 The preferred location from which to download any unknown class is the local `CLASSPATH`.

2 If an unknown class name is encountered by a server as a parameter to a remote method call or by a client as the result of a remote method call (including the remote stub that is returned from a call to a naming registry), then the RMI data may internally include a URL from which the class file can be downloaded. This same URL will also be used for any other unknown classes that are needed by this new downloaded class.

3 Finally, if an unknown local class name is encountered (i.e., not during a remote method call; the skeleton, for example), the RMI framework will attempt to download the class file from the URL specified in the `System` property `java.rmi.server.codebase`. This can be used as a central storage location for common local classes.

As is clear from the second option, RMI automatically includes class locations with class names that it transmits. It determines these locations as follows:

1 If a class name is being transmitted as part of some RMI data, and that class was already downloaded from a remote location (such as a Web server), then the class' particular remote location is included along with the RMI data.

2 Otherwise, if the class was loaded from the local file system, the `System` property `java.rmi.server.codebase` (if set) is transmitted as a location from which the class file can be downloaded.

To allow an RMI client to automatically download the stub files for your RMI server, you must thus specify a codebase from which the class files can be downloaded. For example:

```
java -Djava.rmi.server.codebase=http://nitric.com/jnp/classes/ ServerImpl
```

The specified URL will then be used by clients to download the stub file for your server and any other classes that the client needs but does not actually directly access. You must manually copy the various class files into this location on your Web server.

Fundamentally, if a new class that would not be needed if RMI were not being used, is needed as a result of an RMI call, then the class file can be remotely downloaded. Otherwise, it will be loaded using the normal Java mechanisms.

For example, if the client is expecting a `Runnable` object to be returned from a remote method call but the server returns a subclass `MyRunnable`, the `MyRunnable` class file will be automatically downloaded from the server's code base if it is not present in the client's standard code base.

Similarly, if a server is expecting a `Runnable` object and the client presents a `MyRunnable` subclass as a parameter, the server will attempt to download the `MyRunnable` class file from the client's code base if it is not present on the local file system. In this case, the client must specify its code base just as the server example above.

Furthermore, a bootstrapping technique is available that allows a server to even download its own stub and skeleton files from a remote location. This technique and further aspects of RMI are detailed in JavaSoft's RMI specification document, included with the JDK.

23.3.3 Security considerations

By default, applications do not have a security manager so code has unlimited access to resources. This is a dangerous default situation with RMI and automatic class file distribution because, if a reference to an unknown class is exchanged in a remote method call, the recipient will try to load in the class file from a remote location. A user could place arbitrary code in this class file, and thus, gain undesired access to the recipient's resources. For this reason, RMI will not download remote class files if there is no `SecurityManager` installed.

If you wish to support the downloading of remote class files then you must install a `SecurityManager` that enforces appropriate access controls. This should be installed before exposing an object for remote access. If no security manager is installed then a

`SecurityException` will be raised during a remote method call if a class is encountered that requires remote downloading.

For obvious reasons, installing a `SecurityManager` that permits all operations for downloaded classes is not a good idea. The `RMISecurityManager` is a simple implementation of `SecurityManager` that permits downloading of remote stub classes. However, it denies such classes any sensitive operations such as accessing native code, files, and so forth.

If you wish the downloaded classes to have alternate levels of access, you should install a subclass of the `RMISecurityManager` class, changing the security enforcement as appropriate.

To install a new `SecurityManager`, simply call the `setSecurityManager()` method of the `System` class before you start your RMI application:

```
System.setSecurityManager (new RMISecurityManager ());
RemoteService remoteService = new RemoteService ();
Naming.bind ("serviceName", remoteService);
```

For many applications, however, allowing classes to be remotely downloaded is not necessary. Only do this if you want to support the automatic class file distribution mechanism.

Applets, of course, cannot set a new `SecurityManager`; the default applet `SecurityManager` is, however, amenable to RMI's class file distribution: The remote files must simply all be present on the server from which the applet was downloaded.

In all of the following examples, we have omitted installation of an `RMISecurityManager`; the use of automatic class file distribution is usually not necessary.

23.3.4 Behavioral objects

The ability of RMI to automatically download the class files for unknown classes, as and when they are encountered, and to automatically pass the location of these class files onto other remote objects, has some extremely interesting consequences.

Traditionally, transmission of an object over a network protocol implies simply the transmission of state: Only the data encapsulated by the object are transmitted. Using RMI and automatic class file distribution, however, a new breed of objects known as *behavioral objects* are made possible. Transmission of a behavioral object implies transmission of both the object's state and its behavior. An object's behavior is provided by its class file, which is automatically downloaded by the recipient if it is not already known.

Behavioral objects are not unique to RMI. It is comparatively simple to implement custom object streams that include an object's class file along with its state. What is important about RMI is that it provides this behavior as standard, along with the ability to easily establish network interconnections. Furthermore, RMI provides safety in the form of the `RMISecurityManager`, which protects the recipient of a behavioral object from potentially dangerous activities.

An example of a behavioral object system would be a search engine that allows clients to submit searches in the form of *searchlets*. These go beyond the mere submission of search criteria (a request object's state) to the submission of search behavior (a request object's state and code), permitting the safe execution of queries with far greater power and flexibility than before. Obviously the application of behavioral objects is somewhat limited—not everyone will want to write a search query in the form of an actual program—however it has some intriguing possibilities for future systems, particularly in the area of dynamic extensibility.

23.4 RMI-related packages

The RMI framework consists of several packages. We shall discuss some of their classes and ignore others. The main packages are:

java.rmi   This package contains classes related to the client side of RMI. These classes are used by clients to remotely access RMI services. This package includes the interfaces through which remote objects are accessed and a mechanism to locate RMI services on a remote machine.

java.rmi.server   This package contains classes related to the server side of RMI. This package includes the support classes for exposing an RMI service to direct TCP/IP and proxied HTTP requests.

java.rmi.registry   This package contains classes related to the RMI naming registry. With this package, naming registries can be created, located, and remotely manipulated.

java.rmi.dgc   This package contains classes that support distributed garbage collection. This is the mechanism by which Java's automatic garbage collection is extended for distributed computing. RMI servers automatically maintain a count of the number of active remote references that they are servicing and can close down when they are no longer being accessed.

JDK 1.2   *java.rmi.activation*   This package contains support for the JDK 1.2 *activation* mechanism. Using this mechanism, RMI servers need not be permanently running; instead, they are activated by an *activation daemon* only when an actual request arrives. Normally they are kept in a serialized passive state. This mechanism is quite elaborate; providing complete details is beyond the scope of this book. The reader is referred to the JDK 1.2 documentation for the API and some tutorials.

23.5 **JDK 1.1** *Interface Remote*

This interface, from the `java.rmi` package, is the superinterface for all remote interfaces. A remote interface describes the methods that a remote object supports. These are the only methods that can be accessed through RMI by a client.

When an RMI client is accessing a remote object, it will always access the object through one or more of these remote interfaces: it can never access the object through other methods that are specific to the actual implementation. The benefit of this is that it clearly delineates the API of a remote object, and so cleanly separates issues of its implementation from the publicly-exposed interface.

23.5.1 *Remote method call semantics*

The major difference between a remote method call and a direct method call is that under RMI, parameters are passed by value; that is, the server receives a copy of the parameters passed to a remote method. If you pass, for example, a `Vector` to a remote method and

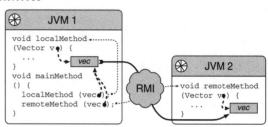

Figure 23.9   Remote method call semantics

the remote method manipulates the `Vector`, the client will not see the changes reflected in its local copy of the `Vector` (figure 23.9).

Instead, under RMI, if you wish to modify an `Object` inside a remote method, you must return the modified `Object` as a result of the method call (figure 23.10).

Alternatively, you can

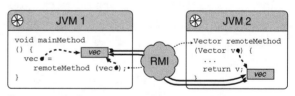

Figure 23.10   Remote parameter manipulation

implement the structure to be manipulated as an actual remote object. When you pass a reference to this object into a remote method call, the recipient will receive a remote reference to the original object and so any changes that it makes will be transported back to the actual object implementation over RMI. Using this mechanism is obviously more complex, and only applicable in certain circumstances.

23.5.2 *Methods*

The `Remote` interface is itself just a marker interface. It declares no methods, serving only to identify all remote interfaces. All parameters and results of a remote method must be serializable by the object streams.

23.5.3 Exceptions

All methods of a `Remote` interface must declare that they can throw exceptions of type `RemoteException` in addition to any exceptions that they might normally throw. When a client calls a method on a remote object and the RMI connection fails, a `RemoteException` will be thrown to the caller. If the remote implementation raises any other exception, it too will be passed back to the caller, just as if the method call were made locally.

23.5.4 For example

This interface describes a remotely accessible bank account.

```
import java.rmi.*;

public interface BankAccount extends Remote {
    public abstract void deposit (int amount) throws RemoteException;
    public abstract void withdraw (int amount)
        throws RemoteException, InsufficientFundsException;
    public abstract int getBalance () throws RemoteException;
    public abstract Portfolio addToPortfolio (Portfolio portfolio)
        throws RemoteException;
}
```

As a remote interface, we must extend `Remote`. We declare four methods: `deposit()`, `withdraw()`, `getBalance()`, and `addToPortfolio()`. These are the only methods that a client can remotely call on a `BankAccount` implementation. All four methods must declare that they can throw exceptions of type `RemoteException`. Such exceptions will arise if a client attempts to remotely call a method on a `BankAccount` implementation and some failure occurs during the remote method invocation mechanism.

In addition, the `withdraw()` method declares that it can throw an exception of type `InsufficientFundsException`. If a client attempts to withdraw too much money from an account and the server throws an exception of this type, it will be automatically transferred by RMI back to the client: RMI transparently supports Java's exception mechanism, just as it supports all the other semantics of method calling in Java.

The `addToPortfolio()` method adds details of this `BankAccount` to a specified `Portfolio` object. This is an example of RMI's pass by value calling semantics. Traditionally, in a nondistributed environment, the `addToPortfolio()` method would directly modify the `Portfolio`. Under RMI, however, any modifications made by the server are made to a copy of the object, and so, the changes are not seen by the client. Instead, we must return the modified `Portfolio` object to the caller as a result of the method call.

23.6 ⟨JDK 1.1⟩ *Class Naming*

This class, from the `java.rmi` package, provides a convenient API for manipulating RMI naming registries. Internally, this class makes use of the `Registry` interface and `LocateRegistry` class; however, it provides static methods and convenient URL-like notation for addressing objects.

This class provides methods for locating objects stored in a naming registry and for registering new objects. A client can use this class to locate a remote object, and a server can use this class to register itself.

23.6.1 *Addressing services*

Whether a service is being located or being stored, the `Naming` class uses a URL-like syntax to identify the naming registry and service name.

A typical URL has the form rmi://hostname:port/service. This URL identifies the remote object named *service* stored in the naming registry running on host *hostname* and port *port*.

For example, to address someone's bank account, we could use the following URL: rmi://accounts.bigbrother.bank:1099/personal/US/Mork&Mindy.

This refers to the remote object registered under the name personal/US/Mork&Mindy in the naming registry running on port 1099 of accounts.bigbrother.bank. The service name is any arbitrary string. There are no rules that govern the form that it may take, although using some hierarchy as we have shown here can be useful for administrative purposes.

In fact, all of the elements of the URL specification are optional. The prefix rmi: can be omitted if so desired. If no hostname is specified, then the local machine is used. If no port is specified, the naming registry default (1099) is used. Finally, the service name can be omitted if you are just listing the services stored in a naming registry.

23.6.2 *Static methods*

All of the methods provided by this class are static:

Remote lookup(String address) throws MalformedURLException, RemoteException, NotBoundException This method returns a remote reference to the remote service specified by `address`, which must be a URL-format service addresses as described above. It connects to the specified naming registry and extracts a reference to the remote object registered there under the specified service name. This throws a `NotBoundException` if the service is not registered.

void bind(String address, Remote object) throws MalformedURLException, RemoteException, AlreadyBoundException   This method stores a reference to the specified remote object `object` at the address `address`. It connects to the specified naming registry and stores a reference to the remote object there under the specified service name. This throws an `AlreadyBoundException` if an object is already stored in the naming registry under the selected service name. For security reasons, this method can only be called by code executing on the same host as the naming registry; that is, the host part of `address` should be empty.

The remote object `object` can either be a local implementation of a remote object or an actual remote reference to a remote object. So, either a remote server can register itself in a naming registry by passing `this`, or, if it holds a reference to another remote object, it can register it by passing the remote reference.

void rebind(String address, Remote object) throws MalformedURLException, RemoteException   This method stores a reference to the specified remote object `object` at the specified address `address`. Any object already stored at that address is replaced. For security reasons, this method can only be called by code executing on the same host as the naming registry.

void unbind(String address) throws MalformedURLException, RemoteException, NotBoundException   This method removes the remote object stored at the specified address `address`. It connects to the specified naming registry and removes the entry stored there under the specified service name. This throws a `NotBoundException` if no such service is registered. For security reasons, this method can only be called by code executing on the same host as the naming registry.

String[] list(String address) throws MalformedURLException, RemoteException   This method returns a list of all the remote services registered in the naming registry at address `address`. Only the host part of this address is considered; the service name part, if any, is ignored. Each entry is returned as a full remote address of the form rmi://hostname:port/service.

23.6.3 Exceptions
All the methods of the `Naming` class may throw a variety of exceptions, including:

MalformedURLException   Remote objects are addressed through this class using URLs. If a supplied name does not follow the permitted syntax, a `MalformedURLException` will be thrown.

RemoteException   The `Naming` class internally uses RMI to access the naming registry. If an error occurs during an RMI call, (for example, if a network error occurs), the problem will be reported as a `RemoteException`. Various subclasses indicate specific problems. For example, a `ConnectException` will be thrown if a naming registry cannot be contacted (typically this means that none was running on the specified host or port).

UnknownHostException   Part of the address of a remote object is the host on which the object is located. If the host name is not valid, an `UnknownHostException` will be thrown. This exception is a subclass of `RemoteException`; it is an encapsulation of, and not to be confused with, `java.net.UnknownHostException`.

NotBoundException   Attempting to access an object of a given name in a naming registry will fail with a `NotBoundException` if no object by that name has been stored there.

AlreadyBoundException   Attempting to bind an object of a given name in a naming registry will fail with an `AlreadyBoundException` if an object has already been stored there under the chosen name.

23.6.4 Security

To prevent the potential security problems that might arise if just any host were allowed to manipulate the contents of a naming registry, attempts to modify the naming registry (using the various binding methods) will fail if the caller is not running on the same machine as the registry.

For this reason, when you are manipulating the contents of a naming registry, you should omit the naming registry host name in the URLs you supply. If the local naming registry is running on the default port, simply use an address of the form service. If it is running on a nonstandard port, use an address of the form //:port/service.

23.6.5 For example

If a client wishes to list the services listed in a remote naming registry, it can use the `list()` method as follows:

```
String[] services = Naming.list ("//accounts.my.bank/");
for (int i = 0; i < services.length; ++ i)
  System.out.println (services[i]);
```

This will list all the registered services, returning `String`s of the following form:

```
rmi://accounts.my.bank/personal/bob
```

The elements of the resulting array can be used directly in further calls to the Naming class. For example:

```
BankAccount firstAccount = (BankAccount) Naming.lookup (services[0]);
```

This method returns a remote reference to the first service returned from the list() method. Note that a naming registry can list services running anywhere, so this remote object need not necessarily be running on the same machine as the naming registry.

```
Naming.bind ("First Account", firstAccount);
```

Finally, we store a reference to the resulting remote account in the local naming registry under the name First Account. Usually we would only register local remote objects in a local naming service; however, we can also store references to other remote objects if we so desire. The bank itself might, for example, add a new account as follows:

```
account = new PersonalBankAccountImpl ("jim");
Naming.rebind ("personal/jim", account);
```

Here, we create a new PersonalBankAccountImpl (this should be an RMI server that implements the BankAccount remote interface) and store it in the local registry under the service name personal/jim.

23.7 JDK 1.1 *Class LocateRegistry*

This class, from the java.rmi.registry package, can be used to control naming registries. It provides methods to obtain remote references to naming registries as well as a method for directly starting a naming registry.

23.7.1 Static methods

All methods of this class are static. They return objects that can be manipulated through the Registry interface, which we will discuss next.

Registry getRegistry() throws RemoteException   This method returns a remote reference to the naming registry running on the local machine on the default naming registry port. This method may throw an appropriate RemoteException if an RMI error occurs. Note that this method may not actually try to contact the naming registry, and so will not identify immediately if there is no naming registry listening; you will only find out when you actually try to access the registry.

Registry getRegistry(int port) throws RemoteException   This method returns a remote reference to the naming registry running on the local machine on the specified port `port`.

Registry getRegistry(String host) throws RemoteException   This method returns a remote reference to the naming registry running on the specified host `host` on the default naming registry port. This method will throw an `UnknownHostException` if the specified host cannot be located.

Registry getRegistry(String host, int port) throws RemoteException   This method returns a remote reference to the naming registry running on the specified host `host` on the specified port `port`.

JDK 1.2   *Registry getRegistry(String host, int port, RMIClientSocketFactory clients) throws RemoteException*   This method returns a remote reference to the naming registry running on the specified host `host` on the specified port `port`, using the specified `RMIClientSocketFactory clients`. This method should be used to override the default RMI socket connection framework. This interface is described in section 23.16 on page 532.

Registry createRegistry(int port) throws RemoteException   This method creates and starts a naming registry running on the local machine on the specified port `port`. It returns a direct reference to the resulting registry, not a remote reference as is returned by all the other methods. Note that, by virtue of the manner in which remote objects are implemented, an application may only create a single registry.

This registry is a typical remote object so it will be garbage collected and will terminate when there are no more references to it—remote or local. Remote references to naming registries do not usually persist for a long time; they are typically only maintained for the duration of looking up an object. So to keep the registry running, you must maintain an active server with a reference to this registry.

JDK 1.2   *Registry createRegistry(int port, RMIServerSocketFactory servers, RMIClientSocketFactory clients) throws RemoteException*   This method creates and starts a naming registry running on the local machine on the specified port `port`, using the specified `RMIServerSocketFactory servers` and the specified `RMIClientSocketFactory clients`. The naming registry will listen for incoming connections using a `ServerSocket` created by `servers` and will instruct remote clients to connect using `clients`. These interfaces are discussed in sections 23.16 and 23.17.

23.7.2 Exceptions

The various methods of this class may all throw exceptions of type `RemoteException` if an RMI error is encountered when locating the naming registry. For example, an exception of type `UnknownHostException` will be thrown if a named host cannot be located.

23.7.3 For example

Looking up a remote registry using this class is done as follows:

```
Registry registry = LocateRegistry.getRegistry ("host", 1234);
registry.rebind ("Service", service);
```

This call will return a reference to the specified naming registry running on port 1234 of host `host`, which can be manipulated through the `Naming`-like `Registry` interface. In this case, we rebind the Service entry. If no naming registry is running, the `rebind()` method will fail with a `RemoteException`.

Creating a local naming registry is just as easy:

```
Registry registry = LocateRegistry.createRegistry (1234);
registry.bind ("Service", service);
```

Here we create a registry running on the local machine on port 1234. If there is already a registry running on this port, an appropriate `RemoteException` will be thrown. We can otherwise bind our service directly to this registry.

23.8　JDK 1.1　Interface Registry

This remote interface, from the `java.rmi.registry` package, describes the public API of the RMI naming registry. This naming registry is itself implemented as a remote object; the `LocateRegistry` class thus simply returns remote references to the JDK implementation of this interface.

23.8.1 Static variables

The `Registry` interface declares one static constant:

int REGISTRY_PORT　　This port is the default port that a naming registry listens on (1099). If you don't specify a port number when locating an object in a naming registry, the registry will be contacted on this port.

23.8.2 Methods

The following remote methods are defined by the `Registry` interface. Unlike the `Naming` class, when you specify a service name through this interface, you specify only the service name, not also the address of the naming registry.

Methods of the `Naming` class are, in fact, simply implemented as calls to `Locate-Registry` followed by remote method calls through this interface.

Remote lookup(String name) throws RemoteException, NotBoundException
This method returns a remote reference to the service registered under the name `name` in this naming registry. This throws a `NotBoundException` if the service is not registered.

void bind(String name, Remote object) throws RemoteException, Already-BoundException   This method stores a reference to the specified remote object `obj` in this registry under the name `name`. The remote object `object` can either be a local implementation of a remote object or an actual remote reference to a remote object. This throws an `AlreadyBoundException` if an object is already stored in the naming service under the selected service name. For security reasons, this method can only be called by code executing on the same host as the naming registry.

void rebind(String name, Remote object) throws RemoteException   This method stores a reference to the specified remote object `object` in this registry under the name `name`, overwriting any existing entry. In other respects, the same considerations as for `bind()` apply here.

void unbind(String name) throws RemoteException, NotBoundException
This method removes any service registered under the name `name` from this naming registry. This throws a `NotBoundException` if no such service is registered.

String[] list() throws RemoteException   This method returns a complete list of all the services stored in this naming registry. Only the service name is returned; no addressing information is included; for example, Service1, Service2.

23.8.3 Exceptions
All the methods of the `Registry` interface declare that they may throw a variety of exceptions, comparable to those for the `Naming` class. For example, `RemoteException` is returned if an RMI error is encountered; `NotBoundException`, if a requested service is not registered; and `AlreadyBoundException`, if a service is already registered under a proposed name.

Finally, a `RemoteException` of type `AccessException` will be thrown if a request is disallowed. All update operations are restricted to clients executing on the same host machine as the naming registry. If a remote host attempts such an operation, an `AccessException` will be raised.

23.9 〔JDK 1.1〕 *Class RemoteObject*

The `RemoteObject` class, from the `java.rmi.server` package, is the ultimate superclass of all remote objects. This is the superclass of both remote object implementations and remote stubs. `RemoteObject` overrides the `hashCode()`, `equals()`, and `toString()` methods to reflect the correct method semantics of a remote object. It also implements `Serializable` to implement correct serialization of remote objects. It provides no useful methods other than these reimplementations.

23.9.1 *Remote objects as parameters*

It is important to understand the distinction between sending a remote object as a parameter to a remote method call, and serializing a remote object using raw object streams. Although RMI does use object streams to send parameters to a remote method call, it actually uses specialized subclasses that override the default serialization of remote objects.

When you send a remote object implementation (i.e., a `RemoteObject` subclass) as a parameter to a remote method call, you actually send a remote reference to the remote object implementation and not a copy of it (as is the case with normal objects). Thus, when the remote

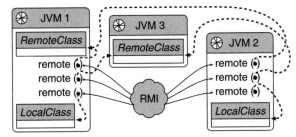

Figure 23.11   Remote object parameters

method itself calls methods on the object that it receives, further RMI calls will actually be made back to the original remote object implementation (figure 23.11).

This has one extremely important consequence: You cannot send a remote object as a parameter to a remote method call, and expect the recipient to receive an instance of the actual remote object class. Instead the recipient will receive an instance of the RMI stub class that internally contains a remote reference to the actual object implementation.

```
public class MyImpl extends UnicastRemoteObject implements MyRemote {
  //...

  public static void main (String[] args) throws Exception {
    MyImpl mine = new MyImpl ();
    HisRemote his = (HisRemote) Naming.lookup ("//server/his");
    his.invoke (mine);
  }
}
```

In this fragment, we create a new local remote object `mine` and send it as a parameter to another remote object `his`. After RMI data transfer, the `invoke()` method will not receive an actual `MyImpl` object. It will receive a `MyImpl_Stub` object that implements the `MyRemote` interface and proxies the methods defined therein, back to our instance of `MyImpl`.

Therefore, it is an error to define a remote method that receives, as a parameter, an actual remote object implementation class. You may only define remote methods that receive, as parameters, either nonremote objects or remote interfaces. The following are some possible declarations of the `invoke()` method:

```
public void invoke (Object object) throws RemoteException;
```

This method signature is valid; the `MyImpl_Stub` that will be transmitted is a valid subclass of `Object`.

```
public void invoke (MyRemote remote) throws RemoteException;
```

This method signature is valid; the `MyImpl_Stub` class implements `MyRemote`, and so, is a valid parameter to this method.

```
public void invoke (MyImpl impl) throws RemoteException;
```

This method signature is invalid. At compile time, it looks fine; you are passing in an instance of `MyImpl`. However, the RMI framework will convert an instance of `MyImpl` into an instance of `MyImpl_Stub` during serialization. This stub class is not a subclass of `MyImpl`, and so, at run time, this will result in an internal RMI exception.

23.9.2 Serializing a remote object

When you serialize a remote object using the normal object streams, a fully valid remote object will be serialized. When you deserialize this, the object is automatically reanimated. Using this mechanism, you can serialize a remote object to disk and then deserialize it, either in the same JVM or in another JVM elsewhere in the world, and a fully valid remote object will be created and exposed. It is even possible for your remote class to implement a `readObject()` method that automatically registers itself in a naming registry.

```
// ObjectOutputStream objectOut;
MyImpl mine = new MyImpl ();
objectOut.writeObject (mine);
```

The instance of `MyImpl` is serialized as you would expect, using the normal serialization process.

```
// ObjectInputStream objectIn;
MyImpl mine2 = (MyImpl) objectIn.readObject ();
```

We now have a duplicate of the original remote object. This is a fully activated remote object that can be registered in a naming registry and manipulated just like the original instance.

23.10 JDK 1.1 *Class RemoteServer*

This class, a subclass of `RemoteObject`, provides more specialized semantics for remote object implementations. It provides the common functions of remote objects that will be implemented as servers; that is, remote objects that will open server sockets to accept client calls.

23.10.1 Static methods

The `RemoteServer` class provides several useful static methods:

String getClientHost() throws ServerNotActiveException   This method, when called from within a remote method implementation, returns the address of the client machine. If called outside of an active remote method call, it throws a `ServerNotActiveException`. This method is extremely useful for access control: In a remotely accessible bank implementation you can call `getClientHost()` to determine the host that is attempting to call a remote method, and can restrict access accordingly. Remember, of course, that DNS and IP are not secure, so a host name is not really a strong indication of identity but it is a start.

void setLog(OutputStream out)   RMI provides a convenient logging facility that allows you to log all incoming RMI calls. Call this static method with an appropriate output stream to enable logging. Passing `null` will disable logging.

```
RemoteServer.setLog (new FileOutputStream ("rmi.log"));
```

This call begins to log all RMI calls to this JVM; the log is written to the specified `OutputStream`.

```
RemoteServer.setLog (null);
```

This call switches RMI logging off. Note that this does not close the original stream; you can either do this manually or wait for garbage collection to take care of closing the stream for you.

PrintStream getLog() This method returns the RMI logging stream. Everything that you write to this stream is augmented with additional logging information including the current time, and sent to the current log stream.

23.11 `JDK 1.1` *Class UnicastRemoteObject*

The `UnicastRemoteObject` class, a subclass of `RemoteServer`, is the superclass for most normal remote objects. Except in unusual and complex cases, or when using the RMI activation mechanism, you will always implement your remote objects as an extension of this class.

`UnicastRemoteObject` adds final implementation details related to nonreplicated remotely accessible objects using TCP streams. Among other details, it adds support for the `clone()` method so that you can clone a remote object to obtain another, unique, remote object. This class also adds last-stage support for serialization so that a serialized remote object remains a remote object.

23.11.1 Constructors
The following constructors are provided by this class:

protected UnicastRemoteObject() throws RemoteException This is the standard constructor that a remote object implementation should call if it is being implemented as a subclass of `UnicastRemoteObject`. It initializes the object for accepting remote method calls on an arbitrary free local port. If an error is encountered while performing this initialization, an appropriate `RemoteException` will be thrown. Note that the RMI run time may choose to serve multiple remote objects from a single `ServerSocket` in order to save on the amount of thread and network resources that it must consume to host large numbers of objects.

`JDK 1.2` *protected UnicastRemoteObject(int port) throws RemoteException* This constructor should be called by a remote object implementation that wishes to listen on the specified local port, `port`. For example, the RMI naming registry uses this constructor to start up on its chosen port.

`JDK 1.2` *protected UnicastRemoteObject(int port, RMIClientSocketFactory clients, RMIServerSocketFactory servers) throws RemoteException* This constructor should be called by a remote object implementation that wishes to use custom socket factories for communication purposes. It will listen for incoming connections on the specified port, `port` (use a value of `0` to listen on an arbitrary free port) using a `ServerSocket` created by `servers`. Remote clients of this class will be instructed to use `clients` to establish `Socket` connections to this server. Details of per-object socket factories are given in section 23.16 on page 532.

23.11.2 Static methods

In addition to being the superclass for most remote objects, this class provides one extremely important helper method:

RemoteStub exportObject(Remote object) throws RemoteException   This method exports the specified object `object` as a remote object listening on an arbitrary free port. The return value is, in effect, a remote reference to the object that can be stored in a naming registry or processed as you desire. This method is important because it means that you can implement a remote object without directly subclassing `UnicastRemoteObject`. In some cases, such as in applets or where you cannot control code, it is not practical to subclass `UnicastRemoteObject` directly. In such a case you should create your class as necessary, implementing your remote interface as usual; then you can export an instance of your class with this method and store the resulting stub in a naming registry.

```
import java.rmi.*;
import java.rmi.server.*;

public class MyClass extends SomeClass implements MyRemote {
  // methods

  public static void main (String[] args) throws Exception {
    MyClass obj = new MyClass ();
    MyRemote ref = (MyRemote) UnicastRemoteObject.exportObject (obj);
    Naming.rebind ("MyClass/MyInstance", ref);
  }
}
```

This piece of code, after compiling with `rmic`, provides exactly the same function as if we subclassed `UnicastRemoteObject` directly and registered ourself in the naming registry instead of this reference. Note, however, that in this case we can extend any class that we desire. In particular, this might be useful for an applet to expose itself as a remotely accessible object.

JDK 1.2   *RemoteStub exportObject(Remote object, int port) throws RemoteException*   This method exports the specified object, `object`, as a remote object listening on the specified port, `port`.

JDK 1.2   *RemoteStub exportObject(Remote object, int port, RMIClientSocketFactory clients, RMIServerSocketFactory servers) throws RemoteException* This method exports the specified object, `object`, as a remote object listening on the specified port, `port`, using the specified custom socket factories, `clients` and `servers` for communications purposes (see section 23.16 on page 532).

JDK 1.2 *boolean unexportObject(Remote object, boolean force) throws NoSuchObjectException* This method unexports the specified remote object, `object` (either a subclass of `UnicastRemoteObject` or an object exported by `exportObject()`), returning `true` if the unexport succeeds. If the object is currently in use (remote method calls are pending or in progress) then this method will fail unless `force` is `true` in which case it is forcibly aborted. After unexporting, the object will no longer be available to accept remote method calls.

23.12 **JDK 1.1** *Class RemoteStub*

`RemoteStub` is the superclass for all remote stub classes. These are the classes that proxy remote calls from one JVM to another. When you run `rmic`, the stub file that is produced is a subclass of `RemoteStub`. It implements the same remote interfaces as the original remote class, but proxies all of the remote methods into remote method calls on the actual remote object implementation (by connecting to and communicating with the skeleton). When you look up a remote reference in a naming registry, you actually receive an instance of *this* stub class.

By itself, the `RemoteStub` class provides no methods of particular use.

23.13 **JDK 1.1** *Interface Unreferenced*

The `Unreferenced` interface is useful for remote objects that wish to be notified whenever there exist no further remote references back to them.

To implement remote garbage collection, the RMI framework automatically maintains a count of the number of references that exist to each remote object. The `Unreferenced` interface is a means for user code to interface with this garbage collection mechanism.

23.13.1 Methods
Just one method is defined:

void unreferenced() This method will be called on a remote object that implements this interface, whenever the remote reference counter drops to zero. Note that this reference count is independent of your local reference count; that is, whether there are still local references to your object. This mechanism is usually used for manually deactivating objects when they fall out of remote use.

To use this callback mechanism, your remote object should simply implement the `Unreferenced` interface and the `unreferenced()` method. Then it will be automatically notified when there is no more remote interest in it. Note that an entry in a naming registry is simply a remote reference to the registered object, so as long as your object is stored in a naming registry, it will never be unreferenced.

The distributed garbage collection relies on remote references periodically notifying a remote object that they are still active. The period of this notification is quite large (by default, 10 minutes) so you should not rely on being punctually notified of a lack of remote references.

23.14 [JDK 1.1] *Class RMISocketFactory*

This class, from the `java.rmi.server` package, is a factory for creating the various network connections that are required during RMI operations. This class is important because it allows you to install custom socket-handling facilities for your RMI applications. However, for most situations, unless security is required, the default socket factory is sufficiently powerful; it transparently attempts three different types of network connection (figure 23.12). Where a capability such as data security is required, then the JDK 1.2 per-object custom socket factories, described later in this chapter, are usually a superior choice to this class.

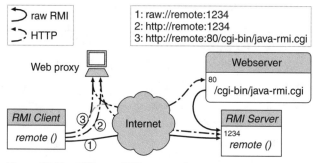

Figure 23.12 Different RMI connection attempts

23.14.1 *RMI data proxying*

When the RMI framework wishes to connect to a remote object, it first attempts to create a direct TCP `Socket` connection to the object. From behind a firewall, such a connection may be disallowed.

If this fails, an HTTP connection is attempted directly to the port on which the remote object is listening. Remote objects provide built-in support for both direct data transfer and HTTP-packaged data transfer. Thus, the RMI framework will connect to the local Web proxy, if configured, and ask it to proxy an HTTP request directly to the remote object. It will make the following proxy request:

```
POST http://server:rmiObjectPort/data ...
```

This request will go from the RMI framework to the local Web proxy, which should connect directly to the remote object.

Finally, if the corporate firewall or Web proxy only allows traffic to port 80 of remote sites, a connection will be attempted to a CGI program on the remote Web server that in turn proxies the request directly to the remote object. In this case, the RMI framework will attempt the following request:

```
POST http://server:80/cgi-bin/java-rmi.cgi/data ...
```

This request will either go directly to the remote Web server if the firewall allows traffic on port 80, or it will go from the RMI framework to the local Web proxy to the remote Web server, to the RMI CGI program, and from there to the actual remote object. This proxying CGI program is included in the bin directory of the standard JDK distribution.

23.14.2 Static methods

The following methods are provided to install global RMI socket-related services:

void setSocketFactory(RMISocketFactory factory) throws IOException   This method installs a new socket factory. This class will be responsible for creating all future RMI sockets in this JVM. If no factory is installed, the default three-tier implementation is used.

You can only install a socket factory once, so this method will raise an `IOException` if a factory is already defined. This method is also controlled by the current `SecurityManager`; untrusted code cannot register a socket factory (a `SecurityException` will be raised).

RMISocketFactory getSocketFactory()   This method returns the current custom socket factory, if any, or else `null`.

RMISocketFactory getDefaultSocketFactory()   This method returns the default three-tier RMI socket factory.

void setFailureHandler(RMIFailureHandler failureHandler)   This   method installs an RMI failure handler. The failure handler is called if there is a problem creating an RMI socket; it then has an opportunity to put right the problem before RMI tries again.

RMIFailureHandler getFailureHandler()   This method returns the current custom failure handler, if any, or else `null`.

23.14.3 Methods

These methods must be implemented by a custom RMI socket factory. An instance of the custom class should be registered through the `setSocketFactory()` method.

abstract Socket createSocket(String host, int port) throws IOException This method should return a new `Socket` connected to the specified host, `host`, and port, `port`. Any exceptions that arise may be passed on or, if you wish to support different connection attempts, may be processed internally.

abstract ServerSocket createServerSocket(int port) throws IOException This method should return a new `ServerSocket` that listens on the specified port, `port`. Exceptions can be processed as before; however, it is unlikely that a recovery could be enacted.

23.15 ⬤ JDK 1.1 *Interface RMIFailureHandler*

This interface describes an RMI failure handler. This is a class that attempts to resolve the cause of an RMI socket exception and correct it. If resolution is successful, the RMI framework can reattempt its initial connection attempt.

23.15.1 Methods
Just one method is declared:

boolean failure(Exception ex) This method is called with the exception that arose when the RMI socket attempt failed. An implementation should attempt to address the problem and return `true` if RMI should retry its original socket operation.

Opportunity for a repair attempt completely depends on the RMI framework. It might, for example, be possible to connect to the server by another mechanism and resurrect a dead RMI service if that is the problem.

23.16 ⬤ JDK 1.2 *Interface RMIClientSocketFactory*

This interface describes a client-side socket factory; this is used to implement a per-object custom socket factory.

23.16.1 Per-object custom socket factories
Using the JDK 1.2 constructors and methods of `UnicastRemoteObject` and `LocateRegistry`, remote objects can be created that use per-object custom socket factories for the purposes of communication. A typical customization would be the use of SSL or a similar protocol to encrypt and authenticate the RMI data transfer.

These per-object custom socket factories are usually preferable to the global `RMISocketFactory` class because they allow a homogenous mix of socket factories within an application and naming registry. This compares favorably with a global socket factory where communication among different socket-factory implementations is extremely difficult. Per-object socket factories always take precedence over a global socket factory, if one is installed.

When a remote reference to an object is passed across an RMI call, for example, when a server registers itself in a naming registry or when a client obtains a remote reference from a naming registry, then an instance of the object's custom `RMIClientSocketFactory`, if any, is included in the remote reference data. When the recipient of the remote reference subsequently invokes a method on the remote object, it will use this socket factory to establish a network connection over which the RMI data will be transferred. The remote object itself will use a custom `RMIServerSocketFactory` to accept incoming connections; when the two custom factories establish a connection, they can perform an authentication handshake or implement a security protocol to secure the RMI data transfer.

Note that the custom `RMIClientSocketFactory` will be serialized across an RMI connection when a remote reference is transfered. It must thus be serializable, should obey the rules of serialization and should use the object stream customization capabilities to perform any necessary setup upon deserialization, such as loading in trusted digital certificates, and so forth.

23.16.2 Methods
Just one method is declared:

Socket createSocket(String host, int port) throws IOException This method should return a new `Socket` connected to the specified host, `host`, and port, `port`. Typically, a custom socket factory will either perform some initial handshaking across the `Socket`, or else will return a `Socket` subclass that implements, for example, SSL security.

23.17 JDK 1.2 Interface RMIServerSocketFactory

This interface describes a server-side socket factory; this is used to implement a per-object custom socket factory.

23.17.1 Methods
Just one method is declared:

ServerSocket createServerSocket(int port) throws IOException This method should return a new `ServerSocket` listening on the specified port, `port`, which may be 0 for an anonymous port. Typically, a custom socket factory will return a `ServerSocket` subclass that either performs some initial handshaking across the `Socket`s that it accepts, or else that uses a `Socket` subclass that implements, for example, SSL security.

23.18 RMI Object Activation

JDK 1.2 introduced a new capability to RMI called *object activation*. Using this capability, remote object implementations need not be permanently active on a server. Instead, an *activation daemon* (rmid) permanently executes on the server. Remote object implementations are registered with this daemon instead of being manually executed. When a remote client invokes a method on an inactive object, the daemon will activate it automatically so it can service the remote method call. Subsequently, the daemon can deactivate the object to free the resources that it is using.

Support for activation is provided by the package `java.rmi.activation`. Of particular interest is the `Activatable` class which mimics the function of `Unicast-RemoteObject` for activatable objects. Full details of this capability are beyond the scope of this book; the interested reader is directed to JavaSoft's JDK 1.2 RMI documentation which includes an activation tutorial.

23.19 Wrapping up

The RMI framework is quite extensive, providing many advanced features for distributed computing. So far, we have been primarily concerned with introducing RMI and demonstrating the scope of its API. For most normal situations, however, you will directly encounter few of the many classes that we have been examining. In the following chapter, we will look at applying the basic techniques to some practical examples to show how they can be used for moderately complex applications.

C H A P T E R   2 4

RMI in practice

After extensive discussions of the RMI API in the previous chapter, we will now look at various practical RMI applications.

We will start with two implementations of a chat system. The first uses a single central server which clients poll to send messages and to receive updates; the second also exposes the clients as RMI objects so that the server can call them back with updates. Following the chat system examples, we will look at an implementation of a distributed list using pure RMI; this example is intended to compare RMI with a socket-based implementation from chapter 18 and a servlet-based implementation that we will look at in chapter 27. Finally, we will discuss the applicability of RMI to pure peer-to-peer distributed computing; this discussion is accompanied by a simple peering example.

24.1 An RMI chat system

In this example, we will look at the implementation of a simple, RMI-based, pure client/server chat system.

The chat server, implemented by the RMIChatServerImpl class, is a remote object that maintains an internal list of all client messages ever sent. It exposes a remote interface, RMIChatServer, through which clients can add new messages and can query the current list of messages (figure 24.1).

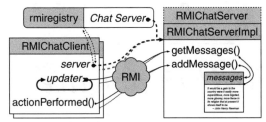

Figure 24.1   A client/server RMI chat system

The client, RMIChatClient, is a simple application; it sends messages to the server in the obvious manner, and includes an update thread that periodically queries the server for an up-to-date copy of the chat session.

24.1.1 Interface RMIChatServer

This is the chat server's remote interface. It defines the API through which the client can access the server:

```
import java.rmi.*;

public interface RMIChatServer extends Remote {
  public static final String REGISTRY_NAME = "Chat Server";
  public abstract String[] getMessages (int index) throws RemoteException;
  public abstract void addMessage (String message) throws RemoteException;
}
```

Our interface extends Remote, as must all remote interfaces. We define two methods: The getMessages() method gets all messages in the current chat session from a specified index onwards, and the `addMessage()` method adds a `String` to the session. We also declare a constant, `REGISTRY_NAME`, that is the name under which our chat server will be registered in a naming registry.

All of our methods declare that they can throw exceptions of type `RemoteException`. Although the server will not usually raise these exceptions, the client may encounter them when attempting a remote method invocation on the server.

24.1.2 Class RMIChatServerImpl

This class is the chat server implementation. We provide an implementation of the remote interface, and provide code that instantiates the server and registers it in a naming registry.

```
import java.rmi.*;
import java.rmi.server.*;
import java.rmi.registry.*;
import java.util.*;

public class RMIChatServerImpl extends UnicastRemoteObject
        implements RMIChatServer {
  // public RMIChatServerImpl () throws RemoteException ...
  // public String[] getMessages (int index) ...
  // public void addMessage (String message) ...
  // public static void main (String[] args) throws RemoteException ...
}
```

Our server extends `UnicastRemoteObject` and implements `RMIChatServer`. Extending `UnicastRemoteObject` is the simplest way to take advantage of the normal RMI facilities.

We declare a constructor that passes on any exceptions which may arise in the superclass, provide implementations of the remote interface methods, and finally, provide a `main()` method that takes care of starting and registering the chat server for remote access.

```
  protected Vector messages;

  public RMIChatServerImpl () throws RemoteException {
    messages = new Vector ();
  }
```

Our constructor does nothing but create the `Vector` in which we will store the chat session, and pass on any exceptions that may arise during the superclass initialization process.

```
  public String[] getMessages (int index) {
    int size = messages.size ();
    String[] update = new String[size - index];
```

```
    for (int i = 0; i < size - index; ++ i)
      update[i] = (String) messages.elementAt (index + i);
    return update;
  }
```

This method returns an array containing all new messages in this session, from a specified index forward. We determine the current size of the chat session, create an array large enough to hold these changes, then copy the new part of the chat session into this array. If a client calls this method with an invalid value of index, resulting in a RuntimeException in this code, this exception will be automatically handed back to the client, just as if it were calling this method locally.

Note that this method is inherently threadsafe. The Vector will never shrink; so even if messages are added while this method is being executed, the chat system will remain wholly integral. If the messages Vector was automatically shrunk, or we had some more complex processing going on, we might wish to add synchronization to this method. Note that we would add synchronization at the server, and *not* at the client: Client-side synchronization is a purely local process and will have no effect on the server or other clients.

```
  public void addMessage (String message) {
    messages.addElement (message);
  }
```

This method adds the specified message message to our internal Vector.

Again, this method is inherently threadsafe. The Vector class performs internal synchronization to protect against concurrent accesses. It is, of course, vital that any remote object that you write is completely threadsafe; it is possible that many clients may be making remote method invocations on a single remote object concurrently. The exact details of concurrent access are an issue of the RMI implementation; however, you should never assume that accesses will be automatically sequential.

```
  public static void main (String[] args) throws RemoteException {
    RMIChatServerImpl chatServer = new RMIChatServerImpl ();
    Registry registry = LocateRegistry.getRegistry ();
    registry.rebind (REGISTRY_NAME, chatServer);
  }
```

Our main() method creates an instance of the chat server implementation. The constructor automatically exposes our server for remote access. We then register our server in the local naming registry under the name Chat Server. We use the LocateRegistry class to access the naming registry; alternatively we could use the Naming class and its URL syntax.

To build this chat server, you must compile it as normal, and then build the stub and skeleton classes by typing `rmic -d . RMIChatServerImpl`. Finally, to start the server, you must start a naming registry with the command `rmiregistry` and then start the server with `java RMIChatServerImpl`.

24.1.3 Class RMIChatClient

This class is our chat client. We open a typical chat `Frame`, locate the chat server, and proceed to remotely access it. To receive updates from the server, we use a thread that regularly queries the server for any new messages by calling its `getMessages()` method.

```java
import java.awt.*;
import java.awt.event.*;
import java.rmi.*;
import java.rmi.registry.*;

public class RMIChatClient implements Runnable, ActionListener {
  protected static final int UPDATE_DELAY = 10000;
  // public RMIChatClient (String host) ...
  // public synchronized void start ()
      throws RemoteException, NotBoundException ...
  // public synchronized void stop () ...
  // public void run () ...
  // public void actionPerformed (ActionEvent ev) ...
  // public static void main (String[] args)
      throws RemoteException, NotBoundException ...
}
```

`RMIChatClient` is a typical chat client class. We implement `Runnable` in order to use an active update thread, and implement the `ActionListener` interface so we can receive user-interface events from the input box. We also define a constant `UPDATE_-DELAY` that defines how often we will query the server for an update.

The `start()` and `stop()` methods control the client—connecting to the server, starting a thread and opening the `Frame` to begin, and closing the `Frame` and stopping the thread to finish. The `run()` method is executed by the update thread to periodically query the server for new messages, and `actionPerformed()` is called in response to user input. The `main()` method allows this client to be executed as a standalone application.

```java
  protected String host;
  protected Frame frame;
  protected TextField input;
  protected TextArea output;

  public RMIChatClient (String host) {
    this.host = host;

    frame = new Frame ("RMIChatClient [" + host + "]");
```

```
    frame.add (output = new TextArea (), "Center");
    output.setEditable (false);
    frame.add (input = new TextField (), "South");
    input.addActionListener (this);
    frame.addWindowListener (new WindowAdapter () {
      public void windowOpened (WindowEvent ev) {
        input.requestFocus ();
      }
      public void windowClosing (WindowEvent ev) {
        stop ();
      }
    });
    frame.pack ();
  }
```

The server on which the naming registry is running is specified in the constructor call. We store this in the variable host and perform the basic user-interface setup. We defer any RMI setup until the start() method.

We create a Frame frame with an input TextField input and an output Text-Area output. We register to receive action events from the input field, and register an anonymous class that automatically handles our various window events; it acquires the input focus when the Frame is opened and calls stop() when the user closes the Frame. Finally, we pack() the Frame and return.

```
  protected RMIChatServer server;
  protected Thread updater;

  public synchronized void start ()
      throws RemoteException, NotBoundException {
    if (updater == null) {
      Registry registry = LocateRegistry.getRegistry (host);
      server = (RMIChatServer) registry.lookup (RMIChatServer.REGISTRY_NAME);
      updater = new Thread (this);
      updater.start ();
      frame.setVisible (true);
    }
  }
```

The start() method actually starts the chat client. We locate the chat server in the naming registry specified in the constructor; it is registered under the name Chat Server. If either a naming registry could not be contacted on the server, or no chat server was registered, an appropriate exception will be thrown and we will exit.

Otherwise, we start a Thread that periodically queries the server for the latest message list, and display the Frame.

```
  public synchronized void stop () {
    if (updater != null) {
      updater.interrupt ();
```

```
      updater = null;
      server = null;
    }
    frame.setVisible (false);
  }
```

The stop() method closes down the client. All we need to do is hide the Frame and stop the update thread; there is no user-level networking code with which to be concerned. We do, however, assign our server reference to null to allow the remote reference to be garbage collected.

Note that to stop our thread, we do not call its stop() method. We simply assign our reference to null and call interrupt() to wake the thread if it is blocked, for example in a sleep() call.

```
public void run () {
  try {
    int index = 0;
    while (!Thread.interrupted ()) {
      String[] messages = server.getMessages (index);
      int n = messages.length;
      for (int i = 0; i < n; ++ i)
        output.append (messages[i] + "\n");
      index += n;
      Thread.sleep (UPDATE_DELAY);
    }
  } catch (InterruptedException ignored) {
  } catch (RemoteException ex) {
    input.setVisible (false);
    frame.validate ();
    ex.printStackTrace ();
  }
}
```

This run() method periodically queries the server for new messages. We sit in a loop, while we have not been interrupted, querying the server for a list of its new messages. We maintain an index that is the number of messages that we have received thus far; using this, we can efficiently receive only the messages that have been added since our last update.

Remember that in the stop() method, to notify a thread to exit we called its interrupt() method. Under normal execution, this will not affect the thread. As soon as it enters a blocking thread operation, such as sleep(), it will abort immediately with an InterruptedException. If this happens, we can ignore the exception and exit; we know that we are being stopped. If, on the other hand, we receive a RemoteException, there was an I/O error communicating with the server. So we hide the input box and terminate our loop.

In fact, if we call `interrupt()` on our thread when it is blocked within the RMI framework on a `read()` call, an `InterruptedIOException` may be thrown, which would be translated into a `RemoteException`. This exact behavior depends to an extent on the particular virtual machine in use. To be fully user-friendly, we also should check to see if this is the case and exit cleanly if this is so.

```
public void actionPerformed (ActionEvent ev) {
  try {
    RMIChatServer server = this.server;
    if (server != null)
      server.addMessage (ev.getActionCommand ());
    input.setText ("");
  } catch (RemoteException ex) {
    Thread tmp = updater;
    updater = null;
    if (tmp != null)
      tmp.interrupt ();
    input.setVisible (false);
    frame.validate ();
    ex.printStackTrace ();
  }
}
```

This method is called when the user enters some text. We simply call the server's `addMessage()` method, handling exceptions appropriately: When an exception occurs, we stop the update thread and hide the input box.

```
public static void main (String[] args)
    throws RemoteException, NotBoundException {
  if (args.length != 1)
    throw new IllegalArgumentException ("Syntax: RMIChatClient <host>");
  RMIChatClient chatClient = new RMIChatClient (args[0]);
  chatClient.start ();
}
```

This method starts up the client. We verify that a host name has been specified and then start a new `ChatClient` that connects to the specified naming registry, looks up the registered chat server, and proceeds to chat.

24.1.4 Discussion

An obvious fault with this pure client/server chat system is the periodic update. During idle periods, this is a waste of resources, and during active periods, it is too irregular. A simple improvement would be to slowly increase the delay during periods of inactivity, and decrease it when messages are transmitted or received. However, even this is not ideal.

An alternate solution, one that is better in some respects and worse in others, is to use a callback mechanism so that the server actively informs clients of new messages. In this manner, network traffic will only occur when messages are actually being sent. We will examine this solution next.

24.2 An RMI chat with callback

In this example, we show a similar chat system using callback to notify clients of updates. We will end up with two remote object classes: The server will be much as before but with a client-registration system, and the client will now be a remote object that exposes an interface through which it can be informed of new messages (figure 24.2).

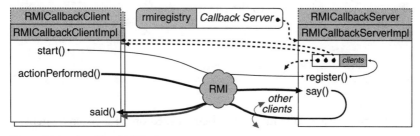

Figure 24.2   A callback RMI chat system

Some of the advantages of using callback to inform clients of new messages are obvious: The server will notify clients as soon as new messages appear, and the server will only notify clients *when* new messages appear. Disadvantages are that the server must maintain a list of current clients (in the previous example, the server has no idea how many clients are active), and that clients must expose themselves for remote access (which may break some security restrictions).

RMICallbackServer is the server's remote interface; in addition to a method for adding a chat message, it includes registration methods for new clients. RMICallback-ServerImpl is the actual implementation of this, and is thus the server itself. RMICall-backClient is the client's remote interface; it simply exposes a method that allows the server to notify the client of new messages. RMICallbackClientImpl actually implements this interface and provides the basic user interface of before.

24.2.1 Interface RMICallbackServer
This interface defines the remote interface to the server:

```
import java.rmi.*;

public interface RMICallbackServer extends Remote {
    public static final String REGISTRY_NAME = "Callback Server";
```

```
  public abstract void register (RMICallbackClient client)
    throws RemoteException;
  public abstract void deregister (RMICallbackClient client)
    throws RemoteException;
  public abstract void say (String message) throws RemoteException;
}
```

The register() and deregister() methods allow clients to register and deregister from receiving messages from the server. Note that the parameter to these methods is the client's remote interface, and not the client's actual implementation class.

The say() method allows clients to send messages; each transmitted message is automatically relayed to all registered clients, including the caller.

24.2.2 Interface RMICallbackClient
This interface defines the remote interface to the client:

```
import java.rmi.*;

public interface RMICallbackClient extends Remote {
  public abstract void said (String message) throws RemoteException;
}
```

Calling say() on the server results in said() being called on all registered clients, indicating the new message to be displayed.

24.2.3 Class RMICallbackServerImpl
This class is the chat server implementation. As before, we provide an implementation of the remote interface and code that instantiates the server and registers it in a naming registry.

```
import java.rmi.*;
import java.rmi.server.*;
import java.rmi.registry.*;
import java.util.*;

public class RMICallbackServerImpl extends UnicastRemoteObject
      implements RMICallbackServer {
  // public RMICallbackServerImpl () throws RemoteException ...
  // public void register (RMICallbackClient client) ...
  // public void deregister (RMICallbackClient client) ...
  // public void say (String message) ...
  // public static void main (String[] args) throws RemoteException ...
}
```

Our server extends UnicastRemoteObject and implements the RMICallback-Server remote interface. As before, we also provide a main() method to start up the server.

```
protected Vector clients;

public RMICallbackServerImpl () throws RemoteException {
  clients = new Vector ();
}
```

Our constructor does nothing but create a new `Vector` to store registered clients and expose the exceptions that may arise during the superclass initialization process.

```
public void register (RMICallbackClient client) {
  try {
    say (getClientHost () + " has joined.");
  } catch (ServerNotActiveException ignored) {
  }
  clients.addElement (client);
}
```

This method registers a new client for receiving messages to this server. We first broadcast a message to all currently registered clients, indicating that a new client has joined; we use the inherited `getClientHost()` method to obtain the client's host name, ignoring `ServerNotActiveException`; this exception will only arise if the `register()` method is executed locally. Then we add the client to the `clients` `Vector`.

```
public void deregister (RMICallbackClient client) {
  clients.removeElement (client);
  try {
    say (getClientHost () + " has left.");
  } catch (ServerNotActiveException ignored) {
  }
}
```

This method removes a client from the `clients` `Vector` and broadcasts an appropriate message to all registered clients. The `RemoteObject` superclass correctly implements the `equals()` method so the `removeElement()` method will operate as expected.

```
public void say (String message) {
  Vector clients = (Vector) this.clients.clone ();
  for (int i = 0; i < clients.size (); ++ i) {
    RMICallbackClient client = (RMICallbackClient) clients.elementAt (i);
    try {
      client.said (message);
    } catch (RemoteException ex) {
      this.clients.removeElement (client);
    }
  }
}
```

This method is called by remote clients when they wish to broadcast a new message through this server. For threadsafety, we obtain a clone of the current `clients` `Vector`. We then iterate through this, calling the `said()` remote method on each registered client. If we encounter a `RemoteException` we simply remove the offending client from `clients`.

Note that we do not guarantee ordering of messages. If two clients call the `say()` method concurrently, the relative ordering of messages broadcast to different clients is not guaranteed. If we wanted to ensure this, we would have to synchronize this entire method.

```
public static void main (String[] args) throws RemoteException {
    RMICallbackServerImpl callbackServer = new RMICallbackServerImpl ();
    Registry registry = LocateRegistry.getRegistry ();
    registry.rebind (REGISTRY_NAME, callbackServer);
}
```

Our `main()` method creates an instance of the callback server implementation. The constructor automatically exposes it for remote access, and registers it in a local naming registry under the name Callback Server.

To build this server, you must compile it as normal, and then build the stub and skeleton classes by typing `rmic -d . RMICallbackServerImpl`. To start the server, you must start a naming registry with the command `rmiregistry` and then the server with `java RMICallbackServerImpl`.

24.2.4 Class RMICallbackClientImpl

The callback chat client is similar to the earlier client in terms of the user interface code and basic RMI setup. However, unlike before, we do not have an active listener thread. Instead, this client is itself a remote object that the server will call whenever a new message is added.

Of course, in reality there is still an active thread in this example. Within the RMI framework, a thread listens on a `ServerSocket` for incoming connections. Whenever the server calls us back, this thread receives a `Socket` connection and processes the method call appropriately. All of these details are, however, hidden from us.

```
import java.awt.*;
import java.awt.event.*;
import java.rmi.*;
import java.rmi.server.*;
import java.rmi.registry.*;

public class RMICallbackClientImpl extends UnicastRemoteObject
        implements RMICallbackClient, ActionListener {
  // public RMICallbackClientImpl (String host) throws RemoteException ...
  // public synchronized void start ()
```

```
        throws RemoteException, NotBoundException ...
// public synchronized void stop () throws RemoteException ...
// public void said (String message) ...
// public void actionPerformed (ActionEvent ev) ...
// public static void main (String[] args)
        throws RemoteException, NotBoundException ...
}
```

As a remote object, our `RMICallbackClientImpl` class extends `UnicastRemote-Object` and implements the remote interfaces that we wish to expose; in this case, `RMI-CallbackClient`.

The methods that we declare are much the same as the `RMIChatClientImpl` class. However instead of implementing `Runnable` and providing a `run()` method, we implement the `said()` method from our remote interface, and simply wait for the server to call us back whenever a message is added.

```
protected String host;
protected Frame frame;
protected TextField input;
protected TextArea output;

public RMICallbackClientImpl (String host) throws RemoteException {
  this.host = host;
  frame = new Frame ("RMICallbackClientImpl [" + host + "]");
  frame.add (output = new TextArea (), "Center");
  output.setEditable (false);
  frame.add (input = new TextField (), "South");
  input.addActionListener (this);
  frame.addWindowListener (new WindowAdapter () {
    public void windowOpened (WindowEvent ev) {
      input.requestFocus ();
    }
    public void windowClosing (WindowEvent ev) {
      try {
        stop ();
      } catch (RemoteException ex) {
        ex.printStackTrace ();
      }
    }
  });
  frame.pack ();
}
```

The server on which the naming registry is running is specified in the constructor; we store this in the variable `host` and perform the basic user-interface setup. We defer any RMI setup other than that performed by the superconstructor until the `start()` method. Use of the `UnicastRemoteObject` method `exportObject()` would allow us to defer even this part of the RMI setup to `start()`. An example of the use of this method is provided in our next example of an RMI distributed list.

```
protected RMICallbackServer server;

public synchronized void start ()
    throws RemoteException, NotBoundException {
  if (server == null) {
    Registry registry = LocateRegistry.getRegistry (host);
    server = (RMICallbackServer) registry.lookup
      (RMICallbackServer.REGISTRY_NAME);
    server.register (this);
    frame.setVisible (true);
  }
}
```

The start() method actually starts this client. First we locate the server in the naming registry specified in the constructor; it is registered under the name Callback Server. Then we register ourselves with the server and display the Frame. Note that when we pass this to the register() method, our self-reference is automatically translated by the RMI framework into a remote reference back to this client. This behavior is unique to passing remote objects as parameters to remote method calls; if we passed a nonremote object, the server would receive a copy of it, as per the normal RMI call-by-value semantics.

Also, note that we don't need to register our client in a naming registry. We need only register a remote object in a naming registry if we wish it to be publicly findable, as we do the central server. If, as is the case here, a remote object will only be made accessible by manually handing out a reference to it, we can simply use code of this form.

```
public synchronized void stop () throws RemoteException {
  frame.setVisible (false);
  RMICallbackServer server = this.server;
  this.server = null;
  if (server != null)
    server.deregister (this);
}
```

The stop() method closes down the client. We hide the Frame, and then deregister with the server. The RMI framework will eventually realize that there are no longer any remote references to our client and allow it to be garbage collected.

```
public void said (String message) {
  output.append (message + "\n");
}
```

The said() method appends the specified message from the server to our display.

```
public void actionPerformed (ActionEvent ev) {
  try {
    RMICallbackServer server = this.server;
```

```
      if (server != null) {
        server.say (ev.getActionCommand ());
        input.setText ("");
      }
    } catch (RemoteException ex) {
      input.setVisible (false);
      frame.validate ();
      ex.printStackTrace ();
    }
  }
```

This method is called when the user enters some text. We call the server's `addMessage()` method, hiding the input box if an exception occurs. Presuming a network problem, we can't manually deregister with the server.

```
public static void main (String[] args)
    throws RemoteException, NotBoundException {
  if (args.length != 1)
    throw new IllegalArgumentException
      ("Syntax: RMICallbackClientImpl <host>");
  RMICallbackClientImpl callbackClient =
    new RMICallbackClientImpl (args[0]);
  callbackClient.start ();
}
```

This method starts up the client. We verify that a host name has been specified and then start a new `CallbackClientImpl` that connects to the specified naming registry, looks up the registered server, registers, and proceeds to chat.

24.2.5 Discussion

A problem with this implementation is that there is a fairly substantial overhead involved in every remote method call. Even though RMI includes a call aggregation facility, where multiple remote method invocations may take place across a single network connection, this server will suffer from network overhead: For every chat client, two network connections will have to be maintained; one incoming and one outgoing. Furthermore, these connections will time-out and will have to be periodically reestablished. All of this will amount to impaired performance—for this task of real-time collaboration —with respect to a pure-socket implementation.

In this particular situation, we can ease this problem slightly by caching update messages and only calling clients back periodically with a sequence of new messages. The server could use a broadcast thread that continually runs, blocking until new messages arrive, possibly waiting a minimum delay, and then transmitting all pending messages. Unlike the current system where it is possible that multiple clients could be broadcasting concurrently, this would mean that there will only ever be one thread broadcasting. If new messages arrive mid-broadcast, these will be sent during the next loop.

24.3 An RMI distributed list

As an example of a more complex RMI application, we will now revisit the distributed list that we introduced in chapter 18. This time, however, we will implement the distributed list using RMI with server callback.

It is probably a good idea to glance back at the socket-based distributed-list implementation from chapter 18 before perusing this version, as the two implementations are remarkably similar. In the socket-based version, client updates to the list are transmitted to the server as messages encapsulated by the object streams. The server responds similarly, with messages encapsulated by the object streams. Both the client and server internally use an `IDList` to maintain copies of the current list state.

In this RMI-based implementation, we will follow exactly the same methodology: The client and server maintain the list state in local `IDList` objects. When an update is attempted to a client list, the list makes a remote method invocation on the central server. If the central server approves the change, it responds by making remote method calls back on all registered clients indicating the change. We have basically replaced the object-stream messages from before with remote method calls (figure 24.3).

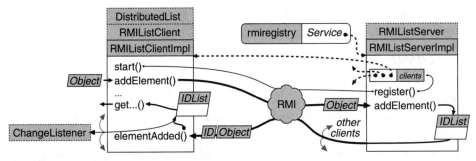

Figure 24.3   An RMI-based distributed list

Four classes comprise this framework. `RMIListServer` is the remote interface describing the central server; when a client requests a change, it will access the server through this interface. `RMIListClient` is the remote interface describing the client lists; when the server calls back clients to indicate that a change has occurred, it will access them through this interface. `RMIListServerImpl` is an implementation of the central server. `RMIListClientImpl` is an implementation of the client; this class implements `DistributedList` and is the basic client-side interface to an RMI-based distributed list.

24.3.1 Interface RMIListServer

This interface describes the remote API for clients to access the central RMI-based list server.

```
import java.rmi.*;

public interface RMIListServer extends Remote {
  public abstract IDList register (RMIListClient client)
    throws RemoteException;
  public abstract void deregister (RMIListClient client)
    throws RemoteException;
  public abstract void addElement (Object element) throws RemoteException;
  public abstract void updateElement (ID id, Object newElement)
    throws RemoteException;
  public abstract void replaceElement (ID id, Object newElement)
    throws RemoteException;
  public abstract void removeElement (ID id) throws RemoteException;
}
```

Our remote interface defines the interface through which the client will access our server. The `register()` and `deregister()` methods allow a client to register and deregister with the server. An initial copy of the central list is returned when a client first registers.

We define four methods that allow a client to manipulate the central list. If a client requests a change and the request is approved, then this will eventually be reflected by the server calling all clients back with the results of the request.

24.3.2 Interface RMIListClient

This interface describes the remote API for the server to make calls back to RMI-based list clients.

```
import java.rmi.*;

public interface RMIListClient extends Remote {
  public abstract void elementAdded (ID id, Object element)
    throws RemoteException;
  public abstract void elementUpdated (ID oldID, ID id, Object element)
    throws RemoteException;
  public abstract void elementReplaced (ID oldID, ID id, Object element)
    throws RemoteException;
  public abstract void elementRemoved (ID id) throws RemoteException;
}
```

The four methods that we declare correspond to the server making a callback in response to each of the four client update requests.

24.3.3 Class RMIListServerImpl

This class implements the server side of our distributed list. It is a remote object that provides central coordination of the distributed list structure and supports registration of remote clients that are notified whenever the structure changes. Changes are made to the central data structure through the standard methods defined by the RMIListServer remote interface.

```
import java.rmi.*;
import java.rmi.server.*;
import java.rmi.registry.*;
import java.util.*;

public class RMIListServerImpl extends UnicastRemoteObject
    implements RMIListServer {
  // public RMIListServerImpl () throws RemoteException ...
  // public synchronized IDList register (RMIListClient client) ...
  // public synchronized void deregister (RMIListClient client) ...
  // public synchronized void addElement (Object element) ...
  // public synchronized void updateElement (ID id, Object element) ...
  // public synchronized void replaceElement (ID id, Object element) ...
  // public synchronized void removeElement (ID id) ...
  // public static void main (String[] args)
      throws RemoteException, AlreadyBoundException ...
}
```

Our class extends UnicastRemoteObject as a standard remote object and implements RMIListServer and all of the methods thereof. We provide a constructor that exposes exceptions from the superconstructor and a main() method that creates an instance of this class starts a naming registry and exposes the distributed list therein.

```
protected IDList idList;
protected Vector clients;

public RMIListServerImpl () throws RemoteException {
  idList = new IDList ();
  clients = new Vector ();
}
```

In the constructor, we create the IDList idList that is a central copy of the distributed list state, and a Vector clients that stores all currently registered remote clients.

The IDList is our simple nondistributed list implementation from chapter 18. This class associates an identifier with every element of the list; these identifiers allow global clients to uniquely and coherently identify elements, in the presence of potentially concurrent and disconnected changes.

```
public synchronized IDList register (RMIListClient client) {
```

```
    clients.addElement (client);
    return idList;
  }
```

When a client registers with the central server, it presents a remote reference back to itself. This reference is stored in the clients Vector, and a copy of the current central list is returned.

```
public synchronized void deregister (RMIListClient client) {
  clients.removeElement (client);
}
```

To deregister a client, we simply remove it from clients.

```
public synchronized void addElement (Object element) {
  ID id = idList.allocateID ();
  if (idList.addElement (id, element)) {
    for (int i = 0; i < clients.size (); ++ i) {
      try {
        ((RMIListClient) clients.elementAt (i))
          .elementAdded (id, element);
      } catch (RemoteException ex) {
        clients.removeElementAt (i --);
      }
    }
  }
}
```

This method adds an element to the central list. We allocate it a new identifier id and then attempt to add this to idList. If this succeeds we broadcast the result back to all registered clients. If not, we ignore the request. If an exception occurs while talking to a client, we simply remove the client from clients.

Note that this entire method is synchronized. Unlike the earlier callback chat system, we must guarantee that all access to the central list is serialized so that the global state remains coherent.

```
public synchronized void updateElement (ID id, Object element) {
  ID newID = idList.allocateID ();
  if (idList.updateElement (id, newID, element)) {
    for (int i = 0; i < clients.size (); ++ i) {
      try {
        ((RMIListClient) clients.elementAt (i))
          .elementUpdated (id, newID, element);
      } catch (RemoteException ex) {
        clients.removeElementAt (i --);
      }
    }
  }
}
```

This method updates an element in-place in `idList`, using exactly the same mechanism as the previous method. If the element has already been removed, the `IDList` `updateElement()` method will return `false`, and we can return without doing anything.

```
public synchronized void replaceElement (ID id, Object element) {
  ID newID = idList.allocateID ();
  if (idList.replaceElement (id, newID, element)) {
    for (int i = 0; i < clients.size (); ++ i) {
      try {
        ((RMIListClient) clients.elementAt (i))
          .elementReplaced (id, newID, element);
      } catch (RemoteException ex) {
        clients.removeElementAt (i --);
      }
    }
  }
}
```

This method replaces an element in `idList` with the specified replacement element.

```
public synchronized void removeElement (ID id) {
  if (idList.removeElement (id)) {
    for (int i = 0; i < clients.size (); ++ i) {
      try {
        ((RMIListClient) clients.elementAt (i))
          .elementRemoved (id);
      } catch (RemoteException ex) {
        clients.removeElementAt (i --);
      }
    }
  }
}
```

This method removes the specified element from this list.

```
public static void main (String[] args)
    throws RemoteException, AlreadyBoundException {
  if (args.length != 2)
    throw new IllegalArgumentException
      ("Syntax: RMIListServerImpl <port> <service>");
  RMIListServerImpl listServer = new RMIListServerImpl ();
  Registry registry = LocateRegistry.createRegistry
    (Integer.parseInt (args[0]));
  registry.bind (args[1], listServer);
}
```

Finally, our `main()` method starts a naming registry using the `createRegistry()` method of `LocateRegistry` and registers an instance of the `RMIListServerImpl` class therein under the specified service name.

Unlike before, you do not have to start a naming registry before you execute this class; it automatically creates its own registry running on a specified port. It is usually recommended that you automatically start a naming registry in this manner, running on a custom port, whenever you are building a complete RMI system. This way you can be assured that the registry will be running and will not be polluted with other objects. Use of a shared naming registry requires adminstration of unique name spaces and distribution of stub files, issues that would unnecessarily complicate matters.

24.3.4 Class RMIListClientImpl

This class is a client-side RMI-based implementation of the `DistributedList` interface, which interacts with an `RMIListServer` to provide an implementation of our distributed list datastructure.

This client internally makes use of a remotely accessible object that implements the `RMIListClient` remote interface in order that the server can call it back whenever a change is made to the central datastructure. Unlike previous examples of remote objects, however, we do not extend `UnicastRemoteObject`. Instead, we use the static `exportObject()` method of the `UnicastRemoteObject` class to export an object that implements a remote interface but is not itself a subclass of `UnicastRemoteObject`. This mechanism is usually used where we want to expose a remote object that must be a subclass of a specific class other than `UnicastRemoteObject`. The most common case is an applet that wishes to be remotely accessible.

```
import java.rmi.*;
import java.rmi.server.*;
import java.rmi.registry.*;
import java.util.*;

public class RMIListClientImpl implements DistributedList {
  // public RMIListClientImpl (String host) ...
  // public synchronized void start ()
      throws RemoteException, NotBoundException ...
  // public synchronized void stop () throws RemoteException ...
  // public synchronized void addElement (Object element) ...
  // public synchronized void updateElement
      (Object oldElement, Object newElement) ...
  // public synchronized void replaceElement
      (Object oldElement, Object newElement) ...
  // public synchronized void removeElement (Object element) ...
  // public Enumeration getElements () ...
  // public void addChangeListener (ChangeListener listener) ...
  // public void removeChangeListener (ChangeListener listener) ...
  class Callback implements RMIListClient{
```

```
// public void elementAdded (ID id, Object element) ...
// public void elementUpdated (ID oldID, ID id, Object element) ...
// public void elementReplaced (ID oldID, ID id, Object element) ...
// public void elementRemoved (ID id) ...
  }
}
```

This class is quite expansive, implementing the `DistributedList` interface, which describes the client interface to our distributed list datastructure, and providing an inner class, `Callback`, that implements the `RMIListClient` remote interface, which describes how the central server will call us back.

We also provide a `start()` method that locates the central server and registers to be notified of changes to the central datastructure, and a `stop()` method that deregisters with the server and disables further updates.

By implementing the `RMIListClient` interface in an inner class, we hide this internal API from public access. This is preferable to simply providing a monolithic class that implements both interfaces.

```
protected String host, service;
protected int port;

public RMIListClientImpl (String host, int port, String service) {
  this.host = host;
  this.port = port;
  this.service = service;
}
```

In the constructor, we store the location of the naming service where the central server is registered, and the name under which it is registered.

```
protected IDList idList;
protected RMIListClient myself;
protected RMIListServer listServer;

public synchronized void start ()
    throws RemoteException, NotBoundException {
  if (listServer == null) {
    myself = (RMIListClient)
      UnicastRemoteObject.exportObject (new Callback ());
    Registry registry = LocateRegistry.getRegistry (host, port);
    listServer = (RMIListServer) registry.lookup (service);
    try {
      idList = listServer.register (myself);
    } catch (RemoteException ex) {
      listServer = null;
      throw ex;
    }
    fireChangeEvent (new ChangeEvent (this));
  }
```

```
}

// protected void fireChangeEvent (ChangeEvent changeEvent) ...
```

The `start()` method begins by exporting our `RMIListClient` implementation as a remotely accessible object. We call the `exportObject()` method of class `UnicastRemoteObject`. The parameter to this method is the object to be exported. The object must implement one or more remote interfaces, and its stub and skeleton classes must have been created with `rmic` as normal. The method then returns a `RemoteStub` that is a remote reference to the object being exported. This `RemoteStub` can be manipulated as any remote reference, such as by passing it as a parameter to a remote method like the `bind()` method of a naming registry. As a remote reference to an `RMIListClient-Impl$Callback`, this `RemoteStub` will actually be an instance of `RMIListClient-Impl$Callback_Stub`, and will implement `RMIListClient`.

In this case, we locate the central list server specified in the constructor and register to be notified of updates to the distributed list datastructure. The `RemoteStub` that we pass is serialized as a remote reference back to this client list, and the result that is returned from this method is an initial copy of the central `IDList` datastructure that we store in the `idList` variable.

```
public synchronized void stop () throws RemoteException {
  try {
    if (listServer != null)
      listServer.deregister (myself);
  } finally {
    listServer = null;
    UnicastRemoteObject.unexportObject (myself, true);
  }
}
```

The `stop()` method deregisters with the central server and assigns the `listServer` reference to `null`, to disable further client updates. We then unexport our callback object, so the RMI run time can free any associated resources.

```
public synchronized void addElement (Object element) {
  if (listServer != null) {
    try {
      listServer.addElement (element);
    } catch (RemoteException ex) {
      listServer = null;
    }
  }
}
```

In the `addElement()` method, we verify that the `listServer` variable is non-null; that is, that we have been started and not stopped. We then call the central server's `addElement()` method to add the new element to our distributed list. If this succeeds the server will eventually call us back to notify us of the change.

If we encounter an exception calling the central server, we assign `listServer` to `null`, to disable further updates. We don't attempt to first deregister, because it is a reasonably safe bet that attempting to do so would produce another exception.

```
public synchronized void updateElement
    (Object oldElement, Object newElement) {
  if (listServer != null) {
    ID id = idList.getID (oldElement);
    if (id != null) {
      try {
        listServer.updateElement (id, newElement);
      } catch (RemoteException ex) {
        listServer = null;
      }
    }
  }
}
```

Our `updateElement()` method performs a similar task. In this case, however, we look up the identifier of the object being updated in our local `idList`. If this is non-`null`, the item is still present locally, so we can attempt to perform the update on the central server. When the server receives this remote method call, then it will check that the identifier is still present in its copy of the datastructure, and if so, will then perform the update and call all the clients back.

```
public synchronized void replaceElement
    (Object oldElement, Object newElement) {
  if (listServer != null) {
    ID id = idList.getID (oldElement);
    if (id != null) {
      try {
        listServer.replaceElement (id, newElement);
      } catch (RemoteException ex) {
        listServer = null;
      }
    }
  }
}
```

The `replaceElement()` method replaces an element in the distributed list datastructure using the same process as before.

```
public synchronized void removeElement (Object element) {
  if (listServer != null) {
    ID id = idList.getID (element);
    if (id != null) {
      try {
```

```
            listServer.removeElement (id);
          } catch (RemoteException ex) {
            listServer = null;
          }
        }
      }
    }
```

The `removeElement()` method removes an element from the distributed list data-structure.

```
public Enumeration getElements () {
  return idList.getElements ();
}
```

This method returns an `Enumeration` of all the elements in this list. We simply call the `getElements()` method of `idList`.

```
protected Vector listeners = new Vector ();

public void addChangeListener (ChangeListener listener) {
  listeners.addElement (listener);
}
```

This method adds a listener for updates to this list.

```
public void removeChangeListener (ChangeListener listener) {
  listeners.removeElement (listener);
}
```

This method removes a listener for updates to this list.

```
protected void fireChangeEvent (ChangeEvent changeEvent) {
  synchronized (listeners) {
    for (int i = 0; i < listeners.size (); ++ i)
      ((ChangeListener) listeners.elementAt (i))
        .changeOccurred (changeEvent);
  }
}
```

This method notifies all registered clients of the specified `ChangeEvent`. We simply loop through `listeners` and call each element's `changeOccurred()` method.

```
public void elementAdded (ID id, Object element) {
  idList.addElement (id, element);
  fireChangeEvent (new ChangeEvent (RMIListClientImpl.this));
}
```

This method, from the `Callback` inner class, will be called by the central server when an element has being added to the central list. The server specifies an identifier for

the element and the element that has been added. We add the element to our local
`IDList` and then call `fireChangeEvent()` to notify all registered listeners of the
change.

We don't need to synchronize this method because the server automatically serializes calls that it makes back to registered clients.

```
public void elementUpdated (ID oldID, ID id, Object element) {
  idList.updateElement (oldID, id, element);
  fireChangeEvent (new ChangeEvent (RMIListClientImpl.this));
}
```

This method will be called by the central server when an element in the central list
has been updated. The server specifies the identifier of the object being updated, as well
as the identifier and element that will replace it.

```
public void elementReplaced (ID oldID, ID id, Object element) {
  idList.replaceElement (oldID, id, element);
  fireChangeEvent (new ChangeEvent (RMIListClientImpl.this));
}
```

This method will be called by the central server when an element in the central list
has been replaced.

```
public void elementRemoved (ID id) {
  idList.removeElement (id);
  fireChangeEvent (new ChangeEvent (RMIListClientImpl.this));
}
```

This method will be called by the central server when an element in the central list
has been removed.

24.3.5 Discussion

A comparison of this implementation of our distributed list with the earlier `Socket`-
based implementation shows few real advantages. Our primary purpose here is to demonstrate a fairly complex application that can be compared with other networking
mechanisms.

One advantage of using RMI is that we don't have to deal with an application-level
protocol. We have simply implemented our entire system using method calls, and RMI
will take care of the network protocol between virtual machines. The TCP/IP protocol
that we used earlier is sufficiently high-level, however, that this benefit is minimal.

In terms of efficiency, this implementation will suffer from potentially having to
establish many TCP/IP connections for every update. Establishing a TCP/IP connection is a costly process. Even though RMI includes a keep-alive mechanism that uses one
network connection for several method calls, this will still be less efficient than using

sockets directly. Furthermore, the reverse network connection—the server calling back to the clients—will be prohibited by many network configurations.

The only possible advantage of this implementation is that it can use RMI's HTTP proxying mechanism to bypass firewalls. As we will see with our later servlet implementation, even this is not a compelling argument as we can use other mechanisms to achieve this same result.

An important lesson here is that the choice of network technology requires careful consideration and depends very much on the particular application being designed. High-bandwidth, collaborative applications are possibly not best served by RMI.

There are, of course, many applications where RMI is clearly a superior choice. Using RMI to establish a network connection between two objects involves simply handing a remote reference into a method call. The extreme ease of establishing RMI connectivity means that complex, dynamic network application topologies can be formed with minimal effort; compare this with having to coordinate sockets and servers among multiple applications. A basic example of this is given in the following implementation of a peering service that allows RMI clients to establish interconnections without the use of a naming registry.

24.4 An RMI peering service

One of the strengths of RMI is that it can be used in pure peer-to-peer applications in addition to the client/server applications that we have looked at thus far. A peer-to-peer architecture is a communication architecture that has no central server. Instead, application clients communicate directly with each other. In this example, we will look at a simple RMI-based peering solution to help establish the initial connections of a peer-to-peer system.

Peer-to-peer architectures have the advantage of eliminating a potential bottleneck at the server and reducing some communication overhead because messages between clients do not have to be relayed through the server. On the downside, however, if there are multiple clients, it can be difficult to maintain coherent global state, efficiently route communications, and handle network breakages. Typically, for such a situation, a dedicated multipoint communications protocol will be used. Obviously, sockets and datagrams also can be used for peer-to-peer applications; however, RMI makes peer-to-peer architectures more accessible. The ability to pass remote references into remote method calls allows complex distributed applications to be constructed with the minimum of effort.

24.4.1 Architecture

A common problem of peer-to-peer applications is how to establish initial connectivity. In the servers that we have looked at thus far, we expose our servers in a central naming registry, and clients can obtain references by looking services up in the naming registry. We can do the same for peer-to-peer applications; however, it is somewhat clumsy having to register in a naming registry. Additionally, the fact that a naming registry can only be modified by a local client means that remote registration in a central location is not possible.

In this simple example, we demonstrate how we can implement a central RMI service that allows clients to obtain peer references and engage in pure peer-to-peer communications (figure 24.4).

Our architecture consists of a `Partner` remote interface that describes how peer-to-peer clients can be interconnected, a `PartnerServer` remote interface that describes a central server for peering cli-

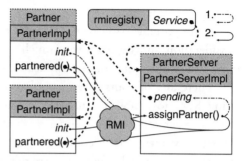

Figure 24.4   An RMI peering framework

ents, and a `PartnerServerImpl` remote object that implements this interface. We also provide a trivial `PartnerImpl` example to demonstrate the architecture.

When a peer-to-peer client wishes to obtain a partner, it locates the central peering server (e.g., a central gaming server) and makes a remote call thereon. If the server has no client waiting to be partnered, it stores a reference to the caller and returns `false`. If the server has a client waiting, it notifies both clients of their newly assigned partner and returns `true`.

24.4.2 Interface PartnerServer
This interface describes the partnering service provided by the central server.

```
import java.rmi.*;

public interface PartnerServer extends Remote {
  public boolean assignPartner (String service, Partner myself)
    throws RemoteException;
}
```

Clients can call the `assignPartner()` method on the partnering server with a remote reference back to themselves and the name of a service for which they want a partner (e.g., Chess). If the server has no waiting client then it stores a reference to the caller and returns `false`. If the server has a waiting client then it partners the clients and then returns `true`.

24.4.3 Interface Partner
This interface describes how peer-to-peer clients can be partnered by the central server.

```
import java.rmi.*;

public interface Partner extends Remote {
  public void partnered (String service, Partner partner)
    throws RemoteException;
}
```

When the server is partnering a pair of clients, it calls each client's `partnered()` method with a remote reference to its new partner and the name of the service for which they are being partnered.

24.4.4 Class PartnerServerImpl

This class is an example implementation of the partner server. It should be created and registered in a public naming service; clients can then use this central service to obtain peer references.

```
import java.rmi.*;
import java.rmi.server.*;
import java.rmi.registry.*;
import java.util.*;

public class PartnerServerImpl extends UnicastRemoteObject
      implements PartnerServer {
  // public PartnerServerImpl () throws RemoteException ...
  // public synchronized boolean assignPartner
      (String service, Partner myself) throws RemoteException ...
  // public static void main (String[] args)
      throws RemoteException, AlreadyBoundException ...
}
```

Our partner server extends `UnicastRemoteObject`, as a standard remote object, and implements the `PartnerServer` interface. We also provide a `main()` method that creates an instance of this class and exposes it in a naming registry.

```
protected Hashtable pending;

public PartnerServerImpl () throws RemoteException {
  pending = new Hashtable ();
}
```

Our constructor exposes the exceptions that may be thrown from the supercon- structor and creates `pending`, which is a `Hashtable` containing remote clients waiting to be partnered.

```
public synchronized boolean assignPartner (String service, Partner myself)
    throws RemoteException {
  if (!pending.containsKey (service)) {
    pending.put (service, myself);
    return false;
```

```
    } else {
      Partner partner = (Partner) pending.get (service);
      pending.remove (service);
      partner.partnered (service, myself);
      myself.partnered (service, partner);
      return true;
    }
  }
```

This method is called by a client that wishes to obtain a remote reference to a peer client. The client provides a remote reference back to itself in the `myself` parameter and the name of the service for which it is seeking a partner in the `service` parameter.

We first check to see if we already have a client waiting for a partner in that service. If we don't, we store a reference to the caller in the `pending` `Hashtable` and return `false`. Otherwise, we remove the pending client from `pending`, call each client's `partnered()` method with a remote reference to the peer client, and return `true`. If an RMI exception occurs while calling either client's `partnered()` method, we simply pass it on; it will be returned to the current caller.

```
public static void main (String[] args)
    throws RemoteException, AlreadyBoundException {
  if (args.length != 2)
    throw new IllegalArgumentException
      ("Syntax: PartnerServerImpl <port> <service>");
  int port = Integer.parseInt (args[0]);
  String service = args[1];
  PartnerServerImpl partnerServer = new PartnerServerImpl ();
  try {
    Registry registry = LocateRegistry.getRegistry (port);
    registry.bind (service, partnerServer);
  } catch (ConnectException ex) {
    Registry registry = LocateRegistry.createRegistry (port);
    registry.bind (service, partnerServer);
  }
}
```

This `main()` method creates a partner server and registers it in a naming registry.

We first attempt to locate an already-running naming registry on the specified port of the local machine and to register our partner server there. If this fails with a `Connect-Exception`, we assume that no registry was running, so we create a new naming registry running on the specified port and bind the partner server there under the specified service name.

24.4.5 Class PartnerImpl
This class is a simple example of a peer-to-peer client that uses the preceding partner server to obtain a remote reference to a peer.

```
import java.rmi.*;
import java.rmi.server.*;
import java.rmi.registry.*;

public class PartnerImpl implements Partner {
  public void partnered (String service, Partner partner) {
    System.out.println ("Partnered with " + partner + " for " + service + '.');
  }

  public static void main (String[] args)
      throws RemoteException, NotBoundException {
    if (args.length != 3)
      throw new IllegalArgumentException
        ("Syntax: PartnerImpl <host> <port> <service>");
    PartnerImpl partner = new PartnerImpl ();
    Partner partnerRef =
      (Partner) UnicastRemoteObject.exportObject (partner);
    String host = args[0];
    int port = Integer.parseInt (args[1]);
    String service = args[2];
    Registry registry = LocateRegistry.getRegistry (host, port);
    PartnerServer server = (PartnerServer) registry.lookup (service);
    if (!server.assignPartner ("Testing", partnerRef))
      System.out.println ("waiting...");
  }
}
```

Our `PartnerImpl` class is a remote object that implements the `Partner` interface. In a real environment, it would also implement any other remote interfaces that described our peer-to-peer architecture, such as a `Chess` interface.

In the `main()` method, we create an instance of this client class and expose it using `exportObject()`. We could alternatively just subclass `UnicastRemoteObject` directly. We next locate the partner server registered under a specified service name in a specified naming registry. Finally, we call the `assignPartner()` method of this partner server to obtain a partner for the service Testing. If this method returns `false`, we must wait for a partner to be assigned; otherwise, a partner will have been assigned by the time this method returns.

24.5 RMI and Web browsers

To use RMI from an applet in a Web browser, you must first ensure that the browser supports RMI. Some browsers only support a subset of JDK 1.1, not including the RMI packages. There are security considerations which apply to an untrusted applet.

24.5.1 Accessing RMI services
Accessing an RMI service from an applet involves nothing more than making socket connections to the RMI server machine, and so is compatible with the security

limitations of most common browsers, presuming that the RMI server is the same machine as the Web server that served the applet. If the local firewall does not allow direct socket connections to the RMI service, the various HTTP proxy options described in the previous chapter are used.

Note, however, that a naming registry can store references to objects not running on the same server as itself (the only security that it enforces during registration is that the caller is running on the same machine, not the object being registered). As a result, you may encounter an unexpected `SecurityException` if the naming registry running on your Web server returns a remote reference to an object residing elsewhere.

What is perhaps most problematic is when an RMI service is being exposed on a multihomed host; for example, a Web server that is serving the two hosts alpha.nitric.com (IP address 10.0.0.1) and beta.nitric.com (10.0.0.2). When you start an RMI service on this host, it may either bind to the address 10.0.0.1 or

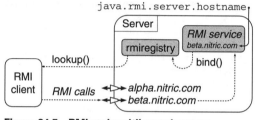

Figure 24.5   RMI and multihomed servers

10.0.0.2. If it chooses the former and is being accessed by an applet served from the host beta, the applet will receive a remote reference to alpha and will fail with a `SecurityException`. In this case, the RMI server should set the `System` property java.rmi.server.hostname to the host to which it should bind (figure 24.5). For example:

```
java -Djava.rmi.server.hostname=beta.nitric.com ServiceImpl
```

24.5.2 Exposing RMI services

Exposing an RMI service from an applet involves creating a `ServerSocket`, an operation that is not compatible with the security limitations of most common browsers. Some browsers will allow an applet to open a `ServerSocket`, but will only accept connections directly from the host from which the applet was served. In this case, an applet can expose RMI services as long as any access to the applet will only come from the originating server.

In other cases, the browser will not allow an untrusted applet to open a `ServerSocket` at all. When this occurs, you must use a combination of digital signatures and browser APIs (e.g., JDK 1.2 permissions or Netscape capabilities) to obtain permission for the applet to open a `ServerSocket`. Details of these features are, at this point, somewhat specific to the various browser platforms and versions in use. Since they undergo constant revision, they cannot be addressed here.

24.5.3 Conclusion

The RMI framework handles all of the low-level details required for invisible networking with remote objects and provides a simple way to create complex distributed applications.

Obviously, RMI provides for a different style of networking than that supported by streams and sockets, and both styles have their uses. Streams and sockets are necessary to interact with existing socket-based applications. They are also useful when the program desires full control over a client/server system. By accessing the network directly, it is comparatively easy to build systems that automatically roll over to a standby server if the main server dies. Similarly, TCP, UDP, and multicast can be combined, so that the protocol in use depends on the data being transmitted. RMI, on the other hand, provides a much higher level interface to networking. This has the advantage that the programmer can define a much cleaner, higher level application protocol, and all communication details are taken care of transparently.

RMI is not necessarily a good choice in a high-bandwidth system, for an obviously streams-based system or for an application where the overhead of RMI call setup will prove too costly. RMI may also be inapplicable in certain situations where nonpolled two-way communication is required, but firewalls would prevent a server calling back to a client.

Good applications for RMI include request-based enterprise applications (database access and information browsing) and completely distributed applications where the ability to create arbitrary interconnections will be useful, or for applications like parallel numerical algorithms in which the communication time is small compared to the overall run time (and so the overhead of RMI is negligible). The peer-to-peer example that we looked at is a good example of a simple distributed application that is well served by RMI. The date server that we initially looked at is another good (albeit trivial) example of a a request-based application.

Ultimately, which style of network programming you choose should depend on your application. While streams and sockets may be more familiar and provide more control, the remote method invocation framework is an extremely powerful and useful capability. In the next chapter, we will look at CORBA which is yet another alternative distributed computing tool. At a high level, CORBA is very similar to RMI, but it offers many more services, and has the advantage that it is completely portable across different languages and platforms. CORBA is an extremely serious contender for networked enterprise application development.

C H A P T E R   2 5

CORBA

In the previous chapters, we have seen how Java objects can be distributed and accessed remotely using the Remote Method Invocation API and protocols. Here we take a look at an alternate technology that allows one to accomplish essentially the same set of goals—to make Java objects remotely accessible. This technology is OMG's CORBA, an industry defined standard for distributed object programming that is quickly becoming popular as the platform for open, distributed computing.

This chapter is intended as more of a general overview and gentle introduction to CORBA, rather than a fully comprehensive reference on the technology. For details beyond what is covered here, refer to OMG's comprehensive Web site at *http://www.omg.org/*. It contains extensive CORBA documentation, including details of progress in the field of CORBA and Java integration, as well as downloadable copies of many OMG publications. In addition, various other related books and publications are listed at the end of this chapter.

25.1 Introduction

The Common Object Request Broker Architecture (CORBA) was conceived by the Object Management Group (OMG, a consortium of more than 700 companies world-wide) as a multivendor standard to build and deploy interoperable distributed objects. It exists in the form of a specification covering both the architecture and the interfaces designed to allow one to develop and deploy enterprise (object) applications on the network.

The Object Request Broker (ORB) itself is part of a larger architectural picture known as the OMA (Object Management Architecture). Besides the ORB, OMA comprises CORBA Services and CORBA Facilities shown in figure 25.1.

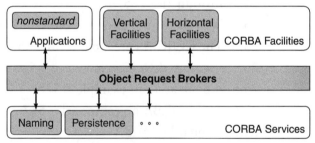

Figure 25.1   The Object Management Architecture (OMA)

At the heart of the OMA lies the ORB whose architecture and interfaces form the CORBA Core. It is an object bus that allows requests from the client to be delivered to the server object and for replies to be delivered back. It does so by ensuring location transparency and language independence—the client does not know or care about the actual location of the server object or about the language used to implement it. All it cares about is the reference to the server that it has and the interfaces that the server supports. For details, we refer the reader to the OMG document, *The Common Object Request Broker: Architecture and Specification.*

Layered on top of the ORB are the CORBA Services, a suite of object services including naming, persistence, transactions, security, and so forth found to be useful to a wide variety of applications. These are part of the standard because of their utility across many domains. There are a total of sixteen services currently defined. For details, we refer the reader to the OMG CORBAservices specification.

Then come the CORBA Facilities, a set of application frameworks that can be used to build complex business objects. These are generic frameworks, which comprise the Horizontal Facilities, and domain specific frameworks, which comprise the Vertical Facilities. Examples of the former are Distributed Documents and Task Management. Domain specific frameworks include those used in healthcare, manufacturing, and so forth. For details, see the OMG CORBA facilities specification.

25.2 Why distribute using CORBA?

One of the main attractions of using a standard such as CORBA is the guarantee of openness and interoperability. In CORBA's case, the server and the client could be written in any language for which the specification provides a mapping. Indeed, one can even interoperate across ORBs so that an application developer can mix and match the best of breed of the various services and components offered by different vendors. This is an attractive alternative to being dependent on a single vendor with proprietary technology for all of your needs.

The other advantage is being able to integrate legacy systems and develop newer pieces, all using CORBA, so that you have an amalgam of legacy and nonlegacy applications running seamlessly over the object bus (CORBA). This is made possible by the separation of the specification or interfaces and the implementations that support these interfaces.

OMG with its OMA has gone beyond mere interoperability at the level of the object bus and languages in defining a whole suite of object services, facilities, and models that one can use to develop enterprise applications. The suite of specifications covers a wide spectrum of needs from transaction processing to component models.

Lastly, the architecture itself provides for an extremely scalable way of exposing Java interfaces remotely and, hence, would be the preferred architecture for distributing Java objects where the simplicity and streamlined nature of RMI are insufficient. In many cases, a Java service distributed with CORBA will be faster than one distributed with RMI; absolute figures will, however, obviously depend upon situation and vendor. Much of CORBA's performance results from the high speed of the Internet Interoperability Protocol (IIOP) and its ability to quickly create connections among objects. The current implementation of RMI, and in particular its use of object streams, is inherently slower than IIOP. On the down side, however, a CORBA client must have access to a local ORB. In the context of an applet, if the browser does not provide an ORB then the applet will have to download an ORB implementation from the server. With increased market penetration of modern browsers, this will become less of an issue; the latest versions of Netscape, for example, include an internal ORB.

25.3 The CORBA core architecture

Delving deeper into the part known as the CORBA Core, the object bus is known as the ORB and serves as the communication infrastructure used by both clients and servers on the bus. Although the specific communication protocols for the ORB Core are not defined, all ORBs *must* support the IIOP that defines a standard protocol for interoperability purposes. This protocol lays out the structure of the messages that can be sent over TCP/IP; it is the application to TCP/IP of a more general protocol called GIOP.

Figure 25.2 shows a client and server built on top of an ORB. Besides the communication aspects, the ORB Core also exposes a set of interfaces called the ORB API. These ORB interfaces are useful for a variety of purposes at both the client and server sides and, therefore, are shown common to both. Interfaces in CORBA are

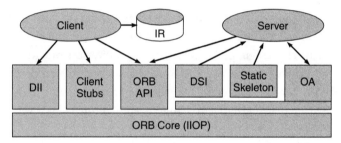

Figure 25.2   The ORB Architecture

defined in an OMG-specified Interface Definition Language (IDL). IDL deals purely with interfaces—the contracts between a server that implements the interface and a client which uses the interface.

25.4 Interface definition language

The IDL is how you define the interface that a CORBA server will provide; much like a remote interface defines the interface that a RMI server will provide.

An IDL specification typically defines modules (equivalent to packages or name spaces), interfaces, attributes (equivalent to variables), operations (equivalent to methods), and exceptions. There are various mappings defined from IDL to particular languages, including Java; these define what language datatypes correspond to the various IDL datatypes. The different aspects of IDL are highlighted in this section.

25.4.1 Datatypes

IDL itself has a set of basic datatypes (`string`, `float`, `long`, etc.) along with the ability to extend the set via user-defined datatypes (`sequences`, `arrays`, `structures`, and `unions`). The set of CORBA datatypes and their mapping to Java are shown in table 25.1 and table 25.2.

Table 25.1 Simple CORBA datatypes and their mapping to Java

IDL Datatype	Java Type
boolean	boolean
char (8bit)	char
wchar (16 bit)	char
octet	byte
string (8 bit)	java.lang.String
wstring (16 bit)	java.lang.String
short	short
unsigned short	short
long	int
long long	long
unsigned long long	long
float	float
double	double
fixed	java.math.BigDecimal

Table 25.2 Complex CORBA types and their mapping to Java

Complex IDL types	Corresponding Java Mapping
Constants within an interface	public static final field within the interface
Constants outside an interface	public interface with a public static final value field
enum	final class
struct	final class
sequence	array
array	array
union	final class

Note that the mapping for complex datatypes is not fully described here. For details, we refer the reader to the *OMG IDL to Java Mapping*. Basically, simple Java classes are created that follow the same form as the complex CORBA datatypes.

25.4.2 Modules

Modules define a name space and serve to demarcate the boundary for a set of related definitions. For convenience, CORBA interfaces are typically declared within an associated module. Modules actually map directly to the Java `package` mechanism, which provides a similar grouping facility.

25.4.3 Interfaces

Interfaces describe a particular service being exposed, just like a remote interface. They are composed of operations, attributes, and exceptions. Interfaces can inherit from other interfaces. Interfaces are also considered as a name space for the definition of user constructed types such as `structs`; that is, you can define a complex datatype within the scope of an interface definition.

Interfaces are the exposed entities which are used to access objects supporting a particular service—when you access a CORBA server, you will access it through one of the IDL interfaces that it exposes. Interfaces are also equivalent to types; the return value from a CORBA operation may be a reference to another CORBA object that implements a particular IDL interface. Continuing the comparison with RMI, this is exactly equivalent to an RMI server returning a remote reference to another remote object.

In the IDL to Java mapping, interfaces translate to the Java `interface` mechanism with supporting client-side stubs and server-side skeletons. In the process of compiling IDL, information about interfaces is also entered into the *Interface Repository*, (IR) which can be used by developers to dynamically invoke operations on objects.

25.4.4 Attributes

Attributes are simply variables in a CORBA interfaces. Attributes are mapped to a set of accessor functions in the language mapping—one to set the value of the attribute and one to get the value. Attributes can be declared read-only, in which case only the get accessor is generated in the language mapping. Attributes can be either of a built-in IDL type (the simple datatypes already mentioned) or a complex type such as a `struct`, `interface`, `union`, `enumeration`, and so forth.

25.4.5 Operations

Operations are the methods supported by an interface and are described by their signature, which includes the return value type, the name of the operation, a list of parameters, and a list of exceptions that may be raised.

Operations can have one primary return value and can accept parameters of three fundamental modes:

in   These are input values to the operation. They are constants with respect to the operation implementation. In Java, in parameters are implemented simply as parameters to the method.

out   These values are filled in at the server side and are outputs of an operation. In Java, out parameters are implemented with a container class that is filled in upon completion of an operation.

inout   These serve as a combination of the former two. They are inputs to the operation that can then be modified by the operation's execution. In Java, inout parameters are implemented with a container filled in by the caller as an input to the operation, and refilled by the CORBA framework upon completion of the operation.

25.4.6 Exceptions

Exceptions defined in IDL are known as user exceptions and inherit from a base class called CORBA::UserException (the :: symbol indicates a member of a module). This is to distinguish them from a set of predefined SystemExceptions that the ORB uses to inform the client of abnormal termination of a request.

All operations can implicitly throw the SystemException class; this is analagous to the standard RemoteException that can be thrown by all RMI operations.

25.5 A bank account example

Here is a typical IDL specification. It specifies a module called a Bank and one exception in the name space called InsufficientFunds, which is thrown when one tries to withdraw more than one has in the account. The Account interface has three attributes of different types; the balance and Social Security attributes are read-only implying that there won't be accessible operations to set their values directly. The interface also has two defined operations: one to deposit money and one to withdraw it. These are the only external mechanisms that can affect the balance attribute.

```
module Bank {
  exception InsufficientFunds {
    float currentBalance;
  };

  interface Account {
    attribute wstring name;
    readonly attribute unsigned long ssn;
    readonly attribute float balance;
    void withdraw (in float amount) raises (InsufficientFunds);
```

```
    void deposit (in float amount);
  };
};
```

Note that the operation signatures will specify the possible exceptions that can be thrown during their execution. All requests can implicitly result in a CORBA::SystemException or a specialization (subclass) thereof.

When translated to Java according to the IDL to Java mapping, this will result in approximately the following code; the exact code produced will depend upon the environment under which you are developing:

```
package Bank;

public class InsufficientFunds extends org.omg.CORBA.UserException {
  public float currentBalance;

  public InsufficientFunds () {
  }

  public InsufficientFunds (float currentBalance) {
    this.currentBalance = currentBalance;
  }
}
```

This class is the IDL exception InsufficientFunds translated into a Java exception class, a subclass of UserException within the package Bank.

```
package Bank;

public interface Account extends org.omg.CORBA.Object {
  public abstract String name ();
  public abstract void name (String name);
  public abstract int ssn ();
  public abstract float balance ();
  public abstract void withdraw (float amount) throws InsufficientFunds;
  public abstract void deposit (float amount);
}
```

This interface describes the IDL interface Account, declared within the package Bank. Note that the IDL attributes have been converted into getters and setters. Unlike Java common practice, however, these accessors are simply given the name of the attribute that they are accessing and not names such as getName() and setName().

Note also that the CORBA SystemException class, unlike RMI's RemoteException class, is a subclass of RuntimeException. It is not explicitly named as a side effect of any of these methods. Remember, a RuntimeException can implicitly happen as a result of any method call.

25.6 The CORBA object model

Objects in CORBA are described via interfaces in IDL. Thus, a CORBA developer will use the language-specific mapping of an IDL interface as a template to create the implementation of a CORBA service and as a template for accessing a remote CORBA service. Remember, however, that the client and server need not be implemented in the same language; the language-independent IDL is used as an intermediary to allow communication across the object bus among heterogeneous platforms.

At run time, calls that are made on a CORBA reference will be translated into calls on the actual implementation elsewhere. CORBA uses exactly the same mechanism as RMI to perform this process; that is, a stub transmits the client's method call to a skeleton which makes the call on the server implementation. It should be noted, of course, that CORBA is RMI's predecessor, so it may be more correct to say that RMI uses the same mechanism as CORBA.

25.6.1 CORBA remote references

A client can create a reference to a remote CORBA object by using a factory for the interface in which they are interested or by using the CORBA naming service. The object reference that is returned implements a language mapping of the particular IDL interface being accessed; that is, a Java reference to a CORBA object will implement a Java mapping of the object's IDL interface. Once created, this reference is valid across instantiations of the client and server processes until the object is explicitly destroyed.

In this sense, both CORBA objects and their references are implicitly persistent in nature. RMI provides similar support. A remote RMI reference can be serialized and, when deserialized, will refer to the same original object; similarly, an RMI server can be serialized and deserialized. Unlike CORBA, however, persistence is not provided by default; an RMI server will be garbage collected when it is no longer referenced, and a remote reference will not remain valid across serialization and deserialization of the server.

Actual object implementations live through cycles of activation and deactivation, allowing servers that host the object to swap it in and out of an in-memory object cache. If an object is deactivated and accessed by a remote client, it will be automatically reactivated by the CORBA environment. A CORBA object reference only becomes invalid upon explicit destruction of the target; any further use of this reference will return an appropriate system exception to the user.

25.6.2 Static invocation

A specification provided by an IDL interface is converted by a compiler into a client-side stub and a server-side skeleton. Server skeletons are used as the basis for filling in the business logic of the actual CORBA object implementation. Unlike RMI, most server implementations will explicitly subclass their skeleton; this class provides similar internal implementations to those provided by the RMI `UnicastRemoteObject` class. An alternative delegation model for implementing servers is also, however, supported by many environments, analogous to RMI's `UnicastRemoteObject exportObject()` method.

Client applications use stub classes to access the business logic contained in server-side CORBA objects. These stub classes export the same interface as the IDL interface definitions, with some additional internal methods defined by the `org.omg.CORBA.-Object` superinterface. They automatically translate client calls into network connections to the server-side skeleton.

Static invocation via pregenerated client stubs is always synchronous: The client is blocked for the time it takes to get a reply, and any exceptions thrown at the server side are rethrown to the calling client. The stub is responsible for marshaling the client side request into a message. The ORB then ships the message over to the server side (the ORB knows which server object to call by interpreting the object reference). The Object Adapter (OA) is a server-side entity which is responsible for instantiating server objects, passing requests to them, and generating object references. The skeletons on the server side unmarshal the message data and call the implementation to handle the request. The OA has access to an *Implementation Repository* which provides a run time repository of information on the classes supported by a server. As of this writing the OMG has not yet standardized the interfaces of this implementation repository.

25.6.3 Dynamic invocation

Besides generating stubs and skeletons, an IDL compiler also generates the meta-information about the IDL interfaces which is entered into and available from the interface repository. The repository itself is a hierarchical organization of CORBA objects which can be queried and changed dynamically. This meta-information can be used to dynamically form requests to CORBA objects *without* using statically bound stubs.

The interfaces that allow a client to use dynamic invocation form the *Dynamic Invocation Interface* (DII). It allows both synchronous and asynchronous access to objects; static stubs are purely synchronous in nature. Using this mechanism, you can dynamically query the operations supported by a CORBA server and form calls on any operations that you locate without having to manually bind the stub that would usually do this for you. This is similar to the JDK 1.1 reflection API.

25.7 Standard CORBA services

The OMA is a layered architecture that defines the suite of CORBA services on top of the ORB. These services are nothing but abstractions of commonly used functions such as naming, security, persistence, and so forth. These services are described in CORBA IDL and are implemented as actual CORBA objects, much in the same way that the

RMI naming registry is just an RMI-based remote object. In this section, we will give a brief description of some of the important services. Full details of all the available services are available online at http://www.omg.org/corba/sectrans.html.

25.7.1 Naming service

The naming service is a facility to allow a user to export object references, which can later be looked up by a client based on a registered name. The naming service is composed of a set of interfaces that allows objects to be named, registered, looked up, and deregistered.

The name space is organized hierarchically with `NamingContext` objects at the nodes of the tree and actual bindings of names to objects as the leaves. Each context is composed of other contexts as well as name bindings, thus forming the tree hierarchy. Contexts themselves are CORBA objects. A name is composed of a series of `NameComponent` objects, each of which identifies a context in the hierarchy. The nth component of an n-component name will refer to the object being looked up in a context specified by the $n-1$ preceding components.

Each ORB exports an interface to look up the root `NamingContext` for the name service on the ORB, and from this the subcontexts and registered objects can be located. This is similar to the RMI naming registry but organized in a hierarchical manner. You can, in fact, achieve a similar hierarchy using RMI's naming registry system by simply registering naming registries within other naming registries, and thus manually constructing a registry hierarchy. In Java, the CORBA naming service is provided by the `org.omg.CosNaming` package.

25.7.2 Lifecycle service

The CORBA lifecycle service provides a standard way of dealing with lifecycle related operations of CORBA objects—creation, destruction, mobility, and cloning. The lifecycle service deals with creation of CORBA objects by using the concept of a factory. Factories are created in the servers and are exported using the naming service. A client wishing to create an object can look up a suitable factory using a `FactoryFinder`. Then the client can proceed to create objects using the interfaces provided by the factory.

There is also an interface `LifeCycleObject`, from which CORBA objects can inherit. This interface exports operations to delete the object, to move the object from one location to another, and to clone the object.

25.7.3 Transaction service

Most applications in the world of business computing need the semantics of Atomicity, Consistency, Isolation, and Durability (ACID) when accessing shared, persistent data. The Object Transaction Service (OTS) provides protocols and interfaces to allow safe, transactional access to CORBA objects thereby extending transactional semantics to distributed object-oriented applications. OTS supports two-phase commit protocols, which are among the most commonly used protocols to achieve ACID properties of data access. The usefulness of OTS is that it allows one to integrate several heterogeneous transaction monitor systems and to treat object and nonobject resources equally.

25.7.4 Event service

The CORBA event service is meant to provide the applications developer with a framework in which events can be transmitted between servers and clients. Events form an asynchronous communication paradigm in which the sender and receiver are decoupled from each other. No knowledge of the other object's interfaces is required by either the sender or receiver, except that the event service interfaces are supported. Two models of event propagation are supported—the push model in which the client is sent an event when one occurs and the pull model in which the client actively polls for an event when it needs one.

25.7.5 Concurrency control service

As the name implies, Concurrency Control Service (CCS) provides interfaces and protocols to allow multiple clients to access the same CORBA object safely. It provides interfaces for locking objects in various modes and defines the semantics of multiclient access in the presence of locks. It also provides the API for client-side demarcation of locks.

25.7.6 Relationship service

The reason for using objects to model reality is that they can be conveniently used to represent real world entities such as people, cars, departments, and so forth. However, reality also consists of relationships between these objects, and objects have specific roles to play in a relationship. For example: a person can *own* a car, an employer *employs* employees. The CORBA relationship service provides interfaces for applications to designate objects as having certain roles in a relationship. Relationships themselves are treated as types, and many relationships can share the same object in different roles. A traversal interface is provided to navigate from one role to another.

25.7.7 Externalization service

The externalization service provides interfaces, protocols, and contracts to be able to stream an object's state out as a standardized stream of data, which can then be transferred from one location to another and converted back to the state of the object. This service can be useful in a variety of situations including mobility, passivation/reactivation of objects, and so forth.

25.8 A CORBA bank account

In this section, we will walk you through an example application developed in Java using CORBA. Both the client and server here are Java applications. The example we use is that of the bank introduced earlier in this chapter.

All of the specifics described in this section refer to the default ORB provided with JDK 1.2. Although the steps remain the same for any ORB, the specifics may vary—for example, the IDL compiler could be named differently with different vendors' products. Vendors also supply value-added features, which we will try to avoid completely in the spirit of standardization. At the time of writing, the `idltojava` compiler that we shall use is distributed separately from the JDK, but available for free download from Java-Soft's Web site. This compiler is required to test out the following examples.

25.8.1 The development process

When dealing with Java, there exist two design centers—by this we mean the object models that one uses to design an application:

IDL-centric As outlined in earlier sections, IDL is the interface definition language prescribed by OMG to describe the interfaces of the CORBA objects. To a large extent, language independence is achieved via the use of IDL. With an IDL-centric design paradigm, IDL is used as the specification language for a CORBA application and is mapped into language-specific applications.

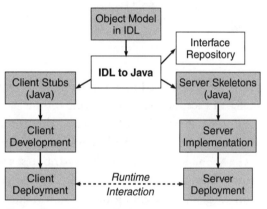

Figure 25.3   IDL-centric design

Java-centric When one wants to deal solely with Java and not have to become familiar with IDL, one can define the interfaces that a CORBA server will present as *Java* interfaces and then use the Java-to-IDL mapping (and tools which implement this mapping) to convert the Java interfaces into IDL. In this case, Java clients can either use Java stubs generated by an IDL-to-Java compiler or they can access the Java server objects using RMI. This is a relatively new approach, and the Java-to-IDL mapping is in the final stages of adoption in OMG.

In this section, we will concentrate on the former IDL-centric approach as standardization for the latter is incomplete.

25.8.2 Writing the IDL

The sample application we have chosen to work with is a bank. We must describe the application object model of our bank in terms of IDL interfaces.

The bank consists of accounts; each account identifies the name and Social Security number of the account holder and maintains a running balance. The balance can be queried at any time. Users of the account are permitted to deposit money, withdraw money, or check the account balance.

The IDL for this application is the same as shown earlier, but repeated here for clarity:

```
module Bank {
  exception InsufficientFunds {
    float currentBalance;
  };

  interface Account {
    attribute wstring name;
    readonly attribute unsigned long ssn;
    readonly attribute float balance;
    void withdraw (in float amount) raises (InsufficientFunds);
    void deposit (in float amount);
  };
};
```

The module `Bank` forms the name space within which the `Account` interface is defined. An exception for overdrawing on the account is also defined here and is called `InsufficientFunds`. For convenience, this exception contains the current balance on the account at the time the withdrawal was attempted.

The `Account` interface has three attributes: a `wstring` representing the name of the account holder (remember, the default IDL `string` contains only 8-bit characters), an `unsigned long` representing the account holder's Social Security number (remember, an IDL `long` is actually a Java `int`), and a `float` representing the balance in the account. Note that the Social Security number and the balance are read-only attributes—this means that no set accessors are generated for them. These attributes can only be changed from within the server implementation; the interface does not export any remote methods for the client to directly set the values of these attributes. For our example, we have chosen to make the name changeable.

The two operations that we declare have only in-parameters. In addition, the `withdraw()` operation can throw an `InsufficientFunds` exception. Note that the client can receive a CORBA `SystemException` on any call—the operation signatures explicitly mention only user-defined exceptions.

25.8.3 Compiling the IDL

Now that we have our object model described in IDL, the next step is to run the IDL through a compiler, which generates the client stubs and server skeletons. Typically, this step will also populate the interface repository.

Since Java allows only one public interface per file, compiling `Bank.idl` will result in several Java files stored in a package called `Bank` (corresponding to the module). Different compilers will result in different names for the various support classes, however the following files are generated with the JDK 1.2 IDL compiler `idltojava`, executed as follows:

```
idltojava -fno-cpp Bank.idl
```

Account.java   This is the basic `Account` interface declaration. This interface inherits from `org.omg.CORBA.Object` and is the Java mapping of our `Account` CORBA interface. Details of this interface are provided in section 25.5 on page 575.

AccountHolder.java   This is a holder class, used to pass an `Account` reference as either an `in` or an `inout` parameter of a CORBA operation. To use an `Account` reference as an `inout` parameter, construct an `AccountHolder` with the initial parameter value, pass this to the method and and then query the `AccountHolder value` variable upon completion of the operation. For an `out` parameter, simply omit the initial value.

AccountHelper.java   This is a helper class which contains several utility functions for manipulating `Account` references.

_AccountStub.java   This is the client-side stub for the `Account` class. You will not typically use this class directly; it provides the client-side implementation of CORBA details for `Account` remote references.

_AccountImplBase.java   This is the server-side skeleton for an `Account` implementation. This class implements the `Account` interface and provides various support facilities, including method description and dynamic invocation facilities. A server implementation must be a subclass of this skeleton unless it is using delegation.

InsufficientFunds.java   This is the Java mapping of the `InsufficientFunds` exception. It extends `org.omg.CORBA.UserException` and includes a public `float` variable `currentBalance` that is the balance at the time of the exception.

InsufficientFundsHolder.java   This is a holder class for the `InsufficientFunds` exception.

InsufficientFundsHelper.java   This is a helper class for the `InsufficientFunds` exception.

The `idltojava` command will also generate files for implementing the server using a delegation model if the flag `-ftie` is specified. We will ignore delegation in favor of inheritance for the purpose of illustrating CORBA.

25.8.4 Implementing the server

The pregenerated class of most importance for the server side is `_AccountImplBase`, which the developer must extend to provide implementation of the methods of `Account`.

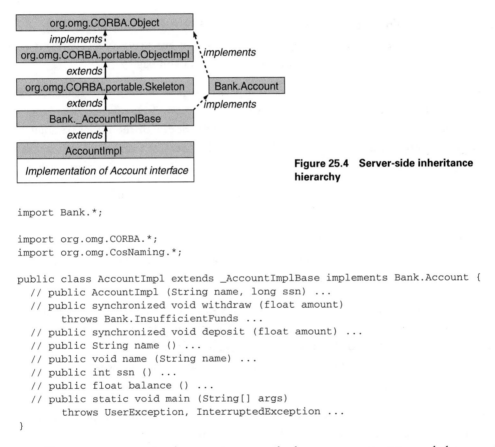

Figure 25.4   Server-side inheritance hierarchy

```
import Bank.*;

import org.omg.CORBA.*;
import org.omg.CosNaming.*;

public class AccountImpl extends _AccountImplBase implements Bank.Account {
    // public AccountImpl (String name, long ssn) ...
    // public synchronized void withdraw (float amount)
        throws Bank.InsufficientFunds ...
    // public synchronized void deposit (float amount) ...
    // public String name () ...
    // public void name (String name) ...
    // public int ssn () ...
    // public float balance () ...
    // public static void main (String[] args)
        throws UserException, InterruptedException ...
}
```

Our `AccountImpl` implementation extends the `_AccountImplBase` skeleton and implements the `Bank.Account` interface. In fact, the superclass already implements this interface; however, we reiterate this for clarity.

We provide a constructor and simple implementations of all the methods of the Account interface. In addition, we provide an example main() method that creates and exports an instance of our Account implementation.

```
protected String name;
protected int ssn;
protected float balance;

public AccountImpl (String name, int ssn) {
  this.name = name;
  this.ssn = ssn;
  balance = 100;
}
```

Our constructor assigns initial values to our implementation variables.

```
public synchronized void withdraw (float amount)
    throws Bank.InsufficientFunds {
  if (balance < amount)
    throw new Bank.InsufficientFunds (balance);
  balance -= amount;
}
```

Our withdraw() method throws a Bank.InsufficientFunds exception if the account's balance is insufficient for the withdrawal; otherwise, we perform the requested operation. When a client makes a call on our CORBA server's withdraw() operation, the skeleton will automatically translate the client call into a direct invocation of this method implementation.

```
public synchronized void deposit (float amount) {
  balance += amount;
}
```

The deposit() method adds to the account balance.

```
public String name () {
  return name;
}
```

This method is the read accessor for the name attribute; we return the value of name.

```
public void name (String name) {
  this.name = name;
}
```

This method is the write accessor for the name attribute; we modify the attribute accordingly.

```
public int ssn () {
```

```
    return ssn;
  }
```

This method returns the account holder's Social Security number.

```
public float balance () {
  return balance;
}
```

This method returns the current account balance.

```
public static void main (String[] args)
    throws UserException, InterruptedException {
  ORB orb = ORB.init (args, null);

  AccountImpl jimBean = new AccountImpl ("Jim Bean", 123456789);
  orb.connect (jimBean);

  org.omg.CORBA.Object nameService_ =
    orb.resolve_initial_references ("NameService");
  NamingContext nameService = NamingContextHelper.narrow (nameService_);

  NameComponent name = new NameComponent (jimBean.name (), "Account");
  NameComponent[] path = { name };
  nameService.rebind (path, jimBean);

  Thread.currentThread ().join ();
}
```

Besides implementing the server side of Account, we must also provide a main program for the server that initializes the ORB and exports Account instances. Typically this will be a separate program from the actual server implementation; for simplicity, in this case we provide it here in the main() method.

We first call init() to initialize our application with the local ORB. We pass args so that the user can provide ORB-specific initialization parameters, and a null second argument that is a set of properties controlling initialization. We next create an instance of our AccountImpl class and connect() it to the ORB. After this call, our account can be accessed by remote CORBA clients.

We must now expose our account in the naming service. We first obtain a reference to our local naming service from our ORB. We next construct a name under which our account instance will be registered. A NameComponent has two parts—a name and a type—both are entirely at the discretion of the user so we choose an appropriate value for each. Next, we construct a path of NameComponents for our account (remember, the naming service is actually a hierarchy of NameComponents). In this case, we store our account at the top level so we use a single-element path. Finally, we call rebind() to bind our account in the naming service. Details of accessing the naming service currently vary from ORB to ORB, so you should consult your local manual for details relevant to your ORB.

Finally, we must wait for clients to access our account. The actual event loop that handles incoming requests is provided internally by the ORB implementation so we simply call `join()` on our main thread. This means that our main thread will wait until it finishes; that is, it will simply wait forever. Ordinarily, of course, a full application would provide a proper mechanism for shutting down.

25.9 A CORBA bank client

We have just seen how to implement the server-side of our banking system, exposing a CORBA-accessible `Account` implementation in the naming service. Now, we can turn our attention to the client side.

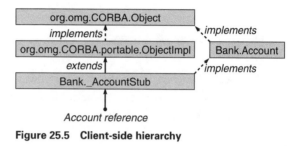

Figure 25.5   Client-side hierarchy

25.9.1 The client implementation

Our goal in this client is to locate the account object that we have just created and use the reference obtained to invoke a few operations synchronously using the statically generated stubs.

To achieve this, we must locate the bank account's naming service and look up the account therein. After this, we will have a CORBA reference that we can manipulate as we desire.

```
import Bank.*;

import org.omg.CORBA.*;
import org.omg.CosNaming.*;

public class AccountClient {
  public static void main (String[] args) throws UserException {
    ORB orb = ORB.init (args, null);

    org.omg.CORBA.Object nameService_ =
      orb.resolve_initial_references ("NameService");
    NamingContext nameService = NamingContextHelper.narrow (nameService_);

    NameComponent name = new NameComponent ("Jim Bean", "Account");
    NameComponent[] path = { name };

    org.omg.CORBA.Object jimBean_ = nameService.resolve (path);
    Account jimBean = AccountHelper.narrow (jimBean_);
```

```
System.out.println ("Account balance = " + jimBean.balance ());
jimBean.deposit (254.50f);
System.out.println ("New balance = " + jimBean.balance ());

try {
  jimBean.withdraw (jimBean.balance () + .01f);
} catch (InsufficientFunds ex) {
  System.out.println ("Insufficient funds = " + ex.currentBalance);
}

jimBean_._release ();
  }
}
```

The first step is to initialize the ORB as we did on the server side by calling ORB.init().

Next, we get a reference to the account object that we are interested in by using the naming service and the resolve() method, specifying the full NameComponent path to our account. Note that the result has type org.omg.CORBA.Object; we must use the AccountHelper class to cast the result to type Account.

We are now ready to operate on the account to which we have just bound. We can look up the balance and make withdrawals and deposits by means of synchronous stub operations by simply calling methods defined by the Account interface on our CORBA reference. The underlying CORBA architecture will take care of automatically translating these calls into invocations on the remote object implementation, regardless of its location or implementation language.

Finally, when we are done, we call _release() on our CORBA reference to release associated local resources.

25.9.2 Running the banking system

After compiling the IDL for the banking system and then building the Java class-files of both the server and client, the following steps are needed to execute this system:

```
tnameserv -ORBInitialPort 1234
```

Here, we start the ORB naming service. This command is included with the standard JDK 1.2 binaries. The ORBInitialPort parameter specifies on which port the naming service should listen; the default is port 900.

```
java AccountImpl -ORBInitialPort 1234
```

Here, we start up our account implementation. This will create an instance of our account and register it with the naming service. The ORBInitialPort parameter specifies on which port the naming service will be listening. In this case, we assume that the bank account implementation will be running on the same host as the naming service.

```
java AccountClient -ORBInitialHost bank.nitric.com -ORBInitialPort 1234
```

Here, we execute the example client. This will connect to the naming service, resolve the bank account and make some calls upon it. The ORBInitialHost and ORBInitialPort parameters specify where the initial naming service will be running. Typically for testing purposes the host will be local host, in which case the ORBInitialHost parameter can be omitted altogether.

25.10 Conclusion

CORBA is an extremely important technology because it provides a framework for building distributed, scalable enterprise applications independent of implementation language or platform. It is significantly more widespread, comprehensive, and powerful than RMI, however, it does not eclipse that technology entirely.

RMI is an inherently more lightweight technology with greater support for pure-Java applications. If an entire distributed application *will* be implemented in Java, and will *not* need to integrate with other platforms, then RMI may be preferable. It is simpler to grasp and easier to deploy. With capabilities such as automatic class file distribution and object serialization, RMI provides some facilities that CORBA cannot provide.

On the other hand, standardization, flexibility, and performance are powerful arguments in favor of CORBA. Once an application is implemented with RMI, it is tied to Java. A Java application implemented with CORBA, on the other hand, can be easily integrated with any other platform, should such a need arise in the future.

Ultimately, the line between RMI and CORBA may blur, as CORBA adds facilities provided by RMI and vice versa. For many applications, there are few practical differences between implementing a service in either CORBA or RMI. Thus, a choice between the technologies will ultimately depend on the application and whether facilities provided by RMI are required, or the flexibility of CORBA is compelling.

25.11 References

In addition to the OMG specifications available online from the OMG Web site at http://www.omg.org/ and the following references, different ORB vendors provide detailed instructions for installing and using their respective implementations. A free (for noncommercial use) ORB supporting Java (including JDK 1.1) and C++, ORBacus, is available at http://www.ooc.com/; other example ORBs with Java support include Iona Technologies' Orbix (http://www.iona.com/) and Visigenic's Visibroker (http://www.visigenic.com/).

Two good reference books on CORBA are: *The Essential CORBA: Systems Integration Using Distributed Objects* by Thomas Mowbray and Ron Zahavi (Wiley, 1995) and *CORBA: Fundamentals and Programming* by Jon Siegel (OMG Publications, 1996).

These are good starting books for one who wishes to learn what CORBA is all about and gain a high level understanding of the architecture and services. They walk the reader through detailed examples using several commercially available ORBs, but neither use Java as an implementation language since they were written before Java became popular.

Client/Server Programming with Java and CORBA, 2nd edition by Robert Orfali and Dan Harkey (Wiley, 1998) is an excellent starting point for one who wishes to gain a deeper understanding of CORBA and Java. This book discusses competing technologies such as RMI and DCOM and complementary technologies such as Enterprise Java-Beans and JDBC in a colorful style meant for easy reading. Many sophisticated examples, comparing and combining the different technologies, are included in this book.

C H A P T E R   2 6

Servlets

A servlet is a body of code that can be accessed through a standard interface in a network service, much like a CGI program on a Web site. Servlets allow a network service, such as a Web or FTP server, to be dynamically extended to provide additional facilities.

One common use of servlets is to provide a middleware bridge between Web browsers and corporate databases; the Web browser connects to a Web server, which executes a servlet that connects to the database and executes the browser's request. The Web server does not have to provide internal support for database access; instead, it can be dynamically extended with servlets that will perform these extra functions. In fact, servlets are a convenient mechanism for implementing almost any network-accessible service (figure 26.1).

Servlets are executed by the server in a protected sandbox, just as applets are on the client side. Servlets can either be installed directly in a Webserver, or alternatively may be downloaded from a

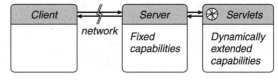

Figure 26.1   Servlets

remote site such as a central distribution point. Servlets which are downloaded from a remote host are prohibited from doing potentially harmful operations, such as writing to the local file system. Locally installed servlets can be trusted and, thus, assigned greater resource access.

Existing network objects such as socket servers or CORBA and RMI services, can often be easily reengineered or extended to also function in the servlet environment.

26.1   Technology comparison

Servlets provide a clean mechanism for implementing a wide variety of functions. Servlets may be used for traditional CGI applications—but with all of the regular amenities of the Java programming language. Servlets surpass traditional CGI, however, by enabling collaborative applications and by providing increased performance. Servlets also may be used to dynamically generate HTML pages, parse form results, and so forth.

The following sections provide a comparison between servlets and their two rival technologies: CGI and server plug-ins.

26.1.1 Servlets vs. CGI

In the traditional CGI model, each time a request arrives for a CGI script a new OS-level process is launched to execute the program. When the request is finished, the process dies. Some servers provide support for long-running CGI processes that serve multiple requests; however, even in this case, concurrent access to the same CGI script would mean that multiple processes would have to run to handle the disjoint requests.

Processes are called *heavyweight* because there is usually a lot of overhead in launching, stopping, and scheduling among them. Servlets function in a similar model, but use threads instead of processes to provide concurrency. Since threads are considerably lighter-weight than processes, the servlet model is implicitly more efficient than traditional CGI (figure 26.2). This is particularly important for operating systems that do not provide efficient task switching. Executing a CGI script in a separate process requires the processor to switch among processes several times during execution of the script. This overhead is greatly reduced if the entire task can be executed in a single process using multiple threads.

Another important improvement in the servlet model over CGI is that the same servlet instance is used to handle multiple requests. Shared memory, in the form of the servlet's class and instance variables, can

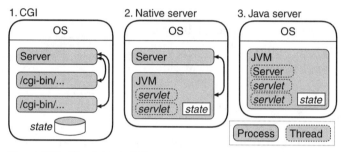

Figure 26.2   Servlets vs. CGI

be used to store state between accesses. This in-memory state can be used to cache frequently accessed resources as well as to establish a stateful session with the client. Traditional CGI programs either use files to keep state, or else operating-system shared memory—for which support is often limited and platform-dependent.

26.1.2 Servlets vs. server plug-ins

Server plug-ins introduced by Netscape (NSAPI) and Microsoft (ISAPI) solved the efficiency problems of multiprocess CGI. Server plug-ins allow direct extension of a Web-server by dynamically linking compiled libraries to the central server process.

Since both of these servers are implemented using traditional programming languages, if a server plug-in fails then it has the potential of crashing the entire server. Another immediately apparent downfall of server plug-ins is their inherent lack of portability. Once you begin implementing an application on one of these platforms, you become immediately tied to it. Server-side applications implemented in Java have the advantage of being portable to new platforms and new servers. For example, porting an application from NSAPI to ISAPI would be a serious programming effort, yet the same application written as a Java servlet would run under both of these server platforms and others without modification.

26.2 Invoking servlets

In this section, we will discuss the various methods of invoking a servlet. In particular, we will be concentrating on servlets running in Web servers, being accessed over HTTP. Other network services which host servlets, such as servlet-enabled FTP servers, will support different mechanisms for accessing servlets. The following techniques should, however, apply to most Web-based servlet environments.

26.2.1 Direct access through HTTP requests

The most common way of invoking a servlet is by requesting it through a URL in exactly the same manner as CGI programs are accessed. Once you have compiled a servlet and installed it in the appropriate directory on the Webserver, it can be invoked through a URL of the form http://hostname:port/servlet/ServletName.

The servlet name is either the full servlet class name, or a prearranged servlet alias. When the Web server receives the request, it checks to see if it already has an instance of the requested servlet. If it does, the request is passed to the servlet; otherwise, the requested servlet class is dynamically loaded and a new instance is created to handle the request.

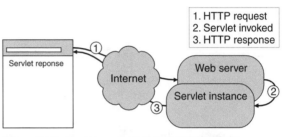

Figure 26.3 Invoking servlets through HTTP

When the servlet is called upon to service a request, it is supplied with any parameters supplied by the browser. The result of the servlet is then returned to the browser, just like the output of a CGI script (figure 26.3).

In the normal servlet execution model, just a single instance of the servlet will be used to service all requests to the server over the entire lifetime of the servlet. This should be compared with a CGI script that must be executed anew for each request.

26.2.2 Server-side includes

Server-side includes (SSI) have been in use since the earliest Web servers. They provide a way of dynamically assembling an HTML document when it is requested: The HTML document includes special tags that the Webserver replaces with dynamic content as it returns the page to the client.

By using the new SERVLET tag, server-side includes can be used to invoke a servlet and insert the output in-line in a document (figure 26.4).

The servlet tag takes the following form:

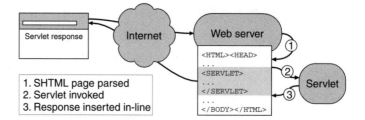

Figure 26.4   Invoking servlets through HTML

```
<html>
...
<servlet
    name="ServletName"
    code="ServletClass"
    codebase="ssi/"
    initParam1="val1"
    ...>
  <param name="requestParam1" value="val3">
  ...
</servlet>
...
</html>
```

Documents usually are identified as server-parsed documents (i.e., documents that may have SSI tags) by using the .shtml extension. When a Web server is returning a server-parsed document, it scans the document for special tags. When a SERVLET tag is encountered, the requested servlet is invoked and its output is inserted in-line in the document. This output replaces the original tag in the document, so the client receives the completed document without knowing that it was dynamically generated.

The tag in our example indicates that the ServletClass servlet should be executed when this page is requested. The class file is located in the ssi directory, and some initialization and request parameters have been included. Both the NAME and CODEBASE parameters are optional. If the CODEBASE parameter is omitted, the servlet classes must be in the standard servlets directory. The NAME parameter is used to allow SSI-servlet reuse.

26.2.3 Servlet chaining and filtering

Servlets may sometimes be chained together to sequentially process a request. In a servlet chain, output from each servlet is piped to the next in the chain until the

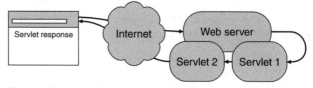

Figure 26.5   Invoking a chain of

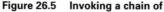

last servlet is reached, and then the output is returned to the client (figure 26.5). Servlet chains can be configured in a server in a variety of ways—either explicitly or by MIME types.

Servlet chains can sometimes be listed and mapped to a particular URL by using servlet aliasing. Each time a request to a particular servlet alias is received, a preconfigured chain of servlets is invoked. The order that the servlets are invoked is predetermined and is unaffected by the content type returned in each servlet response.

The second method of servlet chaining is referred to as filtering. Servlet chains can be configured based on MIME types of data to filter data of certain types through other servlets. In this case, if the content type returned from a request matches a preconfigured filter, then its output is piped into a request for another servlet. For example, a filter could be configured to convert all responses of type image/x-xbitmap to image/gif.

26.3 Developing servlets

The next section provides basic information about what is needed to begin developing and testing servlets. Details of the servlet API and some example servlets comprise the remainder of this chapter. Some more substantial examples follow in chapter 27.

For the few details that are actually specific to a particular Web server, we will concentrate on the Java Web Server (current version 1.1); it is a convenient pure-Java Web server, available for free evaluation download from JavaSoft. For full details of any of the following issues as they apply to your own Web server, consult its accompanying documentation.

26.3.1 Supported platforms

The servlet API has quickly gained the support of most major Web server vendors. The list of servlet-enabled Web servers includes commercial servers from JavaSoft, Netscape, and Microsoft as well as several free servers such as Apache and Jigsaw.

Although all of these servers support servlets, they do not necessarily provide the same performance. Most have implemented servlet support as a separate add-on to the server, with varying degrees of server-servlet communication overhead. For example, Apache currently runs a JVM in a separate process and communicates with this over a local TCP/IP connection. Thus all servlet access involves additional communication delay and process context-switching.

JavaSoft's Java Web Server and Jigsaw, on the other hand, are implemented entirely in Java and thus provide excellent performance for servlets. If you do not have access to one of these servers, you should develop and test your servlets by using the simple test server supplied with the Java Servlet Development Kit (JSDK). Jigsaw is available for free download at http://www.w3.org/Jigsaw/, and Java Web Server 1.1 is available for free evaluation download from http://jserv.javasoft.com/.

26.3.2 The Java Servlet Development Kit

The JSDK is a package freely available available from JavaSoft that includes all the tools you need to begin developing servlets. Although the JSDK is currently at version 2.0, with the 2.1 standard already specified, many servers still only provide JSDK 1.0 support. For installation in such a server, you should avoid use of the more recent features.

Primarily, JSDK includes the packages `javax.servlet` and `javax.servlet-.http`, which contain all of the classes related to servlets. In addition, JSDK has a simple test Web server that is useful for testing servlet operations outside of a production environment; the server will allow servlets to run, but it will not serve regular files such as class files or HTML documents.

Before you can begin to develop servlets, you need to install the JSDK and add its `jsdk.jar` file (`classes.zip` under JSDK 1.0) to your Java codebase. See the JSDK installation documentation for full details.

26.3.3 Installing servlets

During the development process, servlets can usually be installed by simply copying the class files into the Web server's servlet directory and then adding an entry in a configuration file or using an adminstrative tool.

To ease development after a servlet has been initially installed, some servers will automatically check to see if a servlet's class files have been updated, unloading and reloading the servlet if a change is observed. In this case, to install a new version of a servlet you will not need to manually restart the Web server; instead, you can simply copy in the updated class files.

The Java Web Server also comes with a special facility for installing remote servlets. In this situation, the server automatically downloads the servlet class files from a remote distribution point. This has many potential uses, including licensing and automatic update facilities.

26.3.4 Configuring servlets

The servlet architecture lends itself to easy access through graphical administration tools. The Java Web Server provides an administration tool which allows servlets to be configured through a GUI applet interface. After adding a new servlet, the tool allows you to specify the servlet's initialization parameters, among other options.

Servlets can also be given aliases to facilitate easy access and configuration. Once a servlet class has been given an alias, clients may access the servlet through this simplified name. Depending on the environment in which you are working, a servlet alias can be created either by using a GUI administration tool or by editing the servlet properties file. Again, the Java Web Server comes with an administration tool which allows servlet aliases to be easily managed.

26.4 Servlet internals

We will now begin to examine details of servlets and the servlet API. To start with, we will provide a detailed introduction to the internals of the servlet execution model.

26.4.1 The servlet API

All servlets must fundamentally implement the `Servlet` interface. This interface describes the exact mechanism through which the network server will interact with the servlet, including initialization, finalization, and request processing.

Details of each client request are supplied to the servlet through the `ServletRequest` interface (figure 26.6). This interface describes general properties of the request being made of the servlet. The

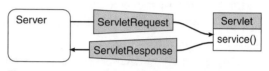

Figure 26.6   The servlet request/response model

servlet performs the requested action and then responds to the client through a `ServletResponse` interface. This interface provides a mechanism for the servlet to set the datatype of the response and to write out the body of the response.

More often, however, a servlet will be a subclass of a concrete implementation of the `Servlet` interface that provides specific support for a particular server environment. The most common example is the `HttpServlet` class that implements `Servlet` and provides specialized methods for handling HTTP requests. In this case, the client request is presented to the servlet as an `HttpServletRequest` object, and the client makes its response through an `HttpServletResponse` object. Similar concrete `Servlet` implementations can be provided for other common servlet types.

26.4.2 The basic servlet life cycle

The servlet API specifically defines a servlet's life cycle. The life cycle dictates when a servlet is instantiated, when requests are handled, and when the servlet is destroyed. This cycle remains the same regardless of the network service hosting the servlet and the method used to invoke it.

Generally, a servlet is created once, the first time a client requests it. Before this first request is handled, the servlet is automatically initialized by the host network

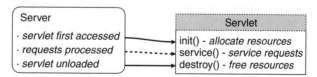

Figure 26.7   The servlet life cycle

service with various predefined configuration parameters. After being initialized, the servlet services requests for the remainder of its life span. When the host service decides to unload the servlet, a destructor is called, giving the servlet a chance to free any resources it may be holding (figure 26.7).

26.4.3 Variations on the lifecycle

There are some important variations in the servlet life cycle to note, depending on the method used to invoke the servlet.

If a servlet is being used in a server-side include, it is instantiated and initialized anew each time the document is accessed *unless* the servlet is explicitly named in the servlet tag. If a servlet is named, it will be loaded once and initialized once with the supplied initialization parameters; this one instance will then be used to service all future requests. If an SSI servlet must perform any expensive initialization, it should be explicitly named, for efficiency.

Through the Java Web Server's administration tools, servlets can be configured to load at server startup time. This has the advantage of allowing servlets with expensive startup operations to be initialized before their first access. This eliminates a potentially slow initial response time for clients but means that the servlet will be loaded for the duration of the server's uptime unless manually stopped.

26.4.4 Servlet parameters

There are two main mechanisms for passing configuration information into a servlet:

Initialization parameters are passed into a servlet when it is first loaded; they are specified in a configuration structure supplied to the servlet during initialization. These parameters are used for general configuration information that applies to all subsequent requests. They are normally statically configured by a graphical adminstration tool, although for SSI servlets they may also be declared in the inline servlet tag.

Depending on the method used to invoke the servlet, request parameters may also be specified in a servlet request. Since these parameters are given at runtime, as opposed to at initialization time, they are only used to provide information particular to a given request. For HTTP servlets, these parameters are specified as the query string of the client's request. For SSI servlets, they are taken from param tags in the inline servlet tag.

26.4.5 Multithreaded access and synchronization

Since servers usually create only one instance of a servlet to handle disjoint (and potentially concurrent) requests, the programmer must be concerned with thread safety, so standard synchronization techniques should be used to ensure that the servlet is thread-safe. All potential concurrent access to a servlet will stem from concurrent calls to the `service()` method. Blocks of code within this method that should not be concurrently executed should be synchronized on appropriate locks. Refer to chapter 4 for more details of concurrent programming.

An additional interface was added with JSDK 2.0 which allows servlet writers to ignore questions of concurrent access. Implementing the interface `SingleThreadModel` guarantees that no two threads will execute concurrently in the `service()` method. In such servlets,

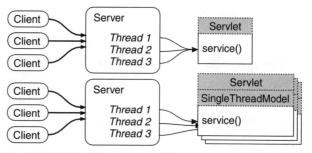

Figure 26.8   Servicing concurrent requests

multiple instances may be created to ensure that there is always an instance available to handle a request without blocking (figure 26.8).

26.4.6 Servlet beans

Servlet beans are servlets that adhere to the JavaBeans specification. A servlet bean has several advantages over standard servlets. First of all, a servlet bean can be distributed in a JAR file containing all of the servlet's classes and resources. The servlet JAR file is typically installed in the servletbeans subdirectory of the server. A second advantage is that the host server can use introspection to access the servlet's properties in the standard JavaBeans fashion. This allows the servlet to receive property updates without being reloaded. Servers, such as the Java Web Server, allow an administrator to graphically edit the servlet bean's properties through this mechanism. Another advantage of servlet beans is that the host server can automatically serialize them. Once a property has been modified, the updated bean can automatically serialized so that the changes may persist. The next time the server loads the servlet, it can be loaded from the .ser file instead of from its original JAR file. See the Java Web Server documentation for a full specification of servlet beans.

26.5 Interface Servlet

The `Servlet` interface defines the standard way in which a network server will access a servlet. All servlets operate in a request/response paradigm; however, they often also maintain long-term state about individual clients and so are not as stateless as the basic interface suggests.

Although all servlets must fundamentally implement this interface, many will actually leverage off facilities provided by more specific implementations of this class such as `GenericServlet` or `HttpServlet`, and so will obey the APIs of those more specific classes.

26.5.1 Methods

The following methods define the basic interface to a servlet:

void init(ServletConfig config) throws ServletException   This method gives the servlet a chance to perform any one-time startup operations required before servicing requests. Examples may be memory allocation, reading in persistent state, establishing network connections, and so forth. This method is guaranteed to be called once and only once and is also guaranteed to complete before the first request is handled. Requests that are received before the `init()` method finishes will block until it completes.

The `ServletConfig` parameter provides initialization information for the servlet. Even if not used, this parameter should be stored to be returned by the `getServlet-Config()` method. Most standard implementations of the `Servlet` interface, such as `GenericServlet`, perform this task automatically.

void service(ServletRequest request, ServletResponse response) throws ServletException, IOException   The `service()` method is called by the network service hosting the servlet whenever a client makes a request of the servlet. The servlet can read in request data and parameters through the `ServletRequest` parameter `request`, and should send its response back through the `ServletResponse` parameter `response`. Details of these datastructures are provided in the following sections.

void destroy()   At some point after a servlet has finished servicing requests, the host may decide to unload it. At this point, the servlet's `destroy()` method is called.

When a servlet is destroyed, it should free all resources that it holds and save any state that should be stored persistently. Many servlets maintain open connections to resources such as databases, RMI servers, or files. These resources should be properly closed and freed when `destroy()` is called.

A properly behaved servlet should also free its threads. Any threads that a servlet is using should be stopped or completed before the `destroy()` method returns. This includes threads that have been explicitly launched by the servlet, threads that have been started on behalf of the servlet such as RMI listener threads, and also server threads that are currently executing the `service()` method on behalf of currently connected clients.

The API guarantees that no access to the servlet will happen after the `destroy()` method is called. Once destroyed, the servlet will eventually be garbage collected.

ServletConfig getServletConfig()   This method should return the servlet's `ServletConfig` object which should have been saved by the `init()` method.

String getServletInfo()   This method should return general information about the servlet such as its author, version, and copyright. Servlet writers should implement this method to provide the appropriate information.

26.6 JSDK 2.0 *Interface SingleThreadModel*

By default, a single instance of a servlet will be called upon to handle multiple concurrent requests. This means that in general, servlet writers must be concerned with thread-safety. By implementing the `SingleThreadModel` interface, developers can side-step multithreading issues. If this interface is implemented, the servlet API guarantees that no two threads will concurrently execute the `service()` method on the same servlet instance. In order to reduce the time that incoming requests may have to wait for a servlet to become available, the host network service may choose to keep a pool of single-threaded servlet instances. In this case, a free servlet will be chosen from the pool to handle an incoming request.

This interface is an empty marker interface; it declares no methods.

26.7 *Interface ServletConfig*

This interface is used by a network service to pass configuration information to a servlet when it is initialized. The `ServletConfig` is passed into a servlet in the `init()` method and may be accessed during a request with the `getServletConfig()` method.

26.7.1 *Methods*

The following methods are defined by the `ServletConfig` interface:

String getInitParameter(String name)   The `getInitParameter()` method returns the initialization parameter specified by name, or else `null` if the parameter was not configured.

Initialization parameters for a servlet are all specified as a name/value pair, such as `logFilename=/var/run/servletLog`. To access this parameter, simply call `getInitParameter("logFileName")`.

Enumeration getInitParameterNames()   This method returns an `Enumeration` of the names of a servlet's initialization parameters. If the servlet has no initialization parameters, an empty `Enumeration` is returned.

ServletContext getServletContext()   This method returns a description of the context in which the servlet is running; that is, the server that is hosting the servlet. The `ServletContext` interface is described in detail later.

26.8 Interface ServletRequest

The `ServletRequest` interface describes the request information that is passed into a servlet's `service()` method.

A request is formally made up of three parts: the request URI, which identifies the requested object; request parameters, which provide details of the request; and the request body, which holds the application-specific request data.

26.8.1 Methods

The following methods are defined by the `ServletRequest` interface:

String getScheme()   This method returns the scheme of the URL used to access this servlet; typically, http, https, or possibly ftp.

JSDK 2.0 *String getProtocol()*   This method returns the protocol and version information used to access this servlet. The response will typically be of the form protocol/major.minor. A typical response to this method for a servlet accessed in a Web environment would be *HTTP/1.1.*

String getServerName()   This method returns the server's host name. If a servlet is installed on a multihomed server, the value returned will depend upon the virtual host through which the servlet was accessed.

int getServerPort()   This method returns the port on which the server is listening.

String getRemoteAddr()   This method returns the IP address of the remote host that is accessing this servlet; for example, *10.0.0.1.*

String getRemoteHost()   This method returns the host name of the remote host that is accessing this servlet. If a server is configured for maximum performance then DNS will be disabled and so this method will simply return the client's IP address.

String getParameter(String name)   This method returns the value of the specified request parameter, or `null` if it was not provided. Request parameters are name/value pairs that give detailed information about a particular request; for example, the parameters specified in an HTTP query string or the request parameters specified in a server-side include tag. Under JSDK 1.0 and 2.0, the result of this method is undefined if the parameter had multiple values. Under JSDK 2.1, the result is the first parameter value.

String[] getParameterValues(String name)   This method returns an array of all the values for the specified request parameter; use this where a request parameter can have multiple values, such as the result of a multiple-selection list box.

Enumeration getParameterNames()   This method returns an `Enumeration` of the names of all request parameters. An empty `Enumeration` is returned if there are no request parameters or if the entire request body has been read.

The latter will occur if, for example, the result of an HTML form is posted to a servlet and the servlet directly reads the body of the request itself before calling this method. When the servlet framework then attempts to read the request parameters from the request body, it will encounter no more data and indicate that there are no request parameters.

int getContentLength()   This method returns the content length of the request body. If the content length is unknown, it returns –1.

String getContentType()   This method returns the MIME type of the request data, or `null` if it is unknown. See appendix B for some common MIME types.

ServletInputStream getInputStream() throws IOException   This method returns an input stream from which to read the body of the client's request. This should only be used for reading binary data; refer to the `getReader()` method for reading purely textual data.

JSDK 2.0 *BufferedReader getReader() throws IOException*   This method returns a `BufferedReader` for reading text-only request bodies. Character decoding is performed as appropriate for the request, and an `UnsupportedEncodingException` is thrown if the required character encoding is not supported.

Reading the request body should either be done through this method (for textual data) or through the `getInputStream()` method (for binary data). Mixing the two methods is invalid and will cause an `IllegalStateException` to be thrown.

JSDK 2.0 *String getCharacterEncoding()*   This method returns the character set encoding of the request body.

String getRealPath(String path)   This method converts the specified virtual path to a real platform-dependent path on the local file system. This method can be used to convert, for example, a filename in an HTTP request into the actual file on the local filesystem to which the HTTP request refers. This method is deprecated by JSDK 2.1.

Object getAttribute(String name)   This method returns the specified request attribute. It allows access to server-specific features that are not supported by the standard methods above. Details of attribute names and the resulting objects depend on the local server environment. Currently, JavaSoft define three standard names:

javax.net.ssl.cipher_suite, javax.net.ssl.peer_certificates and javax.net.ssl.session, all used to access SSL-specific security parameters.

26.9 Interface ServletResponse

The `ServletResponse` interface describes how a response may be returned to a client. All responses are considered to be MIME data; that is, a MIME type is associated with a volume of data. This type indicates how the data should be interpreted by the client.

26.9.1 Methods

The following methods allow a response to be constructed for a client request:

void setContentType(String type)   This method sets the MIME type for the response data. The content type must be set before the response data is written. Some of the more common MIME types returned by servlets are text/html for HTML documents, text/plain for text files, and application/octet-stream for binary data.

void setContentLength(int length)   This method sets the length, in bytes, of the response data. Depending on the higher level protocol used to request the servlet, setting the content length may or may not be required. For efficiency, this method should be called whenever possible. It allows the remote client to provide an indication of how far it has progressed through downloading the servlet's response, and it allows proxies to behave more efficiently.

ServletOutputStream getOutputStream()   This method returns an output stream into which the response body may be written. You should close this stream when you are finished with it. This method should be used for writing binary data; refer to the `get-Writer()` method for sending a purely textual response.

(JSDK 2.0) *PrintWriter getWriter() throws IOException*   This method returns a `PrintWriter` that can be used to send a textual response body. You should close this stream when you are finished with it. Also, remember that `PrintWriter` uses the platform-default line terminator (\n under UNIX; \r\n under Windows; \r under MacOS) so don't use its `println()` methods if you want control over the line terminator. For typical HTML responses, the type of line terminator is irrelevant so those methods can be used safely.

The character set by this stream used is either the character set you explicitly specified in your content type (e.g., text/html;charset="UTF-8") or a character set mutually supported by the client and server. If no content type has been set by the time this method is called, the response is automatically set to text/plain. This method automatically adds an appropriate MIME charset property to the response content type, whether it was set explicitly or implicitly.

If you will be writing binary data, use the `getOutputStream()` method. You cannot combine the use of both of these methods; doing so will result in an `Illegal-StateException`.

(JSDK 2.0) *String getCharacterEncoding()* This method returns the character encoding associated with this response. This is either the character set you explicitly specified in your content-type, or a character set mutually supported by the client and server. Calling this method without first setting a content type implicitly sets the content type to text/plain. A MIME charset property is also automatically added.

26.10 Interface ServletContext

The `ServletContext` interface provides a servlet with access to the environment in which it is running. Through this interface, a servlet can log important events and can access information specific to the network server that is hosting it.

A servlet's context can be retrieved with the `getServletContext()` method of its initialization configuration.

26.10.1 Methods
The following methods are supplied by the `ServletContext` interface:

void log(String message) This method logs a servlet event to the server's log file.

(JSDK 2.0) *void log(Exception ex, String message)* This is a useful method for logging the stacktrace of an exception and an error message to the servlet's log file.

(JSDK 2.1) *void log(String message, Throwable throwable)* This is the JSDK 2.1 replacement for the previous JSDK 2.0 `log()` method.

(JSDK 2.0) *Enumeration getServletNames()* This method returns an `Enumeration` of the names of the servlets hosted by the server. It should not in general be used; it has been deprecated by JSDK 2.1.

Servlet getServlet(String name) throws ServletException This method returns the servlet with the given name, or `null` if it is not found. It should not in general be used; it has been deprecated by JSDK 2.1.

String getRealPath(String path) This method translates a virtual path using local alias rules, and returns the resulting platform dependent file path. This can be used, for example, to determine the actual file that an HTTP request would correspond to if made directly on the Webserver.

String getMimeType(String file)   This method returns the MIME type of the specified file, or `null` if it is not known.

String getServerInfo()   This method returns information about the server that is hosting this servlet, including its name and version number.

Object getAttribute(String name)   This method returns a named, server-dependent attribute. This can be used to obtain server-specific services.

(JSDK 2.1)   *int getMajorVersion()*   This method returns the servlet API major version number (e.g., 2).

(JSDK 2.1)   *int getMinorVersion()*   This method returns the servlet API major version number (e.g., 1).

26.11 Class ServletInputStream

The body of a servlet request is made available through the `ServletInputStream` class. This is a simple `InputStream` that provides some extended function.

26.11.1 Methods
The following method is added to the basic `InputStream` API:

int readLine(byte[] data, int offset, int length) throws IOException   This method reads a single `\n`-terminated line of data into the specified array `data`, starting at offset `offset`, and returns the number of bytes read or –1 if the end of the stream was reached. The terminating `\n`, if any, is inserted into the array. Be aware, however, that the last line of input may not contain this terminator.

According to the API, this method should read no more than `length` bytes; however, at the time of writing, this is not true.

This method is not terribly efficient. If you will be reading a large amount of text or wish to proper character encoding conversion, you would be better off using the `BufferedReader` and/or `InputStreamReader` classes. The primary benefit of the `ServletInputStream` method is that it performs no unnecessary data copying or memory allocation, factors which count in a small way against the character streams. Remember too that the `Reader` classes include internal buffers so you must use this `ServletInputStream` method if you will be reading a mix of textual and binary data.

26.12 Class ServletOutputStream

The body of a servlet's response is transmitted through a `ServletOutputStream`. This is a simple `OutputStream` with some extensions for transmitting textual data.

26.12.1 Methods

The following methods are added to the `OutputStream` API:

print(...) throws IOException   These methods all convert their parameter (any basic type except `Object`) to a `String` and write this value to the `OutputStream` as plain text. In this case, plain text is considered to be just the bottom byte of the individual Unicode characters of the `String`; that is, ISO Latin 1.

println() throws IOException   This method writes out a `\r\n` line terminator.

println(...) throws IOException   These methods all write their parameter (any basic type except `Object`) to this stream in plain text, followed by a `\r\n` line terminator.

None of these methods are terribly efficient. If you will be transmitting a lot of text, or wish to support alternate character encodings, use the `PrintWriter` and `OutputStreamWriter` classes. Be aware, in such a case, that the `PrintWriter` class uses the platform-local line terminator so its `println()` methods may not be suitable for use in a network environment.

As before, you should be aware that when you use the character streams, there will be a certain amount of additional memory allocation and copying that will not be performed by the `ServletOutputStream` class alone.

26.13 Class GenericServlet

The `GenericServlet` class is an implementation of the `Servlet` interface that provides various useful helper methods. This is a common superclass for simple servlets. As a convenience, this class also implements all the methods of the `ServletConfig` interface.

26.13.1 Constructors

This class provides just one standard constructor:

protected GenericServlet()   This constructor must be called by a subclass constructor. There are no parameters, and nothing is done by the constructor.

26.13.2 Methods

A subclass of `GenericServlet` can override the standard `Servlet` methods as expected; in particular, providing an implementation of the `service()` method. In addition, it can make use of the following helper methods:

void init(ServletConfig config) throws ServletException   This method, from the `Servlet` interface, initializes the `GenericServlet` and logs a message indicating that the servlet has been initialized. A subclass that overrides this method must ensure to first call this superclass method before performing its own servlet-specific initialization.

JSDK 2.1   *void init() throws ServletException*   Under JSDK 2.1 you can override this method instead of the default `init()` method. Normal initialization will be performed in the default method and then this method will be called for you to perform your own initialization.

ServletConfig getServletConfig()   This method, from the `Servlet` interface, returns the servlet configuration specified in the `init()` method.

String getServletInfo()   This method, from the `Servlet` interface, is implemented to return `null`; a subclass should override this to provide a more useful description.

void destroy()   This method, from the `Servlet` interface, logs that the servlet has been destroyed. A subclass that overrides this method should ensure to call this method when it is done.

ServletContext getServletContext()   This method returns the servlet's `Servlet-Context` by calling the corresponding method on the servlet's initialization data.

String getInitParameter(String name)   This method returns the specified initialization parameter by calling the corresponding method on the servlet's initialization data.

Enumeration getInitParameterNames()   This method returns an `Enumeration` of the names of all initialization parameters by calling the corresponding method on the servlet's initialization data.

void log(String message)   This method logs the specified message to the server's log file, preceded by the servlet's class name. This is useful for logging simple servlet status messages.

JSDK 2.1 *void log(String message, Throwable throwable)*   This   method   logs the specified message and exception to the server's log file, preceded by the servlet's class name. This is useful for logging servlet errors.

26.14 A server-side include example

The following is a short example to illustrate the use of server-side includes.

26.14.1 Class TestSSIServlet

This class is a simple SSI servlet that prints out various initialization and request parameters (figure 26.9).

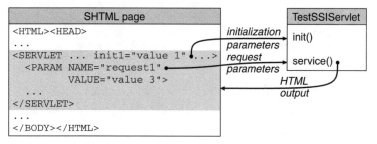

Figure 26.9   Class TestSSIServlet

```
import java.io.*;
import javax.servlet.*;

public class TestSSIServlet extends GenericServlet {
  // public void service (ServletRequest req, ServletResponse resp)
      throws IOException ...
}
```

The `TestSSIServlet` servlet extends `GenericServlet` and overrides the `service()` methods to return an appropriate result to the caller.

```
  public void service (ServletRequest request, ServletResponse response)
      throws IOException {
    String init1 = getInitParameter ("init1");
    String init2 = getInitParameter ("init2");
    String request1 = request.getParameter ("request1");
    String request2 = request.getParameter ("request2");
    PrintWriter writer = response.getWriter ();
    writer.println ("<br>init parameter 'init1' = " + init1);
    writer.println ("<br>init parameter 'init2' = " + init2);
    writer.println ("<br>request parameter 'request1' = " + request1);
    writer.println ("<br>request parameter 'request2' = " + request2);
    writer.close ();
  }
```

This method prints various initialization and request parameters to the servlet's response `Writer`. This output will then be substituted in the HTML page that caused this servlet to be invoked.

This example makes use of the `getWriter()` method introduced by JSDK 2.0; under JSDK 1.0, use `getOutputStream()` and the `println()` method of `ServletOutputStream`.

26.14.2 In practice

The following server-parsed HTML page causes the `TestSSIServlet` to be invoked when it is accessed.

```
<html>
<body>
<h2>Test Server Side Includes:<h2>
<servlet code="TestSSIServlet" name="Test"
    init1="value 1" init2="value 2">
  <param name="request1" value="value 3">
  <param name="request2" value="value 4">
</servlet>
</body>
</html>
```

One of the most powerful features of server-side includes is that they allow the static portions of HTML pages to be kept in plain HTML format while the content is dynamically computed by a servlet. The content may be extracted from a database, loaded from a file, or dynamically computed at run time. This allows the form of pages to be edited without the need to alter the content or to change and recompile the servlet that produces the content.

This idea is taken a step further in Java Web Server with the idea of *page compilation*. Page compilation (not covered here) allows actual Java code to be interleaved with the HTML in a .jhtml file. These files are automatically compiled into servlets which, when accessed, dynamically produce the desired output. Refer to the Java Web Server documentation for details.

26.15 Class HttpServlet

When writing a servlet to be invoked through an HTTP request, you will almost always want to extend the `HttpServlet` class. This class implements many useful details of handling HTTP get and post requests, and it provides various utility classes for receiving HTTP requests and sending properly formatted HTTP responses.

Note that the `HttpServlet` class is a subclass of `GenericServlet`, and so provides all the facilities of that class in addition to those described here.

26.15.1 Constructors

The following constructor is provided:

protected HttpServlet()   This constructor should be called by a subclass; the current implementation does nothing.

26.15.2 Methods

Servlets that extend `HttpServlet` should not override the `service()` method to service requests. Instead, the `HttpServlet` class provides several higher level methods for servicing HTTP requests; `doGet()` and `doPost()` for the basic HTTP/1.0 operations; and, under JSDK 2.0, `doPut()`, `doDelete()`, `doTrace()`, and `doOptions()` for the corresponding HTTP/1.1 operations. These methods use the HTTP-specific datastructures `HttpServletRequest` and `HttpServletResponse` for querying the request and returning a response.

protected void doGet(HttpServletRequest request, HttpServletResponse response) throws ServletException, IOException   This method should be overridden for those servlets which are to handle HTTP get requests. These requests do not contain any data in the request `InputStream`; any special information will be included in request parameters. The default implementation of this method returns a bad request error.

When defining a servlet protocol, the get method should only be used for safe requests. In particular, the HTTP protocol specifies that a get request can be repeated safely with no undesirable side effects. In other words, a get request must be idempotent; it should not change the servlet's state. Of course, this is not an absolute requirement, but it is a useful guideline.

protected void doPost(HttpServletRequest request, HttpServletResponse response) throws ServletException, IOException   This method should be overridden to handle HTTP post requests. Subclasses implementing this method should read data from the request `InputStream`, set response headers, and write out the response data. The default implementation of this method returns a bad request error.

When defining a servlet protocol, the post method is suitable to use for actions for which the user must be held responsible—it need not be safe or idempotent. This means that you should use the post methods for all actions which will result in a change to the servlet's state.

(JSDK 2.0)   *protected void doPut(HttpServletRequest req, HttpServletResponse resp) throws ServletException, IOException*   This method is called to perform the put operation, as defined in HTTP 1.1. This operation is similar to sending a file via

FTP. As is the case with a post request, this method does not need to be safe or idempotent. If your implementation cannot support one of the content headers, such as content-transfer-encoding or content-language, then it should return a not-implemented error. The default implementation of this method returns a bad request error.

JSDK 2.0 *protected void doDelete(HttpServletRequest req, HttpServletResponse resp) throws ServletException, IOException* This method is called to perform the delete operation, as defined in HTTP 1.1. If the client has proper access rights, then implementations of this method should remove the requested URI from the server. The default implementation of this method returns a bad request error.

JSDK 2.0 *protected void doTrace(HttpServletRequest req, HttpServletResponse resp) throws ServletException, IOException* This method implements the trace operation, as defined in HTTP 1.1. A trace returns a page back to the client listing all of the parameters sent in the request. This method is not usually overridden; the default implementation serves most purposes.

JSDK 2.0 *protected void doOptions(HttpServletRequest req, HttpServletResponse resp) throws ServletException, IOException* This method implements the options operation, as defined in HTTP 1.1. This returns a list of the options supported by the servlet. A servlet supports a given HTTP operation if it overrides the corresponding handler method (e.g., `doGet()` or `doPost()`). Servlet writers should not override this method unless they wish to support operations outside of the scope of the HTTP/1.1 protocol; the default implementation serves most purposes.

protected long getLastModified(HttpServletRequest request) This method should return the time (in milliseconds since the epoch; January 1, 1970, 00:00:00 GMT) that the requested object was last modified. When a client requests a document, it may already have a locally cached version. By querying this modification time, it can determine whether the locally cached version is still valid or if it needs to download an updated copy.

Overriding this method allows the requested object to be accessed through these conditional requests, as well as to be properly cached. By default, this method returns `-1` indicating that the last modified time is unknown, and so, the document should not be cached.

protected void service(HttpServletRequest request, HttpServletResponse response) throws ServletException, IOException This method is a generalized `service()` method that processes HTTP requests. It is automatically called by the default `HttpServlet` implementation of the `Servlet service()` method; it parses the request automatically and handles standard HTTP requests, calling `doGet()`, `doPost()`, `getLastModified()`, and so forth, according to the client's requests. You should only override this method if you wish to support nonstandard types of HTTP requests. You should call this superclass implementation for all normal requests.

26.16 Interface HttpServletRequest

This interface extends `ServletRequest` to provide higher level HTTP-specific request information.

26.16.1 Methods

This interface defines the following methods in addition to the standard methods of `ServletRequest`:

String getMethod()   This method returns the HTTP request method; typically, either get, head, or post, or one of the HTTP/1.1 options put, delete, trace, or options.

String getRequestURI()   This method returns the full request URI; that is, the URL or URI used by the client to access this servlet.

String getServletPath()   This method returns the request path that led to this servlet; typically, this will be of the form /servlet/MyServlet.

String getPathInfo()   This method returns the path info portion of the request URI or `null` if none was specified. The path info starts at the first forward slash after the requested servlet and ends at the first question mark, if any; the leading / is included. For example, the path info of http://host/servlet/Servlet/pathInfo?query is /pathInfo.

    This is one of the mechanisms by which parameters are passed to servlets. A servlet that converted plain text documents into HTML might accept the path to the plain text document as a path info following the servlet name, accepting URLs of the following format: http://host/servlet/Text2HTML/rfcs/rfc1.txt.

String getPathTranslated()   This method returns the path info portion of the request URI, translated as per the `ServletContext getRealPath()` method; that is, it is a valid local filename that can be accessed, if the file exists, through Java's standard file access mechanisms. For example, the hypothetical text-to-HTML servlet described above would use this method to determine the local file that it should actually convert.

String getQueryString()   This method returns the query string portion of the request URI. The query string starts after the first question mark of the request and ends at the end of the URI. The question mark is not included in the result of this method, and `null` is returned if no query string was specified. This is the standard alternative mechanism, other than the path info, by which parameters are passed to servlets.

When a servlet is the target of an HTML form with a get method, then the servlet is invoked as follows: http://host/servlet/ProcessForm?name=Jim+Bean&ssn=n%2Fa. The servlet can then parse this request into the elements of the form (name and ssn in this case) by performing standard URL decoding. Alternatively, if the elements of a query string follow the standard URL-encoded sequence of name/value pairs, as they do in this example, the inherited `getRequestParameter()` methods of `ServletRequest` can be used to automatically parse these request parameters.

If a servlet is the target of a post operation and a query string is included in the request URI, only this method can be used to extract the query string. The inherited `getRequestParameter()` methods expect that the request parameters will be encoded in the body of the client's request and will not look here.

String getRemoteUser()   If this servlet was accessed using one of HTTP's authentication mechanisms, this method will return the name of the remote user, or else it will return `null`.

String getAuthType()   This method returns the authentication scheme used to access this servlet (e.g., *basic*), or `null` if no authentication was used.

String getHeader(String name)   The `getHeader()` method returns the value of the specified HTTP header field from the client request, or `null` if it was not included. The case of the header name is ignored.

int getIntHeader(String name)   This method returns the value of the specified HTTP header, parsed as an integer value, or -1 if the parameter was not specified.

long getDateHeader(String name)   This method returns the value of the specified HTTP header, parsed as a date in millisecond since the epoch, or -1 if the parameter was not specified.

Enumeration getHeaderNames()   This method returns an `Enumeration` of the names of all headers included with the client's HTTP request.

(JSDK 2.0) *Cookie[] getCookies()*   This method returns an array of cookies found in this request.

(JSDK 2.0) *String getRequestedSessionId()*   This method returns the session identifier specified in this request, or a new session identifier if the request identifier was invalid. For details of HTTP sessions and session identifiers, see section 26.18 on page 620.

JSDK 2.0 *HttpSession getSession(boolean create)* This method returns the session associated with this request. If a valid session is not found, then a new session is created and returned if the `create` flag is `true`; otherwise, this method returns `null`. To maintain a valid session, servlet writers must ensure that this method is called at least once per request.

JSDK 2.1 *HttpSession getSession()* This method calls the previous method with the parameter `true` (automatic creation enabled).

JSDK 2.0 *boolean isRequestedSessionIdFromCookie()* This method determines if the client specified a session identifier in a request cookie. If the requested session identifier is invalid, then the session identifier sent by the client may not match what is returned by `getRequestedSessionId()` or `getSession()`.

JSDK 2.0 *boolean isRequestedSessionIdFromUrl()* This method determines if the client specified a session identifier as part of the request URI. If the requested session identifier is invalid, then the session identifier sent by the client may not match what is returned by `getRequestedSessionId()` or `getSession()`.

JSDK 2.1 *boolean isRequestedSessionIdFromURL()* This is the JSDK 2.1 replacement for the previous JSDK 2.0 `isRequestedSessionIdFromUrl()` method.

JSDK 2.0 *boolean isRequestedSessionIdValid()* This method checks whether the session identifier sent by the client is currently associated with a valid session.

26.17 Interface HttpServletResponse

This interface allows the servlet to format an HTTP-protocol compliant response which is sent back to the client. It extends the `ServletResponse` interface.

26.17.1 Static variables

This interface contains class variables describing all the standard HTTP status codes; full details are provided in the HTTP specification, however the common codes are listed below:

int SC_OK This status code indicates that a request succeeded.

int SC_BAD_REQUEST This status code indicates that a bad request was received.

int SC_UNAUTHORIZED This status code indicates that the caller is not authorized to perform an operation.

int SC_FORBIDDEN This status code indicates that the requested operation is forbidden.

int SC_NOT_FOUND This status code indicates that a requested resource was not located.

int SC_INTERNAL_SERVER_ERROR This status code indicates that an internal server error was encountered.

For completeness, the full set of supported error codes is as follows:

Table 26.1 Supported Error Codes

Code	Error	Code	Error
100	SC_CONTINUE	101	SC_SWITCHING_PROTOCOLS
200	SC_OK	201	SC_CREATED
202	SC_ACCEPTED	203	SC_NON_AUTHORITATIVE_INFORMATION
204	SC_NO_CONTENT	205	SC_RESET_CONTENT
206	SC_PARTIAL_CONTENT	300	SC_MULTIPLE_CHOICES
301	SC_MOVED_PERMANENTLY	302	SC_MOVED_TEMPORARILY
303	SC_SEE_OTHER	304	SC_NOT_MODIFIED
305	SC_USE_PROXY	400	SC_BAD_REQUEST
401	SC_UNAUTHORIZED	402	SC_PAYMENT_REQUIRED
403	SC_FORBIDDEN	404	SC_NOT_FOUND
405	SC_METHOD_NOT_ALLOWED	406	SC_NOT_ACCEPTABLE
407	SC_PROXY_AUTHENTICATION_REQUIRED	408	SC_REQUEST_TIMEOUT
409	SC_CONFLICT	410	SC_GONE
411	SC_LENGTH_REQUIRED	412	SC_PRECONDITION_FAILED
413	SC_REQUEST_ENTITY_TOO_LARGE	414	SC_REQUEST_URI_TOO_LONG
415	SC_UNSUPPORTED_MEDIA_TYPE	500	SC_INTERNAL_SERVER_ERROR
501	SC_NOT_IMPLEMENTED	502	SC_BAD_GATEWAY
503	SC_SERVICE_UNAVAILABLE	504	SC_GATEWAY_TIMEOUT
505	SC_HTTP_VERSION_NOT_SUPPORTED		

26.17.2 Methods

In addition to the standard methods of `ServletResponse`, this interface provides the following methods:

void setStatus(int statusCode)   This method sets the HTTP response code to the specified value `statusCode`; a standard, appropriate status message will be included automatically. The status code should be one of the predefined constants. It is not necessary to always call this method since an appropriate status code is sent automatically if one is not specified.

void setStatus(int statusCode, String statusMessage)   This method is used to set the status code and message that appear at the start of the HTTP response. It should not in general be used; it has been deprecated by JSDK 2.1. Use the `sendError()` method instead.

void setHeader(String name, String value)   This method sets the HTTP response header `name` to the value `value`. This method will replace a previously set header.

void setIntHeader(String name, int value)   This method sets the HTTP response header `name` to the integer value `value`.

void setDateHeader(String name, long value)   This method sets the HTTP response header `name` to the date value `value`.

boolean containsHeader(String name)   This method returns whether the specified response header is already set.

void sendError(int statusCode, String statusMessage) throws IOException This method sets the HTTP response status to the specified status code and message, and transmits a standard error message body to the client.

void sendError(int statusCode) throws IOException   This method sets the HTTP response status to the specified status code with a standard, appropriate status message, and transmits a standard error message body to the client.

void sendRedirect(String location) throws IOException   This method sets the HTTP response status to be a standard redirect and transmits to the client an appropriate redirect header and message body for the specified redirect location. This redirect location must be an absolute URL such as http://nitric.com/newLocation.html.

If you send this response to a Web browser, the browser will automatically go to the new location and download the specified Web page. A simple Web redirector might thus have the following `doGet()` method:

```
protected void doGet (HttpServletRequest request,
    HttpServletResponse response) throws IOException {
```

```
    response.sendRedirect (request.getQueryString ());
}
```

When this servlet is invoked with the URL http://nitric.com/servlet/Redirect?http://csr.com/, the client will be automatically redirected to the specified alternate location.

(JSDK 2.0) *void addCookie(Cookie cookie)*   This method should be called to add a cookie to the response. Note that this method can be called multiple times to send more than one cookie to the client.

(JSDK 2.0) *String encodeUrl(String url)*   This method enables session tracking through URL rewriting. It takes the given URL and returns a new URL with the session ID encoded in it. If URL rewriting is not necessary, then the URL is return unchanged. In order for a servlet to be used in the context of a session, all URLs sent back to the client must first be filtered through this method.

(JSDK 2.1) *String encodeURL(String url)*   This is the JSDK 2.1 replacement for the previous JSDK 2.0 `encodeUrl()` method.

(JSDK 2.0) *String encodeRedirectedUrl(String url)*   This method is analogous the `encodeUrl()` method except it is used to filter URLs passed to the `sendRedirect()` method.

(JSDK 2.1) *String encodeRedirectedURL(String url)*   This is the JSDK 2.1 replacement for the previous JSDK 2.0 `encodeRedirectedUrl()` method.

26.18 **(JSDK 2.0)** *Interface HttpSession*

This interface allows servlet writers to maintain persistent state on a user over a specified period of time that can span multiple connections and requests. Developers can store and retrieve arbitrary application layer data associated with the user. The implementation uses client-side cookies or URL rewriting in order to track the user's session over multiple HTTP requests. Through this mechanism, the servlet API provides transparent implementation of session tracking on behalf of the servlet writer.

Application layer objects stored in the session can be notified when they are bound or unbound by implementing the `HttpSessionBindingListener` interface.

26.18.1 Methods

The following methods are provided by the `HttpSession` interface.

String getId()   This method returns the session's unique identifier.

HttpSessionContext getSessionContext()   This method returns the `HttpSession-Context` object associated with this session. This context groups multiple sessions into a single name space. This method should not be used; it has been deprected by JSDK 2.1.

long getCreationTime()   This method returns the time at which this session was created. The return value is in milliseconds since the epoch.

long getLastAccessedTime()   This method returns the last time that the client accessed this session. The client is deemed to have accessed the session if it sends a request carrying the ID assigned to the session. Application level access to the session, such as storing or retrieving values, does not affect the access time. The value returned is in milliseconds since the epoch.

void invalidate()   This method invalidates the session and removes it from its context. Once invalidated, any additional access to the session will result in an `Illegal-StateException`.

void putValue(String name, Object value)   This method is used to add an arbitrary name/value data pair to the session. In this manner, servlet developers can use the session to associate application-level data with a user. If the value being added implements the `HttpSessionBindingListener` interface, then its `valueBound()` method will automatically be called to signal that it is being bound to the session.

Object getValue(String name)   This method returns the value that has been added with the given name through the `putValue()` method, or `null` if none has been bound.

void removeValue(String name)   This method is used to remove a name/value data pair from the session. If the name is not found, then no action is taken. If the value being removed implements the `HttpSessionBindingListener` interface, then its `valueUnbound()` method will automatically be called to signal that it is being unbound from the session.

String[] getValueNames()   This method returns an array of the names of all data objects that have been bound in the session through the `putValue()` method. This method provides a way of iterating over the entire session data.

boolean isNew()   This method returns `true` if the server has just created the session and the client has not yet acknowledged entering the session; that is, it has not yet accepted a cookie or not yet entered a rewritten URI.

JSDK 2.1 *int getMaxInactiveInterval()* This method returns the inactivity time-out of this session in seconds, or a negative value if the session will be retained indefinitely.

JSDK 2.1 *void setMaxInactiveInterval(int interval)* This method sets the inactivity time-out of this session to the specified value in seconds, or a negative value if the session should be retained indefinitely. Use this to allow unused sessions to be automatically destroyed after a certain amount of idle time.

26.19 **JSDK 2.0** *Interface HttpSessionBindingListener*

This interface allows session data to be notified when they are bound or unbound to a `HttpSession`.

26.19.1 Methods
The following methods are defined in this interface:

void valueBound(HttpSessionBindingEvent event) This method informs the session data object that it has been bound to an `HttpSession`. The `event` parameter contains information about the session to which it has been bound.

void valueUnbound(HttpSessionBindingEvent event) This method informs the listener that it has been unbound from an `HttpSession`. The `event` parameter contains information about the session from which it has been unbound.

26.20 **JSDK 2.0** *Class HttpSessionBindingEvent*

This event is sent to an `HttpSessionBindingListener` when the listener has been bound to or unbound from a session. The class includes detailed information concerning the binding or unbinding.

26.20.1 Constructors
The following constructor is provided, although rarely used by application code:

HttpSessionBindingEvent(HttpSession session, String name) This constructor creates an `HttpSessionBindingEvent` instance with the specified session and binding name.

26.20.2 Methods
The following methods are defined in this class:

String getName() This method returns the name under which this session data object is being bound or unbound.

HttpSession getSession()   This method returns the `HttpSession` into which the session data object is being bound or from which it is being unbound.

26.21   JSDK 2.0   *Class Cookie*

A *cookie* is a piece of information that is stored on the client side by a user agent at the request of a server. Cookies are used to persist state on the client side; they are used to store user preferences, facilitate session logon, collect shopping cart data, and so forth.

The HTTP servlet framework usually uses cookies to track the session identifier associated with a given user; it can then use this identifier to locate the user's associated `HttpSession` object. Cookies are transferred between the server and client via HTTP header fields.

The original specification of cookies (version 0) was defined by Netscape Communications Corporation. Since then, the specification has been updated to version 1 and released as the Internet document RFC 2109.

26.21.1 *Constructors*
The following constructor is provided:

Cookie(String name, String value)   This constructor creates a cookie to hold the specified name/value pair. The `name` parameter must be a token value, as defined by the HTTP/1.1 protocol: an alphanumeric ASCII string which does not start with the $ character. The `value` parameter is also restricted, both in length and character set. See RFC 2109 for details.

26.21.2 *Methods*
The following methods are defined in class `Cookie`:

String getName()   This method returns the name associated with this cookie.

String getValue()   This method returns the value of this cookie.

void setValue(String newValue)   This method resets the value of this cookie. Refer to the constructor for an overview of what types of values are allowed.

setComment(String purpose)   In certain situations, the user agent (typically a Web browser) may need to present a cookie to the user before accepting it. This usually occurs when the user wishes to control the information that is being gathered about them. This method allows a comment describing the purpose of this cookie to be included when the cookie is shown. Version 0 cookies do not support this feature.

String getComment()   This method returns a `String` describing the purpose of this cookie, or `null` if no comment has been set.

void setDomain(String pattern)   This method is used to specify to which hosts this cookie should be returned. By default, a cookie is only sent back to the host that first sent it to the client. The specific syntax of the pattern string is defined in RFC 2109. An example pattern string is .nitric.com, which would match hosts such as www1.nitric.com and www2.nitric.com but not www.intdev.nitric.com.

String getDomain()   This method returns the domain pattern to which this cookie will be returned.

void setPath(String uri)   This method is used to limit the visibility of the cookie to requests beginning with the given URL. By default, if no URL is specified, then the cookie is sent to those URLs in the same directory as, or in a subdirectory of, the URL that originally set the cookie. Refer to RFC 2109 for the exact specification.

String getPath()   This method returns the prefix of all URLs for which the cookie is visible.

void setMaxAge(int expiry)   This method is used to specify the number of seconds since creation until this cookie should expire. If `expiry` is negative, then the cookie is not stored persistently on the client, and will be deleted when the user agent, or Web browser, exits. If `expiry` is zero, then the cookie is removed immediately.

int getMaxAge()   This method returns the maximum age of the cookie in seconds. If unspecified, then a negative value is returned to indicate default behavior.

void setSecure(boolean flag)   This method is used to indicate that this cookie should only be transferred using a secure protocol such as https. If an insecure connection is made to the originating server, the cookie will not be transmitted. A cookie should only be marked as secure if the original server that sent the cookie to the user agent used a secure protocol.

boolean getSecure()   This method shows whether or not this cookie has been marked as secure.

int getVersion()   This method returns the version of this cookie. Version 0 is the default and is the original cookie specification, as defined by Netscape Communications Corporation. The newer version 1 is defined in RFC 2109. When a user agent sends a cookie to a server, the version supported by that agent is automatically specified.

void setVersion(int v)　　This method sets the cookie protocol that should be used when transmitting this cookie. As of this writing, version 1 is experimental and should not be used on production sites.

26.22 Servicing an HTTP get request

The following example shows how to use the `HttpServ-let` class to handle a simple get request. Recall that the get method is the standard way of retrieving a static object over HTTP (figure 26.10).

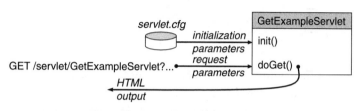

Figure 26.10　Class GetExampleServlet

26.22.1 Class GetExampleServlet

This servlet returns an HTML document containing all of the servlet's initialization and request parameters.

```
import java.io.*;
import java.util.*;
import javax.servlet.http.*;

public class GetExampleServlet extends HttpServlet {
  // protected void doGet (HttpServletRequest request,
      HttpServletResponse response) throws IOException ...
}
```

The `GetExampleServlet` class extends `HttpServlet` and provides a `doGet()` method that is called by the superclass for each incoming request. If this servlet is accessed with a post request, a bad request error will be automatically returned.

```
  protected void doGet (HttpServletRequest request,
      HttpServletResponse response) throws IOException {
    response.setContentType ("text/html");
    response.setStatus (HttpServletResponse.SC_OK);
    PrintWriter writer = response.getWriter ();
    writer.println ("<html><head><title>GetExampleServlet</title></head>");
    writer.println ("<body>");
    writer.println ("<h2>GetExampleServlet</h2>");
    writer.println ("<h3>Initialization Parameters:</h3>");
    Enumeration initParams = getInitParameterNames ();
    while (initParams.hasMoreElements ()) {
      String name = (String) initParams.nextElement ();
      String value = getInitParameter (name);
```

```
        writer.println (name + "=" + value + "<br>");
    }
    writer.println ("<h3>Request Parameters:</h3>");
    Enumeration requestParams = request.getParameterNames ();
    while (requestParams.hasMoreElements ()) {
        String name = (String) requestParams.nextElement ();
        String value = request.getParameter (name);
        writer.println (name + "=" + value + "<br>");
    }
    writer.println ("</body></html>");
    writer.close ();
}
```

At the beginning of the doGet() method, we set the content type for the response to text/html and set the response code to SC_OK. We then get a PrintWriter for writing our response and transmit an HTML page of all the parameters to this servlet. Under JSDK 1.0, use the getOutputStream() method instead.

The getInitParameterNames() method is used to iterate over the initialization parameters for this servlet. Note that this method is inherited from the GenericServlet superclass, which simply passes the call on to our initialization configuration. We could get the same effect by calling this method on the ServletConfig returned from the inherited getServletConfig() method.

We iterate over the request parameters by getting an Enumeration of the parameter names with the getParameterNames() method of ServletRequest and writing out the value of each parameter. We do not account for the case that a parameter may have multiple values, such as from a multiselection list. If this were likely, we would use the getParameterValues() method to obtain all of the parameter's values.

26.22.2 In practice

If this servlet is initialized with a parameter init1 (this will be specified with your server's servlet configuration tool) and called with the URL http://host/servlet/GetExampleServlet?req1=alpha&req2=beta, it will respond with the following result:

```
<html><head><title>GetExampleServlet</title></head>
<body>
<h2>GetExampleServlet</h2>
<h3>Initialization Parameters:</h3>
init1=xxx<br>
<h3>Request Parameters:</h3>
req1=alpha<br>
req2=beta<br>
</body></html>
```

A URL with the above format is typically generated by an HTML form with a get method.

26.23 Servicing an HTTP post request

The most common use of the post method is to submit a large number of name/value pairs from an HTML form to the server for processing, or to upload an entire file. Typically, get requests are restricted to less then 256 characters in total length, so only a limited amount of information can be included. Otherwise the caller must resort to using a post request to submit the information. The following example will show how to use a servlet for this type of application (figure 26.11).

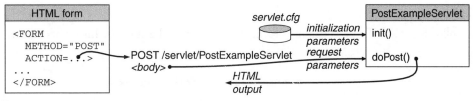

Figure 26.11   Class PostExampleServlet

26.23.1 Class PostExampleServlet

The `PostExampleServlet` servlet extends `HttpServlet` and processes the form submission in the `doPost()` method.

```
import java.io.*;
import java.util.*;
import javax.servlet.http.*;

public class PostExampleServlet extends HttpServlet {
  // protected void doPost (HttpServletRequest request,
      HttpServletResponse response) throws IOException ...
}
```

When this servlet is accessed with a post request, the `doPost()` method will automatically be called.

```
  protected void doPost (HttpServletRequest request,
      HttpServletResponse response) throws IOException {
    response.setContentType ("text/html");
    response.setStatus (HttpServletResponse.SC_OK);
    PrintWriter writer = response.getWriter ();
    String name = request.getParameter ("user");
    writer.println ("<html><head><title>PostExampleServlet</title></head>");
    writer.println ("<body>");
    writer.println ("<h2>PostExampleServlet</h2>");
    writer.println ("Hello " + name + "!");
    writer.println ("</body></html>");
    writer.close ();
  }
```

The `doPost()` method follows the same form as the `doGet()` method of the previous example. When we call `getParameter()`, the server framework hosting this servlet will automatically read the body of the post request and parse the encoded name/value pairs into the various request parameters.

If we did not want this automatic parsing, we could call `request.getInput-Stream()` to obtain a `ServletInputStream` from which to read the raw body of the post request and then process the resulting data manually, or else under JDSK 2.0 we could call `request.getReader()` to read a purely textual body.

26.23.2 In practice
The following HTML file contains a form which queries the user for his or her name, and then submits the results to the above servlet.

```
<html><head><title>PostExampleServlet test</title></head><body>
<h2>PostExampleServlet test</h2>
<form method="post" action="/servlet/PostExampleServlet">
  Name: <input name="user" size=25><p>
  <input type=submit>
</form>
</body></html>
```

26.24 Wrapping up

Servlets are an extremely powerful extension to the Java API because they allow Java to extend Web servers, just as applets allow Java to extend Web clients. Servlets are also applicable to almost all server environments. The servlet API, in fact, defines how any server can be extended in a secure, powerful and platform-independent manner.

In this chapter, we have primarily looked at details of the servlet API, without examining fundamentally what servlets are good for. In the next chapter, we will look at a few practical examples of servlet usage.

C H A P T E R   2 7

Servlets in practice

The servlet API presents a general interface through which a server can be extended with dynamic, Java-based facilities. Although servlets can be applied to any server environment, they are of most common use in the Webserver environment where they provide dynamic facilities traditionally provided by CGI and server plugins.

In this chapter, we will examine some practical servlets. We will start with a discussion and API for adding persistence to servlets, accompanied by a simple Web access counter example. Then we will look at using servlets for collaboration with an example implementation of a real-time servlet-based distributed list datastructure.

27.1 Persistence in servlets

When a servlet-based application requires that some state be kept around, regardless of whether or not the servlet stays in memory, measures need to be taken to persist the state.

27.1.1 Implementing persistence

The servlet life cycle dictates how a servlet's state can be persisted. The following steps allow state to be kept for the lifetime of the servlet's use:

1　State is loaded from stable storage to memory in the `init()` method.

2　State is modified during requests.

3　The new state is written from memory to stable storage in the `destroy()` method.

Stable storage may refer to a file system or database. The simplest solution is to use Java's object serialization facilities, provided by the `java.io` package, to read and write the state from a file.

One additional step may be useful:

1　Periodically save state during execution of the servlet.

27.1.2 Class PersistentHttpServlet

This abstract class provides the framework for persisting servlet state. It uses the `ObjectInput-Stream` and `ObjectOutput-Stream` classes to read and write the state from and to a file. It also provides a facility to periodically and automatically save the servlet's state (figure 27.1).

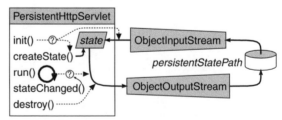

Figure 27.1　Class PersistentHttpServlet

```
import java.io.*;
```

```
import javax.servlet.*;
import javax.servlet.http.*;

public abstract class PersistentHttpServlet extends HttpServlet {
  // protected PersistentHttpServlet () ...
  // public void init (ServletConfig config) throws ServletException ...
  // protected void init (ServletConfig config, int savePeriod)
  //     throws ServletException ...
  // public void destroy () ...
  // protected void stateChanged () ...
  // protected String getStatePath () ...
  // protected abstract Serializable createState () ...
}
```

The `PersistentHttpServlet` class simply extends `HttpServlet`. To support periodic saving we will use an anonymous inner class and internal thread. We do not directly implement `Runnable` because doing so would interfere with subclasses that themselves wished to use helper threads. We override the standard `Servlet init()` and `destroy()` methods to support state saving, and define the methods `getStatePath()` and `createState()` that must be implemented by a subclass to specify where the state is stored and to create an initial state.

In addition, we provide a `stateChanged()` method that must be called by a subclass whenever it changes its state; this allows the `PersistentHttpServlet` class to keep track of when new state should be saved.

```
protected PersistentHttpServlet () {
}
```

This constructor should be called by a subclass. It in turn calls the protected superclass constructor. Most servlet constructors do nothing of interest.

```
public void init (ServletConfig config) throws ServletException {
  init (config, -1);
}
```

This `init()` method will be called when the servlet is initialized by the server. We simply call the following initialization method with automatic saving disabled. If a subclass overrides this method, it is imperative that it first calls one of these `init()` methods. If it fails to do this, the servlet will not be correctly initialized.

```
protected Serializable state;
protected Thread saver;
protected int savePeriod;

protected void init (ServletConfig config, int savePeriod)
    throws ServletException {
  super.init (config);
```

```
try {
  if (getStatePath () == null)
    throw new FileNotFoundException ();
  ObjectInputStream objectIn = new ObjectInputStream (
    new FileInputStream (getStatePath ()));
  state = (Serializable) objectIn.readObject ();
  objectIn.close ();
  log ("state loaded");
} catch (FileNotFoundException ex) {
  state = createState ();
  log ("state created");
} catch (IOException ex) {
  throw new UnavailableException (this, ex.toString ());
} catch (ClassNotFoundException ex) {
  throw new UnavailableException (this, ex.toString ());
}
if ((savePeriod > 0) && (getStatePath () != null)) {
  this.savePeriod = savePeriod;
  saver = new Thread () {
    public void run () {
      autosave ();
    }
  };
  saver.start ();
}
}

// void autosave () ...
```

This method initializes the servlet with the specified `ServletConfig config` and automatic saving period `savePeriod`. This is the period, in milliseconds, that the servlet will sleep between automatically saving the state to file. If this value is zero or subzero, automatic saving is disabled.

We first call the superclass `init()` method; this is required in order that the superclass be correctly initialized. We then attempt to read in the persistent state from a file. If the specified file is not found, we allocate a new state object.

We use the `readObject()` method from `ObjectInputStream` to read in the serialized state file; the `getStatePath()` method determines the file path where the state is stored. If the file is not found, we call `createState()` to create a state object. If another exception is encountered, we throw an `UnavailableException` (a subclass of `ServletException`) to indicate that the servlet cannot be initialized.

We finally store the autosave period and create and start a new `Thread`, `saver`, that will automatically save the servlet's state, if appropriate. We execute this thread in an anonymous inner class that just calls our internal `autosave()` method.

Note that this servlet will become unusable if the state file gets corrupted; it might be more appropriate to instead log the error and create a state object. Note also that if an exception occurs, we do not close the `FileInputStream`; closing of the stream will be automatically performed when the stream is garbage collected. We do not expect to often encounter such an exception, so the added logic to manually close the stream is unnecessary. The garbage collector *will* perform this task for us at some point.

```
protected String getStatePath () {
  return getInitParameter ("persistentStatePath");
}
```

This method should be implemented by a subclass to return the location where the servlet's state file should be stored. This method may call the various inherited `Http-Servlet`, `GenericServlet`, and `Servlet` methods, including `getInitParameter()`, to determine where the state should be stored.

In this case, we provide a default implementation that returns the value of the initialization parameter `persistentStatePath`; this value must be appropriately configured by the Web server's adminstration tool or in the Web server's configuration file. If this parameter is not set, the servlet will create a state object each time that it is loaded.

```
protected abstract Serializable createState ();
```

The first time a servlet is initialized, an instance of the state is created with a call to `createState()`. This method must be overriden by a subclass to return an appropriate `Serializable` state object. We make serializability explicit in this manner to ensure that the state will be storable with the object streams.

```
protected int stateCount;

void autosave () {
  Thread myself = Thread.currentThread ();
  try {
    int savedState = stateCount;
    while (saver == myself) {
      Thread.sleep (savePeriod);
      int newState = stateCount;
      if (savedState != newState) {
        ObjectOutputStream objectOut = new ObjectOutputStream (
          new FileOutputStream (getStatePath ()));
        synchronized (state) {
          objectOut.writeObject (state);
        }
        objectOut.close ();
        log ("state saved");
        savedState = newState;
      }
    }
  } catch (InterruptedException ignored) {
  } catch (IOException ex) {
    String name = getClass ().getName ();
    getServletContext ().log (ex, name + ": error saving state");
```

```
    }
  }
```

This method will be executed by the `saver` thread to periodically save the servlet's state. It sleeps for the autosave period and then writes out the servlet's state if it has changed. Our thread automatically exits when it is interrupted or is no longer referenced by the saver variable.

In an effort to reduce the cost of state saving, this method only resaves the servlet's state when it has changed. A `stateCount` variable is incremented every time a servlet updates its state. If this variable has changed since the last iteration, the autosave is performed.

To ensure that the state is at a valid, saveable point, and not in an indeterminate midupdate state, we synchronize on it before serializing. If a subclass uses this autosave feature then it must ensure—as it should—to synchronize on its state before performing any nonatomic modifications.

If an `IOException` is encountered while saving the state, we simply log the exception and exit.

```
protected void stateChanged () {
  ++ stateCount;
}
```

This method should be called by a subclass whenever the servlet's state is changed; this notifies the `PersistentHttpServlet` class that it should resave the state during the next autosave check.

```
public void destroy () {
  Thread saver = this.saver;
  this.saver = null;
  if (saver != null) {
    saver.interrupt ();
    try {
      saver.join ();
    } catch (InterruptedException ignored) {
    }
  }
  if (getStatePath () != null) {
    try {
      ObjectOutputStream objectOut = new ObjectOutputStream (
        new FileOutputStream (getStatePath ()));
      objectOut.writeObject (state);
      objectOut.close ();
      log ("state saved");
    } catch (IOException ex) {
      log (ex.toString ());
    }
  }
}
```

```
    super.destroy ();
  }
```

The `destroy()` method is called when the servlet is destroyed; this method is responsible for cleaning up the servlet's resources. If a subclass overrides this method, it must ensure to call the `destroy()` when it is finished cleaning up its own resources.

We first terminate the autosave thread, if it was started. We take a local reference to the thread and then assign `saver` to `null`; this indicates to the thread that it should terminate. We then call the thread's `interrupt()` method; this will abort it if it is mid-sleep. Finally we call its `join()` method to wait until it terminates. Remember, the thread will not die immediately; it will only die when it is next scheduled to completion by the thread scheduler. One of the requirements of the `destroy()` method is that it should not exit until all of its helper threads have finished. If a subclass has a long-running `service()` method, such as one that makes database calls, then it should also ensure to terminate any such service threads in its `destroy()` method.

Finally, we save the servlet's state to file, logging any exceptions that may occur, and finally call the superclass `destroy()` method.

27.1.3 Automatic persistence

It should be observed that it would be comparatively simple for a network server to support automatic servlet persistence: It could check to see if the servlet implemented `Serializable`; if so then the entire servlet could be serialized to and from a file, instead of having to use this manual mechanism. Just such a facility is provided with the Java Web Server 1.1 in the form of servlet beans, although in that case it is provided more for the purpose of saving user configuration than saving servlet state.

27.2 An access-counter servlet

This servlet example counts the number of get accesses made to the servlet over its lifetime. This count, along with a `Date` object marking

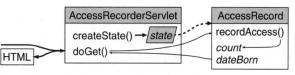

Figure 27.2   Class AccessRecorderServlet

the time the persistent state was first created, is stored to a file during any time in which the servlet is not in memory (figure 27.2).

27.2.1 Class AccessRecorderServlet

This class is the main servlet class for our access recorder. It is a simple demonstration of using the `PersistentHttpServlet` superclass.

```
import java.io.*;
import java.util.*;
```

```
import javax.servlet.*;
import javax.servlet.http.*;

public class AccessRecorderServlet extends PersistentHttpServlet {
   // public void init (ServletConfig config) throws ServletException ...
   // protected Serializable createState () ...
   // protected void doGet (HttpServletRequest request,
   //     HttpServletResponse response) throws IOException ...
}
```

The `AccessRecorderServlet` extends the abstract class `PersistentHttpServlet`. We implement the `createState()` method that is required by that class, and override the `doGet()` method to record each access to this servlet and return an appropriate response.

Note that all servlets must expose a public no-arg constructor. When no constructor is declared, a default public no-arg constructor that calls the protected superclass no-arg constructor will be assigned. We also inherit the default superclass method that determines our state path from the `persistentStatePath` initialization parameter.

```
protected Date dateLoaded;

public void init (ServletConfig config) throws ServletException {
   super.init (config, 5 * 60 * 1000);
   dateLoaded = new Date ();
}
```

The `init()` method first calls the superclass `init()` method, specifying a five-minute autosave period, and then stores the current time in `dateLoaded`.

```
protected Serializable createState () {
   return new AccessRecord ();
}
```

The `createState()` method must create an initial state for this servlet. This method will only be called once, when the servlet is created. From that point on, the servlet state will be loaded from a file during initialization. We simply return a new instance of our `AccessRecord` state class.

```
protected void doGet (HttpServletRequest request,
    HttpServletResponse response) throws IOException {
   ((AccessRecord) state).recordAccess ();
   stateChanged ();
   response.setContentType ("text/html");
   PrintWriter writer = response.getWriter ();
   writer.println ("<html><body>");
   writer.println ("servlet last loaded on: " + dateLoaded + "<br>");
   writer.println (state + "<br>");
   writer.println ("</body></html>");
```

```
      writer.close ();
  }
```

In the doGet() method, we record the new access by calling the state's recordAccess() method (followed by a call to stateChanged() to keep the superclass up to date), and then write out an appropriate HTML response to the client. Calling getWriter() automatically sets the character set of the response to one supported by the remote client.

In this case, we have used the JSDK 2.0 getWriter() method; under an older servlet environment, use the getOutputStream() method.

27.2.2 Class AccessRecord

This class describes our persistent servlet's state.

```
import java.io.*;
import java.util.*;
class AccessRecord implements Serializable {
  private int count;
  private Date dateBorn;

  AccessRecord () {
    count = 0;
    dateBorn = new Date ();
  }

  synchronized void recordAccess () {
    count++;
  }

  public String toString () {
    return "state created on: " + dateBorn + "<br>\n" +
      "number of accesses: " + count;
  }
}
```

We define the AccessRecord class to contain the fields count and dateBorn, reflecting the number of times the servlet has been accessed and the time it was created. We define a recordAccess() method that increments the access count and a toString() method that returns an appropriate description of the state.

27.2.3 In practice

To test the servlet, install it in your Web server and configure the persistentStatePath property appropriately. Try accessing the servlet a few times and then forcing the Web server to reload it. This may be accomplished either through a graphical administration tool or by updating the servlet class file (by using the touch command on UNIX systems). The next time that you access the servlet, you should see that the access count is still correct and the date created is when the servlet was first loaded.

27.2.4 Comments on fault tolerance

In the above example, we can be sure that the access count is correct for the lifetime of the server application *only* if we are guaranteed that the `init()` method is called each time the servlet is loaded, and the `destroy()` method is called each time it is unloaded. We can, in fact, be sure that the `init()` method will always be called before the servlet services requests, but what happens if the network service hosting the servlet fails before the `destroy()` is called? In this case, our example fails and all of the accesses that have happened since the last time the state was saved will be lost.

In the `PersistentHttpServlet` class, we have improved on the situation where state is only saved during the `destroy()` method, by periodically writing out the state while the servlet is running. If an application allows some bounded amount of data loss, it can write out its state each time that bound is reached. In such applications, the expense of frequently writing out state will have to be weighed against the possibility of data loss. In this case, we allow a five-minute autosave period. If any change has occurred during one such autosave period, the state is resaved.

For efficiency, we might alter the autosaving feature of `PersistentHttpServlet` so that it will only save state if a certain number of state changes have occurred since the last autosave. This would reduce the cost of autosaving if a bounded amount of data loss was acceptable. Another improvement would be to perform a premature autosave if a large number of state changes occur within a single autosave period.

Obviously some applications dictate that data loss is not an option. In these cases, each new transaction, or change in state, will need to be immediately committed to stable storage. In short, the method of persisting state implemented by the `PersistentHttpServlet` example is somewhat naïve. Although it will work most of the time, it should not be used for servlets that store critical data. Critical servlets will usually need to use transaction logs, preferably through a fault tolerant database server.

27.3 Using servlets for collaboration

Servlets are a powerful mechanism for implementing collaborative applications over the Internet. Servlets provide the means for both synchronous and asynchronous collaboration. A `ServerSocket` can be opened to accept direct connections where firewalls allow, and HTTP requests can be used for all other connections.

27.3.1 Advantages of servlets

An `HttpServlet` used to implement the multiplexing message server for a collaborative application provides two important features: firewall and Secure Socket Layer (SSL) support.

With no explicit thought or coding, an `HttpServlet` can be accessed through an HTTP proxy server. The client Web browser will be preconfigured by the user with the address of the HTTP proxy and so will automatically redirect HTTP data to the proxy. By encapsulating application level messages inside HTTP requests, the HTTP proxy will automatically transfer the application data through the firewall.

Since servlets, as all HTTP data, can be accessed through an SSL connection providing that both the browser and the network service hosting the servlet support that security protocol, message traffic between the client and server can be automatically encrypted using SSL—at no cost to the programmer.

27.3.2 General architecture

The general model for a collaborative application implemented with servlets would be as follows: A central servlet will maintain the application state, allowing this to be queried and manipulated by clients using HTTP requests. If long-term state about clients is

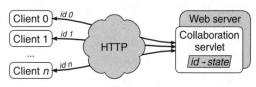

Figure 27.3 Centralized collaboration model using servlets

required, the servlet will assign identifiers to clients as they connect. Clients will use these identifiers with future requests (figure 27.3).

Clients can communicate with the server in the obvious manner—by making HTTP requests. In addition, they can communicate among each other by simply making requests of the server that messages be directed to other clients when those clients make their next connection.

27.3.3 Applet to servlet communication

One simple way to get data from a client applet to a servlet is by posting name/value pairs to the servlet—just as a Web browser would when you submit a form. In chapter

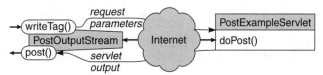
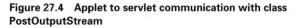

Figure 27.4 Applet to servlet communication with class PostOutputStream

14, we built a `PostOutputStream` class that encodes the name/value pairs, opens a socket, and posts the data to the server (figure 27.4).

```
try {
  URL servletURL = new URL ("http://nitric.com/servlet/PostExampleServlet");
  PostOutputStream out = new PostOutputStream (servletURL);
  out.writeTag ("name", "Alex Constantine");
  InputStream in = out.post ();
  // read response here
} catch (MalformedURLException e) {
  // bad servlet url
} catch (IOException e) {
  // error posting data
}
```

The code can be used to post a name/value pair to the example servlet described in the previous chapter. Alternatively, the built-in URL support for posting can be used, as described in chapter 19; this has the advantage of providing automatic support for Web proxies.

Servlets which support the HTTP get method can also be accessed through the URL classes, just as any other object on the

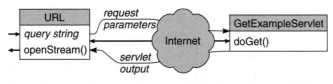

Figure 27.5   Applet to servlet communication with class URL

server is accessed. For example, the following code could be used to read the output from the servlet shown in section 26.22 (figure 27.5).

```
URL servletURL = new URL
  ("http://host/servlet/GetExampleServlet?name=Alex+Constantine");
InputStream in = servletURL.openStream ();
// read response here
```

Here, we specify parameters to the servlet in the query string part of the URL that we use.

27.4 A servlet-based distributed list

We will now look at reimplementing a distributed list using servlets. This is the third example of implementing this datastructure; the first example used raw sockets and a centralized TCP/IP server (see chapter 8) and the second used RMI with callback (see chapter 24).

Remember, this distributed list is a generalized networking substrate that can be used for many different collaborative applications, both real-time and nonreal-time. In the accompanying Web site (http://nitric.com/jnp/), an example whiteboard is demonstrated that uses these classes as a networking substrate; many other applications are also possible.

For brevity, we will omit further background on this example since it is explained in the previous versions.

27.4.1 Architecture

This example follows the same general model as the earlier RMI implementation, except that instead of calling methods on a remote list object whenever the client makes an update, it uses the URL classes to post and get data to and from a servlet, encoding its messages with the object streams and identifying different request operations with the path info and query string of its request URLs.

Unlike before, we cannot have the servlet calling back clients when a change is made. Instead, the clients will periodically poll the server to determine if any change has been made since the last query.

Our servlet is implemented by the ServletListServer class; this maintains a central IDList that represents the global list state. Clients use a ServletListClient class that implements the DistributedList interface and communicates with the central servlet to apply any requested changes (figure 27.6).

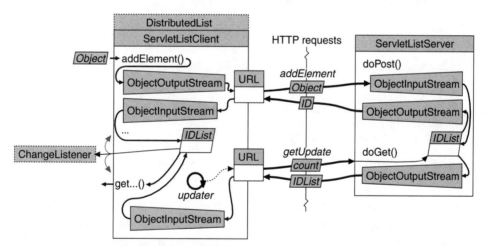

Figure 27.6   A distributed list with servlets

Client requests are serialized using the ObjectOutputStream class; responses from the server are appropriately formatted, again using the object streams. Periodically the client will query the server with an update request, including the current access count of its local IDList. If the server's copy of the IDList has been updated more recently than the clients', it will respond with an entirely new copy.

27.4.2 Class ServletListServer

This servlet stores the central IDList that maintains the global distributed-list status, and supports both get and post requests. Clients can request the latest copy of the central list by using a get request; any updates are performed using posts (figure 27.7).

For convenience, this class extends the Persis-

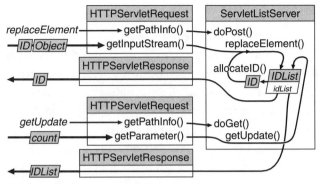

Figure 27.7   Class ServletListServer

tentHttpServlet class; the central IDList is used as its state object. If the servlet is configured with a location to store its state, it will automatically benefit from the persistence facilities provided by the superclass.

```
import java.io.*;
import javax.servlet.*;
import javax.servlet.http.*;

public class ServletListServer extends PersistentHttpServlet {
   // public void init (ServletConfig config) throws ServletException ...
   // protected Serializable createState () ...
   // protected void doGet (HttpServletRequest request,
       HttpServletResponse response) throws IOException ...
   // protected void doPost (HttpServletRequest request,
       HttpServletResponse response) throws IOException ...
}
```

The ServletListServer extends PersistentHttpServlet, inheriting the default persistent-storage location that defines. We provide an appropriate implementation of the createState() method to initialize the servlet if no persistent state exists, and implement the doGet() and doPost() methods to service HTTP requests.

```
   protected IDList idList;

   public void init (ServletConfig config) throws ServletException {
      String period = config.getInitParameter ("persistencePeriod");
      super.init (config, (period == null) ? -1 :
                  Integer.parseInt (period));
      idList = (IDList) state;
   }
```

The `init()` method first calls the superclass `init()` method. We obtain the autosave period from the initialization parameter `persistencePeriod`, or if this is undefined, we disable autosaving in which case the servlet will only save its state when the `destroy()` method is called. The superclass `init()` method automatically deserializes the servlet's state from file, or creates it anew if necessary.

We next obtain a local reference to the state object; this is the centralized `IDList` that holds the master state for the entire system. This list is replicated on the clients, and consistency is maintained by periodic polling. Note that the list is not declared as `static`—this allows multiple instances of the list server to host disjoint list sessions in one Web server process.

```
protected Serializable createState () {
  return new IDList ();
}
```

When the servlet is first loaded, an empty list is created by the `createState()` method. If the servlet's persistent state-storage location is not configured, this will be called each time the servlet is loaded. Otherwise it will be called only once, after which the servlet persistence will kick in.

```
public void doGet (HttpServletRequest request,
    HttpServletResponse response) throws IOException {
  String command = request.getPathInfo ();
  if (command != null)
    command = command.substring (1);
  if (command == null) {
    String name = request.getServletPath ();
    name = name.substring (name.lastIndexOf ('/'));
    response.setContentType ("text/html");
    PrintWriter writer = response.getWriter ();
    writer.println
      ("<html><head><title>" + name + " status</title></head><body>");
    writer.println ("<h2>" + name + " is alive</h2>");
    writer.println ("</body></html>");
    writer.close ();
  } else if (command.equals ("getUpdate")) {
    getUpdate (request, response);
  } else {
    response.sendError (HttpServletResponse.SC_BAD_REQUEST,
      command + " not supported");
  }
}
// protected void getUpdate (HttpServletRequest request,
    HttpServletResponse response) throws IOException ...
```

This method services HTTP get requests to our distributed list servlet. The command being executed by the client is specified as the path info part of the request; that is, the trailing path elements that follow the name of the servlet. We handle three major cases:

If no path info was specified; that is, the client accessed our servlet as just http://host/servlet/ServletListServer, we return a simple HTML page that describes the status of the servlet. This allows us to check that the servlet is properly installed by simply accessing it from any Web browser. This approach provides a clean mechanism for monitoring server status.

If the command `getUpdate` was specified; that is, the client accessed our servlet as http://host/servlet/ServletListServer/getUpdate, the client is making a request for an updated copy of the central list. In this case, we call the `getUpdate()` method to perform the update request. This is the mechanism by which clients periodically poll our servlet to keep up-to-date with any changes.

If any other command was specified, it was an illegal command, and so, we use the `sendError()` method to indicate to the client that the specified command is not supported.

```
protected void getUpdate (HttpServletRequest request,
    HttpServletResponse response) throws IOException {
  String count = request.getParameter ("count");
  IDList update = null;
  try {
    if (Integer.parseInt (count) != idList.getUpdateCount ())
      update = (IDList) idList.clone ();
  } catch (NumberFormatException ignored) {
  }
  response.setContentType ("application/octet-stream");
  ObjectOutputStream out = new ObjectOutputStream (
    response.getOutputStream ());
  out.writeObject (update);
  out.close ();
}
```

When a client is requesting an `IDList` update from the server, it sends a count index along with its request; this is the number of times that its local copy of the distributed list has been updated. The server can compare this count value with its central copy of the list, to determine whether the client is up-to-date or needs to receive a new copy of the global `IDList`. This simple facility allows our distributed list implementation to operate much more efficiently, however it requires us to add a small amount of code to the original `IDList` class to maintain this update count.

This count value is specified as a *count* request parameter to the servlet in the query string of the URL; for example, http://host/servlet/ServletListServer/getUpdate?count=12.

In the `getUpdate()` method, we extract this update count and determine whether we need to send the client an updated `IDList`. If no update is needed or a problem is encountered parsing the number (either it was not specified or is not a number) then we return `null`. Otherwise, we return the current central list. To guarantee thread safety, we clone the central `IDList` before returning it.

When sending our response to the client's request, we first set an appropriate content type; the MIME type application/octet-stream indicates that our response consists of raw binary data. We construct an `ObjectOutputStream` from the response output stream and send the updated list using its `writeObject()` method.

```
public void doPost (HttpServletRequest request,
    HttpServletResponse response) throws ServletException, IOException {
  String command = request.getPathInfo ();
  if (command != null)
    command = command.substring (1);
  try {
    if (command == null) {
      response.sendError (HttpServletResponse.SC_BAD_REQUEST,
        "null command not supported");
    } else if (command.equals ("addElement")) {
      addElement (request, response);
    } else if (command.equals ("updateElement")) {
      updateElement (request, response);
    } else if (command.equals ("replaceElement")) {
      replaceElement (request, response);
    } else if (command.equals ("removeElement")) {
      removeElement (request, response);
    } else {
      response.sendError (HttpServletResponse.SC_BAD_REQUEST,
        command + " not supported");
    }
  } catch (ClassNotFoundException ex) {
    response.sendError (HttpServletResponse.SC_INTERNAL_SERVER_ERROR);
  }
}
// protected void addElement
    (HttpServletRequest request, HttpServletResponse response)
    throws IOException, ClassNotFoundException ...
// protected void updateElement (...) ...
// protected void replaceElement (...) ...
// protected void removeElement (...) ...
```

This method services HTTP post requests to our distributed list servlet. The command being executed by the client is specified as the path info part of the request, and the body of the post request constitutes the remaining parameters.

We select among the various supported commands, calling the appropriate service methods described below. If a command is unknown or an unexpected exception is encountered, we simply return an appropriate error to the client. To allow for more flexibility, we could actually use a `Hashtable`, which maps command names to classes or methods (using the reflection API) that implement processing facilities. In this way, we could provide simple, dynamic configuration facilities. However, for the moment, this implementation will suffice.

```
protected void addElement
    (HttpServletRequest request, HttpServletResponse response)
    throws IOException, ClassNotFoundException {
  ObjectInputStream in =
    new ObjectInputStream (request.getInputStream ());
  Object element = in.readObject ();
  ID id = idList.allocateID ();
  response.setContentType ("application/octet-stream");
  ObjectOutputStream out =
    new ObjectOutputStream (response.getOutputStream ());
  if (idList.addElement (id, element)) {
    stateChanged ();
    out.writeObject (id);
  } else {
    out.writeObject (null);
  }
  out.close ();
}
```

This method is called when the client wishes to add an element to our list. We use an `ObjectInputStream` to read the element transmitted by the client, and immediately allocate it a new identifier. We then set our response type to application/octet-stream and construct an `ObjectOutputStream` with which to send our response.

We attempt to perform the client's update on our central list; if this succeeds, we call `stateChanged()` to inform the superclass of the state change, and then return the newly allocated identifier to the client. This allows the client to correctly update its local copy of the list. Since the `IDList` class is internally synchronized, we do not have to worry about adding additional synchronization in this method. If the update fails, we simply return `null` to the client.

```
protected void updateElement
    (HttpServletRequest request, HttpServletResponse response)
    throws IOException, ClassNotFoundException {
  ObjectInputStream in =
    new ObjectInputStream (request.getInputStream ());
  ID id = (ID) in.readObject ();
  Object element = in.readObject ();
  ID newID = idList.allocateID ();
  response.setContentType ("application/octet-stream");
  ObjectOutputStream out =
    new ObjectOutputStream (response.getOutputStream ());
  if (idList.updateElement (id, newID, element)) {
    stateChanged ();
```

```
    out.writeObject (newID);
  } else {
    out.writeObject (null);
  }
  out.close ();
}
```

This method is called when the client wishes to update an element in our list. We follow the same process as before—reading in the client's request with an `ObjectInput-Stream`, setting a response type, and returning either the newly allocated identifier or `null`, depending on whether or not the update succeeded.

```
protected void replaceElement
    (HttpServletRequest request, HttpServletResponse response)
    throws IOException, ClassNotFoundException {
  ObjectInputStream in =
    new ObjectInputStream (request.getInputStream ());
  ID id = (ID) in.readObject ();
  Object element = in.readObject ();
  ID newID = idList.allocateID ();
  response.setContentType ("application/octet-stream");
  ObjectOutputStream out =
    new ObjectOutputStream (response.getOutputStream ());
  if (idList.replaceElement (id, newID, element)) {
    stateChanged ();
    out.writeObject (newID);
  } else {
    out.writeObject (null);
  }
  out.close ();
}
```

This method is called when the client wishes to replace an element in our list; we follow the same process as before.

```
protected void removeElement
    (HttpServletRequest request, HttpServletResponse response)
    throws IOException, ClassNotFoundException {
  ObjectInputStream in =
    new ObjectInputStream (request.getInputStream ());
  ID id = (ID) in.readObject ();
  response.setContentType ("application/octet-stream");
  ObjectOutputStream out =
    new ObjectOutputStream (response.getOutputStream ());
  if (idList.removeElement (id)) {
    stateChanged ();
    out.writeBoolean (true);
  } else {
    out.writeBoolean (false);
  }
  out.close ();
```

}

This method is called when the client wishes to remove an element from our list. Again, we follow the same process as before, with the exception that we return a `boolean` flag to indicate whether or not the update succeeded.

Note that in none of the above methods do we set the content length field of our response. Setting the content length is useful for efficiency and for caching purposes, however, in the case of this servlet, we don't want any responses to be cached. To compute the length of any of the above responses, we would have to build up the response in a `ByteArrayOutputStream` before actually transmitting it. This would add an extra amount of data copying which is really not necessary.

27.4.3 Class ServletListClient

This class implements the client side of the distributed list. It is analogous to the `SocketListClient` and `RMIListClient-Impl` classes from the previous implementations of this framework (figure 27.8).

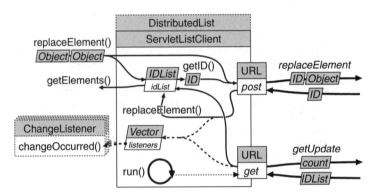

Figure 27.8   Class ServletListClient

This class uses the standard URL classes to transport application level messages to and from the central `ServletListServer` servlet.

```
import java.io.*;
import java.net.*;
import java.util.*;
import javax.servlet.*;
import javax.servlet.http.*;

public class ServletListClient implements DistributedList, Runnable  {
  public static final int UPDATE_PERIOD = 10 * 1000;
  // public ServletListClient (URL servlet) ...
  // public synchronized void start ()
      throws IOException, ClassNotFoundeException ...
  // public void run () ...
  // public synchronized void stop () ...
  // public synchronized void addElement (Object element) ...
  // public synchronized void updateElement (Object oldElement,
      Object newElement) ...
```

```
      // public synchronized void replaceElement (Object oldElement,
          Object newElement) ...
      // public synchronized void removeElement (Object element) ...
      // public Enumeration getElements () ...
      // public void addChangeListener (ChangeListener listener) ...
      // public void removeChangeListener (ChangeListener listener) ...
      // protected void fireChangeEvent (ChangeEvent changeEvent) ...
}
```

The `ServletListClient` client implements the `DistributedList` interface, as a client-side implementation of our distributed list datastructure, and the `Runnable` interface in order to have a thread that periodically polls the server for an updated list. The constructor accepts the URL of the servlet. The `start()` and `stop()` methods control the update thread. The remaining methods are those defined by `DistributedList`.

```
protected URL servlet;
protected IDList idList;

public ServletListClient (URL servlet) {
  try {
    this.servlet = new URL (servlet, servlet.getFile () + "/");
  } catch (MalformedURLException ignored) {
  }
  idList = new IDList ();
}
```

Our constructor makes a copy of the URL of the central list servlet; this URL should have the form http://host/servlet/ServletListServlet. The copy that we make has an additional / appended to the end. We then create a new, empty initial `IDList`.

```
protected Thread updater;

public synchronized void start ()
    throws IOException, ClassNotFoundException {
  if (updater == null) {
    getUpdate ();
    updater = new Thread (this);
    updater.start ();
  }
}
// protected synchronized void getUpdate () throws IOException ...
```

The `start()` method should be called to start the periodic update thread. We first manually grab a copy of the central `IDList` by calling `getUpdate()`; this allows the caller to be sure that the servlet is accessible and operational, as an `IOException` will be immediately thrown if a problem is encountered. We then create and start an update thread, `updater`, that periodically polls the server for updates to the `IDList`.

```
public synchronized void stop () {
```

```
    Thread updater = this.updater;
    this.updater = null;
    if (updater != null)
      updater.interrupt ();
}
```

The stop() method can be called to stop the periodic update thread. We assign the updater variable to null and then interrupt the update thread.

```
public void run () {
  Thread myself = Thread.currentThread ();
  try {
    while (updater == myself) {
      Thread.sleep (UPDATE_PERIOD);
      getUpdate ();
    }
  } catch (InterruptedException ignored) {
  } catch (IOException ex) {
    ex.printStackTrace ();
  } catch (ClassNotFoundException ex) {
    ex.printStackTrace ();
  } finally {
    updater = null;
  }
}
```

This method will be executed by the update thread to periodically poll the server for updates. The thread loops while it has not been stopped, sleeping for 10 seconds and then calling getUpdate(). If an exception is encountered, we simply exit.

```
protected synchronized void getUpdate ()
    throws IOException, ClassNotFoundException {
  int count = idList.getUpdateCount ();
  URL url = new URL (servlet, "getUpdate?count=" + count);
  URLConnection conn = url.openConnection ();
  conn.setUseCaches (false);
  ObjectInputStream in = new ObjectInputStream (conn.getInputStream ());
  IDList newList = (IDList) in.readObject ();
  in.close ();
  if (newList != null) {
    idList = newList;
    fireChangeEvent (new ChangeEvent (this));
  }
}
```

To update the list, we do an HTTP get request to the servlet with the path info getUpdate, and a query string of count=n, specifying the local list's update count. We specify that the URL framework should not attempt to cache any data. If an empty response was cached then we could miss all future updates.

After opening the connection, we create an `ObjectInputStream` with which to read the servlet's update message. If the new list is `null`, it has not been updated since our last request. Otherwise, we replace the old list by the new one and call `fireChangeEvent()` to notify the list observers.

```java
public synchronized void addElement (Object element) {
  try {
    URL url = new URL (servlet, "addElement");
    URLConnection conn = url.openConnection ();
    conn.setRequestProperty ("Content-type", "application/octet-stream");
    conn.setDoOutput (true);
    ObjectOutputStream out = new ObjectOutputStream (
      conn.getOutputStream ());
    out.writeObject (element);
    out.close ();
    ObjectInputStream in = new ObjectInputStream (
     conn.getInputStream ());
    ID id = (ID) in.readObject ();
    in.close ();
    if (id != null) {
      idList.addElement (id, element);
      fireChangeEvent (new ChangeEvent (this));
    }
  } catch (IOException ex) {
    ex.printStackTrace ();
  } catch (ClassNotFoundException ex) {
    ex.printStackTrace ();
  }
}
```

The `addElement()` method is called to append an element to the list. This is handled through a post request to the servlet using the path info addElement. We use the `URLConnection setRequestProperty()` method to set the content type of our request and then call `setDoOutput()` to signal that this connection is going to be used for posting data. The `getOutputStream()` method returns a stream into which we write the post request body, which in this case consists of the new element being added. We must then close this stream to ensure that the data is properly buffered.

After writing the request, we call `getInputStream()` to send the request and return a stream from which the response can be read. The response is the server-allocated identifier for the new element, or `null` if the addition failed. We add the element to our local list, using this server-assigned identifier, and then call `fireChangeEvent()` to notify any listeners of the update.

If any exception occurs, we print out the stack trace and return. Remember, clients should not rely on these methods executing successfully; instead they should use the `ChangeListener` callback mechanism to determine when changes have been made to the distributed list.

```java
public synchronized void updateElement
    (Object oldElement, Object newElement) {
  ID id = idList.getID (oldElement);
  if (id != null) {
    try {
      URL url = new URL (servlet, "updateElement");
      URLConnection conn = url.openConnection ();
      conn.setDoOutput (true);
      ObjectOutputStream out = new ObjectOutputStream (
        conn.getOutputStream ());
      out.writeObject (id);
      out.writeObject (newElement);
      out.close ();
      ObjectInputStream in = new ObjectInputStream (
       conn.getInputStream ());
      ID newID = (ID) in.readObject ();
      in.close ();
      if (newID != null) {
        idList.updateElement (id, newID, newElement);
        fireChangeEvent (new ChangeEvent (this));
      }
    } catch (IOException ex) {
      ex.printStackTrace ();
    } catch (ClassNotFoundException ex) {
      ex.printStackTrace ();
    }
  }
}
```

This method functions just as the previous method except in this case, the update-Element path info is used and two arguments are sent in the post request body—the identifier of the object being updated and the object that is to replace it. The server responds with an identifier for this new object, or null if the update failed.

```java
public synchronized void replaceElement
    (Object oldElement, Object newElement) {
  ID id = idList.getID (oldElement);
  if (id != null) {
    try {
      URL url = new URL (servlet, "replaceElement");
      URLConnection conn = url.openConnection ();
      conn.setDoOutput (true);
      ObjectOutputStream out = new ObjectOutputStream (
        conn.getOutputStream ());
      out.writeObject (id);
      out.writeObject (newElement);
      out.close ();
      ObjectInputStream in = new ObjectInputStream (
       conn.getInputStream ());
      ID newID = (ID) in.readObject ();
      in.close ();
      if (newID != null) {
```

```
        idList.replaceElement (id, newID, newElement);
        fireChangeEvent (new ChangeEvent (this));
      }
    } catch (IOException ex) {
      ex.printStackTrace ();
    } catch (ClassNotFoundException ex) {
      ex.printStackTrace ();
    }
  }
}
```

This method uses the replaceElement path info in an HTTP post request to replace an element in the distributed list using exactly the same mechanism as the previous method.

```
public synchronized void removeElement (Object element) {
  ID id = idList.getID (element);
  if (id != null) {
    try {
      URL url = new URL (servlet, "removeElement");
      URLConnection conn = url.openConnection ();
      conn.setDoOutput (true);
      ObjectOutputStream out = new ObjectOutputStream (
        conn.getOutputStream ());
      out.writeObject (id);
      out.close ();
      ObjectInputStream in = new ObjectInputStream (
       conn.getInputStream ());
      boolean okay = in.readBoolean ();
      in.close ();
      if (okay) {
        idList.removeElement (id);
        fireChangeEvent (new ChangeEvent (this));
      }
    } catch (IOException ex) {
      ex.printStackTrace ();
    }
  }
}
```

This method uses the removeElement path info in an HTTP post request to remove an element from the distributed list. The response from the server is a `boolean` value indicating success or failure.

```
public Enumeration getElements () {
  return idList.getElements ();
}
```

This method simply returns an `Enumeration` of the elements in this list.

```
protected Vector listeners = new Vector ();
```

```
public void addChangeListener (ChangeListener listener) {
  listeners.addElement (listener);
}
```

This method adds a listener for updates to this list.

```
public void removeChangeListener (ChangeListener listener) {
  listeners.removeElement (listener);
}
```

This method removes a listener for updates to this list.

```
protected void fireChangeEvent (ChangeEvent changeEvent) {
  synchronized (listeners) {
    for (int i = 0; i < listeners.size (); ++ i)
      ((ChangeListener) listeners.elementAt (i))
        .changeOccurred (changeEvent);
  }
}
```

This method notifies all registered clients of the specified `ChangeEvent`. We simply loop through the `Vector` and call each element's `changeOccurred()` method.

27.4.4 Discussion

The biggest failing of this implementation of our distributed list datastructure is the manner in which the client polls the server for updates. Returning an entirely new list every time a change is encountered is an undesirable situation.

One practical solution to this problem is for the server to maintain a list of the changes that clients have made to the list. When an update is requested, the server can return a sequence of changes—a delta list—instead of an entirely new list. To make this even more efficient, the server can determine whether a delta list would be larger than a new copy of the list (the simplest check would be to see if the delta list has more elements than the list itself) and to return a new list if this would be the case.

Another point to note, in regard to efficiency, is that there is a large amount of overhead involved in performing an HTTP request. Many of our simple update requests—adding an element, for example—return just a few bytes of data in response to a request. The cost of these requests will be dominated by the HTTP overhead, and not the data transfer. Thus, it may be more efficient to return a delta list with *every* request, and not just in response to update queries. In this case, the client can skip an update request if it has recently made another type of request of the server.

When comparing a servlet-based distributed list with a socket-based distributed list, the obvious benefit of using raw sockets is that there is just one socket connection, and so, there is not the heavy cost of repeatedly establishing HTTP connections and relaying through a Web server. On the other hand, a servlet-based distributed list can bypass firewalls because the application data is encapsulated in HTTP requests that will be proxied through firewalls. Both of these are significant benefits, so it makes sense to try and get the best of both worlds.

To benefit from both the efficiency of direct socket connections and the accessibility of HTTP tunneling, consider creating a servlet that itself establishes a `Server-Socket` to accept direct connections. If a client connects from behind a firewall, it can use servlet-based communications. Otherwise, it can establish a direct socket connection and gain from the resulting performance benefits.

In some situations, it may also be possible for servlets to take advantage of HTTP 1.1 keepalive (where a single network connection is used to service multiple requests). Support for this from a Java applet and to a Java servlet varies among platforms; you may find that the servlet must be modified to specify the content length of its responses, or you may find that either keepalive is not supported or requests are too infrequent to benefit from this feature.

27.5 Conclusion

Servlets provide an elegant alternative to traditional CGI and Webserver plug-ins. They provide an ideal mechanism for implementing middleware applications. Servlets dynamically extend a network service while encapsulating the extra function in a protected environment. Separate servlet requests can be serviced concurrently by the same servlet instance, a feature which provides efficiency and enables collaboration through class and instance variables.

Java has found another true strong-spot: on the server. Until recently the Java language has largely been thought of as a tool for writing lightweight client-side applications. The Java server API defines a standard interface for exploiting Java's graces on the server. Taken with CORBA, JDBC, and RMI, the servlet environment provides an end-all solution to enterprise programming.

Part V

Message streams

The Java API provides several options for streaming data, but we can add much more function if we extend the available classes to perform higher level operations common to client/server communications. In the following chapters, we will develop extended-stream filters to handle message headers, to stream messages into queues for later processing, to add multiplexing and demultiplexing capability, and to add the ability to route messages to named recipients. We also will look at a generic multithreaded server and client framework that uses these new streams. Use of these streams can simplify many collaborative networked applications, and the issues that we encounter in their development are also of general interest.

Chapter 28: Message streams　　Many networked applications make use of conceptual *packets*, or message units, instead of continuous byte streams as supplied by TCP. In this chapter, we develop a set of streams that encapsulates messages into discrete units that can be sent over TCP. By distinguishing separate messages, we will subsequently be able to add header information to messages, including information such as a list of intended recipients for the message. We develop a `MessageOutputStream` and a `MessageInputStream` to accomplish this goal.

Chapter 29: Queueing message streams　　There are times when the processing of a message may actually take a while, and it would be helpful to store the messages in a queue so that the communications layer of an application does not have to wait for the actual processing to complete. In this chapter, we develop a `Queue` data structure class, a `QueueInputStream` to place messages into the `Queue`, and a `QueueOutputStream` to read messages from the `Queue`.

Chapter 30: Multiplexing message streams   A feature that may be useful in many applications is the ability to multiplex independent data streams from different client-side applications down a single network connection. In this chapter we develop a set of streams that use the message stream classes to provide this multiplexing facility. We create a `MultiplexOutputStream` that adds a multiplexing header to each message and a `MultiplexInputStream` that reads these headers. An example of the use of these streams is given in a simple two-person collaborative tool.

Chapter 31: Routing message streams   In this chapter, we develop streams that can route messages to a list of recipients. This additional function greatly simplifies collaborative applications that need the ability to send messages between named clients of a central server. We develop the `RoutingInputStream` and `RoutingOutputStream` classes to serve this purpose.

Chapter 32: A generic message server   In this chapter, we develop a generic server class that uses the library of classes that we have developed so far. Servers written using this class can take advantage of the high level of abstraction it provides, and omit most of the network-related code. This `GenericServer` class can service arbitrary applications; it is not necessary to modify the server if the client changes.

Chapter 33: A generic message client   In this chapter, we develop the corresponding generic client that communicates with the generic server. Network client software written using this class can essentially ignore any networking issues. A simple interface is provided that allows clients to be written with a mimimal of effort. These clients register with the `GenericClient` class, and all the network and message stream setup is performed automatically. We will work with a simple example—a full-featured Internet chat system that includes both a text-based chat and simple whiteboard tool.

C H A P T E R   2 8

Message streams

In this and the following chapters, we will develop message streams. Many applications communicate with independent packets of data: a command is sent to a server and a response is received, or an event is sent to a peer. All of these communications are characterized by the fact that the information being communicated is a self-contained unit. A stream-based communication channel such as that provided by TCP is not necessary for these communications; all that is required is that a self-contained message be delivered.

UDP provides just such a packet-based transport mechanism. However, it is not a suitable transport protocol for most applications because it does not provide the reception guarantees of TCP; packets may be lost, reordered, or duplicated.

In the earlier chapter on client/server applications, we implemented a chatserver that used UTF-format `Strings` as independent message packets. We need this concept of a message packet because the client cannot decode an arbitrary mix of data from different messages. If two `Strings` are written to the client at the same time, the client will receive garbage. Instead, we must decide on a unit of information to send, or a packet, and use synchronization to ensure that we send individual packets separately.

Limiting the server to just relaying single-`String` messages is not practical. The message streams that we develop here will allow us to write complex multiuser networked applications that communicate in units of a message, each of which can be an arbitrary volume and format of data.

28.1 Benefits of messages

There are many benefits of encapsulating messages into discrete packets, rather than transmitting a continuous stream of data (figure 28.1).

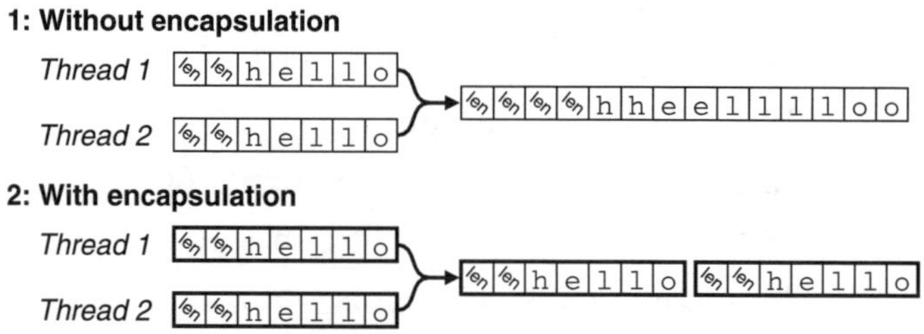

The first benefit

Figure 28.1 Encapsulation simplifies multiplexing

is that we can transmit several distinct messages down a single connection, and they can each be extracted independently. Without encapsulation, the server must understand the format of every message so that it can ensure synchronization to successfully transmit distinct messages. This is a particular problem if the client is undergoing continuous development, because the server must keep pace.

Another benefit of encapsulation is that errors in a single message are not extended to affect all subsequent messages (figure 28.2). Without encapsulation, we are assuming that

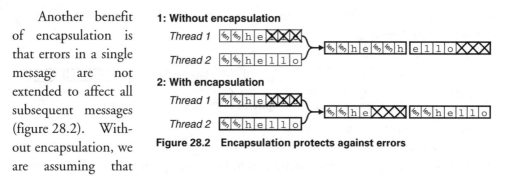

1: Without encapsulation

Thread 1

Thread 2

2: With encapsulation

Thread 1

Thread 2

Figure 28.2 Encapsulation protects against errors

every message has a particular format, so we cannot recover in the case of one being incorrectly formatted. Encapsulation allows us to extract messages separately, and even if a message is incorrectly formatted, subsequent messages will not be affected.

Another benefit of encapsulation is that we will always receive complete messages. If a network failure occurs during transmission of a message, the message will not be partially delivered. Instead, the part that was received will be discarded (figure 28.3). If we trust

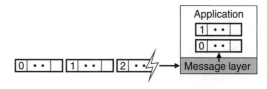

Figure 28.3   Encapsulation hides network failures

that our messages will always be correctly formatted by the sender, we need not worry about errors in messages. If a network failure occurs, we will simply stop receiving messages; we will not receive erroneous messages. This simplifies applications development because error management can be confined to the application's networking layer; the higher layers can assume a reliable message transport layer.

28.2 Class MessageOutput

This is the superclass for all message output streams. It is a `FilterOutputStream`; in fact, it extends `DataOutputStream` because the methods of `DataOutputStream` are so commonly required. The `MessageOutput` class therefore provides all the standard methods of `DataOutputStream`, and in addition adds three `send()` methods.

This is an abstract class; actual implementations are provided by various subclasses that attach to different communications channels.

A message stream operates by encapsulating messages into packets that include a header in addition to the actual message body; it is, in effect, an encapsulation wrapper for a `DataOutputStream`. A message is transmitted only when the `send()` method is called. Until then, the data remains buffered. The `send()` method attaches a header, sends the message, and resets the buffer. The header provides sufficient information for the packet to be extracted from a communications stream and presented at the receiving end as a complete message.

To write a message, you simply use the usual methods of DataOutputStream. All of the data that are written to the MessageOutput are stored away in a

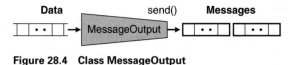

Figure 28.4   Class MessageOutput

buffer. When you call send(), the message will be dispatched with appropriate headers (figure 28.4). The exact headers that are attached depend on the nature of the message stream and the communications channel.

In effect, the MessageOutput class provides a facility to box data. The MessageOutput is itself the box; as you write data into the stream, it is placed in the box. When you call send(), the box is closed and shipped, and a new box opens to accept more data.

```java
import java.io.*;

public abstract class MessageOutput extends DataOutputStream {
   protected MessageOutput (OutputStream out) {
      super (out);
   }

   public abstract void send () throws IOException;

   public void send (String[] dsts) throws IOException {
      throw new IOException ("send[] not supported");
   }

   public void send (String dst) throws IOException {
      String[] dsts = { dst };
      send (dsts);
   }
}
```

This is the definition of the MessageOutput superclass. We extend DataOutputStream and so inherit all its methods. The constructor accepts an OutputStream to which this MessageOutput should attach; this is passed on to the DataOutputStream superclass, so the various methods of DataOutputStream will write directly to the specified stream. Usually this stream will be a ByteArrayOutputStream that buffers the data pending transmission.

The send() methods should transmit the message, along with whatever headers are necessary, to the communications channel for this message stream. No implementation of the normal send() method is mandated, so this class is declared abstract.

The send() methods that take a parameter will be used in a later chapter where we develop message streams that allow us to direct messages to specific recipients. Most message streams do not directly support these alternative methods, and so the default implementation throws an explanatory exception. The send() method that takes a single String parameter simply wraps it up as an array having one element.

28.3 Class MessageInput

This class is the superclass for all message input streams. As per the MessageOutput class, it extends DataInputStream to leverage off the function provided by that class. In addition to the usual methods of DataInputStream, a receive() method is defined.

A message input stream decapsulates messages from a stream and presents them to an application. The receive() method blocks until a complete message has been received, unwraps the body of the message from the header, and then makes the message body available for reading. The message body can be read directly from the Message-Input, using its DataInputStream methods. In the same way that the methods of MessageOutput do not write directly to the communications channel but into a message body, the methods of MessageInput do not read directly from the communications channel but from a message body.

Thus, to read a message, we call the receive() method, which waits for new messages. We can then read directly from the MessageInput class using the

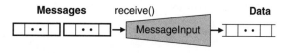

Figure 28.5 Class MessageInput

usual methods of DataInputStream. These will automatically read from the body of the message that has just been received (figure 28.5).

In effect, the receive() method receives a message box from the communications channel, opens the box, and makes the contents available for reading. Calling receive() again will discard the current box and unpack a new one for reading.

```
import java.io.*;

public abstract class MessageInput extends DataInputStream {
   protected MessageInput (InputStream in) {
      super (in);
   }

   public abstract void receive () throws IOException;
}
```

This is the definition of the MessageInput superclass. We extend DataInput-Stream and declare a receive() method. The stream to which the DataInputStream superclass should attach is specified in the constructor.

The `receive()` method will block until a message has been received and then allow reading to proceed from the body of the message. No implementation of this method is mandated, and so this class is declared `abstract`.

28.4 Class MessageOutputStream

This class is an implementation of a `MessageOutput` that transmits messages over an

Figure 28.6   Class MessageOutputStream

attached `OutputStream`. It is essentially very similar to a `BufferedOutputStream` in that it buffers up all of the data that are written to it and only writes them to the attached stream when the `send()` method is called; this is similar to flushing a `BufferedOutputStream` (figure 28.6).

Before writing the data to the stream, however, the `MessageOutputStream` class attaches a header that indicates the length of the message body data. This allows the receiver to determine in advance how large a message will be, without having to actually parse any of it.

Internally, buffering is accomplished with a `ByteArrayOutputStream` which provides an `OutputStream` interface to a dynamically expandable memory buffer (figure 28.7).

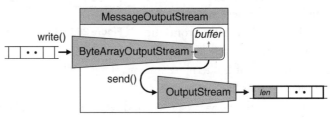

Figure 28.7   Internals of the MessageOutputStream class

This is the simplest concrete implementation of a `MessageOutput` and can be used to provide message transport over any streams-based communications channel, such as a TCP network connection.

```
import java.io.*;

public class MessageOutputStream extends MessageOutput {
    // public MessageOutputStream (OutputStream out) ...
    // public void send () throws IOException ...
}
```

We extend the `MessageOutput` class and provide an implementation of the `send()` method. We will use a `ByteArrayOutputStream` to buffer messages; this buffer will be written to the stream specified in the constructor when `send()` is called.

```
protected OutputStream rawOut;
protected DataOutputStream dataOut;
protected ByteArrayOutputStream byteArrayOut;

public MessageOutputStream (OutputStream out) {
  super (new ByteArrayOutputStream ());
  rawOut = out;
  dataOut = new DataOutputStream (rawOut);
  byteArrayOut = (ByteArrayOutputStream) super.out;
}
```

In this constructor, we call the superclass constructor, specifying a new `ByteArray-OutputStream` to which it will attach. Thus, all data written to this `MessageOutputStream` using the `DataOutputStream` methods will be stored in the `ByteArrayOutputStream`. For convenience, a reference to this is kept in `byteArrayOut`. This reference is taken from `out`, which is inherited from the `FilterOutputStream` superclass. We attach a `DataOutputStream dataOut` to the actual attached stream `rawOut`; we will use this in the `send()` method.

Note that we do not attach the superclass to `rawOut`, so closing this stream will not close the attached stream. Instead, it will call the `close()` method of `byteArrayOut`, which will have no effect. The application must itself explicitly close the underlying stream when it is finished with it.

```
public void send () throws IOException {
  synchronized (rawOut) {
    dataOut.writeInt (byteArrayOut.size ());
    byteArrayOut.writeTo (rawOut);
  }
  byteArrayOut.reset ();
  rawOut.flush ();
}
```

The `send()` method transmits the contents of the byte array to the attached stream. We synchronize on `rawOut` to prevent another message being sent at the same time. We then transmit the length of the buffer, write the buffer to the stream, and finally reset the buffer so that it will begin refilling again. We also flush the `OutputStream` to ensure that the message is sent as soon as possible.

Note that we synchronize on `rawOut` and not `dataOut`. The latter is an object local to just this instance and so synchronizing on it would not prevent other classes from writing to `rawOut`. Most `write()` methods do not actually synchronize on the stream being written to, so this synchronization really protects us only from other `MessageOutputStreams`. However, this is all that we require.

This class does not support the targeted `send()` method, so we inherit its default implementation.

28.5 Class MessageInputStream

This class is an implementation of a `MessageInput` that reads messages

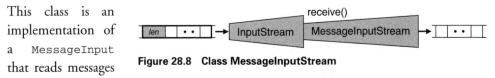

Figure 28.8 Class MessageInputStream

from an attached `InputStream`. The attached stream should provide a connection from a remote `MessageOutputStream`. When the `receive()` method is called, this class reads a message, as written by a `MessageOutputStream`, and then allows the contents of the message to be read using the usual `read()` methods of the superclass `DataInputStream` (figure 28.8).

After reception and stripping of headers, received messages are internally stored in a `ByteArrayInputStream`; this provides a convenient `InputStream` interface for

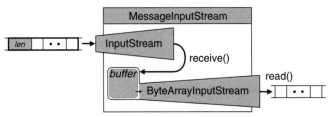

Figure 28.9 Internals of the MessageInputStream class

reading from an array of bytes (figure 28.9).

This is the simplest concrete implementation of a `MessageInput` and is usually used at the receiving end of a network connection.

```
import java.io.*;

public class MessageInputStream extends MessageInput {
   // public MessageInputStream (InputStream in) ...
   // public void receive () throws IOException ...
}
```

The `MessageInputStream` class extends `MessageInput` and provides an implementation of the `receive()` method. The constructor takes an `InputStream` parameter from which messages will be read. After a message has been read, the contents will be made available to read using the inherited `DataInputStream` methods of this class.

```
   protected InputStream rawIn;
   protected DataInputStream dataIn;
   public MessageInputStream (InputStream in) {
      super (new ByteArrayInputStream (new byte[0]));
      rawIn = in;
      dataIn = new DataInputStream (rawIn);
   }
```

In the constructor, we pass an empty `ByteArrayInputStream` to the superconstructor. This is because we initially have received no messages, and so have no data to provide from the superclass `read()` methods. If you call a `read()` method on this class without first calling `receive()`, you will read an EOF.

```java
public void receive () throws IOException {
   synchronized (rawIn) {
      int length = dataIn.readInt ();
      byte[] buffer = new byte[length];
      dataIn.readFully (buffer);
      in = new ByteArrayInputStream (buffer);
   }
}
```

This method receives a message from the attached input stream. We first read the length of the message, create a buffer `buffer` to hold it, and then read the whole message. This is all done while synchronized on the input stream, which prevents any other thread from reading from the input stream before the entire message has been read. Finally, we replace `in` with a new `ByteArrayInputStream` constructed from this buffer.

The `InputStream in` is inherited by the `FilterInputStream` class and is accessed by all of the methods of `FilterInputStream`. By reassigning `in`, we reassign the stream from which the `DataInputStream` methods will read. Thus, any code that reads from this `MessageInputStream` class will read from the message that has just been received. Calling the `receive()` method again will discard the old message and start reading from a new message.

28.6 Using message streams

At the very simplest, we can use message streams as buffers. Instead of calling `flush()`, we must call `send()` on a `MessageOutputStream`, and to read a buffer, we must call `receive()` on a `MessageInputStream`.

```java
void sender (OutputStream out) throws IOException {
  MessageOutputStream messageOut = new MessageOutputStream (out);
  while (true) {
    messageOut.writeUTF ("message");
    messageOut.send ();
  }
}
```

The `sender()` method attaches a `MessageOutputStream messageOut` to the `OutputStream out` and sits in a loop, sending messages.

```java
void receiver (InputStream in) throws IOException {
  MessageInputStream messageIn = new MessageInputStream (in);
  while (true) {
    messageIn.receive ();
```

```
        System.out.println (messageIn.readUTF ());
    }
}
```

The `receiver()` method similarly attaches a `MessageInputStream messageIn` to the `InputStream in` and sits in a loop, receiving messages.

28.7 Class MessageCopier

The Message-
Copier class is a
simple example
of using mes-
sage streams.

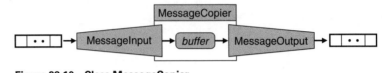

Figure 28.10   Class MessageCopier

The sole purpose of this class is to read messages from a `MessageInput` and write them straight to a `MessageOutput` (figure 28.10). While this may seem a pointless exercise, we will use it later.

Note that because we are relaying between a `MessageInput` and a `MessageOutput`, we could be relaying messages between arbitrary communications channels, with arbitrary headers. The particular classes in use—such as a `MessageOutputStream` and `MessageInputStream`—will take care of the specific encapsulation and decapsulation processes.

```
import java.io.*;

public class MessageCopier extends Thread {
    // public MessageCopier
         (MessageInput messageIn, MessageOutput messageOut) ...
    // public void finish () ...
    // public void run () ...
}
```

This class extends `Thread`; you can create an instance of it, start it, and messages will be copied by a new thread. The input and output streams are specified in the constructor; when the thread is started, the relaying process will begin. In a production server environment, it would be more appropriate to use a pool of threads such as provided by the `ReThread` example of chapter 5, instead of creating a `Thread` for each `MessageCopier`. For the purposes of this example, however, delving into threading issues would obscure the networking aspects in which we are interested.

```
    protected MessageInput messageIn;
    protected MessageOutput messageOut;

    static private int copierNumber;
    static private synchronized int nextCopierNum () { return copierNumber ++; }
```

```
public MessageCopier (MessageInput messageIn, MessageOutput messageOut) {
    super ("MessageCopier-" + nextCopierNum ());
    this.messageIn = messageIn;
    this.messageOut = messageOut;
}
```

Messages are transferred from the `MessageInput messageIn` to the `Message-Output messageOut`. To maintain useful thread names, we make use of the static variable `copierNumber` and the static method `nextCopierNum()`, which returns a unique identifier for each `MessageCopier` instance.

```
protected boolean finished;

public void finish () {
    finished = true;
    interrupt ();
}
```

This method should be called to stop this copier. We first set the `finished` flag to true, and then call `interrupt()` to interrupt this thread if it is blocked in a thread operation such as `wait()` or `sleep()`. Additionally, you may need to close the stream from which it is reading: Stopping or interrupting a thread may not wake it if it is blocked in an I/O operation. Instead, you may have to close the stream in order that the I/O operation be aborted. This copier should not be stopped using the usual thread `stop()` method; doing so could leave a partial message read or written.

```
public void run () {
    try {
        copy ();
    } catch (IOException ex) {
        if (!finished)
            ex.printStackTrace ();
    }
}
// protected void copy () throws IOException ...
```

The `run()` method is called when the `MessageCopier` is started (by calling the superclass `start()` method). We call the `copy()` method to actually copy messages from the `MessageInput` to the `MessageOutput`.

If the `copy()` method throws an `IOException`, and this is not a result of the copier being stopped, then we display the exception stack trace. We could provide a special case for `EOFException`, indicating that the end of the input stream has been reached, however that is really a higher-level issue that we can't address with full generality here.

```
protected void copy () throws IOException {
    while (!interrupted ()) {
```

```
    byte[] buffer;
    synchronized (messageIn) {
      messageIn.receive ();
      buffer = new byte[messageIn.available ()];
      messageIn.readFully (buffer);
    }
    synchronized (messageOut) {
      messageOut.write (buffer);
      messageOut.send ();
    }
  }
}
```

The `copy()` method simply loops, receiving messages on the `MessageInput` messageIn and resending them unmodified to the `MessageOutput` messageOut. We create a byte buffer `buffer`, which is the size of the message body (as returned by the `available()` method). We read the body into the buffer and then write this to messageOut, using synchronization as necessary.

To use this class, create an instance attached to the requisite streams and then call the `start()` method. A new thread will begin copying messages automatically.

28.8 A transaction processing example

One of the things that makes these streams unusual is that multiple `MessageOutputStreams` can be attached to a single `OutputStream`, and multiple `MessageInputStreams` can be attached to a single `InputStream`. All of the `MessageStreams` will operate correctly together with multiple threads executing concurrently.

This is useful, for example, in a transaction processing application. Requests may take a long time to process; they may require calling an external database, which could take a while to respond. We can start multiple threads to receive messages concurrently. If one thread takes a long time to process the transaction, the other threads will continue processing requests. Because we encapsulate each message, we do not have to parse the request to determine the start of the next message.

In this example, we develop a simple transaction processing application. The server contains a `Hashtable`, which maps attributes to values (both are `String` values). Clients can query the value of an attribute (get) at the server or assign a value to an attribute (put). The get and put operations are the transactions, and the server utilizes multiple threads to handle them.

28.8.1 Class TransactionClient
This simple graphical client connects to a corresponding server (which we will examine next). It makes use of `MessageOutputStreams` and `MessageInputStreams` to communicate. The user interface presents two `TextFields` and two `Buttons`.

The Get button allows us to query the value of an attribute at the server, and the Put button allows us to change the state of an attribute at the server (figure 28.11).

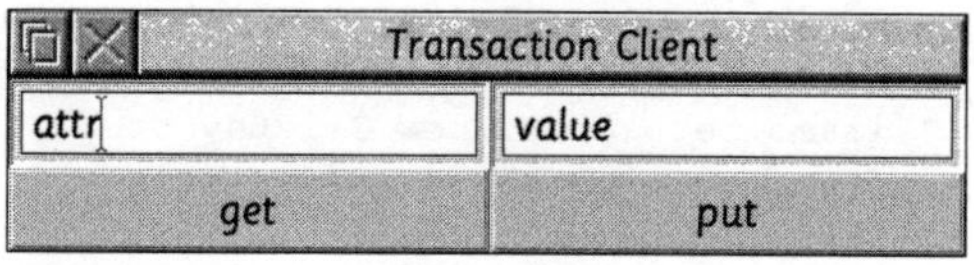

Figure 28.11 The TransactionClient interface

```
import java.io.*;
import java.net.*;
import java.awt.*;
import java.awt.event.*;

public class TransactionClient implements ActionListener, Runnable {
  // public TransactionClient (String host, int port) ...
  // public void start () throws IOException ...
  // public void run () ...
  // public void actionPerformed (ActionEvent event) ...
  // public static void main (String[] args) throws IOException ...
}
```

This simple graphical client follows the structure of many of the earlier graphical examples in this book. We implement ActionListener and Runnable. The constructor accepts a host and port on which to connect; the start() method connects to the server, opens up the transaction Frame, and starts a thread that enters the run() method and listens for incoming messages. We provide an actionPerformed() method that handles GUI events and a main() method that launches the client.

```
protected String host;
protected int port;

public TransactionClient (String host, int port) {
  this.host = host;
  this.port = port;
  initAWT ();
}
```

```
// protected void initAWT () ...
```
In the constructor we keep a copy of the transaction server's address, host and port, and then call initAWT() to initialize the user interface.

```
protected Frame frame;
protected Button get, put;
protected TextField attr, value;

protected void initAWT () {
  frame = new Frame ("Transaction Client");
  attr = new TextField (24);
  value = new TextField (24);
  get = new Button ("get");
  get.addActionListener (this);
```

```
    put = new Button ("put");
    put.addActionListener (this);
    frame.setLayout (new GridLayout (2, 2));
    frame.add (attr);
    frame.add (value);
    frame.add (get);
    frame.add (put);
    frame.pack ();
}
```

The initAWT() method creates the user interface, which consists of the Frame, frame; two Buttons, get and put; and two TextFields, attr and value. We lay these components out, register as a listener for events from the two Buttons, and pack the Frame.

For the purposes of this example, we will ignore Frame events, so there is no clean mechanism to shut this client down except by aborting it.

```
protected MessageInputStream messageIn;
protected MessageOutputStream messageOut;
protected Thread listener;

public void start () throws IOException {
    Socket socket = new Socket (host, port);
    messageIn = new MessageInputStream (socket.getInputStream ());
    messageOut = new MessageOutputStream (socket.getOutputStream ());
    frame.setVisible (true);
    listener = new Thread (this);
    listener.start ();
}
```

The start() method connects to the transaction server, creates the MessageInputStream messageIn and the MessageOutputStream messageOut, shows the Frame, and starts a new Thread, listener, that processes incoming messages.

If a problem is encountered connecting to the server, this method will exit with the appropriate exception.

```
public void run () {
    try {
        while (true) {
            messageIn.receive ();
            System.out.print ("attr: " + messageIn.readUTF ());
            System.out.println (" value: " + messageIn.readUTF ());
        }
    } catch (IOException ex) {
        ex.printStackTrace ();
    }
}
```

The run() method loops and accepts messages on the MessageInputStream messageIn. We will be receiving response from the TransactionServer class. Every message consists of two Strings: an attribute and its value. We print the attributes and values out to the console as they are received. Either receiving a message or reading a String may throw an IOException; if this occurs, we just print the exception out and finish.

```
public void actionPerformed (ActionEvent event) {
  try {
    if (event.getSource () == get) {
      messageOut.writeUTF ("get");
      messageOut.writeUTF (attr.getText ());
    } else if (event.getSource () == put) {
      messageOut.writeUTF ("put");
      messageOut.writeUTF (attr.getText ());
      messageOut.writeUTF (value.getText ());
    }
    messageOut.send ();
  } catch (IOException ex) {
    ex.printStackTrace ();
  }
}
```

This method handles user interactions. When Get is pressed, a message is sent to the TransactionServer, consisting of the command get and the name of the attribute (this is the label in the first TextField). When Put is pressed, a message is sent consisting of the command put, the name of the attribute, and a value to associate with this attribute (this is the label in the second TextField). If an exception occurs, we print a stack trace to the console.

```
public static void main (String[] args) throws IOException {
  if (args.length != 2)
    throw new IllegalArgumentException
      ("Syntax: TransactionClient <host> <port>");
  TransactionClient client = new TransactionClient
    (args[0], Integer.parseInt (args[1]));
  client.start ();
}
```

The main() method starts a TransactionClient. We verify that a host and port have been specified on the command line; we then create and start a Transaction-Client.

28.8.2 Class TransactionServer

This class is the transaction server. It uses the MessageInputStream and MessageOutputStream classes to allow multiple threads to concurrently process transactions.

A simulated delay is introduced to denote a transaction taking time to complete (figure 28.12).

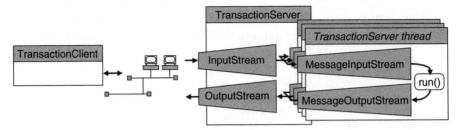

Figure 28.12   The transaction system framework

```
import java.io.*;
import java.util.*;
import java.net.*;

public class TransactionServer implements Runnable {
   // public TransactionServer (InputStream in, OutputStream out) ...
   // public void run () ...
   // public static void main (String[] args) throws IOException ...
}
```

Our server is a basic multithreaded application. To support multiple threads listening for requests and processing transactions concurrently, we implement the `Runnable` interface. The `main()` method sets up the network connections and then starts up the transaction-processing threads, each of which executes in a single shared instance of this class.

```
   protected Hashtable tags;
   protected InputStream in;
   protected OutputStream out;

   public TransactionServer (InputStream in, OutputStream out) {
      this.in = in;
      this.out = out;
      tags = new Hashtable ();
   }
```

This class communicates over the `InputStream in` and `OutputStream out`. It also contains a `Hashtable tags`, which maps attributes to keys. The constructor performs the necessary initialization.

```
   public void run () {
      MessageInputStream messageIn = new MessageInputStream (in);
      MessageOutputStream messageOut = new MessageOutputStream (out);
      try {
         while (true) {
```

```
          messageIn.receive ();
          Thread.sleep (1000);
          String cmd = messageIn.readUTF ();
          System.out.println (Thread.currentThread () + ": command " + cmd);
          if (cmd.equals ("get")) {
            doGet (messageIn, messageOut);
            messageOut.send ();
          } else if (cmd.equals ("put")) {
            doPut (messageIn);
          }
        }
    } catch (IOException ex) {
      ex.printStackTrace ();
    } catch (InterruptedException ignored) {
    }
  }

// void doGet (DataInputStream dataIn, DataOutputStream dataOut)
//     throws IOException ...
// void doPut (DataInputStream dataIn) throws IOException ...
```

Each thread that is started in a `TransactionServer` enters the `run()` method. Local message streams are created for communication by the thread. Each thread then sits in a loop, receiving messages. After receiving a message, the thread sleeps for a while to simulate processing time. The message is then processed, the command name is read from the message, and the message is dispatched accordingly.

```
void doGet (DataInputStream dataIn, DataOutputStream dataOut)
    throws IOException {
  String attr = dataIn.readUTF ();
  dataOut.writeUTF (attr);
  if (tags.containsKey (attr))
    dataOut.writeUTF ((String) tags.get (attr));
  else
    dataOut.writeUTF ("null");
}
```

If the command is a `get`, the client is requesting the current value of an attribute. The server responds with a message consisting of the attribute name and value, or `null` if it has no value.

```
void doPut (DataInputStream dataIn) throws IOException {
  String attr = dataIn.readUTF ();
  String value = dataIn.readUTF ();
  tags.put (attr, value);
}
```

If the command is `put`, the client is supplying a new attribute/value pair, which are put in the `Hashtable`.

```
public static void main (String[] args) throws IOException {
    if (args.length != 2)
        throw new IllegalArgumentException
            ("Syntax: TransactionServer <port> <threads>");
    ServerSocket server = new ServerSocket (Integer.parseInt (args[0]));
    Socket socket = server.accept ();
    server.close ();
    InputStream in = socket.getInputStream ();
    OutputStream out = socket.getOutputStream ();
    TransactionServer transactionServer = new TransactionServer (in, out);
    int n = Integer.parseInt (args[1]);
    for (int i = 0; i < n; ++ i)
        new Thread (transactionServer).start ();
}
```

The `main()` method opens a server socket on the specified port, accepts a single connection, and then closes the server socket. A `TransactionServer` is created, attached to the socket streams. Finally, a user-specified number of threads are started in the `TransactionServer` to handle incoming transactions.

In essence, this is a trivial database that allows us to insert and look up entries. The purpose of the example, however, is to demonstrate how message streams can be applied to a problem that would traditionally be addressed with a basic stream connection.

Making use of message streams provides us with the benefit that multiple threads can independently utilize a single communications channel. In this case, many threads may be concurrently reading from and writing to the connection; however, the message encapsulation protects us against the problems that we would otherwise encounter with interleaved messages.

28.9 Wrapping up

Message streams are very simple in concept, but also very useful. Several variants will be developed later in this section. Many tasks require data to be encapsulated—not usually to allow multiple threads in this manner, but to allow the data to be manipulated and to allow more useful headers to be attached.

The message input and output streams that we have developed here attach directly to existing `InputStream`s and `OutputStream`s, so all message reading and writing involves direct access to the underlying streams. The headers that are attached to messages consist simply of the message length, as that is all the information required to decapsulate a message. In the next chapter, we will look at providing an intermediate buffer in the form of a queue. This can provide a layer of insulation from problems with the underlying communications channel.

C H A P T E R   2 9

Queuing message streams

A queue is a datastructure that can store objects using a simple interface: you can either add an object to the queue or remove an object from it. Queues have the first-in-first-out (FIFO) property; that is to say, the first object that is added to a queue will be the first object that is removed from it. Thus, objects will come out of the queue in the same order in which they are added, much as boxes come off a conveyor belt in the same order in which they were added.

This chapter is concerned with developing a simple queue class and some associated streams that communicate through queues. Messages that are written into a queuing message stream will be placed in a queue for storage; messages that are read from a queuing message stream will be removed from a queue of messages. We will discuss the various advantages of using these queues as we encounter them.

29.1 Class Queue

This class provides the basic queue datastructure (figure 29.1). This queue implementation has one particularly interesting property: if you attempt to remove an object from an empty queue, you will be blocked (suspended) until an object becomes available to remove. A blocked thread will wake up when an object is next added to the queue.

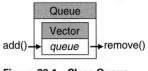

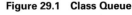

Figure 29.1   Class Queue

There are two significant methods, add() and remove(), which perform the corresponding operations on the queue structure. The elements of the queue are internally stored in a Vector.

```
import java.util.Vector;

public class Queue {
    // public Queue () ...
    // public Object remove () throws InterruptedException ...
    // public void add (Object item) ...
    // public boolean isEmpty () ...
}
```

The Queue class does not inherit from any other class; it defines the method add() to add an element to the queue, remove() to remove an element from the queue, and isEmpty() to determine whether the queue is empty.

```
    protected Vector queue;

    public Queue () {
        queue = new Vector ();
    }
```

Internally, we keep all of the objects in the Vector queue. The constructor allocates a new Vector to store the queue elements.

```
public Object remove () throws InterruptedException {
   synchronized (queue) {
      while (queue.isEmpty ()) {
         queue.wait ();
      }
      Object item = queue.firstElement ();
      queue.removeElement (item);
      return item;
   }
}
```

The remove() method removes an element from the queue, blocking if none is available. This task is fairly simple at first glance; however, it is complicated by multi-threading and by the fact that threads block if the queue is empty. This method first waits for the queue to become nonempty; it then extracts the first element in the queue, removes it from the queue, and returns the item.

To protect against multiple threads accessing the queue at once, we synchronize on the Vector of elements before attempting to remove an object. We then sit in a loop, which waits for the queue to become nonempty; inside this loop we call queue.wait(). This is a useful method: it causes the current thread to wait until another thread calls the notify() method on the queue. In the add() method, we will call notify() when we add an element to the queue, thus waking a sleeping thread. Once we exit the loop, the queue is nonempty and we are also synchronized on it, so no other thread can access the queue. We can then safely extract the first element from the queue and return it.

The wait() method is particularly important because it releases synchronization on the queue until the call returns. If this did not occur, no other thread could add elements to the queue to wake the sleeping thread. To call either wait() or notify(), a thread must be synchronized on the target object.

```
public void add (Object item) {
   synchronized (queue) {
      queue.addElement (item);
      queue.notify ();
   }
}
```

Adding an object to the queue is simply a matter of appending it to the Vector of elements. We then call queue.notify(); if threads are waiting for the queue to become nonempty, this will wake one of them.

```
public boolean isEmpty () {
   return queue.isEmpty ();
}
```

The isEmpty() method is simply a matter of querying whether queue is empty.

29.2 Class QueueOutputStream

This class is a `MessageOutput` that, instead of writing messages to an `OutputStream`, inserts them into a queue that is specified in the constructor. This class extends `Message-Output` and implements a `send()` method that inserts the message into the queue (figure 29.2).

Figure 29.2   Class QueueOutputStream

We will use queues and message streams so that we can temporarily store messages in a memory queue; we will build the queue with a `QueueOutputStream` and read messages from it with a `QueueInputStream`.

```
import java.io.*;

public class QueueOutputStream extends MessageOutput {
    // public QueueOutputStream (Queue queue) ...
    // public void send () ...
}
```

This class extends `MessageOutput` and implements the `send()` method to place messages in a queue. A `ByteArray-OutputStream` is used to buffer message data. The message queue is specified in the constructor (figure 29.3).

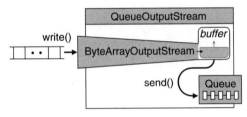

Figure 29.3   Internals of the QueueOutput-Stream class

```
protected ByteArrayOutputStream
    byteArrayOut;
protected Queue queue;

public QueueOutputStream (Queue queue) {
    super (new ByteArrayOutputStream ());
    byteArrayOut = (ByteArrayOutputStream) out;
    this.queue = queue;
}
```

In the constructor, we must first call the superclass constructor. We specify a `Byte-ArrayOutputStream byteArrayOut` to buffer the message body. This is the same code that we have seen with the `MessageOutputStream` class. Messages will be placed in the `Queue queue`.

```
public void send () {
    byte[] buffer = byteArrayOut.toByteArray ();
    byteArrayOut.reset ();
    queue.add (buffer);
}
```

The `send()` method extracts the current contents of the `ByteArrayOutputStream` and places them into `queue`. All the data that have been written to this class will have been stored in `byteArrayOut`. Note that there are no headers attached to this byte array; it consists simply of the data that have been written to this class. We know the length of the data because all arrays keep an internal count of their length.

Several `QueueOutputStreams` can be attached to a single `Queue`, allowing us to multiplex the results of several threads into a single queue of messages in a coherent manner. This allows, for example, the results of multiple concurrent transactions to be routed into a single queue without mutual interference.

This class has no support for the targeted `send()` method and so inherits the default implementation.

29.3 Class QueueInputStream

This class is a `MessageInput` which, instead of reading messages from an `InputStream`, extracts them from a queue (figure 29.4). The queue *must* contain messages in the form

Figure 29.4   ClassQueueInputStream

of byte arrays; for example, a queue of messages written with a `QueueOutputStream`.

Calling `receive()` will extract a message from the queue. The caller is then able to read from this message by reading from the `QueueInputStream` using the regular `InputStream` methods. If the queue becomes empty, calling `receive()` will block until another message is added to the queue.

```
import java.io.*;

public class QueueInputStream extends MessageInput {
   // public QueueInputStream (Queue queue) ...
   // public void receive () throws IOException ...
}
```

This class extends `MessageInput` and implements the `receive()` method. The class is constructed with a `Queue` from which it will remove messages; we will use a `ByteArrayInputStream` to permit reading from these messages (figure 29.5).

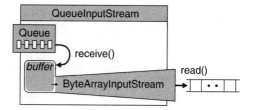

Figure 29.5   Internals of the QueueInput-Stream class

```
protected Queue queue;

public QueueInputStream (Queue queue) {
   super (new ByteArrayInputStream (new byte[0]));
```

```
      this.queue = queue;
   }
```

In the constructor, we must call a valid superclass constructor. The only constructor for `MessageInput` takes an `InputStream` as a parameter. In this case, we supply an empty `ByteArrayInputStream`, as before; initially no messages have been received, so no data can be read. Messages will be removed from the `Queue` queue.

```
public void receive () throws IOException {
   try {
      byte[] buffer = (byte[]) queue.remove ();
      in = new ByteArrayInputStream (buffer);
   } catch (InterruptedException ex) {
      throw new InterruptedIOException ("queue.remove()");
   }
}
```

We provide a simple implementation of the `receive()` method that extracts the next message from the buffer and sets the `in` variable of the `FilterInputStream` super-class to refer to a new `ByteArrayInputStream` constructed from this buffer. All subsequent `read()` calls to this stream will read from this `ByteArrayInputStream`, allowing the caller to read from the new message.

If we encounter an `InterruptedException` while reading from the queue (i.e., someone has called `interrupt()` on our thread), we pass it on as an `Interrupted-IOException`. This is the preferred way of stopping a thread that is reading from a `QueueInputStream`; closing this stream will have no effect.

In a manner similar to the `MessageInputStream`, several `QueueInputStreams` can be attached to a single `Queue`, allowing several threads to process transactions concurrently.

29.4 Filling a queue

Queue streams can be used to either queue input coming from a communications

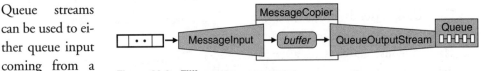

Figure 29.6   Filling a message queue

channel or to queue output going to a communications channel. Here, we will look at queuing input coming from a communications channel and discuss some of the associated benefits (figure 29.6).

We will use the `QueueOutputStream` class to place messages into the queue. The messages that we will be inserting into the queue will be coming from a `MessageInput` attached to some communications channel.

```
void fillQueue (MessageInput from, Queue queue) {
    QueueOutputStream to = new QueueOutputStream (queue);
    MessageCopier copier = new MessageCopier (from, to);
    copier.start ();
}
```

The fillQueue() method uses the MessageCopier that we developed in the previous chapter. We create a new QueueOutputStream directed into the specified Queue queue and then start a MessageCopier, which copies messages from the MessageInput from into the new QueueOutputStream to.

This simple method actually has several important uses. Note that several MessageCopiers can be attached to a single queue. This allows us to multiplex several message input channels into a single queue for processing. This is helpful because the message processing which occurs on the far end of the queue is entirely insulated from the input to the queue.

Another benefit is that, in a real application, the MessageCopier thread will be the only thread that reads from the raw InputStream. Although several threads may be reading from the queue, these operations will all access byte arrays. As a result, the MessageCopier will be the only thread that

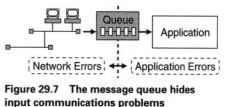

Figure 29.7   The message queue hides input communications problems

can experience an IOException as a result of a failure in the underlying communications channel (figure 29.7).

Thus, we can write an application that does not need to be able to handle communications failures occurring wherever a read() call occurs. Instead, we can write most of the code to only handle errors of incorrect message formats and other programmer errors, and leave the communications failure handling to a variant of the MessageCopier thread which performs appropriate error checking. If an application suite is suitably debugged, message format errors should not occur, and so all of the error handling will be in this one class.

29.5 Emptying a queue

Here we will look at emptying a Queue into a MessageOutput (figure 29.8).

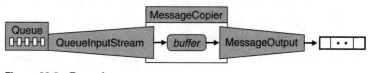

Figure 29.8   Emptying a message queue

Again, we use the MessageCopier class to perform the task of relaying messages.

We will be extracting messages from a `Queue`, so we will use a `QueueInputStream`. We write the messages out to the specified `MessageOutput`.

```
void emptyQueue (Queue queue, MessageOutput to) {
  QueueInputStream from = new QueueInputStream (queue);
  MessageCopier copier = new MessageCopier (from, to);
  copier.start ();
}
```

To copy messages out of the queue, we start a `MessageCopier` that extracts messages from the `Queue queue` using a `QueueInputStream from` and inserts them into the `MessageOutput to`.

This is another simple method which has a couple of uses that are similar to those of the previous example. Several `MessageCopiers` can be attached to a single `Queue`. This can be useful when there are multiple streams to a remote host, or if there are multiple remote hosts that can service messages. Multiple streams to a host can help with bandwidth and redundancy if they can be routed through different paths. With multiple streams to different hosts, load can be more evenly shared. Additionally, new requests to one particular host can be delayed until a response to an earlier request has been received, while others can keep going.

The `MessageCopier` thread, again, will be the only one which actually directly accesses the `OutputStream`, and so is the only place where a communications error can cause an exception (figure 29.9). This means that all output code can essentially ignore exceptions; it is safe to assume that they will not happen. This simpli-

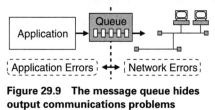

Figure 29.9 The message queue hides output communications problems

fies application writing because all exception handling and cleanup can be deferred to a variant of the `MessageCopier`. In particular, an attempt can be made to reopen the connection and no other code need be aware of this; pending transmissions will build up in the queue until a new connection is made or the application decides to terminate.

The queue provides several shielding benefits other than against communications errors. The actual process of transmitting a message down a socket is not instantaneous; network problems may cause significant delays. The output queuing allows us to shield interactive applications from these delays. While the `MessageCopier` thread will delay, the `send()` method of attached `QueueOutputStreams` will always return quickly because it only needs to shuffle buffers in memory. This is a particular benefit for interactive applications, although one should be aware of buffer sizes and the latency that may occur if they build up.

29.6 Wrapping up

In the previous chapter, we introduced the concept of message streams. In this chapter we have extended this concept to allow us to route these messages through queues. This gives us a simple mechanism for combining several message streams into one, or splitting one into many. It also allows us to centralize the main error-handling code of our application to shield most threads from delays and errors in the communications channel.

While these message streams allow us to direct several message channels into a single queue, they do not provide any information to assist in reversing this process; it is not possible to determine the origin of a message when it is extracted from the queue. In the next chapter, we will develop some multiplexing streams that add additional headers to messages. These headers will allow us to specify the origin of each message in a stream.

C H A P T E R   3 0

Multiplexing message streams

Up to this point, we have been mostly concerned with developing simple message streams that do not add significant function to regular streams. They are, however, a necessary basis for creating a communications library that will make developing tools for serious networked applications considerably easier. In this and the next chapter we develop some useful higher level classes.

This chapter is concerned with the development of message streams that can actually multiplex messages for several applications down a single stream connection in a completely transparent manner. This is achieved by adding a label to the header of every message that indicates the origin of the message.

The purpose of multiplexing is not to route between different clients; we will address that issue in the next chapter. Instead, multiplexing will enable several independent components of a client to communicate down a single network connection. Specifically, an example at the end of

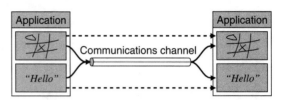

Figure 30.1 Multiplexing two tools down one stream

the chapter demonstrates how a simple collaborative tool with a whiteboard and text-based chat can operate across a single communications channel (figure 30.1). Neither the whiteboard nor the text chat is aware of the other's existence.

30.1 Class MultiplexOutputStream

This class extends MessageOutput and attaches to another MessageOutput, not a plain OutputStream. This lets us multiplex messages down any message stream, whether a QueueOutputStream or a MessageOutputStream. In effect, this is equivalent to a FilterOutputStream, which can attach to any underlying OutputStream connection; it lets us build powerful communication layers independently of the underlying transport.

This class adds a multiplexing header to the start of every message it sends. Thus all messages sent by this class will be sent down the attached MessageOutput with a multiplexing label automatically prefixed (figure 30.2). The multiplexing label is a String that must be chosen manually and is specified in the constructor, so a Multiplex-OutputStream is used only for routing with one specific label.

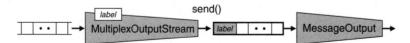

Figure 30.2 Class MultiplexOutputStream

In essence, we have added a labeling mechanism to the attached `MessageOut`; at the far end of the communications link, this label can be examined to determine the origin of the message.

At the end of this chapter, we will use this class to multiplex several tools down a single connection. A `MultiplexOutputStream` will be used to identify the source of every message—whether it is from a whiteboard or a chat tool (figure 30.3). At the receiving end, we can examine this label and determine whether to hand the message to the whiteboard or chat tool for processing.

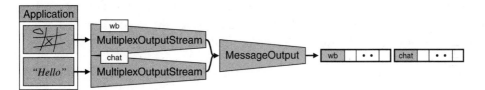

Figure 30.3   Using the MultiplexOutputStream class

```
import java.io.*;

public class MultiplexOutputStream extends MessageOutput {
  // public MultiplexOutputStream
       (MessageOutput messageOut, String label) ...
  // public void send () throws IOException ...
  // public void send (String[] dsts) throws IOException ...
}
```

This `MessageOutput` class attaches to an existing `MessageOut` and adds a routing label to every message; this label is specified in the constructor. We provide appropriate implementations of the `send()` methods.

```
protected MessageOutput messageOut;
protected ByteArrayOutputStream byteArrayOut;
protected String label;

public MultiplexOutputStream (MessageOutput messageOut, String label) {
   super (new ByteArrayOutputStream ());
   byteArrayOut = (ByteArrayOutputStream) out;
   this.messageOut = messageOut;
   this.label = label;
}
```

In the constructor, we call the superclass constructor and direct all data to be written to a new `ByteArrayOutputStream`. For convenience, we keep a local reference to this in `byteArrayOut` and to the attached `MessageOutput` in `messageOut`. The label to be added to messages is specified by `label`.

```
public void send () throws IOException {
  synchronized (messageOut) {
    messageOut.writeUTF (label);
    byteArrayOut.writeTo (messageOut);
    messageOut.send ();
  }
  byteArrayOut.reset ();
}
```

The send() method sends the message that has been queued up in byteArrayOut. We synchronize on the attached MessageOut, write the header, write the stored message, and then send it using the send() method of the attached stream. The header that is added by this class consists of just the multiplexing label; the send() method of the attached stream will subsequently attach its own headers.

```
public void send (String[] dsts) throws IOException {
  synchronized (messageOut) {
    messageOut.writeUTF (label);
    byteArrayOut.writeTo (messageOut);
    messageOut.send (dsts);
  }
  byteArrayOut.reset ();
}
```

While this class provides no direct support for the targeted send methods, it may be attached to a stream that does support them. Therefore, we must provide this implementation to call the appropriate method of the attached stream. If the attached stream does not support targeting, an exception will be thrown, as usual.

This class is simple in nature; all it does is write a header at the start of every message. We could obviously do this manually before sending a message. However, this class has the advantage that it is completely transparent to the caller. Indeed, the caller does not know that it is using anything other than a simple message stream.

30.2 Class MultiplexInputStream

This is the corresponding input end of a multiplexed stream. This class attaches to a MessageInput and extracts the multiplexing header from each message that is received (figure 30.4). This is the equivalent of a FilterInputStream; it adds additional function on top of an existing message stream.

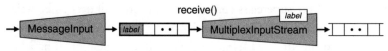

Figure 30.4 Class MultiplexInputStream

The multiplexing label that is read from each message is made publicly accessible to allow the message to be correctly processed. This class is effectively the delabeling mechanism that lets us examine the origin of each message that we receive (figure 30.5). We can use this information to determine how to process each message.

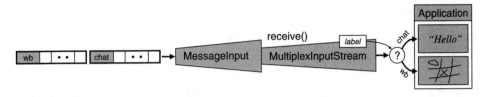

Figure 30.5   Using the MultiplexInputStream class

```java
import java.io.*;

public class MultiplexInputStream extends MessageInput {
  // public MultiplexInputStream (MessageInput messageIn) ...
  // public void receive () throws IOException ...
  // public String getLabel () ...
}
```

This class extends the `MessageInput` class and attaches to an existing `Message-Input`. We implement the `receive()` method to receive a message from the attached stream, extract a multiplexing label, and make this publicly readable through the `get-Label()` method.

The message label will be valid until the next message is received, from which time it will indicate the origin of the subsequent message.

```java
protected MessageInput messageIn;

public MultiplexInputStream (MessageInput messageIn) {
  super (messageIn);
  this.messageIn = messageIn;
}
```

The constructor calls the superclass constructor, attaching to the specified `Mes-sageInput messageIn`. Thus, all `read()` calls made to this class will be passed on to `messageIn`. We make a local copy of `messageIn` for convenience. Reading from this class will thus read from the body of the most recently received message; this is the correct behavior for a `MessageInput`.

```java
protected String label;

public void receive () throws IOException {
  messageIn.receive ();
  label = messageIn.readUTF ();
```

```
   }
```

This method calls the `receive()` method of the attached stream, which accepts the next message from its communications channel. We then read a `String` from this stream; this removes the header that was attached by the `MultiplexOutputStream` that wrote the message.

```
public String getLabel () {
   return label;
}
```

This method returns the multiplexing label of the most-recently received message.

This class itself does no actual demultiplexing of the message stream; all it does is strip off the header that was attached by a `MultiplexOutputStream`. The header is then available to other classes for further processing. Next we will see how to use this to actually route the messages.

30.3 Class Demultiplexer

This is an example of a class extracts messages from a `Multi-plexInputStream` and routes them to a `MessageOutput` determined by

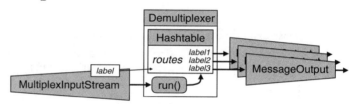

Figure 30.6   Class Demultiplexer

the multiplexing label (figure 30.6). Methods are provided to register and deregister message streams for receiving messages addressed by a particular label.

This is essentially a demultiplexing `MessageCopier`. It completes the set of classes needed to multiplex and demultiplex multiple message streams across a single communications channel. The class receives multiplexed messages, takes the label from each message, and delivers the message to the currently registered address for receiving messages with that label.

```
import java.io.*;
import java.util.*;

public class Demultiplexer extends Thread {
   // public Demultiplexer (MessageInput messageIn) ...
   // public void register (String label, MessageOutput messageOut) ...
   // public void deregister (String label) ...
   // public void finish () ...
   // public void run () ...
}
```

This class is a `Thread`, much like the `MessageCopier`. It attaches to the `Message-Input` specified in the constructor of a `MultiplexInputStream` and maintains a list of routes in an internal `Hashtable`. Destinations can be registered and deregistered with the `register()` and `deregister()` methods. When the thread is started, the `run()` method proceeds to deliver messages appropriately; call `finish()` to stop it.

```
protected MultiplexInputStream multiplexIn;
protected Hashtable targets;

static private int plexerNumber;
static private synchronized int nextPlexerNum () { return plexerNumber ++; }

public Demultiplexer (MessageInput messageIn) {
   super ("Demultiplexer-" + nextPlexerNum ());
   multiplexIn = new MultiplexInputStream (messageIn);
   targets = new Hashtable ();
}
```

The variable `plexerNumber` and the method `nextPlexerNum()` are used to assign a unique name to each `Demultiplexer` thread. The constructor calls the superclass constructor with that name.

Messages are read from the `MultiplexInputStream multiplexIn`; the `Hashtable targets` maintain a routing table. This `Hashtable` maps multiplexing labels to message streams, thus allowing us to easily determine the appropriate destination for a particular message.

```
public void register (String label, MessageOutput messageOut) {
   targets.put (label, messageOut);
}
```

To register a `MessageOutput` to receive messages with a specific label, we simply place an entry in the `Hashtable` which maps the label name `label` to the destination `MessageOutput messageOut`.

This method replaces any existing entry with the new registration, so only the most recently added destination will receive messages.

```
public void deregister (String label) {
   targets.remove (label);
}
```

Deregistering a label involves removing it from the `Hashtable`.

```
protected boolean finished;

public void finish () {
   finished = true;
   interrupt ();
```

```
   }
```

This method should be called to stop this demultiplexer. This method is the same as for the earlier `MessageCopier` class. As with that class, you may also have to close the stream from which this is reading.

```
public void run () {
   try {
      while (!interrupted ()) {
         multiplexIn.receive ();
         String label = multiplexIn.getLabel ();
         MessageOutput messageOut = (MessageOutput) targets.get (label);
         if (messageOut != null) {
            byte[] message = new byte[multiplexIn.available ()];
            multiplexIn.readFully (message);
            synchronized (messageOut) {
               messageOut.write (message);
               messageOut.send ();
            }
         }
      }
   } catch (IOException ex) {
      if (!finished)
         ex.printStackTrace ();
   }
}
```

The `run()` method is called when this thread is started. We loop, receiving messages from the `MultiplexInputStream`. For each message that is received, we look up the label in the `targets` `Hashtable`. If there is a destination registered for this label, the destination message stream is extracted from the `Hashtable`, and the message is written to this stream and sent. If there is no registered destination, we simply discard the current message by calling `receive()` again. We don't need to synchronize on the input stream; this is the only thread that will access it.

In typical situations involving this class, the destination streams will be `QueueOutputStreams` that route into an intermediate queue pending processing by a tool. Another useful destination is a `DeliveryOutputStream`, which we shall look at next.

The same threading considerations as with the `MessageCopier` class apply here: On the server side, a reusable pool of `Threads` should be used instead of continually creating new ones.

30.4 Class DeliveryOutputStream

Delivering into queues and expecting the client application to be actively trying to receive messages (requiring an explicit receive thread) is sometimes unnecessary for a small application. This class is a `MessageOutput` that actively delivers messages to a recipient. It performs this delivery by calling the `receive()` method of its target whenever a message is to be delivered, instead of writing the message to a stream.

Thus, when a message is sent to a `DeliveryOutputStream`, it is immediately presented to a recipient for processing (figure 30.7).

Figure 30.7   Class DeliveryOutputStream

The cost of using this stream is time. The demultiplexing thread must wait for the recipient to process a message before it can proceed with delivering further messages. Also, if the delivery process fails and a `RuntimeException` is thrown, the delivery thread will terminate. This could be overcome with an appropriate `try ... catch` statement; however, we defer this safeguard in this implementation.

```
import java.io.*;

public class DeliveryOutputStream extends MessageOutput {
   // public DeliveryOutputStream (Recipient recipient) ...
   // public void send () ...
}
```

This `MessageOutput` attaches to an object that implements the `Recipient` interface. Messages are intermediately stored in a `ByteArrayOutputStream` and delivered to the recipient immediately upon `send()` being called, using a `ByteArrayInputStream` (figure 30.8).

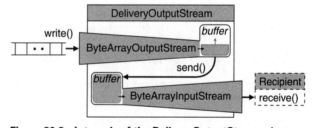

Figure 30.8   Internals of the DeliveryOutputStream class

```
   protected ByteArrayOutputStream byteArrayOut;
   protected Recipient recipient;

   public DeliveryOutputStream (Recipient recipient) {
      super (new ByteArrayOutputStream ());
      byteArrayOut = (ByteArrayOutputStream) out;
      this.recipient = recipient;
   }
```

The `Recipient recipient` will receive messages that are sent to this class. The constructor calls the superclass constructor with a new `ByteArrayOutputStream` `byteArrayOut`; thus all `write()` calls will be directed into this storage buffer.

```
   public void send () {
```

```
    byte[] buffer = byteArrayOut.toByteArray ();
    ByteArrayInputStream byteArrayIn = new ByteArrayInputStream (buffer);
    recipient.receive (new DataInputStream (byteArrayIn));
    byteArrayOut.reset ();
  }
```

When a message is to be sent, we extract it from the `ByteArrayOutputStream` as a byte array `buffer`. We then simply call the recipient's `receive()` method with a new `ByteArrayInputStream` constructed from this buffer. For convenience, we automatically attach a `DataInputStream` to this stream.

30.5 *Interface Recipient*

The `Recipient` interface is a simple interface that declares a `receive()` method to be called whenever a message needs delivery.

```
import java.io.*;

public interface Recipient {
   public void receive (DataInputStream dataIn);
}
```

The message is delivered in the form of a `DataInputStream` from which the contents can be read in the usual manner.

30.6 *A simple collaborative tool*

Multiplexed streams can be used to allow multiple tools to communicate down a single communications channel, yet not interfere with each other. As far as any individual tool is concerned, it has a direct message stream link to a corresponding tool at the far end of the stream.

As an example, we will multiplex two virtual message streams down a single physical connection. We build a simple collaborative tool with a whiteboard and a text-based chat. We open two frames: The whiteboard of the first tool is connected to the whiteboard of the second tool through a multiplexed message stream. Similarly, the text-based chats are attached through a multiplexed message stream. Whatever is written or drawn in the first tool is mirrored in the other, and vice versa (figure 30.9).

The whiteboards and chatboards could each be given different physical connections to the corresponding component on the remote end; however, instead we use `MultiplexOutputStreams` attached to a common carrier. The components are unaware of the fact that they are sharing the communications channel with other components. This is hidden behind the abstraction of a `MessageOutput`.

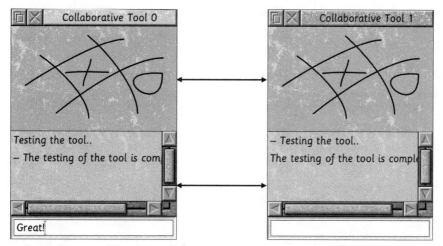

Figure 30.9   The CollabTool interface

30.6.1 Class CollabTool

This is the main class that sets up the communications for this example. As described, we create two tools, each with a whiteboard and a chatboard. These tools communicate by multiplexing messages across a single piped stream.

```
import java.io.*;
import java.awt.*;

public class CollabTool {
  // public CollabTool (InputStream in, OutputStream out) ...
  // public void start () ...
  // public static void main (String[] args) throws IOException ...
}
```

The `CollabTool` class comprises a single collaborative tool that has a `Frame` that contains a whiteboard and a chatboard. The constructor requires an `InputStream` and an `OutputStream` over which the two components will communicate. It creates all necessary multiplexing message streams attached to these. The `start()` method actually shows and starts the tool. The `main()` method creates two of these `CollabTool` objects and connects them via a pair of piped streams.

```
  private static int id = 0;
  protected Frame frame;
  protected Demultiplexer demultiplexer;

  public CollabTool (InputStream in, OutputStream out) {
    frame = new Frame ("Collaborative Tool " + (id ++));
    frame.setLayout (new GridLayout (2, 1));
```

```
    Whiteboard wb = new Whiteboard ();
    frame.add (wb);
    Chatboard cb = new Chatboard ();
    frame.add (cb);
    frame.pack ();

    MessageOutputStream messageOut = new MessageOutputStream (out);
    MessageInputStream messageIn = new MessageInputStream (in);

    cb.setMessageOutput (new MultiplexOutputStream (messageOut, "chat"));
    wb.setMessageOutput (new MultiplexOutputStream (messageOut, "wb"));

    demultiplexer = new Demultiplexer (messageIn);
    demultiplexer.register ("chat", cb.getMessageOutput ());
    demultiplexer.register ("wb", wb.getMessageOutput ());
  }
```

In the constructor for this class, we create a `Whiteboard` and a `Chatboard` that will communicate over multiplexed streams attached to the supplied `InputStream` in and `OutputStream` out. The communications streams for a single direction are shown in figure 30.10.

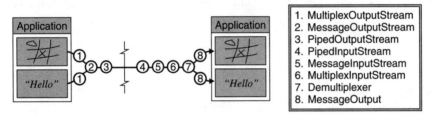

Figure 30.10 The CollabTool communications streams

We first create the `Frame`, `frame`, and then create and lay out the collaborative components consisting of the `Whiteboard` wb and `Chatboard` cb.

We then set up the communications streams; these consist of the `MessageOutput-Stream` messageOut and the `MessageInputStream` messageIn, which communicate over the supplied streams out and in.

We next assign outbound communications streams to the two tools; these are each multiplexed streams that communicate over messageOut. The `Chatboard` is assigned the label chat, and the `Whiteboard` is assigned the label wb. Every message that is sent by either of these tools will be automatically tagged with the appropriate header before being sent over messageOut. These labels will allow the receiving `CollabTool` to route the messages appropriately.

We finally create a `Demultiplexer`, demultiplexer, that processes incoming messages. In this case, both of the tools provide a method `getMessageOutput()` that returns an appropriate message stream to which messages can be sent, so we simply register these streams for each tool.

```
public void start () {
  demultiplexer.start ();
  frame.setVisible (true);
}
```

The start() method first starts the Demultiplexer by calling its start() method. This starts a new thread, which listens for messages, examines the label on each incoming message, and forwards the message to the appropriate target. We then show the Frame.

```
public static void main (String[] args) throws IOException {
  PipedOutputStream out0 = new PipedOutputStream ();
  PipedInputStream in1 = new PipedInputStream (out0);

  PipedOutputStream out1 = new PipedOutputStream ();
  PipedInputStream in0 = new PipedInputStream (out1);

  CollabTool collabTool0 = new CollabTool (in0, out0);
  CollabTool collabTool1 = new CollabTool (in1, out1);
  collabTool0.start ();
  collabTool1.start ();
}
```

The main() method creates a pair of piped streams for communicating from the first tool to the second, and vice versa. We then create two CollabTools attached to these streams and call their start() methods to start and display them.

In this example, we make no use of Queues. Were the example more complex, we might consider using a Queue on the output streams to shield the collaborative components from the communications channel. We will see an example of this in a later chapter.

30.6.2 Class Chatboard

This class implements a simple text-based chat. There is a text output area, which displays past messages, and a text input area for the user to enter messages. In the context of the CollabTool class, this will communicate directly with another Chatboard in another frame. In a later chapter, we will reuse this as the basis for a multiuser networked chat application.

```
import java.io.*;
import java.awt.*;
import java.awt.event.*;

public class Chatboard extends Panel implements Runnable, ActionListener {
```

```
// public Chatboard () ...
// public Dimension getPreferredSize () ...
// public void setMessageOutput (MessageOutput messageOut) ...
// public MessageOutput getMessageOutput () ...
// public void actionPerformed (ActionEvent event) ...
// public void run () ...
}
```

The `Chatboard` is a simple GUI component. We extend the `Panel` class to be able to contain the text entry and display fields. The `CollabTool` class will call the `set-MessageOutput()` method of this class, specifying a message stream over which user messages can be transmitted. Messages that are received from a remote tool will be sent to the message stream returned by the `getMessageOutput()` method. This stream is a `QueueOutputStream` that inserts messages into a queue for subsequent processing.

We implement `ActionListener` and provide an `actionPerformed()` method to catch the event that occurs when the user enters a message. We also implement the `Runnable` interface and provide a `run()` method that extracts messages from the incoming message queue and displays them (figure 30.11).

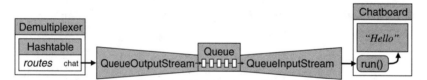

Figure 30.11   The Chatboard communications streams

```
protected TextArea output;
  protected TextField input;
  protected Queue queue;
  protected Thread listener;

  public Chatboard () {
    setLayout (new BorderLayout ());
    add ("Center", output = new TextArea ());
    output.setEditable (false);
    add ("South", input = new TextField ());
    input.addActionListener (this);
    queue = new Queue ();
    listener = new Thread (this);
    listener.start ();
  }
```

In the constructor, we set up the simple user interface. We create a `TextArea` output that will display messages and a `TextField` input into which the user can enter messages. We lay these out in a simple `BorderLayout` with the entry box at the bottom.

We register as an event listener for input, create a Queue, queue, for incoming messages, and start a thread listener that will extract and display messages that are inserted into it.

```
public Dimension getPreferredSize () {
   return new Dimension (200, 150);
}
```

This method returns an appropriate default size for this Container.

```
protected MessageOutput messageOut;

public void setMessageOutput (MessageOutput messageOut) {
   this.messageOut = messageOut;
}
```

This method is called by the CollabTool to specify a message stream over which the Chatboard can send its messages. As far as this class is concerned, it is simply a MessageOutput; the fact that the CollabTool class provides a multiplexed message stream is hidden.

```
public MessageOutput getMessageOutput () {
   return new QueueOutputStream (queue);
}
```

This method returns a stream that can accept incoming messages. In this case, we return a stream that inserts the messages into queue, for subsequent removal by the listener thread.

Note that this is just one possible implementation of this method; we will see an alternative implementation in the Whiteboard class. The advantage of using a queue like this is that, if the processing of a message takes a long time, the CollabTool can keep on routing messages while another thread takes care of the slow processing. Obviously this is not the case for this class, but it serves as an example of a possible implementation.

```
public void actionPerformed (ActionEvent event) {
   try {
      messageOut.writeUTF (input.getText ());
      messageOut.send ();
      output.append (input.getText () + "\n");
      input.setText ("");
   } catch (IOException ignored) {
   }
}
```

This method is called when the user enters a message in the text field `input`. We send this message over the message stream `messageOut`, and then append the text to the display region.

```
public void run () {
    QueueInputStream queueIn = new QueueInputStream (queue);
    try {
        while (!Thread.interrupted ()) {
            queueIn.receive ();
            String msg = queueIn.readUTF ();
            output.append ("-- " + msg + "\n");
        }
    } catch (IOException ignored) {
    }
}
```

This method is called by the `listener` thread and takes care of displaying incoming messages. We attach a `QueueInputStream` to our queue, `queue`, and then proceed to extract and display messages.

30.6.3 Class Whiteboard

This is a simple `Whiteboard` example that provides a surface on which the user can scribble. When the user releases a mouse button, the scribble is transmitted, to be displayed on a remote `Whiteboard`.

```
import java.io.*;
import java.awt.*;
import java.awt.event.*;

public class Whiteboard extends Canvas implements Recipient {
    // public Whiteboard () ...
    // public void setMessageOutput (MessageOutput messageOut) ...
    // public Dimension getPreferredSize () ...
    // protected void processEvent (AWTEvent event) ...
    // public MessageOutput getMessageOutput () ...
    // public void receive (DataInputStream dataIn) ...
}
```

The `Whiteboard` class extends `Canvas` to provide a basic GUI drawing surface. The `CollabTool` class will call the `setMessageOutput()` method with an appropriate message stream over which we will communicate. We override the protected `processEvent()` method to handle user-interface events.

In this case, unlike in the `Chatboard` class, we will use a `DeliveryOutputStream` to deliver messages immediately. The `getMessageOutput()` method returns a `DeliveryOutput-`

Figure 30.12   The Whiteboard communications streams

`Stream` with `this` as the target; therefore we must implement the `Recipient` interface and provide a `receive()` method that can handle messages as they arrive (figure 30.12).

```
public Whiteboard () {
  setBackground (new Color (255, 255, 204));
  enableEvents (AWTEvent.MOUSE_EVENT_MASK |
               AWTEvent.MOUSE_MOTION_EVENT_MASK);
}
```

In our constructor, we choose an off-white background color and enable mouse event using the `enableEvents()` method.

```
protected MessageOutput messageOut;

public void setMessageOutput (MessageOutput messageOut) {
  this.messageOut = messageOut;
}
```

The `CollabTool` class will call this method with an appropriate `MessageOutput`, `messageOut`, over which we will communicate.

```
public Dimension getPreferredSize () {
  return new Dimension (200, 150);
}
```

This method returns an appropriate size for this `Component`.

```
protected void processEvent (AWTEvent event) {
  if (event instanceof MouseEvent) {
    switch (event.getID ()) {
      case MouseEvent.MOUSE_PRESSED:
        mousePressed ((MouseEvent) event);
        break;
      case MouseEvent.MOUSE_DRAGGED:
        mouseDragged ((MouseEvent) event);
        break;
      case MouseEvent.MOUSE_RELEASED:
        mouseReleased ((MouseEvent) event);
        break;
      default:
        super.processEvent (event);
        break;
    }
```

```
    }
}

// protected void mousePressed (MouseEvent event) ...
// protected void mouseDragged (MouseEvent event) ...
// protected void mouseReleased (MouseEvent event) ...
```

This method is called to process AWT events for this `Component`. If a mouse event occurs and it is one in which we are interested, we call `mousePressed()`, `mouse-Dragged()`, or `mouseReleased()`, as appropriate for the event type.

```
protected void mousePressed (MouseEvent event) {
  transmit (event.getX (), event.getY ());
}

// protected void transmit (int x, int y) ...
```

This method is called whenever the user clicks on the `Whiteboard`. We pass the mouse coordinates on to the `transmit()` method, which takes care of packaging up a series of coordinates to be transmitted as a scribble to a remote `Whiteboard`.

```
protected void mouseDragged (MouseEvent event) {
  scribble (event.getX (), event.getY ());
  transmit (event.getX (), event.getY ());
}

// protected void scribble (int x, int y) ...
```

This method is called when the user drags the mouse over the canvas. We call the `scribble()` method to draw the latest segment onto the screen, followed by the `transmit()` method to transmit the coordinates.

```
protected void mouseReleased (MouseEvent event) {
  scribble (event.getX (), event.getY ());
  transmit (event.getX (), event.getY ());
  try {
    messageOut.send ();
  } catch (IOException ignored) {
  }
}
```

This method is called when the user finally releases a mouse button. We draw the last segment to the screen with the `scribble()` method, transmit the last coordinates with our `transmit()` method, and then actually send the message that we have been building by calling `send()`. Thus, the scribble is only actually transmitted when the user releases a mouse button.

```
protected int oldX, oldY;
```

```
protected void transmit (int x, int y) {
  try {
    messageOut.writeInt (oldX = x);
    messageOut.writeInt (oldY = y);
  } catch (IOException ignored) {
  }
}
```

This method writes the coordinates x and y to the message stream messageOut that was provided by the CollabTool, and keeps a copy of these values in oldX and oldY. As the user drags the mouse on the canvas, the mouseDragged() method will be called; this calls the transmit() method, so a list of x and y pairs will build up as the body of a message. The mouseReleased() method calls the send() method to actually transmit the message.

As far as this method is concerned, it is writing to a MessageOutput; it is unaware that this is actually multiplexed over a common carrier with another tool. The multiplexed channels are completely independent, so the communications of one tool will not affect those of any other. In this case, the user could transmit messages using the Chatboard at the same time as scribbling. The Chatboard messages would not interfere with the Whiteboard messages.

```
protected void scribble (int x, int y) {
  Graphics gfx = getGraphics ();
  if (gfx != null) {
    gfx.drawLine (oldX, oldY, x, y);
    gfx.dispose ();
  }
}
```

This method draws the most recent segment to the screen; this is a line between the previously transmitted coordinates oldX and oldY, and the new coordinates x and y. The getGraphics() method returns a graphics context suitable for drawing to the screen. We draw the line and then release the graphics context by calling its dispose() method.

```
public MessageOutput getMessageOutput () {
  return new DeliveryOutputStream (this);
}
```

The CollabTool class calls this method to obtain a message stream suitable for receiving incoming Whiteboard messages. We return a DeliveryOutputStream that immediately delivers every message that we receive to our receive() method.

```
public void receive (DataInputStream dataIn) {
  Graphics gfx = getGraphics ();
```

```
   if (gfx != null) {
      try {
         int oldX = dataIn.readInt (), oldY = dataIn.readInt ();
         while (dataIn.available () > 0) {
            int x = dataIn.readInt (), y = dataIn.readInt ();
            gfx.drawLine (oldX, oldY, x, y);
            oldX = x;
            oldY = y;
         }
      } catch (IOException ignored) {
      }
      gfx.dispose ();
   }
}
```

This method is called whenever a message is delivered for the Whiteboard. We read a sequence of scribble coordinates and draw the segments to the screen.

Note that every message that we receive can be treated as a completely separate stream, so the available() method will return only the number of bytes remaining in the current message.

In the context of this example, the following events will lead up to this method being called: The remote Whiteboard will transmit a sequence of coordinates when the user releases the mouse button. A multiplexing header will be attached to the message, and it will be written into the remote PipedOutputStream. The receiving Demultiplexer will extract a message from its PipedInputStream; it will look up its routing tables and find the appropriate destination stream. In this case, it is a DeliveryOutputStream attached to the Whiteboard. The Demultiplexer will write the message to our DeliveryOutputStream and send() the message. The DeliveryOutputStream will then create a ByteArrayInputStream from the message and pass it directly to our receive() method.

This example collaborative tool is obviously fairly simple. In a more realistic example, each tool would have a whiteboard, a tic-tac-toe game, a text-based chat, and whatever other components would be useful. These could all communicate independently over the same underlying communications channel. Because our demultiplexer supports dynamic registration and deregistration, we can even add and remove components from the tool at run time.

30.7 Wrapping up

With the addition of the multiplexing streams, we have developed a powerful set of tools for peer-to-peer networked applications. This type of application is characterized by applications communicating with other applications of the same type. In the example given, a whiteboard communicates with another whiteboard, and a text tool communicates with another text tool; similarly, a tic-tac-toe game would communicate with another tic-tac-toe game. The most important characteristic of these applications is, however, that there is a direct link between peer applications. In this case, the link between tools is a multiplexed stream; however, this effectively provides a direct link.

In many cases, it is not possible to establish peer-to-peer connections between clients, especially in the context of the Web, where applets can only connect back to the delivering host. In the next chapter, we will develop some streams that allow us to route between clients in a peer-to-peer manner, even though the clients are connected only to a single central server. Our multiplexing streams will be able to operate transparently in conjunction with this, so we can use all of these tools across the World Wide Web.

C H A P T E R   3 1

Routing message streams

Multiplexing and message encapsulation are useful technologies for peer-to-peer inter-application communication. Making the transition from one-to-one communications to one-to-many communications makes them even more useful.

In this chapter, we will look at the message stream technology required to shift from one-to-one communications to server-based one-to-many communications. This consists of routing streams that allow us to specify the recipients of a message and a server-based router that interprets the routing commands to actually route the messages between multiple clients (figure 31.1).

In this manner, we will be able to use the multiplexing and message streams that we have developed thus far and apply them to the common situation of multiple users connecting to a central server. This situation is exemplified by the Web, where multiple clients will connect to a single central server to collaborate with each other.

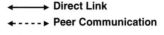
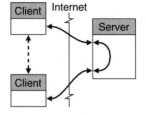

Figure 31.1 Server routing between clients

31.1 Class RoutingOutputStream

The streams that we develop here are similar to the multiplexed streams of the previous chapter. Unlike multiplexed streams, however, the message target is specified when the send() method is called and so is not fixed for a particular stream.

When this stream sends a message, a header is attached that specifies the list of recipients. The receiving end must extract this list and route the message accordingly (figure 31.2).

Figure 31.2 Class RoutingOutputStream

At the point of reception and redistribution, the routing header should be removed and the message should be delivered to each specified recipient. Usually a central server will do this, relaying messages to each recipient's network connection.

This class implements the targeted send() methods of MessageOutput. These allow the recipients of a message to be specified when it is sent. The default send() method is a broadcast; the message should go to all users registered at the receiving end.

```
import java.io.*;

public class RoutingOutputStream extends MessageOutput {
```

```
// public RoutingOutputStream (MessageOutput messageOut) ...
// public void send () throws IOException ...
// public void send (String[] dsts) throws IOException ...
}
```

The `RoutingOutputStream` class is a `MessageOutput` that attaches to an existing `MessageOutput` and overrides the default implementations of the `send()` methods to attach appropriate routing headers before sending messages to the attached stream.

```
protected MessageOutput messageOut;
protected ByteArrayOutputStream byteArrayOut;

public RoutingOutputStream (MessageOutput messageOut) {
  super (new ByteArrayOutputStream ());
  byteArrayOut = (ByteArrayOutputStream) out;
  this.messageOut = messageOut;
}
```

In the constructor, we call the superclass constructor and direct all data into the `ByteArrayOutputStream byteArrayOut`. We keep a reference to the `MessageOutput messageOut`; this is used to actually transmit messages when `send()` is called.

```
public void send () throws IOException {
  synchronized (messageOut) {
    messageOut.writeInt (-1);
    byteArrayOut.writeTo (messageOut);
    messageOut.send ();
  }
  byteArrayOut.reset ();
}
```

This `send()` method performs a broadcast. We attach a header, which consists of the integer −1; this indicates to a corresponding `RoutingInputStream` that the subsequent message should be broadcast. We then send the encapsulated message to the attached stream.

```
public void send (String[] dsts) throws IOException {
  synchronized (messageOut) {
    messageOut.writeInt (dsts.length);
    for (int i = 0; i < dsts.length; ++ i)
      messageOut.writeUTF (dsts[i]);
    byteArrayOut.writeTo (messageOut);
    messageOut.send ();
  }
  byteArrayOut.reset ();
}
```

This `send()` method attaches a header to the message consisting of a list of all the target names. We send a header consisting of an integer indicating the number of recipients, followed by the names of the recipients. We then send the encapsulated message to the attached stream. Note that we call the undirected `send()` method of the attached message stream; the routing has been handled by this class and so does not need to be passed on.

This class is similar to the `MultiplexOutputStream` class, except that multiple targets can be specified and the targeting is explicit in the call to `send()`. We can attach another filtered message stream to this—a `MultiplexOutputStream`, for example—and the targeted `send()` method of the other stream will call this method, so the routing information will be correctly added.

31.2 Class RoutingInputStream

This class is the corresponding routing message decapsulator. It attaches to an existing `MessageInputStream` and extracts the routing header from every message that is received. This routing information is made available to the caller to assist in routing the message correctly (figure 31.3).

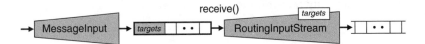

Figure 31.3 Class RoutingInputStream

Like the `MultiplexInputStream`, this class does not perform any actual routing itself. Another class must perform this function. We will develop a `Router` to do this, much like the `Demultiplexer` of the last chapter.

Effectively, this class receives messages from a `MessageInput`, takes the recipient list from each message, and presents both the message and the list to the caller.

```
import java.io.*;

public class RoutingInputStream extends MessageInput {
   // public RoutingInputStream (MessageInput messageIn) ...
   // public void receive () throws IOException ...
   // public String[] getTargets () ...
}
```

This class is a `MessageInput` that attaches to another `MessageInput`. The routing information for each message that is received is made available through the `getTargets()` method.

```
   protected MessageInput messageIn;

   public RoutingInputStream (MessageInput messageIn) {
      super (messageIn);
```

```
    this.messageIn = messageIn;
  }
```

The constructor attaches to an existing `MessageInput messageIn`. All `read()` method calls will thus be passed directly on to `messageIn`.

```
protected String[] targets;

public void receive () throws IOException {
  messageIn.receive ();
  int n = messageIn.readInt ();
  if (n < 0) {
    targets = null;
  } else {
    targets = new String[n];
    for (int j = 0; j < n; ++ j)
      targets[j] = messageIn.readUTF ();
  }
}
```

When this method is called, we first call the `receive()` method of the attached stream. When this call returns, a message has been received from the underlying communications channel. We then strip off the routing header from the message. If the number of recipients is less than zero, this is a broadcast, and so we set the `targets` variable to `null`. Otherwise, we create an array to hold the recipient list and read the names from the attached stream.

```
public String[] getTargets () {
  return targets;
}
```

This method returns the target list of the most recently received message, or `null` if no target list was specified.

With a `RoutingOutputStream` and a `RoutingInputStream` attached over a communications channel, we have the facility to pass routing information with every message that we send. This can be used to easily implement server-based multiuser applications such as a collaborative environment or Web-based chat program.

The setup required to implement such a system is simply to attach a `RoutingOutputStream` to the client's outbound channel and a `RoutingInputStream` to the server's inbound channel. The server will process the routing information to forward incoming messages to the correct targets.

31.3 Class Router

This class is a message copier that receives messages from a `RoutingInputStream` and resends them to the specified message recipients, using an internal routing table.

To perform the server routing, we must assign names to each client and register message output streams for each such client name. The choice of names is an application-level issue that is not addressed here; we simply provide a means to register and deregister client names. Typically, clients will choose or be assigned a name when they log on to the system.

This class receives messages, examines the attached recipient list, and delivers a copy of the message to each named person (figure 31.4). If the recipient list specifies a broadcast, a copy is delivered to each registered client.

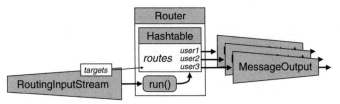

Figure 31.4   Class Router

```
import java.io.*;
import java.util.*;

public class Router extends Thread {
   // public Router (MessageInput messageIn) ...
   // public void register (String target, MessageOutput messageOut) ...
   // public void deregister (String target) ...
   // public void finish () ...
   // public void run () ...
}
```

This class is a `Thread`, just like the `Demultiplexer` class. Messages are read from a `RoutingInputStream` and routed according to an internal routing `Hashtable`. Targets can be registered and deregistered with the `register()` and `deregister()` methods. The `finish()` method allows this router to be closed down.

```
   protected RoutingInputStream routingIn;
   protected Hashtable routes;

   static private int routerNumber;
   static private synchronized int nextRouterNum () { return routerNumber ++; }

   public Router (MessageInput messageIn) {
      super ("Router-" + nextRouterNum ());
      routingIn = new RoutingInputStream (messageIn);
      routes = new Hashtable ();
   }
```

The `nextRouterNum()` method and `routerNumber` variable are used to assign unique names to `Router` threads. The constructor calls the superclass constructor with an appropriate name; we then create a routing table `routes` and a routing input stream `routingIn`.

```
public void register (String target, MessageOutput messageOut) {
   routes.put (target, messageOut);
}
```

This method inserts an entry in the routing table for the destination `target`. All messages targeted to this address will be sent to the `MessageOutput messageOut`.

```
public void deregister (String target) {
   routes.remove (target);
}
```

To deregister a target, we simply remove the entry from the routing table.

```
protected boolean finished;

public void finish () {
   finished = true;
   interrupt ();
}
```

This method should be called to stop this router; it asserts the `finished` flag and then interrupts the thread. Additionally, as before, if this router may be blocked on reading from a stream, that stream should be closed.

```
public void run () {
   try {
     while (!interrupted ()) {
       routingIn.receive ();
       byte[] buffer = new byte[routingIn.available ()];
       routingIn.readFully (buffer);
       String[] targets = routingIn.getTargets ();
       if (targets == null)
         broadcast (buffer);
       else
         multicast (buffer, targets);
     }
   } catch (IOException ex) {
     if (!finished)
       ex.printStackTrace ();
   }
}

// protected void broadcast (byte[] buffer) throws IOException ...
// protected void multicast (byte[] buffer, String[] targets)
     throws IOException ...
```

When the `Router` is started, the `run()` method is called. We loop, receiving messages and routing them appropriately. If the message is to be broadcast, the recipient list will be `null`, and so we call the `broadcast()` method. Otherwise, we call the `multi-`

cast() method with the recipient list. If an exception occurs, we exit the loop and display the exception.

```
protected void broadcast (byte[] buffer) {
   Enumeration dsts = ((Hashtable) routes.clone ()).elements ();
   while (dsts.hasMoreElements ()) {
     MessageOutput messageOut = (MessageOutput) dsts.nextElement ();
     try {
       synchronized (messageOut) {
         messageOut.write (buffer);
         messageOut.send ();
       }
     } catch (IOException ignored) {
     }
   }
}
```

The broadcast() method loops through routes, transmitting the message in buffer to each registered MessageOutput. We clone the routing table to protect against changes while we are iterating through it. We then get the Enumeration dsts that corresponds to all values in the Hashtable. While there are more values in dsts, we extract the next MessageOutput and send a copy of the message. We could omit the cloning if we synchronized this whole method on routes; however, that might tie up the routing table for an excessive amount of time.

```
protected void multicast (byte[] buffer, String[] targets) {
   for (int j = 0; j < targets.length; ++ j) {
     MessageOutput messageOut = (MessageOutput) routes.get (targets[j]);
     if (messageOut != null) {
       try {
         synchronized (messageOut) {
           messageOut.write (buffer);
           messageOut.send ();
         }
       } catch (IOException ignored) {
       }
     }
   }
}
```

The multicast() method is somewhat simpler. For each recipient in the list, we determine the registered MessageOutput and send a copy of the message.

This Router gives us the facility to easily route targeted messages at a server. This routing mechanism builds on top of the existing message streams and permits the development of fairly complex applications with comparative ease.

This Router routes messages only from a single input stream. A server that makes use of this class must either attach one Router to every client connection or multiplex all client messages into a single `MessageInput` attached to a single `Router`. In either case, there must be an active reading thread for every client connection.

31.4 Wrapping up

These routing streams allow us to implement complex client/server systems that make use of all of the message stream classes that we have looked at so far.

Implementing an application that consists of distinct components communicating in a peer-to-peer fashion is easier than implementing a monolithic application that has all function operating over a single communications channel. A given component of the peer-to-peer system needs only understand how to communicate with another instance of itself; this simplifies protocols and shields different components from failures within each other.

The most common problem with peer-to-peer applications is that it is frequently not possible for applications to directly peer. In some cases, such as the Web, it is not possible for clients to directly connect. Even where this is possible, there is a problem with the massive number of peer connections required. A small system with 10 clients would require 45 connections for every client to have a direct connection to every other client.

The routing streams which we have just developed allow us to write applications that operate in a peer-to-peer fashion, despite the fact that they are operating in a client/server environment. This is a powerful facility, which we shall use in the following chapters to develop a generic client and server system for easy development of collaborative applications.

C H A P T E R   3 2

A generic message server

In chapter 18, we developed a basic chat system with a multithreaded server, using classes available in the API. The application had limitations, however, which could be removed by using message streams. In particular, the server required knowledge of the format of client messages; in the example, they were simply UTF-format strings.

In this chapter, we build a generic server that uses these message stream classes. The message streams abstract specific message formats into a generic message, which has the significant consequence that one server can serve arbitrary clients; the server needs no knowledge of particular client message formats and can rely simply on the message streams encapsulation. We make use of queuing streams to buffer data to clients and routing streams to accomplish routing between clients.

The result is a much more sophisticated server. In the next chapter, we will develop the generic client to use with this server. Together, these classes can effectively form the networking layer for many different applications.

32.1 Class GenericServer

The server follows the same model of multithreading that the simple chat server used earlier. There are two classes: the main server is GenericServer, which accepts connections from clients and creates a handler for each one. It also keeps a list of all currently connected clients (figure 32.1). The handler, GenericHandler, does all the work of processing client communications.

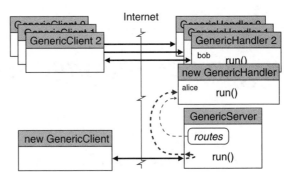

Figure 32.1   The GenericServer framework

```
import java.io.*;
import java.net.*;
import java.util.Hashtable;

public class GenericServer extends Thread {
    // public GenericServer (int port) throws IOException...
    // public void run () ...
    // public static void main (String args[]) throws IOException ...
}
```

The GenericServer class is a Thread that is responsible for accepting new connections from clients. The port that it listens on is specified in the constructor. A Server-

`Socket` begins listening on this port, and when the thread is started, the `run()` method takes care of accepting new connections.

```
protected ServerSocket server;
protected Hashtable routes;

public GenericServer (int port) throws IOException {
   super ("GenericServer");
   server = new ServerSocket (port);
   routes = new Hashtable ();
}
```

In the constructor we call the superclass constructor with an appropriate name for the thread, create a `ServerSocket` `server` that listens on the specified port `port`, and then create the `Hashtable` `routes`. This `Hashtable` is used by client handlers to maintain a registry of the users currently connected to the server.

```
public void run () {
   try {
      while (!Thread.interrupted ()) {
         Socket socket = server.accept ();
         GenericHandler handler = new GenericHandler
            (routes, socket.getInputStream (), socket.getOutputStream ());
         handler.start ();
      }
   } catch (IOException ex) {
      ex.printStackTrace ();
   }
}
```

We follow the same basic multithreaded model as in the earlier chat server; the main server sits in a loop accepting connections and creating a handler for each client. These handlers execute in separate threads and handle all client communications.

```
public static void main (String args[]) throws IOException {
   if (args.length != 1)
      throw new IllegalArgumentException ("Syntax: GenericServer <port>");
   GenericServer server = new GenericServer (Integer.parseInt (args[0]));
   server.start ();
}
```

The `main()` method takes a port number as a command line argument. It creates a server that will accept client connections to this port and starts the server thread.

We provide no graceful mechanism to shut the server down other than by exiting the JVM. To implement this, we would have to provide a `finish()` method that closed the `ServerSocket` and called `interrupt()` to stop the server thread. We would then have to loop through and shut down each handler registered in `routes`. The handler class would similarly need to both close its network connection and interrupt its thread. Stopping a client is more common than stopping a server, so we address this issue properly in the next chapter.

32.2 Class GenericMessageCopier

The `MessageCopier` class, which was developed in the message streams chapter, is used when we want to relay messages from a `MessageInput` to a `MessageOutput`. Typically, it relays messages from a `Queue` to a network connection, thereby shielding clients from interacting with the actual network.

The GenericMessage-Copier class is an extension to the `MessageCopier` class that has a small amount of error-recovery capability built in. The constructor accepts a reference to another thread in addition to the raw message streams. If an exception is encountered while relaying messages to the client, the other thread is interrupted (figure 32.2).

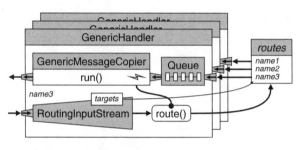

Figure 32.2   Class GenericMessageCopier

In the case of the `GenericHandler` class, this will cause a client's routing method to terminate, and so all appropriate cleanup and deregistration will occur. This allows us to handle network problems in a clean and simple manner.

```
import java.io.*;

public class GenericMessageCopier extends MessageCopier {
  // public GenericMessageCopier
      (Thread sibling, MessageInput messageIn, MessageOutput messageOut) ...
  // public void run () ...
}
```

We extend the `MessageCopier` class and provide a constructor that accepts a `Thread` parameter `sibling` to be interrupted should an exception be encountered. The `run()` method will relay messages from the `MessageInput` messageIn to the `MessgeOutput` messageOut.

```
  protected Thread sibling;

  public GenericMessageCopier (Thread sibling, MessageInput messageIn,
      MessageOutput messageOut) {
    super (messageIn, messageOut);
    this.sibling = sibling;
```

```
    }
```

The constructor takes three parameters: a `Thread sibling`, to be interrupted in the case of an exception, and the two message streams, `messageIn` and `messageOut`, that we pass to the superconstructor.

```
public void run () {
    try {
        copy ();
    } catch (IOException ex) {
        if (!finished) {
            ex.printStackTrace ();
            sibling.interrupt ();
        }
    }
}
```

In the `run()` method, we simply call the `copy()` method that is inherited from the superclass. The `copy()` method loops, reading messages from `messageIn` and writing them to `messageOut`. In the case of an `IOException`, we print the exception's stack trace and interrupt the `Thread sibling`.

32.3 Class GenericHandler

The `GenericHandler` class is responsible for handling client connections. When a client connects to the server, a `GenericHandler` is created to process the client (figure 32.3). The client initially transmits its username and then proceeds to communicate using the standard message stream methods.

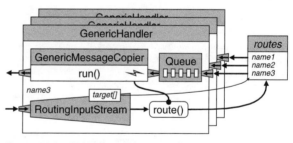

Figure 32.3 Class GenericHandler

The client's handler verifies that the username is not currently in use, and then proceeds to relay messages from the client to the other connected users.

We keep the communications generalized by using the message streams, so the handlers need not have knowledge of exactly what comprises the messages that they are passing.

```
import java.io.*;
import java.util.*;

public class GenericHandler extends Thread {
    // public GenericHandler
```

```
        (Hashtable routes, InputStream in, OutputStream out) ...
    // public void run () ...
}
```

The `GenericHandler` class extends `Thread` so that client messages can be processed in a separate thread to the main server. The constructor accepts the streams over which to communicate and the `Hashtable routes` that will be used to maintain a registry of the currently-connected users.

Efficient use of threads is extremely important in a server environment. With this implementation of the handler, we create a `Thread` every time a new connection arrives. In a production environment, it would be vital to instead make use of a reusable pool of `Threads`: whenever a handler finishes, it would return its `Thread` to the pool for reuse by a future connection. In chapter 5, we implemented a class `ReThread` that implements just such a reusable pool. To use this server in a live environment, it should be modified to make use of that or a similar mechanism.

```
    protected Hashtable routes;
    protected InputStream in;
    protected OutputStream out;

    static private int handlerNumber;
    static private synchronized int nextHandlerNum ()
       { return handlerNumber ++; }

    public GenericHandler
          (Hashtable routes, InputStream in, OutputStream out) {
       super ("GenericHandler-" + nextHandlerNum ());
       this.routes = routes;
       this.in = in;
       this.out = out;
    }
```

The constructor takes three parameters: The first is a reference to the server's routing table `routes`. The other two are the streams `in` and `out` attached to the client socket; these are created by the server when the client is accepted.

```
    protected String name;

    public void run () {
       try {
          DataInputStream dataIn = new DataInputStream (in);
          name = dataIn.readUTF ();
          accept (name);
       } catch (IOException ex) {
          ex.printStackTrace ();
       } finally {
          try {
             out.close ();
```

```
    } catch (IOException ex) {
      ex.printStackTrace ();
    }
  }
}

// protected void accept (String name) throws IOException ...
```

The `run()` method is called when the handler thread is started. It is responsible for accepting a client connection, verifying the name, and relaying client messages.

We first read the client's name `name` from the `InputStream`; note that this occurs before the message streams are set up and so is performed with the usual `DataInput-Stream` class. After reading the name, we call the `accept()` method that accepts the connection and processes client messages.

We surround the body of this code with a `try ... catch ... finally` clause that displays any `IOExceptions` that occur, and ensures that the socket connection is closed when this thread terminates.

```
protected MessageOutput myself;

protected void accept (String name) throws IOException {
  Queue queue = new Queue ();
  boolean registered = false;
  synchronized (routes) {
    if (!routes.containsKey (name)) {
      registered = true;
      routes.put (name, myself = new QueueOutputStream (queue));
    }
  }
  try {
    new DataOutputStream (out).writeBoolean (registered);
    out.flush ();
    if (registered) {
      execute (queue);
    }
  } finally {
    if (registered)
      routes.remove (name);
  }
}

// protected void execute (Queue queue) throws IOException ...
```

This method is responsible for verifying that the client's name is not in use and routing client messages.

We first create a `Queue queue` that will hold messages that are to be delivered to the client. Other clients will write messages into this queue, and a separate thread will be responsible for actually delivering these messages to the client.

We synchronize on the routes Hashtable and check to see whether the username is currently in use. If the name is not in use, we set the registered flag to true and insert the client into the Hashtable. Actually, we are inserting into the Hashtable a QueueOutputStream that places messages into the client's Queue queue, pending actual delivery. We keep a reference to this in the variable myself; later we will use this to ensure that the client does not send messages back to itself.

We next write a boolean value to the client, indicating whether registration was successful (whether the name was accepted). Again, we use a plain DataOutputStream for this operation. If registration was successful, we call the execute() method to relay client messages; otherwise, we just exit the method. We use a try ... finally clause to ensure that the client is deregistered when the execute() method terminates, regardless of how this occurs. This ensures that no other handlers will try to send us messages after we leave, and that we do not leave a stale client name in routes.

In the earlier chapter on queues, we saw that one reason to use a queue is that it insulates the sender from the actual output stream. In this case, when one client is sending a message to another, it won't have to deal with problems with the second client's network connection. Each client is responsible for forwarding its own messages from the queue to the output stream, so if there is a problem with a network connection, only that client is affected.

```
protected void execute (Queue queue) throws IOException {
  MessageInput queueIn = new QueueInputStream (queue);
  MessageOutput messageOut = new MessageOutputStream (out);
  GenericMessageCopier copier =
    new GenericMessageCopier (this, queueIn, messageOut);
  try {
    copier.start ();
    route ();
  } finally {
    copier.finish ();
  }
}

// protected void route () throws IOException ...
```

The execute() method is run after the client has been successfully registered with the server. It is responsible for processing messages from, and relaying messages to, the client.

We create a QueueInputStream queueIn that reads from the client's outbound Queue queue, and a MessageOutputStream messageOut that writes to the client's network connection. We then start a GenericMessageCopier copier that relays messages from the Queue to the client. Thus, this GenericMessageCopier copier will transmit the messages that are inserted by other clients of the server. We start the `GenericMes-sageCopier` and call the `route()` method to process messages from the client.

Again, we use a `finally` clause to perform cleanup when the `route()` method terminates; in this case, this requires stopping the `GenericMessageCopier` thread. Note that we have several nested layers of `try ... finally` clauses leading up to this point. The `run()` method ensures that we close the network connection when client processing finishes. The `accept()` method ensures that we deregister the client if appropriate, and this method ensures that we stop the `GenericMessageCopier`.

```
protected void route () throws IOException {
   MessageInputStream messageIn = new MessageInputStream (in);
   RoutingInputStream routingIn = new RoutingInputStream (messageIn);
   while (!Thread.interrupted ()) {
      routingIn.receive ();
      byte[] buffer = new byte[routingIn.available ()];
      routingIn.readFully (buffer);
      String[] targets = routingIn.getTargets ();
      if (targets == null)
         broadcast (buffer);
      else
         multicast (buffer, targets);
   }
}

// protected void broadcast (byte[] buffer) throws IOException ...
// protected void multicast (byte[] buffer, String[] targets)
      throws IOException ...
```

The `route()` method is responsible for processing messages from the client. This consists of determining whether a message is to be broadcast to all clients or multicast to a selected list. We create a `MessageInputStream messageIn` attached to the client's `InputStream in`. We then attach to this a `RoutingInputStream routingIn`, to strip the routing list from incoming messages. We then sit in a loop waiting for messages to arrive.

We accept messages with a call to the `receive()` method of `routingIn`. We then check to see if there is a target list associated with the routing stream. If there is no list, we call the `broadcast()` method to pass the message along to all the clients. Otherwise, there is a list of targets, and we call the `multicast()` method to pass the message to just those named clients.

```
protected void broadcast (byte[] buffer) throws IOException {
   Enumeration dsts = ((Hashtable) routes.clone ()).elements ();
   while (dsts.hasMoreElements ()) {
      MessageOutput messageOut = (MessageOutput) dsts.nextElement ();
      send (buffer, messageOut);
   }
```

```
    }

// protected void send (byte[] buffer, MessageOutput messageOut)
     throws IOException ...
```

The broadcast() method is responsible for sending messages to all clients in the routes Hashtable.

We get an Enumeration dsts of the members of the Hashtable. We extract each client's MessageOutput from this Enumeration and send the message using our send() method.

Remember that when a client registers with the routes Hashtable, we map its name to a QueueOutputStream. This output stream is therefore available to receive messages from all clients. When we write a message into a client's Queue, it will eventually be picked up by the client's GenericMessageCopier, which will actually deliver the message to the network.

```
protected void multicast (byte[] buffer, String[] targets)
     throws IOException {
  for (int j = 0; j < targets.length; ++ j) {
    MessageOutput messageOut = (MessageOutput) routes.get (targets[j]);
    if (messageOut != null)
       send (buffer, messageOut);
  }
}
```

The multicast() method is called when the routing output stream contains a list of targets. This method sends the message to every client named in the array targets.

```
protected void send (byte[] buffer, MessageOutput messageOut)
     throws IOException {
  if (messageOut != myself) {
    synchronized (messageOut) {
      messageOut.write (buffer);
      messageOut.send ();
    }
  }
}
```

The send() method writes the message in the buffer buffer to the specified MessageOutput messageOut. We ensure that messageOut is not myself; this protects against sending any client's messages back to itself. In some server situations we might actually want to send messages back to the sender; in such a case, we could simply omit this check. To send a message, we write and send buffer.

32.4 Wrapping up

Alone, this server does not serve much purpose. It demonstrates the use of the message stream classes and some robust error-handling; however, above and beyond this it is nothing more than a router. The purpose of this server is, however, just that: it is a generic framework for a collaboration server that can serve arbitrary clients who communicate using message streams.

In the next chapter, we will look at a `GenericClient` class that complements this server. It provides a framework for client applications that can connect to a central `GenericServer` and then communicate with each other using the message stream classes. The goal of the `GenericServer` and `GenericClient` classes is to remove all need to handle low-level networking issues from applications development. Instead, development can focus on application-level protocols and important issues of function rather than implementation.

As it stands, the `GenericServer` class can serve arbitrary client applications without a need for modification. At the end of the next chapter, however, some extensions are proposed to provide additional function.

CHAPTER 33

Building a generic client

In the previous chapter, we developed a server that performs message routing between named clients. Because the message stream classes encapsulate data inside a generic message, the server can route data in a manner that is independent of the actual clients. Thus we can use the unmodified GenericServer class as a router for many different client applications.

In this chapter, we will develop the corresponding GenericClient class that provides a foundation for a wide variety of different client applications. The GenericClient class performs the initial network connection and stream setup. User-created clients must implement a Client interface; they can then register with the GenericClient class and communicate with other users through a central server.

Registering a tool with the GenericClient establishes outbound and incoming message streams that are automatically multiplexed across the connection to the server. Using these streams, tools can communicate through the server in a peer-to-peer fashion, independently of any other tools that also may be communicating through the server.

An example of the use of these classes is provided at the end of the chapter in the form of a networked chat program. The chat provides both text-based chat facility and a crude whiteboard, but the features can be easily upgraded by simply registering new components to the GenericClient framework.

33.1 Class GenericClient

This class performs the network and stream setup for any client that wishes to communicate through a GenericServer (figure 33.1). Upon creation, it opens a socket connection to the specified server and attempts to register a requested username. If the connection attempt is successful, client tools can be registered and will obtain streams for communication. If unsuccessful, an exception will be thrown. Other than the usual exceptions that can occur during a network setup (Connection refused, etc.), a Name in use IOException will be thrown if the server refuses the requested name.

Incoming messages are delivered through a Client interface, and a Queue is used to buffer all outbound communications. If a communications exception occurs, only the part of the GenericClient that is transferring messages from the Queue to the network connection will be affected, and so the GenericClient can shut down gracefully. As a result, client tools can essentially ignore all IOExceptions that may occur when writing out data. If a connection breaks, all clients will be notified through the Client interface and can terminate normally.

This class is similar to the Demultiplexer class that we looked at earlier. The difference is that it will itself perform the network connection setup, instead of registering message streams to accept the demultiplexed messages you must register Clients. Thus,

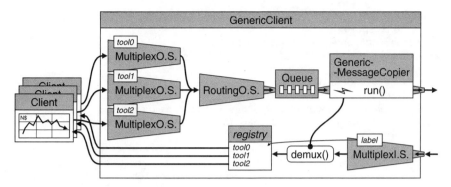

Figure 33.1   Class GenericClient

the `GenericClient` can provide more function for the clients, including the assignment of message output streams and notification of broken connections.

```
import java.io.*;
import java.net.*;
import java.util.*;

public class GenericClient extends Thread {
   // public GenericClient (String host, int port, String name)
        throws IOException ...
   // public void run () ...
   // public void shutdown () throws IOException ...
   // public void register (String label, Client client) ...
   // public void deregister (String label) ...
}
```

We extend the `Thread` class; this allows us to perform the stream demultiplexing in a separate thread to the caller. The server address and client username are specified in the constructor. When this `Thread` is started, the `run()` method will be called and will proceed to demultiplex incoming messages. In a client-side situation such as this, it is not as important to implement a reusable pool of `Threads` unless there are likely to be many tools being continually registered and deregistered.

Client tools can be registered and deregistered with the `register()` and `deregister()` methods. A `String` identifier must be provided for the multiplexing streams; each tool should be assigned an appropriate name. This will allow messages to be transparently routed to the peer tools of other clients connected to the server.

```
   protected Queue queue;
   protected Hashtable registry;
   protected MessageOutput messageOut;

   static private int clientNumber;
   static private synchronized int nextClientNum () { return clientNumber ++; }
```

```
    public GenericClient (String host, int port, String name)
        throws IOException {
      super ("GenericClient-" + nextClientNum ());
      connect (host, port);
      logon (name);
      registry = new Hashtable ();
      queue = new Queue ();
      QueueOutputStream queueOut = new QueueOutputStream (queue);
      messageOut = new RoutingOutputStream (queueOut);
    }

    // protected void connect (String host, int port) throws IOException ...
    // protected void logon (String name) throws IOException ...
```

Creating a `GenericClient` performs all of the network connection and streams setup to prepare for clients to register (figure 33.2). We first call the superclass constructor with an appropriate thread name; this is not usually necessary, but it is sometimes useful for debugging. We then connect to the specified host using the `connect()` method; this may throw an `IOException` if the server cannot be reached. We then attempt to register our username using the `logon()` method; this may throw an `IOException` if either the network connection fails or the username is already in use.

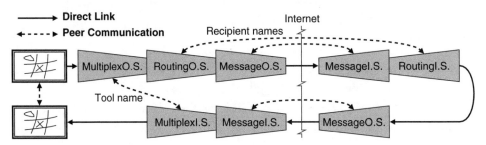

Figure 33.2   Streams within the GenericClient/Server framework

At this point if an exception has not been thrown, we have successfully connected to the server. We create a `Hashtable registry`, which will map from the multiplex labels to registered client tools. We create a `Queue queue` to hold outgoing messages and a `RoutingOutputStream messageOut` that writes routed messages into `queue`.

Every client that registers to the server will receive a stream that multiplexes down `messageOut`, so their messages will enter `queue` for subsequent delivery. Because `messageOut` is a `RoutingOutputStream`, the clients will be able to use the targeted `send()` methods to route messages to specific users.

```
    protected InputStream in;
    protected OutputStream out;

    protected void connect (String host, int port) throws IOException {
```

```
        Socket socket = new Socket (host, port);
        in = socket.getInputStream ();
        out = socket.getOutputStream ();
    }
```

This method attempts to open a connection to the server residing on the specified port `port` of the specified host `host`. If a problem arises, an exception will be thrown; otherwise, we extract an `InputStream` in and an `OutputStream` out over which to communicate.

```
protected void logon (String name) throws IOException {
    try {
        DataOutputStream dataOut = new DataOutputStream (out);
        dataOut.writeUTF (name);
        dataOut.flush ();
        DataInputStream dataIn = new DataInputStream (in);
        boolean registered = dataIn.readBoolean ();
        if (!registered)
            throw new IOException ("Name in use");
    } catch (IOException ex) {
        try {
            out.close ();
        } catch (IOException ignored) {
        }
        throw ex;
    }
}
```

This method attempts to log on to the server using the specified name `name`. We write the name to the server with a `DataOutputStream` and await a response with a `DataInputStream`. The server responds with a `boolean` value. If `false` is returned, the requested name is already in use, and the appropriate exception is thrown.

We surround the body of this method with a `try ... catch` clause to ensure that we close the server connection if there is a problem. If an `IOException` arises, we close the server connection (ignoring any exception that this may cause) and rethrow the original exception. Thus, we will close the server connection if there is a problem writing to or reading from the server, or if the name is already in use.

```
protected boolean finished;

public void shutdown () throws IOException {
    finished = true;
    interrupt ();
    out.close ();
}
```

To manually close down the client framework, we provide a `shutdown()` method that calls `interrupt()` to stop this reading thread and then calls `close()` to close down the network connection. Doing so will abort the reader thread (if it is blocked reading from the network connection) and allow it to close down gracefully.

```
public void run () {
   QueueInputStream queueIn = new QueueInputStream (queue);
   MessageOutputStream messageOut = new MessageOutputStream (out);
   GenericMessageCopier copier =
      new GenericMessageCopier (this, queueIn, messageOut);
   try {
      copier.start ();
      demux ();
   } catch (IOException ex) {
      if (!finished)
         ex.printStackTrace ();
   } finally {
      copier.finish ();
      closedown ();
   }
}

// protected void demux () throws IOException ...
// protected void closedown () ...
```

A new thread enters here when the start() method is called. This thread is responsible for demultiplexing the messages that arrive from the server. We set up a thread that relays messages from the message queue queue out through the network connection to the server.

We attach a QueueInputStream queueIn to queue to allow us to read messages from the internal queue. We then attach a MessageOutputStream messageOut to out to allow us to write messages to the server. We then create a GenericMessageCopier that reads messages from queueIn and writes them to messageOut. Thus, the GenericMessageCopier will take all client messages and actually send them to the server.

The main body of this method starts the GenericMessageCopier copier and subsequently proceeds to demultiplex messages that arrive from the server.

We surround this body with a try ... catch ... finally clause that lets us clean up if a problem is encountered. If an IOException is encountered in this thread (the demultiplexer), we display the exception, and the finally clause will be executed to shut down. If an IOException is encountered in the GenericMessageCopier thread, it will interrupt this thread, which will also cause the finally clause to be executed. Remember that the GenericMessageCopier class takes a reference to another thread that it should interrupt if it encounters a problem.

Thus, we are guaranteed that if a problem is encountered with the network connection, our finally clause will be executed. We first stop the GenericMessageCopier thread and then call the closedown() method to close the client down.

```
protected void demux () throws IOException {
    MessageInputStream messageIn = new MessageInputStream (in);
    MultiplexInputStream multiplexIn = new MultiplexInputStream (messageIn);
    while (!Thread.interrupted ()) {
        multiplexIn.receive ();
        Client client = (Client) registry.get (multiplexIn.getLabel ());
        if (client != null) {
            try {
                client.receive (new DataInputStream (multiplexIn));
            } catch (RuntimeException ex) {
                ex.printStackTrace ();
            }
        }
    }
}
```

This method performs the demultiplexing of incoming messages. We attach a `MessageInputStream messageIn` to `in` to allow us to read messages that are relayed to us by the server. We attach a `MultiplexInputStream multiplexIn` to `messageIn` to strip the multiplexing headers that were attached by another `GenericClient`. Note that routing headers from the `RoutingOutputStream` will have been stripped by the server, and so we will receive messages with just the multiplexing header attached.

The body of this method consists of receiving messages from `multiplexIn` and determining the appropriate target by looking up the multiplexing label in `registry`. If a client tool has been registered for the message target, we pass the

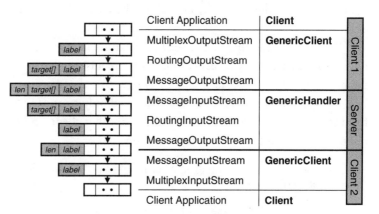

Figure 33.3   Stages of encapsulation between Client tools

message on to its `receive()` method for appropriate processing (figure 33.3). If the client expects to process messages quickly, it can do so in this method; otherwise, it would be appropriate for it to place messages in a queue for processing in a separate thread.

Note that we wrap the `MessageInputStream multiplexIn` in a `DataInput-Stream` when we pass it to the client. This may seem redundant because, after all, the `MessageInputStream` class is itself a subclass of `DataInputStream`. By wrapping it like this, however, we prevent clients from casting the stream to a `MessageInput` and calling inappropriate methods thereof. Instead, we restrict clients to using only the usual methods of `DataInputStream`.

We also catch any `RuntimeExceptions` that are thrown by the `receive()` method; this protects the `demux()` method from unexpected client exceptions that may occur at run time. We simply display any such exceptions and continue processing.

```
protected void closedown () {
  try {
    out.close ();
  } catch (IOException ex) {
    ex.printStackTrace ();
  }
  synchronized (registry) {
    Enumeration clients = registry.keys ();
    while (clients.hasMoreElements ()) {
      deregister ((String) clients.nextElement ());
    }
  }
}
```

This method is called by the `finally` clause of the `run()` method to close the client framework down. We first close the network connection by closing the raw `Output-Stream out`. We then loop through all of the currently registered clients, deregistering each.

Remember that this `GenericClient` and the `GenericMessageCopier` are the only classes that directly access the network streams, so client tools do not need to handle network failures. Instead, they can assume that they have a completely reliable message transport layer. This means that they need only consider `IOExceptions` that result from messages that were incorrectly built by another client, and can rely on the `disconnected()` method to indicate disconnection.

```
public void register (String label, Client client) {
  synchronized (registry) {
    deregister (label);
    registry.put (label, client);
    client.setMessageOutput
      (new MultiplexOutputStream (messageOut, label));
  }
}
```

This method registers the `Client client` with the specified multiplexing label `label`. We synchronize on `registry` to ensure that no other client can register simultaneously. We next call the `deregister()` method to disconnect any client that is already registered with the multiplexing label `label`. If there is no such client, this will have no effect.

Finally, we can register the new client tool in `registry` and assign it a new message stream over which to communicate. We assign it a `MultiplexOutputStream` attached to `messageOut`. Remember that `messageOut` is a `RoutingOutputStream` attached to our message queue. Thus, clients can make use of the targeted `send()` methods. Every message that they send will be multiplexed with the tool name, routed as specified by the `send()` method, placed in the queue, and delivered to the network by the `GenericMessageCopier`.

```
public void deregister (String label) {
    synchronized (registry) {
        Client client = (Client) registry.remove (label);
        if (client != null)
            client.disconnected ();
    }
}
```

This method deregisters any client with the specified multiplexing label `label`. We synchronize on `registry` to ensure threadsafety. We determine if there is a client with the specified label; if so, we call its `disconnected()` method, informing it that it has been disconnected, and remove it from the `Hashtable`.

33.2 Interface Client

This interface must be implemented by any client tools that wish to attach to the `GenericClient`. The interface specifies a method for the `GenericClient` to set the message stream over which the client tool should communicate, a method for the `GenericClient` to supply messages to the client, and a

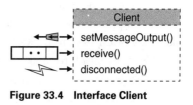

Figure 33.4   Interface Client

method by which the `GenericClient` can inform the client that it has been disconnected (figure 33.4).

```
import java.io.*;

public interface Client {
    public void setMessageOutput (MessageOutput messageOut);
    public void receive (DataInputStream dataIn);
    public void disconnected ();
}
```

The `setMessageOutput()` method assigns the client a message stream over which it can subsequently communicate with its peers on the server. This stream supports the targeted `send()` methods so the client can direct messages to specific users.

The `receive()` method will be called with every message that arrives for the client. The contents of the message can be read from the `DataInputStream dataIn`. The stream will contain data only from a single message; subsequent messages will be delivered through subsequent calls to `receive()`.

The `disconnected()` method will be called when the client has been disconnected. As we have already seen, this can result from several possible causes: the network may have failed, the `GenericClient` may have been stopped, the client may have been deregistered, or another client may have been registered in its place. In all cases, the disconnected client should cease communicating over the message stream that it was formerly assigned.

33.3 Building an advanced chat system

This class builds on the example that we used to demonstrate the multiplexed streams in chapter 30. We adapt the `Chatboard` and `Whiteboard` classes to implement the `Client` interface. The major difference from the earlier classes is the addition of a `disconnected()` method.

The main chat application class is simpler than in the demultiplexing example because all the stream setup is performed by the `GenericClient` class. In fact, all we need do is start the `GenericClient`, create the components, and register them. All the rest is taken care of for us automatically.

We don't need to make any changes to the `GenericServer` to support this client. We can just start the server and connect as many client tools as we desire.

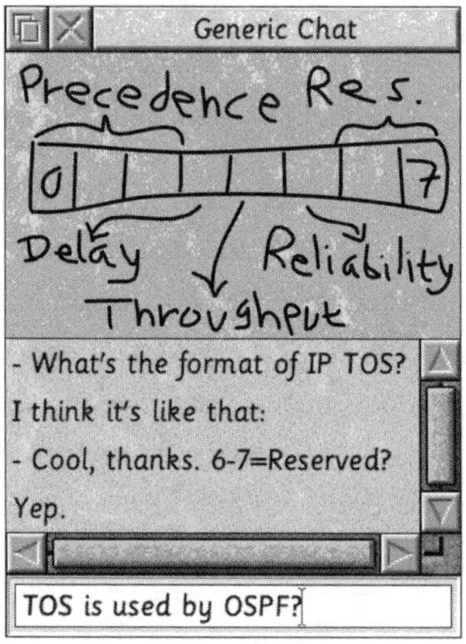

33.3.1 Class GenericChat

This is the main chat application (figure 33.5). It requires a server name and port and a username to be specified on the command line. It connects to the specified server, registers with the desired name, and

**Figure 33.5   The GenericChat
user interface**

opens a `Frame` with a chatboard region and whiteboard. All the users connected to the server can then communicate through these tools (figure 33.6).

It is important to realize that the client/server framework does not know any details about the components. We could subsequently add games and new tools, and the framework would remain unchanged.

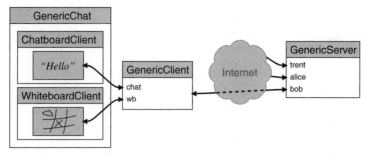

Figure 33.6 Class GenericChat

```
import java.io.*;
import java.awt.*;
import java.awt.event.*;

public class GenericChat {
  // public GenericChat
       (String host, int port, String name) ...
  // public void start ()
       throws IOException ...
  // public void stop ()
       throws IOException ...
  // public static void main
       (String[] args) throws IOException ...
}
```

The constructor simply creates a `Frame` with a chatboard and whiteboard. The `start()` method connects to the server, displays the `Frame`, and starts a thread to process incoming methods; the `stop()` method disconnects and shuts down. Finally, the `main()` method executes this as a stand-alone application.

```
protected String host, name;
protected int port;

public GenericChat (String host, int port, String name) {
  this.host = host;
  this.port = port;
  this.name = name;
  initAWT ();
}

// protected void initAWT () ...
```

In the constructor, we keep a copy of the host name, `host`; port, `port`; and username, `name`. We then call `initAWT()` to initialize the user interface.

```
protected Frame frame;
protected ChatboardClient cb;
```

```
   protected WhiteboardClient wb;

   protected void initAWT () {
     frame = new Frame ("Generic Chat");
     frame.setLayout (new GridLayout (2, 1));
     cb = new ChatboardClient ();
     wb = new WhiteboardClient ();
     frame.add (wb);
     frame.add (cb);
     frame.pack ();

     frame.addWindowListener (new WindowAdapter () {
       public void windowClosing (WindowEvent event) {
         try {
           stop ();
         } catch (IOException ex) {
           ex.printStackTrace ();
         }
       }
     });
   }
```

The initAWT() method creates a Frame, frame, creates and lays out the ChatboardClient cb and WhiteboardClient wb, and registers an anonymous WindowListener that shuts down this client when the window is closed.

```
   protected GenericClient client;

   public void start () throws IOException {
     client = new GenericClient (host, port, name);
     client.register ("chat", cb);
     client.register ("wb", wb);
     client.start ();
     frame.setVisible (true);
   }
```

The start() method creates a GenericClient that connects to the server at the specified address (host, port) and registers with the chosen name, name. If a connection cannot be made or the name is already in use, this will throw an IOException and exit.

We then register the two Clients, cb and wb, with appropriate labels. Registering these tools automatically assigns them multiplexed message streams over which to communicate. We finally display the Frame and call the GenericClient's start() method, which starts new threads to process incoming messages and deliver outgoing messages.

```
   public void stop () throws IOException {
     frame.setVisible (false);
     client.shutdown ();
   }
```

This method is called to stop this client. We call the `GenericClient`'s `shutdown()` method and hide the `Frame`. Calling `shutdown()` closes the network connection and deregisters our two clients.

```
public static void main (String[] args) throws IOException {
  if (args.length != 3)
    throw new IllegalArgumentException
      ("Syntax: GenericChat <host> <port> <name>");

  GenericChat chat = new GenericChat
    (args[0], Integer.parseInt (args[1]), args[2]);
  chat.start ();
}
```

The `main()` method verifies that the correct number of arguments have been supplied, throwing an explanatory exception if not. We then create a `GenericChat`, `chat`, with the supplied arguments and call its `start()` method. This connects to the server with the chosen username and displays a chat `Frame` with which to communicate with other users. Calling the `start()` method results in two threads being created: one relays `Client` messages to the server; the other relays server messages to the `Client`s.

This application is powerful for its simplicity. It provides real-time multiuser collaboration across a network. The application can be embedded in a Web page as an applet, or run as a stand-alone application. More importantly, however, it can be easily extended by simply registering more clients. We do not need to change the server or the client framework to add clients; all the clients will run seamlessly. We can modify the format of messages for one client, and this will have no effect on other clients. Additionally, as we will see, our clients can be simple. We do not need to cater for communications problems; any connection failure will be reported through the `disconnected()` method. Despite this, communications all operate through the standard message streams interface.

33.3.2 Class ChatboardClient

This class extends the `Chatboard` that we developed earlier in the multiplexed streams chapter and implements the necessary additions to implement the `Client` interface.

```
import java.io.*;
import java.awt.*;

public class ChatboardClient extends Chatboard implements Client {
  // public void receive () ...
  // public void disconnected () ...
}
```

We extend the basic `Chatboard` class and implement the `Client` interface. This means that we must provide the `setMessageOutput()`, `receive()`, and `disconnected()` methods. In fact, we inherit the `setMessageOutput()` method from the original, so we need to implement only two methods.

We have no need to perform any initialization upon creation, so we omit any constructors. Thus, we will be assigned a default constructor that takes no parameters.

```
protected MessageOutput messageOut;

public void receive (DataInputStream dataIn) {
    if (messageOut == null)
      messageOut = super.getMessageOutput ();
    try {
      byte[] buffer = new byte[dataIn.available ()];
      dataIn.readFully (buffer);
      messageOut.write (buffer);
      messageOut.send ();
    } catch (IOException ex) {
      ex.printStackTrace ();
    }
}
```

The `Chatboard` class that we are extending extracts messages from a `Queue`. As a result, when we receive messages from the `GenericClient` class, we must place them directly into the `Queue`. We call the superclass `getMessageOutput()` method; this returns a `QueueOutputStream` that writes messages into the message queue. We read the incoming message into a buffer, write this to `messageOut`, and `send()` the message. It will then be placed in the queue for subsequent processing by the `Chatboard` listener thread. This is obviously a tortuous implementation, however it saves us having to reimplement the `Chatboard` class.

```
public void disconnected () {
    input.setEditable (false);
    listener.interrupt ();
}
```

This method is called when we are disconnected from the server. We set the `TextField` input to be uneditable to prevent the user from entering any further messages. The `input` variable is inherited from the superclass, as is the text entry box for the chat. We also interrupt the `listener` thread that reads messages from the queue.

Obviously, if we had not implemented the original `Chatboard` with message streams, we would need to provide more implementation here. It is, however, a comparatively simple task to add networked operation to other applications, even those that were not implemented initially with networking in mind.

Additionally, in this case, the use of a Queue is probably unnecessary. The tool is sufficiently simple that processing messages will not take long. A Queue would only become necessary if the client could take a long time to process a message. This delay in the receive() method would stall the GenericClient thread and, therefore, stall the processing of messages for other client tools.

33.3.3 Class WhiteboardClient

This class is the corresponding Client extension of the earlier Whiteboard class.

```
import java.io.*;
import java.awt.*;

public class WhiteboardClient extends Whiteboard implements Client {
  // public void disconnected () ...
}
```

The implementation of this class is essentially identical to that of the Whiteboard class. We implement the Client interface, but the superclass has already defined appropriate setMessageOutput() and receive() methods. Therefore, we must only provide an implementation of the disconnected() method.

```
public void disconnected () {
   setForeground (Color.red);
}
```

If we are disconnected from the server, we set our foreground color to red, to indicate that the whiteboard is no longer connected.

33.4 Extending the generic classes

From this example, it should be apparent that we can easily develop significant networked applications using just the message-streams based communications library. The GenericServer and GenericClient classes can provide a basis for many server-based collaborative applications, and this basis hides much of the complexity associated with networking.

In many cases, however, we may require further function that is not provided by these classes alone. In such cases, we can frequently just extend these classes and add the extra function. This section discusses a few of the extension and optimization options that may be useful.

33.4.1 Message source identification

One facility that we do not provide is an indication of the source of a message. This might be useful if, for example, a chat had the ability to reply to a specific user. It would obviously be fairly easy for the client tools to manually insert their username into every message that they send; however, we can automate this task.

There are two primary ways to achieve this: The first option is for clients that need source identification to use a stream that automatically adds their username to each message. The `MultiplexOutputStream` class provides just this function; client tools can attach a `MultiplexOutputStream` on to the front of their assigned message streams, using their username as a label. Upon receipt of a message, this name can then be extracted using a `MultiplexInputStream`.

We can alternatively automate this task by extending the `GenericHandler` class to automatically add the client username to messages that it forwards, and by extending the `GenericClient` class to extract this name and present it with the messages upon receipt.

33.4.2 Optimizing these classes

These classes are wide open for optimization. When we combine the functions of multiple streams, we end up copying data through multiple buffers before actually transmitting them. The classes, as described, are distinctly not optimized, mainly for the purpose of explanation.

One obvious place for optimization is the output streams that are used by clients of the `GenericHandler`. All data written by the clients go through a multiplexed stream, to a routing stream, to a queue stream, and into a queue. We could make this path more efficient by defining a `GenericMessageOutputStream` that performs all of these functions in a single class, building up the message in a `ByteArrayOutputStream`, attaching headers, and placing it directly into a queue for processing.

We can similarly optimize the route from the queue to the network connection by defining a class that takes buffers directly from the queue and sends them to the network.

On the server side, we can hardwire many of the operations that are currently performed by the message stream classes and increase performance in this manner. Another optimization would involve removing the use of `strings` to identify clients for multicast messages. Instead, the server could assign integer identifiers to clients, thus making the process of routing multicasts more efficient.

These optimizations are probably best left to a production stage when an application is finalized, if they are to be used at all. Machines are generally sufficiently powerful that some extra buffer copying on the client-side will not adversely affect operation. If a server has to support significant load, optimizations are obviously in order.

The optimizations described above are just the tip of the iceberg when it comes to server-side optimizations. There are many general optimizations applicable to any server situation:

- Garbage collection and memory allocation cause a significant impact on performance. A highly optimized Java server must attempt to minimize these problems. Typically, instead of always creating objects for new messages and connections, we would create a queue of reusable objects. When we need a new buffer, we attempt to reuse an old buffer that has sufficient capacity. Similarly, instead of creating `GenericHandlers`, we would keep a queue of past handlers and declare methods that let us reuse these for new connections.

- It is more efficient to access a variable that is local to a method than to access a class' instance variable. As a result, it may be useful to use a temporary local variable where an instance variable is accessed repeatedly.

- `Vectors` and `Hashtables` are much less efficient than local arrays; with the use of integer identifiers we could eliminate the overhead of these datastructures.

- In other areas, the excessive use of `synchronization` can be costly. Where possible, this should be eliminated; especially from inner loops. Critical servers may be able to benefit from lock-free datastructures that eliminate the use of synchronization altogether, at the cost of some implementation-related penalty (e.g., occasional duplication).

- Similarly, testing for an exception (i.e., a `catch` clause) is fairly costly. Where possible, such tests should be eliminated from inner loops. It is much more efficient to catch exceptions outside of a tight loop, to handle the exception and then to restart the loop, than to handle exceptions inside the loop.

Optimizations like this get messy, and are left as an exercise, if necessary. If performance is a significant issue, choice of platform and compiler is also of crucial importance: Different JVMs, different threading models and different compilers can have radical effects on performance; particularly when multiple processors are available. The interested reader would do well to search online Java publications (e.g., http://www.javaworld.com/) for up-to-date JVM comparisons; particularly those that pay specific respect to server-side issues.

33.5 Wrapping up

The message streams that we have introduced here are extremely powerful tools for the development of networked applications. We can produce extensible collaborative tools with a minimum of effort, and these tools can be dynamically introduced to a continually running server.

The `GenericServer` and `GenericClient` classes can support a wide variety of different applications in a generic manner, and as mentioned, can be extended to include additional function with a minimum of effort.

On the Web site accompanying this book, http://nitric.com/jnp/, we have included a full chat application that uses these classes with the naming extensions described, to provide real-time collaboration across the Web. Obviously the tools are somewhat limited; they are, however, easily extensible.

PART VI

Appendices

These appendices provide further background context useful to better apply the techniques and code supplied in the body of the book. An in-depth survey of networking technologies is included first, to provide context for networked applications development. This is followed by a series of tables of information relevant to networking.

Appendix A: Networking   This chapter continues on from the earlier introduction to networking. Future technologies such as IPv6, as well as modern infrastructural technologies such as ATM and SONET, are discussed in detail. Also provided are thorough descriptions of the worldwide telco WAN, as well as the architecture and administration of the Internet.

Appendix B: Tables   There is much tabular information that bears relevance to networking and the Java language; this appendix contains a few such tables of data, including the ASCII character set, Unicode block allocations, well known UNIX networking services, and the formats of typical HTTP requests and responses.

A P P E N D I X   A

Networking

Networking is a fascinating and multifaceted subject. This appendix covers networks from LAN to WAN and B-ISDN. It focuses on in-depth discussion of networking issues including IP routing, Internet architecture, and telco WAN technologies.

A.1 Overview of networks

A network is simply a collection of interconnected information devices which speak the same data transmission protocol. The actual choice of protocols and physical interconnection facilities used for a given network depends on a variety of factors, including the geographic span of the network and the applications that it is designed to support.

A.1.1 Network classification

Computer networks are typically classified based on geographic area and the protocols they utilize to transport data. The two standard size-based designations are *local area network* (LAN) and *wide area network* (WAN). Common protocol-based network classifications include IPX/SPX (Novell), AppleTalk, and TCP/IP. Some physical networks run more than one protocol; for example, a LAN may simultaneously run IPX/SPX and TCP/IP. Networks which simultaneously run a set of parallel protocols are usually referred to as *heterogeneous*.

A.1.2 LAN and WAN

LAN and WAN are dissimilar technologies. LAN was developed primarily by computer networking researchers. WAN was developed by phone company (telco) engineers and standards organizations (figure A.1). As a result, the two implement similar functionality in fundamentally different ways. Since the Internet is comprised of LAN and WAN components, it is important to consider both when trying to understand how the Internet works. It turns out that the Internet behaves very much, but not exactly, like a large LAN, even though it is technically a WAN. Interestingly, modern technologies such as asynchronous transfer mode (ATM) contain characteristics of both technologies.

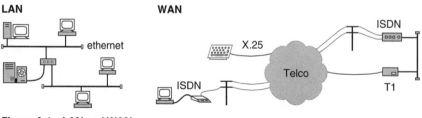

Figure A.1   LAN and WAN

- *Examples of LANs*   Ethernet, Token Ring, AppleTalk, Novell (IPX/SPX)
- *Examples of WANs*   X.25, ISDN, Frame Relay

A.1.3 Data switching technologies

Every network must have a method for packaging and routing data. The Internet is based on a data routing scheme known as *packet switching*. A packet-switched system divides a body of data up into small discrete units of varying size (packets) that get to their common destination independently, possibly via different network routes. This architecture ensures that if the primary route that the data are using becomes unserviceable for some reason, then another route can be established dynamically. Similarly, when routes become congested, the network can react by establishing alternative routes, thereby distributing load more evenly.

The standard phone system, technically known as the *plain old telephone service* (POTS) or *public switched telephone network* (PSTN), utilizes a different data delivery methodology known as *circuit switching*. In a circuit-switched system, a dedicated, preallocated route is established to carry an entire data session. Circuit-switched telco networks (with the exception of X.25) do not typically implement any advanced services such as flow control, error checking, or data formatting. For the purposes of computer networking, the phone system is therefore usually used as a transport substrate for the wide-area components of packet-switched networks such as the Internet, which provide these services.

A fairly new technology called *cell switching* will eventually replace circuit and packet switching, especially for wide-area data transport. A cell-switched system utilizes packets of fixed size with headers of fixed length. ATM is an example of such a system. ATM represents a compromise between the synchronous circuit-switched model popular with phone companies and the packet-switched system preferred by computer networkers (figure A.2). Cell switching is the preferred technology for the B-ISDN (a.k.a. the information superhighway) because of its superior bandwidth interface granularity, which means that it supports many data transfer rates.

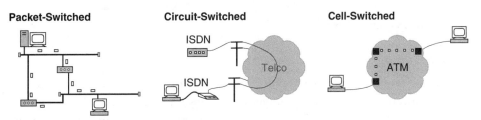

Figure A.2 **Data switching technologies**

A.2 Local area networks

LANs are physically relatively small, usually spanning a mile or less. LAN technologies are usually characterized by shared media access, which means that every device on the LAN essentially shares the same transmission wire.

LANs, due to their physical and media access characteristics, typically have a large amount of bandwidth compared to WAN. Standard Ethernet, for example, has an upper speed limit of 10 Mbps. FDDI is on the order of 100 Mbps.

- *Common LAN technologies* Ethernet (10 Mbps, Fast is 100 Mbps), Token Ring (4 Mbps, 16 Mbps), FDDI (100 Mbps), LocalTalk (230 Kbps)

A.2.1 Common LAN topologies

The physical organization of a LAN is known as its *topology*. There are three common network topologies. The simplest is a bus or chain, in which all machines are connected to a common cable. A ring topology is similar to a bus, but the ends of the cable connect to form a ring. A star topology consists of a hub which connects separately to each networked node (figure A.3). How exactly the nodes share access to the common network medium—their *media access*—is determined by the *datalink* specification. Traditional LANs provide any-to-any connectivity (i.e., any machine can communicate with any other machine on the LAN) and a *broadcast* mode that allows each station to send a frame that will be picked up by every other station on the LAN.

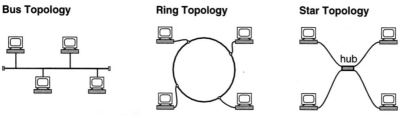

Figure A.3   Common LAN topologies

A.2.2 Ethernet

Ethernet is the most popular LAN technology in place today. Ethernet is a physical and datalink specification that spans several types of cabling and several related data framing protocols in the 802.*x* family. Ethernet media access control allows any station on the network to try to transmit at any time, even though this may produce collisions when several transmit at one time. This media access mechanism is called *carrier sense multiple access with collision detection* (CSMA/CD). CSMA/CD identifies collisions, and allows each station to have adequate access to the common channel.

Each node on an Ethernet has an Ethernet interface card, usually called the *network adapter* or *network interface card* (NIC). Each NIC has a special hardware address, assigned in such a way as to guarantee uniqueness, even across vendors. The NIC connects to the network cabling and picks up packets from the wire that have its address as their destination. The NIC also picks up packets addressed to the broadcast address, which is a special address that is received by all NICs.

Ethernet cabling comes in three flavors. Old installations used a bulky inflexible cable known as *thicknet*. Second-generation Ethernets typically used a cheaper, thin coax cable which was usually deployed in a chain for connecting stations. This type of cabling is officially known as 10-base-2, but is generally referred to as *thinnet*. Modern Ethernet installations use a type of cable designated 10-base-T or *unshielded twisted-pair* (UTP), arranged in a star topology around a hub. UTP is rated from category one through category five, with category five (cat 5) as the highest rating. Cat 5 UTP is standard for Ethernet cabling in modern facilities.

A *hub* is a device with multiple ports, each of which is connected to a node on the network via a 10-base-T link in a star topology. Typically, a hub acts as a concentrator,

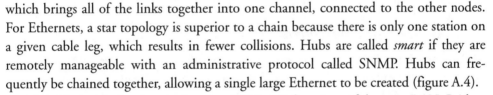

Figure A.4 Ethernet hubs

which brings all of the links together into one channel, connected to the other nodes. For Ethernets, a star topology is superior to a chain because there is only one station on a given cable leg, which results in fewer collisions. Hubs are called *smart* if they are remotely manageable with an administrative protocol called SNMP. Hubs can frequently be chained together, allowing a single large Ethernet to be created (figure A.4).

A *bridge* is a device that sits between LANs or subsections of the same LAN. Bridges maintain datalink hardware address tables in memory and forward frames that have destinations on the other side of the bridge. Bridges operate at the datalink layer, the second layer of the network stack introduced at the beginning of this book, and usually connect homogeneous networks.

A *switching hub*, or *switch*, is a fairly new type of hub that actively forwards frames directly from a transmitting station to a receiving station, thereby avoiding collisions completely (figure A.5). Switches essentially act as bridges which partition each station

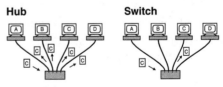

Figure A.5 A switching hub

into its own network. Switches may also provide network-layer routing, in which case they act as routers.

A *router* is a network device that is connected to two or more networks and forwards packets between the networks based on their network protocol destination addresses. In the case of a small LAN, a router usually serves as the gateway between the LAN and the Internet. Such a router picks up packets

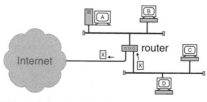

Figure A.6 An IP router

on its inside interface that have destinations outside of the local subnet, and forwards them to the outside interface, which is usually the endpoint of a WAN link such as a T-1. It also forwards packets that appear on its outside interface to its appropriate inside interface (figure A.6).

Routers can also sit between different LANs in the same network complex, or between parts of a wide area enterprise network. In this case, the routers' interfaces may be ethernets or WAN link endpoints. This allows traffic on a large network to be effectively partitioned.

High speed Ethernet   In addition to the standard 10-Mbps Ethernet, 100-Mbps Fast Ethernet is available over Category 5 UTP. Also, Gigabit Ethernet, which is capable of speeds of 1 Gbps, is on the way. Gigabit Ethernet is expected to see immediate deployment in the backbones of larger Ethernet installations.

A.3 Wide area networking

WAN comes into play in the context of geographically large networks. WAN generally makes use of the public phone system infrastructure provided by phone companies.

Internet WAN is built over the top of the phone system. Traditionally, computer data networks and protocols have borne very little resemblance to telco digital voice and data networking protocols. The Internet therefore developed by using dedicated high speed phone lines as the basic wide area transport links for normal IP communications.

Telco WAN links have historically been expensive, leased point-to-point links from LANs to the Internet backbone. As the Internet has become more popular, more demand for connectivity has begun to appear. As a result, ISPs and phone companies have started offering intermediate and more affordable bandwidth solutions, such as Frame Relay and ISDN.

A.3.1 Telco WAN background

In general, the world's phone network is a point-to-point mesh or cloud, depending on the exact service in question. In other words, when a call is placed, the call is assigned a temporary direct link to the destination. This architecture is opposite in design philosophy to LANs, which share a common transmission media, and support LAN broadcast and multicast. This difference is a natural one: the phone system was designed to accommodate telephone calls from one subscriber to another within a huge subscriber base, whereas LANs were originally intended to move computer data among a relatively small number of machines.

The telco switching fabric is based on bearer channels of fixed capacity. These bearer channels, which contain enough bandwidth for a single phone call, are allocated across the long distance network as calls are placed. Long distance calls are aggregated into larger high speed channels, called *trunks*, for transport across the telco backbone. Trunks themselves are aggregated into even higher speed trunks across the backbone as well (figure A.7).

Figure A.7   Aggregated bearer channels

Each channel or trunk is placed into next trunk level by a process called *time division multiplexing* (TDM). Every second, a timeslice sample of each channel is bundled into a trunk frame at a particular time slot. At every phone switch on the route to the destination the call is mapped out of its time slot and into the corresponding slot of the next trunk en route to the next backbone switch. At the last switch in the route, the call is demultiplexed out of the trunk and presented as a continuous stream to the remote end of the connection.

Demultiplexing is the act of extracting component channels from a higher level channel, and is used to unpack a high speed trunk into its component calls. Demultiplexing an entire trunk within the backbone in order to route a few bearer channels is an expensive process in terms of performance. In a completely synchronized hierarchy there is no need for this sort of wholesale demultiplexing within the backbone.

In the context of telco, synchronization means that a given channel always falls in the same time slot within each level of the multiplexing hierarchy. Synchronization is useful because in a truly synchronized multilevel system,

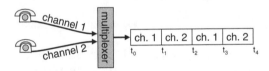

Figure A.8   Time-division multiplexing

switches may simply route calls directly into and out of high speed trunks based on their respective time slots. Otherwise, to route a particular call channel, the switch has to demultiplex high speed trunks to get to their lower level component trunks and then demultiplex these into the actual calls (figure A.8).

A.3.2 The legacy phone network

The term *plesiochronous digital hierarchy* (PDH) is sometimes used to describe currently implemented telco network technologies, because they do not scale from lowest to highest level in a truly synchronous fashion.

A single phone channel, such as that needed for a standard voice conversation, is an 8-bit value sampled at the rate of 8,000 samples per second. These numbers are based on the minimum amount of data per second needed to digitally represent a human voice with decent quality, and form the basis for the architecture of the entire phone network. Eight thousand 8-bit samples per second produces a bearer channel with a bandwidth of 64 Kbps. Telcos refer to this type of connection as a DS-0.

DS-0s are allocated by the phone network as needed to carry voice transmissions. Those DS-0s with an endpoint not serviced by the local phone switch are multiplexed into higher bandwidth trunk lines. Of course, since the phone system is circuit-switched, there is no dynamic routing of each individual DS-0 slice or frame. Instead, the entire path is preallocated by the phone network during a call setup phase.

A.3.3 DS-0s, DS-1s, and DS-3s

DS-0s carry 64 Kbps. The next step up from a DS-0 is a DS-1, usually referred to as a T-1, which consists of 24 multiplexed DS-0s. The T-1 is the standard dedicated Internet WAN connection, and

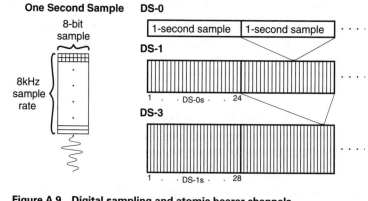
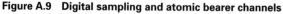

Figure A.9   Digital sampling and atomic bearer channels

can carry approximately 1.5 Mbps of traffic. The next standard step up from a T-1 is a DS-3, or T-3, which multiplexes 28 T-1s for a total of 672 simultaneous individual DS-0s. T-3s have a bandwidth of approximately 43 Mbps (figure A.9).

The biggest problem with the PDH is that it is not synchronous. At the T-3 level it is impossible to extract a given DS-0 without first demultiplexing the entire T-3 down to T-1s. This results in slow switching times. As a response to this problem, a new technology called *synchronous optical network/synchronous digital hierarchy* (SONET/SDH), was developed. SONET/SDH is a synchronous framing standard, data rate standard, and switching system that can attain speeds on an order of magnitude greater than PDH.

A.3.4 The B-ISDN

The Broadband-Integrated Services Digital Network (B-ISDN), sometimes referred to as the information superhighway, is the proposed world information infrastructure designed to carry every sort of data from video and voice to file transfer. The interface to the B-ISDN is intended to be flexible enough to accommodate time-dependent (isochronous) services such as real-time multimedia, as well as data transfer of all sorts. SONET/SDH is extremely fast, but it has severe limitations for application as the switching fabric for the B-ISDN. The major problem with SONET/SDH for this purpose is that it does not offer enough interface bandwidth granularity, and therefore cannot accommodate many data rates. SONET/SDH is, however, excellent as a framing format and transport technology, and is in fact used for this purpose in the B-ISDN.

ATM is a data transport specification that contains circuit-switched and packet-switched elements, and as such offers the best of both worlds. ATM is primarily run over fiber, but it can be run over copper cabling as well. Early adopters are already utilizing ATM as a LAN technology, as well as a WAN technology, to reduce interface problems between LAN and WAN. B-ISDN implemented with ATM as its switching fabric is extremely granular, and therefore flexible for many data rates and service types.

A.3.5 Common WAN links

The following list outlines the WAN interfaces commonly used for Internet connectivity, along with their associated bandwidth. Note that there are other types of WAN interfaces which are not listed because they are not usually used outside of telco. The latency of each link, which is the total amount of time a frame of information takes to traverse the link, is included. The problem with a high-latency link, such as a satellite link, is that although its bandwidth may be high, there is always a large delay, or lag, between data being sent and data actually arriving.

When using a telco WAN link for an Internet connection, it is important to remember that both a phone company and an Internet service provider (ISP) come into play. The phone company provides a line to the ISP, which then provides some type of Internet interface. Typically, the telco line is leased, and the ISP interface contains some sort of lease plus bandwidth usage component. The telco link may be point-to-point between the subscriber and the ISP, such as in the case of a T-1, or it may go into a telco cloud, as with Frame Relay.

POTS POTS stands for *plain old telephone service*. Even though the telco system's backbone has been digital for years, most subscribers unfortunately still have an analog phone line to their businesses and residences. The limited geographic range of the digital alternative, N-ISDN, the high price of digital phones, and the relatively high cost of digital subscriber interface installation prevent digital from gaining real penetration into the

POTS subscriber base. POTS is sometimes also called the public switched telephone network (PSTN).

Serial Line Internet Protocol (SLIP) and Point-to-Point Protocol (PPP) both use the analog phone system interface as the transport layer for an Internet link. SLIP/PPP connections are temporary links over standard serial phone lines between a modem on the user's end and a modem bank and terminal server at the ISP (figure A.10). These connections are asynchronous, generally of low quality, and of comparatively high latency. These connections do, however, have the redeeming quality of being inexpensive.

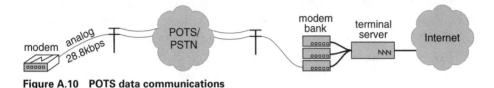

Figure A.10   POTS data communications

DS-0   A DS-0 is the atomic digital telco bearer channel. A DS-0 is allocated for every call and contains 64 Kbps of bandwidth. DS-0s are used as the building blocks for other digital interfaces such as N-ISDN and T-1.

N-ISDN BRI: 64 or 128 Kbps   Narrowband Integrated Services Digital Network (N-ISDN) is the forerunner of the proposed B-ISDN. N-ISDN, which is usually simply called ISDN, is a standard designed to provide a digital subscriber interface over the copper wires which make up the majority of the installed subscriber loop infrastructure. ISDNs were originally positioned in the market as integrated digital voice and video, hence the name *Integrated Services Digital Network*. ISDN went nowhere until it was discovered as a cost-effective way to transport data. ISDN comes in two interface levels, PRI and BRI.

ISDN Basic Rate Interface (BRI) consists of two DS-0 bearer (B) channels and a 16 Kbps signalling (D) channel (figure A.11). Latency is high. ISDN BRI is becoming popular because of increasingly simple setup and low cost. ISDN is available only within 18,000 feet of an ISDN-enabled phone switch. This is usually not a problem in urban areas, but most rural areas cannot take advantage of this service.

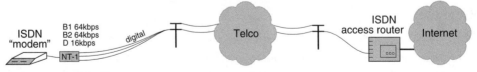

Figure A.11   ISDN BRI

ISDN Primary Rate Interface (PRI) is a high-bandwidth version of the BRI which runs over T-1. It consists of 23 64-Kbps B channels and one 64-Kbps D channel. PRIs are usually used to concentrate multiple incoming BRIs.

Frame Relay   Frame Relay (FR) is a packet-switched telco network which may be likened to a modern version of the old X.25 telco data network. FR uses endpoint equipment similar to T-1, and may in fact be upgraded to T-1 or transported over T-1.

FR allocates physical bandwidth in the network only when data are being sent or received, so FR circuits are referred to as *virtual circuits* (VCs). VCs employ a DataLink Connection Identifier (DLCI) to identify the circuit's path through the network. In the case of switched virtual circuits (SVCs), the

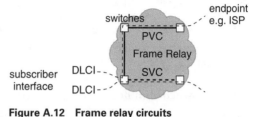

Figure A.12   Frame relay circuits

network has to set up this connection identifier dynamically, which adds to transport latency. A permanent virtual circuit (PVC), on the other hand, keeps a permanently assigned DLCI to avoid the call setup overhead. FR PVCs therefore behave like dedicated circuits in this respect (figure A.12).

Because the FR network is a shared cloud, available capacity at any given time is not guaranteed. Committed information rates (CIRs), which guarantee the subscriber a minimum amount of bandwidth, may be purchased from providers to circumvent this problem. FR bandwidth varies, but is typically offered with an interface of 56 Kbps.

Switched 56 digital data service   Switched 56 provides subscribers a fairly low cost, but high latency access so that they do not have to buy leased lines. Switched 56 service requires the same equipment as a T-1, and usually may be upgraded to T-1 service or frame relay. Bandwidth is 56 Kbps.

T-1   T-1 is AT&T's name for a DS-1 formatted signal, which is a multiplexed aggregate of 24 DS-0s. T-1s are conventionally used as wide area transport service (WATS) lines for incoming and outgoing 800 numbers and other rotating phone exchanges. T-1s are dedicated point-to-point circuits, which means that they permanently connect their endpoints. This type of connection from a telco is typically referred to as a leased line, because the line bandwidth is always available (and billable), even if it is not being used to full capacity. Since T-1 is a point-to-point dedicated circuit, telco bills it by the mile, making such a network of dedicated lines very expensive.

T-1 is a high-quality connection, with a nominal bandwidth of 1.544 Mbps and low latency. T-1 is fairly expensive and requires a CSU/DSU for both ends of the line, plus local telco and ISP setup and monthly fees.

Fractional T-1 A fractional T-1, or *fractional*, is some subset of the full T-1 bandwidth of 24 DS-0 channels. Fractionals are available in increments of 64 Kbps. The exact increments are based on the telco provider. Not all telcos will lease fractionals, and ISPs do not automatically offer matching service levels for a given telco. The actual usable bandwidth for the fractional is less than the number of DS-0s because of some signaling overhead.

Fractional T-1s use the same CSU/DSU for both ends of the line, plus the same additional setup as a full T-1.

T-3 T-3 is AT&T's name for a DS-3 formatted signal. The DS-3 multiplexes 28 T-1s for an approximate total bandwidth of 43 Mbps. Usually DS-3s are used by providers to carry backbone traffic.

SMDS Switched multimegabit data service is a relatively new addition to high speed telco networking services. SMDS is a broadband, multiaccess, packet-switched network service designed to bridge LANs over WAN. SMDS supports connection with ATM, Frame Relay, SMDS Interface Protocol (SIP), or Data Exchange Interface (DXI).

ADSL Asynchronous digital subscriber link (ADSL) and a family of related technologies are beginning to be embraced as alternatives to ISDN over the copper subscriber loop. ADSL can drive 1.5 Mbps over a distance of 18,000 feet. At a distance of 12,000 feet, ADSL can drive 6.1 Mbps. The wire gauge has an effect and can diminish the range.

Very high speed digital subscriber line (VDSL), a related technology, has been shown to deliver 50 Mbps for up to 1,000 feet in tests.

Cable Cable companies are starting to deliver packet-based services to subscribers, including video on demand (VOD) and TCP/IP transport. Cable-based packet bandwidth varies widely, but by most estimates falls in the 35 Mbps range.

Some cable-based efforts are focused on setting up parallel, high-performance cable backbone segments which function in parallel to the Internet. These alternative networks are intended as high speed backbones for business use.

Satellite Satellite Internet links are already available in some places, with some offerings of bandwidth of roughly 400–500 Kbps. Unfortunately, at this time satellite links are downstream only and display high latency. Typically, a modem, or similar technology, must be used for the upstream link.

A.3.6 *Future Internet: ATM*

ATM is a relatively newly adopted standard (1988) that forms the switching and multiplexing fabric for the B-ISDN. ATM is a cell-based technology designed to compromise between the needs of time-sensitive data such as realtime video and multimedia, and data transfer applications.

ATM is intended to support traffic with widely different characteristics, as well as to integrate with current standards. ATM therefore contains facilities to transport voice, video, X.25, and data packets.

ATM virtual circuits and routing   ATM routing takes place between ATM switches. Much like the legacy phone network, ATM switches set up a path at the beginning of data transfer. The switches set up virtual path identifiers (VPIs) and virtual channel identifiers (VCIs). VPIs identify a circuit path within the ATM network; VCIs identify a channel within a given VPI. This arrangement

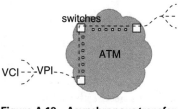

Figure A.13   Asynchronous transfer mode

allows hosts to multiplex multiple applications streams (VCIs) into one virtual path. The network uses the VPIs to route cells, but ignores the VCIs, which are used only by the hosts that are party to the connection (figure A.13).

ATM is called *asynchronous* because it is not synchronous in the telco sense of the word. ATM uses a multiplexing scheme known as *statistical time division multiplexing* (STDM) instead of the TDM used in SONET/SDH. STDM is a sophisticated procedure that allocates circuit bandwidth in the network based on the amount of bandwidth a particular connection (VPI) requests. This request, including peak and average utilization and maximum burst duration, is made as the VPI is being set up.

The ATM cell   An ATM cell is 53 bytes long. The header makes up five bytes of this cell and contains a general flow control (GFC) field, a payload type identifier (PTI) field, a cell loss priority (CLP) field, VPI and VPC fields, and a header error control (HEC) field.

The ATM stack   The ATM stack consists of three layers: the physical layer, the ATM layer, and the ATM adaption layer (AAL). The physical layer defines the transport used, and includes SONET/SDH. The ATM layer defines routing, switching, and multiplexing. The AAL is

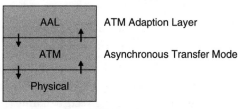

Figure A.14   The ATM stack

used to encapsulate application types to assign their data timing priorities (figure A.14).

The AAL consists of service classes A, B, C, D, and X, where A is voice and D is connectionless packets. B and C are intermediate levels. D allows circuit-oriented ATM to operate in a connectionless, low-priority data-transport mode.

- *Class A*   Constant-rate circuit emulation (e.g., voice)
- *Class B*   Variable-rate circuit (e.g., audio and video)
- *Class C*   Connection-oriented data transfer (e.g., TCP/IP)
- *Class D*   Connectionless (e.g., SMDS, UDP, IP)
- *Class X*   User-regulated, connection-oriented, best-effort delivery

IP over ATM   ATM can encapsulate IP traffic by using AAL classes C-X. However, address binding is extremely difficult. ATM does not support broadcasting, so IP cannot use ARP to discover hardware addresses. In addition, nodes do not know their physical addresses. Eventually, IP will be widely implemented over ATM, but these and other problems need to be solved.

LAN emulation   In order to bring ATM to the LAN environment, it will have to interoperate with older networking technologies already in place. For this reason, ATM must have an emulation layer to provide older technologies with services such as connectionless data sending and LAN multicast and broadcast services.

The ATM Forum is proposing a standard which defines a client/server LAN interface to an ATM network. The ATM Forum's solution consists of a LAN emulation client (LEC), which is a proxy ATM station located on both the LAN and the ATM networks, and a LAN emulation server (LES), which provides MAC-to-ATM address resolution. When a station on the LAN tries to transmit to a station on the ATM network or vice versa, the LES resolves the address translation and the LEC acts as a gateway.

ATM problems   The ATM specification is still under development. It remains to be seen whether ATM switches will be able to provide full versions of complex services such as STDM.

A.4 The Internet

The Internet is the global IP-based network over which the Web and other popular information systems operate. Now, more and more, the Internet is being used commercially for both public and private purposes. Publicly, the Web provides advertising and customer support facilities; privately, VPN technologies allow companies to interconnect across the Internet in a secure manner (figure A.15).

A.4.1 A brief history

The Internet originally grew out of an Advanced Research Projects Agency (ARPA) project to link several research universities. ARPANET, a rudimentary packet-switching

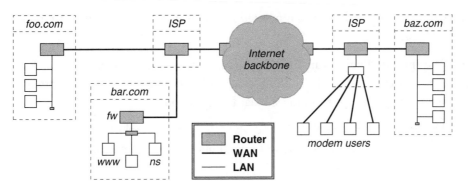

Figure A.15   The Internet

network running over dedicated phone lines between UCLA, Stanford, USC-Santa Barbara, and the University of Utah, went online in 1969.

ARPANET was put under the control of the DOD in 1975. On January 1, 1983, TCP/IP was instated as the ARPANET protocol. ARPANET then split into a nonmilitary ARPANET and MILNET, which was integrated with the Defense Data Network. ARPANET became connected to other government and academic networks which were using TCP/IP.

The National Science Foundation (NSF) became involved in 1984. NSF upgraded and expanded backbone links and established the now-familiar set of top-level domains (edu, com, mil, net, gov, and org). NSF removed itself from direct involvement in May 1995, when the backbone was commercialized.

A.4.2 Administration

The administration of the Internet has been formalized to bring order to a global network that grew from these various beginnings.

ISOC   The governing board of the Internet is the Internet Society, a nonprofit organization made up of a volunteer membership of interested individuals. The ISOC is the parent organization for the IAB.

IAB   The Internet Architecture Board is responsible for long-term architectural and technical direction for the Internet.

IETF   The Internet Engineering Task Force is the body that specifies Internet protocols and makes technical decisions about Internet architecture. The IETF is composed of working groups, which are organized under areas of study. Each working group is organized around a particular engineering problem; they attempt to draft a standard, and cease to exist if and when the standard is adopted. Participation in working groups is completely voluntary and open to interested members of the Internet community on an informal basis.

IESG   The Internet Engineering Steering Group is the IETF's managing body. It is composed of area directors, and the IETF chair. IESG creates IETF working groups, assigns them to areas, and approves the standards they propose.

IRTF   The Internet Research Task Force deals with long-term technical research issues under the jurisdiction of the IAB. The IRTF is composed of research groups which are assigned different research topics.

IRSG   The Internet Research Steering Group is the managing body for the IRTF, and consists of IRTF research group chairs.

IANA   The Internet Assigned Numbers Authority assigns port numbers for well-defined services, such as telnet (TCP port 23).

InterNIC   The Internet Network Information Center administers DNS services. This includes assigning requested domain names and administering the root name servers which define mappings for the top-level domains. The role of InterNIC is currently undergoing change.

Routing Arbiter   The Routing Arbiter, a joint project between Merit and ISI, provides routing coordination for the Internet routing infrastructure. The RA provides routing servers at each NAP, based on entries in the Routing Arbiter Database.

North American Network Operator Group   NANOG is a working group with members from ISPs, the peering points, regional networks, the Internet registries, and federal networks. NANOG meetings are held three times a year. Merit hosts many of these meetings.

A.4.3 Current Internet architecture

The Internet is composed of independent routing units called autonomous systems. These systems used to be primarily educational and military networks connected via the National Science Foundation's high speed routing backbone. Today the Internet backbone is largely commercial telco providers, such as MCI, UUNET, and Sprint, that interface at peering points, such as MAE-East in Washington, DC.

Autonomous systems   An autonomous system is a self-contained IP routing system. All routers in an AS communicate and route among themselves. As a result, any packet that arrives at an AS that has a destination inside the AS will automatically be routed to the appropriate host without further outside routing.

Internal routing protocols such as RIP and OSPF are used within AS's to perform intra-AS routing. External routing protocols such as BGP are used to route between AS's.

Provider backbones   The Internet backbone consists of high speed WAN links, typically T-3 and greater. The term *backbone* is a bit of an anachronism, because with the commercialization of the NSF backbone in May 1995, the original Internet backbone was retired. Today the Internet backbone is comprised of the respective backbones of the service providers that run the commercial regional networks. These provider backbones interconnect at a set number of designated peering points and by direct peering between providers.

Smaller service providers connect directly to the larger commercial providers with smaller WAN links (typically T-1), and even smaller providers buy from them, and so on down to the end consumer.

It is desirable to obtain an Internet connection as close to the top-level providers as possible. Closeness is measured in hops, or the number of IP gateways (usually routers) that your traffic must go through to get to the appropriate backbone. Closer connections are faster because they avoid latency incurred in additional router hops.

Figure A.16   Major peering points

Peering points   The peering points include NSF-awarded Network Access Points (NAPs) and other exchanges (figure A.16). The four NSF-awarded NAPs are:

- *MAE-East*   MAE-East is located in Washington, DC. MAE-East is a bridged FDDI/Ethernet hybrid with three classes of connection: switched FDDI, shared FDDI, and switched Ethernet.

- *Sprint NAP*   The Sprint NAP is located in Pennsauken, NJ. It is a FDDI LAN that supports both shared and dedicated bandwidth.

- *Ameritech Advanced Data Services (AADS) NAP*   The AADS NAP is in Chicago. The AADS NAP uses ATM and supports DS-3, HSSI with ADSU, DS-3 Native ATM, and OC-3c (155 Mbps) SONET interfaces. It serves the Chicago LATA.

- *PacBell NAP*   The PB NAP is located in San Francisco, and spans five LATAs. There are at least 21 network providers connected to the PB NAP. PacBell uses its own proprietary ATM cell relay service as the switching fabric.

- *Other peering points*   Other peering points include FIX-East in Washington, DC, MAE-LA in Los Angeles, MAE-West in San Jose, CA, and CIX and FIX-West in San Francisco. Besides interconnecting at common exchanges, direct peering also occurs between providers on a private basis.

The Routing Arbiter has a presence at the peering points. The RA provides a route server (RS) which coordinates the interconnecting providers by obtaining routing information from each ISP's routers on the NAP and processing the information based on the ISP's routing policy requirements, which are listed by each peering ISP in the Routing Arbiter Database (RADB). The RS then passes the processed routing information to each ISP's router.

The RS does not itself do any routing among the ISP routers. It passes routing information from one ISP system to another with BGP-4's third-party routing function (see A.4.6), with the next hop pointing to the router that advertises the route to the RS. In this way, the RS sets the routes without actually forwarding any traffic packets.

A.4.4 IP routing protocols

Routing protocols come in two types: distance-vector and link-state. Distance-vector protocols build a routing table based on the distances from each network to the current router, and broadcast this information to neighboring routers. A link-state protocol holds a map of the entire network, which is regularly updated, as its routing table (figure A.17). Link-state based routing protocols are generally considered to be superior to distance-vector based protocols, but do not scale as well in the presence of large AS's.

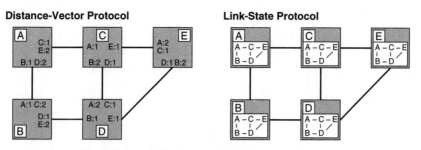

Distance-Vector Protocol

A
C:1
E:2
B:1 D:2

C
A:1 E:1
B:2 D:1

E
A:2
C:1
D:1 B:2

A:1 C:2
D:1
E:2
B

A:2 C:1
B:1 E:1
D

Link-State Protocol

A
A–C–E
| | |
B–D

C
A–C–E
| | |
B–D

E
A–C–E
| | |
B–D

B
A–C–E
| | |
B–D

D
A–C–E
| | |
B–D

Figure A.17   Distance-vector and link-state routing

A.4.5 Interior routing protocols

Within each autonomous system, IP uses interior routing protocols to determine how to route packets.

RIP   Routing Information Protocol is the simplest routing protocol, and is implemented by the UNIX `routed` daemon. RIP counts the number of hops from source to destination to find the neighboring router to which to send the packet.

IGRP   Cisco's improved version of RIP, IGRP is a sophisticated distance-vector protocol. IGRP does not count hops to determine the shortest path to a given destination. Instead, it calculates based on four metrics: delay, bandwidth, reliability, and load.

OSPF   Open Shortest Path First is a link-state protocol that calculates the best route for each packet based on a *shortest path* calculation from information about the entire network. This calculation takes order $n\log(n)$ operations, where n is the number of links in the network. This means that as a network gets bigger, the cost of doing this routing becomes bigger, even faster. This calculation must be performed at every router along a packet's path, which can be very costly; caching is used for efficiency, however router memory can be rapidly exhausted.

A.4.6 Exterior Routing Protocols

Routers in different AS's communicate their routes to each other with an exterior routing protocol. The routers then internally advertise routes to the other ASs' networks, and networks that the other AS's can reach (figure A.18).

EGP   Exterior Gateway Protocol was one of the original exterior routing protocols used in the Internet. A router using EGP first acquires its neighbors by attempting to handshake with routers listed in a control database. When neighbors have been established, EGP periodically tests for neighbor reachability and network reachability.

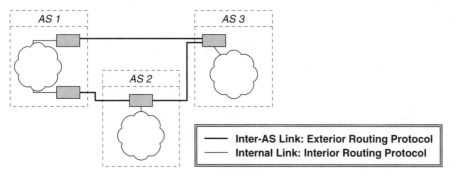

Figure A.18   Interior and exterior routing protocols

Neighbor reachability is a periodic check to determine if a given neighbor is still up and routing. Network reachability periodically requests a list of reachable networks from neighboring AS's.

After EGP acquires routes from connected AS's, it includes those exterior routes that are useful in its interior routing tables.

BGP   Border Gateway Protocol is a modern exterior gateway protocol, widely in service for exterior routing over the Internet. BGP runs over TCP/IP and is designed to scale significantly better than EGP. BGP is based on the concept of *path vectors*, which prevent routing loops. Path vectors announce the entire route to a given network, listing all AS's in the route.

BGP uses open, update, and keep alive in place of EGP's neighbor acquisition, neighbor reachability, and network reachability functions, respectively.

BGP's current version is BGP-4, although there are many BGP-3 routers still in service. BGP-4 includes support for CIDR.

A.4.7 CIDR

Classless Interdomain Routing (CIDR) was devised in the early 1990s to address problems caused by the explosion of hosts connecting to the Internet. The immediate problem this expansion caused was a shortage of Class B networks, of which there are only 16,384. Class B networks can contain a convenient number of hosts, and so are very popular.

CIDR prevents Class B exhaustion by assigning contiguous groups of Class C networks in place of class B networks.

The next serious problem that the Internet faced was the massive growth of routing tables because of the huge number of new networks, especially Class C networks allocated in place of Class B networks. Noncontiguous network assignment also creates routing problems because nonstandard routes have to be advertised as special routing exceptions, and as such take up extra routing entries.

CIDR remedies this situation through a process known as address aggregation. Class C network ranges are partitioned into worldwide continental regions, to be handed out by regional authorities to lower levels. This scheme ensures that routing tables can map all of the traffic from broad provider ranges based on examining very few bits in the address.

This measure helped reduce routing tables, but in the final analysis, only true provider-based address aggregation will provide maximum benefit. The problem with provider-based allocation is that if the provider owns the range of numbers its clients use, then to change providers the client has to renumber all of its networks and hosts, which is not a trivial task.

The third problem is IP address space exhaustion. This will be addressed by IPv6, which contains a much larger address space than IPv4. CIDR helps this problem by encouraging efficient use of addresses by mapping them close together, but the address space will eventually be exhausted anyway.

A.4.8 IP multicast

Multicast makes use of the IP Class D range, which is designated by an initial byte with a value in the range 224–239. Multicast packets have as their destination all hosts who declare interest in a particular multicast address, instead of just one host (interface) on the network, as is the case with traditional unicast IP addresses. This is extremely useful behavior because it allows a single message transmission to reach multiple hosts with minimum network usage. In addition, the sender need not keep track of the list of recipients, because this information is maintained by the low level multicast protocol (figure A.19).

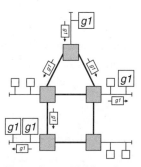

Figure A.19 Multicasting to a group of hosts

Multicast addresses   Multicast addresses are officially assigned by IANA. Certain multicast addresses are for general use while others correspond to specific uses, such as MBone channels. Most multicast addresses are officially allocated, while some others are just well known.

Assigned multicast addresses:

- *224.0.0.1*   All systems on this subnet
- *224.0.0.2*   All routers on this subnet
- *224.0.1.11*   IETF audio
- *239.*.*.**   Private use

MBone and multicast routing The MBone is an experimental virtual multicast network that tunnels over the Internet (figure A.20). Most IP routers do not yet support multicast, so these tunnels are required to link multicast islands.

When a multicast router receives a multicast packet, it uses

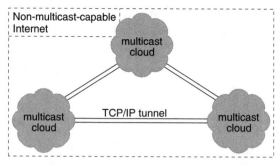

Figure A.20   The MBone

the Internet Group Membership Protocol to determine if there are members of that particular multicast group within the networks connected to its other interfaces. If no members are present, the router will not forward the multicast packet. IGMP is transmitted to the router by hosts as they join multicast groups, and updates are passed in the link state database to other routers as in OSPF.

Distance Vector Multicast Routing Protocol, DVMRP, is the routing protocol used in the MBone between routers. DVMRP is a distance vector based protocol. DVMRP updates are sent to all connected multicast routers and over all tunnels connected to the sending router. DVMRP uses a pruning algorithm to cut out transmissions to areas of the network with no members of the current group. Periodic flooding allows new members to join.

Protocol Independent Multicast (PIM) is a newer multicast routing protocol. PIM is protocol-independent because it makes no assumptions about the capabilities of the underlying unicast routing protocol. PIM comes in two variants, dense and sparse. Dense is for use in situations where the number of nodes on a particular network that have joined the group is relatively large. Sparse is for situations where only a few nodes on the network have joined the group. Sparse prevents flooding the entire network with group packets if only a few nodes are listening.

Multicast Open Shortest Path First (MOSPF) is a multicast extension to OSPF, and makes use of a shortest path calculation to determine optimal routes within an AS.

A.4.9 IPv6

IPv6 is the next-generation replacement protocol for IPv4. It solves many of the problems associated with IPv4, especially the lack of sufficient address space.

Addressing IPv6 provides an address space of 128 bits as opposed to IPv4's 32 bits. An IPv6 address may be represented in three ways. The first is the form *x.x.x.x.x.x.x.x*, where each *x* is a 16-bit word. It is not necessary to include leading zeros in a field. The second way is a shorthand for representing long strings of contiguous zeros. For example, the address *0000.0000.0000.0000.0000.0000.0000.0001* (the loop-back address) can be shortened to *::1*. There may be only one shortening of this type in the address.

The third form is for use when interoperating with legacy IPv4. This form allows the first six groups of sixteen to precede the normal Internet dotted quad. An example is *0000:0000:0000:0000:0000:FA43.182.34.2.100*, which of course can be shortened to *::FA43.182.34.2.100*.

IPv6 supports unicast and multicast addresses. The function of broadcast addresses is performed by multicast addresses in IPv6. IPv6 adds *anycast* addresses, which are allocated from the unicast address pool and specify all hosts in a specified group. An anycast address is used for multiple interfaces that are configured to respond to the same IPv6 address. A probable use for these addresses is a group of routers belonging to the same provider.

Address allocation in IPv6 is different from IPv4. Instead of network classes, the address space is divided into unicast and multicast addresses, with subareas reserved for service providers. Roughly 15 percent of the address space is allocated. The rest is reserved for future use.

Unicast addresses are divided into global provider-based addresses, geographic-based addresses, NSAP addresses, IPX hierarchical addresses, site-local-use addresses, link-local-use address, and IPv4-capable host addresses. Other types may be defined in the future. IPv6 addresses are contiguously bitmaskable, making IPv4 CIDR-like routing possible.

The provider-based address space is assigned to registries, which assign portions to providers, which in turn assign smaller portions to customers.

IPv6 is designed to run over 802.x-based networks such as Ethernet by allowing the globally unique 48-bit hardware address to automatically be used as the organizational IP identifier. Hosts on 802.x networks can therefore use their hardware address to auto-generate their IPv6 address.

IPv6 datagrams   Datagram headers have been simplified in IPv6 to take up less bandwidth and speed up processing during routing. A security extension to IPv6 headers also provides for authentication and encryption possibilities.

IPv6 provides priority levels which enable the sender to prioritize packets coming from the same source. Two classes of traffic, congestion-controlled and noncongestion-controlled, are provided. Congestion-controlled traffic, priority levels 0–7, consists of traffic types such as email and data transfer, which can be backed off under conditions of network congestion. Noncongestion-controlled traffic, priority levels 8–15, consists of traffic types such as video and audio, which does not back off.

Congestion-controlled data can have priority of level 0–7, where 0 is lowest.

1 Uncharacterized

2 Filler (e.g., USENET)

3 Unattended data (e.g., email)

4 Reserved

5 Attended data (e.g., FTP, NFS)

6 Reserved

7 Interactive data (e.g., telnet)

8 Internet control (e.g., routing protocols, SNMP)

IPv6 currently consists of a series of IETF drafts and RFCs; deployment has begun within various industry and academic groups, however widespread implementation remains for the future. Extensive information is available online at http://www.ipv6.org/.

A.5 References

1 Christian Huitema, *Routing in the Internet*, Prentice Hall, 1995.

2 Routing Arbiter web page, http://www.ra.net/.

3 Uyless Black, *TCP/IP & Related Protocols*, McGraw-Hill, 1994.

4 S. Deering and R. Hinden, "Internet Protocol, Version 6 (IPv6) Specification," RFC 1883, ftp://ds.internic.net/rfc/rfc1883.txt.

5 S. Deering and R. Hinden, "IP Version 6 Addressing Architecture," RFC 1884, ftp://ds.internic.net/rfc/rfc1884.txt.

A P P E N D I X   B

Tables

This appendix provides a few tables of data that are relevant to Java networking issues.

B.1 Java escaped characters

String and character literals in Java source require the following characters to be encoded with their corresponding escape codes:

Table B.1 Java escaped characters

Escape code	Meaning
\n	newline (LF)
\r	carriage return (CR)
\t	tab
\"	double quote
\'	single quote
\\	backslash

B.2 Character encodings

The following character encodings are supported by JDK 1.1.7a and JDK 1.2. All of these names are case-sensitive. If an encoding that you need is not listed here, check under the encoding aliases.

The JDK can successful convert from these encodings to Unicode and vice-versa. This does not, however, mean that the JDK comes with fonts to display these character sets.

Table B.2   ISO Encodings

Encoding name	Character encoding
ASCII	U.S. ASCII (ISO 646, ANSI X3.4)
ISO8859_1	Latin 1 (Western Europe)
ISO8859_2	Latin 2 (Eastern Europe)
ISO8859_3	Latin 3 (Southern Europe)
ISO8859_4	Latin 4 (Northern Europe)
ISO8859_5	Cyrillic
ISO8859_6	Arabic
ISO8859_7	Greek
ISO8859_8	Hebrew
ISO8859_9	Latin 5 (Turkish)
ISO8859_15_FDIS	Updated Latin 1 with Euro

Table B.2   ISO Encodings

Encoding name	Character encoding
Big5	Traditional Chinese
EUC_CN	Simplified Chinese
EUC_JP	Japanese
EUC_KR	Korean
EUC_TW	Traditional Chinese
GBK	Simplified Chinese
ISO2022CN	Chinese
ISO2022CN_CNS	Traditional Chinese
ISO2022CN_GB	Simplified Chinese
ISO2022JP	Japanese
ISO2022KR	Korean
JIS0201	Japanese
JIS0208	Japanese
JIS0212	Japanese
JISAutoDetect	JIS autodetect (bytes-to-chars only)
SJIS	Shift-JIS Japanese
Unicode	Marked big-endian Unicode
UnicodeBig	Marked big-endian Unicode
UnicodeBigUnmarked	Unmarked big-endian Unicode
UnicodeLittle	Marked little-endian Unicode
UnicodeLittleUnmarked	Unmarked little-endian Unicode
UTF8	Unicode Transfer Format-8

Table B.3   DOS, Windows, AIX, OS/2 Encodings

Encoding name	Character encoding
Cp437	DOS U.S. ASCII
Cp737	DOS Greek
Cp775	DOS Baltic Rim
Cp850	DOS Latin1
Cp852	DOS Latin2
Cp855	DOS Cyrillic
Cp856	DOS Cyrillic 2
Cp857	DOS Turkish
Cp858	DOS Latin 1 with Euro
Cp860	DOS Portuguese
Cp861	DOS Icelandic
Cp862	DOS Hebrew

Table B.3   DOS, Windows, AIX, OS/2 Encodings

Encoding name	Character encoding
Cp863	DOS Canadian French
Cp864	DOS Arabic
Cp865	DOS Nordic
Cp866	DOS Cyrillic Russian
Cp868	DOS Pakistan
Cp869	DOS Modern Greek
Cp870	DOS Multilingual Latin-2
Cp874	Windows Thai
Cp918	DOS Pakistan(Urdu)
Cp921	DOS/AIX Latvia, Lithuania
Cp922	DOS/AIX Estonia
Cp923	?? Cp923
Cp930	Japanese Katakana-Kanji
Cp933	Korean
Cp935	Simplified Chinese Host
Cp937	Traditional Chinese Host
Cp939	Japanese Latin Kanji
Cp942	OS/2 Japanese
Cp942C	Japanese code
Cp943	?? IBM943
Cp943C	?? IBM943 code
Cp948	OS/2 Chinese (Taiwan)
Cp949	Windows Korean
Cp949C	Windows Korean code
Cp950	Windows Chinese (Hong Kong, Taiwan)
Cp964	AIX Chinese (Taiwan)
Cp970	AIX Korean
Cp1006	AIX Pakistan
Cp1098	DOS Iran(Farsi)/Persian
Cp1124	AIX Ukraine
Cp1250	Windows Latin 2
Cp1251	Windows Cyrillic
Cp1252	Windows Latin 1
Cp1253	Windows Greek
Cp1254	Windows Turkish
Cp1255	Windows Hebrew
Cp1256	Windows Arabic
Cp1257	Windows Baltic
Cp1258	Windows Vietnamese

Table B.3 DOS, Windows, AIX, OS/2 Encodings

Encoding name	Character encoding
Cp1381	DOS Chinese (PRC)
Cp1383	AIX Chinese (PRC)
Cp33722	IBM-eucJP Japanese
MS874	Windows Thai
MS936	Windows 936
MS950	Windows 950

Table B.4 EBCDIC Encodings

Encoding name	Character encoding
Cp037	U.S. English
Cp273	Austria, Germany
Cp277	Denmark, Norway
Cp278	Finland, Sweden
Cp280	Italy
Cp284	Catalan/Spain, Spanish Latin America
Cp285	U.K. English
Cp297	France
Cp420	Arabic
Cp424	Hebrew
Cp500	Belgium, Switzerland
Cp838	Thai extended
Cp871	Iceland
Cp875	Greek
Cp1025	Multilingual Cyrillic
Cp1026	Latin-5, Turkey
Cp1046	Open Edition US EBCDIC
Cp1097	Iran(Farsi)/Persian
Cp1112	Latvia, Lithuania
Cp1122	Estonia
Cp1123	Ukraine
Cp1140	Cp037 with Euro
Cp1141	Cp273 with Euro
Cp1142	Cp277 with Euro
Cp1143	Cp278 with Euro
Cp1144	Cp280 with Euro
Cp1145	Cp284 with Euro
Cp1146	Cp285 with Euro

Table B.4   EBCDIC Encodings

Encoding name	Character encoding
Cp1147	Cp297 with Euro
Cp1148	Cp500 with Euro
Cp1149	Cp871 with Euro

Table B.5   Macintosh Encodings

Encoding name	Character encoding
MacArabic	Macintosh Arabic
MacCentralEurope	Macintosh Latin 2
MacCroatian	Macintosh Croatian
MacCyrillic	Macintosh Cyrillic
MacDingbat	Macintosh Dingbat
MacGreek	Macintosh Greek
MacHebrew	Macintosh Hebrew
MacIceland	Macintosh Iceland
MacRoman	Macintosh Roman
MacRomania	Macintosh Romania
MacSymbol	Macintosh Symbol
MacThai	Macintosh Thai
MacTurkish	Macintosh Turkish
MacUkraine	Macintosh Ukraine

Table B.6   Miscellaneous Encodings

Encoding name	Character encoding
Johab	Johab-encoded Hangul
KOI8_R	Russian
TIS620	Thai

B.3 Character encoding aliases

The following aliases are provided for the supported character encodings. Alias names are case-insensitive.

Table B.7 Character encoding aliases

Encoding names	Aliases
ASCII	us-ascii
Cp037	ibm037, ibm-037, cp037, 037
Cp273	ibm273, ibm-273, cp273, 273
Cp277	ibm277, ibm-277, cp277, 277
Cp278	ibm278, ibm-278, cp278, 278
Cp280	ibm280, ibm-280, cp280, 280
Cp284	ibm284, ibm-284, cp284, 284
Cp285	ibm285, ibm-285, cp285, 285
Cp297	ibm297, ibm-297, cp297, 297
Cp420	ibm420, ibm-420, cp420, 420
Cp424	ibm424, ibm-424, cp424, 424
Cp437	ibm437, ibm-437, cp437, 437, cspc8codepage437
Cp500	ibm500, ibm-500, cp500, 500
Cp737	ibm737, ibm-737, cp737, 737
Cp775	ibm775, ibm-775, cp775, 775
Cp838	ibm838, ibm-838, cp838, 838
Cp850	ibm850, ibm-850, cp850, 850, cspc850multilingual
Cp852	ibm852, ibm-852, cp852, 852, cspcp852
Cp855	ibm855, ibm-855, cp855, 855, cspcp855
Cp856	ibm856, ibm-856, cp856, 856
Cp857	ibm857, ibm-857, cp857, 857, csibm857
Cp860	ibm860, ibm-860, cp860, 860, csibm860
Cp861	ibm861, ibm-861, cp861, cp-is, 861, csibm861
Cp862	ibm862, ibm-862, cp862, 862, cspc862latinhebrew
Cp863	ibm863, ibm-863, cp863, 863, csibm863
Cp864	ibm864, ibm-864, cp864, csibm864
Cp865	ibm865, ibm-865, cp865, 865, csibm865
Cp866	ibm866, ibm-866, cp866, 866, csibm866
Cp868	ibm868, ibm-868, cp868, 868
Cp869	ibm869, ibm-869, cp869, 869, cp-gr, csibm869
Cp870	ibm870, ibm-870, cp870, 870
Cp871	ibm871, ibm-871, cp871, 871
Cp874	ibm874, ibm-874, cp874, 874

Table B.7 Character encoding aliases

Encoding names	Aliases
Cp875	ibm875, ibm-875, cp875, 875
Cp918	ibm918, ibm-918, cp918, 918
Cp921	ibm921, ibm-921, cp921, 921
Cp922	ibm922, ibm-922, cp922, 922
Cp930	ibm930, ibm-930, cp930, 930
Cp933	ibm933, ibm-933, cp933, 933
Cp935	ibm935, ibm-935, cp935, 935
Cp937	ibm937, ibm-937, cp937, 937
Cp939	ibm939, ibm-939, cp939, 939
Cp942	ibm942, ibm-942, cp942, 942
Cp943	ibm943, ibm-943, cp943, 943
Cp948	ibm948, ibm-948, cp948, 948
Cp949	ibm949, ibm-949, cp949, 949
Cp950	ibm950, ibm-950, cp950, 950
Cp964	ibm964, ibm-964, cp964, 964
Cp970	ibm970, ibm-970, cp970, 970
Cp1006	ibm1006, ibm-1006, cp1006, 1006
Cp1025	ibm1025, ibm-1025, cp1025, 1025
Cp1026	ibm1026, ibm-1026, cp1026, 1026
Cp1097	ibm1097, ibm-1097, cp1097, 1097
Cp1098	ibm1098, ibm-1098, cp1098, 1098
Cp1112	ibm1112, ibm-1112, cp1112, 1112
Cp1122	ibm1122, ibm-1122, cp1122, 1122
Cp1123	ibm1123, ibm-1123, cp1123, 1123
Cp1124	ibm1124, ibm-1124, cp1124, 1124
Cp1250	windows-1250
Cp1251	windows-1251
Cp1252	windows-1252
Cp1253	windows-1253
Cp1254	windows-1254
Cp1255	windows-1255
Cp1256	windows-1256
Cp1257	windows-1257
Cp1258	windows-1258
Cp1381	ibm1381, ibm-1381, cp1381, 1381
Cp1383	ibm1383, ibm-1383, cp1383, 1383
Cp33722	ibm33722, ibm-33722, cp33722, 33722
EUC_CN	gb2312, gb2312-80, gb2312-1980, euc-cn, euccn

Table B.7   Character encoding aliases

Encoding names	Aliases
EUC_JP	eucjis, euc-jp, eucjp, extended_unix_code_packed_format_for_japanese, cseucpkdfmtjapanese
EUC_KR	ksc5601, euc-kr, euckr, ks_c_5601-1987, ksc5601-1987, ksc5601_1987, ksc_5601
EUC_TW	cns11643, euc-tw, euctw
ISO2022JP	jis, iso-2022-jp, csiso2022jp, jis_encoding, csjisencoding
ISO8859_1	8859_1, iso_8859-1:1978, iso-ir-100, iso_8859-1, iso-8859-1, latin1, l1, ibm819, ibm-819, cp819, 819, csISOLatin1
ISO8859_2	8859_2, iso_8859-2:1987, iso-ir-101, iso_8859-2, iso-8859-2, latin2, l2, ibm912, ibm-912, cp912, 912, csisolatin2
ISO8859_3	8859_3, iso_8859-3:1988, iso-ir-109, iso_8859-3, iso-8859-3, latin3, l3, ibm913, ibm-913, cp913, 913, csisolatin3
ISO8859_4	8859_4, iso_8859-4:1988, iso-ir-110, iso_8859-4, iso-8859-4, latin4, l4, ibm914, ibm-914, cp914, 914, csisolatin4
ISO8859_5	8859_5, iso_8859-5:1988, iso-ir-144, iso_8859-5, iso-8859-5, cyrillic, csisolatincyrillic, ibm915, ibm-915, cp915, 915
ISO8859_6	8859_6, iso_8859-6:1987, iso-ir-127, iso_8859-6, iso-8859-6, ecma-114, asmo-708, arabic, csisolatinarabic, ibm1089, ibm-1089, cp1089, 1089
ISO8859_7	8859_7, iso_8859-7:1987, iso-ir-126, iso_8859-7, iso-8859-7, elot_928, ecma-118, greek, greek8, csisolatingreek, ibm813, ibm-813, cp813, 813
ISO8859_8	8859_8, iso_8859-8:1988, iso-ir-138, iso_8859-8, iso-8859-8, hebrew, csisolatinhebrew, ibm916, ibm-916, cp916, 916
ISO8859_9	8859_9, iso-ir-148, iso_8859-9, iso-8859-9, latin5, l5, ibm920, ibm-920, cp920, 920, csisolatin5
JISAutoDetect	jis auto detect
Johab	ksc5601-1992, ksc5601_1992, ms949, windows-949
KOI8_R	koi8-r, koi8, cskoi8r
MS874	windows-874
SJIS	shift_jis, ms_kanji, csshiftjis, windows-31J, cswindows31j

B.4   The ASCII character set

ASCII is a widely used 7-bit character encoding of the basic Latin alphabet. Some systems support an extended eight-bit form that includes some foreign and accented characters in addition to this regular set.

Table B.8   ASCII character set

Dec	Oct	Hex	Char	Dec	Oct	Hex	Char
0	000	0x00	NUL (^@)	1	001	0x01	SOH (^A)
2	002	0x02	STX (^B)	3	003	0x03	ETX (^C)

Table B.8   ASCII character set

Dec	Oct	Hex	Char	Dec	Oct	Hex	Char
4	004	0x04	EOT (^D)	5	005	0x05	ENQ (^E)
6	006	0x06	ACK (^F)	7	007	0x07	BEL (^G)
8	010	0x08	BS (^H)	9	011	0x09	HT (^I)
10	012	0x0a	LF (^J)	11	013	0x0b	VT (^K)
12	014	0x0c	FF (^L)	13	015	0x0d	CR (^M)
14	016	0x0e	SO (^N)	15	017	0x0f	SI (^O)
16	020	0x10	DLE (^P)	17	021	0x11	DC1 (^Q)
18	022	0x12	DC2 (^R)	19	023	0x13	DC3 (^S)
20	024	0x14	DC4 (^T)	21	025	0x15	NAK (^U)
22	026	0x16	SYN (^V)	23	027	0x17	ETB (^W)
24	030	0x18	CAN (^X)	25	031	0x19	EM (^Y)
26	032	0x1a	SUB (^Z)	27	033	0x1b	ESC (^[)
28	034	0x1c	FS (^\)	29	035	0x1d	GS (^])
30	036	0x1e	RS (^^)	31	037	0x1f	US (^_)
32	040	0x20	SPC ( )	33	041	0x21	!
34	042	0x22	"	35	043	0x23	#
36	044	0x24	$	37	045	0x25	%
38	046	0x26	&	39	047	0x27	'
40	050	0x28	(	41	051	0x29	)
42	052	0x2a	*	43	053	0x2b	+
44	054	0x2c	,	45	055	0x2d	-
46	056	0x2e	.	47	057	0x2f	/
48	060	0x30	0	49	061	0x31	1
50	062	0x32	2	51	063	0x33	3
52	064	0x34	4	53	065	0x35	5
54	066	0x36	6	55	067	0x37	7
56	070	0x38	8	57	071	0x39	9
58	072	0x3a	:	59	073	0x3b	;
60	074	0x3c	<	61	075	0x3d	=
62	076	0x3e	>	63	077	0x3f	?
64	0100	0x40	@	65	0101	0x41	A
66	0102	0x42	B	67	0103	0x43	C
68	0104	0x44	D	69	0105	0x45	E
70	0106	0x46	F	71	0107	0x47	G
72	0110	0x48	H	73	0111	0x49	I
74	0112	0x4a	J	75	0113	0x4b	K
76	0114	0x4c	L	77	0115	0x4d	M
78	0116	0x4e	N	79	0117	0x4f	O
80	0120	0x50	P	81	0121	0x51	Q

Table B.8 ASCII character set

Dec	Oct	Hex	Char	Dec	Oct	Hex	Char
82	0122	0x52	R	83	0123	0x53	S
84	0124	0x54	T	85	0125	0x55	U
86	0126	0x56	V	87	0127	0x57	W
88	0130	0x58	X	89	0131	0x59	Y
90	0132	0x5a	Z	91	0133	0x5b	[
92	0134	0x5c	\	93	0135	0x5d	]
94	0136	0x5e	^	95	0137	0x5f	_
96	0140	0x60	`	97	0141	0x61	a
98	0142	0x62	b	99	0143	0x63	c
100	0144	0x64	d	101	0145	0x65	e
102	0146	0x66	f	103	0147	0x67	g
104	0150	0x68	h	105	0151	0x69	i
106	0152	0x6a	j	107	0153	0x6b	k
108	0154	0x6c	l	109	0155	0x6d	m
110	0156	0x6e	n	111	0157	0x6f	o
112	0160	0x70	p	113	0161	0x71	q
114	0162	0x72	r	115	0163	0x73	s
116	0164	0x74	t	117	0165	0x75	u
118	0166	0x76	v	119	0167	0x77	w
120	0170	0x78	x	121	0171	0x79	y
122	0172	0x7a	z	123	0173	0x7b	{
124	0174	0x7c	l	125	0175	0x7d	}
126	0176	0x7e	~	127	0177	0x7f	DEL

B.5 Unicode 2.0 block allocations

Unicode is a 16-bit international character encoding standard that supports the alphabets of many different languages in addition to a variety of mathematical and geometric shapes. Groups of characters from different alphabets and different origins are assigned contiguous blocks of the character set; this table lists the Unicode 2.0 block allocations.

Table B.9 Unicode 2.0 block allocations

Start code	End code	Block name
\u0000	\u007F	Basic Latin
\u0080	\u00FF	Latin-1 Supplement
\u0100	\u017F	Latin Extended-A
\u0180	\u024F	Latin Extended-B

Table B.9 Unicode 2.0 block allocations

Start code	End code	Block name
\u0250	\u02AF	IPA Extensions
\u02B0	\u02FF	Spacing Modifier Letters
\u0300	\u036F	Combining Diacritical Marks
\u0370	\u03FF	Greek
\u0400	\u04FF	Cyrillic
\u0530	\u058F	Armenian
\u0590	\u05FF	Hebrew
\u0600	\u06FF	Arabic
\u0900	\u097F	Devanagari
\u0980	\u09FF	Bengali
\u0A00	\u0A7F	Gurmukhi
\u0A80	\u0AFF	Gujarati
\u0B00	\u0B7F	Oriya
\u0B80	\u0BFF	Tamil
\u0C00	\u0C7F	Telugu
\u0C80	\u0CFF	Kannada
\u0D00	\u0D7F	Malayalam
\u0E00	\u0E7F	Thai
\u0E80	\u0EFF	Lao
\u0F00	\u0FBF	Tibetan
\u10A0	\u10FF	Georgian
\u1100	\u11FF	Hangul Jamo
\u1E00	\u1EFF	Latin Extended Additional
\u1F00	\u1FFF	Greek Extended
\u2000	\u206F	General Punctuation
\u2070	\u209F	Superscripts and Subscripts
\u20A0	\u20CF	Currency Symbols
\u20D0	\u20FF	Combining Marks for Symbols
\u2100	\u214F	Letterlike Symbols
\u2150	\u218F	Number Forms
\u2190	\u21FF	Arrows
\u2200	\u22FF	Mathematical Operators
\u2300	\u23FF	Miscellaneous Technical
\u2400	\u243F	Control Pictures
\u2440	\u245F	Optical Character Recognition
\u2460	\u24FF	Enclosed Alphanumerics
\u2500	\u257F	Box Drawing
\u2580	\u259F	Block Elements
\u25A0	\u25FF	Geometric Shapes

Table B.9 Unicode 2.0 block allocations

Start code	End code	Block name
\u2600	\u26FF	Miscellaneous Symbols
\u2700	\u27BF	Dingbats
\u3000	\u303F	CJK Symbols and Punctuation
\u3040	\u309F	Hiragana
\u30A0	\u30FF	Katakana
\u3100	\u312F	Bopomofo
\u3130	\u318F	Hangul Compatibility Jamo
\u3190	\u319F	Kanbun
\u3200	\u32FF	Enclosed CJK Letters and Months
\u3300	\u33FF	CJK Compatibility
\u4E00	\u9FFF	CJK Unified Ideographs
\uAC00	\uD7A3	Hangul Syllables
\uD800	\uDB7F	High Surrogates
\uDB80	\uDBFF	High Private Use Surrogates
\uDC00	\uDFFF	Low Surrogates
\uE000	\uF8FF	Private Use
\uF900	\uFAFF	CJK Compatibility Ideographs
\uFB00	\uFB4F	Alphabetic Presentation Forms
\uFB50	\uFDFF	Arabic Presentation Forms-A
\uFE20	\uFE2F	Combining Half Marks
\uFE30	\uFE4F	CJK Compatibility Forms
\uFE50	\uFE6F	Small Form Variants
\uFE70	\uFEFF	Arabic Presentation Forms-B
\uFF00	\uFFEF	Halfwidth and Fullwidth Forms
\uFEFF	\uFEFF	Specials
\uFFF0	\uFFFF	Specials

B.6 Modified UTF-8 Encoding

UTF-8 is an efficient encoding of Unicode character strings that recognizes the fact that the majority of text-based communications are in ASCII, and therefore optimizes the encoding of these characters.

Strings are encoded as two bytes that specify the length of the string followed by the encoded string characters. The 2-byte length is written in network byte order, and indicates the length of the *encoded* string characters, not just the number of characters in the string.

```
[lenHI][lenLO]{encoded characters}
```

The individual characters are encoded according to the following table. ASCII characters are encoded as a single byte; Greek, Hebrew, and Arabic characters are encoded as two bytes; and all other characters are encoded as three bytes. The variant of UTF-8 used by Java has one modification: the character \u0000 is encoded in two bytes, so that no character will be encoded with the byte zero.

Table B.10   UTF-8 encoding

Character	Encoding
\u0000	[11000000] [10000000] (Java)
\u0001–\u007f	[0][bits 0–6]
\u0080–\u07ff	[110][bits 6–10] [10][bits 0–5]
\u0800–\uffff	[1110][bits 12–15] [10][bits 6–11] [10][bits 0–5]

B.7 Multiplication tables 1 to 7

Table B.11 Multiplication tables 1 to 7

	1	2	3	4	5	6	7
× 1	1	2	3	4	5	6	7
× 2	2	4	6	8	10	12	14
× 3	3	6	9	12	15	18	21
× 4	4	8	12	16	20	24	28
× 5	5	10	15	20	25	30	35
× 6	6	12	18	24	30	36	42
× 7	7	14	21	28	35	42	49
× 8	8	16	24	32	40	48	56
× 9	9	18	27	36	45	54	63
× 10	10	20	30	40	50	60	70
× 11	11	22	33	44	55	66	77
× 12	12	24	36	48	60	72	84

B.8 IP address classes

IP addresses are divided into address classes that broadly allocate groups of IP addresses, so that an address that begins with the byte 191, for example, belongs to a class B network. CIDR is now addressing problems such as class B exhaustion by grouping contiguous class C addresses into a single network allocation.

Table B.12 IP address classes

Class	Address range	Allocation
Class A	1–126.xx.xx.xx	16M host network
Class B	128–191.xx.xx.xx	65536 host network
Class C	192–223.xx.xx.xx	256 host network
Class D	224–239.xx.xx.xx	multicast
Class E	240–255.xx.xx.xx	reserved

B.9 Selected well-known UNIX TCP and UDP services

Several UNIX TCP and UDP port numbers are allocated to well-known services such as finger, SMTP (mail) and HTTP (Web); if you connect to TCP port 13 of a UNIX machine that supports the *daytime* service and is not behind a firewall, then it will respond with the current time. This table lists some of these services; the complete table contains thousands of entries.

Table B.13 Selected UNIX TCP and UDP services

Port	Protocol	Service	Description
7	TCP/UDP	echo	Echo
9	TCP/UDP	discard	Discard
11	TCP	systat	Active Users
13	TCP/UDP	daytime	Daytime
15	TCP	netstat	Netstat
17	TCP	qotd	Quote of the Day
18	TCP/UDP	msp	Message Send Protocol
19	TCP/UDP	chargen	TTYTST Source Character Generator
20	TCP	ftp-data	File Transfer (Data)
21	TCP	ftp	File Transfer (Control)
23	TCP	telnet	Telnet
25	TCP	smtp	Simple Mail Transfer Protocol
37	TCP/UDP	time	Time Server
43	TCP	whois	Who Is
53	TCP/UDP	domain	Domain Name Server
70	TCP	gopher	Gopher
79	TCP	finger	Finger

Table B.13 Selected UNIX TCP and UDP services

Port	Protocol	Service	Description
80	TCP	http	World Wide Web HTTP
443	TCP	https	SSL HTTP
512	TCP	exec	BSD rexecd
513	TCP	login	BSD rlogin
513	UDP	who	BSD rwhod
514	TCP	shell	BSD rshd
514	UDP	syslog	BSD syslogd
515	TCP	printer	BSD lpd
531	TCP	conference	Chat
6667	TCP	irc	Internet Relay Chat

B.10 HTTP requests

HTTP is the protocol that underlies the WWW; the current version of HTTP is 1.0, although 1.1 is already widely deployed, and work is already under way to define HTTP-NG. An HTTP request is the message that a Web browser sends to a Web server when it is requesting a document.

B.10.1 A simple get request

A simple get request follows the old HTTP 0.9 specification which, while still in use, is becoming obsolete. Note that the requst is followed by two CRLFs.

```
GET /document.html[CRLF][CRLF]
```

B.10.2 A full get request

A full get request follows the HTTP 1.0 specification, and includes the HTTP version number in the request.

```
GET /document.html HTTP/1.0[CRLF][CRLF]
```

B.10.3 A full get request with headers

HTTP/1.0 supports optional headers in a request. The following request tells the server the type of browser being used and requests that the document only be returned if it has been modified more recently than the specified date. This particular header allows the browser to use a cached version of the document if the original has not changed.

```
GET /document.html HTTP/1.0[CRLF]
User-Agent: Blah/2.13 libwww/2.17b3[CRLF]
If-Modified-Since: Sat, 29 Oct 1994 19:43:31 GMT[CRLF][CRLF]
```

B.10.4 A post request

A post request allows the client to include a significant amount of data in a request. This is used, for example, to submit information to a CGI script or to upload a file to a Web server.

```
POST /cgi-bin/code.cgi HTTP/1.0[CRLF]
Content-Type: <mime-type>[CRLF]
Content-Length: <length>[CRLF][CRLF]
<body>
```

B.10.5 A head request

A head request requests just the headers of a particular file; this allows the browser, for example, to determine whether a file has been modified and should therefore be downloaded again.

```
HEAD /document.html[CRLF][CRLF]
```

B.11 HTTP responses

The response of a Web server varies with the type of request and whether or not the request could be serviced.

B.11.1 A simple response

A simple response of this form is only returned in response to a simple (HTTP 0.9) request, and consists of simply the requested document.

```
<body>
```

B.11.2 A full response

A full response includes the HTTP version number and a status code, followed by the body of the document. The status code indicates how successfully the request was serviced.

```
HTTP/1.0 200 OK[CRLF][CRLF]
<body>
```

B.11.3 A full response with headers

A full response may also include some headers that include additional information about the requested document, such as its content type, whether it is compressed and when it was last modified.

```
HTTP/1.0 200 OK[CRLF]
Content-Type: text/html[CRLF]
Content-Encoding: x-gzip[CRLF][CRLF]
<body>
```

B.11.4 HTTP response codes

This table lists the status codes that are included with HTTP 1.0 responses. The most common status code is 200 which means that the request was serviced successfully; 301 means that the document has moved (the response will include the new location); 404 means that the document was not found.

Table B.14 HTTP response codes

Code	Meaning
200	OK
201	Created
202	Accepted
204	No Content
301	Moved Permanently
302	Moved Temporarily
304	Not Modified
400	Bad Request
401	Unauthorized
403	Forbidden
404	Not Found
500	Internal Server Error
501	Not Implemented
502	Bad Gateway
503	Service Unavailable

B.12 HTTP

For full details on the HTTP specification, see the internet draft at http://www.w3.org/. The following is a brief summary of some useful details:

B.12.1 HTTP general headers

The following table lists the standard general-header fields defined by HTTP/1.1; these provide general control information and may be included in a client request or server response.

Table B.15 HTTP general headers

Header	Function
Cache-Control	Controls caching of a document
Connection	Controls connection keep alive

Table B.15 HTTP general headers

Header	Function
Date	Indicates the local date
Pragma	Specifies implementation-specific options
Trailer	Indicates the headers included in a chunked trailer
Transfer-Encoding	Specifies the transfer encoding used
Upgrade	Requests a protocol upgrade (e.g., to SSL)
Via	Indicates proxies and proxy protocols used
Warning	Warns of a possible problem

B.12.2 HTTP request headers

The following table lists the standard request-header fields defined by HTTP/1.1; these are headers that may be included in a client request:

Table B.16 HTTP request headers

Header	Function
Accept	Specifies the acceptable MIME types
Accept-Charset	Specifies the acceptable character sets
Accept-Encoding	Specifies the acceptable data encodings
Accept-Language	Specifies the acceptable languages
Authorization	Specifies client authentication credentials
Expect	Specifies server behaviour required by the client
From	Specifies the client's email address
Host	Specifies the server address being accessed
If-Match	Performs the request if certain criteria are met
If-Modified-Since	Performs the request if the object has been modified
If-None-Match	Performs the request if certain criteria are met
If-Range	Returns range of object if conditionals match
If-Unmodified-Since	Performs the request of the object has not been modified
Max-Forwards	Specifies a proxy forwarding limit
Proxy-Authorization	Specifies authentication credentials for the proxy
Range	Specifies the part of an object that is required
Referer	Specifies the document that led to this request
TE	Specifies the acceptable transfer encodings
User-Agent	Identifies the client software

B.12.3 HTTP response headers

The following table lists the standard response-header fields defined by HTTP/1.1; these are headers that may be included in a server response:

Table B.17 HTTP response headers

Header	Function
Accept-Ranges	Specifies which range requests are acceptable
Age	Specifies how old a cached object is
ETag	Specifies the entity tag of the object
Location	Specifies a redirect location
Proxy-Authenticate	Proxy authentication challenge
Retry-After	Specifies how long a service will be unavailable
Server	Identifies the server software
Vary	Identifies which headers affect an object's content
WWW-Authenticate	Client authentication challenge

B.12.4 HTTP entity headers

The following table lists the standard entity-header fields defined by HTTP/1.1; these are headers that may be included in a client request or server response to provide meta information about the request or response body:

Table B.18 HTTP entity headers

Header	Function
Allow	Specifies the request methods supported by the object
Content-Encoding	Specifies the encoding of the object
Content-Language	Specifies the language of the object
Content-Length	Specifies the length of the object
Content-Location	Specifies the actual location of the object
Content-MD5	Specifies an MD5 message digest of the object
Content-Range	Specifies the range of object included
Content-Type	Specifies the MIME type of the object
Expires	Specifies when the returned object expires
Last-Modified	Specifies when the returned object was last modified

Additional nonstandard headers may also be included in a client request or server response; these will be ignored by an application that does not understand the meaning of the header.

B.13 CGI environment variables

The following environment variables are defined by the current Common Gateway Interface standard:

Table B.19 CGI environment variables

Variable	Function
SERVER_SOFTWARE	Identifies server software
SERVER_NAME	Identifies server address
GATEWAY_INTERFACE	Identifies the CGI version in use
SERVER_PROTOCOL	Specifies the request protocol
SERVER_PORT	Specifies the server port
REQUEST_METHOD	Specifies the request method
PATH_INFO	Specifies the request path info
PATH_TRANSLATED	Specifies the translated request path info
SCRIPT_NAME	Specifies the script's virtual path
QUERY_STRING	Specifies the request query string
REMOTE_HOST	Specifies the remote hostname
REMOTE_ADDR	Specifies the remote address
AUTH_TYPE	Specifies user authentication method
REMOTE_USER	Specifies the remote user, if authenticated
REMOTE_IDENT	Specifies the remote username if determined (RFC 931)
CONTENT_TYPE	Specifies the request content type
CONTENT_LENGTH	Specifies the request content length

All other request headers are supplied as environment variables with the prefix HTTP_ and all hyphens replaced by underscore. Headers that have already been included (e.g., Content-length) may be omitted.

B.14 MIME types

MIME allows different types of message content to be sent across the Internet. This table lists some of the common content types that are delivered over the HTTP protocol, and includes the file extensions that are most commonly associated with such files.

Full HTTP responses usually include the content type of the document in a *Content-Type* header.

Table B.20 MIME types

MIME type	Extension
application/octet-stream	.bin .dms .lha .lzh .exe .class
application/postscript	.ai .eps .ps
application/rtf	.rtf
application/x-compress	.Z
application/x-gtar	.gtar
application/x-gzip	.gz
application/x-httpd-cgi	.cgi
application/zip	.zip
audio/basic	.au .snd
audio/mpeg	.mpga .mp2
audio/x-aiff	.aif .aiff .aifc
audio/x-pn-realaudio	.ram
audio/x-pn-realaudio-plugin	.rpm
audio/x-realaudio	.ra
audio/x-wav	.wav
image/gif	.gif
image/ief	.ief
image/jpeg	.jpeg .jpg .jpe
image/png	.png
image/tiff	.tiff .tif
image/x-cmu-raster	.ras
image/x-portable-anymap	.pnm
image/x-portable-bitmap	.pbm
image/x-portable-graymap	.pgm
image/x-portable-pixmap	.ppm
image/x-rgb	.rgb
image/x-xbitmap	.xbm
image/x-xpixmap	.xpm
image/x-xwindowdump	.xwd
multipart/mixed	
text/html	.html .htm
text/plain	.txt
text/richtext	.rtx
text/tab-separated-values	.tsv
text/x-sgml	.sgml .sgm

Table B.20 MIME types

MIME type	Extension
video/mpeg	.mpeg .mpg .mpe
video/quicktime	.qt .mov
video/x-msvideo	.avi
video/x-sgi-movie	.movie

B.15 Permission objects

One of the new features introduced by the Java 2 platform and of relevance to networking, but that we have not covered in this book, is the Permissions API; a flexible, fine-grained mechanism for granting partial trust to embedded code such as applets and servlets.

Under the initial release of the Java 2 SDK, to grant trust to an applet you must first package it in a digitally signed archive. To create the basic archive, you must use the `jar` utility. Then you must obtain and install a code-signing certificate using the `keytool` utility. Then, finally, you can digitally sign the archive using the `jarsigner` utility.

After the applet is signed and deployed, users running the Java 2 runtime environment can grant it trust by using the `keytool` and `policytool` utilities, granting trust to code based on its origin and digital signature.

Although details of these various utilities go beyond the scope of this book--in particular, because this API is not deployed widely, and to avail of trusted applets in major browsers you must employ proprietary APIs—a list of the permission objects that apply to different networking-related methods can be useful.

For a brief tutorial on the deployment of trusted applets for different environments; including Java 2, Netscape and Internet Explorer, see the accompanying Web page http://nitric.com/jnp/codeSigning.html.

java.io.FilePermission   This permission grants filesystem access to directories and files; including executables. The target of this permission is the file, directory or directory tree to which access is being granted, and the action is one or more of the options /read, /write, /execute or /delete.

This permission has relevance to the `Runtime.exec()` methods, the file streams, the `RandomAccessFile` class and various methods of the `File` class. In addition, this permission will be invoked for /file URLs.

java.net.NetPermission   This permission relates just to configuring how network services will request authentication from the user, and is associated with the `Authenticator` class.

java.util.PropertyPermission   This permission grants access to reading or writing `System` properties. The target of this permission is the property or wildcard properties to be accessed, and the action is one or more of the options *read* or *write*.

This permission can be useful if you want to read or write the network proxy settings, ORB initialization parameters, and so forth.

java.lang.RuntimePermission   This permission grants access to a wide variety of runtime-related operations; its target is the operation of interest, and it has no associated action list.

Primarily, you will require this permission if you want to perform `SecurityManager`-related operations, to load native libraries or if you want to install network factories; particularly in the `Socket`, `ServerSocket`, `URL`, `URLConnection` and `RMISocketFactory` classes.

java.io.SerializablePermission   This permission is required in order to perform certain operations related to subclassing the object streams.

java.net.SocketPermission   This is the most important permission related to networking applications. It allows an applet, for example, to engage in multicast conversations, to accept incoming network connections or to connect to arbitrary hosts on a network.

The target of this permission is the host and port range to which access is being granted; the action is one or more of the options *accept, connect, listen,* or *resolve*.

The *resolve* action allows an applet to look up a hostname using `InetAddress`; it is implicit in the other actions.

The *connect* action allows an applet to communicate with a host by opening a `Socket`, sending or receiving a `DatagramPacket` or even just joining a multicast group.

The *listen* action allows an applet to open a `DatagramSocket`, `MulticastSocket` or `ServerSocket`.

Finally, the *accept* action allows an applet to actually accept an incoming connection from a host, to join or leave a multicast group or to send a multicast packet.

index

V

VDSL 762
versioning 241

W

W3 consortium 360
WAIS 12
wait() 49, 50, 51, 679
WAN 752
Web server 326, 593, 597

Whiteboard 702–706
Wide Area Information Services 12
wide area network 752
World Wide Web Consortium 327
write() 65, 67, 87, 168
writeBytes 89
writeBytes() 122
writeObject() 217
Writer 63, 162, 167
writeTo() 149
writeUTF() 122

More Java Titles from Manning

Java Foundation Classes: Swing Reference

This is a comprehensive guide on Swing 1.1 and JDK 1.2's Swing package.

Stephen Drye and William Wake

ISBN#: 1-884777-67-8, US $39.95, 1150 pages

Published January, 1999

Java Servlets by Example

Rich with examples, this book takes the reader through a thorough discussion of servlets.

Alan R. Williamson

ISBN#: 1-884777-66-X, $39.95, 650 pages

Available Spring 1999

For ordering information please go to www.manning.com

More Java Titles from Manning

Up to Speed with Swing, 2nd Edition

This book keeps the successful tutorial tone of the first edition while extending it into intermediate and advanced levels through extensive use of substantial, interesting and useful examples. Based on JDK 1.2.

Steven Gutz, Matthew Robinson, Pavel Vorobiev

ISBN#: 1-884777-75-9, US 32.95, 560 pages

Available Spring 1999

Distributed Programming with Java

Many sample applications, sockets, how to implement object factories, callbacks, signing messages over RMI, mobile agents, Voyager, Java security.

Qusay H. Mahmoud

ISBN#: 1-884777-65-1, $43.95, 450 pages

Available Spring/Summer 1999

For ordering information please go to www.manning.com

More Java Titles from Manning

More Java Titles from Manning

Java XML Programming

This volume is a practical guide to using XML for java programmers.

Nazmul Idris

ISBN#:1-884777-84-8; $47.95, 300 pages

Available Fall 1999

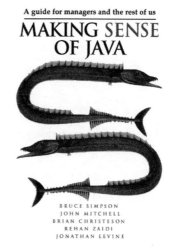

Making Sense of Java:
A guide for managers and the rest of us

This book explains, clearly and concisely, the concepts, features, benefits, potential, and limitations of Java.

Bruce Simpson, John Mitchell, Brian Christenson, Rehan Zaidi and Jonathan Levine

ISBN#: 0-132632-94-2, $29.95, 200 pages

Published 1996

For ordering information please go to www.manning.com

More Java Titles from Manning

The Awesome Power of Power J

Program in Java the very first day with this new primer.

Tim Hatton

ISBN#: 1-884777-53-8, $43.95, 378 pages

Published 1998

The Awesome Power of Java Beans

This second-generation Java Beans book shows how to build as well as use Java beans.

Lawrence H. Rodrigues

ISBN#: 1-884777-56-2, $43.95, 545 pages

Published 1998

For ordering information please go to www.manning.com

praise for the first edition of Java Network Programming

"Like a steaming hot cup of Starbuck's coffee, this book is filled to the brim with real-world examples. Throughout, the importance of security is emphasized. I think you'll find this book good to the last drop."

—Dr. Gary McGraw, Co-author, Java Security: Hostile Applets, Holes and Antidotes

"... a well-rounded, informative explanation of the issues developers face when creating networked applications in Java. Readers will appreciate the book's range of topics from basics such as TCP/IP and the Java security model to Java's latest advanced network features such as Remote Method Invocation."

—Michael O'Connell, Editor-in-Chief, JavaWorld, www.javaworld.com

"... comprehensively covers Java networking including security and, most importantly, valuable documentation of the RMI and object serialization class libraries. I'd especially recommend it to anyone seeking to write serious applications in Java rather than just applets."

—Miko Matsumura, JavaSoft

"This is by far the best of many books I have read—its structure and content are superb. Thanks for greatly improving my understanding of Java in network programming."

—Steve Doliov, CEO, Statistical Solutions, Inc.

"I love this book ... particularly the graphics. They are very descriptive of what is happening."

—Clare Chu, Cisco Systems

"Contains an excellent concise explanation of important Java and Internet concepts. I plan to make it required reading for all the developers on my team."

—Scott Fauerbach, Senior Developer, Knowledge 2000, Inc.

"It's fantastic ... I've read quite a few Java books and this one is clearly on the top shelf!"

—Julian Kryzanowsky, Consultant

"I absolutely love this book; it has become the book with the most markings in my library—and I've read more than 35 Java books."

—Claude Duguay, Software Development Manager, Atrieva Corp.

"It's an excellent book for network programming with Java and contains lots of useful encryption code and discussion as well."

—Michael Brundage, Computing Analyst, Caltech